The Psychology
of Rigorous Humanism
Second Edition

THE PSYCHOLOGY OF RIGOROUS HUMANISM
SECOND EDITION

Joseph F. Rychlak
Loyola University of Chicago

NEW YORK UNIVERSITY PRESS
New York and London

Library of Congress Cataloging-in-Publication Data

Rychlak, Joseph F.
  The psychology of rigorous humanism.

  Bibliography: p.
  Includes indexes.
  1. Psychology—Philosophy. I. Title.
BF38.R93 1987   150   87-22054
ISBN 0-8147-7402-4

Printed in the United States of America

Clothbound editions of New York University Press books are
Smyth-sewn and printed on permanent and durable acid-free paper.

To my teachers and my students

ACKNOWLEDGMENTS

I am grateful to the following copyright holders for granting me permission to quote from their books:

Albert Bandura, *Principles of Behavior Modification* © 1969 by Holt, Rinehart & Winston, Inc. Reprinted by permission of Holt, Rinehart & Winston, Inc.

Richard I. Evans, *B. F. Skinner: The Man and His Ideas* © 1969 by Richard I. Evans. Reprinted by permission of E. P. Dutton & Co., Inc.

Richard I. Evans, *Dialogue with B. F. Skinner* © 1981, Praeger Publishers, New York. Reprinted by permission of the author.

Thomas S. Kuhn, *Structure of Scientific Revolutions* © 1962, 1970 by the University of Chicago. Published 1962. Second edition enlarged 1970. Reprinted by permission of the University of Chicago Press.

Ulric Neisser, *Cognitive Psychology* © 1967, pp. 3, 4, 10, 16, 94, 103, 104, 173, 281, 285, 286, 287, 295. Reprinted by permission of Prentice-Hall, Inc., Englewood Cliffs, N.J.

B. F. Skinner, *About Behaviorism* © 1974. Reprinted by permission of Alfred A. Knopf, Inc.

E. C. Tolman, *Purposive Behavior in Animals and Men* © 1967. Reprinted by permission of Irvington Publishers, Inc., New York.

Adrian van Kaam, *Existential Foundations of Psychology* © 1966 by Duquesne University. Reprinted by permission of the author.

CONTENTS

The Psychology
of Rigorous Humanism
Second Edition

INTRODUCTION

A decade has passed since the first edition of this book made its appearance. The intention in 1977 was to provide the reader with a clear understanding of what it means to be a human being, as well as solid arguments to be used in opposition to the contending "wings" of psychology. The traditional humanists on the left wing seem ever ready to jettison what they take to be dehumanizing scientific efforts to prove something empirically about human behavior. The traditional mechanists on the right wing seem ever ready to jettison the descriptive concepts that have always predicated what it means to be a human being. *The Psychology of Rigorous Humanism* was written as a counterbalancing position to these contending sides, in which a middle ground is taken enabling a teleological theory of the person to be advanced in the context of rigorous empirical validation. To achieve this goal, the first six chapters trace themes from the history of ideas, as well as the significant developments in the rise of science in general and psychology in particular.

This historical background and the arguments enumerated therein enable us to frame a sound, humanistic theory of behavior. We refer to this teleological alternative in modern psychology as "logical learning theory." Chapters 7 and 8 are devoted to this topic, which we take to be a Kuhnian confrontation with the perennial mechanisms of psychology. All of the issues that we have mentioned to this point are as relevant today as they were ten years ago. Therefore, we did not revise the first eight chapters. However, the remaining three chapters of the volume have been thoroughly revised to meet the shortcomings of the first edition.

The original Chapters 9 and 10 had presented a highly detailed accounting of the research conducted on logical learning theory, with explicit details concerning sample description, experimental design, statistical tests, graphs, and so on. This was done in order to remove all doubt that a humanistic theoretician could be just as rigorously precise as the most hard-headed mechanistic theorist. As friendly critics were to point out, this detail amounted to an overkill, detracting from the flow of the presentation that we had achieved in the earlier chapters. Hence, in the present edition we have placed the empirical findings on logical learning theory in Chapter 9. This includes all of the studies referred to in the original edition, as well as several experiments conducted since 1977. We also give a sense of the direction that research in logical learning theory will be taking in the future.

Chapter 10 is an entirely new contribution, written in order to meet a cogent criticism of the first edition. That is, we had not addressed the fact that there are other rigorous approaches in psychology which purport to explain behavior teleologically—as purposive, intentional, self-determining, and so on. Readers of the first edition frequently asked the writer about these alternative approaches. We have taken up the most frequently mentioned of these alternative approaches in Chapter 10, raising questions concerning their merits, pointing to strengths as well as weaknesses, and aligning our views with certain outlooks more than with others. This should give the reader a good sense of just where the computer analogue, social learning theory, attribution theory, and several other such approaches which psychologists are prone to consider teleological fit into the overall picture of rigorous humanism. We learn in all of this comparing and contrasting of views that there is indeed a vigorous expansion, a growing field in psychology that may be described as *rigorous humanism*.

Chapter 11 is an expanded version of the defense that we made of our rigorous humanism in the first edition. We try to meet the most frequent objections voiced by critics who find it somehow incorrect or even improper to begin a line of rigorous theorizing on the assumption that human beings are agents of their own behavior. The tenets of a rigorous humanistic psychology are spelled out. Finally, we have greatly extended the glossary of terminology in the second edition.

Theories of behavior in psychology are difficult to evaluate. On what grounds can we say that "a" theory has merit? Surely, the matter of standing up to empirical evidence is a major reason for theory selection. But, as recent trends in psychology have made clear, some of our most well-researched, valid theories of behavior are no longer in favor. We are said to be in a period of change, if not revolution, moving away from the earlier conditioning theories to the modern cognitive theories of behavior. The writer takes some satisfaction in the fact that logical learning theory, as worked out over a generation ago and as presented in the 1977 version of this book, is not only unchanged in its claims but is even more relevant today than it was twenty-five years ago.

It is the conditioning theories of yesterday, which logical learning theory first opposed, that are slipping from the scene in this age of cognitive science. Logical learning theory also has some questions to raise about today's cognitive theories; but the point of importance is that we have found nothing in the empirical literature or in the rise of computer analogues to adversely affect the tenets of our rigorous humanism. It is hoped that the new generation of psychologists being trained today in the language of cognitive science will appreciate that a view that can hold steady during a time of much indecision and uncertainty has something to offer. Humanistic theorizing in a rigorous research context is most assuredly a viable position to maintain as modern psychology moves forward in preparation for the twenty-first century.

J. F. R.

CHAPTER ONE

An Historical Survey
and Its Lessons

All fields of knowledge achieve distinctiveness based on the objects or events to which they are descriptively applied and the manner in which their resultant conceptualizations are tested for legitimacy. We might be tempted to say that even the objects or events described are theoretical constructions, but this would presume an idealistic interpretation of knowledge. The realist prefers to believe that objects and events exist independent of a theorist's conceptualization, and the challenge is to find accurate representations for what is "really there" in experience. Both realists and idealists must accept the fact that knowledge is impossible without a knower—an organism that processes descriptive information, tests it, and then expounds on what is true or what is inaccurate. Psychology's challenge is to know the knower, and there are surely many pitfalls in this descriptive effort.

To begin such a study a proper first step might be to survey the descent of Western thought, selecting from among its leading thinkers those who seem to have most influenced the ideas that were in existence at the beginning of the twentieth century, when psychology was newly emerging as a scientific discipline. What would such a survey reveal about the knower, the human being on whom our interests ultimately focus? One cannot be strictly empirical in such a survey, of course, because recorded history is not based on samplings from a parameter. Furthermore, if an historical comparison of thinkers (theorists) is to make any sense, we have to employ an organizing scheme. Because schemes prearrange (bias) what we have to say about things, the reader must be assured that the orienting scheme selected here was not arbitrarily concocted by the writer to prove a point from the outset; it has been woven into the fabric of history that we are unfolding.

The writer has employed precisely such a scheme in other contexts, based on Aristotelian terminology, which involved organizing the meaning of theoretical terms under four *causes*, or conceptual frames, having nonoverlapping meanings (see Rychlak, 1968, 1969, 1970, 1972, 1973). Though Aristotle assembled these meanings into four metaconceptions and named them he did not "think them up." We see these meanings in the earliest philosophical accounts. Aristotle did not even limit his framing of causes to the four meanings we review below. (For example, he suggested that change and spontaneity might be thought of as additional "chance" causes of events.) We are in no way committed to Aristotelian philosophy simply because we employ an aspect of his theory of knowledge as a starting point for our survey of Western theoretical history.

The first cause is a *material* cause, which we take to be the substance that comprises a thing. Theories of substance vary, but in general there is some assumption made about an underlying matter, or universal palpability, which lends the essential meaning to an object or event in experience. As further evidence that we are not using "pure" Aristotle in our historical scheme, we should note that he distinguished between primary and secondary substances. Primary substances were viewed as underlying entities that went as potentiality into the construction of all that is. Secondary substances, however, were the more recognizable species of beings, such as a man or a horse. The form (outline, shape) of the latter objects gave their substantial essence additional significance. According to our scheme, Aristotle thus added a formal-cause term to his material-cause account when he defined the secondary substance. When we equate substance with material cause we establish an independence from strict Aristotelian theory.

The second cause is the *efficient* cause, which gets at the *impetus* of or in events—for example, the push, thrust, flow, bringing-about-in-motion aspect of experience. The usual phrasing indicates that an antecedent event invariably and necessarily causes a consequent event, which is called an effect. Thanks to natural science, most people immediately think of *this* meaning of *cause* when we use the term. We often find this efficient cause-effect tandem used in opposition to some other term (e.g., *spontaneity or transcendence*) which lacks the meaning of an invariant antecedent-to-consequent push across the face of time.

The third cause in our scheme is the *formal* cause, which refers to a pattern, shape, outline, or recognizable organization in the flow of events or in the way that objects are constituted (*formed*, as in

Aristotle's secondary substance). Natural objects and behavioral sequences are clearly patterned outlines, recognizable styles of this or that significance to the viewer, who comes to know them as much by these features as by their substantial nature (material cause) or the fact that they are assembled (efficient cause). The very meaning of abstraction or construction in theorizing or in logico-mathematical reasoning comes down to some such patterning of our conceptions into recognizable, albeit abstract, designations. Without a pattern we are adrift and rudderless on the sea of knowledge.

The fourth cause is the one Aristotle specifically coined and made central to his physics, even though the concept of a cause as a reason for behavior had already been employed by Socrates. Aristotle said that before we had fully explicated the nature of anything, we had to state—if possible—its *final* cause. This is best defined as *that, for the sake of which* something happens or comes about. Is there a reason, purpose, intention, or premising meaning that acts as *that* for the sake of which a substance is formed into some recognizable shape, or a line of efficient causation leads to some end result? The emphasis on the direction, goal, or end of events is why theories that employ final-cause meanings are called telic or teleological descriptive accounts (from the Greek word *telos*, meaning end).

This brief introduction of the four causal meanings will suffice for now. Because we make extensive use of these terms throughout the following chapters, they will become increasingly familiar to the reader. Our purpose is not to work out a way of describing human behavior in terms of the causes lying at its root. We must not hypostatize these conceptual categories. Any two theorists might lay equal emphasis on the same cause yet differ dramatically in what they have to say about things. However, the causal scheme as a metaconception permits us to array historical figures for comparison, and it also allows us to diagnose the basic differences that exist in theories of human behavior across varying disciplines.

A Survey of
Western Intellectual History

A survey was conducted following three rules: (1) Select approximately 100 recognized thinkers from across the centuries (we included 104 individuals); (2) analyze one or more constructs of each thinker in terms of the four causes; (3) avoid psychologists *per se* (the history of psychology is discussed in Chapters 3 and 4), although William James and John Dewey had to be considered for their roles in philosophy. The concepts selected were all representative of the person in question. They made possible insightful comparisons among the individuals selected for historical consideration.

The reader will find the names and concepts of the thinkers arrayed in Table 1 (pp. 8–31). This table is organized from left to right as follows: (a) name and life dates of an historical figure; (b) construct(s) or general idea for which he is recognized (numbered consecutively if more than one); (c) definition of the construct or brief description of the idea (numbered consecutively in matching order to the constructs listed); (d) causal meaning(s) employed in the construct designated by an X under the headings Material, Efficient, Formal, and Final. Because more than one causal meaning can be used in a single construct, each X placed under a causal designation is numbered from one through four. Thus, if a theorist's construct employed the meanings of two or more causes, by examining the subscript the reader can get some idea of the predominant meanings employed. For example, in Aristotle's substance conceptions discussed above, primary substance would be given an X *only* under the Material Cause heading of Table 1. However, secondary substance would receive an X_1 under the Formal and X_2 under the Material Cause headings, because Aristotle was using the formal cause meaning as a major emphasis here.

The following sources were used in doing the research for Table 1: Alexander and Selesnick (1966), Becker and Barnes (1952), Burtt (1955), Edwards (1967), Eves (1969), Forbes and Dijksterhuis (1963), Frazer (1959), Kondo (1969), Magill and McGreal (1961), Russell (1959), Sarton (1968), Schwartz and Bishop (1958), Wiener and Noland (1957), and Wightman (1951).

Discussion of Table 1

Note that the most frequently checked cause in Table 1 is the *formal*. This is doubtless due to the fact that one cannot speak about *meaning* without thereby implying a form, pattern, or organization in whatever is being referred to. Letters are patterns, and combined into various words, they acquire symbolic value in meaning expression. The same is true for numbers, and we cannot overlook the logical proposition and syllogism in which a discernible pattern (Wittgenstein's propositional variables) is to be noted. When we see objects (Avicenna), their recognition value (meaningfulness) hinges upon the degree to which the form perceived in nature matches the form we already have in mind (*continued on* p. 32).

Table 1 A Survey of Western Intellectual History

Name and Life Dates	Construct	Definition	Causes			
			Material	Efficient	Formal	Final
Thales of Miletus (c. 640–c. 546 BC)	Water	Universal substance, making up all things and on which the world floats.	X			
Anaximander of Miletus (c. 611–c. 547 BC)	Boundless	Undifferentiated matter entering into the constitutive nature of everything in the world.	X			
Pythagoras (?–c. 497 BC)	Order	In nature, as reflected in numbers; indeed, "things are numbers!"	X_2		X_1	
Heraclitus (c. 540–c. 480 BC)	Logos [rationale]	Rational order in universe, so events follow a discernible [lawful] pattern [incl. "reason"].			X_1	X_2
Parmenides (c. 515–c. 456 BC)	Change is illusion	All appearances of change and motion are illusions. Reality is eternal and indestructible.	X			
Anaxagoras (c. 500–c. 428 BC)	Mind	A "thin and pure" form of matter, which orders other matter into what "is."	X_1		X_3	X_2
Empedocles (c. 493–c. 433 BC)	1) Four roots	1) Earth, air, fire, and water, as constituent elements out of which everything in the world is made.	X			
	2) Motion	2) Due to the interaction of love and strife.		X_2	X_1	
Hippocrates (c. 460–c. 377 BC)	Four humors	Blood, black bile, yellow bile, and phlegm; combine to determine a person's temperament.	X		X_1	

	Concept	Description	(1)	(2)	(3)	(4)
Democritus (c. 460–c. 370 BC)	1) Atom	"Uncuttable"—i.e., indestructible substrate, differing in shape; atoms move and collide.	X_1		X_3	X_2
	2) Nonrandomness	Because of rationale order, events and motions are never random; mechanical actions also take place.			X_2	X_1
Socrates (c. 470–399 BC)	1) Eidos	A single unequivocal designation in mind; hence an "absolute form" or essence; a universal!				X
	2) Good	Purpose or intention of an act.				
	3) Cause	Reason (grounds, premises, etc.) an action is carried out.				X
	4) One and many	Participation of universals in particulars.			X	X
Plato (427–347 BC)	1) Forms	Universal (a la Socrates); immaterial and eternal, signifying the "real nature" of things.			X	X
	2) Idea	That which is apprehended by intelligence.	X_1		X_2	X_2
	3) Pleasure	Instrumental; unrelated to the end sought.	X_2	X_1		
Aristotle (384–322 BC)	1) Syllogism	Sequencing of proofs in reason—i.e., logic.			X_1	X_1
	2) Soul	Living potentiality and actuality, incl. mind.		X_3	X_1	X_1
	3) Good	That at which all things aim [telos or "end"].				X
	4) Theory of causes	Material, efficient, formal, final.	X		X	X

Table 1 A Survey of Western Intellectual History (cont.)

Name and Life Dates	Construct	Definition	Causes			
			Material	Efficient	Formal	Final
Euclid (c. 300 BC)	Axioms	Definitional premises of a geometrical system, based on abstract order and common sense.			X_1	X_2
Epicurus (c. 342–270 BC)	Pleasure	Physical standard by which "good" is always to be judged.	X_1		X_2	X_3
Archimedes (287–212 BC)	Applied mathematics	Empirical demonstrations of mathematical reasoning, as in law of lever, body density, etc.			X_1	X_2
Lucretius (c. 96–55 BC)	Atomic materialism	No purpose in events, as all motions are due to the palpable flow of atoms, bumping into each other.	X_2	X_1	X_3	
Marcus Aurelius (121–180)	Freedom	From the human's capacity to assent or dissent in life's requirements. Virtue is self-control.			X_2	X_1
Galen (130–200)	Vital and animal spirits	God-created enlivening forces that interact with the ebb and flow of blood to stimulate life.		X_2		X_1
Ptolemy (2nd Century)	Geocentric universe	The earth is immobile and at the center of our universe.			X	
Origen (c. 185–c. 254)	Biblical fall of divine powers	Malignant powers of evil arose by free choice, in opposition to the good which God had created.		X_3	X_2	X_1

Thinker	Concept	Description			
Plotinus (c. 205–c. 270)	Soul	More perfect than body; lends meaning to sensations of body, organizing them via [Platonic] forms.		X₁	X₂
Saint Augustine (354–430)	1) Evil	Absence of good.		X	X
	2) Holy Trinity	Three divine persons in "one" God.		X	
	3) Free will	A self-cause; man must will to act.			X₂
Avicenna (980–1037)	Imagery	Possible only when the form perceived by a mental faculty matches the form manifested in matter.	X₃	X₁	X₂
St. Anselm of Canterbury (1033–1109)	First cause proof of God	All efficient effects have antecedent causes; hence, there must be a First Cause (i.e., God).	X		
Peter Abelard (1079–1142)	Predication	A precedent meaning, lending meaning to other things known (e.g., a genus to a species) [Aristotelian].		X₁	X₂
Averroës (1126–1198)	Unmoved Mover	Pure intelligence, outside of time, but within which motion occurs; both first and final cause of things.	X₃	X₂	X₁
Maimonides (1135–1204)	1) Metaphorical meaning	Grasping inexact symbols through a sense of preliminary conviction (i.e., faith).		X₂	X₁
	2) Negative theology	Description and coming to know God by elucidating His negative attributes (i.e., what He is not).		X	
Roger Bacon (1214–1294)	Experimentation	Empirical experience provides facts, which are far superior to reasoned explanations.	X₃	X₁	X₂

Table 1 A Survey of Western Intellectual History (cont.)

Name and Life Dates	Construct	Definition	Causes			
			Material	Efficient	Formal	Final
Saint Bonaventura (1221–1274)	Mystical transcendence	Mind is self-reflexive: It turns back on senses to contemplate them rationally and turns back on rationality to fix attention on God mystically.			X_2	X_1
Saint Thomas Aquinas (c. 1225–1274)	1) Argument from order	A divine intelligence must have been necessary to work out the order and purpose in nature: God.			X_1	X_2
	2) Truth	The final end of the universe, which is telic.				X
	3) Evil will	Due to erring reason.			X_2	X_1
	4) Last, fixed end	Never goods of the body or humanly created good, but only the vision of the Divine Essence.			X_2	X_1
John Duns Scotus (c. 1265–1308)	1) Simplicity in explanation	Unity of conception is to be preferred to plurality, which is never to be posited needlessly.			X	
	2) Being	As matter, which is more fundamental than form.	X			
	3) Contingent cause	An efficient cause made dependent upon an act of will, and therefore not a necessary action.		X_2		
William of Ockham (c. 1300–c. 1349)	Razor	An explanation involving fewer assumptions than an alternative is to be preferred at all times.			X	

Person	Concept	Description				
	2) Intuitive cognition	2) Sense experience of things; i.e., literal inputs of sensory experience.	X_1	X_2		
	3) Abstractive cognition	3) Mental reflections on experience, but comes only after intuitive cognition is input.	X_3	X_4	X_2	X_1
Copernicus (1473–1543)	1) Heliocentric universe	1) Sun is immobile and planets rotate in our universe.	X_2	X_3	X_1	
	2) Gravity	2) The result of matter, forming into spheres.	X_1	X_2	X_3	
Niccolo Machiavelli (1469–1527)	Imitation	Patterning one's behavior on another, by design.			X_2	X_1
Vesalius (1514–1564)	Human vs. animal anatomy	Empirical demonstration of similarities and differences, running counter to Galen's ratiocinations.	X_1		X_2	
William Gilbert (1540–1603)	1) Force	1) A magnetic or electrical field of attraction and/or repulsion.	X_2	X_1		
	2) Experimental method	2) Patterned on a machine analogue, in which the efficient cause played a major conceptual role.		X_1	X_2	
	3) Gravity	3) A reflection of the "force of attraction."		X		
Francis Bacon (1561–1626)	1) Scientific explanation	1) Must be confined exclusively to efficient and material cause meanings.	X_2		X_1	
	2) Proof	2) Inductive always preferable to deductive.		X		
	3) Simple natures	3) Nature has a limited number of forms, and every body can be understood as a compound of these.	X_2	X_1		
Galileo (1564–1642)	1) Law of uniform acceleration	1) Bodies of unequal weight fall the same distance in the same period of time.	X_2	X_1		

Table 1 A Survey of Western Intellectual History (cont.)

Name and Life Dates	Construct	Definition	Causes			
			Material	Efficient	Formal	Final
	2) Law of inertia	Moving bodies, free of friction, will move until deflected by something else.	X_2	X_1		
	3) Proof	Mathematics esteemed as a "new rationalism," but often empirical experimentation must supplement.			X	
Johannes Kepler (1571–1630)	Planetary motion	As elliptical, hence not conforming to the "perfection" thesis of circular motion.		X_2	X_1	
William Harvey (1578–1657)	Blood circulation	Did not "ebb and flow" as Galen had claimed, but was pumped through body mechanically by heart.	X_1	X_2		
Thomas Hobbes (1588–1679)	1) Motion	The central factor in life.		X		
	2) Thought	Computation—i.e., adding and subtracting ideas.		X_2	X_1	
	3) Scientific method	Find [efficiently caused] effects in the movement of events.		X_1	X_2	
	4) Geometry	The most abstract science of motion.		X_1	X_2	
	5) Proof	A hypothetico-deductive procedure.			X	
	6) Time	The "phantasm of before and after in motion."		X		
	7) Hard determinism	Denial of contingency causation.		X		
	8) Association of ideas	Lawful and capable of determination as one aspect of motion.		X_1	X_2	

Philosopher	Concept	Description				
René Descartes (1596–1650)	1) Proof	Via reason (deduction), not senses or imagination.			X₂	X₁
	2) Idea	Whatever the mind perceives directly.			X₁	X₂
	3) Innate idea	As the idea of perfection, which by definition is beyond man; hence, placed in reason by God.			X₁	X₂
	4) Free will	Judgment in the sense of assent or dissent.				X
	5) Reality	Like classical mechanics, with matter not needing to exist (except in God's eye); a machine world.		X		
	6) Animals vs. humans	Humans have souls, which are not machine-like but teleological; animals lack souls and are machines.		X₃	X₂	X₁
Blaise Pascal (1623–1662)	1) Thought	Independent from the body.				X
	2) As if . . .	Doubters in God's existence can act "as if" He does exist, and profit in this "wager."				X
Thomas Sydenham (1624–1689)	Empirical medicine	Complete commitment to the empirical approach of Bacon and Locke; "rational" discourse is abjured.	X₂	X₁		
Robert Boyle (1627–1691)	Pressure and volume in gases	Boyle's Law: At a given temperature, pressure is inversely proportional to the volume of a gas.	X₂	X₁	X₃	
Christian Huygens (1629–1695)	1) Centrifugal force	Due to the circularity of motion in planets.	X₂	X₁	X₃	
	2) Light	"Matter in motion;" waves of force that can summate to gain impact.	X₁	X₂		

Table 1 A Survey of Western Intellectual History (cont.)

Name and Life Dates	Construct	Definition	Causes			
			Material	Efficient	Formal	Final
Benedictus de Spinoza (1632–1677)	1) Will	1) Not free, but reason's ability to see a true idea.			X_1	X_2
	2) Emotion	2) In body, not mind, a passion that is ill-defined because we can have no clear idea of feelings.	X			
	3) Intelligible extension	3) Only ideas can be known certainly, not physical things—e.g., $3 \times 3 = 9$ must follow in rationality.			X_2	X_1
John Locke (1632–1704)	1) Idea	1) Comes exclusively from sensations (inputs).	X_2	X_1	X_3	
	2) Hierarchy	2) Ideas begin as simple and combine quasi-mathematically to form higher-level more complex ideas.			X	
	3) Mind	3) Begins *tabula rasa*, but can reflect on inputs and thereby mediate knowledge.		X_1	X_2	
	4) Knowledge	4) Perception of the agreement or disagreement of two ideas; dependent on frequency and contiguity.		X_2	X_1	
	5) Reality's qualities	5) Primary qualities reside in object (solidity, extension), and secondary qualities reside in mind (color, odor).	X_1	X_2		
	6) Intuition	6) Direct associative perception of agreement or disagreement of any two ideas; results in knowledge and furthers mental mediation [re. Ockham].	X_1	X_2	X_3	

		X₂	X₁	X₃
Isaac Newton (1642–1727)	1) Mechanization of nature — Brought laws of motion, attraction, and force into a unified picture, relying exclusively on inanimate materials, functioning with mathematical precision and without regard for teleological or aesthetic considerations [except, in his informal theory of the world as perfection due to its functioning "within God"].			
	2) Absolute time & space — An anchoring point against which motion and change could be conceptualized mathematically.			X
	3) Motion — A mathematical fiction based on Cartesian geometry.			X
Gottfried Wm. von Leibniz (1646–1716)	1) Free will — A willful act is not necessary, because its opposite does not involve a logical contradiction; hence, contingent causation is possible.			X
	2) Preestablished order — That God's plan and man's (free-willed) volition should coincide was predestined.	X₂		X
	3) Mind — Not *tabula rasa* but like a block of marble, with innate veins that experience must accomodate.	X₂	X₁	X₂
	4) Apperception — "Active" perception, in which humans must bring to bear an intellectual effort in order to "see" or otherwise grasp sensory input [contra-Locke].	X₂	X₁	X₂
	5) Monad — A substance, analogized from logical predication. Indivisible and complete; cannot be explained by reference to other substances. Due to preestablished order, monads combine to make up matter. Are also purposeful, according to Divine Plan.	X₂	X₃	X₃

17

Table 1 A Survey of Western Intellectual History (cont.)

Name and Life Dates	Construct	Definition	Causes			
			Material	Efficient	Formal	Final
Giovanni Battista Vico (1668–1744)	1) Man, as measure of all things	Whenever men can form no idea of unknown things, they judge them by what is familiar and at hand.			X_2	X_1
	2) Cultural stages	Age of Gods, heroes, and then man.			X	
George Berkeley (1685–1753)	Being	Is "being perceived." Contra-Locke, if mind fashions secondary qualities, it also fashions primary.			X_2	X_1
Joseph Butler (1692–1752)	Hierarchical order of human nature	Impulses, passions, and desires at base, with self-concern at higher level and conscience at the apex.			X	
Jonathan Edwards (1703–1758)	Will	Always determined by the greatest apparent good. Good essentially means "whatever draws the will."		X_3	X_2	X_1
Julien Offray de La Mettrie (1709–1751)	All animals are machines	Humans as well as lower animals are machines, differentially modified throughout the universe.	X_2	X_1		
David Hume (1711–1776)	1) Attraction	Principle of association: Ideas attract each other due to similarity, contiguity in time, etc.		X		
	2) Habit as cause	Contiguous experience united in imagination by habit leads to our impression of cause-effect.		X		

Thinker	Concept	Description			
	3) Prediction	Probability that one object or event will be in contiguous relation with another.	X_1	X_2	
	4) Determined judgment	Nature determines all of man's judgments, just as it determines his breathing and feeling.		X_2	X_1
	5) Value	Utilitarian view: That has value which ends in pleasure. To ask why pleasure is sought is absurd (i.e., nontelic).		X_2	X_1
Thomas Reid (1710–1796)	1) Cause in reality	Every event in material reality is efficiently caused.		X	
	2) Reason	As influenced by final causes, incl. truth, duty.	X_2		X
Jean Jacques Rousseau (1712–1778)	Social contract	The basis of society; the contract transforms man and makes him intelligent.	X_2		X_1
Adam Smith (1723–1790)	Sympathy	Putting oneself in imagination in the place of another to experience his feelings.	X_1		X_2
Immanuel Kant (1724–1804)	1) Synthetic a priori	A truth due not to definition (analytic) or to facts (a posteriori); necessary because no sense experience can confute them—e.g., mathematics.	X		X
	2) Categories of understanding	Twelve dialectically framed dimensions, which lend meaning to sensation (i.e., input).	X		
	3) Knowledge	Begins in experience, but does not arise from experience; categories make this possible.	X_2		X_1
	4) Intuition	A form, applied to sensory input, organizing it into a perception.	X		

Table 1 A Survey of Western Intellectual History (cont.)

Name and Life Dates	Construct	Definition	Material	Efficient	Formal	Final
	5) Sensation	Would be meaningless unless framed by space-time factors in perception.			X	
	6) Noumena (thing-in-itself)	Substantiality, outside space and time, accounting for objectivity in perception among human beings.	X			
	7) Phenomena	Appearances of things, made possible through perception and understanding.			X_2	X_1
	8) Faculty	Those aspects of mind that are active (e. g., reason and understanding).			X_1	X_2
	9) Judgment	Faculty of thinking the particular as contained under the universal [see predication, above].			X_2	X_1
	10) Will	Cause that acts in accordance with concepts.			X_2	X_1
	11) Concept	Contains its purpose within its form.			X_1	X_2
	12) Purpose	Concept of an object insofar as the concept is regarded as the cause of the object. Human reason provides the purpose in active conceptualization.			X_2	X_1
Antoine Lavoisier (1743–1794)	Table of chemical elements	Substrate elements of oxygen, hydrogen, azote [nitrogen], sulphur, phosphorous organized as substrate building blocks in the Lockean fashion.	X_1	X_2	X_3	

This page is a rotated comparison chart. The concept descriptions and the marking columns are transcribed below.

Philosopher	Concept	Description					
Jeremy Bentham (1748–1832)	1) Principle of utility	All actions of men are directed toward pleasures or away from pains.	X_2		X_1		
	2) Disposition or choice	The sum of motives, drawing man in different directions. One's will is his motive(s).	X_2	X_1	X_1	X_3	
	3) Intention	Consists of motivation (will) and knowledge of the consequences of an act. Only consequences are properly good or evil.	X_2	X_1	X_1	X_3	X_4
Johann Gottlieb Fichte (1762–1814)	1) World as self-construed	Rejection of noumenal construct of Kant; the world is an unconscious self-created construction.			X_2	X_1	X_1
	2) Self [or ego]	Posits [premises] own existence, then dialectically posits nonself as a "world of experience."			X_2	X_1	X_1
Georg Wilhelm Hegel (1770–1831)	1) Ground	Allows for unity because it provides relational contrast to self; hence, "not-self."			X		
	2) Spirit	Opposite to matter; freedom in essence; self-reflective and seeks to know and actualize.			X_2		X
	3) Alienation	Creations stand free in meaning from creator.			X_2	X_1	X_1
	4) Actualization	Makes mere possibility a reality; creation.			X		X
	5) Historical stages	History moves in stages, like individual life.			X		X
Arthur Schopenhauer (1788–1860)	1) Causation	Because the world is man's idea, all causal relations are formed by his understanding.	X_2		X_2		X_1
	2) Will	A force, making things what they are—e.g., our body is "objectified will." It lacks purpose and is desire personified (yearning, striving, etc.).		X_1	X_3		

Table 1 A Survey of Western Intellectual History (cont.)

Name and Life Dates	Construct	Definition	Causes — Material	Efficient	Formal	Final
Michael Faraday (1791–1867)	Field	An altered space, containing moving lines of electrostatic force.	X_3	X_2	X_1	
Auguste Comte (1798–1857)	Historical stages	History moves through theological, metaphysical, and positive stages.			X	
Peter Gustav Lejeune Dirichlet (1805–1859)	Function and variable concepts	Variable y is function of x when value assigned arbitrarily to latter automatically assigns value to the former. The x variable is thus "independent" and the y variable is "dependent" by (ratio) definition.			X	
John Stuart Mill (1806–1873)	Canons of logic	Agreement, residue, difference, and concomitant variation. Helped elucidate efficient causes in events.		X_1	X_2	
Charles Darwin (1809–1882)	Natural selection	Nontelic, accidental principle in organic evolution.	X_2	X_1		
Søren Kierkegaard (1813–1855)	1) Existence	1) A subjective predication in that life must be created through individual's decision and choice.				X
	2) Choice	2) A dialectical either/or in existence.				X
	3) Authenticity	3) Passionate self-commitment in the face of alienation (i.e., severance from past and future).			X_2	X_1
	4) Truth	4) A mode of existence; engagement, earnestness.			X	

	5) Individual	5) All that there is; humanity does not exist.				
Rudolph Hermann Lotze (1817–1881)	"From within" vs. "from without"	Behavior viewed "from within" is purposive; viewed "from without" it is mechanical.	X_1	X_2	X_2	X_1
Karl Marx (1818–1883)	Class struggle	An inevitable clash between alienated groups, defined by the internal contradiction of dialectical materialism unfolding in history.	X_1	X_3	X_3	X_1
Herbert Spencer (1820–1903)	Evolution	Change, from indefinite to definite, confused to ordered and equilibrated.	X_1	X_2	X_1	
Louis Pasteur (1822–1895)	Disease	Empirically shown to be due to micro-organisms.	X_1	X_2		
Thomas H. Huxley (1825–1895)	Life	Like a game, in which happiness depends upon knowing the rules; nature is amoral.			X	
Ernst Heinrich Haeckel (1834–1919)	Biogenetic law	Ontogenesis is a brief and rapid recapitulation of phylogenesis. No teleology is involved.	X_3	X_2	X_1	
Ernst Mach (1838–1916)	Phenomenological physics	The world consists solely of sense impressions. Scientific concepts are useful fictions, acting as names for complexes of phenomena.	X_3	X_4	X_1	X_2
Charles Sanders Peirce (1839–1914)	Mind	Irritation, arising from indecisiveness, causes a sensed uneasiness until a mode of action is settled on.	X_1	X_2	X_2	X_3

Table 1 A Survey of Western Intellectual History (cont.)

Name and Life Dates	Construct	Definition	Causes			
			Material	Efficient	Formal	Final
Eduard von Hartmann (1842–1906)	Evolution of consciousness in history	Telic; working from instinct to intelligence, to higher and higher levels of consciousness —i.e., from out of unconsciousness to consciousness.				X
William James (1842–1910)	1) Faith	Acting as premising [predicating] hypothesis, can make a possibility "come true."				X
	2) Tough-minded theorists	Sensationalists and mechanists.		X_2		
	3) Tender-minded theorists	Rationalists and free-willists.	X_1		X_2	X_1
	4) Truth	Working, permitting believer to have satisfactory relations with experience; "cash value" of an idea. Meaning is true if it leads to observable consequences. Ultimately, tied to sensations.	X_3		X_1	X_2
	5) Free will	Humans have; involved with chance and possibility, concepts that determinisms do not handle well.			X_2	X_1
Friedrich Wilhelm Nietzsche (1844–1900)	1) Life	In command of oneself; will to power.				X
	2) Will to power	Expansive, assimilating, positive, value-creating tendency in existence.		X_2		X_1
	3) Cause	A fiction—i.e., used by thinkers to account for things, but not necessarily in nature.			X_2	X_1

Philosopher	Concept	Description		X_1	X_2
	4) Value of non-truth	Certain untrue ideas are more valuable to knowledge than are true ideas.		X_1	X_2
	5) Human nature	Basically valuational, even though absolutes no longer exist. (God is dead!)		X	X
Jules Henri Poincaré (1854–1912)	Reality	Mathematical laws held to represent the sole objective reality for science.		X	
Henri Bergson (1859–1941)	1) Duration	Succession of qualitative time changes, melting into each other with no clear outline.	X_2	X_1	
	2) Self	Pure duration, including contradictions such as "caused" and "free." Dynamic and not static.		X_2	X_1
	3) Freedom	Relation of the self to the act it performs. It is a quality of the act, recognized that if same antecedent is enacted, same consequent follows.		X_2	X_1
	4) Intuitive method	Intellectual sympathy, whereby one understands an object by placing oneself within it [incl. people].		X_2	X_1
	5) Élan vital	Telic life force. History is a record of life trying to free itself from domination by matter.			X
Edmund Husserl (1859–1938)	1) Noeisis	Act of perceiving; essentially intentional.			X
	2) Noema	That which is perceived.		X	
	3) Phenomenology	Study of immediate spontaneous experience.		X_1	X_2
	4) Suspension of natural bias	To apprehend things spontaneously "as they are."		X_2	X

Table 1 A Survey of Western Intellectual History (*cont.*)

Name and Life Dates	Construct	Definition	Causes Material	Causes Efficient	Causes Formal	Causes Final
John Dewey (1859–1952)	1) Freedom	When a person acts through planning, he can vary the plan to meet changing conditions and has a conviction that choice and desire are involved.			X_2	X_1
	2) Human conduct	Can be understood only in terms of purpose.				X
	3) Art	Nature, organized; clarifies by intensifying experience for the human being.	X_2		X_1	X_3
	4) Scientific method	Based on controlled change and observation of the effects in an empirical context.		X_1	X_2	
George Santayana (1863–1952)	1) Preferences	Nonrational; things are good because we prefer them.	X_2			X_1
	2) Reason	Order in nature.			X	
	3) Beauty	Positive, intrinsic, objectified pleasure, attributed to things by a person as if it were a quality of the thing observed. Form is a major feature of beauty.			X_1	X_2
	4) Matter	Changes, but beauty in form does not.	X_1	X_2	X_3	
George Herbert Mead (1863–1931)	1) Meaning	Found in significant symbols, which emerge objectively in social relations. We need not be aware of these meanings in social relations.			X	
	2) Idea(s)	Anticipations of future expected actions, made possible via use of significant symbols.			X_1	X_2

Philosopher	Concept		X₂	X₁	X₂
	3) Role	Reflected appraisals that others define for us.	X₂	X₁	
	4) Self	Not unique, but a role defined via others.		X	
Harold Henry Joachim (1868–1938)	Coherence theory of truth	An idea is true if it fits in with other ideas to form a coherent whole.		X	
George Edward Moore (1873–1958)	Common sense	The sense of knowledge as experienced by the ordinary man, as embodied in his use of language.		X	
Bertrand Russell (1872–1970)	1) Mathematical truths	Are tautologies, having nothing to do with the "facts" of reality. Purely formal in nature.		X₁	X₂
	2) Primitive propositions	Undefined presumptions to which a proof must be reduced. Ultimate truths are impossible because everything is grounded in self-evidence.		X₁	
	3) Self-evidence	Not "merely" psychological factors, but at heart a special case of the tautology.		X₁	X₂
	4) Tautology	Propositions in opposition to empirical propositions. We know these without appeal to experience.		X	
	5) Correspondence theory of truth	Defined by events, not percepts. Truth of a proposition is established by its verifier (i.e., independently established evidence corresponding to the proposition).	X₂	X₁	
	6) Logic	In pure mathematics the only constants—giving relations between terms—are logical constants. Hence logic and mathematics are one!		X	

Table 1 A Survey of Western Intellectual History (cont.)

Name and Life Dates	Construct	Definition	Causes			
			Mate-rial	Effi-cient	Formal	Final
Ernst Cassirer (1874–1945)	Knowledge	Emerges as mind discriminates between external and internal senses and between sense contents and affective tones.	X_3		X_2	X_1
Martin Buber (1878–1965)	1) I-Thou	1) A living relation in the "filled present."			X	
	2) Love	2) A sense of responsibility of an I for a Thou.				X
	3) Encounter	3) The total accepting relationship between I and Thou.			X_2	X_1
Albert Einstein (1879–1955)	1) Relativity	1) There are no constants or absolutes in time, space, or motion. These concepts must be measured in relation to reference frames, which in turn can be arbitrarily assigned or presumed [predicated].			X_1	X_2
	2) Principle of equivalence	2) Tautological principle, allowing identities in conceptualization; hence gravitation *is* inertia, matter *is* energy, and gravity *is* curved space.			X_1	X_2
Curt John Ducasse (1881–1969)	1) Freedom	1) Of choice, consists in awareness of alternatives of choice being determined by one's preferences.				X
	2) Volition	2) Determined by the circumstances facing a person, the consequences he judges that volition to have. Freedom of will is "freedom of efficacy" and not necessarily freedom to act.			X_2	X_1

			X_2	X_1
Karl Jaspers (1883–1969)	Consciousness	A relationship of man to the world of ideas. Ideas are permanent and timeless (within time).	X_2	X_1
Percy W. Bridgman (1882–1961)	Operational definition	The concept studied is synonymous with the corresponding operations.	X	
Paul Tillich (1886–1965)	Ontological reason	The structure of mind that enables it to grasp and thereby to shape reality.	X_2	X_1
Martin Heidegger (1889–1976)	1) Phenomenon	1) That which shows itself in primitive disclosure.	X	
	2) Dasein	2) Commitment to life, concerned about existence.	X_2	X_1
	3) Authenticity	3) Choosing for the whole of one's past, present, and future being-in-the-world (i.e., Dasein).		X
Ludwig Wittgenstein (1889–1951)	1) Atomic facts	1) Incapable of analysis into more elemental facts.	X	
	2) Reality	2) Totality of atomic facts.	X	
	3) Modeling	3) Logical picture of a fact (a proposition).	X	
	4) Language	4) Cannot express anything that contradicts logic.	X	
	5) Tautology [contra-Russell]	5) Fails to say anything about the world, for it is true of all possible states of affairs (e.g., "It is raining, or it is not raining").	X	
	6) Logical necessity	6) Is the only form of necessity that does not "exist" in the world.	X	
	7) Words	7) Tools. They do not "stand for" objects.	X	

Table 1 A Survey of Western Intellectual History (cont.)

Name and Life Dates	Construct	Definition	Causes — Material	Effi-cient	Formal	Final
	8) Language games	Rules of procedure, having no necessary base in reality.			X	
	9) Meaning	The use of a word in a language; words do not reflect a mental activity.		X_2	X_1	
	10) Propositional variable	The form of a proposition, which remains constant even though the word content changes.			X	
Rudolph Carnap (1891–1970)	Meaningful languages	Either logic and mathematics (analytical propositions) or science (empirically verifiable synthetic propositions). Logical analysis is logical syntax.			X	
Karl Barth (1896–1968)	1) God	Always subject and never object. God cannot be known to reason, but only when the Divine Subject reveals Himself and wills a human response.		X_2	X_1	
	2) Christ	Because God regards man through Christ, only in Christ can man understand himself. To understand is to be as Christ.			X_1	X_2
Jean-Paul Sartre (1905–1980)	1) Other	Affirms his freedom by rendering us as an object. We assert our freedom by doing the reverse.			X_1	X_2
	2) Will	The manifestation of man's primordial freedom.				X

Alfred Jules Ayer (1910–)	1) Verification principle	1) Asserts that something has meaning only if the thinker can say what observations would lead to a verification of his concept.		X
	2) Self	2) A " logical construction " out of the sense experiences that constitute the actual and possible sense history of the individual.	X_2	X_1

Even beauty (Santayana) has been interpreted as a distinctive arrangement of preferential features of the environment, bringing pleasure to the beholder because of the resultant order—or the contrast of disorder!

We would be mistaken to check *every* construct in Table 1 under the formal cause simply because each thinker relied upon the patternings of language to express his ideas. We must not confound the meaning of the construct with the meanings of the words used to convey this construct. A similar problem arises with formal causation when we discuss teleologies. Although we have examples of "pure" final causation in Table 1, such as Socrates' conception of the good, or Aquinas' idea of truth, to think of a line of telic *behavior* in which the formal cause meaning is not included is virtually impossible. This is because the *that* in the "that for the sake of which" phrasing invariably comes down to some plan, scheme, mathematical assumption, frame of reference, analogue, and the like—all of which take meaning from formal causation. The major premises of syllogistic reasoning are therefore likely to be most readily subsumed under formal causation, but the fact that an organism reasons "for their sake" is what brings the final cause meaning into play.

The scheme we have employed in Table 1, for example, defines a pattern of interrelated meanings and is applied consistently across several different realms of knowledge. Yet it cannot be said to have a purpose as a useful frame of reference. There is a purpose for the scheme to fulfill as an end to *our* reasoning, but the scheme itself has no way of coming to an end—that is, *intending* its purpose. It can only "be" our purpose, as a metaconception. Thus Aristotle properly added the fourth cause to his scheme, because he could see that simply being a schematic pattern, or being part of a schematic pattern, did not necessarily mean that the object under description is behaving for the sake of this pattern.

Although Table 1 purports to present Western intellectual history, it contains important thinkers from the Middle Eastern world such as Avicenna and Averroës because of their acknowledged influence on Western thought. Had we included Oriental thinkers in Table 1 the scheme would have worked perfectly (Fehl, 1964). For example, the *Tao Te Ching* (author unknown, possibly Lao Tzu, c. 600 BC) makes reference to the *tao* (the "way" to various ends, combining formal and final cause meanings) as well as to the *yin-yang* principle (complementary forces of passivity and activity, implying formal and efficient cause meanings). Confucius' (c. 551–c. 479 BC) thought was heavily laden with formal cause meanings—for example, in his concept of *jen* (ideal human relationship) or *li* (rules of propriety). King-Sun Lung (c. 330–250 BC) had a formal-cause conception of universal names very similar to the Platonic-Socratic conceptions. And Han Fei (c. 280–c. 233 BC) had a Bentham-like utilitarian view of human behavior—that is, under the "two helms" of punishment (pain) and reward (pleasure) (implying material- and efficient-cause meanings). Space considerations prevent us from including many Oriental thinkers, but this restricted sampling should be enough to demonstrate that our scheme is viable in Eastern as well as Western thought. We now turn to four distinct lessons Table 1 has to teach us about the nature of theory and method in our intellectual history.

The Concern for Precedents

A significant number of constructs in Table 1 were aimed at finding the possible functioning of precedent assumptions, essences (God), definitions, and the like, "for the sake of which" other beliefs, existences, or necessary implications thereby followed. It is almost as if a common recognition occurs that to know anything demands a background fundamental of some sort. Philosophy is often characterized as a search for some such list of universals or first principles, which enter into all that can be known for all time. This search begins in the ordered universe of a Pythagoras or Heraclitus. We see it in the realm of Being postulated by Socrates and Plato, where Universals or Forms resided in a timeless existence to lend meaning to the round of lived days called Becoming. Related ideas occur in Aristotle's concern with the basic premises of syllogistic reasoning, in Plotinus' conception of the soul as organizer of meanings; and it is most helpfully defined for us in the *predication* construct of Peter Abelard, as adapted from Aristotle. This meaning has remained with us, suggesting that in all arguments or lines of thought a predicate frame must be presumed for meaningful extension to take place. The scheme of Table 1 acts as such a predication in this volume.

In the medieval period theologians commonly contended that life must be predicated on a creation by some Divinity, who could thus bring existence into being but was not Himself subject to creation (predication). This Supreme Being was called an Unmoved Mover (Averroës) or a First Cause (St. Anselm) because His existence was based on an efficient-cause "proof" which suggested God as the *first* precedent to all existence, who got the string of cause-effects underway. A claim often made in medieval times was "The First Principle does not fall under a Genus." That is, God cannot be subsumed by some overriding conception lending meaning to Him, because He *is* the Beginning (the Word). So unfathomable was this Creator that one could not directly stipulate His nature, but rather must resort to a *negative theology* (Maimonides, St. Bonaventura, St. Thomas Aquinas) to approximate an account (i.e., say what God *is not*). In more recent times the elevation of the Creator construct to the highest most active meaning-endowing position possible is to be seen in Barth's claim that God is always a subject and never an object.

Concern for basic assumptions is also to be seen in the descent of mathematics. Pythagoras took a mystical view of numbers as constituting reality in some inscrutable fashion, but Euclid's approach was quite straightforward in its preoccupation with the axiomatic assumptions one need presume for other meanings to follow sequaciously. Archimedes then applied this knowledge to the world of events, and later mathematicians built this "language" into a major descriptive tool. Ptolemy and Copernicus made different assumptions concerning the universe and employed mathematical language with equal success to support their respective views. Galileo's assumptions about motion and the consequent empirical checks he made were also to be supported with mathematical commentary, as were the proofs of Newton and others who followed in the rise of modern science. When Mach, Einstein, and others made even more dramatic changes in the predications of science, a truly revolutionary view of familiar reality was brought about. In this realm of mathematical reasoning we must not overlook Russell's discussion of primitive propositions, which also seem ever to "be there" as precedent assumptions in the reasoning of a logician or a mathematician. One literally can *never* reach back far enough to reason mathematically without making some primitive assumption!

This idea of underlying meanings which are ever "there" has reflected itself in the debates over the human image, and what we can or cannot know as human beings *from birth*. Sometimes a theological point is being made. For example, the innate-idea concept was employed by Descartes and Leibniz to say that certain life assumptions are compelling yet clearly beyond man's true understanding. How could man know that something like perfection was the case, unless a (perfect) God had put this idea into man's *imperfect* mentality. Another form of the innate idea was simply a mathematical proof. This ability to work out—entirely within reason—mathematical consistencies by what Spinoza called intelligible extension was proof enough for some thinkers that human intelligence was innately endowed with ideas (or ideations). The term *idea* becomes vague here, because it is as much the *process* of proving a point as the finished product of this process which is being referred to. Kant's categories of the understanding are pictured more in this "process" sense; though they are not precisely ideas, they do represent supposed innate capacities of the human mind to order sensory input and thus create meaning, which would include mathematical proofs.

Not all thinkers who held that mathematical reasoning was fundamental to human intelligence agreed that mind *qua* mind created anything. Both Hobbes and Locke believed that human thought was essentially identical to mathematical calculation, but this did not suggest a creative intelligence. The human intellect was said to be *tabula rasa* at birth; though it could calculate influences from out of the past as probabilities for the future, it could not be said to in any way conceptualize knowledge from birth. Poincaré's reality, as consisting of mathematical laws, is seen to function within human reason to influence the course of mind as much as it functions lawfully within inanimate events. The meaning-endowing role for mind is almost lost in the modern analyses of Wittgenstein, Carnap, and Ayer, who suggest that a word is not an expression of anything until that meaning is observed functioning, as an empirically demonstrable tool, preferably with a mathematically predictable regularity.

Teleologies Prompt
Introspective Theoretical Descriptions

When we speak of assumptions an "assumer," who predicates his line of argument or reasoning with some such precedent meaning, naturally follows. By focusing on the actual process of this precedent assumption to sequacious inference, deduction, induction, implication, and the like we necessarily tilt our theoretical account to a *first person* exposition. A theory written from the slant or point of view of the object of this theory (i.e., the "data" needing explanation) can be said to be written from an *introspective* theoretical perspective (Rychlak, 1968, p. 27). However, a theory can be written from the slant or the point of view of an observer, looking outward in *third person* terms, about "that, over there." In this case, we can speak of an *extraspective* theoretical perspective (*ibid.*, pp. 27–28).

When we speak about the philosopher's quest for universals, our theoretical reference draws us to the introspective perspective. A human being is making this intellectual effort to find the universal *that* for the sake of which mankind can know anything. But when we speak about the *fruits* of such intellectual effort, we may or may not be speaking about constructs in an introspective sense. Euclid's axioms, for example, are framed to show how the mathematician's line of reasoning may correctly proceed. Granting *this* (for the sake of this), *that* will follow. Each time the mathematician proceeds "for the sake of" such axioms, he may indeed begin a line of teleological reasoning, leading to newly created insights. However, because the axioms and the principles and proofs that can be drawn from these assumptions can be written down and listed for memorization by students of geometry, we can speak of them in third-person or extraspective terms. The product of what seems accurately described in final-cause terms (mathematical reasoning) becomes a nontelic formulation. We have shifted over to that nontelic reliance on formal causality, which is what happens in the theories of Wittgenstein, Carnap, and Ayer. This "double-duty" capacity of mathematics has led to considerable ambiguity in the formulations of so-called hard scientific theory.

Teleological description thus prompts us to employ an introspective perspective. The theological accounts of a Divine Power (efficient cause), creating the palpable world (material cause) to meet some predicating Divine Plan (formal cause) forces us to look for a Divine Intention (i.e., the introspectively viewed end of God's purpose). Though the theologians of history do not presume to speak for God, they clearly choose to see his purposes *in* events. What is the *intent* of sexual intercourse? If the modern theologian sees in this act *only* a Divine Intention for species procreation, any use of contraceptives would represent a subversion of "God's Will." If, however, the theologian can see in the sexual union an alternate Divine Intention —possibly the highest expression of love among human beings—he will be more likely to accept a contraceptive device as consonant with God's Plan, just as he has already accepted the use of the menstruation cycle as a "natural" form of contraception.

Our point here is not to weigh the respective merits of such theological debates, but to demonstrate that invariably a teleological account reaches for the introspective perspective. This is what Lotze meant when he noted that behavior viewed "from within" (introspectively) could be purposive, although "from without" (extraspectively) it might be described in a mechanical fashion. Aristotle (1952a) felt it was important to include in one's science the end to which events moved as telic causes (p. 500). He therefore theorized that leaves exist for the purpose of providing shade for the fruit on trees, and thus that "nature is a cause, a cause that operates for a purpose" followed (1952b, pp. 276–277). Nature had the good intelligence to fashion leaves for the sake of shading fruit. This was, of course, backed up by a God-in-nature view, but even in his discussion of motion and gravity we find Aristotle's telic formulations giving a sense of intelligence to inanimate events (what was later to be called animism, or the anthropomorphization of nature). For example, he explained the motions of objects as due to internal urges by all bodies to seek the places "proper" to them in the world design. This could be interpreted as the movements within a pattern we referred to above—that is, as lacking a true "that for the sake of which" intentionality. Newton's extraspectively framed theory of gravity retained this formal-cause meaning of objects moving within a mathematized space entirely without intentions. However, Aristotle lent a decidedly anthropomorphic (introspective) quality to his theory of gravity when he suggested that something like Newton's "falling apple" would be *seeking* its natural state—union with the earth from which it had sprung.

This (introspective) self-seeking or self-directing side of behavior is what free-will advocates have tried to capture over the centuries—not without some confusion. We can see in the constructs of Marcus Aurelius, Descartes, Ducasse, and William James the common view of human nature as being capable of self-control through assent or dissent. If there are predications in life, presumably one can either affirm or deny certain of these precedent environmental demands. Human beings are not simply efficiently caused, said John Duns Scotus, but rather behave according to *contingent* causes, which are actions determined by the foreseen consequences of a preselected action. In other words a final cause *is* a contingent cause. The behavior carried out depended on what the individual preferred to have follow "this" way or "that" way in the future course of his behavior.

Origen's account of the fall of divine powers suggested that these identities or beings could exercise a choice by dissenting from the God-created goodness of life. This dissenting capacity proved an embarrassment to theological teleologies because if God permitted dissent He must have indirectly allowed for or created evil. Yet how could the Ultimate Goodness (i.e., God) create evil? The strategy since this time in history has been for theologians to remove God as having a direct active tie to the creation of evil. For example, St. Augustine claimed that evil was the *absence* of good—that is, it was not an active principle but the absence of a God-created active principle. St. Thomas Aquinas claimed that an evil will was due to erroneous reason. If a man had all of the correct information (truth) and was reasoning properly, he could not do otherwise but end up in life where God would have wanted him if He had made the succession of choices for this man.

This common end of man's and God's decisions has led to difficulty in final-cause theory about the meaning of free will. It is complicated by the fact that since the time of the Greeks good has been presumed to be that toward which all acts intend (Socrates, Aristotle). The teleologist is therefore erroneously presumed to be speaking about good ends when he introduces his final-cause terminology. This has served theology well, of course, because the intention is to raise the likelihood of morally correct behavior in the human being. But if man is frozen into a Divine Plan, so that his free-will decisions must ever end up where God would have him end up, how can we speak of true behavioral freedom? Is this behavior not simply another one of those formal-cause within-the-design eventualities lacking in true purpose? Leibniz tried to resolve such questions by suggesting that a preestablished order existed, in which both man's volitional course of free action and God's divine ends happened to coincide. The problem of free will is yet to be solved to everyone's satisfaction.

There are a number of introspective telic accounts (see Table 1) that do not call for a necessary tie of decision-making to "good" outcomes. Machiavelli's patterning of the self on the actions of others does not imply that a good outcome is guaranteed, either for the self or for those manipulated as a consequence of this often "selfish" patterning. Vico's man as measure of all things, opting for the sake of what is already known to understand what is still possible to know, does not preclude a mean and harmful teleological outcome. Kant's conception of judgment allowed for the weighing of selfish and evil alternatives, although Kant tried to explicate more altruistic grounds for the sake of which behavior ought to proceed in his *categorical imperative.* Nietzsche's transvaluation of values made clear the idea that humans could opt for the very opposite of the traditional good. Santayana's preferential judgment suggested that reason may never be fully rational, and Sartre's teleological image of man is not dependent upon the concept of a "higher" nature.

Even so, introspectively framed teleologies are more likely to be theories aimed at retrieving the dignity of man than at painting him in the darker hues of existence. We see this in Adam Smith's concept of sympathy, which is the assured basis for equity in human relations, and in Buber's concept of encounter, in which by taking the feelings and outlooks of a "Thou'" into consideration, a truly loving relationship is achieved between people. As a general philosophical point of order, existentialism has underscored the harm that is done when we fail to appreciate the individuality of others. Kierkegaard and Heidegger wrote extensively on the need for people to be genuine, authentic, and self-responsible in interpersonal relations, taking the introspective slant of the other into account at all times. If one views the other as a third-person "object" of manipulation, he effectively turns the other into a freedomless being (Sartre). This is the great danger of extraspective conceptualization, and it can be seen as an ominous likelihood in natural-science models.

The Rise of
Extraspective Theory in Science

If there is a tie uniting ancient to modern thought in science it has to be the rationalistic heritage of mathematics—a realm of knowledge that we have already said can be described either introspectively (in the mental activity of a Euclid) or extraspectively (in his finished system). Historians commonly refer to prescientific or nonscientific philosophies as rational philosophies or simply as rationalism. The theological arguments about God's necessary creation of the good would represent such rational philosophies. However, we must distinguish between philosophical rationalism and mathematical rationalism, because the same style of intellectual speculation and conviction through self-evidence functions in both realms. Evidence of this is to be seen in the fact that very often the same individual made significant contributions to both realms of knowledge.

The origins of rationalism can be seen in Pythagoras' and Heraclitus' assumptions of an ordered universe. Pythagoras saw everything as made up of numbers, and Heraclitus provided the initial justification for a belief in natural law by speaking of a *logos* or the rationale in events. Thus, from these early days rhyme and reason in nature was presumed; usually it was said to be due to the creations of the Deity. This belief in natural lawfulness (*logos* or numerical regularity) then permitted subsequent thinkers such as Democritus and Lucretius to say there is no chance happening in the universe. Though Aristotle referred to chance as one type of cause, a chance event would not follow a fixed or predictable pattern (formal cause); hence, if one holds to a rationale order, chance as illusory follows. This concept of 100% predictability in events because of a Divine Plan was to represent a major tenet of both the philosophical and the mathematical rationalist for centuries. Hard determinisms therefore actually began in the teleological presumption that order in the universe is perfect due to its creation by a Perfect Being. As an informal tenet, even Newton held to this view (see Table 1). The other source of a belief in 100% determinism stems from the material cause. For example, if one sculpts the form of a human person from a block of marble, one will have a statue of a "marble person." The same goes for human beings giving birth to offspring of comparable flesh and blood and so forth.

Concepts of perfection have always preoccupied thinkers as one aspect of their concern for precedents. The Platonic realm of Being was a mental sphere housing perfect forms called universals. When Plato speculated on the nature of the universe he suggested that planets must move in a circular orbit, for this is the most perfect of all geometrical forms. Here was a case of uniting the precedents of philosophical with mathematical rationalism. God was a Perfect Mathematician, so why should he not construct a world in which the most perfect of geometric forms was prominently displayed? This tendency for scientific explanation to assume a world of geometric elegance and simplicity was to predominate for centuries; when Kepler eventually proved that the paths of planets were in fact elliptical, he had to confront severe criticism. Leibniz was also a rationalist in both the philosophical and mathematical sense. We do not scoff at his unquestioned mathematical brilliance (mathematical rationalism), but when he concluded that this was the best of all possible worlds because as a Perfect Being the God who made it could not settle for *less*, we find his philosophical rationalism humorous (as did Voltaire).

Yet from presuming the shape of a planet's orbit or the perfection of a universe is but a short step to the mathematical proof of a Pythagorean theorem or a law of gravity. Rational self-evidence is at play in both realms, and the sense of conviction achieved is psychologically identical. Another offshoot of philosophical rationalism stems from attacks made on this style of theorizing, as employed by the Scholastics. Both Duns Scotus' call for simplicity in explanation and Ockham's razor were aimed at denigrating such rational proofs of God as the First Cause (St. Anselm) or the argument from order (Aquinas), not to mention the irrationalisms of negative theology (Maimonides, Bonaventura, and Aquinas). The only basis for a belief in God, said Ockham, was faith based on *empirical* revelations (miracles). Hence fanciful rational arguments amount to nothing by comparison.

This empirical attitude in theology was a reflection of the historical mood, for a growing dissatisfaction with verbal argumentation in philosophy and the emerging sciences was evident. Roger Bacon had called for empirical experimentation as early as the thirteenth century, and by the turn of the seventeenth century there was a firmly established scientific method and *attitude* on the rise. One could no longer sit in his library and reason his way to the proof of a deity, a world of circular orbits, and a perfectly fixed finite heaven put there for the edification of mankind. The methodological procedures of William Gilbert and the telescope of Galileo were changing the ground rules for knowledge.

We should not naively assume that all rationalism had been foresaken at the birth of science. Mathematical rationalism continued and grew in importance, becoming, as we have already seen, the exclusive "language" of modern science (Poincaré, Carnap). The mystical side to Pythagoras had been dropped, but the world as mathematical reality became one of those monumental precedent assumptions that moved man's thought along to new and exciting implications. Although he was an empiricist, Galileo felt an experiment was essential only when mathematical reasoning failed to end in a clear-cut answer to some problem.

In construing the world as mathematical the early scientists were not trying to account for their own reasoning. The double-duty feature of theoretical perspective in mathematics becomes particularly important in this context. What we find is an *externalization* of the formal-cause properties of mathematics without worrying about the mathematician *qua* human being who is doing the reasoning, making the assumptions, drawing the implications, and so forth. The resultant extraspective perspective meshed beautifully with the machine analogue on which Gilbert was to base the scientific method. We observe "that," in its regularity, and track the effect some antecedent manipulation has on a consequent. This is the spirit of the new science, and Sir Francis Bacon was to give it philosophical justification.

Bacon led the attack on teleological description in natural science. He pointed to Aristotle's erroneous assumptions and the fallacious physical accounts that resulted. There were no reasons for why leaves existed on trees or why bones held up muscles on the frames of bodies. To speculate on these matters was to ensure a dead end for science, which could never hope to establish a (God's) purpose in nature through empirical investigations. Teleological factors are simply unscientific considerations, and such descriptive accounts of things must be confined to aesthetics and ethics (including religion) but *never* mixed into science. By this time in history the Inquisition had provided Bacon and others with sufficient grounds for separating science from religion—which is another way of saying science from teleology! Though other factors were involved, the burning of Bruno at the stake in 1600 was a terrifying example of what can happen when theology and science clash on an empirical question (in this case the finitude or infinitude of the universe). If one considers Bruno a poor example of the scientist, there was Galileo's unhappy experience with the Inquisition to ponder as well.

Teleology was definitely on its way out of scientific description in the seventeenth century. William Harvey's empirical studies in blood circulation, Boyle's work on gases, and Huygens' speculation on centrifugal force did not require a "that for the sake of which" phrasing. At least in their formal role natural scientists since the seventeenth century have discounted questions of why (the end or purpose in patterns) in preference for questions of how (the mechanism of patterns). Bridgman's operationism is the modern heir of Ockham's razor, and the verification principle of Ayer and other logical positivists is also aimed at avoiding anything that might circumvent a purely efficient or material cause explanation of experience.

British Empiricism enveloped the human image in mechanism, aided by the view of mind as mathematical—as in Hobbes' contention that "thinking is reckoning [calculating]." The British revived the "atomic" model that Democritus and Lucretius had first propounded. This interest in the elements that might go to make up anything has been a continuing preoccupation with thinkers across the ages. In one sense this tactic is really a variation on the search for precedent factors discussed above. Plato looked to universals (Being) which supposedly *lent meaning to* particulars (Becoming), and Democritus looked to particulars (atoms) which then constituted general things (all in the universe). There is a decided similarity here in the concern for what precedes what, with one side conceptual (Plato) and the other constitutive (Democritus). But in moving from conceptual to constitutive explanations, a necessary shift takes place in the theoretical account.

Whether we think of Thales' water, the boundless of Anaximander, the roots of Empedocles, Hippocrates' humors, or the atoms of Democritus and Lucretius, the descriptive perspective we *necessarily* assume is third person! We describe what "that" is made up of, even though we may include ourselves in this extraspective designation. The "that" of a final cause is *not* third person. As a premise, we must necessarily take the meanings of the "that" into consideration as we come at life to behave "for its sake." But in theories of elements—including the periodic table of Lavoisier—the account is entirely extraspective. We lose a sense of intelligence in the commentary that only the final-cause meaning can capture, as it moves our explanation to an introspective slant.

John Locke's model of human reason is the most complete phrasing of this third-person constitutive explanation of behavior. We make considerable reference to Locke in the succeeding chapters of this volume, but the point for now is that he viewed ideas as input copies of an immutable reality. Ideas were like water, filling a glass. The mind at birth was *tabula rasa* (no innate ideas), and only after several mental glasses had been filled from experience, did a combination of such simple ideas begin to form into more complex ideas. Mind was thus constituted in this hierarchical sense, with meanings contained therein having been input at the base of the hierarchy (Ockham's intuitive cognition). Talk of a Platonic universal lending conceptual structure (meaning) to some particular makes no sense at all in the Lockean view. Mind is not conceptual. It is a constituted organization of meanings, "associated" together based on principles of contiguity and the frequency of certain occurrences in the life history of an individual.

David Hume was to build on this conception of behavior, reducing telic considerations to efficient-cause repetitions (practice), worn into Lockean habits by way of pleasurable consequences. Bentham's principle of utility then completed the picture of human behavior as entirely mechanical, moved along by pleasurable motives calculated mathematically to result in "so much" satisfaction, assuming that such and thus were to be done. Judgment is relegated to an (efficiently caused) effect on this model, and behavior is presumed to flow with a sort of Heraclitian pattern of complete predictability. Human existence amounts to being a pattern, because there is no way to break out from the hierarchy as shaped by input factors. An exclusive formal causality has replaced final-formal causality. The modern cybernetic image of behavior is the epitome of British Empiricistic thought.

There were those who demurred from this efficent-cause image of human reason. Descartes drew a distinction between human behavior, which he claimed was capable of judging via a free will, and the behavior of lower animals, which he held to be without a soul and hence completely machinelike. (La Mettrie subsequently rejected this distinction). All of the free-will advocates discussed above can be taken as opponents of the mechanistic image of man. Undoubtedly the most sophisticated counter to British Empircism was Kant's. Continuing in the line of descent stretching back to Plato, in which something precedent (universal form) is assumed to lend conceptual meaning to something following (particulars of life), Kant argued that mind is *not* a *tabula rasa* or empty-container process to be etched upon or filled with experience in a fundamentally passive sense. The mind takes raw materials from sensation and, using certain innate categories of the understanding, lends meaning to this meaningless input. We return to a more detailed consideration of the Lockean-Kantian models of mind or behavior in Chapter 2.

Although the actual founders of the new science were not all committed to the machine analogue for human behavior (Gilbert is a prime example), the evolving explanations of nature combined with the empirical style of providing evidence for scientific arguments led to a significant confusion taking place. We now turn to this aspect of Table 1.

A Confounding of Theory and Method

There is no more significant development in Western thought than the rise of modern natural science. Let us review the essentials of this scientific revolution. We have said that it involved the dropping of philosophical rationalism, and the retaining of mathematical rationalism. Science also represents a strategy of logical steps to be taken in proving something to be the case, one that *must* end in an empirical demonstration of the claims on knowledge being made. This empirical test thrusts the attention of the scientist outward, so that to think of his observations in extraspective rather than introspective terms is considerably easier. As an observational frame we have noted that Gilbert employed a machine analogue. Machines are the quintessence of efficient causality, in which some antecedent factor moves or brings about a consequent factor over time. The basic meaning of an efficient cause involves this cause-effect occurrence over time. One cannot have an efficient cause explanation outside of a time frame. But this is not true of a logical proof, in which circles are readily drawn within circles (the "this-is-a-man" circle is drawn within the "all-mortal-beings" circle) and a *necessary* conclusion is visualized immediately, *within time* (a man in the inner circle *must* be a mortal being). There is no antecedent force bringing about this evidence as a consequent over time. If this be true, as we look outward to track events across time via Gilbert's method, is the proof we seek always and only of an efficient-cause nature (e.g., that a certain temperature level causes ice to melt), or could we be engaged in a *logical* line of evidential development as well?

This question is extremely important, because if we overlook the fundamental contribution of noneffficient-causality in our methodological verifications, possibly we may misinterpret that very evidence on which we claim the rigor of our science depends. Surely we appreciate that not every idea a scientist has is *true*, simply because he has experienced or formulated it. This holds for all reasoners, of course, but by stating the obvious here we underscore the fact that a distinction exists between one's theory and the means or manner whereby he establishes a sense of acceptance or conviction in the truth of his theory (recognizing of course that "truths" are never fixed for all time). This sense of conviction obviously requires a second step, an activity by the theorist that is not precisely theorizing but more on the side of proving or providing evidence in support of or against the theoretical statement he has framed (hypothesized, suggested, thought up, etc.).

Therefore we must distinguish between *theory* and *method* in knowledge accural. A *theory* is the uniting of meaningful relations between designated terms (constructs, abstractions), often framed as propositions or hypotheses (Rychlak, 1968, p. 42). Theoretical statements can be framed with great seriousness or purely fancifully and playfully, without regard for the actual truth-value of the speculation. Theoretical propositions are eventually tested, however, and the *methods* by which they are assessed take us into our second step. There is a purely cognitive method that can be used, entirely within mind, as typified by the rational tests of both philosophical and mathematical rationalism. The evidence suggested in such cognitive tests we have called *procedural* (ibid. p. 74), for it allows thinking to go forward by steps of plausibility and common sense. Joachim's presentation of the coherence theory of truth (Table 1) defines procedural evidence for us as a formal-cause conception. We test our ideas against the internal consistency of other ideas, and then, because of the plausibility afforded by the common sense of the totality, we proceed in thought with confidence if not conviction. The search for ultimates and related assumptions discussed above is an effort based on procedural evidence. The power of mind to know self-reflexively seems a compelling truth, although in recent philosophies (Wittgenstein, Carnap, Ayer) this has been stated as the power of mind to know language rules.

Natural science was to call for more stringent evidence. It did not drop reliance on procedural evidence, of course, because this is what mathematical rationalism relies on. Since, as Russell has taught us, logic and mathematics are at one level identical enterprises, we must appreciate that logical analysis is also based on procedural evidence. But what science called for was an extension, a development beyond complete reliance on procedural evidence to the employment of a *research* method. The experiment was a "trial run" in which the theory as framed might be put into an extraspective frame and tested for its capacity to meet empirical reality. Philosophical rationalism could retain those theories of geometric simplicity and perfection in the heavens only because the reasoners in this tradition blinded themselves to the opportunity of looking "out there, to the evidence of observation." Rather than logically arraying or controlling his alternative explanation of things and then, based on such clearly stated premises, making a prediction to the facts of empirical reality, the philosophical rationalist (Scholastic) made arguments "from definition" much as we have done above in the example of logical reasoning (with the circles and the necessary conclusion of *a* man's mortality). Thus granting a Perfect Being as architect, perfect figures in planetary motions *must* follow. Hence all empirical observations to the contrary are erroneous.

This new form of evidence that science ushered in is best called *validating;* it is based on the prearrangement of events taking place in a prescribed succession and based on the predicted and subsequently observed outcome of this succession, either supporting or failing to support the prediction (hypothesis) made (*ibid.*, p. 77). The prescribed succession of events we recognize as our experimental design (trial run) and the phrase *control and prediction* is well suited to describing the essential features of validating evidence. Russell's discussion of the correspondence theory of truth (Table 1) encompasses validation, because one's hypothesis (prediction) must correspond with the subsequent outcome of his experimental paradigm. Of course a scientist often stumbles onto a discovery he has not predicted. In this case he is usually working on some hypothesis that provides the Nietzschean negative value of contrast, for what he sees is not what he expects to see. Dropping the incorrect hypothesis, he then pursues the new discovery in the more typical fashion of controlling and predicting over several studies (called *cross-validation* of scientific findings).

We thus have *three* terms to consider in the generation of scientific knowledge: *theory, procedural evidence* (via cognitive method), and *validating evidence* (via research method). Having distinguished these terms, we can now analyze an historical development that blurred the distinction between what was a theoretical- and pro-cedural-evidence-based proof and what was a validation in the con-trol-and-prediction sense across a time span. It begins in the recog-nition that mathematical proofs are no more dependent upon time than are logical proofs. Russell has shown that mathematics and logic are identical ratiocinations. We can have mathematical assump-tions made about time, of course, as in Newton's (absolute) mathe-matical time (Wightman, 1951, p. 116). But the sense of conviction of a mathematical or logical proof does not wait on the prescribed suc-cession of events to generate "data" in support of one's contention, as is the case in validation.

When Russell tells us that, in the final analysis, all of mathemat-ics (as well as logic) reduces to tautologies he is saying that this is a procedural-evidence form of truth, one that functions outside of time flow. Though we take time to "figure out" or to diagram a mathe-matical proof, the role of time itself in this proof, as in the sense of conviction that follows, is nonexistent. Tautologies are immediately apparent (once perceived), true by definition, and analyzable into a repetition of the inherent "given." They cannot be efficiently caused because they are like internally consistent patterns, which are only to be recognized and not brought about or made to happen. Mathe-matical proofs are therefore always coherence theories (procedural evidence), relying on the internal consistency of a tautology to bring conviction rather than on their correspondence with externally (effi-ciently) caused events.

Even so, thanks to Newton, the machinelike methodology of Gil-bert, the laws of motion proposed by Galileo, and the efficient-cause emphasis of Francis Bacon were all brought together into a formid-able coalition that was to make Newtonian formal causes into nat-ural-science efficient causes. What Newton did was to take the more dynamic approach to geometry that Descartes had begun and apply it as a model to the description of the universe. Cartesian geometry was no longer a Euclidian study of the innate properties of given shapes, for it had acquired dynamic moving propensities. A circle for Euclid was a plane figure, bounded by a line, all of whose points are equidistant from a given point called the center. For Descartes the circle became a plane figure, bounded by a line formed by the *motion* of a point moving in such a way to be always at a constant distance from the center point. Hence when Newton looked at the universe, he, following Galileo's lead, fixed on the *moving* parts—literally the motion—which were then mathematized (*ibid.*, pp. 88–89).

Although we are still in the realm of mathematics when we speak about the motion of points in a line, the implication here is easily drawn that movements are taking place *across time,* particularly because subsequent predictions made from the mathematical theory and proof (procedural evidence) were seen to take place in the time-bound world of real events. When Newton's law of gravity not only explained the motions of known planets and stars but also predicted the existence of stars that were not yet seen (only their presumed gravitational fields were seen to operate on the gravitational fields of observable stars), the impact of this purely mathematical conception on our interpretation of moving reality was inestimable. Numbers were coming to life! To presume that Newton's *formal-cause* proofs (theoretical speculations outside of time and based on procedural-evidence) were actually *efficient-cause* proofs (validation by way of empirical study within actual time) was an easy misunderstanding.

When we look at Newton the man (introspectively) and attempt to describe *his* behavior what do we see? Based on the plausibilities and tautologies of mathematics, Newton works out a *fiction* called gravity to account for certain mathematical relations that hold between points in motion (or one point in motion relative to a fixed point). The fictionalized construct is *not* theorized as somehow created by antecedent events, generated within matter, bursting forth to push consequent events across the face of time. Motion is happening as a given in mathematical space, which means all at once in a formal-cause complex of theoretical mathematical relationships, tested on the basis of tautological self-evidence (procedural evidence). Whether gravity *is* happening in the real world or not is irrelevant to Newton's mathematical ratiocinations. Unless we are prepared to say that the firing of neurons (material-efficient causes) in Newton's brain "caused" the style (formal cause) of his mathematical reasoning, an efficient-cause explanation of Newton's law of gravity is absurd. Newton personally appreciated that he was not speaking about efficient or material causes in his entirely mathematical law of gravity. He once noted in a letter to a colleague Richard Bentley: "You sometimes speak of gravity as essential and inherent to matter [as a material-efficient cause construct]. Pray do not ascribe that notion to me; for the [material-efficient] cause of gravity is what I do not pretend to know" (*ibid.,* p. 101)).

Of course we do not wish to suggest that Newton was in any way an idealist in his recognition of a difference between the events that mathematical theory accurately tracked and the reality itself. He was most assuredly a realist, who put his trust more securely in the efficient-cause regularity of natural lawfulness as Deity-based (see Burtt, 1955, p. 289) than he did in the formal-cause regularities of mathematical reasoning (*ibid.*, p. 214). As fundamentally more empirical than Galileo (see above), Newton looked to Gilbert's experimental methods as the ultimate source of truth. So long as a scientist could empirically demonstrate natural lawfulness—helping the effort along the way through mathematics—he was doing his job properly. He was in the empirical realm of *how* things really happened even though admittedly (and properly!) he could not always say in his formal theory *why* these predictions held up in the world of palpable events. Though admirably empirical, this Newtonian brand of "natural" science actually survived on the blurring of a necessary distinction in the generation of knowledge.

Newton's concept of gravity was purely formal, a mathematical prediction of moving points in timeless mathematical space. But, thanks to the efficient-cause machine paradigm of Gilbert's scientific method and the call for efficient (and material) cause description in natural science by Bacon, a *confounding* took place between what was *method* (Gilbert) and what was *theory* (Bacon, Newton). There were two general results of this confusion: (1) *Only* efficient causes were assumed to be involved in the Newtonian explanation of gravity (motion, movement, then force); and (2) Observations of natural phenomena made through experiments were given an exclusively efficient- (and material-) cause explanation. Although presumptions of natural lawfulness and mathematical regularity had nothing to do with the efficient-cause meaning, a "natural scientist" looking (extraspectively) out to the "facts" could take these unnamed presumptions in his approach and report back *nothing but* the flow of efficient cause across time. His method confirmed his presumptions again and again, for it could not do otherwise. For him to see other than efficient causes in events that took place over time was impossible *in principle*. As Burtt so marvelously expressed it, the Newtonian physicist thereby succeeded in making "a metaphysics out of his method" (*ibid.*, p. 229).

Further evidence of the confusion of (formal-cause) theory with (efficient-cause) method can be seen in the altered interpretation of the statistical "function" that has taken place in our time. Leibniz adopted the convention of referring to a stipulated relationship between two numerical values as a functional relationship. This was a mathematical (formal-cause) term, and when Dirichlet subsequently enlarged on the meanings of an independent and a dependent variable in this functional relationship, he in no way departed from formal- and final-cause phrasing. Thus, as noted in Table 1, an independent variable (x) is one to which the mathematician assigns a value *at will,* and the dependent variable (y) is thereby automatically given a value thanks to the functional (ratio) definition existing between variables.

When this mathematical conception was analogized to the machinelike sequence of validation, in which an experimenter *does* lay his hands on an antecedent "variable" to (efficiently) cause a predicted effect on a consequent "variable" over time, the confusion between formal- and efficient-cause terminology was furthered. The convention in experimentation has since been to call the antecedent variable the *independent* (the one the experimenter manipulates) and the consequent variable the *dependent* (because it supposedly records the effects of an antecedent efficient-cause). Here again, though the mathematical definition of a function is the "relations among numbers occurring *all at once,* by definition" (outside of time factors), the definition of an experimental function is the "impact of an antecedent event on a consequent event." Because experimental data are not only conceptualized but tested in terms of statistical theory (mathematics), the ironic fact is that with each formal-cause proof of this sort the "empirical" observer believes that he is finding further evidence for a universe of *only* efficient causes.

The confounding of methodological with theoretical meanings in science was not serious so long as descriptive accounts were limited to inanimate or subhuman descriptions. But when La Mettrie and others took the mechanistic ideology to the extreme of claiming that human beings were *proven* to be machines, a counterforce began to take place in the history of thought. Kierkegaard and Nietzsche pointed to the subjectivities of life, noting the importance that such ephemeral, often unprovable, and telic factors have on the meaning of life as actually lived. Bergson and Husserl attacked the methods of science, claiming that an alternative method along intuitive lines must be fashioned if human nature was to be properly circumscribed. Such criticisms have merit, although the solutions proffered are not always helpful. We will have our own recommendations in the following chapters. For now, we simply observe in consonance with such critics that when a method precludes the testing of teleological hypotheses it forgoes the claim of being an objective vehicle for the exercise of evidence. A method that dictates acceptable terms for theory is as repressive as a theory that dictates terms for a method. The notorious Inquisition made the latter error; one must hope that modern science will not repeat history by making the former error.

Concluding Suggestions for an Objective Psychology

We must surely be impressed with the common efforts expended by the thinkers listed in Table 1. Across all areas of knowledge we see the search for precedents, the concern with rational orders, and the call for increasingly convincing evidence. We cannot escape the suggestion that there is a common humanity reflected in the intellectual preoccupations of the individuals surveyed. Analogizing to Wittgenstein's "propositional variable," we might say that the form of human nature reflected in Table 1 remains constant although the intellectual content of our thinkers has varied. Yet looking at the major approaches to descriptive explanation in the *science* of psychology today, the conceptual tools now in use would not seem to permit an accurate and fair presentation of the totality of Table 1. As a supposed "natural" science, psychology has committed itself to only *certain* of the Table's contents. How *objective* has this commitment allowed psychology to be in the description of human behavior?

No suggestion is made here that psychology need answer problems framed by theology, or art, or critical philosophy. Harking back to our double-duty feature of mathematics, we can now appreciate the important distinction between the problems as put and then solved *and* those who put such problems for solution. The introspective theorist can see a commonality across all members listed in Table 1 because he is thinking in terms of the *people* sampled there, working as identities to ask and then to answer questions. Is not the greatest form of objectivity to begin our quest in the description of man by looking at all men? We cannot study like a natural scientist if we are studying *the* natural scientist and find his ground rules tripping us. We have to rethink the rules of scientific description, fully appreciating the problems a seventeenth-century scientist faced, but arraying these alongside our twentieth-century problems, arrive thereby at a plausible resolution for our time that will meet the needs of both yesterday and today.

The common themes of Table 1, of which we have only scratched the surface, serve as continuing guidelines for the approach to psychology that is developed in detail in the next several chapters and more generally in later chapters in this volume. We follow this procedure on the assumption that there is nothing in Table 1 that is undeserving of our interest and attention. These are our "data" calling for description, and we return to them whenever appropriate as ready examples for the reader's edification. All of the constructs mentioned in Table 1 are products of a *human* mentality; and in that spirit of complete objectivity which typifies the genuine scientist, we hope to suggest needed conceptual changes so that psychology might more accurately describe the kind of individuals who populate Table 1.

Summary

A survey of 104 outstanding individuals in the history of Western thought is described in Chapter 1. Major conceptions were taken from these thinkers and arrayed into a table, in which definitions and an analysis of these constructs into material, efficient, formal, and final cause meanings were accomplished preliminary to the drawing of certain conclusions regarding the descriptive terminologies surveyed. Study of this table revealed a general concern for the precedent assumptions or premises made in all areas of thought. Thus, whether a theologian or a mathematician, the outstanding thinker of history has devoted considerable attention to the predications of his speciality. Teleologists have formulated theories from an introspective slant, whereas the rise of modern natural science, which has been in principle opposed to telic description, has tilted this frame of reference to an extraspective slant. Efficient-cause and material-cause accounts are invariably extraspective in nature, whereas final-cause description demands an introspective theoretical statement. The formal-cause meaning is used most often by thinkers, undoubtedly due to the fact that "to conceptualize" involves patterning and organization—for example, in the idea or the image of a mental content.

The rise of modern science is shown to parallel a shift in the demands for evidential support in accruing knowledge. Rather than resting his case with the plausibilities of procedural evidence (coherence theory of truth), the modern scientist demands that an additional step be taken to validate theories experimentally (correspondence theory of truth). Although the theories are what attract our interest, the fundamental issue dividing science from other realms of knowledge has to do with *methodological* factors. Though science employs procedural evidence in the mathematical justification it gives to observed events, the translation of such purely formal proofs into experimental designs has caused scientific evidence to appear to support *only* efficient- or material-cause "findings." The formal-cause basis of mathematics, as well as the final-cause reasonings of the mathematician, are rendered incomprehensible in this blurring of distinctions between theory (what human behavior is like) and methodological proof (cognitive methods of the scientist as well as research methods of science). The psychologist more than any other scientist must not let his thinking be prejudiced by the historical remnants of a seventeenth-century struggle between theology (telic accounts) and natural science (mechanistic accounts). The goal is set for a psychology to be unfolded in this volume in which all of the concepts expressed in the historical survey are readily subsumed and taken seriously as "data" reflecting the human condition.

References

Alexander, F. G., & Selesnick, S. T. *The history of psychiatry: An evaluation of psychiatric thought and practice from prehistoric times to the present.* New York: Harper & Row, 1966.

Aristotle, *Metaphysics.* In R. M. Hutchins (Ed.), *Great books of the western world* (Vol. 8). Chicago: Encyclopedia Britannica, 1952. Pp. 499–626. (a)

Aristotle. *Physics.* In R. M. Hutchins (Ed.), *Great books of the western world* (Vol. 8). Chicago: Encyclopedia Britannica, 1952. Pp. 257–355. (b)

Becker, H., & Barnes, H. E. *Social thought from lore to science* (2 vols.). Washington, D.C.: Harren, 1952.

Burtt, E. A. *The metaphysical foundations of modern physical science.* Garden City, N.Y.: Doubleday, 1955.

Edwards, P. (Editor in Chief), *The encyclopedia of philosophy* (8 vols.). New York: Macmillan and Free Press, 1967.

Eves, H. *An introduction to the history of mathematics* (3rd ed.). New York: Holt, Rinehart & Winston, 1969.

Fehl, N. E. *History and society.* Hong Kong: Chung Chi College Publication, 1964.

Forbes, R. J., & Dijksterhuis, E. J. *A history of science and technology* (2 vols.). Baltimore: Penguin Books, 1963.

Frazer, J. G. (abridged by T. H. Gaster). *The new golden bough.* Great Meadows, N.J.: S. G. Phillips, 1959.

Kondo, H. *Albert Einstein and the theory of relativity.* New York: Franklin Watts, 1969.

Magill, F. N., & McGreal, I. P. (Eds.). *Masterpieces of world philosophy* (2 vols.). New York: Salem, 1961.

Russell, B. *Wisdom of the west.* Garden City, N.Y.: Doubleday, 1959.

Rychlak, J. F. *A philosophy of science for personality theory.* Boston: Houghton Mifflin, 1968.

Rychlak, J. F. Lockean vs. Kantian theoretical models and the "cause" of therapeutic change. *Psychotherapy: Theory, Research and Practice,* 1969, **6**, 214–222.

Rychlak, J. F. The human person in modern psychological science. *British Journal of Medical Psychology*, 1970, **43**, 233–240.

Rychlak, J. F. Communication in human concordance: Possibilities and impossibilities. In J. H. Masserman & J. J. Schwab (Eds.), *Man for humanity: On concordance vs. discord in human behavior*. Springfield, Ill.: Charles C Thomas, 1972. Pp. 91–101.

Rychlak, J. F. *Introduction to personality and psychotherapy: A theory-construction approach*. Boston: Houghton Mifflin, 1973.

Sarton, G. *Introduction to the history of science* (4 vols.). Baltimore: Williams & Wilkins, 1927. [Reprinted 1968]

Schwartz, G., & Bishop, P. W. (Eds.), *Moments of discovery: The origins of science*. New York: Basic Books, 1958.

Wiener, P. P., & Noland, A. (Eds.), *Roots of scientific thought*. New York: Basic Books, 1957.

Wightman, W. P. D. *The growth of scientific ideas*. New Haven: Yale Univeristy Press, 1951.

CHAPTER TWO

On Meaning and Models in Human Behavior

The Meaning of Meaning

Meaning as a Relational Concept

In beginning the historical survey in Chapter 1 through the employment of four causal meanings we put off a question that must be confronted: What do we mean by the meaning of anything? This question and the issues it generates recur throughout many of this volume's topics, but we must now deal with it in a preliminary way as one of those predication investigations that so preoccupied the historical thinkers listed in Table 1. If we were to follow the procedures employed in Table 1, the term *meaning* would be listed as primarily a final-cause designation, with probably a second check for the formal cause. The word *meaning* has Anglo-Saxon roots in "to wish" and "to intend." This suggests a directional pointing or inference whereby some "given" heralds "something else," joining the two factors into a patterned totality. Language expressions are framed in this way in that words act as patterned instrumentalities for the meaning extensions a speaker or writer is intending to convey. Meanings therefore always reach beyond the specific and suggest, imply, connote, or clearly signify something beyond simply the given. This means that a *relation* or *relationship* is being emphasized whenever we speak about the meaning of anything. Most experts in this area of study are prone to call meaning a *relational* term, though what is meant by this varies considerably among them (see Creelman, 1966).

There are several ways of speaking about the relations involved in meaning, but we can best organize theories of meaning into two broad classifications based on our introspective versus extraspective distinction. Extraspective relations can be seen in what we have called the tie between a given and the something else to which it points. We might call the former an *item* and the latter its *referent*. Thus, a word like *dog* or *chein* can be termed an item bearing a stipulated relationship to the animal referent we recognize in perceptual imagery as "a certain kind of four-legged creature." The reason we call this relation extraspective is because it is formulated in third-person terms, so that whether or not the person understands French we have a clear tie of "that" collection of letters (*chein*) to "that" image of a canine animal. In this sense language terms are purely formal designations, patterned signs that—strictly speaking—lack a purpose as all formal-cause designs lack purposes. Even so, because there *is* a relational tie here and because many students of language in psychology refer to these extraspective relational ties as reflecting meaning, we have to consider them as such. Let us refer to such theoretical usages as being *sign meanings*. A sign is merely a surrogate image or collection of letters, numbers, and so on, that stand for something else (Cassirer, 1944, pp. 80–84). A sign meaning is therefore important to the process of conveying meanings, but it takes no active, creative, or expressive role in this process.

Turning now to the introspective view of meaning, we might consider the plight of an English-speaking person who does not understand French. Though he knows the word [item] *dog,* as well as its referent, canine image, he does *not* find meaning in the word *chein* (aside from idiosyncratic meanings that he might ascribe to the word in an autistic sense). In this case we are viewing a slightly altered relationship between the individual in the *process* of understanding or conveying meanings and the items he has available (or that he can fashion) in this active process. We learn, therefore, that an item can be related to introspectively just as it can be tied to extraspectively. The heuristic scheme of four causes employed in Chapter 1 is a perfect example of this multiple relatedness in all meanings. We began by defining the four causes as sign meanings (pp. 5–6). These relational ties of four items to four different referents stand whether or not a person is employing the causal terms as a sort of premising meaning for his theoretical conceptions. But when we now look at the thinking of 104 outstanding individuals we find that the relation between a premising or predicating causal meaning and the specific concept that each thinker actually framed makes the *distinctive* difference in what is being meaningfully expressed. Even when the thinker coins an original expression, it is framed through our highly abstract metaconstructs of the four causes.

There is still a meaning relation here, of the sort one finds between the major and minor premises of a syllogism, with the flow of meaning-extension developing from the former to the latter. Using the signs as instrumentalities, this active extension of meaning takes place in the thinker's (introspective) cogitations. Let us refer to this usage as dealing with *symbolic meanings.* A symbol is never a mere surrogate, but is framed to mean something itself and in a new, unique, or idiosyncratic way (Langer, 1948, p. 46). Symbolic meanings *are* teleological in that they *do* intend something or purport to express something. We say "they do" when in fact the action must always be found introspectively in the framing of a symbol *by a person.* Symbolical expression is therefore by definition an introspective theoretical account of meaning. For example, when the number 7 is used by people as a surrogate for *seven things,* this shorthand notation serves a purely sign function. However, when 7 is taken by the individual as representing *luck,* there is a new meaning emerging in the use of this number that was not initially defined as a referent of this item. Of course, in time the numeral 7 can be employed for *luck* by others routinely, who do not really believe (intend that) luck follows this item as an inevitable referent. But at this point in time we would say that the symbolical meaning has given way to a sign meaning. In this sense Jung (1956) has accurately observed how true symbols must "come alive" in the telic activity of a person (or a people).

We might now define meaning as follows: The word [item] *meaning* refers [relates] to the relations between items and their referents as well as to the relations between a user of such meaningful ties and the items he employs for the understanding of experience. An *item* can be a verbal language term (letter, word, sentence, etc.) or a purely sensory image (visual, auditory, etc.). Its relation to a referent signifies [points to] something of importance, relevance, or general understanding to the person involved or to an aspect of his personality. The proviso *to an aspect of his personality* is added because we do not wish to foreclose on the possibility of unconscious symbolical expressions developing, which express significant meanings that are not consciously understood. The term *meaningfulness* can be used to describe the extent of significance, import, or general understanding that an item has for an individual. *Meaningfulness* is thus a measure or metric of the extent of meaning—i.e., clarity, centrality, import, value—the item holds for the individual or part-personality structure.

Extraspective formulations of meaning are framed so that all individuals can learn their relations. We can think of this as an objective meaningful relation between items and their referents. The more generally understood an item is among members of a specified group (language system, culture, civilization, etc.), the more objective is that item. However, when we now look at the introspective appli- cation of meanings we can see that people often use items (which the culture has defined) quite incorrectly or as colored by their pecu- liar (symbolical) connotations. Because two people use the same word does not mean that they are expressing the same meaning. As meanings become idiosyncratic and difficult for all members of a specified group to understand, they can be termed *subjective* (Rych- lak, 1968, pp. 22–27). Newly created terms are thus born in the sub- jective meaning-realm of an individual who strives to say something that cannot yet be stated in the language terms made available by the culture in which he lives. He thus coins a new term, often through a precedent analogy or root-language term. In time, through use of examples and by explicating the concept he has in mind, the individual can make his subjective notions known, and to that extent they become objective. If he cannot, although they continue to have subjective meaning for him, they fail to become objective items for the rest of us.

In speaking of meaning as a relation we are forced to think about the polar factors involved in this relation—what we have to this point called the item (one pole) and its referent (a second pole). Is this tie between the polar ends of a relation something that comes about through the joining of separate and distinct *unipolarities*? Or is the seeming conjoining of unipolarities illusory in some cases, so that what seems to have been "joined" parts into a totality is actu- ally a totality from the outset, now drawn out into intrinsically related parts? In short, can meaning be—at least sometimes—a bipo- larity (or multipolarity) in which implicit relations between terms exist *by definitional implication*? The conceptualization one has of language expression, thinking, and human behavior in general will vary depending upon whether he views the relations of meaning as always unipolar identities brought together into a relationship, or whether he views at least certain of these ties as essentially discri- minations between bipolarities having intrinsic unity.

A unipolar theorist would claim that we have an item [word] *dog* as a unipolar designation, joined through association or practice by the individual to an image of a canine animal as a unipolar referent. These unipolarities have been joined definitionally by the culture "to mean" something, and this is all any meaning-relation can amount to—a tying together of unipolar designations. A theorist who

would favor the bipolar view of meaning would question the universality of such unipolar bondings and point to word relations such as
up and *down* or *left* and *right*. Can we truly learn what *up* is without
necessarily understanding what *down* is? Is this really just an associative bonding of unipolarities, or is there something implicit in the
relational tie of at least certain bipolar meanings in language usage
(as well as in perceptual imagery, because one image can often bring
to mind its opposite quite spontaneously—for example, in a dream
or a reverie). In a sense the unipolar theorist of language fixes on the
poles *per se*, whereas the bipolar theorist keeps his attention focused
on the relation *per se*; and because there are these two sides to meaning, we cannot say which theoretical emphasis is more correct.
Indeed, we are back to precedents, and as with all such predicate
assumptions, we find that they have a history.

Dialectical versus Demonstrative
Theories of Meaning: The Beginnings.

The first *recorded* philosophical debate of history stemmed from our
unipolarity-versus-bipolarity issue (Magill & McGreal, 1961, pp. 1–2).
Thales had begun philosophical explanation by claiming that all
things originated from water.[1] His student Anaximander felt that
such a unipolar substance, having infinite existence, would have
made impossible the multiplicity of what we now call elements to
have arisen in the universe. His concept of the boundless was substituted as a kind of neutral undifferentiated stuff that was no more
wet than dry nor no more hot than cold. But such identities as this
did exist in life, and hence Anaximander argued that they were held
together by an opposition within the very nature of things—for
example, air is cold, fire is hot, water is moist, and so forth. The
boundless could exist as a sea of opposition because it served a
relational or "in-between" role in this theory of substantial reality.
   This theme of opposition as a bonding agent was carried further
by Heraclitus, who added the idea that opposites were fundamentally in strife, and therefore life was a dynamic affair. Heraclitus
liked to point out that we could not grasp certain meanings unless
these meanings were oppositionally united. For example, *justice* is
meaningless unless we also recognize that injustices exist. Stressing
that the totality of dynamic events to be seen within the rationale

---

[1] The names and theoretical constructs mentioned in Chapter 2 without specific
life dates or book citations are taken from the historical survey of Table 1 (pp.
8–31).

could not be unipolar and clear, Heraclitus observed: "Things taken together are wholes and not wholes; being brought together is being parted; concord is dissonance; and out of all things, one; and out of one, all things" (Magill & McGreal, 1961, p. 13). We see here the widely cited one-in-many or many-in-one thesis. The celebrated universality of the Graecian intellect was in part due to this capacity to see interlacing meanings in all things (Becker & Barnes, 1952, ch. 4). A comparable thesis had arisen even earlier in the philosophies of India and China (Nakamura, 1964). There is no evidence of direct cultural transmission here, but none is required because, as with the causal usages discussed in Chapter 1, the question of unipolar versus bipolar interpretations of meaning confronts any thinker—Eastern or Western—once he begins to contemplate this intricate subject. The one-in-many thesis doubtless had separate origins in the history of thought.

Introduction of the term *dialectic* to represent the bipolar emphasis in theories of meaning is proper at this point. There is no one definition for this term, as there is no one school of dialectical usage (see Rychlak, 1968, 1973, 1976 for other treatments of this topic). In the present context a dialectical formulation of meaning would always look to the *relations* between things (items and their referents) or to the opposite of what was being pointed to as *the* referent of a word, and so on. This kind of reverse emphasis to what is being expressed naturally results in a Heraclitian dissonance and confusion from time to time. The dialectical side to meaning is always *implied* by the fact that some given meaning is being affirmed in a statement or proposition. In the example of Heraclitus given above, to stipulate *justice* implies *injustice*. He also spoke of *up* implying *down*. We say *implying* here, but of course the dialectical thesis holds that justice-injustice and up-down are literally one (and also many, considered separately). When a unipolar designation is made, as in the case of a noun such as *tree*, for example, the bipolarity would occur on the question of its existence; in this case the opposite implication would be *nontree* or *no tree*.

There is a fluid quality about opposite meanings in this sense, because we cannot stay with a single "what-is" item without thereby suggesting literally any number of "what-is-not" items. We can ignore alternatives as implied opposites of other opposites, of course. But the inkling and the potential for meanings to "move on" to something else is always there. This motile side to dialectical meaning-generation was used by Heraclitus and Empedocles to say that change itself depended upon the clash of opposition. Empedocles narrowed this clash down to love and strife, which he felt caused all motion in the world through a kind of running confrontation in events (leading some modern thinkers to suggest that he had anticipated the Freudian eros-versus-death instinct theories). The concept of dialectic has altered in this treatment. It has been given a motivating-power role in explanations of life, and a sort of "thrust" quality of efficient causation has therefore been added to the purely formal-cause meaning of opposition within a totality (rationale).

Running counter to the dialecticians of early Greece, the philosophy of Parmenides emphasized the clear and the certain over the multiplex and the dissonant. Although he proffered several arguments favoring the view that nothing changes (itself a kind of unipolarity or fixedness in events), Parmenides is more respected for his beginning efforts toward the founding of what is now called formal logic. Starting his philosophical career as a Pythagorean and much drawn to the clarity and unipolar certainty of numbers, Parmenides framed what might be seen as an early version of Aristotle's Law of Contradiction. Parmenides was attacking the dialecticians when he observed that we can never prove that what-is-not is, because a nothing cannot be a something. Aristotle was later to prove the major force in formal logic, and he stated this unipolar rule of thumb as, "A is not not-A." Note that the focus has again shifted, for now we are considering the matter of *proof* in relation to dialectical meanings.

The early Greeks were much taken with this question of how to know truth in the generation of knowledge. Modern science takes root from their efforts. When Socrates and Plato came onto the historical scene a group of teacher-philosophers had formed called the *sophists*. These men were dedicated to instruction, the pursuit of knowledge, and in a more practical vein, often served as what today might be called lawyers before the courts in service of a client. Facile and clever, if a little superficial, the sophists relied on a procedure of questioning others to extract desired admissions from them in debate or during court appearances. The cunning placement of certain questions enabled a sophist to establish some point he had set out to prove or to teach to a student. This procedure of questions-and-answers was termed dialectical discourse or the dialectical method, and it is said that as a young man Socrates was once befuddled and made to look the fool by the crafty questions of a sophist who had the young man's head spinning, answering affirmatively to points with which he did not agree. Though he found the dialectical procedure of questioning useful in his subsequent philosophical ac-

tivities, Socrates more than anyone else helped to make the word
sophist stand for a specious, insincere, or fallacious reasoner
(debator).

The sophists had perverted dialectic, said Socrates, by pointing
it unidirectionally (unipolarly) toward a predetermined end, whereas
the essence of true dialectical discourse is to be open to *any* direction as the meanings being explored unfolded. The participants need
have no idea of where their discourse would take them at the outset.
Even if they were to begin in error, through a continuing question-
and-answer procedure in which questions were prompted by the
meanings opposite to the answers "just given" by the student, Socrates felt that he could come to know truth; for were not truth and
error *one* (many-in-one thesis)? If the student took position A, following Socrates' first question, as questioner he defended position
not-A; if the student had answered with position not-A, Socrates
would have gone to position A. It was all the same in this procedure
of intellectual inquiry. Plato later showed how this procedure occurred in the thinking of a single person, thus removing the absolute
necessity for two people in the dialectical effort. When we wrestle
with a problem calling for creativity, mulling things over in an internal examination of the factors concerned, we behave very much like
the Socratic exploration carried on by two people. Through an internal dialogue of opposition we gradually stumble upon a "possible"
then "likely" then "certain" course of knowledge. Plato held that we
could reason our way from the lived realm of *Becoming* (our normal
life experience) to the realm of *Being* (where the universals, pure
truth or forms resided) by way of such a dialectical procedure.

Unfortunately, in recording the Socratic dialogues for posterity,
Plato has given many individuals today the attitude that Socrates
was himself a sly questioner who manipulated his counterpart in the
discussion through clever questioning in order to end up at a predetermined point in the discussion. The step-by-step frozen quality that
Plato's account gives us of the dialogues reads like a scenario that
had been written and then enacted. The clearest example of this
would be in the questioning of Meno's ignorant slave boy, who
comes, through Socrates' leading questions, to construct a difficult
geometrical proof. The reason Socrates conducted this exercise of
leading questions was to show Meno that the boy, who had no idea
of what direction to take in this problem solution, could find a proof
if only the proper questions were raised for him in an intellectual
inquiry. The questioning is not so oppositional in this case, because
the various "dead ends" that a completely open dialectical discourse

would engender are obviated as a kind of "shortcut" effort. In his preliminary remarks before the demonstration, Socrates makes clear that in the case of a newly created discovery he would be as ignorant as the slave boy. His partner in the dialectical questioning process would also be ignorant of the needed directions to take, but because the dialectic is open to *all* implications and each statement suggested in the discourse can be evaluated as it emerges, in time a gradual progression to truth would be accomplished. To interpret Socrates as using questions like prongs to extract what he desired from a counterpart in the discursive exchanges he so loved is therefore quite improper.

Aristotle (1952) gave the most sophisticated counter to dialectical examination as a proper method of true science (p. 142). He felt that the dialecticians were falling into the same specious argumentation that the sophists had engendered. He could not see how mere talk could alter the fact that two individuals were floundering in error "from the outset." To clarify his criticism, Aristotle proposed a scheme for describing how all human beings reason. This is the well-known syllogism, in which thought is said to move from a major premise (e.g., all men are mortal) through a minor premise (e.g., this is a man) to a conclusion (this man is mortal). In the tradition of Parmenides, Aristotle was trying to work out some formal rule of how such syllogistic steps might be taken without erroneous conclusions being drawn. We might emphasize here that the discussion of meaning at the opening of Chapter 2 is relevant to the structure and sequencing of propositions in the syllogism. That is, meaning continues to be seen as a relational term. Within a proposition (statement), there is the relation of an antecedent (men) to a consequent (mortality) term. There is also the relation of one proposition (premise) to a second, culminating in the implied meaning-enrichment of man as mortal in the conclusion. Meaning-relations take place within and across propositional statements, just as they take place between a single item (word) and its referent.

Having outlined the syllogism as a model for human reason, Aristotle next distinguished between two ways in which thinking might proceed, basing his distinction entirely on how a person comes to believe in the meaning(s) of his major premise(s). This is where all reasoning must begin, and what meanings are to be furthered necessarily flow from the meanings with which one begins as a major premise or "predication" (a term Aristotle as well as Peter Abelard helped fix into our vocabulary). In contrast to Socrates, Aristotle now states that any discourse that *begins* in error *ends* in error. As in his elucidation of the law of contradiction, Aristotle effectively draws a unipolar distinction between truth and error (i.e., these two meanings are *not* intrinsically related).

When we reason *dialectically,* said Aristotle, we begin a line of meaning-extension by posing an alternative to a partner in discourse (or to ourselves, in that Platonic sense of internal dialogue mentioned above). Based then on what the partner selects as a meaningful alternative, the discourse proceeds to some eventual conclusion even if the opening question (which delimits the area of study) as well as its answer are entirely specious. To ask a question may appear to legitimatize the area of investigation, but this is not necessarily true—as it was not in the case of the notorious query drawn from the Middle Ages of "how many angels can dance on the head of a pin?" Aristotle therefore argued that dialectical examination rests on *opinion* rather than primary and true major premises. When Socrates asked a student some opening question such as What is the nature of honesty? there is no necessary reason to suspect that his fumbling answer will put the discourse on the road to truth. The student's answer might encompass truth but it could just as well embody error; and according to the rules of the syllogism, an erroneous major premise (all men are honest) must of necessity result in erroneous conclusions.

Fortunately, as a counterweight to the dialectical pattern of reasoning, Aristotle contended that we also have a *demonstrative* reasoning capacity. This more ironclad premising of the syllogism is possible because we can delimit our predications to a unipolar designation. Aristotle called such premises "primary and true," and there are two general cases of this type: a truth by tautological definition —for example, when we state "All bachelors are unmarried males" —or a truth that states the "facts" as empirically (demonstrably) known. Centuries later Kant (1952) called the former analytical propositions and the latter synthetical propositions (p. 16). An analytical proposition's truth value can be determined through analysis of the meanings of its antecedent and its consequent terms. The meaning of bachelor thus embraces the meaning of unmarried male tautologically. A synthetical proposition must be shown to be true empirically because the antecedent and consequent terms are not tautologically related in this fashion. For example, claiming that firstborn children make excellent community leaders in adulthood is a synthetical tie of birth order to community leadership. We cannot find the truth here by an examination of concepts, but must go to empirical experience and prove our claim through some form of validation.

Aristotle recognized that dialectical examination helped in determining the truth value of analytical statements. He specifically noted that everyone—including the scientist—must resort to dialectical strategies when major premises could not be established as "primary and true" at some given point in time. But he adamantly denied that a dialectical examination of synthetical propositions had merit. Why? Because such examination relied exclusively on what we have called procedural evidence—or the coherence theory of truth (Joachim). As one of the first tough-minded philosophers of history, Aristotle's theory of knowledge is pitched at the need for validating evidence— or the correspondence theory of truth. One's statements had better meet the facts, said Aristotle, or all he knows for certain is that a subjective and opinionated view is making sense for the present. But the work of knowledge has not yet been completed. It is significant in light of modern developments to note that Aristotle's commitment to methodological rigor did not dissuade him from describing events teleologically. He founded a science of biology but also assigned purpose to nature.

Dialectical versus Demonstrative Themes in Western Thought

We can now employ Aristotle's terminological distinction to retrace our steps across history, pointing to the various uses thinkers have made of either a dialectical (bipolar meanings, reasonings) or a demonstrative (unipolar meanings, reasonings) formulation of events.

In general the mathematicians of history have served to elevate the role of demonstrative reasoning, especially since about the time of Descartes. But a mathematical inclination was not always anathema to a dialectical outlook on the nature of things. The "father of mathematics," Pythagoras, who held to the view that the world was comprised of numbers (as reflections of universals), *also* believed that all things were comprised of opposites and nothing in nature was therefore simple and unmixed (atomic or unipolar) (Untersteiner, 1954, pp. 19–26). Pythagoras was simply reflecting the widely held one-in-many thesis of his age, and though he had many so-called mystical thoughts on the role of numbers in life, his mysticism invariably drew from a dialectical rationale (a fact that is true of all mysticisms). The general belief is that the revival of (neo-) Pythagoreanism in Italy during the fifteenth century influenced Copernicus, in the idealistic sense of the universe conforming to a series of mathematically precise (unipolar) laws (see Burtt, 1955, p. 42). Unfortunately, by this time the dialectical side of Pythagoras had been lost to history. Mathematicians, like all natural scientists, now wanted to explicate what "is" and not what oppositionally "might be" (is not).

There are other indications of a dialectical emphasis in mathematics. The word *algebra* derives from the title of an Arabic treatise (about 825 A.D.) on the subject by *al-Khowarizmi*, which translates "the science of the reunion and the opposition" (Eves, 1969, p. 195). We use the more familiar and equally correct translation "transposition and cancellation" today, but there is a decided implication here of the one-in-many thesis, with the view that mathematical reasoning harmonized the totality through joining the many subparts by oppositions. Today we do not conceptualize the numbers flanking an equation sign as reflecting bipolarity, because the sign represents a tautological identity between the two values. Though identical, there are many ways of viewing the "same" (unipolar) equation by way of moving values about in opposition (bipolar) to each other. We might ponder at this point whether this facility would really be possible in an organism that could reason *only* demonstratively.

The concept of a substrate unity that in turn might constitute all things is to be seen in the atomic conceptions of Democritus and Lucretius. Along with unity in mathematics, this atomic notion has been of immense historical importance to the rise of demonstrative concepts and reasonings. Here we have a belief in the reducibility of all things to a certain unipolar substrate (i.e., atom as the uncuttable or indivisible hence unipolar unit), which in turn formed into complex assemblages of things, reflecting as a consequence (efficient cause) of this assemblage an overriding pattern of recognizable order. Though Heraclitus had seen his rationale (order) as a mixture of clashing oppositions, Democritus and Lucretius changed this multipolar conception to one of a concatenation of unipolar items, joined fixedly into a hierarchy of determinate order. By determinate in this case we mean unidirectional. Events moved as they did because they were "made" to work in that way "and that way only" (law of contradiction). Both Democritus and Lucretius were easily led into a hard-deterministic position based on their demonstrative interpretation of the rationale. This perfection in the rational order was subsequently buttressed by theologians who ascribed things to a "Grand Mathematician" (God).

Of course, this did not mean that theology could rest with a demonstrative tactic. Anyone who studies religious theory will be impressed by the frequent dialectical formulations of many theologians. The foremost dialectician of the Roman Catholic Church is undoubtedly Saint Augustine. He not only called for the free use of dialectical argumentation to buttress our faith in God's existence (even if this amounted to sophistry!), but he also resolved some problems in theological conceptualization through dialectical constructs. The Holy Trinity is the most celebrated of these solutions (Jaspers, 1962, pp. 196–197). Negative theology is also a dialectical formulation.

Theologians and others frequently rely on dialectical formulations to deal with the question of free will. Origen's concept of the fall of divine powers was of this sort. The good—as created by God —would have no meaning without its opposite evil as a potentiality. It was simply a question of time before the opposite possibility was affirmed by Divinities who had this option open to them as dialectical beings. A similar theme is seen in the philosophy of Marcus Aurelius. He argued that the nature of life demanded that each person either affirm (assent) or deny (dissent) certain directions in which meaningful events were unfolding. Life events are not unidirectional, but they call for a contribution from the individual in this sense; this self-initiated affirmation or negation is at the root of human freedom. In the seventeenth and eighteenth centuries we see this theme in the writings of Leibniz. How different this is from the unidirectional determinisms of Democritus and Lucretius! Once we begin our line of thought with a dialectical rationale, there is room in conceptualization for the inconsistencies, the turn of events, the so-called indeterminate features of life (Rychlak, 1976).

Throughout the Medieval period and into recent times the concept of dialectic was also cultivated in the practices of oratory, polemics, and disputation. Rhetoric as a skillful use of speech in persuasion has generally been interpreted as a form of "acceptable" sophistry, much to be admired in individuals who have such abilities (propaganda and modern advertising are further steps down this often sophistical path). In the evolution of law and courtroom procedures a form of questioning arose to counteract such rhetorical manipulations—especially as pressed by a witness before the bar. The witness in today's courtroom is therefore not given the freedom of an open dialogue with the attorney who is putting questions to him in quasi-cybernetic fashion. Witnesses are instructed by the court to behave demonstratively—to answer questions with a unipolar statement of meaning. The questioner must make this possible by limiting his questions to relevant (unipolarly precise) points. Equivocation, qualification, and related human practices of a more dialectical nature arise in the courtroom only through the exchanges of the opponent attorneys, each of whom is out to manipulate the proceedings to reach their predetermined ends of guilt or innocence (amounting to a form of Socratic sophistry when viewed from either end). The jury should weigh whatever evidence is presented; make allowances for the sophistry in the advocacy procedure; and through a more open colloquy, arrive at a reasoned affirmation of guilt or innocence.

The theories of history which we are prone to call "mystical" because we have no way of conceptualizing them via customary logic, often come down to a variant of the dialectical theme. For example, Jung (1953) found that the alchemists believed every form of matter contained within its identity an inner antithesis (p. 268). Lower identities therefore contained the potentials for higher manifestations of their being. As in the transubstantiation of a lower matter (bread and wine) into a higher matter (body and blood of Christ) in the rites of the Catholic Mass, the alchemists tried to convert lead into gold as a concrete proof of God's existence. At least the earliest alchemists tried. In time the symbolical meanings of the alchemical investigations were lost to posterity and the essentially spiritual practices of the founders were eclipsed by purely materialistic efforts (symbols into signs). Another example of mysticism is to be seen in the introspective religious practices of Bonaventura, who theorized as follows: Man can obviously turn back on his senses and contemplate rationally what he receives from vision, hearing, and so on. He is therefore no slave to illusion. But if he can turn back on the senses, why can he not *also* turn back on his rationality and fix thereby on the nonrational? This is possible, said Bonaventura, and he asked that the effort be made to turn inward and away from the rational to a mystical communion with God, a Being so fantastic that He transcends all rational insight in any case.

Saint Thomas Aquinas cast a jaundiced eye at the excesses of dialectical formulations. Though he gave some credence to negative theology and held, as Aristotle had, that all people reason both demonstratively and dialectically, Aquinas did *not* feel it was proper to give free vent to dialectical speculations. In this he countered the more Platonic tradition of Saint Augustine. Aquinas sought to reason from premises that were primary and true (analytical) to the indubitable conclusion in support of God's existence. Arguments from the first cause, order, and purpose in nature represent his efforts in this regard. This intellectual approach was to be called Scholasticism, and it became a form of philosophical rationalism that was eventually to conflict with the rise of natural science in the seventeenth century.

The Age of Science was already presaged in the thirteenth- and fourteenth-century theologies of John Duns Scotus and William of Ockham, both of whom were instrumental in raising the stature of *empirical* demonstration in religious debate. Duns Scotus opposed Scholasticism and belittled the role of analytical philosopher in theology. Explanations must end in simplicity and unity, said Duns Scotus; intricate and subtle accounts of God's existence are therefore suspect on the face of things. Ockham was highly suspicious of the power of mind to know anything about God's existence that was not directly perceived in experience as a miracle (the only legitimate proof, for it was empirical). He distinguished between the *intuitive cognition*, which takes in such empirical information from the environment, and the *abstractive cognition*, which deals with such information mentally after it has been acquired. All knowledge is therefore grounded in experience, outside of mind; hence no amount of introspection or fanciful argumentation concerning God's existence can equal the weight of one empirical demonstration (miraculous happening). All else is and must remain based on faith. A more modern rephrasing of this theme occurs in Karl Barth, who denies that God can be known through human reason and looks to Christ as a corporeal manifestation of proof. Ockham's contention that all knowledge is extramental was to provide an important justification for the school of thought known as British Empiricism, of which he must be seen as a precursor if not an actual founding father.

The denigration of mind reflected in the theologies of Duns Scotus and Ockham did not extend to mathematics, which in the sixteenth and seventeenth centuries was making great strides. Dialectical reasoning was obviously in jeopardy when a great dialectical effort like Descartes'—in which he opened his examination with the question How do I know that I exist? and went on from there in the style of a Platonist—could be completely misunderstood and unappreciated by the man who made it. Descartes (1952) felt that dialectical logic was completely devoid of meaning (p. 17). Though he accepted free will and spoke of assent and dissent in the style of Aurelius, he like most mathematicians—with notable exceptions like Pascal (see Cassirer, 1944, p. 27)—did not think of such mental judgments as due to reasonings by opposition in meaning. Descartes would be placed on the tougher side of the line of descent stemming from Aristotle through Aquinas, because he really was not rejecting the possibility of a dialectical reasoning capacity in man; it was not in principle impossible to reason in this fashion, but when carried out it was without objective meaning. When we move on to the mathematicians of British Empiricism, the *very possibility* of an organism that can reason dialectically drops from view.

The preliminaries for a demonstrative image of human behavior were put down by Bacon and Gilbert, both of whom placed Ockham's intuitive cognition uppermost in defining science as an inductive procedure. The scientist must ever seek to find what "is" in experience as "truth" and avoid what "is not" as an "error." An error is thus basically *nothing*. Only truth has existence. Copernicus and Galileo now add to this strategy the extraspective utility of mathematical reasoning, which is in this sense the quintessence of demonstration. A mathematician may reason dialectically in thinking through his proofs, but as sketched on the blackboard there is no more beautiful example of demonstrative reasoning than a mathematical derivation (recall our double-duty role for mathematics, p. 36). Thomas Hobbes was to take this conception and apply it directly to human reason. Thinking, said Hobbes, is nothing more than "reckoning"—that is, the addition and subtraction of ideas. This meant *all* thinking, so that demonstrative reasoning was no longer just one of at least two ways in which human beings might employ meanings. Man's stomach and liver functioned in only one way, and his brain or mind *also* worked in but one way! John Locke gave us the clearest statement of this demonstrative image of man. Because we use the Lockean model as prototype for all of the demonstrative theories across history we forego further consideration in the present context and take it up in detail below (pp. 86–88).

From this time forward in history there was a growing conviction that all things scientific can be dealt with through demonstrative formulations. Newtonian science is a prime example of this attitude. The fact that Newton dabbled in alchemy for years and subscribed to a religious view of the universe does not alter the fact that he, more than anyone else, gave credence to the view that a science must not only be demonstrative in methodological approach, but scientists must deal with and think in terms of demonstrative theoretical meanings alone!

The most sophisticated counter to this image of man embodied in British philosophy was given by Immanuel Kant, but since we also discuss him below (pp. 88–92) as a prototype model in opposition to Locke, we overlook his approach in the present context. Suffice to say that Kant picked up on Bonaventura's thesis about mind turning back on itself and accounted for such transcendent capacities by way of what he called the transcendental dialectic. Though he put the dialectic back into man's image, Kant was as suspicious of its extensive use as Aristotle and Aquinas had been (yet not so pessimistic as Descartes). Johann Gottlieb Fichte had no such compunctions. Fichte was a subjective idealist, who believed that as selves we first posit our own ego and then through an innate dialectical capacity posit the world of experience. This meant that he reversed the order of merit in Ockham's two realms of cognition. Sensations could not be the source of knowledge, said Fichte, because they were nothing more than phenomenal constructions, projected onto so-called reality rather than taken from it.

G. W. F. Hegel then so dominated dialectical theory in the late eighteenth and early nineteenth centuries that today one can hardly use the term *dialectic* without one's listeners presuming that this is the historical precedent to which one is referring. Some have claimed that every twentieth-century philosophical movement is either a continuation of the Hegelian philosophy in modified form (e.g., Marxian theory) or a reaction against it. Hegel's dialectical formulation takes us back to Heraclitus and Empedocles, because he used it as a rationale for the flow of history. Hegel referred to this as a dynamic unfolding of successive clashes between the opposites of a thesis and an antithesis, resolving itself into a synthesis, which in turn acts as a new thesis to an antithesis, and so forth. What was unfolding here was the mind of a God, coming to self-consciousness as a final "negation of a negation." (In the case of Hegelian theory, it occurred in the balance of an enlightened Prussian monarchy.) Once the divine spirit of this pantheism had achieved self-consciousness, the historical march of the dialectic ended. It is as if Plato's individual, dialectically mulling things over in his mind's eye, trying to work through a problem of some sort, had finally solved the complex riddle and no longer sensed the inner turmoil of creation. Note that this is an introspective formulation of history. History is the reflection of an individual God's dialectical mullings, with the clash of civilizations and the alternations of national characters to be seen among different people of the earth acting as "way stations" along the evolutionary course to divine self-consciousness.

This tendency to view a resolution of thesis-antithesis into a synthesis suggests to many dialecticians *prima facie* evidence that an advance or a development has occurred in events over the three-step process. A synthesis is assumed not to have occurred unless the best of both sides (thesis-antithesis) were fused into one, indicating thereby that an improvement (development, maturation) over the initially contradictory or inconsistent circumstances had taken place. The dialectical conception of change is considerably different from demonstrative conceptions, and we defer for a later topic more detailed consideration of this difference (see ch. 6, pp. 240–241). But in the present context we should note that neo-Hegelian interpretations of the dialectic borrow this suggestion of a developmental advance across stages or levels of either psychological or physical development. A modern example of this use of dialectic can be seen in Riegel's (1973) theory of development.

Hegelian philosophy was idealistic, viewing the material products of a culture as the result of its ideology or the spirit of its age—what Herder had called the *Geist* or *Zeitgeist* (Becker & Barnes, 1952, pp. 487–490). Marx reversed this by turning the Hegelian dialectic to say that ideas always flow from the material realities of a culture's economic forces. Ideas are class linked, and they always reflect the justifications and rationalizations of a group seeking to gain advantage in the dialectical class struggle. This use of the dialectical conception is *extraspective*, putting the thesis, antithesis, and synthesis into the fabric of reality as what Marx and Engels called dialectical materialism. Like Hegel, the Marxian dialectic is also seen to end in the so-called classless state which flows from the final negation of a negation in the realities of socioeconomic evolution. The founders of communism were quite aware of how their conception of events countered the typical demonstrative world views then in ascendance. Marx (1952) pointed out how the logic of dialectics continually upset the doctrinaire professors of his time, who swept its truths under the carpet at every turn and refused to give it legitimacy (p. 11). Engels (1966) noted how dialectical conceptualizations befuddled the Newtonian physicists, who seemed to feel that what they could not understand must necessarily be erroneous (pp. 201–202). Whether or not we favor their economic theory, the observations of these two eminent champions of the dialectic are *surely* correct. An impartial survey of history must convince us that the dialectic as a useful heuristic scheme of animate as well as inanimate nature has been drummed out of natural science.

Dialectic is employed in certain religious formulations, however, as well as in the more humanistic psychologies and philosophies of our time—sometimes without being named as such. The religious critic and founder of existentialism, Søren Kierkegaard, employed a concept of the dialectic which was personal and subjective. This was quite in contrast to the sweeping conception that Hegel employed, but Kierkegaard specifically wanted to put the turmoil and personal decision between opposites back into the individual human being rather than claim that humans were mere pawns in the pantheistic evolution of a divine consciousness. His subjective dialectic has lent the humanistic psychologies of our time a rationale for their concepts of personal action, authenticity, and commitment in life. We see here modern reflections of the Origen-Aurelius-Leibniz line of descent. Continuing in this vein, Paul Tillich's religious theory is dialectical in essence, stressing the need for a self-affirmation on the side of being or nonbeing. Martin Buber's I-Thou concept of encounter is also clearly dialectical in meaning.

Another founder of existentialistic philosophy, Friedrich Nietzsche, was drawn to the tactic of looking at the other side of our most hallowed values and scientific truths. Demonstrative theories of knowledge are fixed only on what is true and not on what is false, but Nietzsche stressed that the value of an idea cannot always be measured by its truth. If man is a telic animal, he can—as Socrates would have said—learn from the reverse of facts. If this were not the case, people would be unable to turn what "is not" into what "is" by way of telic commitment to creation, change, and innovation. The one-sidedness of demonstrative reasoning worried Nietzsche, for he feared that man's valuational capacities could be weakened by the unwillingness to commit oneself to a value judgment in science (an issue that has returned to haunt us in the modern age of atomic physics). Man is a valuing animal, yet natural science has taken away this (final-cause) side of his description as well as fostered an attitude of "who can say?" on moral questions.

This question of valuation is central to dialectical judgment, because clearly if there are two or more meaning-implications in any given situation facing the individual he is forced to find some grounds for the sake of which (final cause) his behavior ought to proceed. George Santayana contrasted the demonstrative physical sciences, which deal with unipolar facts, and the dialectical sciences, which deal in bipolar ideas. Art was viewed as one such dialectical science, in which the objective grounds for a judgment of beauty were constantly under study. As with ethical or religious decisions, the judgment of beauty in art must be actively affirmed (symbolical meaning) for it to come about. Beauty is the antithesis of a sign meaning, for no one could possibly have an esthetic experience if an art object were nothing more than a sign. Rather than coming in through the senses by way of Ockham's intuitive cognition, beauty must be created through an evaluative act. This stems from a dialectical effort made by the individual, who must judge and thereby objectify the grounds for the sake of which one object can be said to be more beautiful than another.

The humanistic philosopher, Henri Bergson, took the Heraclitus-Empedocles-Hegel line of dialectical theory further in his teleological conception of mankind. Rather than supraindividual, the dialectic was said to function within each person (*a la Kierkegaard*) as a vital force (*élan vital*) which dynamically and creatively evolved in nature by way of contradictions. Life and matter were seen as the inverse of each other, even though they had a common origin in an energic reservoir (one-in-many thesis). Following a Hegelian line, Bergson claimed that history was the telic account of life (formal-final causation) trying to free itself from the domination of matter (material-efficient causation) and thereby to achieve self-consciousness. Although he did not give his dialectical conceptions this evolutionary emphasis, the theories of Edmund Husserl retained the self-created and subjectively unique emphases of Bergson, Nietzsche, and Kierkegaard.

The spirit of our age (*Zeitgeist*) is surely not in tune with such dialectical formulations. Societies that embrace dialectical materialism are ironically unsympathetic to minority and divisive ideas. In the philosophies of our time there is little fascination expressed with error, confusion, or inefficiency. Pragmatism (William James), pragmaticism (Charles S. Peirce), instrumentalism (John Dewey), and logical positivism (Rudolph Carnap, Alfred Jules Ayer) are all on the side of demonstrative reasoning. Mathematical and related formal-logic positions (Bertrand Russell, Ludwig Wittgenstein) are similarly construed. The greatest strides in human reason these past four centuries (the Age of Science) have been made with the clear recognition that demonstrative strategies have been employed. But there is a stunning ignorance of the comparable role dialectical conceptions have *also* played in this advance. One of the purposes of this volume is to underscore the forgotten and overlooked side to reason—the one that capitalizes on the bipolarities of meaning and *also* must be elucidated if we are to have a well-rounded picture of the *human* situation.

Dialectical versus Demonstrative Themes in Eastern Thought

In Chapter 1 we stressed that the causal meanings were to be seen in Eastern as well as Western theories of knowledge and that therefore the image of humanity we were reviewing was not culturally regional in nature. Our dialectical-versus-demonstrative distinction can also be seen in Indian and Oriental thinking. To characterize a whole civilization as predominantly one way or the other is risky scholarly business, but we would not be too far from the truth to state that whereas Western thought was to hone the edges of demonstrative reasoning to a fine point, Eastern thinkers have given equal care to the refinement of dialectical thinking (see Kuo, 1976, for additional evidence on this point). This comes as a great revelation to many Western modernists, who see in the Eastern philosophies an almost superhuman magical alternative to their own world views.

The role of Buddhism in shaping Eastern thought is often stressed by scholars, who characterize the peculiarities of Indian, Chinese, and Japanese thought by the ways in which these peoples have assimilated Buddhistic concepts (see, e.g., Nakamura, 1964). Buddhism was founded in its first form in India, of course. The view is generally accepted today that Buddhism was an offshoot of the Upanishadic philosophies of the Vedic literature (Raju, 1967, p. 44). This Hindu philosophy gives a major emphasis to our one-in-many thesis (Saksena, 1967, p. 31). The predominant theme running through both the Hindu and Buddhistic philosophies of India is the necessary search for a oneness in nature, the breaking down of false dichotomies, and a unity in the totality of experience that results in liberation (moksa) or nirvana. The Brahman (Hindu) or Buddha (Buddhistic) constructs are both views of a universal soul to which we must relate by way of an internal search. This inward effort is reminiscent of the Platonic dialectic at work (Raju, 1967, p. 52). The Buddhists seem to have been the first great synthesizers of history, and the Indian mind in general is said to be less analytical than synthetical (ibid., pp. 44 and 62). But this does not mean that synthetical relations are studied empirically, in demonstrative fashion; rather the Indian synthesis is achieved by adoption of a dialectical attitude that suggests that all theories of knowledge are equally correct "from their particular point of view" (Moore, 1967a, p. 14). Hence any ultimate truths must of necessity be a "one" of the Heraclitian sort, in which inner contradictions will naturally exist. Or a further insight might emerge in which what were initially taken as contradictions would be found to be noncontradictions after all.

Buddhism has thus been a philosophy based on the theory of negation as the proper means for arriving at truth: "Accordingly, all the Buddhist schools which rested chiefly on some dialectic arguments can be designated as those of negative Rationalism, the static nature of 'Thusness' [ultimate truth] being only negatively arrived at as the remainder" (Takakusu, 1967, p. 87). We can see a Bonaventura-like tendency to deny rather than affirm as a method for coming to truth in the Eightfold Negation of the great Indian Buddhistic philosopher, Nāgārjuna (c. 100–150 AD). He denied or negated the world of phenomenal experience through four paired oppositions: neither birth nor death, neither permanence nor extinction, neither unity nor diversity, and neither coming nor going (*ibid.*, p. 112). We have a variation here of that negation of negation theme noted in Western thought, so that the Buddhistic monk achieves the middle path (nirvana) by slipping into the totality of existence that is ever rent apart by the tensions of opposition. The dichotomies Nāgārjuna rejected have in a sense set him free of this tension as he effectively becomes one within these many sides to experience.

In contrast to the Western demonstrative presumption that perception is unipolar—for example, we see what is "there" or we see nothing at all (law of contradiction)—the Indian mentality has it that man sees nonexistence just as clearly as he sees existence: ". . . looking at the table, we can say that there is no cat there, just as we can say that there is a book there" (Datta, 1967, pp. 129–130). Even in the Hindu approach to meditation, where the goal is to focus attention on the nondual Brahman, the steps to be taken follow a dialectical path (Nikhilananda, 1967, p. 147). We come to Brahman by the dialectical steps of dismissing ideas of body, senses, mind, and ego which are oppositional to his identity. Once our focusing on Brahman is complete, we find the nodal point of perfect harmony and unity— as a kind of enlightenment by way of removing the irrelevancies from our awareness. Considered in the logic of dialectics, we again have that negation-of-a-negation principle that both Hegel and Marx wove into their conceptions of society as enlightened monarchies or classless states. The golden mean of Greece or the middle path of India are identical notions when looked at through the strategy of dialectical reasoning.

In Chinese thought a comparable synthesizing tendency is seen with great emphasis placed on the one-in-many thesis (Moore, 1967b, pp. 6–7). There arose in China a clear parallel to the demonstrative versus dialectical counterplay we have found in Western history. The renowned Chinese text, the *Tao Te Ching* (c. 600 BC, probably of multiple authorship) is replete with dialectical conceptions, the most famous of which is the *yin-yang* principle (see Chapter 1, p. 32). The *yin* force or element is pictured as passive, receiving, and meek (on the face of things); yet like the female or mother, *yin* represents the potential for infinite creation in the world. In this sense, *yin* is closer to *tao* or the "way"—that is, the universal principle underlying all things as an ultimate pattern of growth (formal-final cause meaning). The *yang* force is more active and bold, reflecting its power overtly in a more masculine sense. Harmony as a kind of dialectical balance between *yin* and *yang* is most desirable, although the Chinese Sage, who is closer to *tao* than others, refuses to display his powers openly and thus appears overly passive to the Western intellect.

In contrast to this dialectical text, the school of thought that devolves from Confucius (551–479 BC) is clearly demonstrative in tone. Confucius was a pragmatic man, more oriented to innovation and change in the world of affairs than to the rejection of this world in contemplation of an inner life. He was critical of the rulers of his time, whom he felt were disdainful of the humanity of their citizenry. He wanted to change things, and the strategy of innovation he followed was to gain the lines of control in the society, either directly by trying to get a position of great authority (at which he was not successful) or indirectly through placing his students in positions of bureaucratic influence. Having taught these men in a way that would ensure their character, Confucius believed that their education would translate into better conditions for the people. His sayings are still quoted as guidelines for the right, proper, and humane way in which to live. He taught respect for tradition and parental authority. He believed that there *is* a right and a wrong way in which to behave. The demonstrative flavor of this style of thought is clear, and therefore we are not surprised to learn that there is no dialectical side to the classical philosophy of Confucius (Kuo, 1976).

Confucius was not alone in his concern for people. Chinese thought has always been humanely oriented (Chan, 1967a, p. 26). Much of the philosophy recorded in China has dealt with the problems of good government, cordial relations between people, family life, and so on. In the fifth century BC Mo Ti (c. 470–391 BC) presented a challenge to Confucianism and at the same time helped found what has since been called the Dialectician School in Chinese philosophy. The dates of his life span are almost identical to those of Socrates (who lived c. 470–399 BC), a remarkable parallel in the history of dialectical conceptualization. Mo Ti's definition of the dialectic brings together humanistic with more purely abstract considerations, for he defined it as an effort to distinguish right from wrong, good from bad government, similarity from difference, name from actuality, benefit from harm, and certainty from uncertainty. These various oppositions cover much of what we have seen con-

sidered in the descent of Western dialectical thinking. Mo Ti's outlook on life was more pedestrian and egalitarian than that of Confucius (as was his personal geneology). He stressed the basic
equality of all men and rejected the Confucian acceptance of fate—
a unidirectional, demonstrative conception—holding instead that
every person must have an equal opportunity to influence his own
destiny. He was particularly harsh in criticizing the Confucian fascination with ritual. Mo Ti's attitudes remind us of the revolutionary
inclinations of a Marx or a Nietzsche, not to mention the individual-
istic focus of a Kierkegaard.

A notable difference between the demonstrative philosophies of
the West and those of China was that the former were invariably
realisms, whereas neo-Confucianism evolved at least one idealism,
thanks to Mencius (c. 372–c. 289 BC). Confucius encouraged man to
be humane toward others so that society would be peaceful; Mencius
encouraged man to be kind to others because that was man's innate
propensity, but one which needed cultivation. Man must practice his
innate "senses" (propensities) to humanity, or they will wither away
as does a limb that is never exercised. Hence goodness (humaneness)
is something which is idealistically created in each individual lifestyle, rather than something that is shaped by the realities of the
external (real) environment. The good man acquires an all-pervading
force (*ch'i*) by practicing the principles of humanity and morality.
He must constantly subject his sense perceptions to the control of
mind, cultivating his innate tendencies to be humane and thereby
come to know Heaven in his lifetime. Although idealistic and spiritual, there is no dialectical formulation in this philosophy. Mencius
is not as distinctively demonstrative as Confucius, but his stress on
the good as innately given (primary and true) hence knowable to all
who make the effort is surely in this general direction.

Not all Confucians accepted this idealistic strain, of course. Han
Fei (c. 280–233 BC) was educated a Confucian but took a more
realistic position on the nature of reality. He was a social philosopher
with an extremely materialistic, even Machiavellian, outlook on
things. Nothing interests man, said Han Fei, except the material
advantages he can gain in life. Men are controlled, not by Mencius'
assumption of an innate goodness needing cultivation, but by the
external sanction of laws that are backed by the power of a ruler.
The effective ruler must maintain a strong state by extending rewards
to those who help his sovereignty and using punishment for those
who fail to submit to his control. Punishment and reward are the
"two helms" that guide man's behavior, and they do so from without
in the extraspective sense we have seen employed in the utilitari-

anism of British Empiricism. Han Fei is thus a demonstrative spokes-man for the ruler, whereas Confucius had in a sense been the spokesman for those who are ruled (at least the middle-class mem-bers of this society). Both Han Fei and Confucius perceive the lines of control in the society as unidirectionally devolving from a position of authority. Neither is a revolutionary thinker, but each seeks to work within the constraints of the power structure to make things happen by way of this unidirectionality.

But the more characteristic spirit of Chinese thought is dialectical, focused on the individual, and directed inwardly. The rise of Bud-dhistic philosophy was an instrumental factor in this world view. Chuang Tzu (c. 370–c. 285 BC) wrote a famous theory of the equality of all things; he liked to point out that right is only right because of the existence of wrong (Chan, 1967b, p. 54). Kung-Sun Lung (c. 330–250 BC) devoted considerable effort to an explication of what we in the West call the Socratic-Platonic universals. He was a leader of the dialecticians, held to the one-in-many thesis, and formulated many intricate philosophical arguments, some of which are considered sophistical. The founding of Zen Buddhism in China (c. 600 AD) was to give even greater prominence to dialectical formulations. The transfer of Zen to Japan in the twelfth and thirteenth centuries was to exert an immense influence on the philosophical outlook of that country.

It is said that in ancient Japanese philosophy there was very little argumentation or dispute (Nakamura, 1964, p. 539). A kind of prac-tical acceptance of events was characteristic of these early thinkers, who had a one-in-many view that the phenomenal reality as known by each person was tantamount to reality. Concern over differences or the existence of an independent reality to which everyone's con-ception must conform simply made no headway in early Japan. Nakamura has shown how the forms of expression in the Japanese language are oriented more to emotional factors than to the truth value of a demonstrative logic (*ibid.*, p. 531). Hence Zen Buddhism and the dialectical outlook on which it depended found a ready intellectual atmosphere when in 1227 Dogen (1200–1235) brought the Sōtō Zen sect of Buddhism to Japan. We find in his writings the paradoxical statements so typical of this philosophy. Muso (or Soseki, 1275–1351) followed, and the general style of master-student instruc-tion in Zen was perfected under his leadership and example.

A comparison of the dialectical exchanges of the Zen Buddhists to the exchanges carried on by Socrates in the dialogues is interest-ing. In the latter case Socrates as teacher always initiated and kept the exchanges going through a series of questions that were suggested as the dialogue unfolded. The teacher takes an active (yang) role and seems to be the one who is leading the way to a discovery of knowledge, although he does not pretend to have information stored in his head for transmission to the student's head. The Zen master, however, is always pictured in a passive (yin) role, and invariably the student must take the initiative by asking the opening question. When the student does this, his teacher responds in a most unusual manner. He might give an answer that is completely unrelated to the question asked; he might simply raise a finger or a fist as a kind of reply; or he might pick up a small stick and throw it at the student. Often he remains silent. If the student prods for a question from the Zen master long enough, he might be treated by what is—on demonstrative grounds—a totally meaningless query; the most popularly cited example is "What is the sound of one hand clapping?"

In the literature of Zen one commonly reads of students going from one master to another, trying various questions on them, getting assorted replies or queries of the type cited, all the while suffering a sense of almost unbearable frustration. Suzuki (1962) tells the classic tale of a student physically striking his teacher for the latter's seeming obtuseness, but to no avail because a conventional answer was still not forthcoming (p. 40). Socrates at times frustrated his students, but this was the result of a sense of confusion due to the many interlocking issues on which his questioning touched. The Socratic dialogues did not always end in clear-cut solutions, and occasionally they led to unexpected paths that created more problems for the student than they solved. But the Zen student's irritation stemmed from the frustration of "not even getting started" on his road to knowledge. The Zen master, of course, was not refusing to aid in the student's education. His paradoxical or *non-sequitor* answer *was* an answer; even his silence said something in reply. He was essentially suggesting to the student that in the act of framing questions we create meaningless problems for ourselves. All questions regarding nature must necessarily disrupt the totality of nature, because they focus on the bits and pieces of experience in order to be answered. Even if a question can be answered, that the answer is *worthy* of expression does not follow—particularly because all it can lead to is a further question, hence more unnatural dichotomization and destruction of the totality that is life.

By answering questions in a seemingly ridiculous fashion the Zen master therefore teaches the student that a senseless question, which can lend no lasting satisfaction to the seeker of enlightenment, must be answered in kind. The posing of a self-contradictory question about the sound of one hand clapping is simply the reverse of this. People who put questions must learn that their precedent conceptualizations are already foisting onto the answering party an arbitrary scheme that might well distort the very thing they are seeking to understand. There is also the implication through all of this that in a final all-encompassing sense the *end* of knowledge is to lend an air of satisfaction and contentment to the educated or enlightened person. By focusing on the ultimate of knowledge, arriving there more through denial or negation of the question–answer dichotomies of life than through the temporary possession of "answers," the Zen master is hoping to exemplify a higher truth for his student.

When he achieves Perfect Enlightenment the student resigns himself completely to what *is*. He no longer raises questions about life and death, truth or falsehood, beauty or ugliness, and so on, because he now appreciates that these are *all* Buddha. He has no anxiety about such questions, for there is nothing to fear in a realm of totality. As the trees do not analyze the clouds and there is no night *versus* day in the earth's rotation, he does not draw oppositional dichotomies to split up nature in some arbitrary fashion. Rather, he slips into the totality that is nature and exists with contentment, having now made the journey that Buddha made and coming to the end at which Buddha arrived. Of course we are making enlightenment appear to be solely an intellectual understanding when in fact the effort of introspective study and contemplation associated with the quest for wisdom in Zen Buddhism must be seen as important *per se*. That is, the student must in effect rediscover the same—highly subjective—experience Buddha had lived through as he made his way to liberation. As Suzuki (1962) notes: "The Buddha's experience of Enlightenment . . . could not be understood by referring it to the intellect which tantalizes but fails to fulfill and satisfy" (p. 84). Hence there is an ineffable, highly personal, and subjective side to the achievement of Buddhahood—the oneness in spirit with humanity—taking us beyond the scope of the present book. Even so, it is not improper to have shown that the *logic* of this so-called mystical school of thought is our familiar brand of dialectical reasoning and conceptualization.

Conclusions and Implications

What are we to conclude from our review of meaning? There is probably little new for the reader to learn in the overview of demonstrative interpretations of meaning. We are educated in the West to think clearly and rigorously in our mathematics and logic classes, not to mention in our personal affairs. We think of science as clear and explicable, whereas art or religion is considered inscrutable and personal, more a mystery than something that can be understood through the objective methods of science. Knowledge has been equated with scientific knowledge so that everyone believes that what is "really factual" will be circumscribed by science someday, whereas all the other business will remain nonscientific, hence weaker or cheaper, by comparison. The harmful effect of this great valuation of demonstrative reasoning is that if we, as human persons, now behave inconsistently or fail to see only one set of "facts" in an event, we are made to feel somehow "outside the pale" of respectable conceptualization as rationalizers, illogical beings, or simply stupid—as if we are not living up to some underlying characteristic of our natures.

Yet anyone who has taken the time to familiarize himself with dialectical logic can immediately make sense of much of this diversity and inconsistency in the error variance of a scientific investigation on human behavior. Error becomes as active a principle in his outlook as accuracy, and he no longer feels responsible for *only* the manageable (predicted) portion of his observations. More to the point, how can we as students of humanity overlook the centuries of evidence which make abundantly clear that a dialectical logic is at work in the *conscious* (nonillusory) efforts of human beings to make sense of their experience? To found science on one of two opposing traditions and then dismiss the other as nonexistent or as unimportant simply because it cannot be subsumed by its opponent is a circular argument at best and an intellectually lazy solution at worst. We in scientific psychology must carefully examine and come to some position on that aspect of behavior we now forego completely —the dialectic!

What, then, can we say the dialectic *is*? In answering, we must surely conclude: *There is no one definition of the dialectic* (see Rychlak, 1976, Chapter 1). Anyone who claims to speak for *the* dialectic is either poorly informed or playing the sophist. The only common characteristic of dialectic is the point we began this chapter with— the use of bipolar meanings in the theoretical account as a *central* emphasis. To speak of the dialectic without such opposition would be impossible. Following this, all kinds of theoretical developments flow. We can emphasize the opposition *per se* and speak of the dynamic clash, strife, class struggle, internal tension, and so on or harmonize this opposition and see it as a one-in-many developmental synthesis, advance, or rationale. The dialectic can be thought of extraspectively, as moving across history in the material substance of the universe as a world principle, or it can be placed introspectively as an individual's peculiar way of coming at life through the affirmation of opposites, hence alternatives, open to him. Strictly speaking, all alternatives begin in the poles of opposition when we view them introspectively (as opposites of opposites *ad infinitum*).

We can limit our talk of dialectic to the fact that "a" concept has more than one meaning-implication; or we can speak of the flow of this meaning-implication as an extension of one, the other, or both of the polar references concerned. When we use the dialectic as a single-identity construct—for example, in Saint Augustine's Holy Trinity conception—the bipolarity is limited to a fixed "something." We do not have to speak of the dialectic as a dynamic flow of meaning-extension in reasoning or as a series of developmental stages. However, this dynamic step is easily taken, particularly when our singular conceptions are framed introspectively (which the Holy Trinity is not). This brings us to a significant point concerning the type of logical statement that flows from one or the other of our two views of meaning.

We noted in Chapter 1 that mathematics served a double duty in that it could be employed as a conceptualization with equal facility both extraspectively and introspectively. Mathematics is simply one example of demonstrative reasoning, and therefore this double-duty feature holds for *all* forms of demonstrative reasoning—for example, classical or so-called Aristotelian logic with its use of the syllogistic frame to capture the steps of accurate (truthful) reasoning. But how often do people begin a line of *their* reasoning from premises that are "primary and true?" Though *in principle* we might all be capable of this, few of us actually do so in our routine thinking. Hence, as a theoretical statement of what people introspectively actually do in life, the demonstrative conception is probably a rather poor reflection of the human reality.

However, this does not detract from the fact that demonstrative reasoning is a supreme example of what human thought could be—and sometimes is—particularly when we frame it extraspectively, as perforce on a blackboard. If we systematically record a planned sequence of life steps, or if we design a scientific experiment by putting down our thoughts in writing this way, anyone who understands our language symbols can see immediately what is being projected sequentially. Anyone other than us could therefore *predict* what must be done to comply with the extraspectively-framed steps

recorded on the blackboard. In fact another person could even enlarge upon what obviously was called for in the *unidirectional* logic
progression. The steps of this logic are necessarily there in the
Aristotelian manner.

The sequential flow of dialectical logic, however, proves difficult
if not impossible to capture in exclusively extraspective terms. For
example, let us contrast the extraspective world principle used by
Marx (dialectical materialism) with the introspective world principle
of Hegelian dialectical theory. The Hegelian formulation (on which
the Marxian was based) comes off much clearer and true to form.
This is so because in dialectical reasoning we are always concerned
with the premise *eventually* taken and never simply with the implications to flow from this opening affirmation. As Aristotle correctly
stated, in the logical progression of dialectic you never know what
direction will be followed until *after* it has been selected. There is
no point in graphing a dialectical syllogism extraspectively by beginning with, "Now, in the major premise we have 'this' affirmation
acting as predicate-assumption, which in turn calls up 'that' opposition" because *no one can say* what is to be initially affirmed or what
the opposite as conceptualized will be! In fact, there may be a succession of oppositions so that after reasoning from an opposite to an
opposite to an opposite, when the syllogistic steps are undertaken the
meanings under extension could well be far from where we had begun. This means that the essential strategy of analysis in dialectical
logic is *post hoc.* We retrace our steps and try to look at the dialectical proceedings from *within* the (first person) cogitations of an
individual who is approaching some problem with the attitude, "Now,
let's see, just what is going on here, what are the possibilities, what is
this all about?"

Hence the most accurate representation of how a dialectical logic
flows is to be seen in introspective formulations, and the analysis on
which we must of necessity rely is "after the fact" of having set a
course of meaning-extension. Hegel's view of history was correctly
post hoc in this fashion, retracing its steps to determine what premises the Divine Spirit affirmed as He moved historical events along.
After all, who can foretell what a God will do? All we can assess is
what He *did.* This search for His premises pushes our account to an
introspective perspective. Although Marx retained this *post hoc*
tendency in his efforts to reinterpret history, the rational counterplay
in events was lost to his theory. Dialectical materialism has become
less the active principle in events than the step-by-step rationale for
the energies expended in the class struggle. Hegelian dialectic was

teleological, with God making the *free* decision to halt events—each of which might have gone otherwise—at that point when He had achieved a level of Self-consciousness to His satisfaction. The Prussian monarchy was God's choice, now made actual in reality and therefore seen by Hegel through *post hoc* examination. Though the Marxian dialectic leads to a certain end (classless state), it has lost this telic character as it was made just another "predetermined" force of nature. Harking back to Socrates, we might say that Marx used the dialectic sophistically. He tried to make it predict events to a foregone conclusion. But one cannot simply draw the course of the dialectic on a blackboard and say where it must necessarily end.

Since the direction taken is *not* predetermined in free dialectic, the direction *actually* taken can be evaluated vis à vis the options open to the identity affirming one way or another at the outset. Finding the grounds for this selection is what interests the artist (Santayana) as well as the religious thinkers of history. We might characterize the logic of dialectic as a *logic of implication*. And though such implications often create "decision problems" and related devisiveness in the topic under consideration, the dialectic as a one-in-many thesis permits us to see how such articulated differences are again brought together. There is almost a reverse implication of "maybe these are the same?" or "maybe there is something identical about these?" based on the initial affirmation of "these are all different."

Dialectical machinations are also well suited to theoretical speculation, but they leave something to be desired in the realm of method, which in this case must ever remain cognitive due to the reliance on *post hoc* analyses. Demonstrative strategies are quite amenable—indeed we might say that they provide the backbone—to research methods of experimentation. Dialectical accounts are thus heavily laden with procedural evidence. Problems arise when, because of this, a scientist thinks that he cannot devise some demonstrative experiment that would support the *fact of* dialectical meanings or reasonings functioning among human beings. This is, of course, quite absurd, and in Chapters 9, 10, 11 of this book we review a decade's work on one such dialectical conception. To appreciate that one might not always predict the course of a dialectical meaning-extension does not mean that we are unable to show the effects of a dialectical intelligence on the course of learning. We must first entertain the possibility that this (dialectical) side to behavior exists before we can begin to design experiments that might test predictions (meaning-extensions) which flow therefrom.

Lockean versus Kantian Models

We can now bring the essentials of the nature of meaning and its uses together into two models of explanation (though the term *paradigm* as employed by Kuhn [1970] would be equally applicable). We can think of these as prototypes for all demonstratively inclined (Lockean) models and dialectically inclined (Kantian) models—with the proviso that we mean "in relation to human description." That is, an impersonal world principle of the Marxian sort cannot be subsumed by what we will term the Kantian model, though Hegel's view is somewhat consonant with this model because he had a personlike identity (God) in mind as one aspect of his world-principle formulation. History does indeed repeat itself, and although certain refinements in the basic pattern of a metaconception might change over the centuries, there is enough fundamental meaning in all human thought styles to justify the coining of two prototypes. Hence we can correctly refer to philosophies that predated Locke's and Kant's lifespan—even in an altogether different culture—as Lockean or Kantian formulations. We use these individuals as symbols of the thought styles we have observed across both Eastern and Western history (for alternate discussions of these models see Rychlak, 1968, pp. 274–283, and Rychlak, 1973, pp. 8–13).

The Lockean Model

John Locke's conception of the human mentality was totally demonstrative—a constitutive model that begins in the atomic theories of Democritus and Lucretius and is carried forward in time to its most thorough phrasing in British Empiricism. Drawing on the precedents of Bacon and Hobbes, Locke held that the contents of mind could only be those (primary and true) items that came into this repository of sensory input "from the outside." Each mental content (unipolar meaning) was embodied in its own discrete unit or a combination of such "idea units" (comparable to the "uncuttable" concept of the atom). At the base of experience we have the *simple ideas* which embody inputs from an independent reality and etch a mental imprint upon what Locke called the *tabula rasa* intellect (a term Aquinas had used in another context). At birth the mind is like a smoothed (blank) tablet and all that comes into mind is put there by the inputs from experience.

Note that the initiative here in meaning generation is put onto the exterior environment. Meanings devolve from outside to inside, and therefore a realistic thesis is highly compatible with the Lockean model. The real world exists "out there," sending inward certain information by way of what Ockham had called the intuitive cognition. *After* this input has been registered on the smoothed-tablet mind we then can see mental operations taking place in terms of what Ockham had called the abstractive cognition. Locke (1952) therefore held that insofar as mind has any power of creation, it is the power to deal with past inputs (i.e., occurring since birth) through memory and by thus recalling ideas, comparing them, affirming or suspending their import for our lives, a contribution of sorts is made to our sequence of behavior (p. 200). This is as active as mind can get in the Lockean view. There is no possibility for mental conceptualization at the point of birth, no organizing or construing potential in the idea whatsoever

The unipolar inputs from reality initially etched onto mind (i.e., simple ideas) are analogical to the lowest whole number (unity) in mathematics, except that a simple idea cannot itself be further subdivided. In other words, at the base of experience an idea is a discrete unit (atomic) having an either-or characteristic mapping reality accurately or inaccurately by way of sensory inputs. The mind records and then recollects this most basic of all information input, combining it in time via a quasi-mathematical (demonstrative) form of reasoning into higher and higher levels of information units called *complex ideas.* Complex ideas *are* divisible, of course; they are similar to complex numbers—for example, when we add three ones and then multiply this by the total of two ones to get six, and so forth. Harking back to Democritus and Lucretius, the simple idea is like an atomistic building block, which combines *in the beginnings* of thought with other atomistic bits of information to constitute a mathematical totality as the mind stores more and more information. These combinations of ideas were called habits or habits of association by Locke, but they were determinate habits based on an analogy to the "thinking-is-reckoning" suggestion of Hobbes. In this sense all meanings issue "from below," from the substrate reality which is the source of input-information. Locke specifically said that the mind could not invent or frame one new simple idea, nor could it subdivide or destroy those simple ideas which have already entered (*ibid.,* p. 128). Quite obviously, no dialectician could agree that "a" simple idea was indivisible by nature because he would see two meaning implications, ready for bifurcation, in many if not all of these so-called simple ideas.

Dialecticians would also disagree on the question of how meanings are input. According to Locke, the meaning *left* enters mind as a simple idea and the meaning *right* enters as a completely different simple idea; in time through frequent (habitual) association of left to right in our experience we learn the concept of directionality as a complex idea. This input frequency is thought of in purely efficient-cause terms (after Bacon). Both the input and the associative tie to other ideas occur purely as efficient-cause connections. Because the input information is conveyed by a sensory apparatus, we find that the Lockean model also makes good use of material-cause description. We can even view the patterning of more and more complex ideas as a kind of formal cause. However, the pattern *qua* pattern is never the source of meaning; it does not organize what is developing meaningfully below, but is merely the determinate end-result (effect) of the coalescing of the lower-order inputs (efficient-causes). Because the pattern does not endow things with meaning, there is no way possible to express human thought as behaving "for the sake of" this organization. Hence a final-cause conception does not enter into this model at all.

How might Locke account for dialectical machinations such as doubt, distrust, rejection, disbelief, wavering between affirmation and negation, conjecture, the concoction of possibilities, and so on? He would claim that such subjectively felt experiences, which we take to be the operations of our active intellects, were actually due to the kinds of frequency distributions of inputs on either or both sides of a question. Moderate or considerable input on "this" side of a point is sensed as opinion, belief, or conviction; fairly equal inputs on both "this" and "that" side of a point result in so-called indecision, or doubt; little input on either side of the point would constitute negation or disbelief and so forth (*ibid.*, p. 369). A possibility is simply a complex idea that has been calculated out of the memory storage of individual inputs, indicating a statistical probability or likelihood that certain events will flow if certain steps are taken.

The Kantian Model

Immanuel Kant aimed much of his commentary at the British empiricist and philosophical skeptic, David Hume, whose writings are in the Lockean tradition. For example, concerning the supposed power of mind to act on experience Hume (1952) observed: ". . . all this creative power of the mind amounts to [is] no more than the faculty of compounding, transposing, augmenting, or diminishing the materials afforded us by the senses and experience" (p. 456). We recognize the spirit of Ockham in this quote as well as the quasi-mathematical view of thought promoted by Hobbes and Locke. Kant favored a conceptual model of mind, one in which meaning devolved from above, framed in by certain inborn capacities that actively function to endow experiences with meaning. We see here a philosophical predilection that stretches back to Plato and Socrates, whose realm of Being within which the universals (forms) resided is a parallel conception to the model of mind that Kant embraced. Kant considered himself a critical realist, but he sounded a note for idealism just as Plato had done centuries earlier. We could easily consider this a Platonic model, just as we might call its contrast a Lucretian or Democritan model.

Kant agreed that there were two sides to knowledge—one having to do with sensation and the other with something more mental—but he disagreed with the passive input view of these activities that the British had proposed. Was sensation, for example, really an outside-to-inside input, or were there certain frames of reference that had to be applied to this process for a meaningful understanding to take place? Ockham had made intuitive cognition seem a completely unstructured or unorganized affair, when actually, Kant argued, sensations are always framed in terms of both time and space. Space and time factors are not *in* the input but are placed onto the input messages to provide them with a meaningful organization. Kant was putting his opening emphasis on a formal-cause usage in countering the strictly efficient- and material-cause usages of the Lockean model.

But this capacity for organization is even more important when we consider the higher mental processes, such as reasoning and understanding. We have mental ideas at both these levels, and particularly in pure reason we have ideas that *transcend* sensory experience entirely (Kant, 1952, p. 115). Knowledge can begin in experience, as organized by sensory factors, but it does not always arise out of experience because in pure reason—completely free thought—ideas are possible that were never input and bear no conceivable relationship to experience. This can occur because of the functioning of a *transcendental dialectic* in mind (dialectical reasoning), permitting us to concoct fanciful and highly distorted versions of that which we perceive daily through reasoning by opposites and the opposites of opposites, until we have removed ourselves from the realm of familiar events and known "facts." Sometimes these fantasied distortions result in workable ideas, which are innovated and put into experience by the person so that a creation comes about. If the head of a man and the body of a lion are combined into a sphynx symbolizing certain things about its originator, can we say in truth that this mixing of man-animal, lower-higher, strength-frailty, and so on is due to input influences alone? Who has ever seen such a figure in nature? Or could it be that a human intelligence is doing something to the input in a way only *it* can manage and that the patent reality of the sphynx is material evidence of this dialectical human capacity? Kant would have held to the latter interpretation.

The emphasis in Kantian thought on the formal cause as lending meaning to—rather than being constituted of—input items in experience is seen in his distinction between the noumenal and the phenomenal aspects of experience. External reality or a "thing in itself" cannot be known directly because of the sensory barrier that comes between us and the palpability of matter. This physical substrate Kant called the *noumena*. What we know of the noumenal realm comes through the combined orderings of our sensations and our cognitive understandings of it via mind. This latter organization of noumenal inputs into meaningful understanding Kant termed *phenomena*. Man cannot escape the fact that his only knowledge of the external world is through his sensory and cognitive shield of phenomenal understanding. Kant called himself a (critical) *realist* because, though he was aware of the drawbacks in speaking about how reality supposedly determined mental behavior, he did accept on faith that the noumenal world really existed.

If we were to describe the phenomenal realm as Lockeans, we would say that the simple ideas became, through repetitions, complex ideas of an habitual nature that provided a kind of higher-order pattern through which subsequent life events might then be interpreted. But this was not Kant's view. He said that just as sensation was organized along space and time lines, so too was the higher understanding organized by *a priori* "categories" which lent meaning to experience *from birth*. Although we need not detail these categories of the understanding that Kant felt all humans had as an aspect of their innate equipment "to know," the observation that he formulated these conceptions in a dialectical fashion is interesting. For example, modality was said to involve possibility-impossibility, existence-nonexistence, and necessity-contingency. Quantity was framed in terms of unity, plurality, and totality. Kant's view of mind was greatly influenced by dialectical metaconceptions. He effectively reversed the Ockham-Lockean line by suggesting that far from being the *source* of all knowledge, intuitive cognition is *meaningless noumenal noise* without the organizing function of space and time at the level of sensation and the categories of the understanding at the level of cognition (knowing). In the Kantian model, rather than an "after" function, abstractive cognition becomes a necessary preliminary activity to the accrual of knowledge. Mind is not *tabula rasa*, but *pro forma*.

With the capacity to reason dialectically in free thought (pure reason) we have quite a contrast to the Lockean model. Kant's model subsumes the meaning of final causation, because the idea here is not a determinate effect of some unidirectional (efficient) cause. Because of the transcendental dialectic in mind, we can even turn back on the evidence of our senses or deny the validity of our categories of reason. We must not think that Kant felt one could not rise above the focusing propensities of the phenomenal realm. When Einstein later challenged our popular conceptions of space and time he did something Kant felt any person could do—that is, "in principle" look to the other side of any designatable meaning-affirmation and thereby propose an alternative. This would not mean that the way in which the organism spontaneously experienced events would necessarily change. Einsteinian theory may be true although the average person is little affected by the fact that there is a relativity to his natural sensations of time. But no person is frozen into his conceptual equipment one way because he can always think to the opposite of what this portends—and to the opposite of this opposite *ad infinitum*.

Though we use the metaphor of a smoothed tablet or a blank sheet to think about Locke's concept of mind, in some ways the metaphor of the water glass is better. Locke thought of each idea as a glass of water in which the water contained therein had been poured in from the outside world. This means that whatever idea is in mind had been put there. If Kant now wants to speak of meanings like modality or quality, Locke would ask him: "Where do these ideas come from if not from the environmental input? How can you speak about such *innate ideas* of things without telling us how they got into mind?" Locke's challenge makes great sense if we view ideas the way he did.

Kant's idea construct was different from a unit of water filling a discrete glass unit, which might then also combine with other glass units of water to form complexities in thought. Kant's idea metaphor was more like a pair of spectacles through which the individual must look to see what is "out there." Our side (as wearers) of the spectacles is the phenomenal realm, and the other side (with which we can never come in contact) is the noumenal realm. The organizing power of these spectacles is never and *never has been* input, anymore than our memory capacity (on which the Lockean model relies) has been input.

In describing our natures we have words for things. We can speak of our memory capacity. There are also words for something we call a possibility or an impossibility as an aspect of what we might call modality. But the only thing that is input about concepts such as possibility-impossibility (modality) is the particular letter collections (words) we employ as items for the referents to which we allude. Kant did not say the words *possibility* and *impossibility* were innate, but rather that the implicit understanding of something like "that can happen" or "that simply cannot happen" are *applied to* experience rather than obtained from it. For example, the child reaches for the moon and then learns that it is not possible to grasp it. But, is the conception of impossibility learned here or the *fact* of what is or is not possible to attain? Kant would contend the latter is input but the former is innate! In time this child will also learn the meanings of the words *possibility-impossibility*; but he will by that time *already know* and indeed can only learn the meanings of these words because he has conceptually experienced what these words refer to. The child has a kind of beginning capacity to organize experience, to contribute something to it *from birth*, and then he builds on this organizational capacity to bring more and more knowledge to bear in an ever-expanding intellectually active sense.

One final point on Kant and the dialectic: Do not conclude that he favored the free use of dialectical speculation. To speculate wildly was perfectly all right, but in science we must take our thoughts a step further and validate them in the most rigorous manner possible. Kant was thus very much in the tradition of Aristotle and Aquinas on the question of dialectical argumentation.

Summary

In Chapter 2 we took up the question of how to interpret meaning *per se*, a concept that was taken for granted in the survey of causation in Chapter 1. As a relational term, meaning can be interpreted as the conjoining of unipolarities or, as a bipolar relationship, within knowledge from the outset. It can also be a combination of both unipolarities and bipolarities. We then suggested that unipolar interpretations of meaning are based on demonstrative conceptualizations, and bipolar interpretations of meaning are based on dialectical conceptualizations. These two approaches to meaning were then traced in the history of both Western and Eastern thought. As in the case of the four causes, this ubiquitous dichotomy is seen to have manifested itself in a number of different areas of knowledge, among all peoples of the earth. By and large, Western thinking has given greater attention to demonstrative and Eastern thought to dialectical strategies and formulations. The rise of mathematics and natural science in the West has virtually eclipsed the dialectic as a conceptual scheme in modern times.

If psychology is to be a science that is representative of the human condition, an appreciation of the dialectical side to behavior must be made. This recognition need not detract from the rigor of the science of psychology. No one theorist can speak for the dialectic, because there are numerous interpretations of the concept with its major emphasis at some point that an oppositional bipolarity in meaning must be presumed by the theoretician in question. Although both forms of conceptualization can be framed from either theoretical perspective, dialectical constructs lend themselves to introspective meanings and demonstrative constructs lend themselves to extraspective meanings. Chapter 2 closes with a discussion of the Lockean and the Kantian models. These metaconceptions nicely subsume the factors discussed in Chapters 1 and 2. The Lockean model is demonstrative, extraspective, prone to the use of material and efficient causation, and fundamentally constitutive in expressive style. The Kantian model is dialectical, introspective, prone to the use of formal and final causation, and fundamentally conceptual in expressive style.

References

Aristotle. *Posterior analytics.* In R. M. Hutchins (Ed.), *Great books of the western world* (Vol. 8). Chicago: Encyclopedia Britannica, 1952. Pp. 95–137.

Becker, H., & Barnes, H. E. *Social thought from lore to science* (2 vols.). Washington, D.C.: Harren, 1952.

Burtt, E. A. *The metaphysical foundations of modern physical science* (rev. ed.). Garden City, N.Y.: Doubleday, 1955.

Cassirer, E. *An essay on man.* Garden City, N.Y.: Doubleday, 1944.

Chan, W.-T. Chinese theory and practice, with special reference to humanism. In C. A. Moore (Ed.), *The Chinese mind: Essentials of Chinese philosophy and culture.* Honolulu: University of Hawaii Press, 1967. Pp. 11–30. (a)

Chan, W.-T. The story of Chinese philosophy. In C. A. Moore (Ed.), *The Chinese mind: Essentials of Chinese philosophy and culture*. Honolulu: University of Hawaii Press, 1967. Pp. 31–76. (b)

Creelman, M. B. *The experimental investigation of meaning: A review of the literature*. New York: Springer, 1966.

Datta, D. M. Epistemological methods in Indian philosophy. In C. A. Moore (Ed.), *The Indian Mind: Essentials of Indian philosophy and culture*. Honolulu: University of Hawaii Press, 1967. Pp. 118–135.

Descartes, R. *Rules for the direction of mind*. In R. M. Hutchins (Ed.), *Great books of the western world* (Vol. 31). Chicago: Encyclopedia Britannica, 1952. Pp. 1–40.

Engels, F. *Dialectics of nature*. Moscow: Progress, 1966.

Eves, H. *An introduction to the history of mathematics* (3rd ed.). New York: Holt, Rinehart & Winston, 1969.

Hume, D. *An enquiry concerning human understanding*. In R. M. Hutchins (Ed.), *Great books of the western world* (Vol. 35). Chicago: Encyclopedia Britannica, 1952. Pp. 446–509.

Jaspers, K. *The great philosophers*. New York: Harcourt, Brace & World, 1962.

Jung, C. G. *Psychology and alchemy*. In H. Read, M. Fordham, & G. Adler (Eds.), *The collected works of C. G. Jung* (Vol. 12, rev. ed.). Bollingen Series XX.12. New York: Pantheon Books, 1953.

Jung, C. G. *Symbols of transformation*. In H. Read, M. Fordham, & G. Adler (Eds.), *The collected works of C. G. Jung* (Vol. 5). Bollingen Series XX.5. New York: Pantheon Books, 1956.

Kant, I. *The critique of pure reason*. In R. M. Hutchins (Ed.), *Great books of the western world* (Vol. 42). Chicago: Encyclopedia Britannica, 1952. Pp. 1–250.

Kuhn, T. S. *The structure of scientific revolutions* (2nd. ed.). Chicago: The University of Chicago Press, 1970. (1st ed., 1962).

Kuo, Y. Chinese dialectical thought and character. In J. F. Rychlak (Ed.), *Dialectic: Humanistic rationale for behavior and development*. Basel, Switzerland: S. Karger AG, 1976. Pp. 72–85.

Langer, S. K. *Philosophy in a new key*. New York: Penguin Books, 1948.

Locke, J. *An essay concerning human understanding*. In R. M. Hutchins (Ed.), *Great books of the western world* (Vol. 35). Chicago: Encyclopedia Britannica, 1952. Pp. 85–395.

Magill, F. N., & McGreal, I. P. (Eds.) *Masterpieces of world philosophy* (2 vols.). New York: Salem, 1961.

Marx, K. *Capital*. In R. M. Hutchins (Ed.), *Great books of the western world* (Vol. 50). Chicago: Encyclopedia Britannica, 1952. Pp. 1–393.

Moore, C. A. Introduction: The comprehensive Indian mind. In C. A. Moore (Ed.), *The Indian mind: Essentials of Indian philosophy and culture*. Honolulu: University of Hawaii Press, 1967. Pp. 1–18. (a)

Moore, C. A. Introduction: The humanistic Chinese mind. In C. A. Moore (Ed.), *The Chinese mind: Essentials of Chinese philosophy and culture*. Honolulu: University of Hawaii Press, 1967. Pp. 1–10. (b)

Nakamura, H. *Ways of thinking of Eastern peoples*. Honolulu: East-West Center Press, 1964.

Nikhilananda, S. Concentration and meditation as methods of Indian philosophy. In C. A. Moore (Ed.), *The Indian mind: Essentials of Indian philosophy and culture.* Honolulu: University of Hawaii Press, 1967. Pp. 136–151.

Raju, P. T. Metaphysical theories in Indian philosophy. In C. A. Moore (Ed.), *The Indian mind: Essentials of Indian philosophy and culture.* Honolulu: University of Hawaii Press, 1967. Pp. 19–40.

Riegel, K. F. Dialectical operations: The final period of cognitive development. *Human Development,* 1973, *16,* 346–370.

Rychlak, J. F. *A philosophy of science for personality theory.* Boston: Houghton Mifflin, 1968.

Rychlak, J. F. *Introduction to personality and psychotherapy: A theory-construction approach.* Boston: Houghton Mifflin, 1973.

Rychlak, J. F. (Ed.), *Dialectic: Humanistic rationale for behavior and development.* Basel, Switzerland: S. Karger AG, 1976.

Saksena, S. K. Relation of philosophical theories to the practical affairs of men. In C. A. Moore (Ed.), *The Indian mind: Essentials of Indian philosophy and culture.* Honolulu: University of Hawaii Press, 1967. Pp. 19–40.

Suzuki, D. T. *The essentials of Zen Buddhism.* New York: Dutton, 1962. [Edited and with an introduction by B. Phillips.]

Takakusu, J. Buddhism as a philosophy of "thusness." In C. A. Moore (Ed.), *The Indian mind: Essentials of Indian philosophy and culture.* Honolulu: University of Hawaii Press, 1967. Pp. 86–117.

Untersteiner, M. *The sophists.* New York: Philosophical Library, 1954.

CHAPTER THREE

The Beginnings: Lockean and Kantian Themes in European Psychology

A thesis of this book is that a running exchange between Lockean and Kantian themes in the image of mankind has permeated the history of psychology, which was to be resolved in the American schools as a victory on the side of Lockeanism (see Chapter 4). In this chapter we begin a documentation of this historical thesis, starting with a consideration of the intellectual climate that had developed in science before psychology's nineteenth-century legitimization in the universities and then carrying forward through the views of important figures in the founding of academic psychology. In a closing section we consider Sigmund Freud's attempted resolution of the same Lockean-Kantian theoretical issues.

Before Psychology:
The Scientific Heritage

Psychology as a formal scientific discipline is usually dated from some point in the latter half of the nineteenth century. The immensely influential historian Edwin G. Boring (1950) has succeeded in fixing the year 1879 as the year in which "the very first formal psychological laboratory in the world" was founded (pp. 323–324). Robert Watson's (1971) historical research would suggest that Wundt's lab—to which this refers—was not actually formalized at the University of Leipzig until later, possibly not until 1894 (p. 272). In basing the birthdate of experimental psychology on such administrative—even bureaucratic—decisions Boring had some justification. He was, after all, addressing himself to the literal place (physical plant) in which experimental research was to be conducted. We know that others (including William James here in America) conducted experiments of a psychological nature before 1879, even in university settings. But this did not mean quite the same thing as being legitimized by a university table of organization. So we can accept Boring's grounds for experimental or "laboratory" psychology, but unfortunately, due to his influence this date has been singled out as the birthdate of *all* psychology (or all "scientific" psychology). One can easily take issue with such a claim.

A newly formalized science does not arrive on the scene without having to adapt its conceptions to sciences that have already staked out proprietary rights. There are certain paradigmatic assumptions (Kuhn, 1970) made by the established sciences that must be conformed to if a fledgling discipline in the university setting hopes to be given its official stamp of creditation. Four tributaries joined at the confluence of scientific thinking predominant in the last quarter of the nineteenth century. We survey these four sources before going on to a detailed consideration of the origins of European psychology *per se.*

The Medical Model

Psychology purports to study the human being, and medicine has traditionally combined fundamental scientific questions with an interest in the total functioning of the human being. The "family of the sciences" rests on the assumption that there are more and less basic disciplines at work within the totality, one resting upon the other and in principle reducible one to the other. Parallels are easier to draw between medico-biological or physiological concepts and human behavior than between chemistry or physics and behavior, and indeed, many of the early figures in laboratory psychology were physicians (e.g., Fechner, J. Müller, Helmholtz, Hering, Wundt).

A basic constitutive emphasis is to be seen in the medical model, as in the humoral theory of Hippocrates who is often called the "father of medicine."[1] Blood, phlegm, black and yellow bile, all served to combine in various portions to make up a person's temperamental and disease proclivities. There was no teleology in such a conception, but Galen was in time to propose that certain "vital" animals spirits *also* intermingled with the ebb and flow of blood to

---

[1] As in Chapters 1 and 2, when names appear in Chapter 3 without life dates or concepts are given without specific book citations the reader can locate them in Table 1 (pp. 8–31). Historical figures not listed in Table 1 are given life dates in the text.

stimulate behavior in living creatures. This was seen as a reflection of God's intention, and Galen's immensely influential anatomical studies of lower animals were conducted as a supposed proof of the Divine Plan. We find, even today, that a tough-minded scientist is likely to accuse the teleologist of wishing to reintroduce vital spirits or vitalism back into science in his talk of intentionality or related final-cause conceptions.

Vesalius later wrote a purely empirical anatomy that used Galen's insights but without the theology. Building on Hippocrates' conception of harmony or homeostasis among bodily fluids (humors), Vesalius' medical model was an essentially mechanical conception of organ systems, structurally interlacing and working without the benefit of a directing vital spirit. Thanks to such nontelic description, Vesalius (as Galileo after him) fell from grace with Church officials and ended his days removed from basic scientific pursuits.

Harvey's discovery that the blood did not "flood and ebb" through the body as Galen had claimed—based on an even earlier analogy drawn by Egyptian physicians to the actions of the Nile River—further advanced the mechanical conception of bodily functioning. The heart acted as a pump, which automatically circulated blood through vessels to nourish the cells of the body. Viewing the bodily cell (or its constituent elements) as something akin to the atomic units (uncuttables) of Democritus or Lucretius was now easy. Little indivisible things entered into and constituted bigger things in all aspects of bodily anatomy and physical functioning. Thomas Sydenham then stripped the last vestige of Galenic religious dogma from medicine in what he called his empirical approach to medicine. Subsequent developments in the medical model incorporated the chemical elements of Lavoisier and others, and the microorganisms of Pasteur's work. Each of these conceptions can also be cast in the building-block or atomic substrate formulations of the classical medical model.

Natural Science

In Chapters 1 and 2 we outlined the rise of natural science, so there is no need to retrace these steps in the present context. Suffice to say that we find a comparable development in physics, astronomy, chemistry, and so on to the evolving extraspective, material-efficient cause models unfolding in medicine. Whether basic or applied, a scientist was increasingly thought of as one who searched for the underlying substrate of factors that went to make up (atoms) or hold together (gravity, chemical union, etc.) the world of palpable (observed) reality.

Mathematics

Although we have already devoted space to a consideration of mathematics in Chapters 1 and 2, we should focus on this historical development in more detail. In doing so we refer to several leaders in the founding of natural science, because obviously mathematics has been taken to be a major ingredient of the scientific ideology.

Recall that Pythagoras adapted a Heraclitian logos-conception of number to the universe, concluding thereby that things are numbers. Based on this assumption of nature as consisting of numbers, Democritus could then suggest that the flow of events was determinately fixed. This tendency to confound a formal cause (mathematics) and an efficient cause (the push of determinate events over time) is a recurring item in the history of thought (see Chapter 1, pp. 41–43, for a somewhat different reflection of this same question). Euclid's axioms have also been thought of as mechanical or efficient causes, particularly because Archimedes was able to put such principles into reality via his law of the lever and concept of body density. If numbers are things, axioms and mathematical laws are the even more refined things of which numbers themselves are constituted. When Ptolemy effectively applied mathematics to the world of experience in his (since discredited) geocentric universe conception, he made the Pythagorean dream a reality.

Roger Bacon's efforts were directed at combining mathematical certainty with the certainty of research experimentation. Bacon was more the advocate of empirical and mathematical study than he was an actual practicing scientist in the sense of propounding researched knowledge *per se*. He helped identify mathematics and research procedures as related aspects of science. Of course not all of the mathematicians of history were enamored with literal experimentation—and *vice versa*! Galileo believed research evidence necessary only when two lines of mathematical reasoning could not solve the problem facing a scientist. Newton's view was the opposite. Even so, there has been a coalescing of roles so that the dream of a perfectly mathematized empirically proven world of reality has been one of the major assumptions of classical experimental science since the time of Roger Bacon.

Burtt (1955, p. 53) has noted that Copernicus owed much to the rebirth of Pythagorean mathematical philosophy engendered by

Roger Bacon, Leonardo da Vinci, Nicholas of Cusa, Bruno, and others in the later Medieval period. Though he reformulated Ptolemaic theory in his heliocentric conception of the universe, Copernicus' victory was still won in the realm of mathematical proof. That is, he did nothing to weaken the grip a mathematized world view had on the imaginations of the budding natural scientists of the seventeenth century. The work of Galileo and Kepler also served to wed the conceptions of mathematics to nature. Descartes frequently put the evidence of mathematical proofs on the side of innate ideas (inspired by God's creation), feeling as he did that this ability to reason abstractly is what distinguishes the higher organisms (humans with spirits) from the lower organisms (animals without spirits) in nature. Newtonian physics construed nature as a mathematized regularity by way of Cartesian geometry. In addition to his purely chemical researches, Antoine Lavoisier next devised a mechanical apparatus for measuring linear and cubical expansions; and before long his friend Pierre Simon Laplace (1749–1827) was speaking exuberantly of the universe as a kind of immense clock, wound to a preset rate of movement, in which "a superhuman intelligence acquainted with the position and motions of atoms at any moment could predict the whole course of future events" (*ibid.*, p. 96).

A major mathematical event of the nineteenth century occurred when James Clerk Maxwell (1831–1879) wrote the mathematical formulae for Michael Faraday's epic experimental achievement of turning magnetism into electricity. Not only stars but the physical phenomena of magnetism and electricity could now be seen to obey mathematical "laws." The role of one "force" on another was effectively thought of as comparable to the impact of the independent variable upon the dependent variable following Dirichlet's refinement of the Leibnitzian function construct. Mathematical certitude was taken to be "in" nature, so that Henri Poincaré could state that in natural science mathematical laws represent the sole objective reality.

Evolution

The final source of influence in the nineteenth century stemmed from the concept of an evolution in nature. It is easy today to think of evolution as a development or forward progression of events. But this idea of a rising progression did not come easily in the history of thought (see Becker & Barnes, 1952). The early Greeks, for example, believed that they had descended from a Golden Age of demigods and heroic figures, and the theological views of a Garden of Eden or a fall of divine powers (Origen) were also not conducive to the picture of an evolutionary advance. Gradually over the ages a dawning of the idea of progress developed, to parallel the advances in scientific and mathematical thought we have already discussed. The distinction Descartes drew between the lower and the higher forms of animal life sounded an early note for an ordering of nature. Giovanni Battista Vico proposed one of the earliest theories of evolution, suggesting that mankind moves through the ages of gods, to heroes, and thence to man—a sequence that is still more or less at the heart of modern theories of social development.

The march of civilization bears the implication of a directed movement, and one of the recurring issues we see raised in discussions of evolution is whether this movement through stages is teleological. Much of the zeal and optimism expressed by the founders of science as to the predictability of events stemmed from their assumption of a perfect order which had been put to design and operation by a Perfect Being. Even when the rationalistic theologian, Joseph Butler, tried to base an ethics on reason rather than exclusively on revelation (in contradistinction to Ockham) the arguments he advanced rested on a conception of man's "higher nature." Man's behaviors were cast in a hierarchical frame, with his impulses and passions at the base and his self-concerns above these, arching ever upward to the highest levels where altruism and conscience were said to rest at the apex of a kind of triangular hierarchy.

Of course not everyone thought of such hierarchies as fundamentally telic. Basing his view of the organism on a Lockean habit conception, Julien Offray de La Mettrie argued that Descartes' distinction between lower and higher organisms was untenable. All behavior is mechanically habituated, and the human being is simply a more complex machine than the subhuman animal. Though such formulations disparaged theological conceptions of free will, the view of organisms as developing from less to more complex mechanical structures, including higher-order reasoning capabilities, was consonant with the idea of evolutionary advance. A growing complexity need not be intelligently aimed to improve from the outset. Fortuitous complexity could, after all, simply "happen" serendipitously.

By the close of the eighteenth century evolutionary concepts were taking rather firm hold in Western thought. Georg Wilhelm Hegel's theory was telic, suggesting that a God was coming to consciousness across dialectical steps in the march of historical events. August Comte took a Vico-like view of history, suggesting that human societies typically move through the three stages of theology, metaphysics, and thence to a "positive" stage of science. The emphasis here was clearly on advance, improvement, and the rising of culture to greater fulfilment under the aegis of empirical science.

The nineteenth-century theory was to crystalize all earlier fumblings into a grand scheme of *physical* evolution, brilliantly uniting the medical model and the budding conceptions of modern natural science as it did so. We refer of course to the theory of organic evolution proposed by Charles Darwin and variations on this theme proffered by Jean Baptiste de Lamarck (1744–1829). The impact of Darwinian thinking on the closing decades of the nineteenth century cannot be overstated—and we mean here on *all* aspects of human knowledge. But its reflections in psychology are striking. Darwin began his studies with some personal inclination towards a telic account of nature, but of course he ended with a decided nontelic or natural-selection view of organic development. He also made use of Herbert Spencer's conception of survival of the fittest which could explain how improvements in animal or plant life might take place without intention or planning. The species that survived weather and the attack of predators could thereby live and multiply. Weaker species must ever succumb to the ravages of the elements and predators. The net effect is an unplanned progression, an improvement in the totality of nature which itself moves blindly. The biogenetic law proposed by Ernst Heinrich Haeckel was also brought into evolutionary theory, suggesting a kind of natural reenactment of evolution by organisms developing *in utero*. The phrase "Ontogeny recapitulates phylogeny" was to capture the imagination of scientists in the closing decades of the nineteenth century.

The Tie That Binds

Is there any tie binding these four root influences on the thinking of an aspiring scientist in the last third of the nineteenth century? Quite obviously they all are easily subsumed by a Lockean conceptualization, stressing as they do the constitutive nature of things. The medical model has cells adding up to larger tissues and bone structures, and beneath this cellular integration level it presumes even more refined chemical and mineral constituents. Though stemming primarily from mathematical calculations, the structure of Newtonian physics is similarly Lockean in conception. As this theory of reality was developed, an image of atomic structures, wound into the very fabric of physical reality, pushed events along according to a Laplacian determinateness. The ultimate source of all things was thus energic, and the core of this energy was to be found in the substrate of atomic structure. The "language of science" (mathematics) was spoken in exclusively demonstrative tongues. This unidirectional style of meaning-extension was also true of evolutionary theory, as a kind of multiplication of lower organisms into higher organisms. Of course one does not claim that a fish "times" a bird "added to" a monkey "makes" a man. But the unidirectional trend line of calculation and constitution from lower to higher organism is clearly in line with the Lockean formulations of our other three sources of influence. And, indeed, we cannot deny that Darwinian biology (eugenics, selection probabilities, etc.) rests on a completely statistical account of transmission and change.

These influences were all conceptualized extraspectively. Science was based exclusively on extraspective theory before the advent of psychology. To the extent that an aspiring scientist of the period considered himself in the mainstream of scientific thought he would be formulating his conceptions in third-person terms. He would hope, if not to work directly with some form of (brass) instrumentation giving immediate evidence of the phenomenon of interest, at least to be able to submit his scientific data to statistical test. In line with the extraspective premise, he would also hope to deal with something palpable—a physical substance that might be dissected, analyzed, or entered into various relationships with other substances leading to clearly discernible outcomes or effects. If he could not work on a "more complex" animal, there was always the opportunity of dealing with "less complex" animals. This strategy was furthered by the Darwinian-Lockean implication that studying simpler organisms was a good first step to the understanding of the more complex organism. This tactic was the reverse of reductive explanation and therefore quite in line with good scientific procedure.

Probably the most comforting aspect of all of this was that, as our well-trained scientist of the late nineteenth century moved about the halls of a first-ranked university, he could expect a *uniformity* in presentation across his classroom lectures and textbook readings. Though the study material changed—from anatomy to mathematics to physics—the model subsuming these various disciplines did not! In time there would be a change taking place in the budding physical theories of Mach, Hertz, Duhem, and eventually Einstein, Bohr, and others (Cassirer, 1950, Ch. 5), but these more Kantian styles of explanation had not yet made their impact on natural science. Psychology emerged at the height of extraspective Newtonian-Lockeanism, and as we now attempt to show, came up against those age-old *intro-spective* and *telic* problems of mind or spirit which had been successfully dropped from this style of explanation. This resulted in a body-mind (-spirit, -soul) confrontation that has to the present day never been satisfactorily conceptualized much less resolved, though it has surfaced regularly under many guises over psychology's brief history. What is not properly grasped in this confrontation is that it is fundamentally a Lockean-Kantian paradigmatic clash!

European Psychological Science

Gustav Theodor Fechner

If we were to name a "father" of experimental psychology based on the design of experimental research instruments (so-called methods) rather than on the founding of a recognized laboratory, Gustav Theodor Fechner (1801–1887) would in all likelihood be our first choice. After an early career in physics, in which he earned a reputation for his work on the quantitative measurement of direct electrical current (Ohm's law was reported in 1826), Fechner turned his attention to the study of consciousness. He was a daring thinker, who believed that mind and matter are merely two ways of speaking about the same thing hence to suggest a mental life for animals or even plants was not a foolish speculation in Fechner's scientific outlook. The problem was one of technique—that is, how can we measure something like the mind scientifically? Ernst Heinrich Weber (1795–1878) had earlier suggested that the perception of a change or a "just noticeable difference" in any stimulus is dependent upon the relationship of this change to the intensity of the stimulation. Adding one candle to two is easily noted, but more than one candle is required to see a change in brightness when a dozen candles are already lighted.

Fechner was to work out a precise mathematical statement of this phenomenon—today often called the Weber-Fechner Law (see Boring, 1950, pp. 287–288)—and he went on from there to devise the psychophysical methods. These experimental devices (average error, constant stimuli, etc.) were his way of proving that mind could be subject to empirical study with as much precision as matter. Fechner considered the mathematization of Weber's speculations and experimental proof in its support (which we now know holds only for a narrow range of stimulation) as sufficient justification that a mind *and* body sphere of experience was true of human behavior. One side (matter, body) worked according to absolute units of energy, but the other side (mind) did not. The mental recognition of a difference is thus *not* one-to-one with the physical stimulus change, but bears a relativistic or ratio function.

According to Boring, Fechner's clearly humanistic interests in founding a "psycho (mind)-physics (body)" area of study were prompted by the fact that he suffered through a period of physical and mental illness (*ibid.*, pp. 275–283). Yet even before his breakdown Fechner delighted in poking fun at the medical model in his satirical writings, under the *nom de plume* of Dr. Mises. Fechner's style is clearly Kantian. We see this in his distinction between inner and outer psychophysics. The question arose: Did the Weber-Fechner ratio hold between a stimulus value in the environment and the raw sensations in the body (outer psychophysics), or did it hold between these bodily sensations and the mind (inner psychophysics)? A Kantian would of necessity take the inner-psychophysics position because of his belief that the sensations entering from the environment were organized according to space-time considerations and then brought into conceptual meaningfulness by the categories of the understanding. Fechner left no doubt that he favored the theory of an *inner* psychophysics, developing arguments to suggest that human beings have a limen of *consciousness* (mentality) rather than a limen of sensory excitation (submentality). Fechner liked to point to the example of dreaming, where there are surely sensations taking place but the dreamer's limen of consciousness has been crossed.

It is prophetic that Fechner should be given historic notice for his experimental techniques even as his teleological theories have been dismissed as misguided spiritual aspirations brought on by mental illness. Invariably experimental designs aimed at validating humanistic theories are subsumed by mechanistic accounts of what supposedly took place in the experimental apparatus (see especially Chapters 4, 5, and 6). Also, each time a theorist has dared to employ final-cause description he has left himself open to the *ad hominem* form of counter which Boring uses in relation to Fechner's telic interests. Obviously, so long as proper techniques are designed to test a humanistic hypothesis, where a theorist's interest springs from in the formulation of this hypothesis makes no difference. Theistic interests are no more suspect than nontheistic interests. But the modern humanist can take heart in the fact that the man who is probably more deserving of the title "father of experimental psychology" than any other was an indominable teleologist, relying on the tactics of a Kantian model to make his case.

Bell versus Müller

The first notable Lockean-Kantian confrontation having implications for an experimental psychology took place even before Fechner's work. In 1791 Luigi Galvani (1737–1798) had proven that nerves were conductors of electrical impulses. In 1811 Sir Charles Bell (1774–1842)—and Magendie in 1822—proved anatomically the dorsal-ventral arrangement of the sensory-motor nerves. This specialization of nerves according to function is also to be seen in the doctrine of specific nerve energies, which Johannes Peter Müller (1801–1855) subsequently proposed, suggesting that not the mode of stimulation but the particular nerve stimulated accounts for the type of sensation a given sensory receptor conveys. Though we have similar anatomical and experimental "facts" cited here about the body's nerve structures, the way in which Bell and Müller theoretically explained these valid findings differed significantly.

As a Lockean, Bell took the position that a person's mental knowledge is the product of dorsal-route sensory inputs, going electrically up nervous pathways to the brain where they are stored as (efficiently-caused) effects to be used in ventral route outputs at the proper times. As Bell said: "All ideas originate in the brain: the operation of producing them is the remote effect of an agitation or impression on the extremities of the nerves of sense" (Boring, 1950, p. 86). Müller, however, held that: "External agencies can give rise to no kind of sensation which can not also be produced by internal causes, exciting changes in the condition of our nerves" (*ibid.*). This is essentially what Fechner meant by inner psychophysics. Müller also noted that the mind has a direct influence on sensation, imparting intensity to sensory receptors by way of focusing attention on one or another. His model is Kantian, in opposition to the Lockean formulations of Bell.

Helmholtz versus Hering

Our next decidedly Lockean-Kantian confrontation in the rise of psychological science was between Hermann von Helmholtz (1821–1894) and Ewald Hering (1834–1918). Helmholtz was educated as a physician but achieved his major reputation as a physicist, an interest he pursued after leaving medical school. His feat of timing the electrical nerve impulse extended the Galvani-Bell-Magendie line of theory. Helmholtz also helped further the constancy principle (first proposed by the physician, Robert Mayer, in 1842) as a style of explanation in physics. This principle held that there is a tendency for energies in a closed system to redistribute themselves (conservation of energy), and hence this force of redistribution could account in an efficient-cause sense for the observed behavior of natural objects. We can see in the following quote from Helmholtz a tendency both to do what Newton found distasteful—that is, reify mathematics into a concept of "force in things" (see Chapter 1, p. 48)—and also to put such forces forward as necessary reductive steps in all physical explanations:

The appointed . . . task of physics is thus to refer natural phenomena to unchangeable attractive and repulsive forces, whose intensity depends upon distance.[2] . . . The work of science will have been completed only when phenomena have been traced back to the simple forces, and when it can be shown also that the given account is the only possible one admitted by the phenomena. Then this would have been proven to be the necessary way of interpreting nature, and it would be the one to which objective truth should be ascribed (Cassirer, 1950, p. 86).

This reductive (and realistic) theory of scientific explanation is completely Lockean in spirit. An energic redistribution of forces amounts to a blind determinism of efficient causes. A role for mental conceptualization (*pro forma*) drops out of such scientific theories *in principle*, because a mental conception would itself represent a kind of "mobilization of forces" blindly uniting into an idea-unit that has flowed into mind rather than been pressed onto awareness by mind. Of course no possibility for dialectical reasoning would exist on this exclusively demonstrative model. Arguing in a decidedly *nondialectical* fashion, Helmholtz can say in his famous paper on physiological optics:

---

[2] This Newtonian translation of mathematical space into physical reality provided the rationale for "associationistic" principles of learning in psychology. The widely heralded Principle of Contiguity was therefore not simply "discovered" in laboratory settings. It was taken as a paradigmatic assumption based on analogy to the Newtonian principle of gravity! That is, the closer two idea inputs are together "in mind" and the more associatively "large" these congeries of inputs might be, the *stronger* is the associative bond between them. See Chapter 4 for a discussion of the frequency and contiguity theses in psychological theories.

My conclusion is, that *nothing in our sense-perceptions can be recognized as sensation which can be overcome in the perceptual image and converted into its opposite by factors that are not demonstrably due to experience.* . . . Whatever, therefore can be overcome by factors of experience, we must consider as being itself the product of experience and training (Helmholtz, 1961, p. 96).

If mind has an influence on itself by way of perceptual under-standing of events, the altering of a current perceptual image is pos-sible only because of former inputs (sensations), which now act as modifiers of ongoing sensation. This procedure followed a kind of unnamed logical premising that Helmholtz referred to as "uncon-scious conclusions" (*ibid.*, p. 83) or "inductive conclusions" (*ibid.*, p. 115) (also translated by Boring, 1950, p. 308, as "unconscious inference"). In the realm of vision these learned inputs were recorded as "local signs" which—through subsequent unconscious inference—provided the individual with grounds for depth perception and the like. Helmholtz was aware of the Lockean-Kantian questions in-volved, for during the decade of the 1860s in which he carried on his debate with Hering, he specifically mentioned the commitment his opponent had to Kantian theory (Helmholtz, 1961, p. 102). Helmholtz called his theory empirical because he supposedly did not go beyond the observed data, and he termed Hering's position "intuition theory" because it supposedly concocted undemonstrable hence unparsimoni-ous innate mechanisms to account for the data of perception (*ibid.*, p. 101).

Hering argued and presented evidence in support of the view that each retinal point has three innate "local signs," one for height, one for the right-to-left position and one for the depth of the visual field. In consonance with Kant he placed a formal-cause notion into the mind structure from the outset of life, claiming that sensation is organized in this fashion without the benefit of input learning. Prac-tice or experience perfects this capacity to see depth and so on, but it does not *cause* it in an efficient-cause sense to come about initially (Boring, 1950, p. 353). Hering's theoretical strategy of bringing a fixed frame to bear in ordering perception is the root of all subsequent phenomenological theories in psychology (gestalt, existential, etc.), although the topics of interest have shifted from vision to cognitive questions of how human beings come to know anything. Helmholtz (1961) admitted that his differences with Hering could not at that time be resolved through experimentation (p. 102), but he implied that systematic data collections would in time clarify things one way or the other. We shall have occasion to question the soundness of this (unconscious or otherwise) inference in the later chapters of this volume.

Wundt and Brentano

We come now to a more mixed-model form of confrontation, in which the protagonists are not so easily aligned as strictly Kantian or Lockean in theoretical outlook. Because it is the most frequently cited confrontation of psychology's history we will go into it in some detail. One of these men finished a major work of his with the following statement:

And this accords with the fundamental character of mental life, which I would have you always bear in mind. It does not consist in the connexion of unalterable objects and varying conditions: in all its phases it [mental life] is *process*; and *active*, not a passive, existence; *development*, not stagnation. The understanding of the basal laws of this development is the final goal of psychology.

If we were to have as multiple choice identifications of this quote Wilhelm Wundt (1832–1920) or Franz Brentano (1838–1917), most psychologists today—having accepted Boring's (1950, p. 385) opposition of Act to Content Psychology—would probably choose Brentano. Yet these lines are the closing statement of Wundt's *Lectures on Human and Animal Psychology* (1907, p. 454).

Wundt's portrayal by Boring (1950) as the father of experimental psychology is not always consonant with statements we read in Wundt's actual writings. For example, Boring claimed that Wundt's view of method held that we must (1) analyze consciousness into elements, (2) determine the manner of connection of these elements, and (3) determine the laws of these connections.

The goal of psychology is the analysis of mind into simple qualities and the determination of the form of their ordered multiplicity. The method, Wundt thought, is adequate to the problem except in the case of the higher processes, where analysis fails and we are reduced to the comparative observation of social phenomena, as when we use the study of language as the key to the psychology of thought (*ibid.*, p. 333).

Wundt (1961) did indeed call for the study of "national units as wholes" (p. 69) through the use of statistics. In fact he seems clearly to have *preferred* such study (*völkerpsychologie*) to physiological experimentation, which he called a "second tool" (p. 70), and not a totally effective one at that. To say, as Boring (1950) does, that

"Wundt fixed the notion of elementism upon psychology" (p. 333) is perplexing when we read again and again in Wundt of the *impossibility* of reducing mind to body and of the many problems involved in such elementary self-analysis in any case. For example, in 1862 Wundt (1961) said:

The psychology based on self-observation, which preferred to designate itself *empirical* [i.e., Brentano's] psychology, must therefore limit itself to an unsystematic juxtaposition of the facts of the consciousness; and, since it is unable to discover an inner connection between these facts, it splits up those components which belong together into a large number of dissociated details (pp. 57–58).

Later, after he had come to define introspection as "internal perception" (Wundt, 1907, p. 245) in which the individual confronts mind (as consciousness) *directly*, Wundt was never convinced that all of the reasons for behavior could be discovered in this way. For one thing, ideas are never completely unique. Ultimately our ideas are subject to cultural influence, and one must therefore look to this supraindividual source for the meanings that enter into behavior (the culture was termed a "collective will"). But even more fundamentally, there was a serious flaw in the method of introspection *per se* (*ibid.*, 1961, p. 427). Introspection permits us to look "at" consciousness, and, if properly trained, we can delineate our emotional and ideational perceptions through this procedure. As such, we can offer scientific accounts of our sensory apparatus in efficient-cause terms (Wundt called these "natural" causes). But when it comes to a complete accounting of behavior as volition or will, introspection must *fail*:

The motives which determine the will are parts of the universal chain of natural causation [i.e., efficient causes]. Nevertheless, the personal character, which alone can constitute volition, cannot be assigned a place in this causal nexus. We cannot therefore decide immediately and empirically that personality in its inmost nature, the source and origin of every difference that exists between individuals and between communities, is itself subject to natural causality (Wundt, 1907, p. 434).

We see reflected in this quote both Wundt's reluctance to reduce character to efficient causes (he claimed that ultimately, personality "is always a riddle," *ibid.*, p. 433) and his acceptance of traditional science which forced him to admit *in principle* that the root source of all behavior is in the efficient causes of nature. Thus an elementism can be inferred in his approach, as it can in all Lockean constitutive models. Yet Wundt believed that reducing mind to body would imply some quasi-material substance that acted like mind yet could never be conceived of in a truly mental fashion:

We conclude, then, that the assumption of a mental substance different from the various manifestations of mental life [as directly perceived internally] involves the unjustifiable transference of a mode of thought necessary for the investigation of external nature to a sphere in which it is wholly inapplicable; it implies a kind of unconscious materialism. . . . What can this "substance" do for us, a substance devoid of will, of feeling, and of thought, and having no part in the constitution of our personality (*ibid.*, p. 453)?

So here we have the generally acknowledged "father of experimental psychology" casting doubts on both efficient (natural) and material (substance) causation as proper descriptive terms for mind. Wundt was in time to be rejected as "mentalistic" by the behavioristic psychologists of this century. He proved an outspoken critic of the "anglo-American utilitarianism and materialism" of his time (Wundt, 1973, p. 17). How is it, then, that we can so readily view him today as an apostle of tough-minded nontelic psychology? Because in his *basic technical position* Wundt fell back on the Lockean models by accepting the "going" definitions of scientific description, statistics, and especially the Darwinian evolutionary models as major heuristic devices. He was influenced by Helmholtz at one point. And we cannot forget the role of Titchener, Wundt's student, who probably did more than any other person aside from Boring (who was Titchener's student) to bring out these fundamentally Lockean themes in Wundt's thought as if they were the only ones held to by the founder of our first psychological laboratory.

The record is gradually being corrected, thanks not in the least to Wundt's son (see Max Wundt, 1944) as well as to some excellent efforts on the part of others (e.g., Blumenthal, 1975; Mischel, 1970). Sometimes Wundt is made out to be almost Kantian in theoretical predilection, which is apparently the course his school took after the Americans had left Leipzig to establish shop in America (see especially Blumenthal, 1975). The position taken in the present analysis is that Wundt was a mixed-model theorist who, for certain technical reasons when he put on his psychologist's cap (i.e., walked across the hall from his philosophical duties), construed experimental research in a way that cemented him to natural science as framed by British Empiricism although as a theoretician he was unhappy with associationistic and mechanistic formulations. This rigorous methodological side to Wundt was the side that Titchener elevated and translated into a supposed Wundtian theoretical outlook for Boring to write into the history books (see Mischel, 1970).

Brentano was not a simple or uncritical Kantian theorist. He owed his greatest inspiration to Aristotle and was critical of Kantian philosophy *per se* (Brentano, 1973, pp. 10–11). Yet there is little doubt but that his fundamental technical stance, and the outlook his famous students Carl Stumpf and Edmund Husserl took from him, was Kantian (in the sense that we have been using this term). Rancurello (1968) notes that Brentano's psychology is fundamentally nativistic (p. 55)—on the order of Hering's view—for he accepted the position that our sensations are by nature spatially organized (a Kantian theme). And who would doubt that Husserl's phenomenology is but a further development of Brentano's Kantian-model concepts of mental life?

Wundt and Brentano both believed in the immediacy of a reality "in mind," making psychology a somewhat different kind of science than the other sciences. Brentano said that sciences like physics must deal with experience indirectly, employing as "data" items that take on indirect significance only as they stimulate and hence cause certain reactions in human beings. Thus color exists only because a perceiving subject reports such an awareness to the physicist. In his early theorizing Brentano insisted that the color experience was *real*, although it existed as an "object" only in the mental cogitations of the person who was having this color-sensation at the moment (called intentional in-existence). Actually, any object in experience bears this kind of reality, as something "immanently objective" or, in other words, something that actually existed *only* in the *mental act* (called a presentation) (Brentano, 1973, pp. 19–20).

Brentano was therefore contending that physical science must deal with *assumed* realities, because these realities were supposedly in the *noumena* (i.e., free of mind *per se*), yet all the physicist has to go on in his work is the phenomenological data reported by a person. Psychology, however, works exclusively at the level of phenomena, meaning it acquires as its subject matter directly relevant data! Mental acts do not stand for anything else, as the phenomenal must stand for the noumenal in physics. Though he intially felt it necessary to insist on the reality (in mental substance) of the "point" of a mental idea (called the terminus or that to which the subjective idea relates as an object), by 1911 Brentano had dropped this realistic position as when he noted: ". . . the thinker is the only object [whose existence is] demanded by the psychical act. The terminus [object] of the so-called relation does not have to be given in reality" (Rancurello, 1968, p. 18).

To call Wundt an evolutionary theorist would not be incorrect. He used this form of theoretical explanation to say that language developed from primitive gestures (Wundt, 1973, p. 148), reflexes were habitual repetitions retained by evolving organisms (*ibid.*, p. 227), emotions were evolutionary remnants of feelings (*ibid.*, p. 387), impulses were developmental precursors of voluntary acts (*ibid.*, p. 423), and mind evolved in parallel fashion to the body from simple associations to a highly complex consciousness (*ibid.*, p. 366, p. 443, p. 451, and p. 454). In drawing out the latter theory, Wundt said that originally man was unaware of himself as a thinking organism. His thought lacked self-reflexivity at an early evolutionary stage, so that man's ideas were taken literally as an object existing in reality much as anything else literally exists (Titchener, 1972, p. 100). The idea was not referential but taken itself as an actuality. As man evolved to a higher stage he gradually became aware of the fact that his ideas were referential (i.e., they made reference to something else), and these latter contents were not therefore necessarily an actuality. This means, of course, that the external reality (say, a given color hue, as measured by objective instruments) and the internal idea of this reality (the actual color hue sensed) need not be entirely in accord. Titchener said this disparity was at the root of the so-called stimulus error. To confuse the object as seen "out there" with the experience actually had "in here" is to commit the stimulus error.

At this point Wundt put forward arguments reminiscent of Brentano. Not only must the physicist himself conceptualize in order to know objective reality, but he must of necessity rely on the indirect evidence proffered by other people about this or that item of information. The psychologist, however, can turn his gaze inward and, through internal perception or *introspection*, gaze directly at the idea as a process and a content (Wundt, 1907, p. 245). The idea is a content in the sense that it makes reference to some form of perceived referent (a tree, a color, etc.). Though mind is parallel to body, Wundt believed that every idea that occurs to us has, at some level, a connection to the physical realm by way of sensation (*ibid.*, p. 445). This assumption of a mind paralleling the body by way of sensory contact was to provide the introspectionist with a justification for the study of two-point thresholds in touch, visual color differences, and so forth. One side (mind) essentially "tracked" the other's (body) actions (psychophysical parallelism). Titchener and Boring referred to the contentual findings of introspection (internal perception) as the elements of Wundt's so-called content psychology. This is a questionable one-sided interpretation of Wundtian psychology.

However, the basic view Wundt took of scientific explanation probably ensured that something like a reductive content psychology would flow from his laboratory in time. The most celebrated example here is his dispute with Brentano's student, Carl Stumpf (1848–1936). Wundt's students had found what they took to be evidence that melodies were actually constituted of elemental sounds, so that a tune was the product or combination of these substrate "contents" of sound. Stumpf pointed out that certain of these so-called scientific findings contradicted what a trained musician's ear would find important to the melody (Boring, 1950, p. 365). Stumpf therefore rejected these findings as simply not reflective of what the musical experience actually entailed. A heated debate with Wundt followed, in which Stumpf argued in the Kantian vein for the total experience and Wundt argued stoically for the "reductionistic" findings of his laboratory students. Two of Stumpf's students were Köhler and Koffka, cofounders along with Wertheimer of the gestalt psychology approach (see Chapter 4). This exchange over the nature of melody can be thought of as a bona fide manifestation of the Lockean-Kantian confrontation.

Though Wundt and Brentano began from a point of agreement on the direct nature of psychological investigation, they ended in a decidedly different psychological account of what was to be seen there. In the interpretation of the facts to be gleaned from the method of psychology we can find our classic difference in outlook taking hold. Wundt drew a firm distinction between the realms of science (pursuit of observed facts) and the philosophical examination of basic tenets (as used by the scientist in beginning his quest or as found by him empirically). Wundt admitted that his acceptance of a psychophysical parallelism created conceptual problems. How are we to think of these two realms relating to each other? Though he thought this was a worthwhile question that required an answer, Wundt did not feel it was one that the psychologist need worry himself over (Wundt, 1907, pp. 450–451). So long as the psychologist in *fact* found a mind-body dualism in human behavior he must proceed on the basis of such observations without concern (just as he must accept evidence that contradicts the practices of musicians in his study of the melody). It was the philosopher who must confront the subtle implications of a psychophysical parallelism! Far from demeaning such philosophical examinations, Wundt believed they were essential to the advance of psychological science because they complemented the work of empirical investigation. In a sense the empiricist led the way and reported the findings that in time the philosopher helped to clarify. But it would be dangerous to confound these two roles.

Brentano was more ready to consider such inscrutable questions, philosophical assumptions, points of view, and so on as the direct province of *psychological* investigation. He had even planned to take up the question of immortality in his formal psychological work (Brentano, 1973, p. 26). One can see Brentano framing a role for such quasi-philosophical study in his distinction between *genetic* and *descriptive* psychology (*ibid.*, pp. 28–29). Genetic psychology is psychophysical; it can take evolutionary themes into consideration, accrue inductive data, and submit such explicit findings to mathematical formulation and test. Descriptive psychology is *not* inductive but seeks to find those abstract presumptions and outlooks of a more deductive nature which cannot be observed or tested with mathematical precision. Indeed mathematics itself rests on such assumptions (axioms, basic concepts). Wundt would find the examination of these and similar world-assumptions in the province of logic and philosophy. Wundt was major professor to 70 doctoral students in philosophy as well as to 116 doctoral students in psychology (Watson, 1971, p. 277). He also *opposed* the tendency, which so many of his American psychology students favored, of removing themselves from Departments of Philosophy to found separate Departments of Psychology (*ibid.*, p. 273). Clearly his concept of the human sciences included equal and cooperative status for psychology and philosophy.

This divergence in professional-role definitions can be seen influencing how Wundt and Brentano talked about *introspection* (Wundt's term) or *inner perception* (Brentano's term). Looked at simply and overtly, both proponents seemed to be doing something alike in that they focused on the sensations and perceptions of mind directly. But the interpretation of what was going on here differed dramatically. For Wundt (1907), introspection was a strictly controlled experimental procedure of "internal perception" (p. 245) in which one presumed that a trained person could observe the functioning of mind (including such things as the awareness of color, the emotional reactions to stimuli, etc.). The steps of this method were taken as replicable and as sensitive to the nuances of changing sensation as was the measurement procedure employed by a physicist (Watson, 1971, p. 269). The only difference is that the introspectionist looks "in here" rather than "out there." Brentano (1973) accurately called Wundt's approach "inner observation" (p. 29) because it seemed to be transferring the empirical attitude of the physicist inwardly.

One of the characteristics of [Brentano's] inner perception is that it can never become [Wundt's] inner observation. We can observe objects which, as they say, are perceived externally. In observation, we direct our full attention to a phenomenon in order to apprehend it accurately. But with objects of inner perception this is absolutely impossible. This is especially clear with regard to certain mental phenomena such as anger. If someone is in a state in which he wants to observe his own anger raging within him, the anger must already be somewhat diminished, and so his original object of observation would have disappeared. The same impossibility is also present in all other cases. It is a universally valid psychological law that we can never focus our *attention* upon the object of inner perception (*ibid.*, pp. 29–30).

To account for internal study Brentano suggested that every mental act is dual, having some object external to it as referent for a primary consciousness, but also a *secondary* act of consciousness in which there is an awareness of itself (*ibid.*, p. 153). Hence, ". . . every mental act, no matter how simple, has a double object, a primary and a secondary object. The simplest act, for example the act of hearing, has as its primary object the sound, and for its secondary object, itself, the mental phenomenon in which the sound is heard" (*ibid.*, pp. 153–154). The upshot here is that every idea is itself a self-presentation, an act of cognition which can be perceived via this secondary act of perception. Brentano rejected unconscious mental acts on the grounds that this would demand a *nonrelation* between an idea and its referent—something that is impossible on the face of things! This is not the same interpretation of the unconscious the Freudians were later to use. Brentano believed that every idea *must* include its terminus, or referent (that to which it meaningfully points). To be conscious therefore meant to be "conscious of something else." Secondary acts of consciousness thus had as their terminus the primary ideas (e.g., seeing items in the environment, having hopes for the future, feeling an emotion, etc.).

Lacking this two-pronged view of internal study, Wundt's method (introspection) amounted to a turning inward of the physical-science approach. As Wundt (1961) suggested in 1862: "As soon as the psyche is viewed as a natural phenomenon and psychology as a natural science, the experimental methods must also be capable of full application to this science" (p. 70). Now, when we turn the natural science approach inward, drawing a direct analogy between the approach dedicated to extraspective study and the approach dedicated to "internal" study, what is likely to happen? Our internal theoretical account will probably be cast in extraspective terms. And this is what actually happened. Though it rests on a so-called introspection, *Wundtian psychology is extraspective in its theoretical account!* Brentano's psychology, however, takes on a more introspective formulation, because he is constantly trying to speak about experience from the slant of the thinking feeling human being. He is "within mind" rather than "looking inward at mind" as introspection was wont to do. Invariably this resulted in a telic account, for Brentano's interest centers on how the person is "coming at life" (in his primary consciousness) rather than in how he is being moved about by the stimuli enervating his sensory apparatus "from without." This is why Brentano placed intentionality at the center of his psychology.

Wundt, who served as an assistant to Helmholtz at the University of Heidelberg, accepted the necessity of science to account for phenomena by reducing the descriptive account to a "simple force" (principle of constancy). Even in 1907, long after he had separated from Helmholtz's direct influence, Wundt could say this about acts of volition: ". . . in giving an account of the particular causes which determine volition, we shall only recognise as *determinate* motives those which give it a definite direction, and which act like simple forces, incapable of further analysis" (Wundt, 1907, p. 231). Indeed, because a force must of necessity act on something that is itself not a force in order to be recognized as such, Wundt's conception of adequate scientific description went beyond the Helmholtzian when he noted, "We must trace every change back to the only conceivable one in which an object remains identical: motion" (Cassirer, 1950, p. 88).

We can see the functioning of forces in the motions of substantial objects. For this reason Wundt did some of his earliest work on the temporal extent of ideation in thinking, bringing him into the "personal equation" phenomenon noted among astronomers (Wundt, 1961, p. 70). Mind takes time to work, because fundamentally it is moved along by efficient causation, even though to isolate "the" causes of behavior is very difficult (Wundt, 1907, p. 434). One can see Wundt making special efforts in his theorizing to bring the idea of a motion into his accounts. For example, an emotional expression was said to be a movement acting as a sign in primitive forms of communication (Wundt, 1973, p. 73), or the instinctive drive was said to act as a motion that propelled impulsive behavior (*ibid.*, p. 147). If he could bring his account down to a motion of some sort, Wundt presumed that he had rendered a full and satisfactory scientific description of events.

Undoubtedly this acceptance of reductive science prompted Wundt's students and interpreters to suggest that he wanted to reduce the mind (psyche) to the body (physical). Furthermore, Wundt's theory of mind simply failed to deal with the teleological issues that a mind construct always raises. He spoke of a parallelism and criticized simplistic efficient- and material-cause accounts of mind, but we do *not* find a satisfactory formal-final cause account issuing in his basic formulations. Wundt suggested that a voluntary action is one in which the "thought of the end to be realised accompanies or precedes it" (Wundt, 1907, p. 387). But this could involve impulsive actions as well, and emotional behaviors were for him *complex* impulsive actions. In fact a volitional act was said always to presuppose a *feeling* acting as antecedent to the behavior that flowed from it (*ibid.*, p. 229). Choice was said to be a complex volition (*ibid.*, p. 228), but there was no freedom of a will to contemplate these choices and select thereby a preferred alternative. The preferred alternative was fixed *first* in the sequence of behavior based on the feelings (emotions, instinctual drives) as follows:

Feeling is not independent of volition . . . impulse is not a process which can be distinguished from will, still less opposed to it; and desire is not the uniform antecedent of will, but rather a process which only appears in consciousness when some inhibition of voluntary activity prevents the realisation of volition proper (*ibid.*, p. 225).

One can see in these beginning theories of behavior a motivation-to-behavior sequence that will someday be formalized in the Lockean drive-to-stimulus-to-behavioral-response style of theorizing that American learning theories were to adopt.[3] There is no way of conceptualizing a truly free choice on this efficient-cause model, because as Wundt observed in the quote cited above: "The motives which determine the will are parts of the universal chain of natural causation [i.e., efficient causes]" (Wundt, 1907, p. 434). Without a dialectical rationale Wundt, like all demonstrative thinkers of history, was forced to concede what Brentano (1973) felt he would be forced to

[3] Blumenthal (1975) places Wundt in the camp of the modern cognitivist or information-processing theorist. This may be correct; however, as discussed in Chapter 5, modern cognitive theory is *still* founded on a Lockean model.

concede—that is, the functioning of mind internally is precisely identical to the functioning of physical events externally (p. 49). Wundt found in his extraspective studies (his theoretical accounts of what he "did") a nontelic albeit highly complex mental machine. Phenomenologists since his time, beginning with Brentano and furthered greatly by the latter's student, Husserl, have tried to call attention to the particular assumptions the Wundtian introspective method makes. But each time the phenomenologist raises one of these most fundamental of all questions, the Lockean thinker in the Wundtian tradition (or is it Titchenerian?) cries, "Foul!" because such questions are for philosophers and not psychologists to answer.

Brentano saw mind as meaning-inducing in that typically Kantian sense—that is, similar to categories of the understanding infusing sensory input with a structure of meaning before anything external can be understood internally. His difficult concept of intentional inexistence gets at precisely this notion of one substance (mind) relating meanings outward to another totally different substance (physical reality) that lacks this conceptualizing facility. Mind is by nature referential, pointing through meaning-extension (ideas) to something (a terminus) other than itself (*ibid.*, p. 97). When it does so it gives this terminus immanent objectivity—that is, although one could not find the terminus of the idea "in reality" it can be located as truly existing "within mind." The existence is "in" mind, we might say, for mind-substance has this capacity intentionally to "inexist" (create extant referents by intending that they exist). As a nonconceptualizing substance that cannot process meanings in this fashion, the physical realm can never, even in *principle*, account for the mental realm. What this calls for then is a reintroduction of formal and final cause description at the level of mind, because the material and efficient causes of natural science's physical reality will *never* prove satisfactory. Brentano turns his back on the natural science which Wundt was only too ready to embrace.

Though more complex than earlier confrontations, the basic and unresolvable differences between Wundt and Brentano stemmed from their respective reliance or emphases on the Lockean and Kantian models.

Ebbinghaus versus G. E. Müller

Another manifestation of our historical confrontation took place in the contrasting ways in which Hermann Ebbinghaus (1850–1909) and G. E. Müller (1850–1934; no relation to Johannes Müller) studied the phenomenon of memory. Ebbinghaus initiated this study, single-handedly devising a method and using himself as subject (following the precedent of introspection here). In searching about for an experimental design to study memory—and in partial reaction to Wundt's belief that higher mental processes could not be brought into the laboratory—Ebbinghaus used as his prototype the method of "natural science," adding:

We all know of what this method consists: an attempt is made to keep constant the mass of conditions which have proven themselves causally connected with a certain result; one of these conditions is isolated from the rest and varied in a way that can be numerically described; then the accompanying change on the side of the effect is ascertained by measurement or computation (Ebbinghaus, 1964, p. 7).

The reference here to causal connection and the strategy of varying an antecedent to note its measurable effect on a consequent are entirely on the side of efficient causality. Equating mathematical (formal) causation with the independent-dependent (efficient-cause) variable sequence Ebbinghaus could next suggest: "A numerical determination of the interdependent changes of cause and effect appears indeed possible if only we can realise the necessary uniformity of the significant conditions in the repetition of our experiments" (*ibid.*, p. 11). A great stress was therefore put on the constancy of experimentation, with strict procedures that involved memorizing a string of (inappropriately named) meaningless nonsense syllables. These were assembled through random combination of a vowel flanked by two consonants, totaling roughly 2300 syllables that were employed in various lists and put to memory. Ebbinghaus laid great emphasis on the importance of a statistical test of the data that issued from his well-controlled procedures.

Every effort was made in the learning trials to avoid fitting nonsense syllables into some prearranged and familiar pattern: "There was no attempt to connect the nonsense syllables by the invention of special associations of the mnemotechnik type; learning was carried on solely by the influence of the mere repetitions upon the natural memory" (*ibid.*, p. 25). This requirement of the method ensured that statistical treatment of the data would be more clear-cut and compelling. All of the precautions taken by Ebbinghaus ensured that a frequency conception of memory, with its length and strength of retentive capacity, would follow statistical summative lines. As such, the methodology is shot through with Lockean presumptions and biases.

G. E. Müller began his theorizing on memory from a more intro-spective slant. Rather than adapting his theory of retention exclu-sively to third-person numerical counts and statistical distributions, he encouraged subjects to introspect after they had achieved learn-ing criterion in order to suggest how it was that they had mastered the task (Watson, 1971, p. 298). Müller felt that Ebbinghaus had made the memorial process appear more mechanical than it actually was. By allowing his subjects to be interviewed in the learning process and to introspect (more in the Brentano sense than the Wundtian), he found that all kinds of already established patterns of meaning were brought to bear by the subjects to organize and hence retain their learning assignments. Subjects looked for meanings in the nonsense materials and *found* them; they fell back on rhyming procedures, used those personalized mnemonic tricks that Ebbing-haus was so careful to avoid in his own case, and so forth. Müller's theory of memory held that the principles of frequency and contigu-ity could not in themselves account for the nature of learning and memory. He took a decidedly Kantian approach, emphasizing the conceptualizing features the individual manifested in preference to the mechanical forces of repetition and reorganization after the input had been banked in memory.

The Wurzburg School of Imageless Thought

From 1900 to approximately 1909 a series of studies was issued from the University of Wurzburg under the leadership of Oswald Külpe (1862–1915). This work has been referred to collectively as the Wurz-burg School of Imageless Thought. Important students and collabora-tors in this work included Ach, Bühler, Marbe, Mayer, Orth and Watt. Külpe had studied under both G. E. Müller and Wundt, but he fol-lowed in the former's Kantian footsteps. In fact Külpe published a short volume, revised twice, on Immanuel Kant's thought, and he published philosophical works of his own dealing with the doctrine of categories. The Wurzburgers did not set out to be a school of "imageless thought." This title devolved on them because of their research findings.

Beginning with the premise of Brentano that it *was* possible— through a kind of secondary consciousness—to examine one's own thought processes, Külpe and his students began to study introspect-ing subjects. When we introspect in this self-reflexive fashion, sub-jective factors such as the flow of certain images in free thought begin to intrude themselves in our associations—a fact that Freud was also to find in working with therapeutic cases. Bakan (1954) has even suggested that one of the main reasons Külpe's finished system lacked a proper treatment of thought was that he and his associates balked at doing what Freud was prepared to do: overcome resistances and plunge into the deeper reaches of mind that come alive because of the kind of free associations upon which the Wurzburgers had stumbled.

What all of this highly personalized recollection by their subjects *did* suggest to the Wurzburgers was that memory was hardly quantitative. There were qualitative, and to that extent, nongeneralizable statements to be made about human memory when people were allowed to be themselves in a methodological procedure. Furthermore, Marbe was to find that subjects who are instructed to judge which of two weights is heavier did not require a *conscious*—analyzable—act of judgment to complete the experimental instruction. This conscious attitude was therefore imageless, and hence the title of the school was born. Watt was to name this conception of the upcoming task *aufgabe*, and the resulting unconscious (imageless) attitude to complete experimental requirements he called *einstellung* (set). Ach referred to this as a *determining tendency*, but all of these concepts come down to the same thing.

The theory is clearly akin to a Kantian category (formal cause) which in turn frames and lends meaning to the task that follows. For Watt, *aufgabe* meant "to behave for the sake of the intended task at hand"—it referred to the subject's *intention* as he came at the experimental procedure. Though Ach was not so clearly telic in his determining-tendency construct, the parallel is clearly there. There was much criticism of the rigor and objectivity of these researches, with Wundt directing the fusillade; but surely we cannot look back from today's perspective and fail to be cognizant of what theory-construction factors were *also* at play.

Galton and Morgan

There is no clearer representative of British Empiricism and its Lockean theory than Sir Francis Galton (1822–1911). His psychological diletantism was characterized by a stress on the statistical investigation of large numbers of individuals. He had no particular theory of behavior to promote, although he did study mental imagery and association through so-called self report techniques. He was also greatly committed to evolutionary theory, due in part to the fact that he was a cousin of Charles Darwin (Watson, 1971, p. 311). He also relied heavily on hereditary transmission concepts so that he was an active proponent of all four of the Lockean precursors mentioned at the beginning of this chapter.

C. Lloyd Morgan (1852–1936) was also a prime advocate of Lockeanism, proposing a famous canon which is similar to Ockham's razor (Chapter 1, p. 12) in that it suggests: "In no case may we interpret an action as the outcome of the exercise of a higher physical faculty, if it can be interpreted as the outcome of the exercise of one which stands lower in the psychological scale" (Boring, 1950, p. 474). This canon meshed nicely with the Helmholtzian and Wundtian reductive conceptions of proper scientific description. It amounts to a denigration of all formal-final cause description in favor of material-efficient cause description. Morgan is usually cited in the history books for having explained the seemingly telic behavior of lower animals *without* relying on final causation. The opprobrious example in this regard is John Romanes (1848–1894) who, relying also on evolutionary theory, held that animals possessed in rudimentary form a self-directive capacity suggesting intelligence. His accounts of animal intelligence were highly anthropomorphized telic accounts, and Morgan's criticisms of this approach were widely disseminated among psychologists who had a commitment to natural science.

Sigmund Freud and the Lockean-Kantian Models

During the nineteenth century the field of applied psychology or psychiatry like the academic centers was faced with problems concerning our historical models. Because he is probably more misunderstood on this question than most, we review the theoretical usages Sigmund Freud (1856–1939) employed to bring together a clinical practice which invited Kantian formulations and a conception of science that demanded Lockean translations. There were three early (pre-1900) sources of pressure on Freud to take a Lockean position on the nature of human behavior and mental illness.

Brücke

The first Lockean influence on Freud was that of Ernst Brücke (1819–1892), his beloved physiology professor at the University of Vienna. Freud attended the lectures of Brentano at this university, and he even translated J. S. Mill into German for Wundt's protagonist (Boring, 1950, p. 358). However, there is no evidence to suggest that Freud was influenced by Brentano, whereas Brücke clearly did have an impact. Of course, as Freud was himself to exemplify, a student does not always follow the complete outlook of his teacher. This seems to have been the case for Brücke, who along with classmates Carl Ludwig, Emil du Bois-Reymond, and Hermann von Helmholtz, failed to adopt the Kantian inclinations of *their* teacher, Johannes Müller. Whereas Müller would have been open to a telic account, in 1845 these four gifted students—all of whom would achieve recognition in science—formed a *pact* to fight against vitalism in scientific explanation (*ibid.*, p. 708). Because vitalism is one type of telic account, the humanistic theorist who would like to think teleologically might be excused if he senses considerable prejudice on the part of those scientists who—like these four quite dispassionate empiricists—look at his efforts as a regression to Galenic medievalism. The constancy principle (conservation of energy) was greatly favored by Brücke, who gave the following version in his published lectures:

Organisms differ from dead material entities in action—machines—in possessing the faculty of assimilation, but they are all phenomena of the physical world; systems of atoms, moved by forces, according to the principle of the conservation of energy discovered by Robert Mayer in 1842, neglected for twenty years, and then popularized by Helmholtz [as the constancy principle]. The sum of forces (motive forces and potential forces) remains constant in every isolated system. The real causes are symbolized in science by the word "force." The less we know about them, the more kinds of forces do we have to distinguish: mechancal, electrical, magnetic forces, light, heat. Progress in knowledge reduces them to two—attraction and repulsion. All this applies as well to the organism man (Jones, 1953, p. 41).

This Lockean constitutive, hence reductive, formulation of behavior followed Freud throughout his career after he left Brücke's laboratory. Though he was to have his fallings-out with many associates over the years, Freud carried a fond affection for Brücke's memory. Trained as a physician, Freud aspired to the role of scientist; in later years he could admit that he was *never* a doctor in the proper sense of putting cure above understanding of the neurosis (and behavior) (see Rychlak, 1968, pp. 169–191). Freud lagged behind his medical school class a full three years, and even after taking the M.D. degree in 1881, he worked for 15 unrecompensed months in Brücke's Institute, doing anatomical and microscopic studies on lower animals. Brücke helped Freud arrange a post-degree travel grant to study with Charcot in Paris. Freud also had great admiration for Jean Charcot (1825–1893), but this was only a brief contact of one year. Though Freud did probably learn from the French that a purely psychogenic explanation of behavior (without reducing behavior to underlying forces) *could* be highly instructive, he did not identify himself as a follower of Charcot.

Breuer

The second Lockean influence on Freud stemmed from his collaboration with Josef Breuer (1842–1925) (Breuer & Freud, 1955). Breuer, who also had attended Brücke's lectures, put much more stock than Freud did in the constancy principle to account for hysterical disorders. For example, the concept of *strangulated affect* as a kind of bound energy that required working-over in order for it to dissipate is Helmholtzian in tone and clearly the favored view of Breuer (*ibid.*, p. 8). The process by which this energy was unbound or redistributed involved taking the patient back in hypnosis to a reconstruction of the unhealthy circumstance in which the emotion had been strangulated (bound) (*ibid.*, p. 17). Reliving such a pathognomic situation after the fact through verbal report was termed an *abreaction* (*ibid.*, pp. 8–11). Freud seems to have accepted this formulation in general terms, but when the collaborators broached the question of the cause of such strangulations of affect, a parting of the theoretical ways proved inevitable.

Breuer fell back on the traditional medical model and said the proclivity to split consciousness and hence to strangulate as hysterics do was traceable to an inborn condition, which he called the *hypnoid state* (Breuer, 1955, pp. 235–236). Freud, however, began to find in his cases a form of defensive avoidance that seemed to trigger the condition without any underlying physiological reason. In discussing one such early case Freud observes: "I was repeatedly able to show that *the splitting of the content of consciousness is the result of an act of will on the part of the patient*; that is to say, it is initiated by an effort of will whose motive can be specified" (Freud, 1962a, p. 46). The reasons motivating such splitting of consciousness into repressed (unconscious) ideas versus active acceptable ones were, of course, to wait on Freud's self-analysis, the sexuality thesis, and so forth. But for appearances sake, the collaborators acknowledged two different forms of the mental disorder—hypnoid hysteria (Breuer's etiology) and defense hysteria (Freud's etiology).

Freud's theory is clearly a departure from the time-honored medical model. His formulation did not even demand that an energic reduction be made. The defense and "wish" defended against were more akin to logical (and especially dialectically logical) maneuvers rather than the running off of an energy to some new redistribution in a closed system. In short, Freud's account has taken on teleological overtones. By looking at the motives of his patients he was moving to the introspective perspective and finding the Kantian formulation of things increasingly meaningful. Breuer was a conventional Lockean thinker, seeing people as constituted of certain genetic structures, influenced by these factors no matter what they might do as human beings to bring things about in life. Intention or will had no place in this completely extraspective account.

If we trace Freud's handling of the hypnoid-state theory, we find a neat demolishment taking place. He begins the process with rather faint praise in 1895 by observing:

I regard this distinction [hypnoid versus defense hysteria] as so important that, on the strength of it, I willingly adhere to this hypothesis of there being a hypnoid hysteria. Strangely enough, I have never in my own experience met with a genuine hypnoid hysteria. Any that I took in hand turned into a defence hysteria. . . . In short, I am unable to suppress a suspicion that somewhere or other the roots of hypnoid and defence hysteria come together, and that there the primary factor is defence" (Freud, 1955, p. 286).

In an 1896 paper on "The aetiology of hysteria" he notes that "there are often no grounds whatever for presupposing the presence of such hypnoid states" (Freud, 1962b, p. 195). He adds that if one only searches deeper into the psyche he will find a repressed defense in time. Finally, in a 1908 paper entitled "Some general remarks on hysterical attacks," Freud reduces the phenomenon of a hypnoid state to the physiological sensation of a protracted pause following a climax of intense sexual release (Freud, 1959, p. 233).

Fliess

Wilhelm Fliess (1858–1928) was a successful nose–throat specialist who practiced in Berlin and with whom Freud, who lived in Vienna, carried on a correspondence between the years 1887 and 1902. Breuer had introduced the two men. By Freud's (1954) personal estimate, Fliess was his "only audience" (p. 337) during the difficult years of the 1890s while he was conducting his self-analysis and putting together his thoughts into the Interpretation of Dreams (Freud, 1953). We cannot overestimate the importance Freud attached to Fliess's friendship and encouragement. No other professional relationship in his life was to have more significance, not even the subsequent contact with Jung. Intermingled with the personal features of the Freud–Fliess relationship was the fact that one man (Freud) had telic leanings as a theoretician and the other (Fliess) was an uncompromising physical determinist, who argued that men as well as women were governed by "periodic cycles" of either 23 or 28 days (like the menstrual cycle) which accounted for both physical and psychological diseases.

Fliess seems to have nagged Freud for physicalistic descriptions of behavior, because there are several points in the correspondence where Freud challenges his friend to suggest how they might in some way explain things physiologically or organically (Freud, 1954, p. 169, p. 265). We have to guess at much of this because Freud did not preserve Fliess's letters; in fact he tried to have the remaining correspondence and drafts destroyed unpublished—more for personal reasons than anything else. Fortunately, he did not succeed, and one quite remarkable document remains called the *Project For A Scientific Psychology* (Freud, 1966b, pp. 283–387). Freud began work on this unfinished psychology on the train while he was returning from a September meeting with Fliess in 1895. We can surmise from the correspondence that Fliess' prompting got the work underway, and Freud worked on it almost feverishly until October of that year, at which point he sent off three parts of a projected book. But by November 1895—one month later—he could say to Fliess in a letter: "I no longer understand the state of mind in which I concocted the psychology [the *Project*]" (Freud, 1954, p. 134). Though he did make a few fitful returns to this work in response to Fliess' urging, he never completed it and, as we have noted, tried to have it destroyed altogether. In the opening lines of the *Project* we read the following:

The intention is to furnish a psychology that shall be a natural science: that is, to represent psychical processes as quantitatively determinate states of specifiable material particles, thus making those processes perspicuous and free from contradiction. Two principal ideas are involved: (1) What distinguishes activity from rest is to be regarded as Q, subject to the general laws of motion. (2) The neurones are to be taken as the material particles (Freud, 1966b, p. 295).

This is (1) the most beautiful Lockean phrasing in *all* of Freud's writings; (2) this is the *only* Lockean phrasing in *all* of Freud's writings. The style here is clearly Helmholtzian; it reveals the fact that Freud knew very well how to take a demonstrative view of behavior, reducing psychological factors to a substrate of efficient (motion) and material (neurones) causation. The fact that he could not complete the *Project* is a mute testimony. It teaches us that this extraspective effort, in which Freud really tries to frame behavior "over there, in the physical functioning of the body" rather than "in here, within the various levels of mind" misfired completely. This was simply *not* the way in which Freud reasoned.

From his very first paper (Freud, 1966a) in which he attempted to explain neuroses without the Lockean interventions of Breuer, Freud proved to be a sagacious *dialectician*. He framed this first in terms of *antithetical ideas*, each generated by the same person at the same time—for example, when we aspire to win but also recognize that we might lose just as readily. In certain instances such negatively framed ideas actually reach the light of day, and the result is an hysterical neurosis (*ibid.*, p. 121). The recognition here is that meanings and meaning-expressions are *bipolar*! Intending more than one thing at the same time is *not* impossible. Yet, in the quote from the *Project* above we have Freud embracing the Law of Contradiction—a most unFreudian affirmation!

The dialectical side to Freud's thought, which enables him to make telic commentary, is patently clear in the Fliess correspondence. Freud learned that antithetical ideas were often the other side of consciously stated intentions precisely because the individual had initially toyed with them as his "true" attitude. They were frequently self-reproaches, voiced by individuals suffering from guilt (a judgment made of one's worth "for the sake of" or on the basis of some principle). In 1896 he could say to Fliess: "Indeed, it appears as though the whole psychical complex—recollection and self-reproach —is conscious at first. Later on, without anything fresh happening, both of them are repressed, and in their place an *antithetic symptom* is formed in consciousness" (Freud, 1954, p. 149). Freud should have named the symptom a synoptic, or synthesized, symptom, for this was the feature of the dialectic he was to arrive at, as have all dialecticians since the beginnings of thought.

What happens when there are two ideas, each antithetical to the other? The dialectician finds that invariably these seeming opposites can be shown to imply a new alternative, or at the very least, they can be brought together in a more or less unhappy alliance for a period of time. And so it was to dawn on Freud that symptoms were compromises! The symptom thus always reflected what Freud was to call the repressed wish (formerly the antithetic idea) and the repressing wish (formerly the intention). A wish is surely a final cause, a hoped-for or merely expected state of affairs toward which the individual feels himself drawn—often, in spite of himself (e.g., Freud would say one can *wish* for punishment). With this new development Freud could now weave the most shocking dialectical twists for Fliess, as in the following:

It turns out, for instance, that hysterical headaches are due to a fantastic parallel which equates the head with the other end of the body (hair in both places—cheeks and buttocks—lips and labiae—mouth and vagina); so that a migraine can be used to represent a forcible defloration, the illness thus again standing for a wish-fulfillment (Freud, 1954, p. 273).

The migraine patient could have her psychic cake and eat it too. Her repressed wish (to be seduced or raped) might be accomplished even as the repressing wish for punishment (the pain of headache) could be satisfied as well. In an alternative case mentioned to Fliess, Freud theorizes that hysterical vomiting in a female patient is to be seen as emanating from an unconscious (repressed wish) to be pregnant—even from an imaginary lover—while also becoming emaciated and undesirable sexually in response to the moral indignation the woman feels (repressing wish) for her lustful sexual phantasies (*ibid.*, p. 277).

Freud thus evolved a model of illness in which the personality structure sought a certain adjustment level, with the ego as the "man in the middle" seeking a balance between the unacceptable intentions (wishes) of the id and the socially more appropriate intentions (wishes) of the superego. These specific constructs were worked out after the turn of the century, of course, but the line of thought is presaged in the correspondence in the all-important period of the 1890s. Considering the oppositional character of mental intentions (due to the bipolarity of meanings), if some form of stalemate were possible, one could speak of mental health. If for any of a number of reasons the personality structure deteriorated and the stalemate was broken, neurosis or psychosis was the result. In Freudian psychology there is a fine line between what is neurosis (illness) and what is simply character (personality structure). In modifying the medical model as he did, Freud put teleology back into the human condition. It was not illness that acquired a final cause, not disease which gained a mentality, but rather the "personality" about whom a judgment of mental normality was being made.

Of course such talk of dialectical twists and wishes bringing about illness fell on unsympathetic ears. Fliess had mental illness springing from a kind of broken biological clock, which distorted the rhythm of the periodic cycles. It was the Breuer theory all over again, a variation on the traditional medical model. He never appreciated the Freudian thought style, and at their final meeting in Achensee in 1900 there was a vitriolic scene in which Fliess called Freud a "thought reader" who projected his own ideas onto clients (a charge that is still made against psychoanalysis) (*ibid.*, p. 324). Freud's bitter response to this assessment left Fliess with little motivation to continue their relationship. There were a few letters after this (Lockean-Kantian) argument, but by 1902 Freud and Fliess no longer corresponded. Thus personal considerations did not prevent Freud from sticking to his theoretical guns. But he did feel the need to give his new psychology a "sound" that might be more harmonious to the natural scientist's ears.

The Freudian Compromise: Libido Theory

Sigmund Freud must be seen as a transitional figure in the history of science, one of those eminent thinkers who have a predilection of what is needed, but yet who strive to retain what they take to be the merits of the older conceptualizations. Much was taking place on the Continent in the closing decades of the nineteenth century, the period when Freud was to mature and put forward his initial views (see, e.g., Feuer, 1974). A "new physics" was being written at this time, drafted from a more Kantian phenomenological frame of reference as exemplified by Ernst Mach (1838–1916) (Cassirer, 1950, p. 93). The emphasis here was on how the physicist himself—as a conceptualizer—might perceive his data, the assumptions made in doing so, the consequent "reality" observed, and so forth. Looked at psychologically, here was a view of science that might have underwritten Freudian thought beautifully. Freud could have jettisoned not only the traditional medical model, but the traditional Newtonian model of science as well!

But this is not how things went. Doubtless out of reverence for Brücke and possibly also out of a certain guilty concern over the "thought reader" charge, Freud viewed the theories of Mach as anathema to science. Indeed Freud apparently avoided the social philosopher Josef Popper-Lynkeus, a man he admired, because the latter had Mach as a friend. He did not want to bestir the waters in his relations with Popper-Lynkeus, who could somehow cultivate a social life with the "intellectual nihilist" Ernst Mach (Rieff, 1959, p. 26). Thus Freud missed an opportunity to move into the stream of a changing physics, a more Kantian physics, as reflected in the thought of men like Mach, Hertz, and Duhem (Rychlak, 1968, p. 116).

In place of this invitation to phenomenological science, Freud reverted to a Lockean reductionistic strategy and raised a mental energy conception to the forefront of his theory. Freud never even mentioned *libido* until late in the Fliess correspondence, and his handling of the construct was strange, to say the least. Though he had other instincts in mind during various formulations of his theory, the energy of the sexual instincts is the only one he ever named. He assigned no name to the energy of the self-preservation instinct (earlier theory) or the death instinct (later theory). Freud sought a continuing focus on sexuality. *Libido,* a term physicians used to refer to sexual promptings, allowed him to keep this focus and also to give his theory the look of natural science. As late as December 1909 Jung could ask Freud in a letter: "I should like to pump you sometime for a definition of libido. So far I haven't come up with anything satisfactory" (McGuire, 1974, p. 270). Freud responds in the same month: "[In answer to] . . . your difficulty regarding 'my' libido. In the first sentence of the *Theory of Sexuality* there is a clear definition in which I see nothing to change: The analagon to hunger, for which, in the sexual context, the German language has no word except the ambiguous 'Lust' " (*ibid.,* p. 277). This is as explicit as Freud would become, even when speaking informally with a friend and ally. There is absolutely no need in a dialectical account to reduce intentions or wishes (formal-final causes) to energies (material-efficient causes), but Freud seems to have felt he would be afforded scientific status if he did so.

There is a certain irony in the fact that a man who began his conceptualizations entirely at the level of intentional analysis, and thereby not only explained but cured neuroses *without* an energy notion, should end up as apostle for instinctive drives and mental energies. A reasoned overview of Freud's intellectual development must surely convince us that libido theory is a superfluous—really metaphorical—account of the workings of mind. It is the remnant of a constancy-principle strategy, but one that is badly distorted and in fact misplaced. There would be nothing uniquely Freudian in viewing mental energies as forces that propel the organism when they rise (bound) and cease this propulsion as they fall off in volume or level (unbound).

What *is peculiar* to Freud's mental energies is the fact that in his theoretical formulations drive power *always* issued from a dialectical ploy, oriented teleologically for conflicting ends, and then rephrased in energy terms *after* the implications were clear. Not merely the instinctual drive or its (efficient cause) energy provided the dynamics of motion; the energy as stimulated and then opposed by another oppositional (antithetical) energy required a resolution or synthesis in repression, projection, sublimation, or whatever. Energies that run to their expenditure in physics are never manipulated with strategies (formal causes) "for the sake of which" (final causes) one side of the mind (id) makes itself known through a devious parapraxis despite the vigilance of an opposing side of mind (ego, superego). In the Freudian unconscious there *is* trickery and deceit, ploy and counterploy, until one's head is set spinning from trying to keep up with the machinations supposedly going on. Each client is a marvel of intricate detail and fascinating motivation.

This is not to say that Freud employed a dialectical strategy consciously, nor that he would in any way have liked to be considered a dialectician—which to him meant sophist (Rychlak, 1968, p. 323). The "thought reader" charge was to haunt Freud throughout his lifetime. Nor did Freud clearly appreciate the addition of final causes in his presentation. He seems to have simply presumed that anyone who rejected his views did so on the basis of their sexualized content. As late as 1915 he freely admitted that his libido theory depended more on an analogy to biology than on the direct evidence of psychoanalysis (Freud, 1957, p. 79). He could always present explanations of the neurosis in *either* psychological (formal-final causal) *or* libidinal-energic (material-efficient causal) terms. As he grew older he even seems to have used the libidinal phrasing more and more, but the basic style of Freudian thought was to remain dialectical and telic. However, Freud must be viewed as a mixed-model theorist. Those who feel he was a physicalistic theorist in the classical medical-model sense would do well to read *The Freud/Jung Letters* (McGuire, 1974) where there are numerous examples of Freud and Jung rejecting traditional medical explanation (see especially pp. 115–116).

Summary

Chapter 3 begins with a discussion of the conceptual forces that served to define natural science for the nineteenth century, the period in which psychology emerged as an independent science. The medical model, Newtonian mechanism, rise of mathematics, and Darwinian evolutionary theory are shown to merge in a fundamental Lockeanism which was to exert an overwhelming influence on natural-science theory. But the founders of psychological science were not all committed to a Lockean model. We surveyed several important figures and found that there always was much sympathy for a more Kantian formulation of human behavior. This was true of Fechner, who because he first devised experimental procedures is probably more deserving of the title Father of Experimental Psychology than is Wundt.

The Bell–J. Müller differences in interpreting nerve functions and mentality are seen to encompass a Lockean-Kantian difference, as did the Helmholtz-Hering disagreement on the nature of visual perception. Helmholtz popularized the constancy principle in psychology, which demanded that for a full scientific account to be rendered the theorist must bring his psychological theory down to underlying physical simple forces. This traditional Lockean form of explanation was also embraced by Wundt, who added that we must explicate these forces in terms of the motions (efficient-causes) within which they are manifested. A detailed comparison of Wundt and Brentano then revealed that the Lockean-Kantian issue defines their differences, albeit in a somewhat more subtle way because there are indications of a leaning toward a mixed model on both sides. Wundt's basic commitment to scientific procedure is what stamps him as predominantly a Lockean, although he was more inclined to make room for humanistic (as opposed to mechanistic) theories than our leading historians have given him credit for. An important conclusion derived from this comparative study is that, whereas Brentano's "inner perception" resulted in *introspective* theory, Wundt's "internal perception" (introspection) resulted in *extraspective* theory. Ebbinghaus (Lockean) and G. E. Müller (Kantian) are seen to take different positions on the historical confrontation of our models in the theories of memory and learning they each advocated. Similar contrasts can be seen between the Wurzburgers (Kantian) on the Continent, and the British psychologists, Galton and C. L. Morgan (Lockean).

Though he refused to think in strictly Lockean demonstrative terms despite pressure to do so from Brücke, Breuer, and Fliess, Freud *did* embrace a form of Lockean reductionism in his libido theory. Though he might have based psychoanalysis on the newly emerging physics of his time, Freud demurred and returned to the Helmholtzian strategy of reducing *psychic* events to *psychic* simple forces. The resultant libido theory is a Lockean-Kantian compromise

of major proportions and one of the least viable aspects of psychoanalytical thought. Ultimately libido theory rests on a dialectical and
telic rationale, though it has succeeded in convincing many people
that Freud was a demonstrative theorist and a biological determinist.

References

Bakan, D. A reconsideration of the problem of introspection. *Psychological Bulletin*, 1954, **51**, 105–118.

Becker, H., & Barnes, H. E. *Social thought from lore to science* (2 vols.). Washington, D.C.: Harren, 1952.

Blumenthal, A. L. A reappraisal of Wilhelm Wundt. *American Psychologist*, 1975,
30, 1081–1088.

Boring, E. G. *A history of experimental psychology* (2nd ed.). New York: Appleton-Century-Crofts, 1950.

Brentano, F. *Psychology from an empirical standpoint.* New York: Humanities,
1973.

Breuer, J. Theoretical selection, section III. In J. Strachey (Ed.), *The standard
edition of the complete psychological works of Sigmund Freud* (Vol. II).
London: Hogarth, 1955. Pp. 185–251.

Breuer, J., & Freud, S. On the psychical mechanism of hysterical phenomena:
Preliminary communication. In J. Strachey (Ed.), *The standard edition of
the complete psychological works of Sigmund Freud* (Vol. II). London:
Hogarth, 1955. Pp. 1–17.

Burtt, E. A. *The metaphysical foundations of modern physical science* (rev. ed.).
Garden City, N.Y.: Doubleday, 1955.

Cassirer, E. *The problem of knowledge.* New Haven: Yale University Press, 1950.

Ebbinghaus, H. *Memory: A contribution to experimental psychology.* New York:
Dover, 1964.

Feuer, L. S. *Einstein and the generations of science.* New York: Basic Books,
1974.

Freud, S. *The interpretation of dreams.* In J. Strachey (Ed.), *The standard edition
of the complete psychological works of Sigmund Freud* (Vols. IV & V).
London: Hogarth, 1953.

Freud, S. *The origins of psycho-analysis, letters to Wilhelm Fliess, drafts and
notes: 1887–1902.* New York: Basic Books, 1954.

Freud, S. The psychotherapy of hysteria. In J. Strachey (Ed.), *The standard edition of the complete psychological works of Sigmund Freud* (Vol. II). London: Hogarth, 1955. Pp. 254–305.

Freud, S. On narcissism: An introduction. In J. Strachey (Ed.), *The standard
edition of the complete psychological works of Sigmund Freud* (Vol. XIV).
London: Hogarth, 1957. Pp. 67–102.

Freud, S. Some general remarks on hysterical attacks. In J. Strachey (Ed.), *The standard edition of the complete psychological works of Sigmund Freud (Vol. IX). London: Hogarth, 1959. Pp. 227–234.

Freud, S. The neuro-psychoses of defence. In J. Strachey (Ed.), The standard edition of the complete psychological works of Sigmund Freud (Vol. III). London: Hogarth, 1962. Pp. 41–61. (a)

Freud, S. The aetiology of hysteria. In J. Strachey (Ed.), The standard edition of the complete pyschological works of Sigmund Freud (Vol. III). London: Hogarth, 1962. Pp. 182–221. (b)

Freud, S. A case of successful treatment of hypnotism. In J. Strachey (Ed.), The standard edition of the complete psychological works of Sigmund Freud (Vol. I). London: Hogarth, 1966. Pp. 115–128. (a)

Freud, S. Project for a scientific psychology. In J. Strachey (Ed.), The standard edition of the complete psychological works of Sigmund Freud (Vol. I). London: Hogarth, 1966. Pp. 283–397. (b)

Helmholtz, H. von Treatise on physiological optics. In T. Shipley (Ed.), Classics in psychology. New York: Philosophical Library, 1961.

Jones, E. The life and work of Sigmund Freud: The formative years and great discoveries (Vol. 1). New York: Basic Books, 1953.

Kuhn, T. S. The structure of scientific revolutions (2nd. ed.). Chicago: University of Chicago Press, 1970. (1st ed., 1962.)

McGuire, W. (Ed.), The Freud/Jung letters. Bollingen Series XCIV. Princeton, N.J.: Princeton University Press, 1974.

Mischel, T. Wundt and the conceptual foundations of psychology. Philosophical and Phenomenological Research, 1970, 31, 1–26.

Rancurello, A. C. A study of Franz Brentano. New York: Academic, 1968.

Rieff, P. Freud: The mind of the moralist. New York: Viking, 1959.

Rychlak, J. F. A philosophy of science for personality theory. Boston: Houghton Mifflin, 1968.

Titchener, E. B. Systematic psychology: Prolegomena. Ithaca, N.Y.: Cornell University Press, 1972.

Watson, R. I. The great psychologists. Philadelphia: Lippincott, 1971.

Wundt, M. Die Wurzein der deutschen Philosophie in Stamm und Rasse. Berlin: Junker und Dunnhaupt, 1944.

Wundt, W. Lectures on human and animal psychology (4th ed.). New York: Macmillan, 1907. (1st ed., 1894.)

Wundt, W. Contributions to the theory of sensory perception. In T. Shipley (Ed.), Classics in psychology. New York: Philosophical Library, 1961.

Wundt, W. The language of gestures. Paris: Mouton, 1973.

CHAPTER FOUR

A Lockean Victory: The Americanization of Scientific Psychology

Because most of the early influential American psychologists had taken advanced degrees in Europe—or at least had spent some time in study there—the issues discussed in Chapter 3 were naturally alive in the academic circles of the United States in the late nineteenth and early twentieth centuries. However, an Americanization of scientific psychology was to take place in relatively short order as the lead in this discipline shifted from Europe to the United States. In Chapter 4 we underscore a few of the predominant themes in psychology's historical development, showing thereby how they solidified into an *institutionalized* outlook on the nature of proper scientific psychology.

Functionalism Versus Structuralism

Caldwell, Titchener, Calkins, Angell

In 1897 Professor William Caldwell (1863–1942) traveled from Northwestern University in Evanston, Illinois, to Ithaca, New York, where the American Psychological Association was holding a December meeting. Caldwell disagreed with the psychology then being advocated by E. B. Titchener (1867–1927), Wundt's student and foremost advocate in America. Indeed, as we suggested in Chapter 3, much of what we know and understand about Wundtian psychology in America derives from Titchener's interpretations of his mentor's outlook (aided and abetted by the writings of Boring, who was the protégé of Titchener). Caldwell presented a small paper at the Ithaca meeting, which was later published in the *Psychological Review*

(Caldwell, 1898). Though he was not aware of it at the time, this brief "point of order" raised by Caldwell was to touch off a major confrontation in early American psychology.

Caldwell's complaint centered on the fact that in his book *An Outline of Psychology* Titchener (1897) chose to speak for *all* of psychology when he held that there was no evidence for mind in the findings of experimental psychology. When Titchener spoke of experimental psychology he was stressing the introspective method, but he also included the work of Ebbinghaus (see Titchener, 1961, p. 231). Titchener viewed the *self* as the total of conscious processes that run their course under the conditions laid down by bodily tendencies (Caldwell, 1898). Based on his own introspective investigations, Caldwell objected to these blanket statements and argued: "There is in us a feeling consciousness of selfhood, or the realization of (as Aristotle puts it) an inward operative (formal or final) purpose which is not expressed by his biological self, his 'sum of tendencies' [a phrase used by Titchener]" (*ibid.*, p. 403).

Based on *evidence* using the same methods proposed by Titchener of internal perception, Caldwell felt that he had observed a "mind or 'will' working from within outwards, conditioning mental process" (*ibid.*, p. 402). Stout (1860–1944) also found this natural tendency for an attitude of mind, utilizing schematic apprehensions in an *active* fashion (*ibid.*, p. 405). Mind is passive when it must confront sensations from without, yet it *also* can be proven introspectively that it is active, schematizing, conceptualizing, and so on. However, "Titchener will not call it both active and passive; he insists that it is passive, consisting merely of sensation and affection" (*ibid.*, p. 405). In this "active" criticism leveled at Titchener Caldwell was to frame for the first time a major distinction in our history when he observed: "Titchener surely separates the 'content' from the 'activity' of attention" (*ibid.*, p. 404).

This seems to be the first explicit statement opposing content (Lockean) to act (Kantian) psychology. Though such differences existed in the outlooks of Wundt and Brentano, the former did not consider himself a content psychologist and the latter called his approach empirical psychology. The point of Caldwell's criticism is that in the Titchenerian-Wundtian use of introspection, what resulted was an *extraspective* formulation of elements—excitations contained in the physical apparatus—totaling "over there" into behavior. As an introspectionist in the tradition of Brentano, Caldwell felt that this account denied the *objective fact* that something like a self-identity brought forward a contribution to experience *in addition to* the simple taking in and collating of such sensation-contents in the physical apparatus of the body to summate or "make up" behavior.

Just as Ebbinghaus had tried to perfect his experimental methods to accomodate a mathematical theoretical formulation (see Chapter 3, p. 120), so too did Wundt and Titchener make every effort to train their introspecting subjects to *avoid* questions of selfhood in the effort. Becoming aware of one's self-identity in the process could contaminate the findings, and introduce subjectivity (recall the Wurzburgers!) hence unreliability, into the procedure. Therefore evidence for selfhood could not be attained in the Titchenerian model of introspection as method. There is also clear evidence that Titchener did not wish to entertain anything smacking of teleological theory. Caldwell even observed that Wundt was more accepting of the mind as an active agent in life than was Titchener (*ibid.*, p. 406). In support of his findings on the self he noted that a physiological text of the period "refers to an ultimate tendency of living matter to act from within outwards, to act in a way that cannot be explained by mechanical or reflex action. There is a self-preservation *nisus* in the life of a biological organism which may be said to constitute its unity, to make it more than the mere sum of tendencies" [One in Many Thesis!] (*ibid.*, p. 406). The entire talk is a beautiful example of a humanistic theorist, leveling his Kantian guns at a leading Lockean thinker of the period.

Caldwell's name is not found in today's major psychology history texts, but his unsung role must not be forgotten, because in charging that Titchener was losing the human person in the assemblage of elements he called a self, Caldwell prompted Titchener to write his famous 1898 paper "The Postulates of a Structural Psychology" (appearing in the *Philosophical Review*, and reprinted in Shipley, 1961, from which we take quotations). In his quasi-reply—where reference to Caldwell is made only in footnotes—Titchener (1961) bases his case on an analogy to biology where the division between morphology, or structure, and the function these various structures serve to the economy of the organism is commonly made (p. 224). The structural approach in psychology is then identified as experimental psychology, and the functional approach is likened to what Titchener called Brentano's descriptive (nonexperimental) psychology. Titchener added a third aspect having to do with the changes in structure or function over time—implying a developmental form of psychological study as an extension of either or both of the basic approaches. No real discussion of this third alternative is carried out.

Titchener employed the structure-function dichotomy in two

ways. The first and major use was to suggest a "pecking-order" distinction in psychology, relegating functionalism to a second-class standing—for example, when he noted: "The methods of descriptive psychology cannot, in the nature of the case, lead to results of scientific finality" (*ibid*, p. 228). That is, in simply describing how things happen the psychological scientist does not base his account on the firm underpinning of a structure; hence, he cannot be a first-rate scientist. Titchener drew no real distinction between functionalism, act psychology, descriptive psychology, and even faculty psychology (*ibid.*, p. 228). All of these approaches settled on explanations that were insufficient and often spurious. We must never forget that "function presupposes structure" (*ibid.*, p. 227). A physical apparatus is required to do the behaving in all behavior! This is especially important for a science of psychology, because: "There is, further, the danger that, if function is studied before structure has been fully elucidated, the student may fall into that acceptance of *teleological explanation which is fatal to scientific advance* . . . [italics added] (*ibid.*, p. 229).

The second use of the dichotomy takes root from this attack on teleological description. Titchener tried to identify all functionalists as teleologists, and vice versa. This included an effort to make this dichotomy a rephrase of what *he now called* the content-act confrontations of his student days. Thus he referred to Brentano's difficult phrase of immanent objectively (see Chapter 3, p. 112) as "language of function, not of structure" (*ibid.*, p. 232) and added: "The 'psychology from an empirical standpoint' is a systematization of mental 'activities,' *i.e.*, of the mental functions of the human organism" (*ibid.*, p. 232). He went on to place William James (1842–1910) in the functionalist camp because of the latter's concept of the "fiat of the will" (*ibid.*, p. 241) and even underscored the Aristotelian and Kantian features of all functionalist psychologies (*ibid.*, p. 242).

The actual postulates of a structuralist psychology amount to three or four points: that sensations (*ibid.*, p. 233) and affections (*ibid.*, p. 234) are the elements of mind, that these are underivable, one from the other (*ibid.*, p. 236), and that they are subject to determination by the factors of intensity and quality (*ibid.*, p. 236). The question of *time* in the workings of mind was also emphasized because Titchener could not conceive of an affective or sensational process that was free of duration (*ibid.*, p. 238). Titchener ends his paper by observing that structuralists are more in agreement with what their approach to psychology involves than are the functionalists (*ibid.*, pp. 241–242).

Caldwell (1899) was to write a rebuttal to Titchener in which he admirably reaffirmed his charges and defended a telic interpretation of selfhood. Subsequently Mary Whiton Calkins (1863–1930) (1906), in her 1905 Presidential Address to the American Psychological Association, also took up the question of a much needed self-construct in psychology. Calkins called for a union of functionalism (her theoretical outlook) and structuralism, with *both* sides accepting as a "basal fact" (*ibid.*, p. 68) the reality of a self in human behavior (based on the evidence of introspection). Calkins directed her commentary primarily at James Rowland Angell (1867–1949) and only secondarily at Titchener. Angell, who was at the University of Chicago at this time (along with John Dewey until 1904, at which time Dewey left for Columbia University), was becoming a leading spokesman for the (more accurately, "a") functionalist outlook. In 1902, during the Decennial celebration of the University of Chicago, Angell delivered a talk on the nature of structural versus functional psychology. In 1903 he published a paper on the relations of structural and functional psychology to philosophy (Angell, 1903). The Chicago School of psychologists (Dewey, Angell, later Carr and others) were conducting experiments on both humans and lower animals. They employed introspection as well as other strictly empirical strategies that we now identify as "the" approach to experimental psychology. Though this would seem to be the province of structural psychology *a la* Titchener, these men at Chicago were calling themselves functionalists!

Understandably Caldwell and Calkins were dissatisfied with structural or content psychology. They were humanists, wanting to see a role for intentionality by way of self-direction in the psychology of their time. Calkins (1906) even charged that Angell had gone over to a structuralist position in his stressing the necessity of providing a physical basis to behavior (p. 71; see Angell's discussion, below). But what the structuralists at Cornell (Titchener's university) and the functionalists at Chicago (Dewey, Angell, Carr) had to argue about is considerably more difficult to appreciate. This was surely a most unusual debate. The humanists, Caldwell and Calkins, soon fell from view in this exchange (relegated to footnote mention by the apparently more eminent protagonists). When he was elected President of the American Psychological Association in 1906, Angell (1907) used the occasion to spell out in detail what he considered was "The Province of Functional Psychology." We will take a close look at this historic rebuttal [sic] to Titchener's 1898 paper.

Angell organizes his presentation around three basic characteris-

tics of the functional outlook, although he notes that there are variations on each of these themes. The first point confronts directly the
Wundtian-Titchenerian use of introspection, for it suggests that functionalists hope to "discern and portray the typical *operations* of consciousness under actual life conditions, as over against the attempt
to analyze and describe its elementary and complex *contents*" (*ibid.*,
pp. 62–63). Angell does not speak of act or of an active mind conceptualizing events; he sees the functionalist as tracking the *operations* of mind, a term which he soon uses interchangeably with *function* (*ibid.*, p. 66). The functionalists at Chicago do not go along with
the Wundtian thesis of a "direct observation of inner experience"
(see Chapter 3, p. 112). They find this artificial, a *post hoc* examination of consciousness: "As a matter of fact many modern investigations of an experimental kind largely dispense with the usual direct
form of introspection and concern themselves in a distinctly functionalistic spirit with a determination of what work is accomplished
and what the conditions are under which it is achieved" (*ibid.*, p. 65).

A second characteristic of the functionalist approach is its commitment to the Darwinian theory of evolution (*ibid.*, p. 62). The
functionalist would like to study "mental activity as part of a larger
stream of biological forces which are daily and hourly at work before
our eyes and which are constitutive of the most important and most
absorbing part of our world" (*ibid.*, p. 68). Combined with the move
away from introspection, this has resulted, said Angell, in a "quasi-
biological field which we designate [as] animal psychology" (*ibid.*,
p. 69). One studies lower animals to gain thereby "the longitudinal
rather than the transverse view of life phenomena" (*ibid.*, pp. 70–71).
This does *not* mean the anthropomorphization of lower animals. The
modern functionalists' observations are "in the spirit of conservative
non-anthropomorphism as earlier observations almost never were"
(*ibid.*, p. 70). Indeed, Angell insisted that most behaviors are formed
through repetitions into a regularity "approximating physiological
automatism" (*ibid.*, p. 72) so that when we contemplate the role of
consciousness in life it is actually a form of "accommodation to the
novel" (*ibid.*, p. 72). The novel, once put into habitual routine, becomes the automatic. But what is the "operation" by which this
routinizing of behavior is made possible? Angell observes:

In the execution of the accommodatory activity [i.e., mental activity] the
instincts represent the racially hereditary utilities, many of which are
under the extant conditions of life extremely anomalous in their value.
The sensory-algedonic-motor phenomena represent the immediate short
circuit unreflective forms of selective response. Whereas the ideational-

algedonic-motor series at its several levels represents the long circuit response under the influence of the *mediating effects of previous experience* [italics added]. This experience serves either to inhibit the propulsive power intrinsic to the stimulus, or to reinforce this power by adding to it its own dynamic tendencies. This last variety of *action* [italics added] is the peculiarly human form of mediated control. On its lowest stages, genetically speaking, it merges with the purely immediate algedonic type of response. All the other familiar psychological processes are subordinate to one or more of these groups. Conception, judgement, reasoning, emotion, desire, aversion, volition, etc., simply designate special varieties in which these generic forms appear (*ibid.*, p. 74).

The term *algedonic* refers to the pleasantness-unpleasantness dimension of hedonic physiological experience. By linking sensory-algedonic-motor phenomena into the overall concept of a response, Angell was pointing to the reflex-arc concept which had by this time been widely discussed in America. But in speaking of the mediating effects of previous experience on such reflex activity Angell was anticipating in striking fashion the line of development behaviorism was to take. We return to this point below in our discussion of the wedding of behaviorism to functionalism.

Although Angell speaks of *action* in the above quote, note that this has nothing to do with what Brentano (or Caldwell or Calkins) would have meant by the term—i.e., as a conceptualizing effort of mind to confront and exert an influence on experience. For Angell, the action of mind is exclusively as an instrumentality: "Mind [is] conceived as primarily engaged in mediating between the environment and the needs of the organism" (*ibid.*, p. 85). Angell lumped actions with functions, and these concepts in turn were both viewed as aspects of control in behavior—a term that issues from the third characteristic attributed to functional psychology.

This has to do with "determining the relations to one another of the physical and mental portions of the organism" (*ibid.*, p. 80). Functionalism takes on a psychophysiological coloring at this point because it does not rest easily with Wundtian psychophysical parallelism (see Chapter 3). It begins with the premise that the bodily side of experience has some *necessary* tie to the mental side. This is what Calkins rebuked in Angell's position, believing that it was proper for psychology to deal exclusively with the workings (Brentano-like acts) of mind *qua* mind. Angell's functionalism had no real appreciation for the phenomenal realm of experience, except as the possible effect of purely physical causes. As he said of human volition:

. . . if one considers the usual accounts of the ontogenesis of human volitional acts one is again confronted with intrinsically physiological data in
which reflexes, automatic and instinctive acts are much in evidence . . . .
volition cannot be understood either as regards its origin or its outcome
without constant and overt reference to these factors (*ibid.*, p. 81).

Though Titchener would have the functionalist resorting to telic
formulations, there is absolutely nothing but efficient causation in
this theoretical treatment of volition.

A vital adjunct to this functionalist interest in the relations of
body-mind involved what might be termed an "argument from
method" rather than from theory in the settling of all scientific disputes. This harks back to the first characteristic of functionalism,
having to do with a discarding of introspection in favor of more "life-
like" studies. Rather than looking inward (introspection *a la* Wundt),
the functionalists at Chicago wanted to look outward to study things
the way any natural scientist studies them. Angell felt that in so
doing they shifted the question of mind-body relations from the
realm of theoretical opinion to that of methodological verification.
Hence he said: "The position to which I refer regards the mind-body
relation as capable of treatment in psychology as a methodological
distinction rather than as a metaphysically existential one" (*ibid.*,
p. 83).

In other words, what was defined as "mind" in an experimental
format and what was defined as "body" depended upon the data an
experimentalist focused on in the design of his study. If confusion
between the two realms of explanations occurred, the proper context in which to resolve such differences is the methodological and
not the theoretical. This strategy of looking for answers to all problems of knowledge in a methodological rather than a theoretical context was important to functionalism—so important that Angell
termed it a "functionalistic metaphysics" (*ibid.*, p. 84). In shifting
all questions of knowledge over exclusively to the side of method
Angell began a long line of arguing from the circumstances (later
called the antecedents) under which behavior takes place rather
than from the mental acts people are (introspectively) aware of while
they *are* behaving. This action of mind came to be known as consciousness, and here is how he framed this still popular functionalistic argument:

They [the functionalists] urge further that the profitable and significant
thing is to seek for a more exact appreciation of the precise conditions

under which consciousness is in evidence and the conditions under which
it retires in favor of the more exclusively physiological. Such knowledge
so far as it can be obtained is on a level with all scientific and practical
information. It states the circumstances under which certain sorts of
results will appear (*ibid.*, p. 84).

Wundt and Brentano (Chapter 3) would have considered this an
indirect form of mind-study, for it leaves things up to an observer
other than the subject under observation to name (induct, presume,
deduce, etc.) those circumstances under which consciousness may
or may not be said to enter into experimental findings. Indeed this
observer need not even ask the subject what *he* thinks is at play in
the succession of "observed events" which have been pre-arranged
entirely at the convenience of the experimental observer in the first
instance. This is a vital question in any research done on human
beings, one Angell did not foresee arising but which was to be resur-
rected generations later in the history of experimental psychology as
an embarrassment of major proportions (see Chapter 6). We must
consider what a subject might be consciously contributing to the
experimental procedure because Angell equated all "circumstances"
under which behavior—both mental and physiological—takes place
with *controls* on behavior. He noted that any account of mind had
to deal with the "manner in which mental processes eventuate in
motor phenomena of the physiological organism" (*ibid.*, p. 86). Only
when consciousness eventuates in bodily action can we state with
scientific assurance that there is such an operation as mind. Mind is
therefore a controlling factor in behavior:

The functionalist's most intimate persuasion leads him to regard consciousness as primarily and intrinsically a control phenomenon. Just as behavior
may be regarded as the most distinctly basic category of general biology in
its functional phase so control would perhaps serve as the most fundamental category in functional psychology, the special forms and differen-
tiations of consciousness simply constituting particular phases of the general process of control (*ibid.*, p. 88).

This word *control* was to become a premiere construct in experimental psychology, albeit a frequently misunderstood one. Angell
is confident that mind controls behavior (body) and that we can
study such factors empirically. But what if, in studying the mind
"indirectly" (to quote Wundt and Brentano), the empirical observer
finds that he can personally *predict* what the subject will or will not
do in an experimental context based on the observer's knowledge of

most famous of which is the *yin-yang* principle (see Chapter 1, p. 32). the antecedent circumstances that also face the subject? Following Angell's prescription to let the empirical methods answer questions of knowledge, would it not then be more accurate to say that the circumstances controlled consciousness (mind) than vice versa? Angell did not anticipate such a ready reversal of his confident belief in the mind as controlling agent, but as we shall see below, because of his denigration of a role for *theory* in knowledge-accrual, this is what actually happened with the advent of behaviorism. He spoke of ethics and logic as a means of controlling behavior (*ibid.*, p. 89) and ended with a summary statement of the functionalist's aim: "to see the mind which he analyzes as it actually is when engaged in the discharge of its vital functions" (*ibid.*, p. 90). In a few years his student, John Watson, would drop the mind (consciousness) construct altogether.

There was no immediate reply by Titchener. Though he returned to the topic of functionalism in his *Systematic Psychology: Prolegomena* (1972; first published in 1929), Titchener did not feel that the dispute needed furthering. He analyzed the functionalism of George Trumbill Ladd (1842–1921), who was cut from the Brentano mold (see Boring, 1950, p. 526), placing him in opposition to the more biological approach of Angell. He then placed C. H. Judd (1873–1946) between these two extremes, as a theorist who tried with little apparent success to preserve both the physical basis of behavior and the self as a "possessor of knowledge" (Titchener, 1972, pp. 159–160). But Titchener had little heart for continuing the debate. His closing views on the subject were as follows:

"Structural" psychology, as its name implies, recognized the existence of a correlative psychology of function; it isolated itself only to the degree that it demanded equal rights for content and activity, and by so doing protested against the autocracy of function. In the "biological" atmosphere of its time the phrase did good controversial service. If the view of my book [*Systematic Psychology: Prolegomena*] is accepted, both "functional" and "structural," as qualifications of "psychology," are now obsolete terms (Titchener, 1972, p. 178).

A Misfired Polemic

Much to psychology's detriment, the humanistic polemic advanced by Caldwell was *never* aired properly, nor given clear acknowledgement in the history books. As a result the significant role teleological questions have had to play in the historical development of psychology has been submerged. Boring (1950, p. 555) suggests that Titchener raised the structural-functional issue as an angular jab at Dewey (who is mentioned once in the article). Hilgard and Bower (1966) go so far as to suggest that Titchener "attacked Dewey's position" (p. 298). Titchener was actually prodded into action by Caldwell, and then he made a first effort to align sides in terms of the same distinctions he felt were at play in his student days between Wundt and Brentano. He skirted the telic theoretical question by disclaiming it as a nonscientific concern, and in the ensuing emphasis on proper scientific procedures he lost the initiative to an even more vigorous approach.

Titchener properly aligned Caldwell and Brentano and then, characterizing these approaches as essentially nonscientific descriptive psychologies, tried to equate his view with the natural-science tradition of experimentation (the "pecking-order" intimidation referred to above). Translating the issue into theory-construction terms, we can see that for him structure meant the material-cause apparatus of the nervous system and so on, and content meant the stimulus complexes (sum of excitations) that were carried by these structures. As nonexperimentalists, Caldwell and Brentano were characterized as likely to speculate telically, falling back on the formal-final cause tandem in accounting for behavior.

If the debate could have been sustained with a leading teleologist (Caldwell did not qualify), Titchener might have succeeded in his alignment of sides—with "his side" being "the" scientific community and the opponents "something else." But a satisfactory opponent to speak for teleology was not forthcoming. Ladd's 10 years in the ministry probably disqualified him (Boring, 1950, pp. 524–526), and by this time in the eyes of American psychologists James had become more the philosopher than the leader of a spirited defense of teleological psychology. And as if to bedevil Titchener or challenge his lead, we have the Chicago group taking the wrong name from his scheme to identify themselves as "the" scientific community! The move from Wundtian introspectionism to overt experimentation proved a boon to psychological science. Its Darwinian justification of animal psychology led to a host of highly instructive experiments. A body of objective knowledge began to accrue having great heuristic value as well as practical implications for the control of human behavior.

Hence, Titchener found himself engaged in two somewhat different arguments: one aimed at the familiar Brentano-like psychologists who wanted to view human behavior as telic, framed introspectively around a self, and one aimed at the Chicago brand of psychologists who were nontelic, extraspective, and just as dedicated to experimental psychology as he was. The former confrontation was a classical Kantian-Lockean one, but the latter was a *Lockean-Lockean nonconfrontation!* Although the question of proper scientific method separated Cornell from Chicago, even this is not without certain qualifications. Because Titchener *did* include the work of Ebbinghaus as an example of structural psychology, the criticism suggesting that he refused to study lifelike researches or that he was committed *only* to introspection did not hold in the broader sense. Furthermore, the Wundtian methods of introspection —which, as we noted in Chapter 3 (p. 117), resulted in extraspective theoretical accounts—even advanced the study of physiological processes or functions (a fact Titchener always stressed).

The oft-cited historical confrontation between functionalism and structuralism was no confrontation at all in one aspect and a misfired polemic in another. It was begun by a humanist, who found the Newtonian interpretations of science brought to this country by Wundt's students lacking in something vital to man's conceptualization. Titchener lost the totality (the one) in the constitutive total of basal elements (the many), and yet this self-organizing principle of mental life is most characteristic of the human experience. Rather than a full airing of the introspective-versus-extraspective *theoretical* slant implied, what developed was a temporary quibble over the rules of *methodological* procedure. There was an implicit assumption held to by Cornell *and* Chicago which Angell made explicit: All problems of a theoretical (philosophical) nature could be answered in time through methodological refinements. The data gathered in psychological science would answer all questions about selves and consciousness and minds, so why play at the role of philosopher in these matters? Get on with the accrual of scientific evidence, which in turn meant (extraspectively) *observe behavior.* The stage was set for a new development.

The Wedding of Behaviorism to Functionalism

The Lockean Advocates:
Watson, Tolman, Hull, Skinner

Although we do not need to go into their work to make the point of this section, we should mention Edward L. Thorndike (1874–1949) and Ivan Petrovich Pavlov (1849–1936) because of the importance of their respective law of effect and reinforcement principles to the development of behaviorism. Every psychologist knows that John B. Watson (1878–1958) formally established behaviorism as an approach to psychology in his classic 1913 paper "Psychology as the Behaviorist Views It." The groundwork for behaviorism had already been presaged in Angell's brand of functionalism. Watson was Angell's student in psychology at the University of Chicago, where he earned a doctoral degree in 1903 (with the physiologist Donaldson as co-major professor) and then stayed on as a member of the faculty. Boring (1950) suggests that what may have set Watson off on his own path was a 1907 monograph he authored on the kinaesthetic and organic sensations of the white rat in the learning of mazes:

The rule of functional animal psychology of that date was that, when you have finished your observations of behavior, you use the results to infer the nature of the animal's consciousness and then show how those processes function in the animal's behavior. Watson rebelled at lugging consciousness in, after he had adequately described the animal's functional behavior (p. 556).

There are three important points entailed in this adjustment made by Watson. First, when he rebelled at lugging consciousness in he was making a *theoretical* shift in emphasis (i.e., selecting which constructs he would use to account for the data). There is *never* anything explicitly in the data of experimentation to dictate for the observer what one and *only* one theoretical explanation must be used to account for the fact pattern under observation. In dropping consciousness Watson was taking the prerogative of an extraspective observer —that is, to employ only the theory which is necessary to account for the data under observation *that interests him!* Second, in giving his *reasons* why he needed to drop consciousness Watson in that typical functionalist way begun by his mentor (Angell), held that the data *compelled* him to do so. In other words, he leveled the argument from method we mentioned above. Because all one can "see" in the T-maze apparatus is a white rat running about in response to certain observed environmental circumstances and other presumed internal circumstances (drives), why impute a consciousness of these circumstances to the rat? This lack of parsimony is unbecoming to science. Why not be *truly* scientific and remain with only that which is observed?

Third, in predicating his argument in this fashion Watson could go on to the *next* issue in the above quote and say: If behavior is a function of environmental (and internal) circumstances, it is *itself* an effect and not a cause. It is under control rather than controlling.

Consciousness is simply the remnant of a medieval mythology about the supposed control that mind has on behavior (this is a repudiation of Angell; see above, p. 144). Because he was of the opinion that his methodological observations and not his theoretical stance is what forced him to limit his descriptions to the behavioral functions at play before his eyes, Watson had no real alternative but to use the language of *efficient causality* (with a secondary emphasis on the material cause to account for internal stimuli). The upshot is that he did what other natural scientists were doing: confounding his theory of functionalism with the supposed functional relationships of antecedent events impelling consequent events in that independent variable-dependent variable (IV-DV) sequence we know of as an experimental procedure. In speaking of this sequence theoretically he took the language of stimulus-response (S-R), a familiar antecedent-consequent succession due to the reflex arc concept that had been given wide consideration by psychologists. Both the IV-DV and S-R conceptions were used in the sense of efficient causality. Watson (1913) was therefore in the position of drawing a startling parallel: "Psychology as the behaviorist views it is a purely objective branch of natural science. Its theoretical goal is the prediction and control of behavior" (p. 158).

The response is a function of the stimulus; some stimuli exist internally and others exist externally in the environment. When a given response is made in reasonable proximity to a given stimulus, and especially if this association is repeated frequently, the resultant S-R regularity persists as a *habit*. Internal responses can be thought of as implicit, and external responses are overt and hence rather than reflecting mental consciousness, human thought is *implicit responding* (Watson, 1924, p. 15). It is controlled and not controlling. So to carry out his program, the "rule, or measuring rod, which the behaviorist puts in front of him always is: Can I describe this bit of behavior I see in terms of 'stimulus and response' " (*ibid.*, p. 6)? Because the stimulus always controls the response, a sagacious behaviorist in time should be able to work out the complete (efficiently) causal network of events of which behavior "is a function" (Watson, 1913, p. 167).

The phrase *control and prediction* has become a rallying cry for rigorous psychologists ever since. Introductory texts often define psychology as "the science of behavioral control and prediction" or a like definition. Mixed into this abstract formulation of a professional goal are the meanings of both a theoretical sort (what kind of determinism is presumed in this word *control*?) and a methodological sort (is not this a standard for validating evidence, and no more?). Many psychologists would prefer to restrict the phrase to the side of our methodological procedures in accruing evidence, because they do not feel that psychology should have as a professional aim the control of the lives of people. To meet such objections we have to spend some time on the theoretical side of knowledge, using our conceptual facilities (procedural evidence) to clarify our directions. But Watson failed to appreciate the theory-method distinction because all there is to life is behavior. Ultimately, behavior is a response that is a motion (reminiscent of the Wundtian reduction; see Chapter 3, p. 110), flowing along as a function of implicit and overt stimulation. He placed his psychology on the confident grounds of Newtonian-Laplacian science. There is probably no clearer call for mechanistic psychology in the literature than Watson's request of his generation: "... let us try to think of man as an assembled organic machine ready to run" (Watson, 1924, p. 216).

Before long this simplistic version of "S to R to habit"—analogized from the reflex-arc cycle—was found wanting as a theoretical statement, although Watson's efforts were paying dividends. Psychology was building a distinctive body of scientific knowledge. Edward Chace Tolman (1886–1961) felt that a refinement was needed in the input-output mechanism of Watsonian behaviorism. Tolman spent time with the gestalt psychologist Kurt Koffka, and although he was not influenced sufficiently to take a more Kantian view of things, he *did* come away believing that behaviorism had to broaden its explanatory range. In his classic work *Purposive Behavior in Animals and Men* (1967; first appeared in 1932), Tolman begins his argument for a revised behaviorism as follows: "It will be contended by us (if not by Watson) that 'behavior-acts,' though no doubt in complete one-to-one correspondence with the underlying molecular facts of physics and physiology, have, as 'molar' wholes, certain emergent properties of their own" (p. 7).

The joining of behavior to act excites our interest, suggesting that Tolman was cognizant of the terminological and conceptual disputes of his predecessors. But by *act* Tolman did not mean anything other than responsivity in the typical behavioral sense. His reference to emergent properties in molar behavior relates to the gestaltist emphasis on the one (gestalt) over the many (elementalism). This formal-cause theme is what Tolman brought to behaviorism to "account for behavior," as the saying now goes. Tolman here initiates a theoretical proclivity that has been cultivated by all subsequent behaviorists. The strategy is essentially to try to explain humanistic terms in other than telic fashion. Of course it is put more professionally than this, as "try to account for all behavior using 'scientific' terminology." Graduate students in psychology soon learn to express—and in time, unfortunately, to think—this way, which comes down to "exclude final causation from your speculations!"

Yet Tolman is known for his founding of a purposive behaviorism (a phrase William McDougall used to describe his work and which Tolman then adopted). He was critical of Watson for wanting to limit the description of behavior to muscle twitches or aimless motions. Behavior has molar properties which emerge to give it a unique quality (the gestaltists had spoken of form qualities). If one looks at these molar patterns, he invariably finds them to be goal oriented. Behavior is always a question of "getting-to or getting-from a specific goal-object, or goal-situation" (*ibid.*, p. 10). And this persistent striving toward or away from goals itself takes on "a specific pattern of commerce-, intercourse-, engagement-, communion-with such and such intervening means-objects, as the way to get thus to or from" (*ibid.*, p. 11). If behavior is thus aimed at ends by its very nature, surely one should be able to observe the course of such actions and to see if a purposive effort is made to improve on the performance *vis à vis* some (equally observable) goal. Hence:

The doctrine we here contend for is, in short, that wherever a response shows docility [i.e., teachableness, improvability] relative to some end—wherever a response is ready (a) to break out into trial and error and (b) to select gradually, or suddenly, the more efficient of such trials and errors with respect to getting to that end—such a response expresses and defines something which *for convenience* [italics added], we name a purpose (*ibid.*, p. 14).

We have italicized the phrase *for convenience* in the above quote to (1) emphasize that this is what we mean by the extraspective theorist describing events "over there" (third person) as *he sees fit*—that is, for his convenience and not for the convenience of the subject—and also to (2) provide another example of the tendency to account for a telic phenomenon in other than telic terms. Tolman is not saying that he is presenting evidence here of what the teleologists of history have meant by purpose. He is saying that to view behavior as purposive seems reasonable, although in truth we can never hope to "see" palpable purposes as we can see a rat's leg, flexing in behavior; but maybe we can use the term anyhow, relating it to the improvement in performance that a rat might show in running the maze, and in this way broaden behaviorism as we "account for" what the teleologists have been wanting us to consider but in a more scientific fashion! Tolman was quite aware of this strategy of explanation. He took special pains to distinguish his data-based view of purpose from other more traditional telic accounts, as in the following discussion of William McDougall:

. . . for us, purpose is a purely objectively defined *variable* [italics added], which is defined by the facts of trial and error and of resultant docility; for Professor McDougall, purpose seems to be an introspectively defined subjective "somewhat," which is a something other, and more than, the manner in which it appears in behavior; it is a "psychic," "mentalistic" somewhat, behind such objective appearances, and to be known in the last analysis through introspection only. This difference between our point of view and McDougall's is fundamental and . . . complete . . . " (*ibid.*, p. 16).

This remarkable passage continues the argument from method which we saw Angell initiate. Note that Tolman here refers to purpose as a *variable*! It is not a theoretical construct, something that is framed by the psychologist and then put to test in a methodology calling for IV-DV regularities and the attendent controls that result in validation or fail to do so. Purpose is itself a "variable" to be captured in the facts of experimental observation. There is a blatant confound here of method-talk with theory-talk. Tolman speaks as if all he were disparaging is the introspective *methods* of the earlier psychologies. Actually, he is also disparaging the *theoretical* constructions a psychologist such as McDougall might have hoped to put to test in the experimental methods of functionalism or behaviorism. McDougall, the humanist, is pictured as a kind of "swami," playing with psychic unobservables, which comes down to nonentities hence nonscientific methodological formulations.

Had he been more circumspect concerning his total procedure as a scientist, Tolman could have seen that he was *not* rejecting McDougall's position on the basis of data—that is, the findings of experimentation! He was defining (or ridiculing) it away exclusively on theoretical grounds. He and behaviorists before and after him made it appear that something like a purpose, in the telic sense of a "that for the sake of which" (theoretical account), could not be put to scientific test. Of course even Angell would have seen the docility of behavior in Tolman's rat-runs as evidence for *consciousness!* And a psychological theory *could* view it as evidence for a genuine "that for the sake of which" characteristic in the rat's behavior. If the steps of control and prediction in validation were followed, there is nothing intrinsically impossible with testing a theory of *teleological* behavior in the IV-DV sequence, so long as we keep clearly in mind what is our *theory* (of purpose in behavior) and what is our *method* of validation. By placing his definition of purpose on the side of method—as a variable to be seen fluctuating in the IV-DV sequence —Tolman effectively negates the possibility of *ever* proving empirically that final causation exists in behavior. Why? Because the IV-DV sequence is taken *by definition* as an efficient-cause sequence of events.

If purpose is a variable, which variable might it be—the independent or the dependent? As a manifestation of behavior it is a response, and therefore clearly it must fall on the side of a dependent variable. Hence, it is by definition an efficiently caused effect and *no purpose at all*, if we mean by this term what the common sense of humanity has meant by it. Tolman wanted to correct the aspect of the humanistic-mechanistic debate on which behaviorism had been vulnerable. He tried to give behaviorism a more relevant formulation, one that would speak more directly to an extrapolation to man's behavior. To "account for" the fact that animals and humans might indeed contribute something to their course of behavior and not simply "muscle twitch" their way through life Tolman next proposed what might be called the *mediation thesis:*

The behaviorism here . . . presented will contend that mental processes are most usefully to be conceived as but dynamic aspects, or determinants, of behavior. They are *functional variables* [italics added] which *intermediate* [italics added] in the causal equation between environmental stimuli and initiating physiological states or excitements, on the one side, and final overt behavior, on the other (*ibid.*, p. 2).

A variant statement bringing in the word *response* follows:

Our system [purposive behaviorism] . . . conceives mental processes as *functional variables intervening* [italics added] between stimuli, initiating physiological states, and the general heredity and past training of the organism, on the one hand, and final resulting responses, on the other. These *intervening variables* [italics added] it defines as behavior-determinants (*ibid.*, p. 414).

This formulation obviated having to name whether purposes were independent or dependent variables. Purposes were *neither*. They "functioned" between a host of stimuli on the one side, and a number of responses on the other. In coining the term *intervening variable* (Int. V) Tolman legitimized the practice of mixing method-talk with theory-talk in experimental psychology. Behavior was now said to involve "S-Int. V-R" or "S-O-R" (with the O standing for organism, as Robert S. Woodworth [1869–1962] was to conceptualize the mediational sequence). What role did such intervening functions have in learning? Tolman suggested: "The process of learning any specific maze is thus the building-up of, or rather a refinement of and correction in, the expectations of such specific (*sign, significate and signified means-ends-relation*)-wholes, or, as we may hereafter call them, *sign-gestalts*" (*ibid.*, p. 136). The sign-gestalt (sometimes called a cognitive map) acts as a mediational aid, and the process is self-corrective so that:

. . . after learning has brought about the . . . changes in the expected sign-gestalts, such changes are going to react upon and modify the "readinesses" to sign-gestalts which the animal is going to carry with him to subsequent problems. The effect is one of reinforcing the propensities for certain types of means-objects as "probable" ways to given types of goals and weakening it for others (*ibid*, pp. 151–152).

We shall have much to say of the mediation model in the remaining pages of this volume. For now a note is sufficient that it makes no difference to a *theory* of behavior as efficiently caused whether we say "today's behaviors (responses) are a function of today's stimulations" or whether we say "today's behaviors (responses) are a function of yesterday's (mediated) stimulations *plus* today's stimulations." The latter account, which is what Tolman (and Woodworth) proposed, adds former efficient causes, but the basic meaning of a quasi-knee-jerk impetus to *all* behavior remains! The individual cannot on this theory opt against the experience he has had in the past. He is unable to go against these probabilities or to circumvent the layout of the sign-gestalt until subsequent experience intrudes and changes his purpose for him. Tolman has built on Angell's mediation idea to strengthen the behavioristic line of theory, but he has failed completely to "account for" what we know of as a purpose in that Brentano sense of reasoning "for the sake of" intended meaning-extensions. As the historical survey of Table 1 has taught us, one cannot say final cause when one really means yesterday's efficient cause.

The next major figure in this line of descent was Clark Leonard Hull (1884–1952). Hull (1943) elaborated on the concept of reinforcement, bringing in drive-reduction as a major explanatory principle. This remained within the material-cause type of formulation. He kept the mediation concept alive, and to "account for" seemingly telic behavior of the sort Tolman would have called purposive, he coined the term *fractional, antedating goal reaction* (later called *anticipatory goal response* by Neal Miller). It was not that an animal was making purposive moves in improving his responses toward the goal. One could see the rat gradually edging along the wall in the direction of the turn he would be making in the T-maze. It may have looked like a purposive maneuver, an intended preparation coming before the actual goal response of eating the food in the goal box, but it was not! What the animal had been learning via his repeated trials in the T-maze is a response of run-turn-eat. As he became more proficient through the practice trials (combining Watsonian frequency with drive reduction), the animal might reflect a "fraction" of the total goal reaction even before it had reached the point in the maze where its reward would be found.

The unique feature of this account is that Hull was to turn responses into stimuli here. That is, the actual stimulus for a fractional antedating goal reaction was the *responses* an animal was making in reaching the eventual goal. A fraction of the behavioral output generated a new kind of "intervening" input, which Hull termed the *pure stimulus act*. These stimuli were pure in the sense that their only role was to guide the course of behavior along the route to eventual reinforcement. They could not result in drive reduction via a consummatory response being made to them directly. Based on such a line of explanation, Hull (1952) developed his more extended theories of secondary reinforcement, habit-family hierarchies, and so on. Our point here is not to give a full presentation of Hullian learning theory, but simply to demonstrate that mediation theory was greatly expanded in the descent of behaviorism and this expansion was *not* an affair of method but rather of theoretical development. Tolman's claims of observing purpose methodologically were simply not defensible. Purpose is a *construct*, entertained theoretically by the observing experimentalist, who obtains empirical evidence favoring his conceptualization or fails to do so.

As Tolman did not reject McDougall based on evidence, Hull did not drop Tolmanian purpose based on evidence but rather on theoretical predilection. All of Tolman's evidence was simply reinterpreted! Hull was trying, in the best traditions of behaviorism, to give behavior a scientific (nontelic) appearance. The great advantage that he enjoyed, as all modern behaviorists enjoy, is the fact that the efficient- and material-cause conceptions are easily moved up and down the levels of abstraction we employ in describing anything (see Rychlak, 1968). The efficient cause in particular is the most multi-ordinal conception we have available to us. Literally *anything* can be seen in terms of its constitution (material cause) or those motions that have brought it about (efficient cause). Because plans of action must be drawn up by someone, rather than focusing on the pattern of behavior resulting (the formal-cause aspects) one can stress the motions that went into this planning by the individual who used a pencil to do (behavior) the drawing (planning). If a person seems to be putting his plans into effect (final-cause behaviors "for the sake of" plans), focus on the motion in behavior rather than on the strategy under presumption. Behaviorism's claim is that the motion *causes* the plans to come about, as well as the eventual intended actions in lieu of the plans. The *reverse* explanation is considered mentalistic, anthropomorphic, and probably spiritual as well.

The final person we wish to mention in this section is Burrhus Frederic Skinner (1904–   ). Because Skinner's thought is examined in detail in other sections of this book (see especially Chapter 6, pp. 255–270), we do not delve deeply into his outlook at this point. Suffice to say that Skinner (1938) *reverses* the classical S-R construct to a kind of R-S regularity in events. A behavioral response is not elicited by fixed stimuli, but rather is emitted as a kind of acting-upon operation. Responses are operators, or *operants*, which bring about changes in the contingent circumstances resulting in positive reinforcements (which are in this case stimuli for the next occasion). This does not mean that Skinner has foresaken the language of mediation. He once said: "As a determinist, I must assume that the organism is simply mediating the relationships between the forces acting upon it and its own output, and these are the kinds of relationships I'm anxious to formulate" (Evans, 1968, p. 23). Once again, clearly in the theoretical realm do we find Skinner eager to make formulations, although to hear him argue the case all of his views would seem to have been pressed on him by the weight of observational evidence (see, e.g., Skinner, 1956).

The Kantian Dissenters:
James, McDougall, Gestaltists, Rogers

William James (1842–1910) did not participate in the debate over functionalism versus structuralism (claiming on one occasion that he did not understand it), but we must surely accept him as an impor-

tant historical figure who would have resisted the trend functionalism was to establish in psychology. He would have considered this
an automation theory of behavior, and he specifically rejected this
point of view (see James, 1952, p. 90). James would have to be considered a mixed Lockean-Kantian theorist. His philosophy of Pragmatism has definite intonations of Lockeanism, in the sense of a
Yankee empiricism and practicality. He also gave the concept of
habit considerable emphasis, and his psychology is heavy with
physiological descriptions. But his fundamental efforts in the description of behavior were to account for it introspectively and,
above all, to include telic factors in the description. His celebrated
distinction between tough-minded (Lockean) and tender-minded
(Kantian) approaches to psychology reflected our historical confrontation. He claimed to have taken a middle position on this dimension, and we agree with that assessment.

The first major spokesman for teleological psychology in America
was probably William McDougall (1871–1938). Though he was to
wage an essentially losing battle, McDougall clearly saw the developing trends of a functional psychology and what this could only mean
for a humanistic image of man. For example, he saw the inevitable
divergence that a mechanistic account of behavior stressing efficient
causes would engender *vis à vis* the more literary descriptions of
human experience (McDougall, 1922, p. 8). Literary psychology demands formal-final cause phraseology, and to be viable our science
must be capable of embracing such descriptions without distortion.
Watson's psychology was being typified as pure science in the 1920s,
but McDougall feared that this form of purification was distilling the
human constants from the behavioral equation.

Though he used the language of instincts in his theories, McDougall saw these as inborn potentials for making self-contributions to
one's behavior, allowing for a true "that for the sake of which"
framing of human experience. The organism does not have to be
taught its instinctive potentials, although through experience such
nativistic tendencies were modified in maturation. But the way in
which these instincts were modified over life was *not* through what
Watson called the shaping of behavior. Only an efficiently caused
behavior can be shaped. Instincts were purposive sequences. Purpose was an introspectively conceived (theoretical) *telic* account of
the organism "coming at" the world with a self-directed contribution
to that course of methodological events under Tolmanian observation. McDougall astutely underscored the newly emerging tendency
in the 1920s for behaviorists to "account for" telic meanings in their

use of terms such as: "motor sets . . . trends . . . drives . . . [and] determining tendencies, all of which are terms of the Purposive Psychology, thinly disguised" (McDougall, 1923, p. 288). He was a committed humanistic psychologist, whose vision of psychology was too
broad to be encompassed in the tightening grips of the antecedent-
consequent vise that was closing in on psychology.

The next group of dissenters, who also fought a somewhat losing
although brilliant battle with the rising functionalism *qua* behaviorism, were the gestalt psychologists: Max Wertheimer (1880–1943),
Wolfgang Köhler (1887–1967), and Kurt Koffka (1886–1941). The
Kantian-Lockean lines of the gestalt-behaviorism disagreements were
more apparent than they had been in the cases of James and
McDougall. Köhler (1961b) reiterated one of the central themes of
the present volume when he observed:

The psychologist no less than other people has learned to see the world
through the eyeglasses of natural science. What he beholds in this manner
seems to him so obvious, he is so little aware of his eyeglasses, that any
other view will appear to him as a distortion of the genuine aspect of the
world (p. 207).

As we know, the gestaltists were to popularize these Kantian spectacles as the *phenomenal field*, which functioned as a gestalt one to
organize the many features within its frame of reference. To suggest that we might be able to "account for" the intellectual life of
man in terms of the "intrinsically blind, connection of mere facts"
according to the frequency thesis or principle of contiguity was to
fill Köhler (1961a) with "a mild, incredulous horror" (p. 11).

The gestaltists based their counter to behaviorism on researches
conducted in sensory modalities, particularly vision, and they extended their views by way of analogy to explanations of higher
mental processes (Wertheimer, 1945), personality (Koffka, 1935), and
social behaviors of all types (Marrow, 1969). They were sophisticated
concerning the rise of the "new physics" in Europe at the turn of the
twentieth century and took from this more dynamic conception of
science a series of terms to help convey their approach to psychology—terms such as *field, vector, force,* and so on. Although not
thought of as a strict gestaltist, Kurt Lewin (1890–1947) must surely
be considered in this light as well (*ibid.*). What the gestaltists actually did in theory-construction terms was to add the formal cause
to the hopper of scientific description; in fact they gave it primary
emphasis! This did not mean they *also* welcomed final-cause descrip-

tion. Though we can at points see what are clearly telic leanings in their writings (e.g., Wertheimer, 1945, p. 215), there are also significant disclaimers, as in the following:

To say: a certain process occurs because it is biologically useful, would be the kind of explanation we have to guard against. For the biological advantage of a process is an effect which has to be explained by the process, but the former cannot be used to explain the latter. A process must find its explanation in the dynamics of the system within which it occurs; the concept of biological advantage, on the other hand, does not belong to dynamics at all. And therefore teleological explanations in terms of biological advantage have no place in gestalt theory (Koffka, 1935, pp. 599–600).

This limits things to biological description, but it is difficult specifying what the gestaltists believed about man's ability to be free from unidirectional controls emanating in the stimulations of the environment or from the "functioning" (as Wertheimer, 1945, liked to call it) of the physical brain processes. The gestaltists were basically realistic in theoretical persuasion. They tried to bring behavior into a uniformity with its biological side or counterpart, but *not* in the Lockean sense of trying to point to the determinate substrate or the substantial constituent of behavior. Rather, the claim was made that a gestalt *identity* (isomorphism!) existed between the molar organization of the (proximal) stimulus as input from the (distal) environmental stimulation *and* the "motion of the atoms and molecules of the brain" (Koffka, 1935, p. 62). Though we have succeeded here in supplanting the efficient-cause (Lockean) building blocks "from below" by the organizing gestalt (Kantian) spectacles "from above," there is no more clear role for the "that for the sake of which" phrasing in the latter than in the former theoretical account. The final cause has been left out of both views.

Although the gestaltists had much to say about the organization of the proximal stimulus of the phenomenal field by way of various principles (figure-ground, closure, good continuation, proximity, etc.), they did not employ the dialectic in their descriptions. The bodily processes on which they based their explanations were best suited to demonstrative terminology, so that what was psychological and what was physical became united through a formal-cause emphasis without the benefit of a bipolar conception keeping the former potentially independent from the latter (at least to some extent!). Meaning for the gestaltist is always organization or structure. (Of course, this has nothing to do with Titchenerian structuralism.) Thinking (hence behavior) must be seen to take place in the layout of the pattern facing a person. As Wertheimer (1945) put it: "When one grasps a problem situation, its structural features and requirements set up certain strains, stresses, tensions in the thinker. What happens in real thinking is that these strains and stresses are followed up, yield vectors in the direction of improvement of the situation, and change it accordingly" (p. 195).

To describe the organization of a phenomenal (proximal) stimulus on the retina according to gestalt principles is one thing. But when we now equate such organizations with the brain material itself (isomorphism) and go on from there to explain thinking as due to the stresses, strains, and tensions of a phenomenal field, definite problems develop for the teleologist. We might now ask the gestaltists: What role does the *person* play in this structural organization and reorganization of the phenomenal field as the tensions are resolved and then reactivated? To say that a person as an ego or self is an "organized portion of the field" (Koffka, 1935, p. 520) does not answer the question, because as we noted concerning the scheme of Table 1 (p. 32) or the organization of letters into words (p. 56), simply being a part of a pattern does not mean that one behaves "for the sake of" this pattern. To speak of "patterns of energies" playing themselves out to a new level of gestalt organization is no more telic than to speak of efficiently caused (S-R) reflexes tying into a chain of associated habits. Though the flavor of each theory is distinctive, neither explanation has the individual-as-contributor active in the flux and flow of behavior.

A similar problem arises in the theorizing of our last major historical dissenter: Carl Rogers (1902–   ). Rogers and Skinner (1956) were to have a series of important debates that helped clarify the incompatibilities of mechanism and humanism. Although he tried to emphasize the person's organization of his *own* (subjective) phenomenal field, Rogers (1951, 1961) took most of his theoretical terminology from neogestalt theories and wound up with some of the same drawbacks to a full and rich humanistic formulation of behavior. There can be no doubt on the commitment Rogers has had to a teleological image of man. Speaking of the Skinnerian world view, Rogers (1961) once said:

I do . . . have strong personal reactions to the kind of . . . world which Skinner explicitly (and many other scientists implicitly) expect and hope for in the future. To me this kind of world would destroy the human person as I have come to know him in the deepest moments of psychotherapy. In such moments I am in relationship with a person who is spontaneous, who is responsibly free, that is, aware of this freedom to choose who he will be, and aware also of the consequences of his choice. To believe, as Skinner holds, that all this is an illusion, and that spontaneity, freedom, responsibility, and choice have no real existence, would be impossible for me (pp. 390–391).

Much as one might agree with Rogers here, the problem for a theoretician is to say how this freedom comes about. Lacking an appreciation of the dialectic as a theoretical tool, Rogers had to base his theory of personality on the *feelings* people have as they organize their phenomenal fields. Feelings teach us about what we value, and our values in turn reflect the organization of our phenomenal fields. If one is psychologically congruent with his feelings, the rest of his phenomenal experience will fall into place. In a sense Rogers holds that an isomorphism between bodily feelings and psychological values is not only possible but is the natural state of human beings. Only when we deny or distort these feeling-based values do we run the risk of personal maladjustment (incongruence). Rogers eventually built this view of man into what might be termed a naturalistic ethic, bringing to the fore again his teleology but in a different context:

Instead of universal values "out there," or a universal value system imposed by some group—philosophers, rulers, priests, or psychologists—we have the possibility of universal human value directions emerging from the experiencing of the human organism. Evidence from therapy indicates that both personal and social values emerge as natural, and experienced, when the individual is close to his own organismic valuing process [i.e., a feeling-based process]. The suggestion is that though modern man no longer trusts religion or science or philosophy nor any system of beliefs to give him values, he may find an organismic valuing base within himself which, if he can learn again to be in touch with it, will prove to be an organized, adaptive, and social approach to the perplexing value issues which face all of us (Rogers, 1970, p. 441).

This feeling-based organismic valuing process is therefore culture free, based on the assumption that any human being, anywhere in the world, at any point in history, would opt the same way as any other person, given only that he would openly and honestly contemplate the circumstances in light of how he felt about them as a human being (congruence) (*ibid.*, p. 440). Though an interesting thesis, the theory leaves unstated how a physical process (the feeling!) can evaluate or be the basis for an evaluation that can go "either way." That is, when an emotion is underway it does not appear to be open to alternatives. The feeling is definite and one-sided; though it can be in opposition to what is transpiring in experience, this is as an adamant opposition—often characterized as an unreasoned ("emotional") prompting. To judge, an organism must align that which is to be assessed "in relation to" some independent standard, and "for the sake of this comparison" arrive at a valued course of action. If the feeling is not the act of assessment, it must be the standard.

But this leaves the account unfinished, for it must surely be true that subhuman animals rely on such direct emotional reactions, yet we do not consider them valuing organisms. Human beings are considered higher animals because of what man has done in relation to his emotional standards, how he has been able to use or—as Rogers' theory points out—*not use* the emotional base as standard against which to assess his course of action. The concept of *feeling* takes its meaning from the material- and efficient-causes, and we might add, a formal-cause meaning in the sense of a patterning of emotions. But to speak of a *value* is to go beyond such considerations and impute some capacity on the part of an organism to evaluate (reason "for the sake of"). Behaviorists describe a value as either some kind of secondary reinforcement, which has presumably "rubbed off" from basic drive reductions, or an (efficiently caused) input via cultural influence now serving a mediating role in the succession of behavior. Rogers feels that this takes the humanity out of behavioral description, and he tries to present us with an alternative. Yet the same difficulties that confronted the behaviorists stymie Rogers: We cannot *say* one thing (feeling, as a material-efficient cause) and *mean* another (value, as a final cause).

Functionalism's Heritage

In the remaining pages of Chapter 4 we review five points that are still relevant to modern psychology as the heritage of functionalism.

Arguments from "Scientific" Method

The functionalists quickly adopted the "argument from method" which permitted them to require empirically demonstrable "facts" *before* they would entertain the likelihood of a given theoretical suggestion. This began as an attack on the "nebulous" humanistic conceptions of ego, spirit, or consciousness (Weiss, 1919) but soon spread to any form of teleological explanation (Kuo, 1928). The use of statistical tests (Calverton, 1924) brought mathematics into the functionalistic approach, and in time a theory of meaning was embraced that took operationalism (Stevens, 1935) as a kind of prerequisite for the possible employment of constructs. What was not operationally definable was, in effect, nonexistent. Hull's (1937) hypothetico-deductive method ensured that theory would not stray too far from the hard facts of observation.

This quarter often contended that mentalistic conceptions were anathema to the necessary determinism a scientific method had to presume for such knowledge to accrue (Boring, 1946). Behavior was just one more item of scientific manipulation in the pursuit of rigorous knowledge (Bergmann & Spence, 1941). To speak of mentalistic phenomena was to speak of the chimerical. Thought is not reality, said the functionalists, and all we can observe to validate is behavior as a palpable reality. Theory, as a product of thought, was not to be cultivated *as* theory. Better to deal in the intervening (methodological) variable than in the hypothetical (theoretical) construct (Meehl & MacCorqoudale, 1948). To contend that the scientist, himself a human being, needs accounting for in some reasonable fashion that may not be readily experimented on is to miss the point. Such speculations on human nature are best done in the nether regions of the arts, not at the hard frontiers of objective science (Spence, 1948). Indeed, a properly worked-out science would not require *any* theoretical speculation whatsoever (Skinner, 1950). Observed reality is before us, and experimental manipulations are predictable. Why then concern ourselves with archaic notions about human nature? We know what science is. Let us practice it!

From the other side, humanism, there came a steady counter to such developing functionalistic positions. Fernberger (1922) suggested that psychology might split into two wings, one devoted to the study of behavior (efficient causes) and the other to the study of consciousness (final causes). A decade later Yerkes (1933) reintroduced this notion of calling for a division between psychology and psychobiology. Although an eminent researcher himself, Yerkes freely admitted that he was never a psychologist in the true sense of the word (*ibid.*, p. 211). Adams (1928, 1937) made many fine arguments in favor of a concept of mind in psychology. Skaggs (1934) noted that the contrived laboratory procedures being used by psychologists bore little relation to life outside the laboratory. And Winter (1936) pointed to the outmoded Newtonian physics on which behaviorism was basing its approach to science. There was much concern expressed over the "mechanicomorphizing" of human behavior (Waters, 1939, 1948) and the overidealization of science (Allport,

1946, p. 132). Miller (1946) emphasized that proof is open to many interpretations, and the control-and-prediction sequence of scientific validation did not always result in complete understanding of the phenomenon studied in any case. Finally, Bakan (1953a, 1953b) uncovered many informal assumptions in behaviorism, assumptions the scientist permits himself to make yet fails to attribute a comparable intellectual facility to the persons under his description.

The unhappy outcome of this steady barrage of humanistic counters to functionalism is that it served to further the very tender-minded stereotype the behaviorists were advancing as characteristic of all teleologists. In donning the mantle of Spokesman and Defender of Science the functionalistic psychologists stole the initiative from the humanists, who were now put in the intolerable position of seeming to argue *against* rigor each time they raised a point of philosophical dispute. The behaviorist *always* begins his line of commentary from what can be observed, or from the hard data, as he calls it. This makes it appear that his arguments are always factual and without interpretations of these facts. In challenging such naiveté, the humanist—even though he is correct—comes off looking the tender-minded critic of science in the process. He could not hope to win in this polemical stance, and surely by mid-twentieth century he had not won much in the way of an innovation to psychological science. The behaviorists have succeeded in making the choice appear to be either *their* rigorous views or the mushy views of arty types who are incapable of conducting proper empirical investigations.

Arbitrary and Miniature Theorizing: The "Accounting For" Argument

A second heritage of functionalism involves the tendency we have already emphasized above, of "accounting for" certain concepts in a supposedly more scientific fashion (see Dollard & Miller, 1950, p. 6, for a typical claim of this sort concerning Freudian theory's translation into S-R terminology). We noted this tendency above—for example, when Tolman suggested that *purpose* was a methodological term or when Hull framed this intentionalism as a supposed fractional antedating goal response. The great stress on operational definitions early in psychology's existence probably hurt more than it helped (Stevens, 1935; Bergmann & Spence, 1941). This "canon" made it appear that by simply defining a conception in terms of the operations required to measure it *always clarified* the meaning of this construct. It also implied that errors in meaning could not be promulgated for any length of time, because everyone would immediately see what is transpiring and the confusions generated would be made plain. Neither of these assumptions are correct.

In fact quite the reverse has *usually* taken place. Rather than taking the responsibility to frame clear theoretical positions and *then* moving to an operationalization (or occasionally reversing this sequence), psychologists have felt that their job was finished if they could simply point to a reproducible "empirical" effect. The trouble is that our theories do not always get translated into research designs clearly, so the observed data really are meaningless unless understood in light of the assumptions which generated them. Operational definitions and empirical observations are *never* free of theoretical interpretations.

For example, in their book *Social Learning and Imitation* Miller and Dollard (1941) defined *stimulus* and *response* as follows: "A response is any activity within the individual which can become functionally connected with an antecedent event through learning; a stimulus is any event to which a response can be so connected" (p. 59). Quite obviously, unless we knew a lot about what psychologists had been considering a stimulus and a response beforehand, this definition would not help us very much. The definitions given in their later effort, *Personality and Psychotherapy*, are not much clearer: "We shall call anything a stimulus that seems to have the functional properties of a stimulus and anything a response that seems to have the functional properties of a response" (Dollard & Miller, 1950, p. 69). Though both definitions have a functionalist rationale, they fail to reflect the broad history of purely theoretical assumptions made by those individuals who "operationalized" the stimulus and response constructs in the first place. We shall see in the next section how this led to a confounding of methods with theories. For now we simply want to stress that the functional properties of stimuli and responses are *not* that easily observed.

Consider the pupillary observations introduced to the literature by Hess (1965) and subsequently elevated into an important experimental topic called pupillometry. If a person looks at a picture of something he likes, as opposed to something to which he is indifferent or dislikes, we can often observe his pupils dilating. According to Dollard and Miller's operational definitions, the liked picture would be a stimulus and the dilation of the pupil would be a response. Though a reasonable (extraspective) theory, this is *all it is!* We are not empirically observing dilations as responses and pictures as stimuli here. We are witnessing the conceptualizations of a particular line of *theory* (stimulus and response are theory terms) being put to methodological test. A teleologist might conceptualize the identical observations differently, so that the pupil dilation does not come out a response to the picture; it is a preparatory, hence *stimulating act* in the tradition of Brentano (see Chapter 3). Attention is being mobilized "for the sake of" an interest, and this mobilization is *not* responsive but prospective—literally stimulating the organism to extend interest and meaning rather than respond to anything.

The teleologist might therefore hold that the picture is merely an instrumentality, conceptualized essentially as a response to the projected interest pattern of the individual now looking at something that he likes. This more Kantian interpretation of the dilation is just as reasonable a(n) (introspective) theory as the one currently accepted which ever frames the pupillary dilation as a response. But the point is that nothing in the observations made can decide which of these two interpretations we take is the "real" one, or even the "best" one. The only reason we take the conventional interpretation is because it is readily grasped by all, and it has the sanctions of our institutionalized paradigm. But there is a price paid for this agreement, because although it is easier to see one's theory directly in one's apparatus than in having to keep these two realms separate, the tendency is to stick with rather mundane theoretical conceptions—variations on not only common but *dull* themes. Irwin [1971] has said this about as well as it could be said: "Identification of the meaning of psychological terms with experimental manipulations may once have had corrective value against extreme looseness of conception, but it has also had the effect of sanctifying dull and superficial work and making thought stop short where it is most needed" (p. 25).

The very ease with which we can become confused about what the "operations" mean forced the functionalists to bring their theoretical commentary closer and closer to the experimental design actually followed in the study. Phrases such as "for the purposes of this experiment, construct X is operationally defined as Y and Z" seemed to meet the criticisms of detractors who felt that the translation of a concept into operations often distorted the meaning as framed. By limiting one's claims to one specific experiment we of course end up focusing our attention on what was actually functioning in the experimental design *per se. Functionalism* came to mean study carefully whatever seems functionally relatable in an experimental format (see, e.g., Woodworth & Sheehan, 1964, pp. 57–58). It has been defined as follows:

Functionalism is empiricist rather than systematic. It eschews inference for established experimental relationships between demonstrable variables. Its laws are quantitative, directly descriptive of data. There is a healthy respect for data, and there is a commendable urge to state issues specifically in a form subject to test (Hilgard & Bower, 1966, p. 330).

Although this definition is aimed at functionalism as merely one school of thought among many, the present argument holds that literally *all* of modern experimental psychology has this value system. The earlier behaviorists—men like Tolman, Hull, Guthrie—tried to explain things systematically. They were the system builders, with Hull achieving the heights of this explanation style. Since his time we have witnessed the rise of so-called miniature theories (*ibid.*, pp. 332–333), supposedly less ambitious but more precise efforts to clarify a delimited area of study. But the truth is, such narrow-gauged theorizing was *inevitable*, once the exclusive focus on method had taken place. Miniature theorizing is the justification given to the fact that we are not permitted to reason (theorize) very much beyond the experimental apparatus *per se*. We find the experimenter saying the same things in various sections of his report—introduction, method, and discussion of results—so that the design becomes the common denominator because this is where the functioning of variables actually took place.

This leaves no room for telic theory, of course, because the paradigm of scientific method is properly devoid of intentional manipulation. The purpose of validation is to remove the plausible rules on which procedural evidence is dependent. Even the most rudimentary theoretical or metatheoretical examination of the course of scientific investigation establishes this fact. But when one expects to learn all there is to know from methods of this sort, methods that have *intentionally* been stripped of intentionality, then through a kind of Ebbinghaus-circularity (see Chapter 3, pp. 119–121) it is impossible in principle to establish the easily discernible role of telic factors in the behavior of human beings—subjects *or* scientists! In the style of Titchener, criticisms of this circular approach were relegated to philosophy by our leading functionalists—an especially telling relegation because unlike Wundt these psychologists saw no use for philosophy at all! There was a rush to data, and anything that might be circumscribed operationally was taken as worthy of study, especially if this empirical definition suggested a simplified version of behavior. Animal study was popular because of the implicit Darwinian view that it could provide insights into rudimentary laws going to make up all forms of behavior.

The Lockean assumption was made that someday these bits and pieces of "well-controlled research" could then be put together and say something meaningful. But this putting together of a data puzzle is *not* a methodological problem in any case. It is a theoretical effort, one that will require some overriding suggestions that cannot be seen directly in any one (or more) experimental design(s). Even if this be true, the functionalist is likely to say that to base one's theory on well-controlled data is better than to speculate from fuzzy conceptions before the facts are gathered. This sounds plausible and is based on the realistic assumption that facts are like apples—fallen from the tree of knowledge. But facts are never quite this palpable or meaningfully discernible, even when we define our experimental terms operationally and test our findings statistically. Indeed, as the next section demonstrates, the functionalists did not even keep clearly in mind what was their *theory* and what was their *method*. In a situation of this sort a call for "the" facts is surely gratuitous.

Confounding Method with Theory

A method is the means or manner employed to advance evidential support for one's theoretical speculations, hunches, predictions, and so on. There are two general cases of method: the *cognitive* method, in which procedural evidence is employed as a test of truth value, and the *research* method, in which validating evidence is taken as the standard for belief in the theory espoused. Experimental evidence is of the latter variety, in which the scientist designs a "trial run" (an experiment) to test his thoughts or simply arranges circumstances so that he cannot *intentionally* tamper with how they might eventuate and watches to see what happens without any particular idea as to what this might be. This control of circumstances and the possible prediction of an outcome is what we mean by experimental validation or research evidence. Ordinarily, if a scientist begins his research by simply watching for an outcome, he tries to crossvalidate whatever knowledge he has accrued by doing his more formal predicting in a follow-up study (usually, a series of studies).

As operational definitions do not always clarify a meaning as originally expressed (recall Tolman's redefinition of purpose), so too validation in an experimental context does not always answer what we want to know. That is, sometimes we can observe a controlled sequence of events (experimental design) and even predict its eventual outcome without understanding what is taking place, how it achieves its predictable outcome, or why it should work under certain circumstances and not others. Functionalists believe that because they might literally observe the antecedents to behavior and, in conjunction with these, the consequents of behavior, the conceptual requirements of understanding will necessarily issue during the experimental course of events. Sagacious observation *per se* will provide explanations for what is empirically known. But this is simply untrue, and it has been untrue for all other sciences in the history of thought.

As the eminent philosopher of science Philipp Frank (1957) has shown, scientific findings (validated predictions or observations) *outstrip* the common sense understanding of them, taking us back to that condition earlier in history where we could control and predict without knowing why, what, or how such regularities in events were really brought about. Man predicted his course of travel under the stars, controlled the crops through practical know-how, and cured himself of certain diseases centuries before there was anything like a scientific account of these beneficial outcomes. With the birth of science, and especially with the advent of modern physics, the kinds of predictions that were possible from the thinking of an Einstein or a Bohr did not make "common sense," although they were found observationally to be valid. In truth the earlier folk theories of stars as baubles, hung in the sky above a flat terrain by a God so that man could find his way about were more plausible than, for example, the notions of gravity *as* inertia, or electrons making quantum leaps.

The obvious lesson is that science is not only a methodological endeavor. Constant attention must be given to theoretical considerations—or, as they might be called, metatheoretical or philosophical considerations. The cognitive test of procedural evidence is all that can be hoped for here, but there is always the counterbalancing requirement in science to return to validation whenever possible. One side need not be ignored in preference to the other, as has happened too often in the history of thought. Recall from Chapter 1 how the medieval theorist, relying exclusively on procedural evidence, came to anthropomorphize nature. Later, in Newtonian science, the uncritical acceptance of empirical data without sophisticated study of assumptions led to a "theorization" of scientific method—that is, the assumptions of the method were projected onto the world as a *necessary* characteristic and then "proved so" by the results of this very same method (Burtt, 1955, p. 229). Though functionalists like to point to the former circumstance as an inevitable outcome of teleology in science, they constantly fall into the errors of the latter variety by confusing what is their methodological commentary with what is their theory of explanation.

This confounding was easy to make because both stimulus-response (S-R) theory and the independent variable-dependent variable (IV-DV) sequence of experimentation can be construed in exclusively efficient-cause terms—even though the IV-DV sequence was introduced as a mathematical formal cause (see Chapter 1, p. 50). Because the functionalists eschewed philosophical analysis as not sufficiently empirical for science to worry about, the almost shocking confounding of terms that was to result went unnoticed in the arbitrariness and practicality of their research efforts. We now turn to an historical documentation of these charges.

In his opening call for behaviorism John Watson (1913) set as his goal the "working out [of] a systematic scheme for the prediction and control of response in general" (pp. 162–163). As we have just reviewed it, the phrase *control and prediction* defines validating evidence. But Watson was not saying that the experimentalist performs this activity to support or refute his theoretical hypotheses, which in turn might account for the observed data. He was controlling not an independent variable, but a "stimulus" (*ibid.*, p. 163) so that he might efficiently cause the organism's movements to go the way he wanted them to go. Rather than validated knowledge, behaviorism sought lawful ties of stimuli to responses: "In a system of psychology completely worked out, given the response the stimuli can be predicted; given the stimuli the response can be predicted" (*ibid.*, p. 167).

Tolman was next to confound theoretical with methodological terminology, and he did so while expressly trying to "cognize" the simplistic efficient-cause approach of Watson. Watson had removed the organism *qua* thinker from the succession of events called behavior, but Tolman reintroduced a modest role for mentality in behavior, as a kind of "middle term" in the efficient-cause sequence. Returning to the quote cited above (p. 153), we find Tolman (1967) saying: "Our system . . . conceives [of] mental processes as functional variables intervening between stimuli, initiating physiological states, and the general heredity and past training of the organism, on the one hand, and final resulting responses, on the other. These *intervening* [italics added] variables it defines as behavior-determinants" (p. 414). A variable, whether intervening or not, is a *methodological* concept, referring specifically to the logic of experimental design. The status of a variable is achieved by translating our theoretical construct into a measurable (demonstrable) factor in the experimental sequence, allowing for an IV-DV succession of events to take place with an hypothesized outcome. To put such evidential measurements into the central nervous system of people (or rats) is to make an unwarranted extension of what is or can be observed in the experimental design.

Stevens (1935) next crystallized an attitude in experimental theoretical description that has continued to the present: "Psychology regards all observations, including those which a psychologist makes upon himself, as made upon the 'other one' and thereby makes explicit the distinction between the experimenter and the thing observed" (p. 517). This should be recorded in the history of psychology as the *principle of extraspection!* Whereas Brentano had a secondary consciousness in his introspective method, observing the observer from an introspective slant, the Americans now assumed that whenever they observed the observation was extraspective. Even when they looked into their own activities as scientists they were describing events in an extraspective sense.

Hull (1937) defined the equation of method to theory for all time. The second rule of his hypothetico-deductive method called for what is effectively a tautological identity of theory (or postulate) and the test of that theory (in the experimental procedure). Bergmann and Spence (1941) then voiced a classic confounding of terms in their reiteration of the Watsonian dream when they observed, "Like every other science, psychology conceives its problem as one of establishing the interrelations within a set of variables, most characteristically between response variables on the one hand and a manifold of environmental variables on the other" (pp. 9–10). To speak of response variables is blatantly to preempt the possible theoretical account of why experimental variables might be said to bear an observed relationship. This paradigmatic preemption effectively *dictates* terms to the experimenter, who must now either see his dependent variable as a response or risk being considered nonscientific by his peers. Meehl and MacCorquodale's (1948) subsequent paper on the distinction between a hypothetical construct (theory) and an intervening variable (method) did nothing to check the developing terminological confusion. The point of this classic paper was to suggest that a methodological construct—the intervening variable—is somehow more meaningful (because it is part of the operations made in validation) than is a theoretical construct (which accounts for the observed data in a less real unobservable fashion).

By mid-twentieth century our leading psychologists easily slipped back and forth between terminologies. Though he does not consider himself an S-R psychologist (and with good reason), Skinner can say of himself: "As an analyst of behavior, I want to relate the probability of response to a large number of independent variables, even when these variables are separated in time and space" (Evans, 1968, p. 12). A scientist who believes he is observing "variables at play," which are efficient causes *only* in the experimental context, will have put himself in the position of being unable to see a role for teleology in behavior *in principle*, so long as he follows this experimental procedure! He will have defined himself into a mechanistic corner which even empirical evidence cannot bring him out of. This takes us into the next heritage of functionalism.

Negating Proof for Teleology:
The S-R Bind

Let us assume that a humanistic psychologist were to follow the strict canons of validation, putting his telic theoretical construct to test in an empirical research effort. He begins by designing an experiment that flows from his premising theory, properly controls the designated variables in consideration of his hypothesis, and then eventually makes the proper empirical observations which are tested statistically and found to be significantly different from a chance array of means in the direction of his predictions. Having found evidence for his telic construct, he drafts his empirical findings as a report and submits it to a leading journal of experimental psychology with appropriate theoretical commentary on the findings embracing the validity of teleological behavior. What does the typical tough-minded referee say upon reading this manuscript? Does he reason as follows: "I'll be darned. There does seem to be grounds here for a belief in teleological accounts. Let's see how this theorist develops his thinking in light of his findings." From personal experience and knowledge of other humanists' experiences, the present writer can answer: *Hardly!* The preponderant odds are that his cogitations will run as follows: "There seems to be a behavioral (S-R) regularity in there, but until we delineate all of the antecedent variables controlling these measured responses the author seems to think are self-initiated intentions, we are unable to say *what* is taking place. One thing for certain: this business about mental intentions and personal directions is unwarranted by the observations. We must find the antecedent determinants (S-R laws) of these mediating intentions. We need a more scientific account!"

The humanist can either change his theoretical account and do what functionalists always do—that is, repeat his experimental design as a pseudotheory in the discussion section—or he can resubmit the manuscript to another journal. But even in this eventuality, the editorial review will probably be the same. If so, are the journal referees proved *correct* in their assessment of humanistic research? Is not the humanist simply demonstrating in his carping about how evidence is to be interpreted what the functionalists have claimed all along? Humanists are unable to accept the judgment of their peers in an objective test of their theories. Nothing could be further from the truth!

The point here is that the *evidence* has been laid down in the original experimental design. Evidence must always be seen in the prediction and control of events *before* data are arrayed. In the demonstrative strategy one always moves from the meaning as originally formulated in theory *to* the predicted succession of events in methodological test. Having so confounded methodological with theoretical considerations, the reviewer honestly believes that the humanist's IV-DV (method) succession supports *his* (the reviewer's) S-R theory. Of course any form of efficient-cause theory would be the same here, such as input-mediation-output, and so on. Terminology changes across journal referees but the efficient causality remains constant, making it impossible *in principle* for a final-cause construct to be tested.

The concept of law in psychology is interpreted so that this efficient-cause empiricism is permitted to flourish. A law is, or should be, considered a stipulated and proven relationship between two or more variables, often expressed in mathematical terms. A law is therefore methodological terminology. When it is graphed or stated as a statistical value the law can be thought of as one of the Leibniz-Dirichlet functions (see Chapter 1, p. 22, and p. 49). But in psychology the confounding of method with theory has resulted in erroneous claims such as "S-R laws are discovered" rather than "lawful relations under methodological observation may be given S-R (efficient-cause) interpretations."

Even today too many psychologists take as self-evident that: (1) antecedent Ss determine consequent Rs in the cause-effect terms of efficient causality; (2) experimental IVs define Ss and DVs define Rs; (3) for all practical purposes IVs *are* Ss and DVs *are* Rs; (4) the relationship between these two "variables" are therefore determinate, as proven by the statistically significant evidence of a predicted outcome; (5) the extent of this efficient-cause determination of an antecedent-to-a-consequent can be expressed mathematically as a(n) (S-R) law or function; and (6) theoretical speculations going beyond such empirically observed facts are unwarranted, unless they make direct reference to further variables which can be concretely manipulated (i.e., efficiently caused to vary).

This functionalistic credo has fooled many into thinking that it is an *objective* approach to science, but ironically it is precisely the opposite. The writer has termed this style of theorizing the "S-R Bind," but it could just as readily be called an "efficient-cause bind," for what it reflects is a circularity in which, because of the confusion of theory and method, any evidence presented in the efficient-cause IV-DV methodological frame is seen, hence "proven," as the S-R theoretical frame (Rychlak, 1968, pp. 57–60). This literally precludes establishing a teleological construct as valid. Without consciously intending to do so, the functionalistic psychologists have devised an approach to science that is nonobjective and essentially repressive, because it cannot leave room for explanations that fail to meet its efficient-cause biases.

Institutionalization of the Lockean Model

The final heritage of functionalism is a clear victory of the Lockean over the Kantian model. Because of Kuhn's (1970, 1st ed., 1962) analysis of the "scientific paradigm," much attention has been devoted to the question of psychology's having or not having a paradigm. We take up Kuhn's work in Chapter 5. For now we simply wish to note that it is commonly believed that psychology lacks a unifying paradigm of this sort. Robert Watson (1967) has argued that rather than functioning under a formal paradigm, psychology splits up into camps under the influence of a series of oppositionally framed "prescriptions," such as our historical functionalism-structuralism debate. Giorgi (1970, p. 165) has suggested that we may be in a preparadigmatic stage in psychology, for we surely have much disagreement over what sort of human image to embrace.

The present analysis holds that we *do* have a formal institutionalized paradigm in psychology, stemming from the confounding of method and theory discussed above. In large measure because of the rise of functionalism, which due to its eclecticism has become a kind of universal outlook among all empirical psychologists, the Lockean model has emerged victorious in the historic confrontation with Kantianism. The Yankee Spirit of hardheaded no-nonsense practicality has made this victory possible. Those psychologists who were attracted to the simplicity and promise of clarity advanced by functionalism were also the individuals who populated the academic centers of America. By stressing empirical data and going easy on the question of theory a number of different viewpoints could be brought together to prove that psychology was a science, like any of the established sciences in the university setting. Lockeanism took hold of psychology as an *officially sanctioned theory of behavior,* even though it gained this status under the guise of scientific method.

This legitimizing of Lockeanism in experimentation ensures that it will not be dislodged until psychologists take a completely new look at what they are doing in the research context. Even if a modern psychologist does not think of himself as an S-R theorist, when he now describes what he is doing in the research context the weight of procedural evidence implying a one-to-one correspondence of IV-DV to S-R is overwhelming. As do the gestaltists, he feels that to speak of "the stimulus" in a behavioral context is objectively correct. This does not make him an S-R theorist. Of course, stimuli stimulate, which means that next we are in the realm of responses. But responses do not have to be mechanical; they can simply be descriptions of behavior. Does not behavior move along? This means it is constituted of responses, does it not? And so it goes. Before two pages have been written, thanks to the paucity of *technical* terms for a telic account of behavior, the modern psychologist finds himself slipping inevitably into the Efficient-Cause (S-R) Bind.

For the teleologist to retain the integrity of what he really wants to say will require the fashioning of a new technical language in the description of behavior. Above all, he will have to take a close look at terms that in the past have been brushed over lightly, dismissed as philosophical, or arbitrarily redefined to meet the needs of experimental design. In the remaining chapters of this volume we make this effort and suggest a more useful terminology for telic description. We do not call for a complete rejection of Lockeanism in this reexamination. Rather, we hope to restore its historical opponent (Kantianism) to a more equal status in the ongoing activity of psychological science. We think this would be good for psychology, bringing back the kind of dialectical confrontation that used to make psychology a dynamic science but has in recent years been lost to the succeeding generations of individuals who enter the profession. There are still such clashes in the realm of basic-versus-applied or clinical-versus-experimental psychology, but we hope to see it restored "right in academia" between those rigorous psychologists who consider themselves humanists and those who do not. In fact we think that much of the necessity for clashes such as basic-applied or clinical-experimental would be removed if there were a viable Kantian alternative to the Lockeanism presently issuing from the psychological laboratory. The applied and clinical psychologists would then have perfectly rigorous psychological principles (laws, functions) of a *telic* variety on which to base their theories of human behavior.

Summary

Chapter 4 carries the historical confrontations of the Kantian-Lockean models in psychology to America. It begins with a consideration of the structuralism-functionalism debate, showing how this historical confrontation was initiated by a humanistic criticism of the Wundtian-Titchenerian approach to psychology (more Titchener than Wundt, actually). Caldwell leveled this criticism and it was subsequently carried forward by Calkins, both of whom might be said to be Kantians in the style of Brentano. However, the major figures to emerge in this debate were Titchener and Angell. Titchener seems to have become embroiled in two different kinds of debate. Because, as the chapter demonstrates, *both* Titchener and Angell favored Lockean formulations, the Kantian-Lockean issue that triggered Caldwell's criticism was never satisfactorily resolved. What is worse, its humanistic theme was lost to the history of psychology. We conclude that the notorious structuralist-functionalist disagreement was in fact a Lockean-Lockean *non*confrontation, an insignificant quibble so far as the basic "image of man" issue is concerned.

We trace the rise of functionalism in America over the first half of the twentieth century, with specific attention given to behaviorism's role in this advance. Watson, Tolman, Hull, and Skinner are presented as major Lockean advocates of the functionalist metaphysics. The growing emphasis given to efficient-cause description in functionalism's rise as well as the tendency to redefine telic terminology to meet the needs of experimental design are underscored. James, McDougall, Wertheimer, Köhler, Koffka, Lewin, and Rogers are then reviewed as the major Kantian dissenters over the first half of the twentieth century. Some of the weaknesses of these latter positions are discussed.

The final third of Chapter 4 is devoted to a consideration of functionalism's heritage. We contend that modern American psychology is based on a functionalist metaphysics. The following characteristics are to be seen in this heritage: arguments from "scientific" method, arbitrary and miniature theorizing, the confounding of method with theory, arbitrarily negating proof for teleology, and the institutionalization of the Lockean model. Before psychology will be in a position to rectify its current one-sidedness, a study will have to be made of the technical language used to describe behavior. This can be achieved if the present Lockeanism is counterbalanced with a more viable Kantianism. Chapter 4 completes the historical background required to understand the revolutionary changes called for in the chapters that follow.

References

Adams, D. K. The inference of mind. *Psychological Review*, 1928, **35**, 235–252.

Adams, D. K. Note on method. *Psychological Review*, 1937, **44**, 212–218.

Allport, G. W. Personalistic psychology as a science: A reply. *Psychological Review*, 1946, **53**, 132–135.

Angell, J. R. The relations of structural and functional psychology to philosophy. *Philosophical Review*, 1903, **12**, 203–243.

Angell, J. R. The province of functional psychology. *Psychological Review*, 1907, **2**, 61–91.

Bakan, D. Learning and the scientific enterprise. *Psychological Review*, 1953, **60**, 45–49. (a)

Bakan, D. Learning and the principle of inverse probability. *Psychological Review*, 1953, **60**, 360–370. (b)

Bergmann, G., & Spence, K. Operationism and theory in psychology. *Psychological Review*, 1941, **48**, 1–14.

Boring, E. G. Mind and mechanism. *American Journal of Psychology*, 1946, **54**, 173–192.

Boring, E. G. *A history of experimental psychology.* New York: Appleton-Century-Crofts, 1950.

Burtt, E. A. *The metaphysical foundations of modern physical science* (rev. ed.). Garden City, N.Y.: Doubleday, 1955.

Caldwell, W. Professor Titchener's view of the self. *Psychological Review*, 1898, **5**, 401–408.

Caldwell, W. The postulates of a structural psychology. *Psychological Review*, 1899, **6**, 187–191.

Calkins, M. W. A reconciliation between structural and functional psychology. *Psychological Review*, 1906, **13**, 61–81.

Calverton, V. F. The rise of objective psychology. *Psychological Review*, 1924, **31**, 418–426.

Dollard, J., & Miller, N. E. *Personality and psychotherapy: An analysis in terms of learning, thinking, and culture.* New York: McGraw-Hill, 1950.

Evans, R. I. *B. F. Skinner: The man and his ideas.* New York: Dutton, 1968.

Fernberger, S. W. Behavior versus introspective psychology. *Psychological Review*, 1922, **29**, 409–413.

Frank, P. *Philosophy of science.* Englewood Cliffs, N.J.: Prentice-Hall, 1957.

Giorgi, A. *Psychology as a human science: A phenomenologically based approach.* New York: Harper & Row, 1970.

Hess, E. H. Attitude and pupil size. *Scientific American*, 1965, **212**, 46–54.

Hilgard, E. R., & Bower, G. H. *Theories of learning.* New York: Appleton-Century-Crofts, 1966.

Hull, C. L. Mind, mechanism, and adaptive behavior. *Psychological Review*, 1937, **44**, 1–32.

Hull, C. L. *Principles of behavior.* New York: Appleton-Century-Crofts, 1943.

Hull, C. L. *A behavior system.* New Haven: Yale University Press, 1952.

Irwin, F. W. *Intentional behavior and motivation: A cognitive theory.* Philadelphia: Lippincott, 1971.

James, W. *The principles of psychology.* In R. M. Hutchins (Ed.), *Great books of the western world* (Vol. 53). Chicago: Encyclopedia Britannica, 1952.

Koffka, K. *Principles of gestalt psychology.* New York: Harcourt, Brace, 1935.

Köhler, W. Gestalt psychology today. In M. Henle (Ed.), *Documents of gestalt psychology.* Berkeley: University of California Press, 1961. Pp. 1–15. (a)

Köhler, W. Psychological remarks on some questions of anthropology. In M. Henle (Ed.), *Documents of gestalt psychology.* Berkeley: University of California Press, 1961. Pp. 203–221. (b)

Kuhn, T. S. *The structure of scientific revolutions* (2nd ed.). Chicago: The University of Chicago Press, 1970 [1st ed., 1962].

Kuo, Z. Y. The fundamental error of the concept of purpose and the trial and error fallacy. *Psychological Review*, 1928, **35**, 414–433.

Marrow, A. J. *The practical theorist: The life and work of Kurt Lewin.* New York: Basic Books, 1969.

McDougall, W. Prolegomena to psychology. *Psychological Review*, 1922, **29**, 1–43.

McDougall, W. Purposive or mechanical psychology? *Psychological Review*, 1923, **30**, 273–288.

Meehl, P. E., & MacCorquodale, K. On a distinction between hypothetical constructs and intervening variables. *Psychological Review*, 1948, **55**, 95–107.

Miller, D. L. The meaning of explanation. *Psychological Review*, 1946, **53**, 241–246.

Miller, N. E., & Dollard, J. *Social learning and imitation.* New Haven: Yale University Press, 1941.

Rogers, C. R. *Client-centered therapy.* Boston: Houghton Mifflin, 1951.

Rogers, C. R. *On becoming a person.* Boston: Houghton Mifflin, 1961.

Rogers, C. R. Toward a modern approach to values: The valuing process in the mature person. In J. T. Hart & T. M. Tomlinson (Eds.), *New directions in client-centered therapy.* Boston: Houghton Mifflin, 1970. Pp. 430–441.

Rogers, C. R., & Skinner, B. F. Some issues concerning the control of human behavior: A symposium. *Science*, 1956, **124**, 1057–1066.

Rychlak, J. F. *A philosophy of science for personality theory.* Boston: Houghton Mifflin, 1968.

Skaggs, E. B. The limitations of scientific psychology as an applied practical science. *Psychological Review*, 1934, **41**, 572–576.

Skinner, B. F. *The behavior of organisms: An experimental analysis*. New York: Appleton-Century, 1938.

Skinner, B. F. Are theories of learning necessary? *Psychological Review*, 1950, **57**, 193–216.

Skinner, B. F. A case history in scientific method. *American Psychologist*, 1956, **11**, 221–233.

Spence, K. W. The postulates and methods of "behaviorism." *Psychological Review*, 1948, **55**, 67–78.

Stevens, S. S. The operational definition of psychological concepts. *Psychological Review*, 1935, **42**, 517–527.

Titchener, E. B. *An outline of psychology*. New York: Macmillan, 1897.

Titchener, E. B. The postulates of a structural psychology. In T. Shipley (Ed.), *Classics in psychology*. New York: Philosophical Library, 1961. Pp. 224–243. Originally published in *Philosophical Review*, 1898, 7, 449–465.

Titchener, E. B. *Systematic psychology: Prolegomena*. Ithaca and London: Cornell University Press, 1972.

Tolman, E. C. *Purposive behavior in animals and men*. New York: Appleton-Century-Crofts, 1967.

Waters, R. H. Morgan's canon and anthropomorphism. *Psychological Review*, 1939, **46**, 534–540.

Waters, R. H. Mechanicomorphism: A new term for an old mode of thought. *Psychological Review*, 1948, **55**, 139–142.

Watson, J. B. Psychology as the behaviorist views it. *Psychological Review*, 1913, **20**, 158–177.

Watson, J. B. *Behaviorism*. New York: Norton, 1924.

Watson, R. I. Psychology: A prescriptive science. *American Psychologist*, 1967, **22**, 435–443.

Weiss, A. P. The mind and the man within. *Psychological Review*, 1919, **26**, 327–334.

Wertheimer, M. *Productive thinking*. New York: Harper, 1945.

Winter, J. E. The postulates of psychology. *Psychological Review*, 1936, **43**, 130–148.

Woodworth, R. S., & Sheehan, M. R. *Contemporary schools of psychology* (3rd ed.). New York: Ronald, 1964.

Yerkes, R. M. Concerning the anthropocentrism of psychology. *Psychological Review*, 1933, **40**, 209–212.

CHAPTER FIVE

What Kind of Scientific Revolution Is Needed in Psychology?

We said at the close of Chapter 4 that psychology's institutionalized paradigm is in fact the Lockean Model. Chapter 5 clarifies what a paradigm is and what it means to say that we can revise or revolutionize this aspect of scientific practice. Because our view is that psychology can never be properly humanistic on an exclusively Lockean model, we must deal with this paradigmatic question. We begin with a clarification of the concept of scientific revolution.

What Is a Scientific Revolution? Kuhn versus Popper

Although novel ideas have always been called revolutionary, the popularization of this term for advances in science must surely be traced to Thomas S. Kuhn's *The Structure of Scientific Revolutions* (1970a; 1st ed., 1962), which has had a great influence on our thinking. Kuhn defines revolutions as "those non-cumulative developmental episodes in which an older paradigm is replaced in whole or in part by an incompatible new one" (*ibid.*, p. 92). If we ask what a paradigm is, the issue becomes clouded; for the term has a broad range of definitional convenience, and for good reason because it relates to the most abstract features of scientific reasoning as well as to the explicit steps to be taken in the observation and description of empirical phenomena. Masterman (1970) has suggested that Kuhn used this term in no less than 21 different senses, but Kuhn (1970a) believes that he had used it in only two general ways.

The first, or sociological, usage refers to the "entire constellation of beliefs, values, techniques, and so on shared by the members of a given community" (*ibid.*, p. 175). The second, which is a less encompassing usage, has to do with "the concrete puzzle-solutions which, employed as models or examples, can replace explicit rules as a basis for the solution of the remaining puzzles of normal science" (*ibid.,* p. 175). Rules are the more formalized, established viewpoints and preconceptions of a school of thought, which derive from paradigms to act as prescriptions for how to proceed in the experimental-design activity of science (*ibid.,* pp. 38–39). However, a paradigm can guide research in the absence of rules (*ibid.,* p. 42).

The heart of Kuhn's (itself revolutionary!) argument is that science does not proceed through the so-called principle of falsification *alone,* and indeed, one wonders if it ever follows this ideologically satisfying conception. One of the foremost spokesman for this view of how science is done, Karl R. Popper (1959), has defined this principle as follows: "*It must be possible for an empirical scientific system to be refuted by experience*" (p. 41). If a statement is put in such a way that it cannot be refuted, it is not a scientific pronouncement. The statement "It will or will not rain here tomorrow" is not scientific, for it cannot be refuted; but the statement "It will rain here tomorrow" can be refuted, hence it is properly scientific. Science can only work through a kind of negating procedure of *falsifying* claims put to nature by the theorist in question. As scientists, says Popper, we never really verify things but continually falsify—or fail to falsify—claims (theories, hypotheses, etc.) expressed by some investigator (recognizing, of course, that serendipitous findings occur as well). This is why the scientist always restates his hypotheses into the null form. Ultimately the reason we must falsify has to do with the logical fallacy of "affirming the consequent" of an "If [antecedent] . . . then [consequent] . . ." proposition.

This error in reasoning occurs as follows: Take the major premise "All men are mortal" (i.e., If a man, then a mortal). Assume we now affirm the antecedent of this proposition by pointing to an animal standing before us and say "man" (i.e., This is a man). Given our major premise it follows *necessarily* that "This man is mortal" (see Chapter 2, p. 63). In this case we have affirmed (in our act of pointing) the antecedent of an "If . . . then . . ." proposition. However, if we were to have affirmed the consequent (i.e., pointed and said "mortal") it would not have followed necessarily from our major premise that the animal standing before us was a man. Obviously there can be several other animals besides humans designated as mortal beings. The principle of falsification simply emphasizes that scientific statements are always of the latter type, because what we do in an experiment is say "If my theory X holds, then the following sequence of Y events (my experiment) will result in findings Z.

Following the sequence of Y events, Z *does* occur! Hence?" We like to think our theory has necessarily been verified, but Popper teaches us that it has not. There will always be, *in principle*, other ways of accounting for the observed data (the facts) than our preferred theory.

As a logician, Popper has devoted himself to clarifying issues such as these and to stipulating certain rules of procedure which he claims all scientists who are doing the work of science correctly will have to follow. He does not concern himself much with how scientists come to their major premises in actual practice, the actual reasons why they may take this or that point of view which is framed in their scientific statements such as "It will rain tomorrow." Popper's concern is therefore more with the *deductions* made by the scientist once he has put his statement (hypothesis) to nature. His opening sentences of *The Logic of Scientific Discovery* reveal this deductive interest of his as the tone of the volume is being established:

A scientist, whether theorist or experimenter, puts forward statements, or systems of statements, and tests them step by step. In the field of the empirical sciences, more particularly, he constructs hypotheses, or systems of theories, and tests them against experience by observation and experiment (*ibid.*, p. 27).

Popper is a great favorite of psychologists who consider themselves rigorous, for they see in his writings a parallel to Hull's (1937) hypo-thetico-*deductive* method [italics added]. When Popper (1959) says ". . . in my view there is no such thing as induction" (p. 40) (except for a possible mathematical induction), he aligns himself with the realistic theories of psychology which have taken the Lockean presumption that ideas are not put onto experience (induced), but obtained strictly through inputs from experience.

Kuhn has come along to challenge this idealized view of science that Popper has promulgated. Kuhn's study of history has convinced him that scientists are usually eager to support in their research efforts the meaning-presumptions made in their theoretical paradigms from the outset. In other words, the practice of science is more *inductive* than Popper has led us to believe. Scientists are seen to go along, defending their paradigmatic presumptions and continuing to do so until some anomaly develops in their findings or a new area of interest in science develops that does not fit these presumptions too well. At such "extraordinary" times in history we see a revolution coming about. Negative instances (falsifications) are at such revolutionary nodal points taken as evidence *against* a paradigm rather than simply as "puzzles," and the sympathies of many (especially the younger) scientists for the predominant paradigm of that period wanes. In these extraordinary times a new paradigm emerges, once again to capture the imagination and explanatory proclivities of the scientists who then further it.

The rest of the time we have what Kuhn calls normal science, and during such stretches the paradigm in ascendance is not really under threat. There is none of that disinterested rigorously deductive effort to disprove the paradigm which Popper believes occurs; at least there is remarkably little of it. What most scientists do during this normal period is to solve fairly limited puzzles generated by the background paradigm (Kuhn, 1970a, p. 82). Some of these are really new anomalies, taking shape gradually, but the "normal scientist" does not see them as such. To use Popper's terminology, he is more the verifier at this point than the falsifier. He designs his study to *support* and not to falsify the already accepted paradigm, although the logic of science still applies in the sense of affirming the consequent. He is a rule follower, doing what his forerunners have done with minor variations on their experimental designs (*ibid.*, p. 10). Sometimes the rules worked out actually hamper the discovery of new facts so that a shift in experimental techniques is required before a significant advance is achieved (*ibid.*, p. 59).

If we now hark back to the terminology of Chapter 1, we see that as an historian, Kuhn's interests are in the *precedents* of the scientific quest. He finds that scientists *do* have such precedent paradigms at play in their work, as overriding inductive inferences, and he cannot bring himself to accept the idealized Popperian view that scientists are interested *only* (or even primarily) in the evidence that may or may not falsify their theoretical statements. As he noted in direct colloquy with Popper, not only is evidence overlooked or reinterpreted out of the anomaly category into the unsolved puzzle category, but sometimes a theory is dropped (e.g., the Ptolemaic) even *before* it is put to satisfactory test (Kuhn, 1970b, p. 10). We cannot hope to judge a whole theory in the same way that we judge the outcome of a single experiment (*ibid.*, p. 12).

Saying "It will rain tomorrow" can easily be seen as true or false, but when we study the more abstract paradigmatic assumptions concerning the nature of rain (why it can be said to fall, for example) they cannot be falsified, nor can the theoretical statements derived from these assumptions. As Frank (1957) has noted, agreement with observations and logical consistency cannot resolve differences in scientific outlook of such a high generality (p. 359). Whether we call it a paradigm or a precedent makes no difference; the point-of-view factor is *always* present because whatever one *states* rests on some other given (as brought to bear "from above" on the ladder of abstraction; see Rychlak, 1968, pp. 12–16). Thus Kuhn has challenged the principle of falsification, stating that it is not a logical rule but more an ideology and methodological rule reflecting one view of the scientific endeavor (Kuhn, 1970b, p. 15). Summing up, Kuhn charges that Popper "has sought to solve the problem of theory choice during revolutions by logical criteria that are applicable in full only when a [precedent] theory can already be presupposed" (*ibid.*, p. 19).

In his reply Popper (1970) admitted that something like Kuhn's concept of normal science existed, but he denied that this was in any way the normal activities of all or even most scientists. Indeed those individuals who practice science this way had been "taught badly" (*ibid.*, p. 52). Science, at any time in its history, ranges on a continuum between the Kuhnian poles of so-called normal and extraordinary scientific activity (*ibid.*, p. 54). No single paradigm ever has the complete grip on a scientific specialty (biology, physics, etc.) as Kuhn implies; at the very least in *certain* sciences there are one or more such paradigms active at the same time. Furthermore, some of the benefits to be accrued from scientific efforts devolve from the interchanges between such competing paradigms. Popper criticized Kuhn for suggesting that there can be no rational discussion between such frameworks, leading to the necessity for a revolution in outlook (*ibid.*, p. 57). Attesting to his belief in absolute, or objective, truth (as opposed to the relativism implied in Kuhn's analysis), Popper reaffirmed his belief that only in the test of empirical evidence will such varied paradigms as are active in science be furthered or dropped (*ibid.*, p. 56).

Despite Popper's belief in rational discussion across conflicting paradigms, the writer has found that we are—as a science of psychology (applied settings not included)—under the unilateral direction of the precedent implications of a single paradigm, the advocates of which have not yet perceived what a minority of humanistic psychologists view as glaring anomalies in their Lockean framework. A change, if not a revolution, is surely called for; but before this is possible, advocates on *both* sides of the question must be clearer on just where the locus of a Kuhnian argument applies.

Revolutions in Theory, Not in Method

If scientific knowledge combines both theory and method, it follows that paradigmatic influences devolve on both sides of the theory-method distinction. Further, to think of Kuhnian revolutions occurring on *either* side without necessarily affecting the other is quite possible. Thus we might revolutionize what we accept as the grounds for belief in a statement (i.e., method) without affecting the kinds of theories we put to test. Or we might alter the kinds of theoretical statements we make in relation to the methods we continue to employ in testing them. Where does Kuhn focus his argument in speaking of scientific revolutions?

That Kuhn (1970a) thinks of revolutions occurring in the *theoretical* realm is clear from many sources in his treatise (p. 7, pp. 17–18, p. 77, and especially, p. 182). Indeed even such a distinctive paradigm as quantum mechanics is said to be open to *various* interpretations by different groups within the science of physics (*ibid.*, p. 50). There are two instances in which Kuhn seems to be driving at method. First, there is the matter of rules, which encompass the "acceptable steps" to be taken in the design of experiments. Resting ultimately on the procedural evidence of an overriding paradigm, rules act as strictures. If the researcher does not follow the rules of proper science, ending in validating evidence, he is not going to be listened to. He also had better stay close to certain research designs, mix his chemicals in the prescribed fashion before conducting the test called for, and so forth. A second type of methodological issue can be seen in Kuhn's (1970a) reference to a preparadigm period in the history of science: "The pre-paradigm period . . . is regularly marked by frequent and deep debates over legitimate methods, problems, and standards of solution, though these serve rather to define schools than to produce agreement" (pp. 47–48).

Except for these two somewhat angular references to a concern over the evidential steps to be taken in the practice of science, Kuhn's emphasis is entirely on the question of what kind of theoretical position are we to take on the nature of our subject matter? The revolutionaries to whom he refers—Copernicus, Newton, Lavoisier, and Einstein (*ibid.*, p. 6)—*did not* revolutionize the paradigm on which rested the assumptions concerning strict research procedures or the need to control and predict events to validate one's claims on knowledge. Revolutions as paradigm confrontations arise purely in the sphere of theory (as buttressed, of course, by the cognitive testing of what is or is not plausible via procedural evidence). The essential ingredient is when a particular scientist is likely to call one man's puzzle—whether solved or not—his anomaly:

Copernicus saw as counterinstances what most of Ptolemy's other successors had seen as puzzles in the match between observation and theory. Lavoisier saw as a counterinstance what Priestly had seen as a successfully solved puzzle in the articulation of phlogiston theory. And Einstein saw as counterinstances what Lorentz, Fitzgerald, and others had seen as puzzles in the articulation of Newton's and Maxwell's theories (*ibid.*, pp. 79–80).

At these subtle points in history an extraordinary scientific event is likely to take place. A paradigmatic shift at the level of theory occurs, and the findings that had stood before as evidence for theory X now fall nicely into place for theory Y (not to mention the entirely new things theory Y teaches us). This can always happen because of that affirming-the-consequent nature of experimental evidence we discussed above. There is frequently a shift in the instrumentation employed by the innovator as well. He does not follow the institutionalized rules of design any more than he has followed the institutionalized form of explanation. This does *not* mean he departs from validating evidence, of course. But so often our technical instruments, our stilted patterns of experimental design, keep us from seeing what could be shown to be valid simply because we fail to theorize beyond our fixed instrumentation. Kuhn (1970a) now asks:

Ought we [to] conclude from the frequency with which such instrumental commitments prove misleading that science should abandon standard tests and standard instruments? That would result in an inconceivable method of research. Paradigm procedures and applications are as necessary to science as paradigm laws and theories, and they have the same effects. Inevitably they restrict the phenomenological field accessible for scientific investigation at any given time (pp. 60–61).

This restriction of theory by method is what we have been driving at in emphasizing the confounding of the former with the latter. But when we are speaking of a Kuhnian revolution we are referring to dramatic shifts in the theoretical viewpoints of scientists. Indeed since the turn of the seventeenth century and the rise of modern science, though there have been a number of quite startling paradigm shifts in scientific theory, *there has never been a paradigmatic shift in the theory of knowledge defining scientific method!* There have been some attempts in this direction, primarily at the philosophical level (Kuhn's preparadigmatic efforts); but insofar as science *per se* has retained an identity, the ground rules for evidence have remained validation. One must of necessity begin with procedural evidence in cognitive tests—which includes mathematical reasoning—but the mark of a true scientist since Newton has been the recognition that ultimately his formulations would have to bear up under the control-and-prediction rule of objective empirical evidence.

How Can a Rigorous Science Be Humanistic?

We are now prepared to understand how a humanistic science can be rigorous. The logic of scientific method need not be altered to achieve a humanistic science of psychology. What we must revolutionize is the way in which we construe the design of our experiments, the manipulations we apply to our independent variables, and the explanations we proffer for the observed changes in the dependent variables. We must recognize that the empirical test of control and prediction in validation is *never* the sole source of descriptive terminology which presumes to say what is going on within the apparatus. It was once believed to be so; for example, when Bergmann and Spence (1941) claimed: "All scientific terms are derived terms, derived from and retraceable to what one might call 'the hard data,' the 'immediately observable' or what Stevens calls the 'elementary operation of discrimination' " (p. 6). We must now say in no uncertain terms that *this functionalist ideology is wrong.* The concept of an elementary operation of discrimination is itself fraught with Lockean (simple-to-complex) presumptions and hence cannot be accepted without question. Psychologists derive their terms from all manner of sources, including analogies to philosophical models that have been woven into the very fabric of their metaphysical outlook "as scientists."

The only thing standing in the way of a rigorous humanistic psychology is the lack of recognition on the part of psychologists that such a theory of man is possible! Lacking this recognition, they do not frame their precedent hypotheses in terms of it, which means that studies are never designed to test this possibility, and evidence which might in fact support it continually goes unrecognized. We do not have to change our ground rules for validation to initiate a rigorous program of empirical research providing evidence for or against the thesis that human behavior is telic. This may occasionally call for some unique experimental designs, or we can go on using the same experimental designs that we have always been using, with the only change being that now we begin with the assumption that a telic animal is in the apparatus. What does this imply about the likely outcome, and how can we check our thinking against a purely mechanistic hypothesis? Starting at this level, researches can be conducted just as they are now except that the introduction and discussion sections of these reports will be more than simply rephrases of the procedure section (see our comments concerning this practice in Chapter 4, p. 167).

The adjustment called for in our revolution is purely technical. Humanism is the desire on the part of a theoretician to employ formal- and final-cause description. Humanists do not ask the functionalist question of how we can more scientifically *account for* what used to be called purpose (i.e., as an efficient cause), but seek to answer a question like how we can prove scientifically that purpose in human affairs actually takes place (i.e., as a final cause). As introspective theorists, humanists fall more naturally into the Kantian line of descent which places emphasis on the inductive capacity of mind to organize or influence its experience in some way *from birth*. Talk of phenomenal fields (Rogers, 1951), world views (Binswanger, 1963), and personal constructs (Kelly, 1955) fills their accounts—all of which are introspectively conceived Kantian spectacles, serving as the *that* (grounds) on the basis of which behavior is being carried out. But once such telic theoretical formulations are translated and verified in the research designs called for, they fall easy prey to the theory-method confound and come out as mediated efficient causes (see Chapter 4, pp. 168–172).

Feuer (1974) has argued persuasively that using *revolution* in speaking of paradigm change in science may be too strong a word, falsely analogized from social upheavals that occur when a class of people is actively repressed. After all, the scientific method is committed to the rule of evidence, so ultimately it must encourage revisions and additions to its knowledge (*ibid.*, p. 265). Sometimes the scientists using the favored paradigm even give credence to the newly emerging paradigm (*ibid.*, p. 275). This is hardly what one finds when we observe the machinations of a vested social class, working to preserve its advantages and actively repressing some disadvantaged class or classes "beneath them." Why then insist upon the more aggressive term when something like *revision* might do as well?

Although we agree with this argument in principle, there are still a few points we must consider before dropping revolution as a proper descriptive characterization of what is needed in psychology. First, as Feuer himself appreciates, there is undoubted merit to Kuhn's arguments concerning the reticence of scientists to accept empirical data that fail to support the precedent assumptions they make as a school of thought (*ibid.,* pp. 330–334). Hence the provisions made in science for a self-correcting revision in outlook are not foolproof and at their best are exceedingly slow in allowing for an alternative idea to take shape. Second, and more to the point for rigorous humanism, *we have had very little need in the natural sciences to revolutionize the basic antipathy felt for teleological explanations.* Though science may indeed accept evidence and ultimately aid the revolutionary paradigm in its ascendancy, the rule-strictures on what is a scientific explanation remain. Whenever a telic commentary enters scientific discourse, it is framed as something other than legitimate science, or the scientist is speaking loosely and we are all quite aware that his references to intention or purpose in events are given *enquotes.*

If we now analogize between groups of scientists advocating telic theory versus natural-science theory and the bourgeoisie versus proletarian classes of Marxian theory, the parallel may not be so extreme after all. When as a young man of 24, Hermann von Helmholtz (see Chapter 3, pp. 123–124) formed a pact with his fellow students (including Brücke, later to be Freud's professor) to fight vitalism in science, he was reflecting the values of his class identity (Boring, 1950, p. 708). Though it is confounded with quasi-materialistic ideology, the vitalistic principle of explanation in physical science is fundamentally telic. By swearing oaths to repress such theory Helmholtz was surely not reflecting the disinterested spirit of a principle of falsification. That is, although Fechner specifically designed his research to test a mind-body question of this type (see Chapter 3, p. 105), the psychologists who followed Helmholtz's lead (including Wundt) were not seen to entertain such possibilities in their subsequent employment of the psychophysical methods. Helmholtz's opposition to vitalism was framed initially in the sphere of physical explanation. But as psychology was then modeled on physical theory, this antiteleology attitude was carried over to psychological explanation as well.

Returning to Feuer's admonition, though he is quite correct that scientific innovations are not generally akin to social revolutions, in psychology we feel the parallel is properly drawn. We do indeed require a scientific revolution in psychology. We hope that the resulting *synthesis* of a new theoretical paradigm with the old methodological paradigm will take the best from both sides. We wish to add telic theories while retaining the same, nontelic, empirical, purely mechanical ordering of events over time known as the *experimental design*. The advantages of objectivity to be gained in the latter procedure are what we feel must be retained. There will be no pacts in this revolution to fight mechanism. We need sophistication following our revolution, not further repression. Some psychologists find this modest suggestion too revolutionary, but others find it not revolutionary enough. There are hopes in certain quarters to revolutionize scientific method *per se*, and we now turn to a few of these views.

Why Humanistic Methodologies Tend to Fail as Rigorous Science

Humanism is a growing movement in psychology and the call for humanistic methods is often heard from these quarters. An Association for Humanistic Psychology now exists, with an accompanying *Journal of Humanistic Psychology*, dedicated to the advancement of humanistic topics such as love, creativity, spontaneity, play, warmth, ego-transcendence, autonomy, responsibility, authenticity, meaning, transcendental experience, and courage (Bugental, 1963; Haigh, 1969; Maslow, 1961). The papers which appear in this journal do not necessarily follow the format of an experiment, with procedure sections and the statistical analysis of data, but are usually discursive surveys, case-history reports, or personal observations. Humanists like to cite Polanyi (1964), because this distinguished philosopher-scientist puts the intuition of the investigator above the validation of an experiment in any rank ordering of steps in the scientific enterprise. Others seek to find an alternative to control and prediction in validation by going to analytical or conceptual procedures such as cultural hermeneutics (Palmer, 1969) or Zen's enlightenment (Suzuki, 1962).

To attempt a survey of the many different strategies employed by humanists in their calling to question or outright rejection of scientific methodology would require a volume in itself. We therefore restrict our comments to two of the better-known and well-done efforts of this nature in the literature—the existentialistic critique of Adrain van Kaam (1969) and the phenomenological critique of

Amedeo Giorgi (1970a). Before turning to these specific presentations, we must clarify where the problems arise in most humanistic revisions of the scientific enterprise.

The Steps in Science as a "Line of Development"

If we were to frame the general steps taken by a scientist in furthering knowledge, the following would be a fair approximation: (1) speculate theoretically at whatever level of formalization (i.e., from rough analogies through involved "systems" of explanation); (2) test the plausibility of such speculations cognitively (procedural evidence) and design thereby an experiment that can show the implications of this theory quite independently of the scientist *qua* theorist; (3) carry out the projected validation. Sharp distinctions between these three steps, especially 1 and 2, are not possible, but the general logic here suggests that only those who move through step 3 *at least some of the time* are participating in a scientific endeavor (see Chapter 1).

We call this sequence the *line of development,* because we recognize the fact that sheer validation is never meaningful in and of itself. There is and always must be some background assumption lending meaning to the findings as seen in the experimental sequence (apparatus, instrument, etc.). We take cognizance here of that affirming-the-consequent issue discussed above even as we raise the significance of theory and procedural evidence in the course of scientific "discovery." Of course not all human beings take our third step and actually validate impartially what they think could be validated if someone would but do the work involved. Hence, though we agree with Conant (1952) that scientists in the laboratory carry out habits of well-ordered inquiry that go back to the caveman (p. 40), we do not entirely agree with Kelly (1955) when he suggests that every man is a scientist (p. 5). The challenge of science comes in when we take our third step, and though potentially capable, not everyone is prepared or willing to do so.

Having now recognized that scientific investigation calls for a line of development, we can acknowledge further that it can be *stretched* somewhat in going from points 1 to 3. To conduct an experiment that was implied by some background theory at point 1 without having this complete theory ensconced in the experimental apparatus at point 3 is not a violation of parsimony. Indeed *in principle* we can never have all of the precedents which function as background factors to our empirical studies nestled in our experimental designs. There will always be some more abstract level from which a premise or paradigm or metaphysical assumption is taking root in our approach to knowledge. What is essential in this process is that we be clear about what our background factors are and that we do the best job we can in logically developing these meanings into our eventual test of our thinking at point 3. In other words, some of the so-called control that becomes prominent at step 3 is already underway in the logical controls being developed across points 1 and 2.

As we hope to show in the examples below, the tendency for humanistic methods is either to stop somewhere around points 1 or 2, falling short of scientific validation altogether, or to go on to 3 with some loosely designed project, often boiling down to a discursive survey of some group of individuals. There is a rationale given for such efforts, but these justifications simply do not salvage the kind of tepid science that ensues. What is so disheartening about these efforts is that they pass by many fine opportunities to show humanistic features of behavior in the laboratory. There is no reason why humanistic constructs cannot be framed and put to test in the most rigidly controlled arid realms of laboratory science imaginable. All one need do is begin at point 1 with the proper assumptions and then, working carefully and rigorously, develop through a kind of extension of the meanings carried by these premises a program of empirical research that can be repeated by anyone who takes an interest in the problem. Rather than a final cause, or an aspiration, as construed in the theory at point 1, we end up at point 3 with some marks on a piece of paper made by subjects who have been put into an experimental design established to test the implications of our theory (at point 1).

One can easily sympathize with the dreams of those who hope someday to find a scientific method which is capable of capturing the richness of lived human experience. The scientific method is clearly aimed demonstratively at restricting and narrowing alternative factors down to the point that any one study is rather a thin soup. This is why paradigms need considerable filling in during what Kuhn (1970a) has called the phase of normal science (pp. 23–42). But this delimitation in each study proves discouraging to many humanists on two counts. First, there is the sense of artificiality that such controlled efforts lend to the theoretical account. It all seems a make-believe game, with either validation sought for some trivia already known or having no true relevance to the lived experience of the man on the street. Second, the humanist who considers himself existentialistic or phenomenological in orientation finds the variables designed for in the experiment to be so far removed from what the individual is actually experiencing at his end of the observer-subject continuum as to be a violation of scientific objectivity on the face of things. This charge of a distortion in the arbitrarily selected dimensions of study by the extraspectionist, who then forces his schemes onto his subjects with total disregard for their actual experience, is what we mean by the *purity criticism* (Rychlak, 1968, p. 390).

The extraspectionist in psychology has been accused of purposely neglecting his responsibility to capture the more introspectively framed account of life that we all live within, each day of our existence. Based on some misguided principle of natural science, the extraspectionist ignores purely spontaneous experience to perpetuate the illusion of a material- and efficient-cause theory of humanity as natural products. Although quite legitimately stated in psychology, the unhappy result of the purity criticism is that it tends to focus on the methods of science rather than on its theories. The nemesis of failing to distinguish proof from theoretical description or explanation continues to dog us. A typical derision of science is to be seen in the following quote from Boss (1963), who is commenting on his more humanistic approach to psychology (Daseinsanalysis):

. . . analysis of *Dasein* urges all those who deal with human beings to start seeing and thinking from the beginning, so that they can remain with what they immediately perceive and do not get lost in "scientific" abstractions, derivations, explanations, and calculations estranged from the immediate reality of the given phenomena (pp. 29–30).

What makes such derision unfortunate is that, if we survey the leading figures in science over this century—for example, Bridgman (1959), Bronowski (1958), Conant (1952), Eddington (1958), Einstein (1934), Oppenheimer (1956), Schrödinger (1957), and Whitehead (1958)—we find much more support for a humanistic theory of behavior than for a mechanistic account. Modern science has become more open to Kantian-like terminology because of its recognition that what one observes in the "hard reality" is due at least in part to what one presumes from the outset. This is clearly a recognition of the telic factors in the work of science or the scientist-human who does the work. A liberal approach to scientific theorizing is more current and appropriate than is the staid and lifeless form of Newtonian science that is still dreamed of in too many psychology departments. To provide our students with a humanistic outlook which is internally hostile to research design seems more harmful than helpful. Furthermore, we tend to attract students who are *in fact* not interested in developing the necessary self-discipline and exerting the effort that a scientific career demands.

Two Examples of a Humanistic "Method:" Van Kaam and Giorgi

We turn now to two distinguished examples of psychological criticism that call for a humanistic approach to method: the existential view of van Kaam (1969) and the phenomenological critique of Giorgi (1970a). Our intention here is to look into each of these views in light of the claim that scientific method (validation, or step 3 above) need *not* be revised, much less revolutionized, to achieve the goals being sought by van Kaam and Giorgi.

In his book *Existential Foundations of Psychology* van Kaam (1969) levels a purity criticism in the opening arguments: ". . . human sciences will never present us with a full understanding of man so long as they are pure speculative knowledge or mere laboratory knowledge without reference to the real, lived world of man" (p. 25). The culprit is developed as more method than theory, with the suggestion that a phenomenological substitution is called for: "Phenomenology as a method in psychology thus seeks to disclose and elucidate the phenomena of behavior as they manifest themselves in their perceived immediacy" (*ibid.*, p. 29).

A distinction between *comprehensive* and *differential* psychological theories (van Kaam's term for theory here is *modes of existence*) is then drawn (*ibid.*, pp. 114–175). The point of this distinction is to say that science tends to discriminate and break down behavior from its totality into differential pieces (in our terms, a Lockean-model reduction), whereas a comprehensive psychological theory tries to retain the wholeness of lived experience. As such, comprehensive theory would retain teleological descriptions of human behavior (*ibid.*, p. 110). Though one might suspect that van Kaam's polemic is solely on the side of theory, when he speaks of his approach as *anthropological phenomenology* he brings in the factor of method as supposedly *also* changed: "Anthropological existential phenomenology is both an attitude [in our terms, theory] and a controlled method. It leads to a comprehensive understanding of intentional behavior as a structured whole which is differentiated in many patterns of behavior" (*ibid.*, p. 252).

Without *phenomenological explication* of scientific endeavors, a science of psychology can be sent scurrying about on meaningless endeavors:

Empirical observation, experimentation, measurement, and accumulation of data should be fostered in all differential psychologies. From the viewpoint of comprehensive psychology, however, much of this admirable effort is wasted if there is no phenomenological explication of *what* it is that is being observed, experimented upon, measured, correlated, and applied (*ibid.*, p. 303).

We can heartily agree with the need for phenomenological explication, *if* what this means is something akin to our steps 1 and 2— thinking about what sorts of speculations are worth making and, in light of this reflective assessment, a procedural-evidence testing of what one's scientific activity is "all about." This sort of preliminary activity is essential to a proper experimental design, and this preparatory effort seems to be what van Kaam is referring to. However, in the familiar style of purity critics he bears down rather severely on the scientific method of step 3 *per se*—for example, in the following excerpt where he is discussing the evidence of so-called differential (typical Lockean) psychology:

. . . the hypothesis that learning is based on a process of conditioning can be verified only by differential-scientific evidence; it cannot be validated directly by either spontaneous or comprehensive-scientific evidence. The evidences of differential psychologies are only indirect evidences. They do not make behavior itself manifest; they are deduced from spontaneous evidences by means of abstract scientific methods. The latter may consist of logical, mathematical deductions or of empirical inductions, the methods of which may differ in each differential psychology. To be sure, the conclusions of differential psychology possess their own type of evidence. Yet such scientific-differential evidences are always less reliable than naive self-evidences (*ibid.*, p. 275).

We learn in the next few paragraphs that what van Kaam means by *less reliable* is less constant or subject to change—for example, when a future scientific account based on new evidence alters our current thinking on some topic, such as human learning in behavior. People 50 years from now will have the same spontaneous phenomenal experience of learning that we have today. However, our scientific theories of the learning process, based on evidence accumulated over the next 50 years, may be vastly different from what it is today. Hence differential scientific evidences are less reliable than the naive commentaries proffered by living subjects (*ibid.*, p. 276). Note what has happened here: van Kaam has also confounded theory with method so that he is uncertain as to what is unreliable and what needs ever to be reliable in the scientific quest. Could not the style of accruing evidence have remained highly reliable over the

50-year span, even as the theories being put to test in this fixed strategy of accruing evidence changed? In fact these theories *could* have changed in the direction of greater congruence with the spontaneous phenomenal accounts of today and tomorrow (which is the revolution we hope to see take place!).

To say that a *method* (evidence source) is unreliable because it tests different theories over time is like saying an aging automobile is unreliable (or unfaithful) because it dependably carried a series of different owners over time. What van Kaam has stumbled upon here is the fact that scientific methods are *always* those last steps of our three-step sequence, which means they always have more than one theory that might account for them. Methods are those consequents we examined above, which are affirmed in the logic of scientific test and to that extent are *never* in one-to-one (necessary) agreement with their antecedent theoretical backgrounds. The empirical findings of scientific method are not unreliable; they are simply subject to change in theoretical description—over time, within time, any time! By confounding what is method with the theory accounting for the resultant findings, van Kaam, like so many humanistic critics, points his guns in the wrong direction.

What kind of actual study would be conducted if we used the phenomenological method? In the example cited van Kaam presents data on a survey of high school and college students who "explicated" their feelings—in writing on a form administered by the experimenters—when they were really "understood by somebody" (*ibid., p. 331*). The sample was then broken down into percentages of subjects expressing various positive reactions to being understood, such as that they felt relieved and satisfied, safe in the relationship, in experiential communion with the person, accepted, and so on (*ibid.. p. 336*). How does this differ from *any* study conducted by a scientist who is going to follow the rules of validation at step 3? Clearly, for the sake of convenience, he would want to construct a scale following such prestudy, and after he had accumulated items dealing with the feeling of being "really understood by somebody" that reflected reliability of a test-retest variety, he would probably search about for other samples of people in order to extend the range of his knowledge about this theoretical construct.

For example, a group of prisoners would probably have a different sense of what it means to be really understood than high school and college students. Though the phenomenal experience is presented very positively, what about those times when we are caught in a lie or some other misbehavior and hence feel "really understood" yet hardly safe, at ease, or in experiential communion with the person or persons who understood us. The survey instructions (*ibid.*, p. 331) do not make such circumstances clear, and there was obviously a very positive demand characteristic or set in this study. But these are precisely the kinds of questions a sagacious investigator would next seek to answer if he is *scientifically* interested in his theoretical construct. This is why the paradigm continues to be filled in by normal science (Kuhn, 1970a). We do not wish to be unfair to van Kaam, because this study was presumably done merely as an example to show how his approach lets the subjects define the construct eventually to be used, rather than coming to them with a preconceived definition of the construct (*a la* the purity criticism); yet, in counterexample fashion we must at least point out that humanists are frequently criticized for the paucity and superficiality of their scientific work.

Giorgi (1970a) begins his critique with a sophisticated review of the tendency in psychology to press natural-science efficient-cause models onto the teleological human being. He argues that there was a kind of choice early in the game between a humanistic theory of man and a scientific methodological approach, with the result that "in the conflict between fidelity to scientific methodology and fidelity to the phenomena (in this case man), almost all early psychologists opted for the methodology" (*ibid.*, p. 92). Once again we find a leading humanist making scientific method appear by definition to be anathema to humanistic theories. Yet, as we demonstrated in Chapter 3, both Gustav Fechner (p. 105) and Johannes Müller (p. 106)—individuals who were important to the founding of experimental methods in psychology—took a clearly Kantian humanistic view of mankind. Only later, as the Lockean thinkers—Helmholtz in particular as well as Wundt—came on the scene was a confounding of efficient-cause method with efficient-cause theory accomplished. Rather than these Lockean scientists having an option in the matter, they were merely encouraged by the hard data being generated in the laboratory that complex human behavior was reducible to underlying simple forces and motions (Cassirer, 1950, pp. 85–91).

The purity criticism plays a central role in Giorgi's polemic:

Let us take, as an example, experiments designed to discover the threshold time for subjects to perceive how many dots are on a screen. This experiment is usually described as "perception as a function of time," meaning that the experimenter is interested in finding out how long it takes the subject to perceive what he (the experimenter) already *knows.* Thus, the

subject must acquire knowledge and express an objective fact—x dots—
and is usually not in any way instructed to relate how he experienced the
phenomenon of tachistoscopic visual presentations. The latter factor is
simply presumed and never taken into account (Giorgi, 1970a, p. 153).

The fault here would seem to lie in the exclusively extraspective
and arbitrary *theory* of the experimenter, who selected the time
dimension as a base-rate standard against which to claim learning
was a function of (see our discussion of functionalism, Chapter 4,
pp. 162–176). Yet Giorgi's continuing analysis places the fault on the
side of the method used to validate such assumptions. He calls for a
phenomenological technique of reduction (*ibid.*, p. 162), which
means that we should try to clarify and delineate the presuppositions
that define our perspective. By *perspective* is meant something akin
to the Kantian spectacles that we bring to bear in formulating a
precedent slant on things, a slant that in turn will determine sequaciously what we will say about them: "The fact of perspectivity is
the main argument against all theories that posit absolute positions"
(*ibid.*, p. 163). Once again this seems more a question of theory than
method. But Giorgi also favors Merleau-Ponty's concept of *structure*,
which is a conceptualized "whole" that is identifiable, analyzable,
and transposable. When clarified or explicated it reflects the psychological meaning a person experiences in relation to it (*ibid.*, pp. 178–
179). This formal-cause concept implies that a procedural-evidence-
based examination of structure can be carried out, due to its Heraclitian order or internal consistency as a total (coherence theory of
truth). Giorgi refers to this analysis of structure as a method (*ibid.*,
p. 192), but in our terms this would represent a cognitive and *not* a
research method (see Chapter 1, p. 46). Because it would stop short
of our step 3, we could not accept it as a genuinely scientific method
—adding, as Giorgi would doubtless want us to, "based on our definition of science!"

An experiment by Colaizzi (1967; see also 1973) is then cited by
Giorgi (1970a) in which subjects in a memory task are interrupted
after one trial and asked what they were thinking about at that time
(p. 192). Rather than learning as a function of time, these subjects
were actually becoming accustomed to the apparatus; some mentioned the unfamiliarity of the learnable materials, others gave their
reactions to the instructions, and so forth. Here again the aim is to
map the course of learning according to the (introspectively conceived) subject's actual experience rather than to the already known
fact that *time* (practice, rehearsal, familiarization, repetition, etc.)

would be required to acquire the materials. Giorgi calls such experimental designs "human scientific procedures" (*ibid.*, p. 193) and adds that they are really not totally existent in modern psychology but that they are possible. Though they may not look scientific, they are just as scientific as any other approach to valid data.

As with our reaction to the van Kaam study above, we are moved to ask: How does this procedure differ from the standard control and prediction sequence? Obviously Colaizzi's design could be repeated, with the data found initially predicted to cross-validate. In fact Colaizzi's work is itself a kind of cross-validation of G. E. Müller's historic findings that (when asked!) subjects in memory tasks may be seen to be doing more than simply acquiring materials mechanically "as a function of time" (as Ebbinghaus might have had it). By asking his subjects, Müller found that they consciously organized their materials after the kinds of preliminary assessments Colaizzi reported taking place in the first few "look sees" of the task at hand had been completed (see Watson, 1971, p. 298). Clearly, there is no strike against the scientific method in Colaizzi's work. What we humanists need is *more of the same*: humanistic theoretical statements put to test in a continuing line of cross-validations, carried on within a *rigorous* experimental context. We actually do have a viable paradigm in the Kantian model. What we need is a core of humanists willing to carry on the work of normal science (Kuhn, 1970a).

Giorgi (1970b) seems to be aware of the theory-leaning basis of the phenomenologist's polemic and of the paucity of research that flows from this general outlook. He noted that after a phenomenological argument has been presented, a critic will generally rise in the audience and say, "There's a phenomenologist for you. They are always telling you what *ought* to be done instead of *doing* it themselves. When will they stop talking and start *doing* something" (p. 96). Admitting that there is a certain truth to this charge, Giorgi then observes that what the phenomenologist is calling for is "a new way of *conceiving* the problem" (p. 96). He then adds:

In other words, the break-through that is demanded [i.e., what we have been calling a revolution in psychology] is essentially a theoretical one—how to *conceive* of new ways of experimenting, or of new ways of looking at phenomena, etc. Thus, we [phenomenologists] are *doing* plenty, even if we are not collecting data. If "doing" is defined narrowly and only in terms of data collection—then our critic is right. But if thinking is a mode of behavior—and empirically oriented psychologists apparently think so, at least so far as experiments are conducted in thinking—then the effort to seek new ways of *conceiving* perennial problems cannot be dismissed as irrelevant (*ibid.*, pp. 96–97).

Although Giorgi and the writer would appear to be *in tandem* on the question of where psychology needs revolutionizing, in our exchanges at the 1974–1975 Nebraska Symposium on Motivation we had considerable difficulty getting together on the program of change called for (see Rychlak, 1975 and Giorgi, 1975). Giorgi continually sought an admission that there was a precedent to *every* meaningful term in the language and that there were—at least possibly—as many precedents as there were individuals thinking and talking and using conceptual language. Yet the facts of history and even of science suggest to the writer that at some point in our search for precedents —for the slants and subjective meanings of unique persons—we *just do* find a realm of objective understanding in the terminological meanings confronted. We have objectivities and we have subjectivities in the precedents to which *every* language term ultimately relates. This objective realm—where a term or conception is understood by more individuals than just the single (subjective) person using it—used to be discussed at the most abstract levels as the question of universals. This ancient preoccupation of thinkers across history (see Table 1) to secure universal verities is hardly *subjective*, because we see again and again those recurring issues of causation, one and many, demonstrative versus dialectical strategies in reason, and so forth, indicating that there is as much commonality as there is difference in the extant or even potential knowledge of mankind. The purity criticism has merit, but it cannot be used in *every* instance without *itself* becoming a universal.

All of this phenomenological or existential talk about revolutionizing the methods of science constitutes a *straw man* argument. There are no inherent conflicts between validation and humanism. Those approaches that profess to fall back on the wisdom of philosophy or on the knowledge to be gained from the arts have failed as science because of their need to rely exclusively on procedural evidence to support their theoretical points of view. This in no way denigrates the role of philosophy or art in existence, and one can often go directly from philosophy and art to a scientifically testable line of development. We must never forget that human beings can create or "think up" possibilities that are not now in existence but which they could indeed "make happen." To say that some experience is phenomenally true but unamenable to scientific validation might simply mean that it has not yet reached creation in overt behavior. This ability to create can of course be studied scientifically. But to expect a scientist to run after each person's phenomenal reality in hopes of capturing each possibility that might be subjectively concocted is surely unnecessary and a waste of time. We need philosophical analysis to clarify our thinking, and artistic creations to enrich our life alternatives. These theory-laden and procedural-evidence-based activities are necessary and important to science. Yet so is validation important to science because there can be no science without it. Science means a stand on evidence *not* a stand on the human image. If science dictates the human image, it is no longer science! But most assuredly, any so-called humanistic methodology that falls short of validation is doomed to failure. Humanists *must* take our third step.

Why Mediational and Related Cognitive Theories Tend To Fail as Humanisms

A humanist making arguments of the sort being presented in this book is often confronted with the following objection:

You seem to be making the differences between humanism and mechanism insolvable by arguing against a behaviorism which no longer exists. Present day cognitive behaviorism or cognitive psychology handles all of the issues you raise about an active intellect and final causes. All we need do here is to acknowledge that the living organism surely *does* have certain processes that contribute to the stimulus input—literally *constructs* the stimulus—and then go on from there to build a more unified science of psychology. There are innumerable ways in which such processes mediate between sensation and behavior, possibly serving a feedback function or whatever. If you want to call these intervening processes (or the long-term memory of items stored in these processes) the "that for the sake of which" newer sensory inputs are constructed, that's your business. Why not say things this way and end all of this divisiveness in psychology by making it appear that humanism and mechanism are so incompatible when they are not!

This objection is actually a rephrasing of the "accounting for" argument discussed in Chapter 4 (p. 164), and it has beguiled psychologists for generations in the rise of the functionalist ideology. Though the writer would love to play the role of arbiter and resolver of psychological theoretical disputes like those of humanism-mechanism, the honest truth is that a mediational model—which is what the objector invariably calls for—simply *cannot* convey the meanings being expressed in the humanistic polemic. The reason for this theoretical intransigence is that we confront the meanings of efficient-formal causation (mechanism) here with the meanings of formal-final causation (humanism). Cancelling what is common to both ends of the confrontation we are left with the fulcrum issue: Can we rely exclusively on efficient causation to account for our data on human beings, or must we add the meaning of a final cause as well? Though it may deflate the scientific self-assurance of the objector to learn that we cannot reduce the meaning of final causation to an underlying efficient causation—that is, treat this matter via the institutionalized Lockean model—the fact will always remain that we *cannot* say one thing (efficient cause) and mean another (final cause).

To be more precise, one cannot do this in a demonstrative presentation, which is the posture taken by the scientist in this context. One could of course say one thing and mean another—for example, by informally analogizing from what is said but not meant to what is meant but not said. This would involve a dialectical maneuver and rely in large measure on sophistry (see Chapter 2). Because a rigorous science should not be based on sophistry or on informally framed analogical arguments in general, we would do well to clarify our thinking on just what is involved in the humanism-mechanism controversy that keeps it from being "handled" to the satisfaction of both sides. A good first step here is to focus on the terminology employed.

Cognitive Theory and Mediation Theory

Along with objections of the sort mentioned above, the humanist is likely to hear of various "new looks" developing in the learning theories or other forms of psychological theory at any given point in time. Colleagues or students are ever ready to reassure the humanist that his concerns over the grip of Lockeanism on psychology are no longer necessary. The most recent saviour theory seems to be a collection of views termed *cognitive* psychology. Because the term *cognitive* has a distinctive history in psychology, the psychologist who is mature enough to recall how prominently it was employed to describe approaches like those of Rogers (1951) in the 1940s and 1950s might be quite surprised to see what sorts of psychologists claim to be cognitive in outlook a generation later. Some even claim to be recapturing this earlier paradigm in their newer versions (e.g., Boneau, 1974). References to Kuhn are prominent in these approaches, and the general impression is usually given that we are on the brink of an extraordinary-science period with the dawning of a new paradigm in the rise of cognitive psychology (see, e.g., Solso, 1974, p. ix). A detailed look at these new theories convinces the writer that, except for intimations of a change in emphasis (to be discussed below), what they have to offer poses no threat to the Lockean model. Though advocates of cognitive psychology like to place themselves in opposition to S-R behavior theory (e.g., Dulany, 1968), on the critical point of *telic description* there is absolutely no difference between such views. Indeed there is about as much difference between modern cognitive and behavior theories as we found between American structuralism and functionalism (Chapter 4).

What does the term *cognition* mean? A dictionary search teaches us that it devolves from Latin roots meaning to become acquainted with or to get a knowledge of. The preferred meaning is "act or faculty of knowing," which suggests that there is a process of some sort going on in coming to know experience. When we get down to the details of describing this process, the point at which it is thought to occur, troubles begin to develop and our familiar divergence results. The British Empiricist (Lockean) interpretation of this process begins in William of Ockham's rules for proper theological debate (see Table 1). In rejecting what he took to be the fanciful theological proofs of the scholastics, Ockham distinguished between two kinds of knowing. Recall from Chapter 2 (pp. 69–70) that there is the *intuitive cognition*, which is tantamount to saying sensory input of experience through the organic structures of the body (eyes, ears, touch, etc.), and there is the *abstractive cognition*, which refers to the purely mental processing that man can accomplish based *solely* on the inputs of intuitive cognition. Proofs of God couched in the abstractive cognition are no better than those items of information that are made available through the intuitive cognition. As such they can never be a substitute for the empirical demonstration of miraculous occurrences—which are also input at the level of sensation. In the final analysis this empirical demonstration at the level of intuitive cognition is the *only* satisfactory evidence for the belief in God. This same question arose later in Locke's attack on the possibility of innate ideas (Chapter 2, p. 91). Mind is on the receptive side of knowledge, taking in rather than creating knowledge or having it stored innately to manufacture at will.

In opposition to this use of cognition, continental philosophy devolving from Kant took quite another view of the knowing process. As if to underscore the central nature of this difference, Kant (1952) takes up the question in the very first paragraph of his first introduction to *The Critique of Pure Reason*. Kant admits that "all knowledge begins with experience" (*ibid.*, p. 14), but adds that it does not necessarily follow from this that all knowledge arises out of experience:

For, on the contrary, it is quite possible that our empirical knowledge is a compound of that which we receive through [sensory] impressions, and that which the *faculty of cognition* [italics added] supplies from itself (sensuous impressions giving merely the *occasion*), an addition which we cannot distinguish from the original element given by sense, till long practice has made us attentive to, and skilful in separating it (*ibid.*, p. 14).

As we noted in Chapter 2 (p. 92), Kant had the level of intuitive cognition *itself* organized by time and space, and then at the so-called abstractive cognitive levels he brought in his concept of the categories of the understanding.

In essence the Kantian faculty of cognition returns to the scholastic model which Ockham was rejecting, because it suggests that there is a unique reasoning potential in mind, one that could well enter into the creation of knowledge *per se*. Kant was not trying to wage theological debate, of course, but his concept of transcendence via the *transcendental dialectic* permitted him to say that mind *qua* mind was not always on the passive side of an intuitive-to-abstractive cognitive course. The *faculty* concept was to become an object of derision in psychology, whereby everything from the Kantian categories of the understanding to Gall's phrenological labels were lumped into the same designation and then dismissed as "innate ideas" (Boring, 1950, p. 53). Those of us who recall using the term *cognitive* to describe Rogerian theory circa 1950 are surely thinking of this descriptive label in its Kantian sense. It was a neo-gestalt term at that time, having to do with the role that purely phenomenal organizations had upon sensory input, not *after* input had been affected, but coming at the same time or possibly even before such input was sensed (see Koffka, 1935, pp. 78 and 382). The distinction between distal (geographical) and proximal (phenomenal) stimuli made by the gestaltists closely approximated Kant's distinction between the noumenal and the phenomenal in cognition. As cognitive faculties the categories of the understanding operated completely in the phenomenal realm.

Having now pinpointed the current use of cognitive as some mixture of Ockham's intuitive and abstractive cognitions, we further argue that there is really no difference here from what in Chapter 4 we outlined as the mediation view of behavior (p. 154). Though this formal designation has been used most often in S-R theories, the study of history teaches that it has always been a vital part of theories relying predominantly on the efficient cause to account for descriptions of behavior. Helmholtz' concept of inductive conclusions or unconscious inference was of this variety (Chapter 3, p. 108). Wundt later employed the concept of apperception in similar fashion: He meant that inputs after birth act in the present as habitual frames determining the actual perception of an object we see before us today (Boring, 1950, p. 329). Indeed John Locke (1952) himself referred to the role of earlier inputs (associated ideas) on later input propensities as "intellectual habits" (p. 250). Such habits of thought give us an illusion of determining our own conceptual understanding, but in actuality the frequency of inputs arraying themselves "this way or that" in our connected habit (mediational) systems are really the determining factors: "Probability upon such grounds carries so much evidence with it, that it naturally determines the judgment, and leaves us as little liberty to believe or disbelieve, as a demonstration does, whether we will know [cognize] or be ignorant" (*ibid.*, p. 369).

This British Empiricist interpretation of cognition can be seen in E. C. Tolman's mediation conception (see Chapter 4, pp. 152–154). Tolman (1967) believed he could observe purposes and cognitions in behavior (pp. 12–13). These aspects of behavior necessarily went together (*ibid.*, p. 13), because in a sense cognitions were the "carriers" of purposes (*ibid.*, p. 27). As such, cognitions were said to be behavior-determinants, acting as intervening variables (*ibid.*, p. 414). In his glossary of terms, Tolman defined cognition as:

A generic term for one of the two classes of immanent determinants . . . of behavior. A cognition (a means-end readiness . . . or an expectation . . .) is present in a behavior in so far as the continued going-off of that behavior is contingent upon environment entities (i.e., types of discriminanda, manipulanda, or means-end-relations) proving to be "so and so." And such a contingency will be testified to whenever, if these environmental entities do not prove to be so and so, the given behavior will exhibit disruption . . . and be followed by learning (*ibid.*, p. 440).

Cognition thus referred to certain judgments and expectations which the organism had functioning as a mediator that "thus and such" would lead to "so and so," and following a purposive act of some sort, if this sequence of events failed to develop in the *contingent* circumstances, a disrupted pattern resulted calling for new learning to occur. This kernal idea of an organism mediating certain purposive or intentional *information* (the most common term employed) is what modern cognitive psychology has retained (e.g., see Broadbent, 1963). We turn now to two fine examples of such cognitive theories

Two Examples of Cognitive Mediation Theories:
Irwin and Neisser

Advocates of teleological theory may find encouragement in the patent efforts being made by modern cognitivists to employ terminology that is usually found in what Skinner (1971) has termed the "literature of freedom" (p. 30). On the surface such terms as *intention, purpose, active* or *constructive perception, optional behaviors, freedom* and *behavioral unpredictability* reassure us that we are moving to something different in psychological theory. In his statement of cognitive behaviorism Boneau (1974) even claims: "A humanistic version of the human individual emerges as a distinct possibility" (p. 308). However, when we look closely at what is being expressed in these views, we invariably find the unacceptable device of using a mediation concept to account for how the person comes today to employ these seemingly intentional behaviors.

The dateline of a theory's appearance in the literature is unimportant to the issues now being raised. These issues will have to be considered in *all* subsequent theories purporting to be cognitive or otherwise humanistic in nature, for they are not subject to the corrective influences of recently gathered data. In other contexts the writer has taken up the views of Boneau (Rychlak, 1975) and Mischel (Rychlak, 1976) on similar counts. The reader is simply being alerted by way of examples to what a humanistic theorist finds unacceptable in mediational efforts "to account for" telic considerations in behavior. Corrective measures are proposed in subsequent chapters of this volume.

In his *Intentional Behavior and Motivation: A Cognitive Theory* Francis W. Irwin (1971) acknowledges a neo-Tolmanian precedent and defines cognition as the knowledge an organism has of the situations and outcomes in which it finds itself (p. 104). His Situation-Act-Outcome (SAO) theory relies on an interlocked triad notion (ibid., p. 75). This triad consists of a preference (oPO') and a pair of complementary act-outcome expectancies ($aa'Eo$ and $a'aEo'$). If an organism prefers one outcome to another (o' to o in this example) and perceives that one act-outcome expectancy will lead to this preference ($a'aEo'$) while also perceiving that another act-outcome expectancy will lead to a dispreferred outcome (*aa'Eo*), a choice will be made by the organism for the former alternative (i.e., *a'aEo'*). The *situation* is essentially a complex of stimuli (ibid., p. 13); the *act* is anything that an organism can be said "to do" (*ibid.*, p. 17); and the outcome is the state of an organism's environment "some time after an act" (*ibid.*, p. 20).

The teleologist would be likely to interpret an act as literally creating or bringing about the outcomes of life, but Irwin (1971) makes clear that an act cannot influence its outcome because the latter is still in the future when the act is initiated. The outcome of an act can affect only *later* occurrences of comparable acts (p. 58). We find here a first intimation of the pseudohumanistic usage of *act* which separates the teleologist from the mediational thinker. How then are we to conceptualize the fact that a later event over time can influence an earlier event? Irwin responds: "The answer of a 'cognitive' theory is that the organism prefers the outcome that it *expects* its act to produce; it prefers the actual outcome only if it coincides with this *expected outcome*" (*ibid.*, p. 58).

Irwin emphasizes that concepts of expectation are central to cognitive theories (*ibid.*, p. 70). His contribution to expectancy theory and what separates him from stimulus-response psychologies is said to be the fact that he employs *two* terms on the "act" side of things, whereas the S-R theories settle for one term (*ibid.*, p. 72). Hull's fractional antedating goal reaction (see Chapter 4, p. 155) is thus a single response made to a stimulus complex, whereas in SAO theory the organism is viewed as formulating two complementary expectancies—one for the preferred and one for the dispreferred outcome. This is where both choice and intention enter: ". . . we take an act to be intentional if and only if its occurrence depends upon the existence of an interlocked triad in which the expected outcome of the act in question is also the preferred outcome and the expected outcome of the alternative act is also the dispreferred outcome" (*ibid.*; p. 78). A choice is the process that eventuates in one of the two alternative acts being carried out (*ibid.*, p. 79). The act chosen is intentional, but even the rejected act is an intentional act (*ibid.*, p. 84).

The upshot is that to speak of a choice on this model depends upon an act first occurring (*ibid.*, p. 89). To speak of possible choices, which might or might not eventuate in overt behavior, has little place in this theory. Irwin keeps his theory close to research paradigms in which terms like choice become operationalized. He sprinkles his presentation with examples in which a subject already *has* a preference or in which a preference or expectancy is established in earlier trials for a subject, who manifests it at some point, and then we bring to bear SAO theory to account for the process of selection *after* such preferential acts have been made (*ibid.,* p. 91). When accounting for how preferences or expectancies arise initially, Irwin falls back on a familiar theme. He says these are "acquired" (*ibid.,* pp. 60, 103) or learned: "It may be remarked that the acquisition and modification of act-outcome expectancies, which is required by our criteria, is obviously a form of learning . . ." (*ibid.,* p. 81). How are we to conceive of this learning process? The mediation-model strategy of this cognitive theory is never clearer than in the following, where Irwin employs a theory-method confound to put his central constructs between what we know as past inputs and present outputs, acting now in succession as fundamentally *efficient causes:*

Preferences and expectancies are dispositional states of the organism, and changes in such states, such as "learning," are processes. Psychology attempts to relate such states and processes to prior and concomitant vari-ables, on the one hand, and to acts, on the other. In a logical sense, then, they are *intervening variables* [italics added] (Irwin, 1971, p. 106).

If we can relate such states and processes to prior and con-comitant variables and if our variables of interest (preferences, expectancies) are intervening variables, of what use are such conceptions as behavioral *originators?* The behavioral determination here is exclusively instrumental, which means fundamentally that it has *itself* been efficiently caused by some antecedent event. Irwin's dispositional states *do not* dispose from birth but are brought in as theoretical analogues to the telic meaning of intentionality in that typical "accounting for" fashion of the functionalist's argument (see Chapter 4). No matter how often Irwin (1971) may use terms like intentions, choices, and even freedom (p. 85), the SAO theorist cannot escape the S-R (efficient-cause) Bind because he is willing to see in his experimental observations a variable mediating between other variables, rather than a telic theoretical construct. Predicating all on the Lockean *tabula-rasa* thesis, he must of necessity make behavior a tail-end affair, under the direction of influences other than those originating in the *pro-forma* possibilities of human creativity.

Ulric Neisser's (1967) *Cognitive Psychology* ranges across the broad discipline encompassed by this designation, but this excellent volume also presents a preferred theory by its author. His many assurances to the reader that, for example, "the world of experience is produced by the man who experiences it" (p. 3) or that "perception is not a passive taking-in of stimuli, but an active process of synthesizing or constructing a visual figure" (p. 16) can lull one into believing that we have something other than the traditional Lockean-mediation model under development in this volume. Neisser apparently believes that his outlook is in the line of descent from Brentano's Act Psychology (*ibid.*, p. 10), and he makes several favorable references to the work of the gestalt psychologists (e.g., pp. 50, 90). However, he primarily bases his approach on the work of Bartlett (1932, 1958). His core definition of cognition would probably be "the flow of information in the organism" (p. 208; taken from Broadbent, 1963).

Neisser (1967) uses the word *mediation* throughout the text, but he does not seem to mean what we have been meaning in the sense of an efficient-cause sequence of events. He seems to use this concept in a more active sense, often equating it with the meanings of *construction* and *synthesis*. In speaking of his preferred outlook he notes: "The central assertion is that seeing, hearing, and remembering are all acts of construction, which may make more or less use of stimulus information depending on circumstances" (p. 10); yet this active contribution to the stimulus input is termed a *mediation* (p. 3), so that in effect "all knowledge of the world is mediated rather than direct" (p. 173). We therefore do not wish to make our case employing quotations from Neisser's writings in which he is employing the word *mediation* in his sense. But at the same time we *do* want to claim that Neisser *is* a mediation theorist in the meaning of our term—that is, having ultimately to fall back on the meaning of *yesterday's efficient causes*. Though he wavers somewhat, this seems clearly to be his *basic* theoretical stance, all humanistic-sounding assurances to the contrary.

Neisser's cognitive approach is more British than continental, a fact we quickly discern in his distinction between a cognitive and a dynamic account of cognition: "Asked why I did a certain thing, I may answer in dynamic terms, 'Because I wanted . . . ,' or, from the cognitive point of view, 'Because it seemed to me . . .'" (*ibid.*, p. 4). In a subsequent discussion, however, we learn that the processes of focal attention in cognition are "very much under the control of developmental and dynamic factors" (*ibid.*, pp. 103–104). Though this might suggest a greater stress on the telic features in cognition (the "wants" of people in knowing) Neisser's treatment of cognitive phenomena does not encompass much in the way of identity concepts—apparently because this is not specifically the province of cognitive psychology. This is especially noticeable in his discussion of the Hoffding function, which he views as primarily a question of "pattern recognition" (*ibid.*, p. 50). Koffka (1935) felt that this phenomenon underscored the active processes in recognition and immediately brought in an identity concept to account for it because "recognizing involves an object-Ego relationship" (p. 594). When Neisser (1967) turns his attention to an identity concept or executive, he does so by way of cybernetic or information-processing analogues (*ibid.*, p. 292), a strategy to which we return below. A good sense of Neisser's preferred theory is to be seen in the following, which is a summary of his figural synthesis conception:

If we allow several figures to appear at once, the number of possible input configurations is so very large that a wholly parallel mechanism, giving a different output for each of them, is inconceivable. To cope with this difficulty, even a mechanical recognition system must have some way to select *portions* of the incoming information for detailed analysis. This immediately implies the existence of two levels of analysis: the preattentive mechanisms, which form segregated objects and help to direct further processing, and the act of focal attention, which makes more sophisticated analyses of the chosen object. . . . This means that the detailed properties and features we ordinarily see in an attended figure are, in a sense, "optional." They do not arise automatically just because the relevant information is available in the icon [transient visual memory], but only because part of the input was selected for attention and certain operations then performed on it. . . . In this sense it is important to think of focal attention as a constructive, synthetic activity rather than as purely analytic. One does not simply examine the input and make a decision; one *builds* an appropriate visual object (*ibid.*, p. 94).

This is surely the core of Neisser's thinking, and he employs this conception of active synthesis or construction in several contexts (e.g., pp. 103, 212–213, 225, 235). We confine our comments to this style of theorizing in his treatment of the higher mental processes (memory, recall and thought). Neisser recognizes that the British Empiricists (Hobbes, Locke, Hume, and especially James Mill) popularized the so-called reappearance hypothesis in memory. This is "the notion that the stored information consists of ideas, suspended in a quiescent state from which they are occasionally aroused . . ." (*ibid.*, p. 281). We are challenged to learn that even the gestalt psychologists accepted this hypothesis, because they spoke of "traces" in memory (*ibid.*, p. 283). A recheck of Koffka (1935) finds him discussing how traces are altered through being assimilated to other patterns so that they frequently never reappear as initially perceived (p. 524). Koffka also reiterates the importance of ego-systems in this context, so that traces may even be actively kept from reappearing in awareness altogether (*ibid.*, p. 525). This does not strike us as a simple reappearance hypothesis, surely.

To understand Neisser's (1967) strategy of explanation we must distinguish between construction (or synthesis) at the level of a sensory receptor (eye, ear, etc.) and construction at the level of the higher mental processes or, as we might call it, *mind*. Neisser seems to be a constructionist at the level of sensation—on the order of Kant's claim that sensory input is organized according to space and time—but at the level of mind he remains a traditionalist (a Lockean mediation theorist). He does not have a paralleling constructive role of mind *qua* mind as Kant did in his use of the categories of the understanding (see Chapter 2, p. 90). Hence, when we come to the higher mental processes, we find Neisser quickly foregoing his act-psychology stance to place a theoretical emphasis where Brentano would *not* have placed it. After noting that perceptual construction takes place, he observes that this requires a certain "raw material" on which to work (*ibid.*, p. 284). Harking back to Kant's view of cognition (refer above, p. 204), we now wonder if this means that sensuous impressions as raw materials give cognition the occasion to act. But this is not the theory of cognition being advanced, for we next read: "Perception is constructive but the input information often plays the largest single role in determining the constructive process. A very similar role, it seems to me, is played by the aggregate of information stored in long-term memory" (*ibid.*, p. 285). We have at this point clearly left the Kantian form of cognition and are now speaking of the influence of intuitive cognition on abstractive cognition in that sense of Ockham discussed above.

The unique feature of Neisser's argument, and where he departs from the reappearance hypothesis, is his claim that the nature of the information stored in long-term memory, which acts mediationally upon the inputs of "today," is *not* the "finished mental event" but rather the "traces of *prior processes of construction*" (ibid., p.285). All learning is response learning—that is, the learning to carry out some coordinated series of acts (*ibid.*). Neisser holds that the mental traces are not simply revived or reactivated by memory processes (recall) but that the recollection is of information concerning previous constructions used in the present to form new constructive acts. We always see and know more (ground) than the focal point of our attention (figure). When we first perceive or imagine an aspect of experience, the process of construction is never limited to the focal point in any case. We tend to build a spatial, temporal, and conceptual framework as well (*ibid.,* p. 287). Admitting that most of his text deals with the constructions in focal attention, Neisser then turns to a discussion of the *cognitive structures* to be found in higher mental processes:

One easily forgets the *occasions* on which one learned how the local streets are oriented, what the Civil War was about, how to shift gears, or how to speak grammatically, but they leave a residue behind. Because these residues are organized in the sense that their parts have regular and controlling interrelations, the term "cognitive structures" is appropriate for them. (This definition is meant to leave the question of empiricism and nativism open. It is very possible that the form and organization of at least some cognitive structures, especially those for space, time, and language, are determined genetically, or otherwise, before any experience has accumulated) (ibid., p. 287).

Though at first blush this parenthetical disclaimer may appear to reflect proper scientific discretion, a moment's reflection will convince the reader that this is *precisely* the question on which Neisser should be taking a stand, for this is what *always* divides the Lockean from the Kantian. We cannot leave such questions open in the context of empirical research without assuring that a Lockean view of things will prevail due to the IV-DV, S-R confound (see Chapter 4, p. 173). Granting that information which has been input since birth plays a role in what a person brings to bear in life, does this mean the capactiy to know such information is *itself* a product of earlier information? If so, how was this earlier information made known? What is often unappreciated is that a Lockean is a nativist on the questions of long- and short-term memory. He makes no assumptions about memory being learned. Since we now find that memory is itself organized by the individual, the question becomes: Can such organizations of memory *also* be innate? To answer yes to this question calls for a somewhat too anthropomorphic formulation to suit the Lockean's empirical tastes. As we have seen with Neisser versus Koffka, for a thinker in this tradition to invoke ego identities as the "constructors" of events is difficult. Yet, cognitive structuring cannot simply "hang there" without some recognition that there is an executive role going begging. Neisser knows full well why modern tough-minded psychologists balk at postulating such executives in their cognitive theories:

They are afraid that a separate executive would return psychology to the soul, the will, and the *homunculus*; it would be equivalent to explaining behavior in terms of a "little man in the head." Such explanations seem to lead to an infinite regress, which must bar further research and frustrate theory. If the actions of the executive account for behavior, what accounts for those actions in turn? Does the ego have an ego (*ibid.*, p. 295)?

This shopworn argument is based exclusively on an efficient-cause premise as regards what "accounts for" behavior. Self-direction is being interpreted here analogously to an individual sitting in an automobile, determining where it will go and what it will do. The machine is nontelic, but the homunculus human being within "accounts for" the actions observed on the roadways. But if the person within is *also* a machine, we need another homunculus to drive this identity about, and then another for the machine within *ad infinitum*. The argument crumbles once we broaden our interpretation of causation to include the meanings of finality. Neisser does not do this, but retaining the essentially efficient-cause extraspective perspective, takes his lead from the instrumentation of modern computer technology:

It now seems possible that there is an escape from the regress that formerly seemed infinite. As recently as a generation ago, processes of control had to be thought of as *homunculi*, because man was the only known model of an executive agent. Today, the stored-program computer has provided us with an alternative possibility, in the form of the *executive routine* (*ibid.*, p. 295).

Modern psychologists often go to cybernetic or information-processing analogues of this nature. One is likely to see a flow chart in their presentations, consisting of a series of boxes arrayed from left to right, labeled with terms such as *selected filters, encoding, search units, sensory buffers, decision channels, long-term and short-term memory storages*, and there is likely to be a feedback loop or two in such characterizations before the input flows through the system to its "output" (see Solso, 1974, for some prime examples). Though there is a pattern in the design of this flow (that is, a formal-cause emphasis is given), the essential characteristic of such informational flow is that it is efficiently causal in nature. The machine never truly behaves "for the sake of" a premise (a "that") because it has no awareness (even in principle!) of the fact that it is reasoning according to predicate assumptions as framed in its program. Lacking a self-reflexive intelligence, its strategy of reasoning is exclusively mediational. In short the machine never really acts, never really constructs anything—if we mean by *active intellect* and *construction* a creative potential to conceptualize possibilities and thereby bring them to bear in actuality. This human prerogative is left to the programmer, and we are back to our question: 'Is he a homunculus or not?' Neisser's treatment of the executive factor in perception and cognition reflects his cybernetic-like theoretical resolution of the identity problem (that is, the synthesizer or constructor of knowledge):

. . . when you see a friend across the street, you are not seeing only him. *He*, a person of a particular kind with a particular relevance to your life, is appearing *there*, a particular place in space, and *then*, at a certain point in time. Similarly, a spoken sentence is not just a string of words to be identified, but it has a particular meaning, is spoken by a particular person, at a particular time and place. These frames of reference can be thought of as a third level of cognitive construction. The preattentive processes delineate units, provide partial cues, and control simple responses; focal attention builds complexly structured objects or movements, one at a time, on the basis thus provided; the background processes build and maintain schemata *to which these objects are referred* [italics added] (*ibid.*, p. 286).

To the Kantian cognitivist, the schemata would be the very *starting* point, because meanings are said to devolve from above, rather than function as a frame of reference to which organized and structured objects from below are referred! Though we do have some changes of emphasis here, the fundamental institutionalized paradigm of psychology has gone essentially unscathed in Neisser's account. Whether we think of the cognitive hierarchy as consisting of focalized *items* or of *processes* makes no difference. So long as we are putting our emphasis on the source of knowledge as exclusively or primarily issuing from below, from the environmental input, which is *then* sequentially arrayed by way of one, two, or three organizational stages into a constitutive totality, we have the familiar Lockean model under espousal. Kantian formulations do not become those dreaded nativisms out of a love which their propounders have for innate mechanisms, but because Kantian theorists know full well that a mediation strategy must necessarily focus on the *processing* (the efficient-cause) of information as it flows from antecedent to consequent circumstance. There is no theory to date that has accepted mediation conceptualizations and avoided this necessary eventually. Some merely hide things better than others. The crux of the issue remains that *initial* capacity, ability, potential, of the organism to contribute something to the knowledge it acquires by way of experience without having "learned" to do so!

Hence we conclude that cognitive-mediational theories fail as humanisms because they simply do not capture the basic meaning of final causation. This inability to account for teleological behavior is also tied to the demonstrative nature of such theories. We have yet to see a cognitive theorist in the tradition of Ockham formulate a model that can subsume dialectical reasoning. However, Irwin's (1971) interlocked triad and his insistence on a complementary expectation, a rejected act to match the intended one, and so on, all suggest a quasi-dialectical formulation (pp. 75–77). Irwin seems to have employed these counterbalancing features primarily for reasons of logical symmetry, but dialectical formulations *could* have been introduced to his thinking at these specialized points of theory development. Neisser (1967) also moves into an area in which dialectical analysis is highly compatible when he begins speaking of the multiplicity of thought or the distinction between primary and secondary (Freudian) processes in thought (pp. 296–303). Neisser will have no little difficulty in accounting for the dialectical twists of dreaming and psychosis on an executive program fashioned exclusively along demonstrative lines.

Another drawback to the human image portrayed by these mediation conceptions is in their limited and simplistic treatment of choice. To see how a true choice is possible is difficult unless—at least some of the time—there is a truly arbitrary decision being depicted. Irwin's model of intentions leading to choices makes this process appear to run like clockwork, as indeed it can be made to do in a neatly devised research context. But is this the way choices arise in life? For example, can one choose an alternative going *against* one's preferences? Can we choose "for the devil of it?" Invariably such theories have choice fixed by the probability distribution of the information being mediated "this way" or "that way" on the question being pondered (not unlike Locke's use of probability quoted above, p. 205). Humanists find that this portrayal does not ring true, for people clearly *do* opt against the odds, standing against pressures, accepting the likelihood of death, taking the short end of a "long shot," and so forth. Is our only recourse to take a demonstrative posture and call all such behaviors illogical, or can we find an alternative logic on the basis of which people are behaving in these circumstances? Surely the humanist's position here is clear.

A further objection the humanist has to cognitive-mediational theories is their light treatment or highly inadequate treatment of *meaning.* No real distinction is made between what is a sign and what is a symbol in thought (Chapter 2). Constructive organizations are *always* seen as playing a sign function in the flow of information and never an expressive meaning-inducing role in the unfolding of events. *Meaning* is a relational term, and the nature of a relation is that it *does induce* an organization among the various elements being united. But cognitive theories fall back on mediated signs rather than on fundamentally expressive meanings in providing their accounts of what is supposedly going on in the experiment.

Putting together the points concerning the arbitrariness in behavior and the processing of meanings, we can see how mediation models find it impossible to capture the novel and the creative in behavior. To see the individual human being as creative we must take an introspective perspective and carefully elucidate what he contributes to the course of events going on within his lifeline. We cannot picture him extraspectively as a series of boxes with feedback loops, moving him along according to a set pattern based upon set input information now fixed into memory storages of various durations. There can be no originating source of control on such a model, in which the term *intention,* or *purpose,* may just as well be seen as a "code-X" carried by a feedback loop or storage box. There is no need for telic commentary on this model, because there is no true chance for creativity in the organism which is cybernetically conceptualized. Humanists prize these ascriptions, such as the person's creative potentials or peak experiences in living (Maslow, 1971, pp. 168–179). They simply cannot accept novelty as another one of those encoded behaviors that just happen to prove successful through serendipity or whatever, to a course of behavior.

We must also remember that the two views reviewed here as modern examples of psychological theory do not exhaust the varieties of mediation concepts presently employed. Space does not permit a thorough review of such *noncognitive* formulations as the admittedly S-R mediation theories or those Lockean formulations in which a physiological substrate is pointed to as the ultimate behavioral determinant. Obviously these mediation theories, many of which rely on drive reductions or genetic transmissions to say how it is that human behavior is determined, are totally unacceptable to a teleologist. The Skinnerian view is a special case, and we devote a full section to operant theory in Chapter 6 (pp. 255–270).

One final caution: We must not allow those who fail to see the retention of Lockeanism in mediational models to present themselves as the true innovators of our time. Although they act in a sincere belief that they are advancing psychology, the prophets of the "new look" of cognitive mediationism must be called to answer the arguments of the present chapter before we let them carry the revolutionary (or evolutionary) banner at our forefront. Mahoney (1974) is a case in point, as when he prepares his reader for the mediational models he is about to advocate following a very telling chapter on the weaknesses of so-called nonmediational (Lockean) models (pp. 35–39). He suggests to his reader: "We are long overdue for some evolutionary progress in our paradigm. The mediational models which we shall now examine may provide some adaptive conceptual mutations in our understanding of complex human behavior" (*ibid.*, p. 49). This seeming advance is a *trap*; it simply perpetuates the efficient causation of (nontelic) Lockeanism at another level of description; and far from being an evolutionary advance, it is an apology for the badly mangled but entrenched model of the academic establishment.

Intimations of a Revolution in Psychology?

Significant changes do seem to be apparent in the thinking of rigorous psychologists in the last quarter of the twentieth century. Not everyone would agree with this assessment, of course. Kausler (1974) notes that the new look in cognition is actually the return to certain unsolved problems dating back to Ebbinghaus. Even so, because these are questions of *theory* and not of *method* (evidence), we have reason to look to the future of psychology with confidence that significant changes in theory will eventuate. The major stumbling block to teleology is proper terminology. The earliest most influential psychologists (including Ebbinghaus) simply refused to take seriously a psychology of telic description (Chapters 4 and 5). The time is now ripe for a serious reevaluation of our terminology in light of our experimental rules of data collection.

There is much talk of rules in modern cognitive psychology, stemming apparently from the writings of the logical positivists (see Table 1). Wittgenstein's influence in particular seems great, because his style of referring to language games and their attendant rules seems to have been adopted in a number of scientific theories, ranging from genetic codes to mathematical language systems. But the problem for psychology is that, although such rules (as all mathematics) are based upon *logic,* the mediation theorist seems to view logic itself as a kind of predetermined ordering that does not require a special "accounting for" in human behavior. Yet, as any logician knows, in the most fundamental of all logical efforts, *predication* (Table 1: Aristotle and Peter of Abelard), what is affirmed by the reasoner into a patterned meaning is *not* fixed and without arbitrariness at some point in the line of reasoning.

Logicians speak of "granting this, that follows" because they know full well the precedent-sequacious line of meaning-extension that human reason generates. And even if they are not dialecticians, they also know the reverse—that is, "granting that, this follows." Though we hear much about the ordering, organizing, and encoding of language terms according to rules from modern cognitivists, they are remarkably mute concerning *this* predicating or premising activity of logic. Logic is surely an ordering, and the resultant rules generated in cognition are most surely empirically demonstrable. But until we have some way of acknowledging that the cognizing individual literally *conceptualizes* (contributes to the form his logical reasoning will take), we will never capture what needs capturing in a psychology of the human being. Mediational models cannot help here because mediational organization always occurs as an *effect* of previous learning. Happily, there are growing signs that modern researchers are finding subject-induced organizations in learning tasks which are anomalous to a Lockean model.

For example, James J. Jenkins (1974) has done an excellent job of explicating the Lockean assumptions in traditional views of memory, assumptions which he notes are losing their grip on this field of inquiry. He and other psychologists have found the writings of Stephen C. Pepper (1970) to be of help in formulating theoretical alternatives to Lockeanism in psychology. Pepper distinguished a series of *world hypotheses*, which are root metaphors that thinkers of all types—from philosophers to scientists—employ in describing their areas of interest. Although the parallels here are not exact, the Lockean model relates to what Pepper calls the *mechanism* root metaphor (Jenkins, 1974, calls this "associationism" in psychology); and the Kantian model comes closest to his *contextualism* on certain crucial points (Pepper, 1970, Chapters 9 and 10). Pepper traces contextualism to the philosophies of Charles S. Peirce, William James, and John Dewey, but one could easily show that contextualism takes from these views the Kantian side of what in Chapter 4 we called a mixed Lockean-Kantian formulation in the philosophy of William James (p. 157).

To find a leading experimentalist of Jenkins' (1974) reputation calling for a shift to contextualism in the field of memory is of no small interest. He may well have named a significant trend in cognitive psychology, one begun in the work of Bousfield (1953) and Tulving (1962) and others, whereby the subject in a learning (memory) experiment is seen to organize his recall of words based upon certain categories—either those made available by the experimenter (for example, providing subjects with names of people vs. names of cities) or actually induced by a subject's idiosyncratic associative proclivities. Jenkins (1974) based much of his argument on a study of Bransford and Franks (1971), in which subjects were seen to *construct* (Neisser's term) complex sentences, which they believed with certainty that they had seen before *but had not*, out of shorter sentences, which were seen and which contained the meanings eventually inferred and organized into the longer sentences.

Thus evidence is accruing that for words (Bousfield, Tulving) and sentences (Bransford & Franks) a subject *does something* to the task at hand in terms of some organizational capacity he has to sort a task out in some way. Psychologists have undoubtedly known this for decades. They probably took this as one of those Kuhnian puzzles, rather than as an anomaly. Let us hope that we have a growing number of psychologists who are now considering the anomalies of a mediating animal which seems an actively organizing animal. Next question: Can this organization be shown to begin early in life, from birth or at least before any learning can be said to have taken place? If so, the mediation model as presently conceived must surely be modified significantly. This would doubtless be a genuine revolution in psychology, and it would be a revolution at the *level of theory*. The integrity of the scientific method would not be challenged.

A Sensible Revolution For All Time

Though there will doubtless always be Kuhnian revolutions in psychology, just as there are in other sciences, we are proposing a single revolution *for all time* which will liberalize psychology on the side of theoretical description even as it keeps us within the bounds of rigorous science. Kantian theories will no longer be pressed into or "accounted for" by the linear strictures of a scientific methodology that itself sprang from Lockean precedents. We will retain the demonstrative rigor of this method even as we recognize the possibility that it can test *other* than Lockean theories. Dialectical and telic formulations will *not* be permitted to affect the strictures of validating evidence. *Rigor* will mean knowing where one comes from theoretically, carefully extending a line of development to the point of empirical testing and then, in the most demonstrative way possible, *proving* what we believe to be the case in the unmolested succession of events known as validation. Because we acknowledge the affirmation-of-the-consequent fallacy in this sequence, a healthy sense of modesty will characterize our claims concerning the facts we presume to discover in the empirical data at play before our eyes. The contribution theory makes to this sequence of events will never be forgotten.

We lose our theoretical way and become "method mad" when we fallaciously believe that theories arise only in the data. Theories, like cognitive structurings of the stimulus, have *other* sources of organization than that which patterns them in the noumenal reality. They have a source that is expressed variously but always comes back to that phenomenal awareness called *mentality*. That scientists behave as they do, according to the meaning-lending structurings of a precedent paradigm, is no mere accident. This is their course of activity because this is their very nature as human beings! We all *must* predicate our thinking on something other than the focal point of our concern. This is not a radical notion, but bears the weight of history as we discovered in Chapter 1 (see Table 1). The difficulty in furthering a revolution in psychology stems from the fact that we lack some appropriate *cognitive category* or *paradigmatic frame* within which to alert our senses to this side of behavior. Lacking this precedent, we cannot discover its effects even when they are involved in our studies, or we let them pass by as puzzles rather than catch them up as anomalies.

Kuhnian anomalies do not "spring forth" from the data, but are "put onto" such events in an empirical study. In the next three chapters of this volume we review a series of issues in an aim to clarify and then extend the terminology introduced to describe the nature of human behavior. In doing so we hope to be writing-in the precedents for a *sensible* revolution, one that will not unseat or repress *any* view on pseudoscientific grounds. We do not need to supplant the Lockean mechanistic model with the Kantian humanistic (contextualistic) model. Anyone who expresses interest in Lockean formulations should be encouraged and supported to continue his study just as he now does. But we hope that he would, if not be humbled, at least made contemplative by the recognition that his historical ties to the machine paradigm of scientific *method* are no longer mandates for a preferred position in the scientific *theoretical* hierarchy.

Telic theoretical accounts are no longer to be dismissed as lacking parsimony, or as departing from the data, or as reflecting a homunculus machine within a machine. No one who is unable or unwilling to take the theoretical viewpoint of another can claim objectivity in science. If the constructs being used are found wanting, they can easily be refuted *within the language realm* of the theory under espousal. But if a critic simply refuses to comprehend a telic theory and in some way claims the rights of preemption as a "genuine" scientist who "knows" what a proper scientific account must be like, something far more serious is taking place. In this case, rather than critical analysis, we are faced with *paradigmatic repression;* the only alternative here is to employ countermeasures to remove the repression. In this book we direct arguments counter to such repressions. If psychology is open to our revolution in theory *versus* method, there shall be no reason ever to repress an idea—that is, a theory or even a theory of knowledge. There *will* remain a repression of sorts on the side of method, because we insist on a validation by way of terminating the theoretical line of development in an objective repeatable experiment!

Summary

In Chapter 5 we try to clarify what is meant by the phrase *scientific revolution,* and in light of this clarification, to propose the type of revolution called for in psychology. Kuhn's position is seen as reflecting more accurately what takes place in scientific work than does Popper's concept of the falsification of scientific theories. Scientists work to further the meanings of certain precedent paradigms to which they owe their very understanding of the area of study in which they are engaged. What is not generally appreciated, however, is that the Kuhnian concept of revolution is *exclusively* on the side of theory and not method. The scientific ground rules of validation are not what is being challenged in a scientific revolution, but rather the ways in which we conceptualize the findings of our empirical observations and experiments.

Indeed the very procedure of science as a line of development entails a necessary logical error—that of *affirming the consequent* of an 'If . . . then . . .'' proposition. This is not fatal to science, but it does signal that for any given fact pattern a series of (literally, N!) theoretical descriptions is potentially capable of accounting for the regularities observed. Psychology can be both rigorous and humanistic if we learn to use telic theories and then put them to test in typical experimental fashion, employing validating evidence. So long as we avoid confounding what is our theory with what is our method, such a rigorous humanism is possible.

We next discussed two kinds of views on how to solve the problems of a humanistic psychology by erring in opposite directions. First, there are the psychologists like van Kaam and Giorgi who indicate that we can derive a new methodology of science that will rectify the difficulties of writing humanistic theory by advancing something other than strict validation in their support. But when we come right down to what these alternative methods suggest, there is no difference between such practices and what would be expected from a more conventional scientific effort—particularly in an early stage of experimentation. So-called phenomenological and existential "methods" threaten to resolve themselves into an exclusively pro-cedural-evidence-based approach to science, and for this reason we cannot accept them as viable alternatives to the current rules of validation.

When we next turn to the cognitive approaches of Irwin and Neisser, which suggest to many psychologists that humanistic issues are now being "handled" adequately, a problem arises in the other direction. Although the rules of evidence are properly adhered to in these approaches, the actual theoretical constructs being put to test are simply *not* adequate to the explanatory task. Ultimately these theories are all mediational in tone and hence must—at the crucial point of behavior's earliest manifestations—accept a *tabula-rasa* rather than a *pro-forma* account of mentation. Mediation theory thus falls short of a genuinely telic theory on at least three counts: (1) Mediators (signs, rules, encoders, models, etc.) are input and hence are past "effects" rather than truly present "causes," which means that (2) a genuine "that for the sake of which" determination in the sequence of motion called behavior is *never* achieved (i.e., there is no arbitrariness in behavior); (3) resulting in exclusively a demon-strative way of describing the course of behavioral events.

A sensible revolution for psychology is to distinguish clearly between what is our theory and what is our method of validating these outlooks and to admit a broader range of theoretical formula-tions. Specifically, we need Kantian as well as Lockean theories of behavior. Neither outlook is to be given preferential status, and the telic formulations that invariably flow from Kantian models will only strengthen psychology as a science of human behavior.

References

Bartlett, F. C. *Remembering.* Cambridge: The University Press, 1932.

Bartlett, F. C. *Thinking.* New York: Basic Books, 1958.

Bergmann, G., & Spence, K. Operationism and theory in psychology. *Psychological Review,* 1941, **48**, 1–14.

Binswanger, L. *Being-in-the-world.* (Translated and with a critical introduction by J. Needleman.) New York: Basic Books, 1963.

Boneau, C. A. Paradigm regained? Cognitive behaviorism restated. *American Psychologist,* 1974, **29**, 297–309.

Boring, E. G. *A history of experimental psychology.* New York: Appleton-Century-Crofts, 1950.

Boss, M. *Psychoanalysis and daseinsanalysis.* New York: Basic Books, 1963.

Bousfield, W. A. The occurrence of clustering in the free recall of randomly arranged associates. *Journal of General Psychology,* 1953, **49**, 229–240.

Bransford, J. D., & Franks, J. J. The abstraction of linguistic ideas. *Cognitive Psychology,* 1971, **2**, 331–350.

Bridgman, P. W. *The way things are.* Cambridge, Mass.: Harvard University Press, 1959.

Broadbent, D. E. Flow of information within the organism. *Journal of Verbal Learning and Verbal Behavior,* 1963, **2**, 34–39.

Bronowski, J. *The common sense of science.* Cambridge, Mass.: Harvard University Press, 1958.

Bugental, J. F. T. Humanistic psychology: A new break-through. *American Psychologist,* 1963, **18**, 563–567.

Cassirer, E. *The problem of knowledge.* New Haven: Yale University Press, 1950.

Colaizzi, P. F. An analysis of the learner's perception of learning material at various phases of a learning process. *Review of Existential Psychology and Psychiatry,* 1967, **7**, 95–105.

Colaizzi, P. F. *Reflection and research in psychology: A phenomenological study of learning.* Dubuque, Iowa: Kendall/Hunt, 1973.

Conant, J. B. *Modern science and modern man.* Garden City, N.Y.: Doubleday Anchor, 1952. (Originally published, New York: Columbia University Press, 1929.)

Dulany, D. Awareness, rules, and propositional control: A confrontation with S-R behavior theory. In T. R. Dixon & D. L. Horton (Eds.), *Verbal behavior and general behavior theory.* Englewood Cliffs, N.J.: Prentice-Hall, 1968.

Eddington, A. *The philosophy of physical science.* Ann Arbor: University of Michigan Press, 1958.

Einstein, A. *Essays in science.* New York: Philosophical Library, 1934.

Feuer, L. S. *Einstein and the generations of science.* New York: Basic Books, 1974.

Frank, P. *Philosophy of science.* Englewood Cliffs, N.J.: Prentice-Hall, 1957.

Giorgi, A. *Psychology as a human science: A phenomenologically based approach.* New York: Harper & Row, 1970. (a)

Giorgi, A. Toward phenomenologically based research in psychology. *Journal of Phenomenological Psychology*, 1970, **1**, 75–98. (b)

Giorgi, A. Phenomenology and the foundational problems of pyschology. In W. J. Arnold & J. K. Cole (Eds.), Nebraska symposium on motivation (Vol. 22). Lincoln: University of Nebraska Press, 1975.

Haigh, G. V. Letter to the editor. *Psychology Today*, 1969, **3**, 4.

Hull, C. L. Mind, mechanism, and adaptive behavior. *Psychological Review*, 1937, **44**, 1–32.

Irwin, F. W. *Intentional behavior and motivation: A cognitive theory*. Philadelphia: Lippincott, 1971.

Jenkins, J. J. Remember that old theory of memory? Well, forget it! *American Psychologist*, 1974, **29**, 785–795.

Kant, I. *The critique of pure reason*. In R. M. Hutchins (Ed.), *Great books of the western world* (Vol. 42). Chicago: Encyclopedia Britannica, 1952. Pp. 1–250.

Kausler, D. H. Continuity of processes across variants of recognition learning. In R. L. Solso (Ed.), *Theories in cognitive psychology: The Loyola symposium*. New York: Wiley, 1974. Pp. 45–75.

Kelly, G. A. *The psychology of personal constructs* (2 vols.). New York: Norton, 1955.

Koffka, K. *Principles of gestalt psychology*. New York: Harcourt, Brace, 1935.

Kuhn, T. S. *The structure of scientific revolutions* (2nd ed.). Chicago: The University of Chicago Press, 1970. (1st ed., 1962.) (a)

Kuhn, T. S. Logic of discovery or psychology of research? In I. Lakatos & A. Musgrave (Eds.), *Criticism and the growth of knowledge*. Cambridge: The University Press, 1970. Pp. 1–23. (b)

Locke, J. *An essay concerning human understanding*. In R. M. Hutchins (Ed.), *Great books of the western world* (Vol. 35). Chicago: Encyclopedia Britannica, 1952. Pp. 85–395.

Mahoney, M. J. *Cognition and behavior modification*. Cambridge, Mass.: Ballinger, 1974.

Maslow, A. H. Eupsychia, the good society. *Journal of Humanistic Psychology*, 1961, **1**, 1–11.

Maslow, A. H. *The farther reaches of human nature*. New York: The Viking Press, 1971.

Masterman, M. The nature of a paradigm. In I. Lakatos & A. Musgrave (Eds.), *Criticism and the growth of knowledge*. Cambridge: The University Press, 1970. Pp. 59–89.

Neisser, U. *Cognitive psychology*. New York: Appleton-Century-Crofts, 1967.

Oppenheimer, R. Analogy in science. *American Psychologist*, 1956, **11**, 127–135.

Palmer, R. E. *Hermeneutics*. Evanston, Ill.: Northwestern University Press, 1969.

Pepper, S. C. *World hypotheses*. Berkeley: University of California Press, 1970.

Polanyi, M. *Personal knowledge*. New York: Harper Torchbook, 1964.

Popper, K. R. *The logic of scientific discovery*. New York: Basic Books, 1959.

Popper, K. R. Normal science and its dangers. In I. Lakatos & A. Musgrave (Eds.), *Criticism and the growth of knowledge*. Cambridge: The University Press, 1970. Pp. 51–58.

Rogers, C. R. *Client-centered therapy.* Boston: Houghton Mifflin, 1951.

Rychlak, J. F. *A philosophy of science for personality theory.* Boston: Houghton Mifflin, 1968.

Rychlak, J. F. A humanist looks at psychological science. In W. J. Arnold & J. K. Cole (Eds.), *Nebraska symposium on motivation* (Vol. 22). Lincoln: University of Nebraska Press, 1975.

Rychlak, J. F. Is a concept of "self" necessary in psychological theory, and if so why? In A. H. Wandersman, P. J. Poppen, & D. F. Ricks (Eds.), *Humanism and behaviorism: Dialogue and growth.* Elmsford, N.Y.: Pergamon Press, 1976.

Schrödinger, E. *Science theory and man.* New York: Dover, 1957.

Skinner, B. F. *Beyond freedom and dignity.* New York: Knopf, 1971.

Solso, R. L. (Ed.), *Theories in cognitive psychology: The Loyola symposium.* New York: Wiley, 1974.

Suzuki, D. T. *The essentials of Zen Buddhism.* (B. Phillips, Ed.) New York: Dutton, 1962.

Tolman, E. C. *Purposive behavior in animals and men.* New York: Appleton-Century-Crofts, 1967.

Tulving, E. Subjective organization in free recall of "unrelated" words. *Psychological Review*, 1962, **69**, 344–354.

van Kaam, A. *Existential foundations of psychology* (Image Books ed.). Garden City, N.Y.: Doubleday, 1969.

Watson, R. I. *The great psychologists* (3rd ed.). Philadelphia: Lippincott, 1971.

Whitehead, A. N. *The function of reason.* Boston: Beacon, 1958.

CHAPTER SIX

Misunderstandings, Confoundings, and Oversights in Modern Psychological Science

The discussion of a revolution in the distinction between theory and method is continued in Chapter 6. We also underscore the role dialectic has *already* played in the rise of modern science, and give detailed consideration to what is frequently held up as a stumbling block to humanism—the concept of determinism in events.

A More Rigorous Use of Terms That Can Mean Theory, Method, or Both

The arguments about the confounding of theory with method can best be documented by arraying a number of terms frequently used by psychologists under these designations in tabular form. We can then easily see that many of these meanings cross over in common psychological parlance. Table 2 pp. 228–229 contains such an array of terms. It has at the top different terms that refer to essentially the same thing whether framed in a *theoretical (model, contiguity, hypothesis)* or a *methodological* context (*design, frequency, prediction*). Near the midpoint of the table we begin to see several repetitions across the two arrays, sometimes with modest differences between theoretical usage (theoretical behaviorism) and methodological usage (methodological behaviorism). But at other times the identical word or phrase is used (*function of* or *law* or *control*). When identical words are used under each array they are in quotation marks.

Table 2 is not exhaustive, and the reader may not agree with all of the parallels drawn. But it can hardly be denied that something of this sort goes on regularly in psychology. Note an essential characteristic of this table: It lacks terminology which might refer to *dialectical* meanings. This is as it should be, for as we argued in Chapter 5, proper science calls for methods that are nondialectical. However, when psychologists consciously set out to *restrict* their range of theorizing to the conceptualizations of Table 2 in the name of rigor we find serious developments taking place. For example, Underwood (1975) has defined model as follows: "As I understand the strict use of the term *model,* it means that a set of empirical relationships developed in one area of discourse is applied to another area of research as a possible explanatory system" (p. 129). Clearly, if a psychologist were to follow this recommendation, he would have to confine his models (left side of Table 2) to analogues drawn from the right side of Table 2. This means that his models must necessarily remain demonstrative (an example of what we call below, p. 245, formal-cause determinism!).

Underwood goes on to recommend certain guidelines for satisfactory theory construction in psychology—the sort of thing one might teach to a student who has asked the question: How do you get a theory? (*ibid.*, p. 128). Two of the three recommendations stress that "The theory must assume at least two intervening processes, and these processes must interact in some way to relate the independent variables to the dependent variables;" and ". . . any assumed process [in the person's behavioral activity] must be tied to at least one independent variable" (*ibid.*, p. 131). We see here *precisely* the concern that humanists have regarding the likely outcome of psychological theory which is confounded with questions of proof. Using these guidelines, Underwood *must* teach his students to think about behavior in exclusively efficient-cause terms. He furthers the tradition of Bergmann and Spence (1941, pp. 9–10) and MacCorquodale and Meehl (1948, pp. 103–105), who taught us that the proper if not the *only* locus in which to consider the role of theory is *between* the independent and the dependent variables of an empirical investigation (i.e., the S-R bind).

Underwood is mistaken on several counts. There are just as many examples in the history of science where *unsuccessful* models have been resuscitated to solve problems as there are of successful models and designs doing so. Arago's proposal of the "crucial experiment" to test the corpuscular theory of light is a famous case in point. Though satisfactorily refuted in 1855, this corpuscular "model" was revived in 1905 by Einstein who employed its heuristic powers in modified form as the hypothesis of light quanta or photons (Frank, 1957, p. 31). To teach that theories serve heuristically only between observable and manipulable variables is simply *not true!* We have seen Kuhn's arguments to this effect in Chapter 5. Robert Oppenheimer (1956)

Table 2 Some Terms Employed in Psychology Having the Meaning of Theory and/or Method

Theoretical terminology	Methodological terminology
Model [paradigm]	Design
Facts	Data
Stimulus and response	Independent and dependent variable(s)
Antecedent [cause]	Independent variable
Consequent [effect]	Dependent variable
Contiguity	Frequency
Hypothesis	Prediction
Demonstration	Control
Parameter	Treatment
Hypothetical	Operational
Interpretation	Generalization
Individual differences	Variance
Relationship	Law (correlation)
Construct	Observation (variable)
Single	Idiographic
General	Nomothetic
Learning	Trials-to-criterion
Habituated	Reinforced
Association	Correlation (law)
Alternatives	Manipulations
Understanding	Evidence
Conviction	Confidence level

once spoke about this directly to psychologists, pointing out how in physics *analogues* as theoretical devices come into play even *before* one sets about to identify what his variables will be. To believe that models emerge from proven methods and that science is therefore merely a question of extending these empirically derived frames of reference to the further reaches of explanation is an injustice to the human capacity for creativity. This is how psychology has come to make an efficient-cause metaphysic of its efficient-cause method (Burtt, 1955, p. 229).

Many readers can recall drafting research reports of the sort "The effect of [variable] X on [variable] Y." Taken in this pristine methodological phrasing, no one can object to the meanings conveyed which speak of evidential relationships between theoretical hypotheses now translated into operationalized variables. A related phrase is the *functional relationship* between variables (see Chapter 4). Combining as it does the meanings of empirical observation with that of statistical analysis, this functional phraseology has an especially

Table 2   Some Terms Employed in Psychology Having the Meaning of Theory and/or Method (*Cont.*)

Theoretical terminology	Methodological terminology
Consequence	Contingency
Descriptive	Actuarial
Reductionism	Operationism
Hypothetical construct	Intervening variable
Theoretical variable	Experimental variable
Theoretical behaviorism	Methodological behaviorism
Theoretical assumptions	Statistical assumptions
Theoretically determined	Statistically determined
"Effect(s) of"	"Effect(s) of"
"Function," "function of"	"Function," "function of"
"Dimension(s)"	"Dimension(s)"
"Findings"	"Findings"
"Results"	"Results"
"Influence(s)"	"Influence(s)"
"Law"	"Law"
"Norm"	"Norm"
"Determined"	"Determined"
"Mediate," "mediation"	"Mediate," "mediation"
"Generalization"	"Generalization"
"Control(s)"	"Control(s)"
"Contingent upon"	"Contingent upon"
"Interaction"	"Interaction"
"Condition(s)"	"Condition(s)"
Etc.	

appealing sound to it, as when Kausler (1974) here argues for the evidence supporting the continuity of learning processes across experimental tasks: "In general, our confidence in continuity increases directly with the number of common functional relationships that performance on the tasks in question bear with relevant independent variables" (p. 61). Looked at in one sense, all this conveys is that our belief in a theoretical position is strengthened with increasing validating evidence in its support. But looked at in another, there is the connoted suggestion that the performance of a subject is functionally related to the independent variables—not to the theory defining these variables, but to the variables *per se!* Kausler may have meant it in either sense, but too many psychologists see in such phrasings what they wish to see. A humanist can agree with the first meaning, which merely emphasizes the role of evidence in research, but he would object to the more theoretical efficient-cause connotations of the second meaning. Although framed in a rigorous context of empirical research, this statement is *not* satisfactorily rigorous because it can be taken in different ways.

The use of certain phrases like *function of* or *effects of* in both a theoretical and methodological sense has given rise to ethical problems in psychology. Because one "sees" the dependent variable as a "function of" the independent variable and because, as an experimenter, one must "control and predict" the "effects of" the latter on the former it seems the purest of logic to conclude that psychology's mission is the "control and prediction of behavior" in general. The chief modern advocate of this view has been B. F. Skinner (1971), of course, but even such a biologically oriented psychologist as D. O. Hebb (1974) has spoken in favor of efforts to control people's behavior (pp. 71–72). If *control and prediction* means that psychology is a science relying on validating evidence, there can be no quarrel with it. This would merely state that all psychologists accept the same ground rules of evidence or proof in their empirical work (methodological usage). However, if this phrase means that psychologists in their professional role have literally to control and thereby predict the course of the lives of people or of social groups, quite another issue is being framed. In this case the language has shifted from purely methodological considerations to a theoretical or metatheoretical question of values and ethics (see Rychlak, 1968, Chapter 6 for a more thorough discussion of this question). Not all psychologists value the role of applied scientist, actuarian, or social innovator; some even find the aspiration to the role of controller in human affairs unethical. Whether we agree with these values or not, once again a lack of precision in terminological usage has confounded and befuddled us all.

The high valuation placed on mathematics by psychologists cannot be overstated. A major feature of our history has been the rise of statistical methods, with names like Galton, Cattell, Spearman, Thorndike, Pearson, and Thurstone distinguishing the pages of our textbooks. Because of what we called in Chapters 1 (p. 36) and 2 (p. 83) the double-duty characteristic of mathematical reasoning, we can both speak about our statistical assumptions and at the same time refer to the statistical (functional) relationship of purely objective variables at play in research experiments. The former assumptive requirements can refer to the introspective theoretical perspective, because a reasoner makes such assumptions, whereas the latter commentary coalesces nicely with the extraspective theoretical perspective. Unfortunately, too many psychologists have forgotten the introspective features of mathematics and simply take as given that the world *is* a Pythagorean reality (see Table 1), functioning independently of man's puny intelligence but responding in certain ways to mathematical assessments.

This extraspective view of mathematics underwrites the frequent assertion by psychologists that they seek out variables to study in behavior. Statistical theory is based on the assumption of distinct parameters, existing as pools from which data can be sampled (albeit entirely in mathematical space). The plausible implication here is that literally *anything* that can be delineated, hence varied in some way (as to weight, patterning, intensity, etc.), *is* such an identity, drawn from a pool, parameter, base rate, and so on of identical variables. It follows from this implication that psychologists *must* be engaged in the study of variables. This reasoning is at the heart of a distinction currently drawn between so-called theoretical behaviorism and methodological behaviorism (not to be confused with Skinner's 1974 usage, pp. 13–16). This distinction asserts that *all* psychologists are methodological behaviorists because we all deal in observed behavior as variables in our (empirical) experiments, even when we disagree with the behavioristic theoretical accounts of such observations (e.g., disagree with conditioning theory). This distinction rests on the improper use of the word *behaviorism* in the methodological context. Observing behavior is not a behaviorism, which implies a doctrinaire adherence to a style of conceptualizing this behavior by all who engage in the methodological activity of validation. Because this is incorrect, the distinction is misleading—and unnecessary in any case.

Psychological scientists can no more study behavior without theoretically conceptualizing it in some fashion than they can study variables without such conceptualization. Saying that we in psychology study variables is method-lingo, correct enough in one sense but seriously overlooking the equally true statement that we make up these variables based on theoretical assumptions and paradigmatic predilections. Because variables do not drop like apples from the tree of knowledge, we never merely *study* variables. How and why have we delineated *this* particular variable to investigate? What is our understanding of *that* particular behavior in terms of causal description? Focusing on the end-state of our line of development from theory to test (see Chapter 5, p. 191) is surely a one-sided characterization of the scientific enterprise. Yet there are those in psychology who frame their complete outlook in terms of variables (method) as equivalent to constructs (theory). For example, Mischel

(1973) has distinguished between person and situational variables, combining these two into a kind of summative interaction as follows: ". . . to predict a subject's voluntary delay of gratification, one may have to know how old he is, his sex, the experimenter's sex, the particular objects for which he is waiting, the consequences of not waiting, the models to whom he was exposed, his immediately prior experience—the list gets almost endless" (p. 256).

When we frame the task of psychology as the prediction of a theoretical construct such as delay of gratification, we make this predicting of a multitude of variables, all "functioning" at once, appear to be what the psychologist must aspire to. Table 2 has the word *hypothesis* as the theoretical equivalent of the methodological term *prediction*. But Mischel is not saying here that we must study by way of a program of research the many hypotheses that seem plausibly related to his theoretical construct of delay of gratification. He is saying in the style of Underwood above that we must literally demonstrate the validity of such a prediction *all at once* by running the appropriately complex experiment. Cronbach (1975) subsequently noted that if such an experiment were actually designed and carried out it would involve 120 statistical interactions in the resulting factorial analysis of variance (p. 120). This complexity of data analysis obviously takes such an experiment out of the realm of possibility.

If we keep the distinction between theory and method before us, this problem vanishes in the recognition discussed throughout Chapter 5 that all scientific investigation affirms the consequent of an if . . . then . . . logical sequence. Unless one hopes to formulate a theory of how predictions are made, and so forth, the use of *prediction* as a theoretical statement of what we must know about the influences on delay of gratification *is simply inappropriate*. Predictions flow from hypotheses and serve as potential evidential supports for the theoretical outlook contained in these hypotheses. The hypothesis carries the antecedent belief (Age may be related to delay of gratification) *not* the prediction (Group A, being older, will delay more readily than group B). The hypothesis is a "may" statement, but the prediction is a "will" statement, and we should not be so ready to equate these two *different* formulations of things. And even if the prediction is sustained, the theory underlying the hypothesis must be held to in light of our affirmation-of-the-consequent limitations. That is, we must never forget that *other* hypotheses might *also* be sustained by the predictions made in validation. Cronbach seems to have appreciated that evidence never proves a theoretical hypothesis true for all time, but he ascribed this fact more to potential changes taking place in the actuarial universe or parameter than to the nature of scientific explanation *per se.* Accepting Mischel's (methodological) usage of "prediction" as proper, Cronbach discussed the changing fortunes of statistical prediction as follows:

The forecast of Y from A, B, and C will be valid enough, if conditions D, E, F, etc., are held constant in establishing and in applying the law. It will be actuarially valid, valid on the average, if it was established in a representative sample from a universe of situations, as long as the universe remains constant. When the universe changes, we have to go beyond our actuarial rule. . . . When we step outside the range of our experience, we have to use our heads (*ibid.*, pp. 125–126).

Although we can "slip in" Mischel's variables into A, B, C, and so on, the theory under discussion here is purely mathematical, sustained by the plausibilities of procedural evidence (cognitive method) and used as an adjunct to the logic of validation (research method). But strictly speaking, we are not dealing in lived reality here anymore than Newton's mathematical conception of gravity was about forces inhering in real things (Chapter 1, p. 48). When we actually do an experiment and secure evidence in support of our delay-of-gratification theory, we are *not* dipping our hands into some existing "universe of situations" in randomly assigning subjects to experimental conditions. An observed experimental difference exceeding the .01 level of significance is based strictly on assumptions concerning the *single* sample we have dealt with, projected against statistical fictions of other samples that might have been selected *at this point in time* under identical conditions. We are in mathematical space *not* real space, so there is no proper expectation or reasonable guarantee that if 99 other samplings of these variables were done on successive days the observed (p.<.01) differences would be significantly identical 99 times out of 100. No one has ever conducted a series of 100 experiments in this fashion to see what would in fact eventuate for such an .01 level finding, except in computer simulations which are themselves "events" taking place in mathematical space and *not* reality!

And we should not be misled by the phrase *holding conditions constant.* This refers to a procedure for checking one's thinking, based on the logic of scientific method. Holding conditions constant is not something that we literally do in life, because conditions frequently cannot be handled this way. But we can still employ the *logic* of balancing off circumstances to observe a consistent variation. Returning to Cronbach's quote above, conditions *are what they are* once we assign theoretical constructs to our symbols A, B, C, and so on. If we can let these construed identities be what they "are" across our methodological group arrangements, while simultaneously requiring that some (usually one) consistent difference(s) across these groups exist(s), an evidential conclusion can be arrived at so long as we have predicted the outcome actually observed (validating evidence). But if we now believe that conditions in life must be held constant so as to increase the predictive power of this method *qua* theory, we not only delude ourselves as to our proper scientific role but also pose what is an impossible task.

We must therefore appreciate that holding conditions constant and making predictions to observed outcomes are purely methodological activities of the psychologist. Believing in these findings and carrying this line of theory forward to do further experiments—each of which is subject to the logical proviso of affirming the consequent —is predominantly a *theoretical* activity (sustained by procedural evidence, of course). We cannot overlook or denigrate this role of theory in science. Here is where our paradigms always come into play (Chapter 5).

Because Cronbach speaks of going beyond the actuarial rule in the above quote, he seems to have reserved a prominent place for the role of theory in his scientific outlook. This is unfortunately not true. He disputes with Suppes (1974), who has argued that a major duty of the psychologist is to theorize. After acknowledging that the theoretical stance one takes influences the prevailing view of man. Cronbach quickly adds: "But a point of view is not a theory, capable of sharp predictions to new conditions" (*ibid.*, p. 123). Cronbach, like Mischel and Underwood, thinks of theories as predictors—that is, he confounds method with theory-talk! Points of view *are* theories, and they not only permit us to isolate and define Cronbach's A, B, C, variables, but they provide the frame within which we must work when such universes change. How other than by the application of a theory can we find our way to new universes of relevance when old predictions crumble to insignificance? This is what *using our heads* means. If we could not delineate the universe of relevance, how sharp could our *methodological* predictions ever become? By continually referring to hypothetical theoretical activity as if it were predictive methodological activity, the leading psychologists of our time perpetuate the unfortunate denigration of theory which has plagued psychology for a century. Let us hope that in the last quarter of the twentieth century we will end this needlessly harmful practice.

Whether a psychologist is using a term in its theoretical or its methodological sense is not always immediately clear. But the writer has found that after moderate study of a written treatise or, if possible, discussion with the psychologist in question, *any* meaning can be clarified in the sense of our examples above. If leaning in the direction of descriptive explanation, we have a theoretical usage; and if leaning in the direction of proof or evidential support for such explanations, we have a methodological usage. Should this practice be made routine, introduction of dialectical theories into psychology would be far easier. As noted at the outset of this section, a science of psychology based exclusively on the meanings of Table 2 could never entertain dialectical theory. Yet dialectic has played a more prominent (albeit unnamed) role in psychological thinking than is now appreciated, and it has been given due recognition as a theoretical paradigm in the rise of physical science. We turn next to this frequently overlooked side of science.

Dialectical Theory and the Rise of Modern Science

The program we have in mind for psychological science would emphasize demonstrative reasoning in the context of validation and allow *either* demonstrative or dialectical reasoning to flourish on the side of theory. So long as the psychologist would move to validate his theories "some of the time" we would accept his approach as scientific. This sequence of theory-to-test places the concept of prediction in proper perspective, because this is *not* something psychologists need do all the time! Psychologists do not have to become actuarians. As we now appreciate, events can be predicted without understanding why they occur as they do. Psychologists have a responsibility to fill in the understanding side of knowledge. Control and prediction is something we do in order to check our understanding by arranging circumstances or stipulating parameters for measurement, and so on, in the context of evidential support. The resultant data collections are often highly artificial in nature, not meant to be predicting life by any stretch of the imagination. If all theories must predict life, by definition a theory in favor of unpredictive life circumstances would be impossible. Yet, clearly, theories of the unpredictability of behavior are within the realm of possibility. The variance accounted for in our studies hardly outweighs the vast variance we *fail* to predict. Hence a theory might indeed speak for this *unpredictive* side to behavior.

One of the ironies of psychology is that there are and always have been dialectical theories underwriting its empirical investigations. These conceptualizations act as unnamed assumptions, and hence their influence goes unrecognized or at least unnamed in the *formal* statement of our "scientific knowledge." Beginning with Wilhelm Wundt, one of the fathers of experimental psychology (Chapter 3), we find that the outlines of his major theoretical contribution—a tridimensional theory of the emotions—are framed within the dialectical dimensions of pleasant-unpleasant, tension-relaxation, and excitement-depression. Mancuso (1976) has surveyed a number of areas in psychology which rely upon the unnamed presumption of a dialectically reasoning subject in experimental investigations. Continuing with the notion of acturial prediction, Mancuso shows how frequently the parameter, or variable, delineated by the statistically oriented psychologist is framed as a dimension within a bipolarity. The ends of the dimension framing a difference in value are opposites or require that the subject know oppositional meanings in order to be assessed, but no cognizance is taken of this fact. Scaling techniques employed by Thurstone (with Chave, 1929) and Sherif (with Hovland, 1961) as well as the *semantic differential* of Osgood's researches are shown to make informal presumptions of dialectical understanding in the subjects who are so assessed (Osgood, Suci, & Tannenbaum, 1957). The developmental psychology of Piaget (with Inhelder & Szeminska, 1964) is also shown to rely heavily on dialectical constructions, a fact to which Riegel (1973) has also pointed.

One of the parameters often cited by the empirical psychologist is social-class level (lower, middle, upper), to which all manner of values, living styles, political attitudes, and so on, are functionally related. Yet the class consciousness or class identity that is simply presumed in framing these socioeconomic levels rests upon the delineation afforded by the social and economic theories of the great dialecticians Hegel and Marx (see Chapter 1). Class concepts are as the one and many, set in opposition (or contradiction) yet constituting a totality. This internal dynamic (force of opposition) provides the motives for social change, as a reorganization or synthesis of the old into the emerging new. Hegelian-Marxian themes of class consciousness have in recent decades been extended by analogy to relations between the races, the sexes, and even between age levels (youth versus aged). The debt owed to dialectical theory in social science is all the more remarkable because of the ignorance of social scientists in general about this style of reasoning and the consequent organization of human affairs that results.

The reader may feel that showing dialectical theories at work in psychology and related social sciences is fairly easy but that no role for dialectic has been demonstrated in the "hard" sciences. This would be an erroneous conclusion, for there are several noteworthy examples of dialectic in the rise of physical science. The most basic rules of rigorous observation and discrimination are framed on a dialectical premise. For example, the Socratic-Platonic method of dichotomy (*Sophist*) holds that any grouping of the so-called genus in observation must be divided into two and only two subgroups: the logical species in which one is characterized by some feature (*differentia*) and the other is not. This rigorous classification scheme was subsequently refuted by Aristotle, who showed that no matter how carefully the differentiae are chosen, there is always overlap, so that *flying* would include some mammals and *not flying* some birds (Wightman, 1951, p. 365). But this general strategy of classification by way of opposition (Plato and Socrates *were* dialecticians!) was to be retained in the rise of science. We see it centuries later in John Stuart Mill's *Canon of Difference*, which was one of several such rules designed to aid a physical scientist in the elucidation of efficient causation (see Table 1). Mill's canon states that when cases in which a phenomenon occurs (A) differ from cases in which it does not occur (not-A) in only *one respect*, that respect, or its absence, is the effect or cause or part of the cause of this phenomenon (A). Mill's rigor is accepted by empirically oriented psychologists today, who reason out what is a stimulus and what is a response on precisely such bases as the Canon of Difference. But they fail to appreciate the underlying dialectical logic which makes such empirically observed regularities observably determinable.

Dialectical reasoning ends when its constructions are frozen into rigid "either-or" categories, of course. As noted in Chapter 2 (p. 85), the dialectician opposes the One and Many Principle to the demonstrative reasoner's Law of Contradiction. However, the ability to get such iron clad differences underway in thought doubtless stems from the human being's dialectical reasoning capacities. Oppositionality is extremely important to that *sine qua non* of demonstrative reasoning—mathematics! We do not always appreciate the fact that an equation sign unites two values in a relation of *identity* which are yet also *opposite* to each other so that it requires a change of sign to move numerical values across the balancing midpoint of $X + 2 = Y - 4$. As noted in Chapter 2 (p. 66)), the word *algebra* devolved from the title of a treatise by *al-Khowarizmi* which meant the "science of the reunion and the opposition" or "science of transposition and cancellation" (Eves, 1969, p. 195). We are more familiar with the latter terminology, but the obvious dialectical phraseology of the former is almost a rephrase of the One and Many Principle. Bakan (1953, 1956) has presented some excellent analyses of another clear reflection of dialectic in the mathematics of probability theory known as the Rule of Bayes. In opposition to the demonstrative frequency theories of probability—in which a distribution of events as "primarily and truly existing" is taken for granted—the Rule of Bayes finds its probability estimate in the comparison of two *opposite* likelihoods or possibilities. No assumption is made here about the reality of an independent frequency (see Rychlak, 1968, pp. 152–156, for a more thorough discussion of Bayes' theorem). Psychological statistics have been based predominantly on a frequency thesis.

Once the view is taken that there is a primary-and-true difference between events, a difference that is merely reflected as an opposite by the human awarenesss but is *not* fundamentally united by a one-in-many relational tie, we lose a dialectical to a demonstrative phraseology. The conceptualization of opposition here literally changes, and this change is often misleading because it appears on the surface that an "opposite is an opposite." Critics of dialectical theory invariably confound a demonstrative opposition with a truly dialectical opposition in this sense. When the dialectician is employing bipolarity or opposition he does not—or should not—suppose that this one distinction to which he alludes is the *only* one possible in the descriptive realm under consideration (see Rychlak, 1976). To think that an opposite is literally either-or is not to reason dialectically, but rather to reason cybernetically (demonstratively). Cybernetic machines reason according to such an either-or binary logic. Just as the machine takes its initial program "seriously" and hence cannot reason beyond what the program directs, so too is the machine frozen into a thinking pattern of unrelated either-or discriminations which are never simply arbitrary separations of the one into the many. A dialectical reasoner, however, is always conscious that other dichotomies can be drawn. His distinctions are made to elucidate the totality by way of oppositionality, *not* to break this totality up to state what is right or true or best and what is wrong or false or worst. C. G. Jung (1958) speaks as a true dialectician when he observes: "We name a thing, *from a certain point of view,* good or bad, high or low, right or left, light or dark, and so forth. Here the antithesis is just as factual and real as the thesis" (p. 305). Demonstrative conceptualizations are seriously wanting in the description of the ineffable in human experience: "Non-ambiguity and non-contradiction are one-sided and thus unsuited to express the incomprehensible" (Jung, 1953, p. 15).

Two kinds of dialectical themes are to be seen in the rise of modern mathematical physics. First, we have the stimulation provided by a thinker relying on dialectical alternatives who acts as a model and a spur for revolutionary conceptions. Einstein (1916) has acknowledged such an indebtedness to Ernst Mach (1893), who must surely be seen as a dialectically oriented theorist and the single person most influential in bringing about the separation of modern physics from classical Newtonian (Lockean) physics. Naming his outlook phenomenological physics, Mach insisted on recognizing the major role that the conceptualizing (theorizing) individual had on the description of nature. This critique was more than simply noting the selective biases in factual description that various physicists manifested. It got to the very core of how we think about reality, and in underscoring the alternatives possible in this conceptualization process, Mach used as examples the dialectical reversals and distortions of his dreams. He liked to show how either Ptolemy or Copernicus were correct, depending upon where one stood in assessing their explanations of the solar system—on the earth or on the sun. Mach rejected conventional views such as the immutability of time, atomic palpability, and the efficient-cause determinism of reality. As we noted in Chapter 3 (p. 130), although Mach readily embraced the speculative theories of Sigmund Freud, the father of psychoanalysis could not stomach what he took to be Mach's "intellectual nihilism" (Rieff, 1959, p. 26).

Feuer (1974) and others have argued that Einstein's willingness to shift his premises and to speculate daringly was influenced by this—what we now claim is a dialectical—style of Ernst Mach's theorizing. Feuer also notes that Einstein's personal friend during his student days, Friedrich Adler, was a Marxian philosopher-physicist who tried to unite Mach's phenomenological physics with the revolutionary dialectical theory of communism (*ibid.*, pp. 18–20). There is probably no better one-and-many phrasing than the following, where Mach is speaking of the primary role of the unifying *idea* over the multitude of isolated (factual) *observations:*

Guided by one's interest for the whole of things again and again one directs one's attention beyond the facts, whether these facts may be straight sensations or belonging to the domain of representations. . . . Then, one would, perhaps, in a happy moment, contemplate the simplifying and fertile thought (Frank, 1957, pp. 319–320).

A second more direct form of dialectical influence is to be seen in the rise of modern physical theory. Feuer (1974) presents a

fascinating argument in this sense for the translation of Kierkegaardian thought into the atomic physical theory of Niels Bohr (p. 138).
Bohr's professor and personal friend, Harøld Hoffding, had once
studied for the ministry before becoming estranged from the church.
The experience had brought him into contact with the philosophy
of Søren Kierkegaard. Like Mach, Hoffding took an interest in the
phenomenal conceptual schemes that physicists employed to explain
their data, speaking of these as various *analogies* which can be
sorted out through dialectical examination and then settled upon.
This type of dialectical examination was based on what Kierkegaard
had termed a *qualitative dialectic* in the psychic identity of human
beings.

This more individualized interpretation of the dialectic was
opposed to Hegel's conception of a World Principle at play in historical events—a kind of objective dialectic that swallowed up the
unique individual (see Chapter 2). Kierkegaard's formulation was
more subjective than this, aimed at the idiographic course of life
each person must follow. He therefore gave his dialectic a developmental interpretation and used it to describe the qualitative changes
made in life as the individual moved from certain fixed stages in
living style (stadia) to other fixed points. Not all people traversed
the three stadia of life, but if they did so the movement followed
through *aesthetic, ethical,* and *religious* manners of spiritual (psychological) living. One cannot relate these stages to physical events,
and natural science is therefore unable to capture this entirely
spiritual development. Physical nature moves through gradations,
linear cause-effects, but the passage across life's stadia are abrupt
leaps or jumps. Kierkegaard, like Mach, was essentially rejecting the
natural scientist's penchant for explanation through efficient-cause
reduction. Rejecting this causal chain, Kierkegaard interpreted
change as dialectically generated through opposition; therefore the
direction taken was based upon a decision, a commitment to one
lifestyle over another, rather than through a uniform impulse or a
seedling growth from the antecedent circumstance.

According to Feuer, based on his study of Kierkegaard (*ibid.,*
p. 132) as well as his reading of the Møller novel *The Adventures of
a Danish Student*, in which dialectical themes are prominent (*ibid.,*
pp. 129–130), Niels Bohr fashioned a rationale for the inexplicable
leaps of the electron across the orbits of the atom:

The Kierkegaardian model of discontinuous leaps became part of Niels
Bohr's deepest emotional-intellectual standpoint. The atom in its "sta-

tionary state" was later like one of Kierkegaard's stadia of existence. And the leap of the electrons from one orbit to another was like the abrupt, inexplicable transitions of the self [across the stadia of life] (p. 136).

Bohr's theory of the atom thus departed from the Newtonian conception, in which the electrons around the nucleus could have traveled in any of an infinity of possible orbits; that is, any circular motion with any radius value would have been satisfactory. Bohr's conception held that only *certain* orbits with specific radii were admissible. Feuer quotes a remarkable passage from Bohr which should be contemplated by all modern psychologists who find telic commentary improper in the scientific context:

. . . the author [i.e., Bohr] suggested . . . that every change in the state of an atom should be regarded as an individual process, incapable of more detailed description, by which the atom goes over from one so-called stationary state to another. . . . We are here so far removed from a causal description that an atom in a stationary state may in general even be said to possess a free choice between various possible transitions to other stationary states (*ibid.*, p. 137).

This marvelous tie that dialectical conceptions have for what Jung called the incomprehensible is what attracts the humanist's attention to this style of reasoning. Other examples of dialectical influences in modern physical science could be noted. For example, Heisenberg learned from Plato's *Timaeus* that alternatives were as fundamental to human thought as were the forms of geometric figures—and such alternatives are born in the contrasting poles of dialectical opposition (*ibid.*, p. 173). But we want now to move ahead in the remainder of Chapter 6 to consider a topic of great concern for many social scientists: the question of determinism in events (including behavioral events). As we shall see, dialectical formulations permit us to justify a stand on behavior as *both* potentially free and yet always determined.

The Meanings of Determinism and Some Applications of This Concept in Psychology

Assume that a man is driving along the highway in his automobile. Though he may not notice from the outset, gradually it dawns on him that more cars are passing his car than *vice versa*. Although he is obeying the posted speed limit, he is a relatively slow driver this day. As he mulls this fact over in his mind, he admits that this has always been the case. Whenever he takes a long trip and therefore has the time to take note of his driving style, he is struck by the high percentage of drivers who seem to be violating the speed limit to which he is holding. Soon the natural implication is suggested: Why not speed up? Because this suggestion is not totally satisfying, the man begins to wonder just what determines his behavior anyway? How could we answer this question?

As a first step we might assess whether his impressions are correct. Do more automobiles pass his vehicle than vice versa? This *observable event* can be tabulated from an extraspective perspective, and because we can extrapolate findings from earlier trips we could have predicted his rate of driving speed on this particular trip. But can we say that he is determined in behavior by the statistical probability which *we* assign to his driving rate? After all, even he knows that for his entire life he has driven at or below the legal speed limit. Surely we cannot believe that this statistical probability level determines his driving speed today. Maybe he has a physical reason for not propelling his car along at high speeds. He may have an inner-ear sensitivity that makes him uncomfortable when a vehicle is moving along too rapidly. He, more than the average person, senses the pitches and rolls of an automobile under high speeds.

Most psychologists would immediately suspect that this man's present driving rate "was a function of" (theory-method confound) his past experience in driving, whereby he had learned (been conditioned) to drive his car at a modest speed. One could even view the inner-ear sensitivity as an aspect of the reinforcement equipment that shaped this man into what is now a relatively slow highway driver. A reasonable hypothesis here is that he was taught to drive by a harsh parent or parent-surrogate, one who impressed on him the importance of driving within the limits of the law. The rigidity and moralistic overtones of such instruction doubtless emanated from a lifelong environment in which strict adherence to rules was required. The man may have been reared in an overly scrupulous religious home atmosphere. Once again we can think of this history of reinforcement in actuarial terms, postulating that if we had the proper observational opportunities of this man in *nondriving* situations, we still could have predicted through a *generalization-of-behavior* principle what would likely take place on the highway. This habitual pattern of behavior is not identical to the actuarial statistic that permits us to predict, of course. Presumably there is something carried by the man as an organism capable of learning to behave which is actually the determinant in this case.

But there is another possible determination of behavior we have not yet entertained. Left to his own devices, this man could well put it forward as follows: "I have thought all of the things over you mentioned. Surely I am not driving this way to maintain a statistic. The point about my inner-ear seems a bit farfetched because I have always been well-coordinated and enjoy rides at the amusement park such as a roller coaster. I suppose you could trace it to my religious instruction if you wanted to, but knowing this today why do I let this earlier influence go on determining me? When I *do* speed up just to show that I *can* do so it all seems very childish. No, the *real* reason I drive as I do today is because, after a careful examination of all these factors, I *choose* to do so. I don't need to save the few minutes or hours that speeding affords. I surely don't need the added tension of racing around other cars. My present rate is satisfactory in that it saves me fuel and that means money. Furthermore, an orderly society is to be preferred over one that lacks reasonable rules. So, all things considered and after careful reflection, I tell you straightout: I drive as I do because I want to!"

The reader has doubtless surmised that with this telic formulation we have covered all four of the causal meanings as they relate to the question of determinism in behavior. Psychologists rarely specify which of these meanings is involved when they refer to the determinations of behavior, but obviously this clarification is important.

The Four Types of Determinism

The word *determine* has Latin roots meaning to set a limit on something. As applied to behavior, the limitations are usually thought of as alternatives that might be carried out in the course of events but are prevented from occurring. To refer to this setting of limitations in terms of the antecedent influences on consequent behavioral events is common in psychology. Antecedents go before consequents in time when we construe events in actual lived space. The puff of air is antecedent to the blinking of an eyelid. However, the definition of an antecedent also bears the meaning of a *precedent*, when applied to conceptual, logical, or grammatical usages. The antecedent of an *If . . . then . . .* proposition need not be thought of as occurring first in time. The total proposition is best viewed as a meaningful pattern, in which the antecedent term (*man*) does not efficiently or materially cause the consequent term (*mortal*) to come about determinately. The pattern (formal cause) of the totality ("If man, then mortal") bears the meaning completely free of time considerations.

The antecedent term in this case (*man*) does force the meaning of mortality into the pattern, but this conceptual necessity is a purely formal-cause eventuality. The precedent-sequacious line of meaning extension in this patterning is outside of time considerations. We have seen other examples of this extra-time feature of determinate relations—for example, in the necessity of mathematico-logical reasoning (Chapter 1, pp. 44–45) and in the use of the function construct in methodological validation (Chapter 1, p. 49 and Chapter 3, p. 100).

Our theory-method confound in psychology makes the introduction of time into every description of behavior easy; indeed to do so is quite necessary, for we have to "account for" the observed behavior of an IV-DV sequence *as* an antecedent-consequent flow of events. But even physical factors such as the inherited proclivity to inner-ear sensitivities can be viewed as antecedents to behavior which are not exactly functioning across time in that cause-effect fashion of the air puff and eyeblink. Thus, a malformed spine at birth is likely to limit the athletic skills of its bearer as a young adult; yet who would claim that the spine determined the restricted athletic ability in adulthood the same way that a foot race, run against a clock, determines our judgments of the athletic ability of even normal adults?

And what of our driver's reasons for proceeding as he does today? Are these not antecedents to his behavior, at least in the sense of precedents? We surely cannot think of the idea containing his reasons as pushing along the nervous impulses which synergistically enervate the muscles of his accelerator foot, efficiently causing it to relax. Mind-body dualisms arise in psychological theory because some of us feel it is desirable to capture this meaning of a determinate intention without identifying it with the actions carried out in its aim. Ideas encompass premises, frame meanings for the sake of which behavior is then carried out. But the carrying out in behavior is *not* the complete intentionality, says the dualist. The monist claims that all there *is* is behavior and hence to assign other causes to the sequence of motion we can observe is to depart from (Baconian) science. Are these views purely assumptive, or can we possibly hope to do research in psychology to settle the question of what determinate causes are at play in human behavior?

The thesis of this book is that we should be able *in principle* to cast light on this issue by way of rigorous empirical research, *after* we have clarified the issues involved, and hence what it means to see or not see telic factors in behavior. We state the proviso "in principle" because obviously to hope for a settled question is a vain and even naive anticipation. To crystallize the causal interpretations of determinism, Table 3 contains an array of the four kinds of antecedent determinants that may be said to arise when we emphasize one or another of these historic terms:

Table 3 Four Types of Antecedent Determinants, Arrayed According to Causal Description

Causal Meanings	Nature of Determining Antecedent	Examples
Material	A substance having certain qualities that set limits on behavior	Genes, drives as chemical agents, sensory experience, organic development, etc.
Efficient	A thrust, push, unidirectional action or necessary inducement limiting one line of behavior in regard to another	Stimuli, signals, cues, reflexes, motions, etc.
Formal	A pattern, form or style of behavior that limits what will be expressed, recognized, or expected	Type, order, paradigmatic frame, actuarial frequency distribution, norm, etc.
Final	A precedent "that for the sake of which" certain alternatives are limited in preference to others	Reason, premise, belief, assumption, bias, implication, conviction, etc.

Granting each of the determining antecedents of Table 3, certain limitations are put upon the behavior to follow. The reader can easily think up examples of the consequents to flow from these antecedents. We must also note that any one line of behavior under description can contain several or *all* of the determinations. We do not mean to suggest that these are mutually exclusive designations, anymore than we felt that the causes of Table 1 were mutually exclusive as regards the theoretical constructs they entered into as descriptive meanings. The point of Table 3 is to dramatize the different uses we can make of the antecedent construct and the form of determinism that is then posited. We turn now to a number of issues having to do with determinism that have arisen in psychology.

Laws and the Generalization of Behavior

There is no more familiar assertion in psychology than "behavior is lawful." This phrase is used as a rationale for prediction, because the assumption is that lawful behavior is under a determination of some sort and that therefore it generalizes across situations. Knowing the laws of one situation, we can predict to a subsequent situation of relative similarity. The problem is that we are not always certain precisely what form of determinism is going on in such predicted generalizations. Etymologically, the use of *law* has *not* meant an efficient-cause regularity. Laws as binding customs in a community were seen as claims put on peoples by a controlling authority. In religious circles this authority was a Supreme Being. This kind of law controls behavior because of final-cause determinism, as a binding premise, belief, or conviction among the loyal citizenry or the faithful. Laws in mathematics or in logic—for example, the Law of Contradiction (A is not not-A; see p. 61)—are similarly *not* determinate influences in an efficient-cause sense, but rather in a formal-cause sense. To be accepted such laws do not require validating evidence. They have a convincing quality based on their immediate expression (due to procedural evidence); once understood they are accepted and act as guiding assumptions which control behavior far more certainly than an antecedent based upon some thrust, push, or unidirectional action.

Levy (1963) observed that if we did not make the assumptions of lawfulness in behavior "there would be no point in performing any research; the results of any given study would have to be considered fortuitous and no generalizations would be possible" (p. 58). Statements of this sort are common in psychology, and they leave one wondering what is being generalized in a research finding. If we think of lawfulness as the relationship between an independent and dependent variable—the sort of thing one could graph and therefore give a mathematical statement of (recall Dirichlet's function construct, pp. 49 and 100)—clearly we should not expect this slope of line or its numerical equivalent to generalize. This is simply a shorthand notation for our empirical finding, which in turn reflects the theory we put to test. We are now using the term *law* in its proper *methodological* sense (Table 2). The *theory* not the law, always generalizes! Indeed the precise slope of line or the exact *p*-level of a lawful relationship between experimental variables are not expected to generalize *per se*. Occasionally the level of significance will even fall below an acceptable level without affecting the generalizability of the theory under test. Hence lawfulness *per se* has no direct tie to the generalizability of an empirical finding. Experimental findings will naturally be extended so long as these findings prove theoretically instructive to the scientist carrying on a line of investigation.

What sort of determination is involved in such theoretical generalizations? Obviously this is a question of formal (e.g., paradigmatic) and final (e.g., belief, conviction) causation. The scientist holds to his theory, filling in his very understanding of a subject matter in terms of such theoretical predilections. No modern scientist can overlook the role of theoretical determinism in his efforts. This point is what we referred to above (p. 234), in noting that though Cronbach was well aware of Mischel's unlikely program of methodological verification he (Cronbach) still felt it necessary to denigrate the role of theory in science. The statistically oriented psychologist is likely to do this because he has already accepted a theory, based on the plausibilities of formal- and (his) final-cause understanding. Mathematics is totally on the side of formal-cause determination, and when entertained by the reasoning intellect of a mathematician, the assumptions accepted thereby act as final-cause determinations of his behavior. Because the focus of attention is on data in these mathematically framed approaches, the psychologist so inclined finds it easy to take potshots at those *who do not* think of their professional role in life as that of a "sampler" of atheoretical data pools (parameters), which mysteriously change empirical definition from time to time, but which always fall neatly into line with statistical *theory.* Other theories are therefore excoriated quite regularly by these statistical "empiricists."

Of course, by keeping their attention focused on what they presume are atheoretical data items, picked from a bagful of natural laws called parameters, these empiricists are likely to end up in a theory-method confound. A case in point is Campbell and Stanley (1963), who after noting that researchers are often conditioned to avoid doing further research because of negative results in their earlier studies, go on to observe:

For the usual highly motivated researcher the nonconfirmation of a cherished hypothesis is actively painful. As a biological and psychological animal, the experimenter is subject to *laws of learning* [italics added] which lead him inevitably to associate this pain with the contiguous stimuli and events. These stimuli are apt to be the experimental process itself, more vividly and directly than the "true" source of frustration, i.e., the inadequate theory (p. 3).

In this quote Campbell and Stanley are not thinking of the *laws of learning* as methodological evidence for a theoretical position. They are using this phrase as a theory of behavior, accepting without question the traditional Lockean explanation of learning as efficiently caused habits, joined together *without* formal-final causation as determinant antecedents. Antecedents and consequents get hooked up in contiguous fashion, and this is what a law is—a tendency to limit alternatives by way of fixing certain determiners (stimuli) to certain determinants (responses). We see here another example of the S-R Bind (p. 173). If psychologists would only distinguish between what is their theory and what is their method, such statements would be judged in their proper light. The point is: It is wrong to present methodological findings as if they were theory free. Evidence *for a theory* can of course be presented, but it must always be understood as supportive of theoretical presumptions.

That this is not an isolated instance in the thinking of Campbell and Stanley is to be seen in their discussion of generalization, a concept equated with induction (*ibid.*, p. 17). They first distinguish between internal and external validity. Internal validity refers to the predicted relationship between independent and dependent variables —for example, proving that practice on a verbal-memory task increases retention of the verbal items under memorization (*ibid.*, p. 5). External validity, however, refers to the applicability of such findings in contexts outside of the research laboratory—for example, in predicting the performance of subjects in an actual classroom (will the better memorizers in the lab also do well in the classroom?) (*ibid.*, p. 17). Problems of internal validity are satisfactorily handled through probability statistics, but generalizing to the classroom— external validity—is more difficult because: "Generalization always turns out to involve extrapolation into a realm not represented in one's sample. Such extrapolation is made by *assuming* one knows the relevant laws" (*ibid.*, p. 17).

Does a scientist make predictions based upon his actual or assumed knowledge of laws so that his inductive generalizations are solely or even primarily from past empirical findings? Doubtless once evidence has been accrued, and therefore lawful relations have been established, a scientist utilizes this evidence in support of the theory that generated the line of study in the first instance. But if scientists literally relied upon laws (methodological meaning) rather than upon a conviction that certain constructs when translated into variables could be shown to be lawfully related (theoretical meaning), there would be very little scientific advance. The history of science is replete with examples of men and women trying endlessly to bring forward evidence for something they believed theoretically to be the case but which could not yet be proven (Wightman, 1951). Believing something to be true—even when it is true!—and then *proving* it are two clearly different activities of the scientist. Saying that laws must be known rather than theories is surely a curious way of putting the scientific quest. Yet so great is their desire to avoid theory-talk that Campbell and Stanley (1963) suggest: ". . . we do, in generalizing, make guesses to yet *unproven laws* [italics added], including some not even explored" (p. 17).

To the psychologist who uses *law* in a methodological sense, speaking of unproven laws is a contradiction in terms. Laws *are* proofs—at least they are when we use this term in its scientific rather than in its logical or custom-bearing sense. Referring to laws which have not yet been explored is at worst a blatant reification of this construct or at best a poetic allusion to the scientific effort— rather 'like pointing to the remainder of our future as "unlived tomorrows." In the former case it is an efficient-cause theory of reality; in the latter it is a final-cause assumption on the part of the scientist which has no meaning until we fill in those variables that will be theoretically delineated and, when tested, constitute *a law* because of the proven relationship between them.

The Behavioristic Concept of Freedom

A major tenet of humanistic psychologies is that the person is a contributing agent to his behavior; so behavioral style is *not* rooted solely in the patternings of the environment, but is patterned to some extent by the identity of the person. This self-induced pattern- ing of behavior is usually typified as *free will*, and as we have seen in the rise of mediation theory (Chapters 4 and 5), psychologists have attempted to account for this autonomy in strictly efficient- cause terms. In presenting his social-learning theory, Bandura (1969) states the typical mediational argument as follows:

. . . social-learning approaches treat internal processes as covert events that are manipulable and measurable. These mediating processes are ex- tensively controlled by external stimulus events and in turn regulate overt responsiveness. By contrast, psychodynamic theories tend to regard in- ternal events as relatively autonomous. These *hypothetical causal agents* [italics added] generally bear only a tenuous relationship to external stim- uli, or even to the "symptoms" that they supposedly produce (pp. 10–11).

As humanists we can easily see Bandura manipulating in his studies what we would prefer to call an independent variable, in order to observe the *effect* of this *stimulus* (his term) on what he calls the *response*, but what we would like to call the dependent variable. Having achieved the predicted outcome, Bandura, as all behaviorists, claims that *he* has determined the organism's behavior because the observed findings show this to be a fact. Humanists go on attributing hypothetical, nonscientific characteristics to behavior in their constructs of mind. Framing things in terms of scientific laws, Skinner (1974) expressed this same attitude as follows: ". . . pure mentalism . . . has dominated Western thinking for more than two thousand years. Almost all versions contend that the mind is a nonphysical space in which events obey nonphysical laws" (pp. 31–32).

Formulations like this characterize the humanist as a medieval cleric, clinging to supernatural beliefs of a spiritual realm without substance in which miraculous events violating natural laws occur. The truth is that when Bandura speaks of autonomous causal agents he is only referring to the autonomy of formal and final causes from merely material and efficient causes in the determination of behavior. This is all that Skinner's comments actually refer to. Formal-final cause constructs are nonphysical because they capture something the Baconian prescription specifically kept out of "natural" science. As we noted above in speaking of dualism, mentalistic positions arise *not* out of any desire on the part of a theorist to revert to pre-scientific theological dogma, but simply because he finds the descriptive utility of material and efficient causes to be limited when it comes to the human condition.

What is fascinating about the behaviorist's presumption that he, by efficiently causing (manipulating) certain environmental stimuli to vary *solely* determines the behavioral responses of his subject, is that both historical and hard research evidence have steadily eroded this position. In the present section we take a look at this erosion from the perspective of what it means to be free in a behavioral sense (as opposed to political freedom). Because natural science advanced a strict or "hard" (100%) determinism of an efficient-cause type, the early tough-minded psychologists in this century found the concept of freedom to be totally incorrect (see, e.g., Kuo, 1928). Gradually, as the "accounting for" proclivities of functionalism were enlarged upon, a position on this conception of freedom in behavior was delineated. D. O. Hebb (1974) summarizes this view colorfully:

I am a determinist. I assume that what I am and how I think are entirely the products of my heredity and my environmental history. I have no freedom about what I *am*. But that is not what free will is about. The question is whether my behavior is entirely controlled by present circumstances. Heredity and environment shaped me, largely while I was growing up. That shaping, including how I think about things, may incline me to act in opposition to the shaping that the *present* environment would be likely to induce: And so I may decide to be polite to others, or sit down to write this article when I'd rather not, or, on the other hand, decide to goof off when I should be working. If my past has shaped me to goof off, and I do goof off despite my secretary's urging, that's free will. But it's not indeterminism (p. 75).

When Hebb states that he is a determinist, we know that he means to say a material- and efficient-cause determinist. As a Lockean thinker he would not consider it proper to assign a determination to formal and final causes in behavior. So he is brought to a conception in which freedom means somewhat free from today's material- and efficient-cause determinations but 100% determined by yesterday's material- and efficient-cause determinations. Bandura's (1969) view of freedom is comparable, although he bases his argument more clearly on mediational theory:

The process of behavioral change will be conceptualized quite differently depending upon whether one assumes that responses are regulated predominantly by external stimulus events or partly by mediating symbolic events. In nonmediational interpretations, learning is depicted as a more or less automatic process wherein stimuli become associated with overt responses through differential reinforcement. By contrast, in mediational formulations the learner plays a far more active role and his responsiveness is subject to extensive cognitive determination. On the basis of salience of environmental events and past learning experiences persons select the stimuli to which they will respond; environmental events are coded and organized for representation in memory; provisional hypotheses regarding the principles governing the occurrence of reinforcement are derived from differential consequences accompanying overt behavior; and after a given implicit hypothesis has been adequately confirmed by successful corresponding actions, the mediating rules or principles serve to guide the performance of appropriate responses on future occasions (p. 45).

We presented several arguments in Chapter 5 for why this "accounting for" mediational conception is inadequate to teleological description (see especially pp. 201–217). Bandura has improved on Hebb's informal account by placing greater emphasis on the formal-cause meaning, speaking as he does of the coding and organizing of environmental stimuli. But there is no more willingness to acknowledge a final-cause determination in his than in Hebb's formulation.

Indeed Bandura makes clear that: ". . . behavior comes to be regulated by antecedent stimulus events that convey information about probable consequences of certain actions in certain situations" (ibid., p. 19). Of course, since the past input information can influence present circumstances, Bandura like Hebb, can speak of a reciprocity between what the person brings forward (mediationally) as determinant influences and what the current environment asks of him: "Psychological functioning . . . involves a continuous reciprocal interaction between behavior and its controlling conditions. Although actions are regulated by their consequences, the controlling environment is, in turn, often significantly altered by the behavior" (ibid., p. 46). Hence: "Some degree of freedom is possible within a deterministic view if it is recognized that a person's behavior is a contributing factor to subsequent causal events" (ibid., p. 88). A person is free to the extent that he can "partly influence future events by managing his own behavior" (ibid., p. 88).

Though Hebb and Bandura are agreed and present us with what is surely the going interpretation of freedom in the behavioristic camp, the humanist cannot accept a characterization of behavior that puts the source of determination solely in the unidirectional control of the environment—whether we think of this environment as taking place yesterday and now reciprocally interacting with the present environment or not. The person, not the environment, always makes the difference in what eventually happens behaviorally. Humanists believe that to speak of efficient-cause determinism after the fact or in the abstract is easy. However, when dealing with people in the spontaneous, informal, nonexperimental atmosphere of everyday life, the telic side to behavior is always more evident. This is probably why psychotherapy practitioners have traditionally been more prone to embrace teleological theories than have experimentalists. As an historic case in point, we can even use a half-decade from the life of Bandura to show how the humanity of people can intrude on the most self-assured interpretations of the lab scientist.

In his 1969 book Principles of Behavior Modification Bandura took up the famous confrontation between Carl Rogers and B. F. Skinner (1956), "Some Issues Concerning the Control of Human Behavior." In this debate the humanist Rogers differentiated between various types of control, two of which were external control and influence. Bandura (1969) discussed the merits of this humanistic distinction:

In the first category [of control], designated as external control, person

A [a prison warden?] creates conditions that alter person B's behavior without his concurrence [a prisoner?]. The second and presumably more humanitarian form, labeled *influence*, involves processes in which A [warden] arranges conditions that modify B's [prisoner's] behavior, to which he gives some degree of consent. This distinction between external control and influence, however, is more apparent than real. In many instances certain conditions are imposed upon individuals without their agreement, knowledge, or understanding, from which they can later free themselves by willingly changing their behavior in a direction subtly prescribed by controlling agents. Thus, for example, persons who have been legally committed to mental hospitals or penal institutions may voluntarily enter into treatment programs to acquire the types of behavior that will improve their living circumstances in the institution and ensure a speedy discharge. A more fundamental ethical distinction can be made in terms of whether the power to influence others is utilized for the advantage of the controller or for the benefit of the controllee, rather than in terms of the illusory criterion of willing consent (p. 82).

In the April 1974 issue of the American Psychological Association's *Monitor* (a newspaper), Bandura's illusory criterion had come back to him with a vengence, for in a front page story entitled "Behavior Modification under Fire" it was reported that two United States Federal Agencies had just announced that they were ceasing to fund behavior-modification projects. The government actions were prompted by congressional inquiries, pressure from civil rights groups, and a recent court victory in which a group of prisoners had successfully blocked a behavior-modification program in their penal institution. We put the words *Warden* and *Prisoner* in the above quotation from Bandura's writings to underscore the parallel between what he had to say vis à vis Rogers' humanistic concerns in 1969 and what he now was to say in 1974. In the *Monitor* (1974) issue under discussion we read that Dr. Albert Bandura, then President of the American Psychological Association, advocated a "rigorous public scrutiny" of all behavior modification programs in the climate of that period. Bandura is quoted as saying: "Society has no moral or legal right to force an individual to change. If I am black and am put in a prison because I'm opposed to the political and social system in this country I sure as hell wouldn't want behavior modification forced on me" (p. 4). Bandura went on to advocate that the prisoners be granted permission to run their own program of behavior modification, saying: "There are risks in granting more responsibility but we must take those risks" (*ibid.*).

Now aside from the obvious point that this is *precisely* what

Rogers was getting at in the first place and why he felt it necessary to distinguish between external control and influence, the talk of moral and legal rights by Bandura can surely *not* be subsumed by his theory of efficient causation in human affairs. A moral principle embodying a right is nothing but an input X in the mediating processes of a person or a people who have been *shaped* into holding to this X rather than, let us say, Y or Z. If we are to speak of truly moral rights in behavior we must find a grounds in some universal (or absolute) on which to base this morality, as in the precedents for which philosophers since the beginning of recorded history have been searching (see Table 1). If Bandura really believes that human beings are determined by such considerations, his *formal* theory of behavior has a few missing terms—terms that can be encompassed only by a "that, for the sake of which" phrasing.

Of course because Bandura's initial theoretical position had a reciprocal relationship envisioned between the person and his environment as freedom, we might contend that all he is now doing in encouraging prisoners to design their own behavior-mod programs is to exercise this freedom. Or we might say that the prisoners' past shaping, which controls them mediationally today as "free" persons, has succeeded in controlling Bandura's behavior—as a member of the social environment of these prisoners—so that he speaks more positively today of negotiation in human relations than he had earlier. Bandura (1974) took the former view in his Presidential Address to the American Psychological Association, presenting a string of statements reminiscent of the cognitivists discussed in Chapter 5—that is, pseudotelic in intonation. But the core idea of mediational control, which in turn inevitably means yesterday's efficient-cause control of today's behavior was retained (*ibid.*, p. 876).

Stepping back from this historical vignette, what are we to make of it? A theorist who is prepared to employ final-cause determinants in his account would find all of this reciprocity business a routine confounding of theory and method. We are back to Mischel's thinking (refer above, p. 232), in which one varying fluctuation of an efficient-cause nature pushes another about and vice versa, so that a patterning emerges and we call variations in this efficiently caused pattern freedom. This extraspectively framed give-and-take is not so absolutely wrong as a characterization as it is simply incomplete. The abstraction is too rarified, so the heart of the matter has been lost to methodological analogues. We have to assume the introspective perspective in theoretical description and look at this in human terms. What happened in the prison was that a group of human beings, who reason "for the sake of" certain assumptions about who they are and what their rights are in a culture founded by people like them, "stood up for" these rights. They could have conformed, because they actually control what is or is not going to be a successful behavior-mod program. But instead they rebelled (see our discussion of freedom vis à vis Skinner's theory, below). The prisoner said: "Look, I don't have to go along with this silly program of handing me chits everytime I meet some institutional requirement. In fact, I don't think this sort of program is proper and humane treatment to begin with. Even if some of these other men agree to go along with it, they shouldn't. It's not right! Let's see what the courts have to say about this."

Doubtless there were all manner of unnamed motivations prompting the prisoner's rejection of behavior modification. We are not so naive as to assume that they were all uniformly concerned with abstract universals of a humane nature. Some were doubtless out to get back at their imprisoners in any way open to them. But such considerations are irrelevant to the point under consideration, which is: We make far better sense out of considering the final-cause determinations in this behavior than we do in clinging to the method analogues of a reciprocal relationship between two kinds of variables or yesterday's inputs versus today's inputs, all somehow totaling to predictable interactions *without* telic considerations entering into them. No psychologist has done more for the promotion of behavior modification than B. F. Skinner, who achieved this feat through a remarkable redefinition of what it meant to respond. We now turn to Skinner's innovation and what it masks.

B. F. Skinner and the Efficient-Cause Reversal

There has been general consensus among behaviorists concerning the locus of a response on the time dimension. Based on analogies to the reflex arc, theorists since the days of Watson have assumed that the stimulus occurs first (afferent stimulation) and the response occurs second (efferent responsivity). The reflex-arc concept was the *sine qua non* of natural-science description, combining as it did the material-cause meaning in the very "meat" of the nervous tissues and efficient-cause meaning in the electrical energy that sent the impulses on their way over time. Behaviorists may have left this literal model, but they still harbor the "in-principle" view that there is a one-to-one relationship between behavior as observed and the existing physical equipment of the behaving organism. In the mid-

1970s, D. O. Hebb (1974) could say with confidence: *"Psychology is a biological science"* (p. 72). In the first half of the twentieth century this biological emphasis was to be seen in the drive-reduction theories that flourished. Body-tissue needs, acting in consonance with other stimuli in the environment, combined to motivate behavior and, when satisfied (drive-reduction), stamped in the S-R regularity known as a habit. We can picture this sequence as follows:

TIME DIMENSION: (SOONER) ————————————————————→ (LATER)

DRIVE *STIMULUS* ———————————→ ENVIRONMENTAL *STIMULI* ———→
RESPONSE(S) ————————————→ DRIVE REDUCTION (REINFORCEMENT)

The drive reduction achieved over time supposedly led to a reinforcement, or an adding to of the behavioral sequence (S-R regularity) that preceded it in the time sequence (English & English, 1958, p. 452). Subsequent modifications of this general model did not alter the sequence of responses occurring after stimuli. For example, in the mediation model of Dollard and Miller (1950) a response that occurred earlier in time could subsequently act as a cue (stimulus) of later behavioral responsivity. This was called a "cue-producing response" (*ibid.*, p. 98), and because of this theoretical maneuver we preserve the proper order of things in a mediation model, as follows:

TIME DIMENSION: (SOONER) ————————————————————→ (LATER)

DRIVE & ENVIRONMENTAL *STIMULI* ————————————→ MEDIATING
STIMULI ————————→ OVERT *RESPONSE*(S) ————————→ REINFORCEMENT

The reason having a stimulus coming first on the time dimension is so important is because, as an efficient cause, the antecedent must—by definition (see Table 3)—push or impel the consequent. Something later in time cannot logically efficiently cause something taking place earlier. Around the turn of the twentieth century Ernst Mach was waging a war on Newtonian conceptions of the universe as supposedly underwritten by not only atoms, but by efficient causes (see our discussion of his influence on Einstein above, p. 239). He was instrumental in cementing the view of modern physics that Dirichlet's function which connected observed dependent to independent variables, was *not* the efficient cause that the Newtonians had made it (see pp. 22 and 49). Mach asked that scientists look at causes *not* as compelling efficient causes, but as *functional* formal-cause patterns of antecedents to consequents. In 1931 the young Skinner, impatient with classical views on the nature of a response, employed Mach's name and arguments in calling for a view of causation in psychology whereby "explanation is reduced to description and the notion of the function [is] substituted for that of [efficient] causation" (Skinner, 1931, p. 446). In his book *The Behavior of Organisms* Skinner (1938) again refers favorably to the "modern theories of causality in which the correlational aspect is emphasized" (p. 443).

Skinner's call for a functionalistic causation would seem to have been welcomed by the functionalistic psychologists forming ranks in the 1930s and 1940s. Unfortunately, the functionalist attitude (see Chapter 4) was of a different type than the Machian functionalism. Recall that the functionalists honestly believed they were observing the literal push of consequents by antecedents in the IV-DV regularities of their experiments. Although he felt his terminology was reflective of a difference from this S-R psychology, Skinner was to prove no exception to this rule. His Machian functionalism did not run very deep. The *formal* opposition to functional causation in psychology was articulated in Spence's (1956) subsequent distinction between so-called *R-R Laws* (response-response or, in our terms, formal-cause laws) and *S-R Laws* (stimulus-response or, in our terms, efficient-cause laws). This was a blatant hypostatization of a methodological term into a theoretical usage, but Spence left no doubt as to where the more functional R-R law fell on the Lockean hierarchy of things: "These R-R laws represent only one small segment of the total framework of a science of behavior, and unfortunately not a very basic one at that" (*ibid.*, p. 9). Thanks to writings such as these, by the 1950s and 1960s, whereas the rest of modern science had become Einsteinian-Machian, psychology had reaffirmed Newtonianism!

Skinner was only too ready to promulgate this antitheoretical outlook, which viewed anything less than a direct manipulation of reality below the efforts of science. As he said during the 1950s: "When we have achieved a practical control over the organism, theories of behavior lose their point" (Skinner, 1956, p. 231). What Skinner had actually sought a generation earlier, and the reason he invoked Mach on those occasions, was a *reversal* of the typical S-R sequence over time. As is well known, Skinner distinguished between the elicited response traditionally employed in behaviorism and his conception of the emitted response, the so-called *operant* response. The core distinction to be drawn here involves placement of the response on the time dimension:

To distinguish operant from an elicited reflex, we say that the operant response is "emitted." (It might be better to say simply that it appears, since emission may imply that behavior exists inside the organism and then comes out. But the word need not mean ejection; light is not in the hot filament before it is emitted). *The principal feature is that there seems to be no necessary prior causal event* [italics added] (Skinner, 1974, pp. 52–53).

This would of course require a revolutionary view of the causal sequence, for if a response has no prior cause, it is a "before" on the time dimension and not an "after." This means it cannot be an efficient cause, and it meets the requirements of functional causation by Mach; to that extent one is left to his theoretical predilections to fill in the details of what is essentially a formal-cause description of *patterns* over time (called schedules by Skinner). Of course when Skinner chooses a phrasing like "there seems to be no necessary prior causal event," we are not sure what he really believes, particularly when he goes on to speak of "the *apparent* [italics added] lack of an immediate cause in operant behavior . . ." (*ibid.*, p. 53). What is seeming or apparent can mean that if we knew more we could discern "the" cause after all.

The picture is further clouded by the fact that in other contexts Skinner clearly states that operants are indeed more like causes than effects—that is, they are something other than efficiently caused responses:

I prefer to use the word "operant" in the sense of behavior which operates on the environment and produces reinforcing effects. You define an operant in terms of its *effects* [italics added], and study it by means of its effects on your apparatus. Operant behavior, as I see it, is simply a study of what used to be dealt with by the concept of purpose. The purpose of an act is the consequences it is going to have (Evans, 1968, p. 19).

Skinner calls the effected consequences *contingencies*: "I use the word 'contingencies' to describe the conditions which prevail at any given time and which relate a bit of behavior to its consequences" (*ibid.*, pp. 19–20).

If the operant *operates* as a purpose does on the environment to produce consequences (effects) and if the relationship between this antecedent operant behavior and the eventual consequents is termed a contingency, Skinner clearly has *reversed* the traditional S-R sequence, as follows:

TIME DIMENSION: (SOONER) ⸻⟶(LATER)

OPERANT *RESPONSE* [BEHAVIOR] ⟶CONTINGENT *STIMULI* AS
CONSEQUENCES ⸻⟶REINFORCEMENT EFFECTS

If the operant response did not act on the environment to effect a change in some way, reinforcement could not follow. If this action leads to a contingent circumstance that increases the probability of of subsequent responding, we can speak of reinforcement taking place. If not, no reinforcement develops. That Skinner sees the parallel between his concept of operant responding and purposivity is fitting, because as we noted in Table 1, the notion of a contingent cause was employed by John Duns Scotus and other medieval thinkers as due to a final-cause determination in which the line of efficient causation was *predetermined* by the patterned intentions of the actor (see Chapter 7, p. 294). This was viewed as something *other* than mere efficient causation. Moral decisions were said to depend upon a person's preliminary examination of the likely consequences of his act. To this extent man was free to act (free will), and the determinism achieved when a course was settled on was "softer" than the actions of noncontemplated, subhuman, or inanimate events.

If we now put the concept of contingent cause together with that of a functional cause in observed events, we could readily understand how even very predictable events of a lawful nature might be accounted for in other than efficient-cause ways (see Table 3). A person's observed behavior could be the (later) contingent effect of an (earlier) operant response termed an *intention*. If Skinner really means that operants are *not* efficiently caused by some antecedent connection thrusting them or eliciting them, his formal theoretical position admits to such a telic formulation!

The Hidden Teleology of Operant Conditioning

Although Skinner may have defined his operant response as producing reinforcing effects, his behavioristic commitment to nontelic description never left him for a moment. It therefore did not seem circular for him to say: "I view the study of operant behavior as essentially an exploration of the effects of all of the contingencies of reinforcement which are around in daily life or can be created in laboratories" (Evans, 1968, p. 20). Now we have the effect of an operant response as supposedly the cause of subsequent operants! Skinner has performed a theoretical maneuver here paralleling Dollard and Miller's cue-producing response, which amounts to a form of mediational role for the contingent stimuli, as follows:

TIME DIMENSION: (SOONER) ————————————————————→(LATER)

OPERANT *RESPONSE*————————→CONTINGENT *STIMULI*
REINFORCEMENT————————————————→INCREASED OPERANT

Skinner conveniently overlooks the fact that he (as theorist) *begins* this sequence over time with an operant response. This means he must believe that either (1) there was a previous stimulus efficiently causing the initial operant response after all, or (2) something that occurs later in time can cause something that happened earlier to increase its occurrence. But how could the latter take place in an efficient-cause frame? In this case we retain the efficient-cause order so that contingent stimuli would be acting as cues triggering operant responses. Skinner has permitted a "kind of" previous-stimulation explanation to sneak into his theory of causation because of what is called the *discriminative stimulus*. Bandura (1969) has also been influential in this development—for example, when he notes: "The discriminative stimuli simply modify the probability that a given response will occur, but they do not elicit it" (p. 25). Skinner's (1974) reference to this possibility goes as follows: ". . . a stimulus present when a response is reinforced acquires some control over the response. It does not then elicit the response as in a reflex; it simply makes it more probable that it will occur again . . ." (p. 74).

When Skinner says: "It [discriminative stimulus] makes it more probable that it [operant response] will occur again" we know that he is confounding method (observed differences in response level) with theory (his behavioristic account of this observation). He does not want to make the discriminative stimulus an efficient cause of the operant level, and we can appreciate this reluctance for it surely cannot be so on his basic theoretical stand. Why not? Because he has already told us that without the emitted operant, *no such stimulus would exist!* If the operant response creates the reinforcing contingent circumstances, *pari passu* it creates the discriminative stimulus which is present when a response is reinforced.

Skinner has tried from his early Machian overtures to bring off an altered (revolutionary?) view of the response in psychology, but he is not fully cognizant of the final-cause possibilities in this move. He seems to have believed that he could subsume these telic factors by what he considered to be a more scientific formulation, one that retained the efficient cause as exclusive in all behavior. How did he achieve this? Over the years Skinner avoided the teleological phrasing of events that was implicit in his theory by analogizing to the style of explanation used in Darwinian evolutionary theory.

If one looks at behavior exclusively on the basis of an extraspective perspective, one can see such events occurring over time as if they were discrete units, aligned in a row much as we might align a series of children's building blocks. This is a reflection of the demonstrative unipolarity common to Lockean formulations. Because behavior is now seen to occur in distinct units over time, one can analogize between the development of organic changes in evolution over time and the successive changes to be seen in the course of these units of behavior over time. In other words, what survives in behavior is what has led to a viable outcome, a good "after" situation for the organism in question. The animal which evolves physically to a point where, for example, following some environmental shift in climate, it continues to survive the change, is in a sense rewarded by contingent circumstances just as the animal which turns over the right stick in the forest is rewarded by a lode of nutritious insects. This is the parallel Skinner (1974) draws; his core argument runs as follows:

Darwin's theory of natural selection came very late in the history of thought. Was it delayed because it opposed revealed truth, because it was an entirely new subject in the history of science, because it was characteristic only of living things, or because it dealt with purpose and final causes without postulating an act of creation? I think not. Darwin simply discovered the role of selection, a kind of causality very different from the push-pull mechanisms of science up to that time. The origin of a fantastic variety of living things [as units] could be explained by the contribution which novel features, possibly of random provenance, made to survival. There was little or nothing in physical or biological science that foreshadowed *selection as a causal principle* [italics added]. . . . There are certain remarkable similarities between contingencies of survival and contingencies of reinforcement. . . . Both account for purpose by moving it after the fact [on the time dimension], and both are relevant to the question of a creative design. When we have reviewed the contingencies which generate new forms of behavior in the individual, we shall be in a better position to evaluate those which generate innate behavior in the species (pp. 36 and 40).

Skinner's contention that Darwin discovered a new causal principle is most assuredly incorrect, because the point of natural selection as a theoretical construct is to suggest that efficient causation can account for improvement and advance through serendipitous and other chance occurrences without invoking final causes (God's intentions) or even formal causes (God's plan)—although there is a definite patterning to be seen in the course of organic structures over time. Having once studied to enter the clergy, Darwin was well aware of the concepts of causation and thoroughly familiar with what *natural selection* meant in these classical descriptive terms. As is well known, Darwin was to base his concept of morality on the role of culture in human life, rather than directly on a moral form of behavior evolving in the very substance of man's physical structures. Skinner employs this cultural natural-selection idea as a corollary to his belief that the environment, not the person, controls the contingencies and hence the behavior to be seen emitted over time. He likes to cite passages from Darwin's (1952) *The Descent of Man* which emphasize the fact that nations which produced the most citizens of intelligence, bravery, patriotism, and moral benevolence through natural selection were those that survived and even prevailed over the less favored nations (see Skinner, 1974, p. 205). But he *fails* to cite the more paradoxical passages in which Darwin is contemplating—now from a more introspective perspective—the involutional side to evolutionary advance:

We civilised men . . . do our utmost to check the process of elimination [natural selection]; we build asylums for the imbecile, the maimed, and the sick; we institute poor-laws; and our medical men exert their utmost skill to save the life of every one to the last moment. There is reason to believe that vaccination has preserved thousands, who from a weak constitution would formerly have succumbed to small-pox. Thus the weak members of civilised societies propagate their kind. No one who has attended to the breeding of domestic animals will doubt that this must be highly injurious to the race of man (Darwin, 1952, p. 323).

Even when we can see how our vaccination practices and related physical therapies are keeping individuals alive who might otherwise succumb, the contingent circumstance here is not so reinforcingly well defined a unit as Skinner would have us believe. Though physical controls can be introduced through eugenics, abortion, and euthanasia, there is hardly agreement on the consequences of such selective acts—whether of positive- or negative-reinforcing value in the long run. But more fundamentally, so long as people do—as did

Darwin—anguish over the implications of their grasp of nature and its evolving status, these studied appraisals cannot be explained in the same way that natural selection is explained. These are clearly ruminations about contingencies *before* they happen, purposive examination of what to do. Efficient causation as the vehicle of natural selection is not the *only* causal determination at play in the evolution of mankind. In truth such introspective concerns cannot be properly analyzed by way of the natural-science theorizing that Skinner has retained.

If we could think of behavior in introspective as well as extraspective terms, the functional cause which Skinner began his career defending is capable of subsuming a *final*-cause meaning as well as the other three meanings (see discussion of introspective perspective and teleology in Chapter 1, pp. 35–39). One could not claim through mere observation that he was seeing an antecedent thrusting or cueing or in any way *necessarily* bringing about a consequent simply because there was a patterned regularity in the course of events being looked at. The observer might even entertain the possibility that an organism behaving over time could bring to bear some "before" unit of behavior "for the sake of which" an "after" unit of behavior followed to effect changes of a contingent variety. But in this case the contingency effected had been known beforehand by the behaving organism. Skinner is surely wrong when he holds that purposes are after the fact on the time dimension (see above quote). One does not look extraspectively *at* an intended purpose *after* some course of behavior has taken place. One looks *through* an intention *before* this eventual behavior occurs—or fails to do so! Skinner's purpose construct is like that of Tolman's (see Chapter 4)—that is, only if behavior actually eventuates in reinforcement or facilitation to some end can it be said to be purposive. An intention that goes awry or a purpose that is not facilitative (Tolman's docility) fails to qualify as either of these terms *by definition*. But is the statement true that man never aspires for the unattainable or, at the very least, the highly doubtful eventuality?

Consider the following quotations taken from Skinner's interview with Evans (1968) from an introspective perspective. Skinner begins with a typical mediational supposition: "As a determinist, I must assume that the organism is simply mediating the relationships between the forces acting upon it and its own output, and these are the kinds of relationships I'm anxious to formulate" (p. 23). He is even willing to characterize his own behavior in these extraspective terms: "I regard myself simply as an organism responding to its environment. This is my environment. It's designed to bring out my verbal behavior with maximal efficiency" (ibid., p. 65). He is not an originating source of control, but is under the control of environmental contingencies. Skinner next opines that a form of reciprocity a la Bandura's argument (refer above) takes place in the operant conditioning of behavior: "Man can control his future even though his behavior is wholly determined. It is controlled by the environment, but man is always changing his environment" (ibid., p. 107). But in elaborating on this reciprocity, Skinner next offers this rule of thumb in how to approach a problem solution: "If you are faced with two courses of action, check off all possible foreseeable consequences [italics added] before making a choice" (ibid., p. 109). If a consequence is foreseeable, it cannot be something that occurs only after the fact, and even if erroneous projections were made leading to no reinforcement following this purposive examination, we would still have to recognize the existence of this initial intentionality of the behaving organism. The capacity to project possible outcomes as contingent circumstances if "such and such" behavior were instituted is precisely what Duns Scotus meant by contingent causation (Table 1). This projection did not exist in the unidirectional immutable controls of the environment, but in man's ability to judge for himself and thereby act for the sake of certain moral principles. Nothing in Skinner's theory negates this kind of behavior from actually taking place.

Thus we can see how Skinner has a hidden teleology in his theory. If organisms are telic, then all that Skinner has experimentally observed in his many studies could still hold. Operant conditioners may be controlling people's behavior today based on what they take to be the nontelic manipulations of an efficiently caused environmental input, while in fact they may be capitalizing on the teleological proclivities of human beings. Control may reflect cooperation, conformity, or submission to authority (scientific and otherwise!). Skinnerian theory is an unknowing teleology. The arguments for environmental control are circular, and even the empirical evidence to which we next turn fails to support the image of man that Skinner demands.

Awareness and the Nature of a Contingency

We know from our study of paradigmatic innovations and revolutions (Chapter 5) that evidence can be adduced for some position only if the precedent theoretical paradigm allows for this alternative in the first place. Evidence is always on the side of an affirmed consequent; without a proper antecedent theoretical stance, one cannot always see even that which is there for the seeing. Operant conditioners, like many other tough-minded psychologists, have reflected this theory-blindness concerning the mounds of evidence accruing in support of the role of awareness in both operant (instrumental) and classical conditioning (see reviews of this work in Bandura, 1969, Chapter 9, and especially Brewer, 1974, which is a most stunning indictment of both classical and operant conditioning on this question). Confining our comments to the operant-conditioning approach, whereas Greenspoon (1955) had claimed that his subjects were unaware of the experimental manipulation (contingent reinforcement) of saying "mmm hmm" following each operant emission of a plural noun, studies by De Nike (1964), Dulany (1962), and Spielberger et al. (1963) were to suggest quite the opposite. The lion's share of the predicted variance was due to those subjects who could identify *not* the contingent discriminating stimulus (see above) of "mmm hmm" but the pattern of "if I say a plural noun then he (the experimenter) hums." *All* subjects hear the contingent stimulus (this can be established with electrical equipment attuned to their inner ears if necessary) but only some of them turn it into a "discriminative" stimulus (or whatever) by catching onto the *pattern* (formal cause) of certain befores (plural nouns) leading to certain afters ("mmm hmms") over the experimental period.

This awareness factor has had several counters by the Lockean establishment in experimental circles. We mention only a few. One of the first denigrations of awareness in operant conditioning was based on Farber's (1963) finding that a significant number of aware subjects never showed a change in their behavior—that is, they failed to emit more plural nouns even when they knew that this was expected of them. Operant conditioners saw in this finding an opportunity to revive the classical distinction between learning and performance, suggesting that because performance was what counted, simply being aware was not always enough to affect overt behavior. That this nonperformance was likely to be evidence *for* rather than against telic behavior was subsequently established by Page (1972), who showed how certain subjects do indeed see the response-reinforcement contingency but who do not necessarily then conform to experimental expectations. Having first established a means for identifying these two classes of subjects—those who were aware and conformed versus those who were aware and did not conform—Page simply stopped the experiment in midrun and asked these subjects to make him (the experimenter) *do the opposite* of what he was then doing ("make me say 'mmm hmm' " or "make me stop saying 'mmm hmm' "). On the *very next trial* these two conditions crisscrossed their so-called emission rates perfectly so that statistical tests were not needed to demonstrate differences. As predicted, the subjects who were not cooperating to that point had the experimenter verbally expressing the contingent reinforcement, whereas the cooperating subjects had him cease this verbalization. And the unaware subjects continued fumbling along at about the same level at which they had been performing to that point.

Another counterargument is to claim that awareness obviously cannot function in response acquisition, although it may be important in response selection. To learn new responses is vitally important, hence here again awareness is secondary in importance to conditioning which shapes actual behavior. Bandura (1969) resorts to this argument in the following: "Acquired insights, no matter how valid they may be, have limited utility for individuals who lack the necessary performance skills. The case is analogous to informing English monolingual students in verbal conditioning experiments that the criterion responses are Hindustani adjectives" (p. 579). The question of what is or is not a limited utility is all important here. Assuming that the base rate of emission for Hindustani adjectives to this point in the experiment was zero, an astute subject, following Bandura's instruction, could increase his rate by 100% through repeating the word *Hindustani*. Furthermore, by simply playing word-rhyming games, he could concoct a series of "ani" endings and thereby further increase the chances of stumbling onto another member or two of this verbal class. Of course this says nothing about the understanding of the language in question; but when we speak of awareness, we do not necessarily mean understanding in this sense either. The operant conditioning of meaningful topics or involved language expressions has been notoriously unsuccessful— for example, that in use by psychotherapists. And the plural nouns (or other words) being emitted in these experiments are hardly meaningfully connected. What we prove in awareness research generally is that a subject must contribute something to the experiment for it to "work," and, he *has an option* to do as he pleases in this regard.

Operant conditioners staunchly deny that the subject has a true option here. The experimental evidence is simply not taken in this way. A common gambit is to "define away" the entire problem of awareness through an S-R-bind kind of reasoning, as follows:

. . . "awareness" must be a defined concept. Ordinarily, its antecedent conditions are the stimulus contingencies relevant to learning while its consequent conditions are verbal reports, behavior, which refer to those antecedent conditions. To be useful, to be a significant concept, "awareness" defined in this manner must be lawfully related to other kinds of behavior (Maltzman, 1968, p. 329).

This places awareness on the "effect" side, a verbal report under the stimulus control of contingencies, and guided by those laws of learning to which behaviorists are so fond of referring. Apparently Skinner (1974) would account for awareness in this way, for he has stated: ". . . the basic fact is that when a person is 'aware of his purpose,' he is feeling or observing introspectively a condition produced by reinforcement" (p. 57). In other words, if a person is aware of the response-reinforcement contingency and then purposively decides to meet the experimental instructions (or not to do so), *this* aspect of his behavior is *itself* produced by previous contingencies. Skinner's confidence in citing this as a "basic fact" in light of the awareness research evidence is clear testimony to the Kuhnian position on what is possible to prove in science and what is not at any one time in its history.

The Overlooked Operant in Operant Conditioning

In psychology teleologists are often pictured as defensively rigid individuals who are unable to face research data objectively because "the facts" can be expected to explode their cherished beliefs in selves or souls. Yet the unabashed confidence the behaviorists express in experimental findings on both classical and operant reinforcement is more dangerous to the integrity of psychological science than any telic hypothesis the humanist might submit to test. Indeed there is reason today to question the objectivity of behavioristic psychology, so ingrained have the S-R bind, theory-method confound, and related "accounting for" maneuvers (see Chapter 4) become in its style of scientific description. As a case in point we present the overlooked albeit empirically demonstrable operant response going unnamed in a host of modern operant-conditioning experiments.

Let us assume from the outset that Skinner is entirely correct in his theory. We do not now hold that he is capitalizing on the human's telic capacity to prove erroneously that all behavior is efficiently caused. But in taking him at his word, we are going to be extremely rigorous and totally empirical. We begin with his definition of the operant response as "behavior which operates on the environment and produces [empirically observable] reinforcing effects" (Skinner, as quoted in Evans, 1968, p. 19). With our construct in mind we next go to the literature or conduct a series of experiments on this question of awareness in operant conditioning.[1] We evaluate the total body of findings *strictly* in terms of what is operationally definable (awareness defined as the subject's overt capacity to emit responses indicating the nature of the response-reinforcement contingency), observable (we can electronically record a subject's emitted plural-noun production and the experimenter's "mmm hmm" reinforcer), and reliable (the record of crossvalidation on awareness findings is second to none in the psychological literature).

Note that we are taking stock of a class of operant responses that is left unmentioned in the operant-conditioner's account. We make no distinction between the operant responses called *awareness* (what subjects tell us about what is going on) and the operant responses called *plural nouns* in the experimental procedure. *All* language expressions are taken as operant responses in the Skinnerian outlook so how could we do otherwise? It is not for us to say what is or is not "the" operant lawfully related to the production of a subsequent, contingent circumstance like the reinforcer ("mmm hmm"). If we are truly rigorous we let the facts determine this for us. This is especially true when we can demonstrate that awareness-operants (as we might call them) are unquestionably under emission during the ongoing data collections of operant conditioning. That is, subjects *do* make these statements preliminary to manifesting learning, if only *given the chance*. They begin giving hypotheses about what the study involves and *then* bring their "learning curves" up in objective manifestation of learning (see Brewer, 1974, for a survey of such findings).

When we take a properly rigorous view of the operant conditioning experiment, we can say with assurance that *only* the awareness-

---

[1] W. T. Roberts (1974), then a graduate student working under the writer, did his master's thesis on the topic of awareness in operant conditioning, following and crossvalidating Page's (1972) work. We note this so that the reader can be assured that the writer has had some firsthand experimental as well as literature-review experience in the topic under discussion. Even if sufficient evidence accrues in the next few decades to negate the current findings on awareness in operant conditioning, the present discussion is still relevant and historically pertinent to the science of psychology. The point of this section is that a vast body of rigorous empirical evidence now exists which readily relates to the theory generating the research but is reinterpreted beyond recognition because of its injurious implications for the model on which the whole approach rests.

operant can be shown literally to produce the experimenter's "mmm hmm" contingent reinforcer. Whatever else it may be, the plural-noun "response" is *not* an operant because—taken alone—it *fails* to produce the "mmm hmm" contingent circumstance. Though they are instrumentalities, the plural nouns *per se* operate on nothing! Contrary to Skinner's (and other's) contention that the reinforcement produces the awareness, the *observed* evidence leaves no doubt that awareness produces reinforcement (i.e., the "reinforcer" of mmm hmm).

How can Skinner say such things, which clearly depart from the facts as observed? He can do this only by leaving the rigor of experimentation to fall back on theoretical speculations about supposed reinforcements that took place in the *unobserved* past of any single organism's life history, thereby retaining awareness as an effect rather than as a cause in the theory espoused. Would it not be more parsimonious at least to begin with the assumption that the proven law of learning (i.e., awareness operants produce reinforcements more efficiently than other operants) holds at *all* times? Why should this law *not* hold early in life as well? We know that if it would indeed hold, the Skinnerian-Lockean paradigm faces a serious Kuhnian anomaly, for awareness is clearly more akin to the Kantian category of understanding than it is to the Lockean building block (see Chapter 2).

The most telling opposition to reasoning from present data to earlier behavior stems from an argument based essentially on intimidation! The operant conditioner points to the fact that both very young humans, who have not yet achieved speech, and lower animals, who cannot achieve speech, *do* reflect operant conditioning. Therefore awareness operants cannot be established in these organisms—that is, we are unable to interview them—and *this* is the kind of parsimony to which the proper psychological scientist is supposed to aspire. Why postulate two kinds of operants, one for humans and one for lower organisms (as well as infants, etc.)? Does the critic of operant conditioning wish to anthropomorphize lower animals? This natural-science admonition is usually enough to end all debate, not on evidential grounds but purely on theoretical grounds. Ironically this weight of influence from the institutionalized Lockean model is itself a clearly formal-final cause type of determinism (see Table 3).

There was a time in psychology's not-too-distant past when such nonempirical contortions of the observed facts to meet a desired belief would have been likened to the vitalist's relying on souls or guardian angels to account for the unpredictable or inexplicable in human behavior. We now find in modern times our foremost champions of scientific rigor reverting to their own type of "guardian-angel" theory. The Divine Plan seems to have been replaced by the reinforcement history.

Summary

Chapter 6 begins with an array of terms that can mean either theory, method, or both in psychological accounts. Examples are given of how psychologists such as Underwood and Mischel denigrate theory in favor of methods by turning their methods into pseudotheories of behavior. The variable concept is particularly misused in this sense. Mathematical formulations also help to restrict theoretical developments by confounding the meaning of prediction as methodological activity with prediction as an actuarial responsibility. In opposition to the views of Cronbach, we argue that psychologists need not be actuaries, with the social responsibility of literally predicting what people will or will not do in life. The remainder of the first half of Chapter 6 deals with the role of dialectical conceptualization in both psychological and physical science. Dialectical propensities in Machian physics and the actual use of a dialectical formulation in the theorizing of Niels Bohr highlight this discussion.

The second half of Chapter 6 is devoted to a detailed consideration of determinism. To determine is to set limits on something, and we show how the antecedents to this limitation vary depending upon which of the four causes we are concerned with in the theoretical description under espousal. In discussion of the law construct we show that lawful determination does not necessarily mean efficient-cause determination. Laws are best understood in a methodological context where they draw their meaning more from the formal than any other causal meaning. The widely heralded generalizations of psychological knowledge are theoretical in nature and *not* literal—entitized—laws spreading across the landscape. Campbell and Stanley are seen to confound theory and method *vis à vis* generalizing lawfulness in this sense.

The behavioristic conception of freedom, as represented in the thinking of Hebb and Bandura, amounts to a claim that if the individual is not under the total control of present stimuli (input), but can modify this influence based on past shaping (mediators), he is to that extent "free." The efficient-cause nature of this argument is underscored, and the whole position is found wanting. Whether the unidirectional control of today or the unidirectional control of yesterday is determining behavior makes no difference; neither instance can represent a proper psychological conceptualization of freedom.

In the closing sections of Chapter 6 on determinism we discuss the reversal that Skinner effected in the S-R construct, making it an R-S succession of events whereby the possibility exists that something other than an efficient-cause antecedent may be at play in the observed regularities of behavioral emission. Skinnerian theory is shown to contain a hidden teleology and to capitalize on the conforming tendencies rather than on the controlled characteristics of human beings in operant-conditioning experiments. The experimental evidence on awareness in support of this suggestion is pointed to, and some of the more prevalent disclaimers made by operant conditioners are reviewed and found wanting. Chapter 6 closes with a discussion of the overlooked operant in operant conditioning.

References

Bakan, D. Learning and the principle of inverse probability. *Psychological Review*, 1953, **60**, 360–370.

Bakan, D. Clinical psychology and logic. *American Psychologist*, 1956, **11**, 655–662.

Bandura, A. *Principles of behavior modification*. New York: Holt, Rinehart & Winston, 1969.

Bandura, A. Behavior theory and the models of man. *American Psychologist*, 1974, **29**, 859–869 .

Bergmann, G., & Spence, K. Operationism and theory in psychology. *Psychological Review*, 1941, **48**, 1–14.

Brewer, W. F. There is no convincing evidence for operant or classical conditioning in adult humans. In W. B. Weimer & D. S. Palermo (Eds.), *Cognition and the symbolic processes*. Hillsdale, N.J.: Lawrence Erlbaum Associates, 1974.

Burtt, E. A. *The metaphysical foundations of modern physical science* (rev. ed.). Garden City, N.Y.: Doubleday, 1955.

Campbell, D. T., & Stanley, J. C. *Experimental and quasi experimental designs for research*. Chicago: Rand McNally, 1963.

Cronbach, L. J. Beyond the two disciplines of scientific psychology. *American Psychologist*, 1975, **30**, 116–127.

Darwin, C. R. The descent of man. In R. M. Hutchins (Ed.), *Great books of the western world* (Vol. 49). Chicago: Encyclopedia Britannica, 1952.

DeNike, L. D. The temporal relationship between awareness and performance in verbal conditioning. *Journal of Experimental Psychology*, 1964, **68**, 521–529.

Dollard, J., & Miller, N. E. *Personality and psychotherapy: An analysis in terms of learning, thinking, and culture*. New York: McGraw-Hill, 1950.

Dulany, D. E. The place of hypotheses and intentions: An analysis of verbal control in verbal conditioning. In C. W. Eriksen (Ed.), Behavior and awareness: A symposium of research and interpretation. Durham, N.C.: Duke University Press, 1962. Pp. 102–129.

Einstein, A. Ernst Mach. Physikalische Zeitschrift, 1916, 17, 101–104.

English, H. B., & English, A. C. A comprehensive dictionary of psychological and psychoanalytical terms. London: Longmans, Green, 1958.

Evans, R. I. B. F. Skinner: The man and his ideas. New York: Dutton, 1968.

Eves, H. An introduction to the history of mathematics (3rd ed.). New York: Holt, Rinehart & Winston, 1969.

Farber, I. E. The things people say to themselves. American Psychologist, 1963, 18, 185–197.

Feuer, L. S. Einstein and the generations of science. New York: Basic Books, 1974.

Frank, P. Philosophy of science. Englewood Cliffs, N.J.: Prentice-Hall, 1957.

Greenspoon, J. The reinforcing effect of two spoken sounds on the frequency of two responses. American Journal of Psychology, 1955, 68, 409–416.

Hebb, D. O. What psychology is about. American Psychologist, 1974, 29, 71–79.

Jung, C. G. Psychology and alchemy. In H. Read, M. Fordham, & G. Adler (Eds.), The collected works of C. G. Jung (Vol. 12). Bollingen Series XX.12. New York: Pantheon Books, and London: Routledge & Kegan Paul, 1953.

Jung, C. G. Psychology and religion: West and east. In H. Read, M. Fordham, & G. Adler (Eds.), The collected works of C. G. Jung (Vol. 11). Bollingen Series XX.11. New York: Pantheon Books, and London: Routledge & Kegan Paul, 1958.

Kausler, D. H. Continuity of processes across variants of recognition learning. In R. L. Solso (Ed.), Theories in cognitive psychology: The Loyola symposium. New York: Wiley, 1974. Pp. 45–75.

Kuo, Z. Y. The fundamental error of the concept of purpose and the trial and error fallacy. Psychological Review, 1928, 35, 414–433.

Levy, L. H. Psychological interpretation. New York: Holt, Rinehart & Winston, 1963.

MacCorquodale, K., & Meehl, P. E. On a distinction between hypothetical constructs and intervening variables. Psychological Review, 1948, 55, 95–107.

Mach, E. The science of mechanics. Chicago: Open Court, 1893.

Maltzman, I. Theoretical conceptions of semantic conditioning and generalization. In T. R. Dixon & D. L. Horton (Eds.), Verbal behavior and general behavior theory. Englewood Cliffs, N.J.: Prentice-Hall, 1968. Pp. 291–339.

Mancuso, J. C. Dialectic man as a subject in psychological research. In J. F. Rychlak (Ed.), Dialectic: Humanistic rationale for behavior and development. Basel, Switzerland: S. Karger AG, 1976. Pp. 113–125.

Mischel, W. Toward a cognitive social learning reconceptualization of personality. Psychological Review, 1973, 80, 252–283.

Monitor, April 1974, 5 (4). Washington, D.C.: American Psychological Association, 1974.

Oppenheimer, R. Analogy in science. American Psychologist, 1956, 11, 127–135.

Osgood, C. E., Suci, G. J., & Tannenbaum, P. H. *The measurement of meaning.* Urbana: University of Illinois Press, 1957.

Page, M. M. Demand characteristics and the verbal operant conditioning experiment. *Journal of Personality and Social Psychology,* 1972, **23**, 304–308.

Piaget, J., Inhelder, B., & Szeminska, A. *The child's conception of geometry.* New York: Harper Torchbooks, 1964.

Rieff, P. *Freud: The mind of the moralist.* New York: Viking, 1959.

Riegel, K. F. Dialectic operations: The final period of cognitive development. *Human Development,* 1973, **16**, 346–370.

Roberts, W. T. *Instrumental effects of causal constructs.* Unpublished master's thesis. Lafayette, Ind.: Purdue University, 1974.

Rogers, C. R., & Skinner, B. F. Some issues concerning the control of human behavior: A symposium. *Science,* 1956, **124**, 1057–1066.

Rychlak, J. F. *A philosophy of science for personality theory.* Boston: Houghton Mifflin, 1968.

Rychlak, J. F. The multiple meanings of dialectic. In J. F. Rychlak (Ed.), *Dialectic: Humanistic rationale for behavior and development.* Basel, Switzerland: S. Karger AG, 1976. Pp. 1–17.

Sherif, M., & Hovland, C. I. *Social judgment: Assimilation and contrast effects in communication and attitude change.* New Haven: Yale University Press, 1961.

Skinner, B. F. The concept of the reflex in the description of behavior. *Journal of General Psychology,* 1931, **5**, 427–458.

Skinner, B. F. *The behavior of organisms: An experimental analysis.* New York: Appleton-Century, 1938.

Skinner, B. F. A case history in scientific method. *American Psychologist,* 1956, **11**, 221–233.

Skinner, B. F. *Beyond freedom and dignity.* New York: Knopf, 1971.

Skinner, B. F. *About behaviorism.* New York: Knopf, 1974.

Spence, K. W. *Behavior theory and conditioning.* New Haven: Yale University Press, 1956.

Spielberger, C. D., Berger, A., & Howard, K. Conditioning of verbal behavior as a function of awareness, need for social approval, and motivation to receive reinforcement. *Journal of Abnormal and Social Psychology,* 1963, **67**, 241–246.

Suppes, P. The place of theory in educational research. *Educational Researcher,* 1974, **3**, 3–10.

Thurstone, L. L., & Chave, E. J. *The measurement of attitude.* Chicago: The University of Chicago Press, 1929.

Underwood, B. J. Individual differences as a crucible in theory construction. *American Psychologist,* 1975, **30**, 128–134.

Wightman, W. P. D. *The growth of scientific ideas.* New Haven: Yale University Press, 1951.

CHAPTER SEVEN

A Teleological Interpretation of Human Behavior

In Search of New Descriptive Terminology

If we are to effect a revolution in the way human behavior is to be explained, a new terminology is required. Although some psychologists distinguish between *description* and *explanation*, an explanation is always a further description of some item or phenomenon, bringing to bear a construct system removed from the latter but aimed at clarifying it (Rychlak, 1968, p. 46). To explain behavior is to describe fully the conditions under which it may be seen to vary or remain constant. Theoretical descriptions come first, and then with proper foreplanning we can even predict the course of this variation in an experimental context. We want to avoid the tendency to accept what we observe and record in the experimental context as *necessarily* explaining (complete description) what is taking place. Henceforth we call this the *empiricist's error*. In other words, we shall always try to keep our methodological descriptions separate and distinct from our theoretical descriptions, although in certain instances the two lines of explanation will be highly similar if not identical. But they do not *have* to be identical.

Psychologists are understandably reluctant to admit new terminology to their specialty, particularly if such terms seem to indicate a reversal to an age of prescientific thinking. The institutionalized Lockean model encourages psychologists to believe that they already have the conceptual tools to "account for" any type of behavioral description (see Chapter 4). We have tried to show that such accounts do not in fact convey the meaning of what they are designed to stand for. Another reason for trying new terminology is because only in this way can we teach ourselves anything. We fashion a new term to frame concisely what we want to develop as a precedent meaning (see Table 1). Because there are always more implications in a new conception than even the innovator is aware of at the outset, the fruitfulness of new terminology is found in the range of explanation afforded as we bring such terms to bear in an ever-widening arc of theoretical description.

The precedent meanings that have been furthered again and again in psychology have devolved exclusively from the institutionalized Lockean paradigm (see Chapter 4). What is needed are terms and background explanations drawn from a more Kantian, dialectical, teleological frame of reference. In this Chapter we aim at doing precisely this.

A Dialectical Conception of Change in Behavior

As a first step in developing a telic account of behavior, we must take a more sophisticated view of stability and change in events. We have seen in Chapter 6 the basic strategy of explanation employed by the behaviorists, who relying as they do on efficient-cause links called habits, use the time dimension as a baseline to all of their explanations. We cannot overestimate the importance of the time dimension to explanations of behavior proffered by the learning theorist (which includes not only S-R but cybernetic and information-processing accounts as well). The very meaning of behavior is as a flow over time, an efficiently caused sequence of what is first change and second a fixing of this change into set patterns or habits that can be neatly graphed as a curve of learning (Kintsch, 1970, p. 61). Note that in this explanation of behavior what is fixed is made secondary, meaning that the pattern of habitual behavior is determined by the antecedent efficient-cause "shaping" of events. Except for biological limitations (e.g., a dog cannot be shaped to fly) the behavior is determined by change rather than *vice versa*. Change is assumed and behavioral regularity is what must be accounted for. This view is consistent with post-Galilean thought, and to that extent it might be said to be "modern" (Wightman, 1951, p. 68). Pre-Galilean thought had taken behavior as the fixed pattern, and change was what had to be accounted for. Natural science reversed this ordering and modern psychology has followed this general lead.

However, if Newton's account of the universe took on motility as a precedent assumption, as noted in Chapter 1 (pp. 47–48), it *also* framed a stability in the mathematical assumptions of Cartesian geometry. Points move in Cartesian geometry whereas they were fixed in Euclidian geometry, but these moving points *do* have patterns which they define albeit in a moving sense (i.e., straight lines, circles, arcs, etc.; see our continued discussion of this below, p. 290). The obvious question implied here is: What is more important to our understanding, the *motion* of the point or the *fixed* pattern it defines in mathematical space? This question can be raised about all so-called *ideas*. That is, can the logos-pattern be explained via motion or must we acknowledge a role for the pattern *qua* pattern in human understanding?

We are reminded here of the ancient debate between the Heraclitians and the Parmenidians, with the former claiming that all in life is change and the latter contending that change is illusory (Table 1). However, this characterization of the disagreement is oversimplified, for it glosses over the core issue here of dialectical versus demonstrative differences in the view of change. Heraclitus was a dialectical theorist; though he said that no one can step into the same river twice, what he was actually getting at was the continuity and identity in events (the river remains a river) even though there is constant change (as the water flows [one-and-many thesis]) (Magill & McGreal, 1961, p. 16). Seeing flux (dialectical opposition) in all things, Heraclitus marveled at the *logos* (rationale) or pattern of recurring continuity (a form of fixity) in all things. Hence this historic debate is not a foolish exercise in primitive thinking. These human beings, as all of the great thinkers cited in Table 1, were contending something that had to do with their very nature, with what we call mentality or the recognition, creation, and maintenance of fixed patterns within lived events.

If fluctuating changes are continually taking place within the fixity of a logos, what then could constitute a change for the dialectician? This would be a matter of altering the given *pattern* in events. Such changes would take place entirely independently of time flow, and as a matter of fact even this conception of time would be the result of some noticeable reordering of events. Something happens and then something else happens. Extending the meaning of the (now quantified) first event to the second event, we can say that a time period has passed because there is a meaningfulness (meaningful relationship) across ordered events, each of which is patterned (into meaning) and the totality of the sequence is itself therefore patterned (made meaningful). There are psychologists who believe that we will always have to explain behavior in terms of time flow (Wolman, 1971), but history records that dialectical thinkers have not accepted this inevitability.

In Chapter 6 (pp. 240–241) we noted the influence of Kierkegaardian thought on the atomic theory of Niels Bohr. We can now appreciate that Kierkegaard's qualitative leaps across the fixed *stadia* of life were dialectical conceptions of change. The aesthetic, ethical, and religious styles of living are like Heraclitian rationales, each quite different from the other, an altered pattern which, when taken on, qualitatively alters all that follows. Kierkegaard interpreted change as dialectically generated through the opposition of an either/ or, calling for a decision or commitment to one life course rather than another (Lowrie, 1961, p. 135). This concept of a discontinuous leap, of a nonincremental sequence resulting in qualitative changes across *stationary* states is what Bohr then used to account for the change of orbits open to an electron moving around the nucleus of an atom. Newtonian physics had accepted the quantified view that any of an infinity of possible orbits with different radius values would be possible. Bohr reversed the sequence, suggesting that only *certain* patterns would hold. That he suggested the atom in a stationary state possessed a "free choice" as to the transition it might follow in moving to the next stationary state is of more than passing interest to us. This is precisely the kind of explanation which is made possible when we take a dialectical view of the nature of change.

The dialectician begins with the assumption of an order in events, a stationary state or fixed pattern that transcends the flux of moving events at any one point in time. *Every* fluctuation in behavior is not change! The etymological roots of the word *change* imply a form of bartering in which there is a give-and-take resulting ultimately in a reordering of possessions across the two (or more) sides doing the bargaining. If this interplay is seen properly as a dialectical matter and if it is understood that without a reordering (repatterning) there is *no change*, we arrive at a more useful conception of change for the description of human behavior than heretofore available.

Tautology as Psycho-Logic Sans Time

If we were to select a term that might capture the opposite meaning of change or difference we could find no better choice than *tautology*. The dictionary definition of this term focuses on redundancy or needless repetition in the meaning of words. Although correct enough in certain circumstances, this definition is surely inadequate to the broader meaning of tautology, and it completely underrates the importance which something like a mental tautology plays in the psychology of human beings. We now propose to raise the *Principle of Tautology* to a status second to none, paralleling it in importance to such classical psychological principles as contiguity, (law of) effect, association, frequency, and isomorphism.

To aid in our understanding of the tautology we must return to the discussion of meaning as a relational term begun in Chapter 2 (pp. 55–59). We defined *meaning* there as a term referring to the relations between items and their referents as well as to the relations between a user of such meaningful ties and the items he employs for the understanding of experience. This definition encompasses a distinction between the extraspective and the introspective theoretical perspective, a distinction we want to emphasize in the present context. Thus when we say that the item (word) *bread* means what it relates to—such referents as flour, oven, milk, butter, and so on—the relational ties can be framed entirely extraspectively, much as we define words in a dictionary by relating them to other words. But what if we were to relate the word *bread* solely to *bread*? In this case the relation would be one of identity or sameness (bread is bread), and as the definition referred to above suggests, we have expressed a tautology. This redundancy is empty only when the question of existence is not at issue. Saying, "That is bread," while looking at a referent in experience is not a needless expression when one is hungry and attempting to define the edibles in proximity to his personal identity. But the phrase, "That is bread," is actually a variant form of tautology meaning "Bread is bread" or "That is that (which I seek)."

Note however that in this latter instance we are speaking of a tautology as it would be expressed from the *introspective* perspective. We are no longer speaking about dictionary definitions, about relations between items and their referents alone, but about the relation between the user of such items (a hungry person) and the item designated (the bread). The tautological expression is made in a psychological fashion, as reflecting what the person is bringing to bear in organizing his experiences. Having a psychological view of the tautology is quite different from having simply a logical view. Classical logicians, who rarely take seriously the importance of dialectical logic due to its sophistical potentials, are prone to think of tautologies primarily in the more extraspective sense. Following Kant, they are likely to say that a tautology is an analytically true statement, which means that it is true by definition. If we analyze the statement "All bachelors are unmarried males," we can determine that it really states "All bachelors are bachelors" or "All unmarried males are unmarried males" because the definition of the antecedent term is contained in the consequent term. This is obviously comparable to our dictionary definition, a relational identity between terms.

If we are *psychologicians* and accept the view that human beings do follow something like a logic of tautology in their reasoning, would there be any difference between "All bachelors are unmarried males" and "All redheads are hotheaded" in the reasoning of a human being? Surely the latter statement can be shown extraspectively to be nontautological. The definition of *redhead* does not include the concept of hotheadedness, much less equal it identically. As psychologists, can we overlook this fallacious tautological relation an individual is drawing between redheadedness and hotheadedness (based presumably on a limited tautological identity of redness and fire, etc.)? To ask us to do so is like asking a physician to deny the usual digestive process when a patient under his treatment has swallowed a handful of sand, which is clearly in violation of the metabolic processes moving nutritious foodstuffs through the body. Erroneous mental conceptions, like bad foodstuffs in the digestive tract, do not alter or negate the process by which such meanings are extended and seen to work an influence on behavior.

We are seeking the process here and want to capture the Heraclitian identity within change. By looking at meaning through the conceptual eyes of the individual who brings such meanings to bear (i.e., introspectively), the concept of tautology permits us to take both a dynamic and a static view of behavior at the same time. There is order in life, because the person can bring certain givens (meanings) forward, tautologizing them from circumstance to circumstance (each redhead encountered is made hotheaded by definition). The very concept of *idea*, which draws historical precedence from logos, rests on the assumption of a tautologizing capacity in mind so that an X can be brought to bear as X repeatedly, even though circumstances always differ. Plato's realm of Being was a comparable notion of timelessness, from which beautifully perfect and unchanging universal ideas threw forth their variegated (imperfect) meanings, as shadows jumping about on the wall of a cave rest upon some more stable form existing between the wall and the light source. This belief in fixed universals was to dominate thought up to the rise of modern science.

Though he no longer sees the patterns of nature being determined by the prepatternings of universals, the modern scientist did find his universal assumptions in the realm of mathematics. Gödel's proof (Nagel & Newman, 1958) has weakened the earlier confidence in the fixed order of mathematics, but scientists still retain a self-assured attitude regarding quantitative arguments—particularly because these arguments do stand up to the empirical tests of validation. But what is not sufficiently appreciated here is that the psychology of mathematics *itself* draws heavily from the tautological reasoning capacities of the mathematician (Eves, 1969). In his *Introduction to Mathematical Philosophy* Bertrand Russell (1919) went into some detail concerning how tautological reasoning seems fundamental to the human mentality (pp. 204–205). As humans we somehow know by the logical order of a syllogism that it is correct, simply through an examination of its internal meaning structure (coherence theory of truth). Russell confessed that to define the tautology was difficult, but he affirmed a conviction that the farthest reaches of knowledge are fringed by such an intrinsic human capacity to know with certainty once a given pattern falls into order. Without this capacity there could be no mathematics and no science. Russell's analysis in this context is purely introspective and—we would add—psychological.

In their *Principia Mathematica* Whitehead and Russell (1963) also proved through extraspective analysis that mathematics and logic were tautological activities. In this case we are not speaking about the psychology of the human being, but of the capacity to translate mathematical symbols into logical symbols (see our discussion of the double-duty character of mathematics in Chapter 1, p. 36). Russell has shown that mathematics *per se* reduces to tautological statements of the analytical variety (i.e., All X is X). In this case we return to a more introspective formulation; for clearly when a mathematician uses the logic of mathematics, the ultimate conviction he personally senses in his *proof* emanates from the fact that he can show how the left-hand side of his equational development is identical to the right-hand side. We overlook the fact that the equation sign in mathematics signifies a tautological identity. In a psychological sense mathematical arguments are like grand analytical propositions, highly complex but subject to definitional analysis in which the left-hand member (analogical to the antecedent) turns up identical to the right-hand member (analogical to the consequent of an if . . . then . . . proposition) even though several transformations have been made.

Ironically, although statistical conceptions such as the Central Limit Theorem or a finding of unity in F- or t-tests are clearly based on tautologies, no psychological learning theorist to date has employed the tautology to explain how human beings learn. The rigorous psychologist who makes use of quantitative measures learns whether he has found something other than a redundancy of "no difference" in the relational ties of an F-test carried out on his data. But his experimental subject is said to learn exclusively on the basis of a frequency thesis or a principle of contiguity. We therefore have at least two theories of learning being advanced in most empirical researches, and no one currently acknowledges the principle of tautology which surely enters into at least one of them.

Skinner (1974) has observed: "All sciences simplify . . ." (p. 231) in propounding knowledge, but he failed to enlarge on precisely what this involves. Ultimately, the simplification achieved through both philosophical and scientific analysis rests upon man's ability to see identities across seemingly disparate events. Euclidian geometry is premised upon only five axioms and five postulates (Eves, 1969, pp. 121–129). Table 1 demonstrates that the four causal meanings can be seen covering centuries of human conceptualization, and the search for unchanging precedents is simply another manifestation of man's tautological capacity in reason. The history of science provides many clear examples of this human ability—for example, when Hooke tautologized between the concepts of sound and light, attributing thereby the known wave properties of the former to the latter as an hypothesis (Wightman, 1951, p. 130). This led to speculations of an ether, which would presumably undulate and thereby bring about the waves of light. Maxwell's theorizing was based upon an equation of electricity with magnetism (ibid., p. 313). Hertz then did experiments to prove his contention that there was an "identity of light, radiant heat, and electromagnetic wave action" (ibid., p. 315). Even Stahl's discredited phlogiston theory rested upon a commonsensical equation drawn between the giving off of a fiery substance by a burning body and the burning of a candle or the calcination of a metal (ibid., pp. 180–183). The conservation of energy principle in science can be viewed as a grand tautology in which there is a fixed constant within change (ibid., p. 279). It is fascinating to observe in Einstein's theoretical development a definite series of tautological extensions, identifying matter as energy (Kondo, 1969 p. 45), inertia as gravity (pp. 69–70), and gravity as curved space (p. 78).

The reader may object to some of these examples because they are more properly analogies than tautologies. This brings up an important feature of the principle of tautology, for we would now point out that what makes an analogy come about is the *identity* found between the two points of the relation—for example, when Copernicus once argued that the sphere was a "natural" shape because as with a drop of water, the sun, moon, and planets assumed this form spontaneously when left to "their own accord to limit themselves" (Schwarts & Bishop, 1958). A tautology is a relation of identity, and an analogy is a relation of likeness short of identity in meaning formation (patterning). Analogies are always based on dialectical reasoning, for beginning our parallel with what *is* identical across referents, we can then base our understanding on what *is not* the same—that is, in the disanalogy. Other so-called figures of speech, such as the metaphor (e.g., a ship plows the sea), allegory (a lengthy metaphor in story form), or synecdoche (e.g., a person typified as a "cutthroat") are the same. Beginning with a purely *psychological* principle, we are thrust into the entire panoply of studies subsumed by such specialties as psycholinguistics, concept-formation, creativity, and language development.

It is important to grasp that all such tautological derivatives are *timeless* theoretical constructions. They occur immediately, in the very delineation of the patterns of meaning premised or predicated, which is why the Kierkegaardian leap becomes qualitatively different so suddenly. This alteration of meaning is not pushed steadily along by efficient causation, but dramatically shifted through the abrupt changes of formal-final causation as when we move along the gallery of an art museum in which each new painting observed is based on its own unique set of premises. The earlier observations do not prepare us or (telically) determine for us what the next aesthetic experience will be although most assuredly we will sense a change in our awareness as we stroll along.

This timeless quality of patterns can be seen to occur in the mathematical tests to which we submit our data in experimentation. Once a psychologist has gathered his data on a sample of subjects, the very *instant* he concludes "this is my sample," the pattern of scores he has derived from his measurements exists as a quasi-stadia so that any of the resultant statistical tests he performs on the data are already determined via formal-cause determinism (Chapter 6). He has to spend time calculating these scores and submitting them to a computer, but the pattern of statistical treatments we know as the correlation coefficient or the analysis of variance is already fixed without regard to such time considerations. By shifting assumptions (formal-final cause determinations) the psychologist can of course alter his tests and thereby the possible meaning of what his data represent. But this "quantum jump" is again entirely outside of time considerations, because whatever rescorings or statistical revisions this may involve *must* be fixed by the patterning of the original array of subjects.

There is no more handicapping theoretical maneuver possible than to require a teleologist to use the language of stimulus and response in his description of behavior. *Response* in particular has been tautologized by rigorous psychologists with *behavior*, so that it is always thought of as motion over time even when this motility is "shaped" into a recurring pattern. We noted in Chapter 5 that not even the modern efforts to cognize psychology avoid the efficient-cause formulation implicit in this view of behavior as motion. Mediation theory simply puts a kind of pulley-and-gears system between yesterday's pushes and today's shoves. To capture the nature of humanity we advocate the coining of a new term, one that infers behavior as manifesting a stability "for the sake of which" motions are *then* seen to take place. Basing our definition on the Greek concept of *telos* as an end or reason for which behavior is to be manifested, we now propose that psychology accept the fact that certain behaviors are *telosponsive* in nature. This construct may be defined as follows:

A *telosponse* is the person's taking on (premising) of a meaningful item (image, word, judgmental comparison, etc.) relating to a referent acting as a purpose for the sake of which behavior is then intended. The *purpose* of the meaningful item can be assumed without question, as in observing factually that "the door out of the room is over there" or it can be difficult to ascertain as in the subtlety of a dream content. When the individual behaves "for the sake of" this purpose he is telosponding or acting intentionally, although this may be exclusively at the level of understanding and not seen in his overt actions. In this sense, concepts have purpose and human beings intend.[1]

In distinguishing between *understanding-intentions* and *action-intentions* we ensure that our outlook does not fall into the empiri-

---

[1] Since introducing this concept the writer has been—quite properly—criticized by even friendly colleagues for the "bastard form" of combining Greek (*telos*) and Latin (*spondere*) language roots. It is hoped that this scholarly failing over precedents on the writer's part may in time be forgiven, since the intent here was to coin a succinct word that would closely parallel the widely used *response* yet keep *telos* in the forefront. As with many bastards in history, our concept began life with decided handicaps—some of which even outweigh the matter of genetic lineage. Judging from the relative ease with which students and colleagues catch onto our meaning, however, the future looks reasonably good. The telosponse may yet achieve legitimacy in proper psychological society.

cist's error (p. 274). Psychologists have for too long accepted the naive functionalist dictum "All we can objectively observe is overt behavior, so all we can talk about is overt behavior." Surely the extensive work done on awareness in psychological experimentation (see Chapter 6, pp. 264–267) should convince us that some *unobservables* in the actual course of an experiment are more important than that which we can literally see in overt behavior. Einstein continually thought about physical phenomena in ways that could not be put to test through literal observations. What is the advantage to so limiting our intellectual scope?

Only a meaning-processing animal can telospond. We discuss the so-called lower animal in organic evolution below, but a conception of the person in which inputs and outputs are not contingent upon the *introspective meaning* as contained in mental conceptions would fall short of telosponsive description. Of course certain behaviors of an organism can be explained telosponsively, but others are not amenable to this type of description. A human being's stomach may undulate and secrete fluids, hence move or "behave," completely without telosponsivity. Various other reflexive behaviors of the organism, such as eyeblinking to certain stimuli, wincing in some circumstances, or the tensing of a muscle under psychological pressure might be said to occur in the classical sense of a stimulus-response regularity. But insofar as we begin to think of *mental* behavior, including those areas of study such as psycholinguistics, mentioned above (see p. 282), we would begin to touch upon the telosponsivity of human behavior.[2]

An important term in the above definition is *premise*. Logicians are likely to define this as a proposition on which, at least in part, the conclusion of an argument is based. This signifies that there are presumptive meanings embraced by a thinker that enter into the beliefs at which he ultimately arrives. What we learn is therefore always a function to some extent of what we have begun with (using function now in a formal-cause, patterning sense). The writer uses the word *premise* in this predicating sense, except that more referents than merely verbal propositions are included. An image can be

---

[2] We begin now to introduce new terminology over this and the next chapter at an increasing rate. To aid the reader's grasp and for quick reference we have provided a glossary of the most unique and repeatedly used terms (please see pp. 499–508). We have tried to elaborate on the definitions of these constructs in the glossary, interweaving meanings a bit more than is possible in the textual presentation.

thought of as a premise, as can the judgmental comparison of saying "X is better than Y" as an opening presumption to meaningful relationships between the evaluator (the person doing the premising) and X or Y. If Kuhnian paradigms (Chapter 6) predetermine to some extent what a scientist can learn about his area of interest, then either a formalized *verbal* statement or a rough analogy between some *visual* occurrence, such as a wave on a lake's surface and the flow of light under study, can serve as such a paradigmatic premise.

Other central terms in the definition of a telosponse include *purpose* and *intention*. These terms are often used interchangeably and so to draw hard and fast rules for distinguishing between them is probably unrealistic. The reader can probably accept the distinction drawn in the above definition, which points out that although one can speak of the purpose of almost anything, we reserve the meaning of intentionality for a living being—usually a higher animal. In Chapters 1 (p. 32) and 2 (p. 56) we indicated that a pattern of events or a pattern of letters called a word lacked purpose. We meant, of course, that in the extraspective use of the meaning concept, a telic possibility does not exist. A word *qua* word has no purpose. A plan *qua* plan has no purpose. However, when an intelligence (introspectively framed) makes use of a plan or word to extend the meaningful implications contained therein, we *do* see the purpose of the plan or word made manifest. Following Kant, we can say that a concept (plan, word) contains its purpose when an intelligence employs it in conceptualization. The concept *pencil*—either as a word or in a visual-image sense—when grasped by a meaning-processing intelligence expresses its purpose as something that can be used for writing, drawing, and other marking activities. The definition of *pencil* is tautologized with this meaning per our discussion above. The pencil, which is defined purely extraspectively, does not know of its purpose. There is no telosponsive intelligence attributed to the pencil as there is no life at all. Human beings, who concocted a symbolizing procedure and now require a means of utilizing this expressive scheme, intend the purpose of the pencil.

We often see or know the purpose of a concept but do not intend that the purpose contained therein be actualized in overt behavior. We do not pick up each pencil that comes into our cognizance and begin writing with it. What actually takes place in overt behavior depends upon a broader conceptualization of the life circumstances made by the individual—that is, the other meanings he is intending at the time. A premise in which pencil markings are part of the organization (pattern)—such as the realization, "I must get a note off to my stockbroker"—brings about the instrumentality of pencil writing in short order. The person might not even say this to himself, but simply picture himself drafting a note to his broker (image as a premise). However, granting this premising necessity, the purpose of the pencil will be actualized in the total pattern (the full meaning) of a person's intentional behavior.

Therefore we must distinguish between action and understanding intentions. If we think of the purpose of a concept as the *aim of the meaning* involved, not all purposes are aimed at overt action even though they *do* play a role in behavior. If we walk into an attractive room, we might be impressed by the decor without necessarily expounding on this pleasant experience. Or we glance out the window while typing letters to friends and see a robin searching for worms on our lawn. This momentary experience is most assuredly meaningful for some of us, but there is nothing called for in this understanding-intention that requires an action-intention on our part. The meanings here of *robin, grass, worm, nature,* and so forth are part of our experience but they need not relate directly to our ongoing letter typing.

In other circumstances the conceptual understanding afforded by telosponsive intelligence does relate to overt behavior. We must leave the room in order to go to our appointed destination and "there is the door." Doors as conceptual items have purposes, hence we behave "for the sake of" this door-purpose and leave the room through an action-intention. Based on our recognition above that dialectical changes take place only when a pattern alters, the present analysis suggests that meaning—an organizational conception *par excellence*—only bears on overt behavioral changes over time when the total emerging pattern calls for it. This pattern can be properly-understood only through an introspective perspective theoretical analysis of the behaving human being.

For example, not every statement made on the order of "I intend to do that" results in the end that has been projected. People aspire to college degrees who never complete their first semester of study, even though they had sincerely intended to do so. There are many reasons why this inability to actualize the aim of the meaning *higher education* comes about, and we do not wish to oversimplify things, but clearly not until we know what the individual really *was* intending can we take every statement as expressed in a literal sense. In the same way that recognizing and naming (intending) a pencil does not mean the person will necessarily actualize the pencil's purpose in behavior, so too just because the person stipulates the intention to achieve some end in life does not mean that he will actualize the purposive meaning of the words "I intend to complete college." This may simply be an understanding-intention and not an action-intention, or even as an action-intention, it might never be carried to the complete end projected.

What then determines when an intention—action or otherwise—will really eventuate in the goal projected? We will be elaborating on this issue throughout the remaining pages of this volume, but surely a good point at which to begin formulating an answer would be by looking at the totality of purposivity in the individual's psychic outlook. Along with questions of native endowment, physical health, and unforeseen setbacks, there well may be telic factors at variance with college success—such as "I intend to earn my way in college by working 60 hours weekly in an all-night restaurant" or "I expect college to be about as easy to get through as high school, which only called for a few minutes of preparation daily." Looked at totally, such ancillary intentions might be militating against successful completion of college. Without intending to fail, the person might be intending behaviors that will ensure failure.

Even if the premising purpose is quite clear—for example, seeing with one's own eyes that "the door is over there"—we are still prepared to call this a premise—as opposed to, for example, a fact of reality. We thus draw a sharp distinction between the way in which humans telospond and the contents of the premises on the basis of which they do so. Whether something exists independent of the premise and whether it is accurately framed in the premise is totally irrelevant to the dynamics of telosponsivity. One of the great misunderstandings of teleology in psychology is that a telic account supposedly deals with ends that literally exist or eventually happen in the future. In Chapter 6 (p. 263) we attributed something like this to Skinner's position, noting that he fell into this erroneous conception because of a confound between efficient and final causation. But the teleologist does not have to put his goals as literally existing down the road of time or as supposedly drawing the human being to them through a force of suction from out of the future (which is tantamount to a "reversed" efficient cause). Future goals, like present sightings of doorways, *both* come into play at the point of a premise—that is, encompassed in the meaning taken on. The process, "for the sake of this, that follows," stamps a mentality as telic, *not* the fact that it has future goals or expectations in mind toward which it works.

Another suggestion in the above definition is that some premises

that the individual might take on are removed from clear understanding—for example, in the case of dream contents (symbols, etc.).
This leaves open the possibility of dualities in consciousness or a
conscious-unconscious "split" in mind. Nothing in the concept of
telic behavior would contradict the possible role of unconscious
influences in behavior. Many dream interpretations are overdrawn
analogies on the part of imaginative analysts, but there are also
valid examples of a dream symbol serving a purpose in the context
of meanings as understood by the individual concerned (i.e., reflecting his understanding-intentions but in a more analogical fashion,
distorted by dialectical oppositionality, and so forth). By taking the
proper introspective perspective and being sensitive to this idiographic meaning complex, a premising attitude at variance with the
conscious outlook of the person may well be discernible. Dialecticians are not stymied by the fact that people hold contradictory
views on life.

There are three more descriptive terms to define before a complete accounting of the telosponse has been rendered. The first has
to do with the fact that a premise comes first, containing some
meaningful item; and then flowing from this as meaning-extensions,
we have the possibility of intentional behavior developing. It has
been customary to speak of the "firsts" or "befores" in psychology
as *antecedents* and the "seconds" or the "afters" as *consequents*
(see Chapter 6, p. 245). However, due to the identification of
antecedent-consequent with the time dimension we have found it
desirable to use the terms *precedent* and *sequacious* to describe the
order of telosponsive events. These terms make reference to the
ordering of meanings, and they are totally outside the time dimension except in the sense that as terms which describe *order* they
could well imply "sooner" and "later," as by analogy between the
ordering of meanings and the presumed flow of time.

A *precedent* meaning is one that goes before others in order or arrangement and establishes the course and nature of the meanings which follow
it. Though it is often manifested first on the time dimension, a precedent
meaning is not to be thought of as related to or a function of time passage.
Order, not time flow, identifies the precedent meaning.

A *sequacious* meaning is one that follows or flows from the meanings of
precedents, extending these in a *necessary* sense according to the principle
of tautology. Though often manifested second on the time dimension, a
sequacious meaning is not to be thought of as dependent upon time flow.
Order, not location in time, identifies sequacious meanings, which are
always slavishly compliant to the meanings established by precedents.

We now see that the premise is brought to bear as a fixed precedent meaning, which in turn influences the sequacious meanings that may develop as the individual advances on life. His concepts (which have purposes) are more than simply predeterminers of meanings; they literally create the sequacious line of meaning-extension which is constantly taking place in life. Human beings are not shaped or otherwise conditioned via past mediators into quasi-intentional animals (see Chapter 5). Humans are intentional organisms by fundamental nature because meanings flow from precedent to sequacious orderings. There is always more meaning in a precedent than initially grasped or circumscribed. There is always a further implication, suggestion, possibility, negation, and so forth, which the sequacious line of meaning-extension in human reason necessarily (telic determinism) enlarges upon. Thus we find that human beings constantly look for the relevance, portent, or significance of life events, often terming these insights, omens, hunches, lucky developments, and so on. The bipolarity of meaning fosters such lines of development, because given that we grasp the precedent X, we must immediately open up the possibilities: So what? or What next? or Well, sometimes not-X might happen too. A precedent meaning is impossible without a sequacious line of development following, although admittedly sometimes the implications are carried out in the dream world. Because we want to emphasize the fact that precedent premises are conceptual (formal-final cause) determinants taking place outside of time it is helpful to speak of the protopoint in this sequence, as follows:

The *protopoint* is always the first point in an ordering of meanings, although it may itself be predicated by other (including unnamed precedent) meanings. We use the term *protopoint* to emphasize that this is the first ordering in a line of meaning-extension or development *without* reference to the passage of time. Premises are brought to bear at protopoints, acting as precedents, and are then tautologized as sequacious meaning-extensions in the course of telosponsivity.

The survey of Table 1 taught us that scholars across history have tried to name the precedents to their current thinking, which was often found to be a sequacious line of development from some highly abstract universal. Plato reified these precedent meanings in his realm of Being. The ideal of universal lawfulness in science also takes inspiration from this search for an overriding precedent which sequaciously determines all else. Whether human beings will ever rise intellectually to name a protopoint level so abstract yet determinately relevant to *all* of thought or experience is an open question.

Most modern thinkers have rejected this possibility, believing as they do that the ladder of abstract conceptualization has no ceiling.

We must not equate such meaning-extension with *deduction*. It is tempting to see in our formulations a justification solely for deductive reasoning, particularly because premises are usually put in the deductive syllogistic frame of "major-premise *to* minor-premise *to* conclusion." Though this is entirely consistent with our theory of meaning-extension, we must not forget that *induction* also demands a precedent meaning-frame "for the sake of which" a generalization is then made. Inductive reasoning is just as premised as is deductive reasoning. The question of paradigms discussed in Chapter 5 is concerned with the inductive possibilities open to one based upon the precedent meanings encompassed in his paradigm. One does experiments to fill out a precedent paradigm in normal science (Kuhn, 1970, p. 23) *not* because this is a peculiarity of the scientific enterprise, but because this is a reflection of the *general human tendency* to extend meanings both inductively and deductively according to a sequacious line of development.

Cognitive Association versus Conceptualization in Human Behavior

By introducing the construct of telosponsivity in human behavior we are seemingly returning to the pre-Galilean form of thought mentioned at the outset of this chapter, and this has particular relevance to the concept of motion in behavior. In the ancient view—for example, as typified in the philosophy of Aristotle—a precedently fixed order was postulated and then all sequaciously derived motions to be seen in nature were presumed to be aimed at restoring this harmony in organization (Frank, 1957, Chapter 4). The order was separate and distinct from the motion, but it determined the course of the motion. This preexisting fixedness was also to be seen in Euclidian geometry, where motion was not conceived as directly in the nature of a spatial distribution of lines and points. A point was defined as that which has no part, and a straight line was then readily seen as the direct distance between two such points. Points and lines were thus separate and distinct conceptions.

This view sufficed through the medieval period, but as noted in Chapter 1 (p. 47), with the advent of Cartesian geometry Newton succeeded in joining mathematics to motion in his assumption that a body (a point) which is not obstructed by another will move with a constant speed along a straight line into the infinite (Burtt, 1955, pp. 208 and 240). As a naive realist, Newton viewed all natural objects in this fashion, so that if a pattern existed in reality, it had to have been fixed in the material substrate of nature or, if manufactured by human effort, the result of modifying and altering the unidirectionality of motion into the observed pattern. Newton was not trying to explain human behavior, of course, but this general style of explanation takes us directly to the behavioristic assumption that behavior flows over time and then *secondarily* gets its patterning after a manipulated intervention. There is growing recognition in recent years of the importance of organization in mental activities such as memory, but the definitions advanced continue to stress the mediational process. For example, Voss (1972) defined organizational processes which supposedly result in memorial clusters, "chunks," or concepts as follows: "Organization is a process that intervenes between input and output in such a way that input is increased in its systematization and in such a way that there is not a 1:1 input-output relation" (p. 176). The basic idea of an individual altering or influencing the order of input to output is compatible with the present chapter's arguments, but the unidirectional (demonstrative) view of behavior reflected in this extraspective mediational model leaves all of our questions raised in Chapter 5 unanswered.

Because our view of the human being emphasizes predicating rather than mediating abilities, we propose that mentation be viewed in terms of the ability to conceptualize life experience. A *conceptualization* does not intervene, but actively creates by organizing experience from the outset (i.e., from the protopoints of mentation). Though the reader may believe that the present chapter is developing a cognitive theory, the writer would prefer to think of it as a conceptual theory of behavior, because as we saw in Chapter 5, the modern usage of *cognition* has been preempted by the Lockean-model advocates. In the style of Kant, we are now suggesting that input *itself* is precedently framed, ordered, patterned, clustered, and so on, and rather than simply intervening, such conceptualizations make the input aspects of mentation possible in the first instance.

Returning to the historical view of motion, there is more evidence for precedent organization in the thinking of Newton than the first law of motion might suggest. To relate his concept of motion to some (precedent) standard against which an object could (sequaciously) be said to move, Newton accepted the idea of absolute space, which amounts to the system of fixed stars (Frank, 1957, p. 106). Some of the Newtonians based motion on a change of location in relation to a fixed mass of "ether" (Kondo, 1969, p. 38). The logical necessity here is the same in both cases: If something is said to move, it must be said to do so in relation to a fixed standard. What Einstein and other physicists did was to challenge this notion of an absolute space (ether theory was discarded on several counts). Suppose that we have two planets, both seeming to move in a straight line relative to each other, as Newton would have it, but far out in space where there are no fixed star coordinates within which to base our claim that motion is taking place. These two planets are passing by each other and drawing farther and farther apart as we observe them. Now, which planet is moving? Are both planets moving? There is no way to answer such questions, for the motion of one body must be judged against the other. Either or both planets could be moving in relation to some third point acting as a (fixed) standard.

Does this mean that Einstein's theory of relativity could do without an anchoring of some sort against which to assess concepts of space, time, and motion? No. He too needed a precedent standard against which to sequaciously develop relational ties of object to object in a relative sense, and he found this in the (constant) speed of light (186,000 miles per second). A similar necessity for human reason to be anchored or grounded in fixity is to be seen in Heisenberg's Principle of Indeterminacy. Looked at psychologically, this amounts to a recognition that if we precedently take an interest in (the meaning of) an electron's position, we sequaciously influence (the meaning of) its velocity and vice versa (Feuer, 1974, p. 176). Hence the speed and direction of an electron are intrinsically (organizationally) related!

What does all of this teach us? For one thing, it suggests that when Newton formulated his laws of motion, laws which were subsequently to track literal events in observed reality, he was *not* basing these on motion over time but on motion *as conceptualized* within what we have termed at other points in this volume (see Chapter 1, p. 48, and Table 1) mathematical space (space without literal extensionality so that motion is *not* literally occurring). Just as one can think of a straight line or circle without introducing a time factor—that is, these forms are visualized "all at once"—so too can one visualize a straight line or a circle being defined by a *moving* point (the Cartesian geometric innovation). But note: We have the *form* of these images in mind precedently, and the moving point is incidental to a description of the form ultimately defined by its motion. Trying to visualize a moving point without putting it in some patterned form is difficult, but who would claim that once a pattern emerges in the imagined moving point, the initial motion of the point is what created the pattern? So although in actual lived reality Newtonian physics *did* accept the laws of (efficient-cause) motion as primary and the (formal-cause) patternings in events as secondary, in the *psychological conceptualizations* of the human being named Newton we see quite a different ordering taking place. Considered psychologically, Newtonian motion is a formal-cause construct first (where geometric relations are assumed) and an efficient-cause construct second (where moving points trace out the precedent geometric forms sequaciously).

The second lesson is comparably psychological, for it speaks to the question of how human beings apply their intentions. Even should we wish to view the person as behaving via what is called a free will, this *cannot* mean free from the necessity of framing his understanding in some way. As Kant appreciated, to understand is to ground one's judgments within a fixed frame (categories of the understanding). Telic determination results *after* such grounding takes place. We understand (limit the alternatives concerning) which of our two planets moves after we have framed the grounds against which we can (meaningfully) relate them. If we want to describe the mind as capable of willing (free) alternatives, this theoretical account will have to be done in light of the fact that mentality *also* works within a fixed and unchanging (determinate!) framework.

The Conservative Role of Meaning and Mind on the Time Dimension

Now that we have a few new terms we can define *mind* and then consider several topics that relate to mental activity. The procedure we follow—as is true of all instructive efforts—is first to put down precedent terminology which then sequaciously extends the meaning encompassed therein to subsequent arguments. Taking the premise of our terminology, the meanings which then flow (extend) do so *necessarily*. To discredit the line of development one must discredit the premising terminology.

A Definition of Mind

Considering the generations of dispute in psychology over this issue, not to mention the centuries of philosophical debate, to propose a definition of mind may be both foolhardy and impertinent. However, we cannot hope to promote a humanistic science by avoiding this technical requirement. This is *not* something that can be dealt with methodologically. We face a theoretical issue here, and, theoretical formulations can always be changed if they prove uninstructive. Our definition of *mind* would be:

Mind is the innate capacity to telospond in relation to patterns of meaning in experience as well as to create these patterns anew through dialectical reasoning. Patterns of meaning are conceptualized through purely sensory experience such as seeing figural shapes, hearing rhythmic sounds, feeling symptomatically, and so on, but they are also the essence of mentation, orient the patterning of precedent-sequacious meaning-extensions, and thereby constitute the rational order of logic as well as the illogic of sophistry. Mind is fundamentally conservative, so that the flux of experience is fixed at the protopoint in conceptual premises which are then tautologized through telosponsivity in upcoming experience. The patterned effort to fix experience into certainty or knowledge is called thinking, and the conceptualizations employed are called ideas.

The humanist customarily argues—and we have so argued at various points in this volume—that human mentality is an *active* process. Yet in the above definition we claim that mind serves a conservative role on the time dimension, trying in this sense to keep things constant, certain, *known*. To appreciate what is meant we must focus on the premising protopoint, for it is here that the active intellect takes root. To *conceptualize* is to put a frame (order, organization, etc.) onto experience, and as such, the frame *fixes* that which can be known—at least insofar as the frame has what William James (1952) called a "cash value" in its organization. George Kelly's (1955) personal constructs or Kuhn's (1970) paradigms reflect this same tendency for organization to precede the behaviors made possible by the conceptualization afforded. This is the conservative tendency of mind—that is, to fix a knowing premise and extend thereby the range of understanding (Kuhn), predictability (Kelly), or practicality (James).

The reference to innate capacities for telosponsivity should not be taken as some kind of innate-ideas theory in the Lockean vein (see our discussion in Chapter 2, pp. 91–92). What is held to be innate is the capacity to recognize or create patterns (meanings), and when in due time the conceptualizations resulting achieve a certain organization, we can speak of them as ideas or idea-units. We therefore follow the Kantian interpretation of ideas as *pro forma* causes of organization rather than as *tabula rasa* effects of (input) organization.

Dialectic as a Logic of Implication, and, Affirmation

To qualify as a genuine teleology a theory must allow for the possibility of behavior to occur in an *arbitrary* fashion. The term arbitrary has been so identified with unreasonableness and caprice that one might erroneously believe it refers to unpremised behavior. Yet what arbitrariness actually signifies is that the grounds for the sake of which behavior is telosponded have shifted. For example, after claiming that no partiality would be shown in hiring practices, an employer places on his payroll a clearly unqualified family member. This is an arbitrary move, in which the grounds of impartiality have been superseded by some unnamed "blood is thicker than water" assumption. To find the precedents of arbitrary actions may be difficult, particularly because they often have such personal involvements, but they are present if we are privy to all of the thinking involved in an individual's actions.

Where does this capacity for arbitrariness in behavior come from? Is it due to the functioning of discriminative mediational aids or to the operation of a variable ratio in the contingent reinforcement circumstances of each situation? The present view would trace it to the human's dialectical intelligence, which always sees a myriad of possibilities in the continually arising experiences of life. Mind works within this flux of possibility and seeks to stabilize it in conceptual regularities. There is a sense of personal control in such stabilization, even if the order applied is inconsistent. Dialectical orders are not necessarily consistent because the bipolarity of meaning suggests alternatives at every turn. One might think of dialectic as a logic of implication. There is always more in sensory experience than meets the conceptual eye.

This quality of open alternatives in experience demands that the human being affirm some protopoint meaning at the outset for the sake of which behavior might then take place (telosponsivity). We can define *affirmation* as a telosponse in which one pole of a bipolar conception is precedently framed (held to be the case, presumed, believed in, chosen, etc.). Affirmation also encompasses the framing of meaningful unipolarities in sensory experience by tautological means. ("That is that." "That is a tree." "I recognize that face.") This affirmative necessity is another one of those active roles assigned to mind by humanists, because which pole of a bipolarity is affirmed or which item of unipolar experience is singled out for identification is up to the individual and *not* to the environment (see discussion of decision-making below). But having affirmed some premise, the individual has possibilities of affirming other premises at the same time. Indeed, it is often *necessary* that he see such alternative possibilities for affirmation due to the reverse meanings of a dialectical dimension of meaning (i.e., an implication which occurs to him via dialectical insight).

Why is it likely that the individual reasoner *will* see the reverse implications to his affirmations in a dialectical complex of meanings? *Because the dialectical relationship in this case is tautological!* Affirming one pole of a dialectical relationship tautologizes with the meaning at its opposite pole. Jung's (1953, pp. 65–66) treatment of the personal unconscious is much like this, in that what is affirmed behaviorally as persona and ego in consciousness dialectically defines what is implied as a potentially conscious behavior in the unconscious as an opposite identity—the shadow complex. Recall from Chapter 3 (p. 128) that Freud's very first theoretical attempt to explain the neuroses—long before he could be called a psychoanalyst—relied upon a similar idea. Referring to antithetic ideas and a counter will in the psyche, Freud (1966, p. 124) argued that whenever we intend to do one thing ("I must be quiet") the antithetic idea springs to mind ("I won't succeed, I'll make a noise") and that in neurotics this latter, reverse affirmation takes over because of fatigue and other unknown factors. There is a remarkable similarity here between Freud's explanation of hysterical symptoms and Jung's account of complex formation, with both theories relying on the surfacing of such reverse affirmations in overt behavior.

But the opposite of every affirmation is not necessarily *ipso facto* made into an unconscious premise. We are often only too aware that our behavior is arbitrary and that we *could* be proceeding according to a different logical position, attitude, or even lifestyle. Why we do not behave more inconsistently than we do is an involved question. One of the primary roles of mentality is to find stable grounds as so-called reasons for why we behave as we do. The same human nature that prompts us to search for precedent universals (Table 1) prompts us to ground behavioral patterns in reasoned or principled actions. Even when there may be no apparent reason for behavior, the human being would often like to know "Why did I do that?" The framing of reasons for behavior reflects an effort on the part of the human being to find the stable, recurring, predictable patterns of existence. And reasoning, or to reason, is in part an effort to find such grounds for the sake of which it can be said that things happen or behaviors occur. This effort could well help stabilize behavior as the person then continues to behave for the sake of such reasons (grounds).

Our definition of *affirmation* is consistent with the classical logical problem of affirming the antecedent or consequent of an *If . . . then . . .* proposition, which played such a central role in the arguments of Chapter 5 (p. 181). There is a precedent-sequacious relation within these propositions, because antecedents always frame consequents. We also have the bipolarity of antecedent and consequent, either of which may be affirmed in the course of reasoning (*sans* time). Specific contents are put into this organizational frame, so that rather than saying, "If antecedent, then consequent," we say "If a man, then a mortal." But the logical frame is still dialectical and which pole here is affirmed determinately influences what can be concluded as a necessity (precedent-to-sequacious) and what can be merely held to as a belief short of conviction.

Terms like *belief* and *conviction* signify the confidence we have in our affirmations. It is as if the human intelligence, knowing intuitively of the bipolarities in meanings, requires this sense of conviction as a reflection of its tautologizing nature. To hold to a factual belief is more reassuring than to confront life on the basis of premises that are "merely" opinion or hypothetical. Yet the present view would suggest that, psychologically considered, the only real difference between the hypothetical and the factual is this sense of conviction achieved through the exercise of an evidential test which is somewhat different mentation from theory. The hankering after truth is due to the recognition that we do *not* know assuredly that which we affirm in one side of a dialectical opposition. The so-called need for faith (religious or otherwise) is similarly an effort to believe in something that *ought* to be true, no matter what the provable facts may dictate. All such human behaviors reflect the important role of conviction in mental life—another form of fixedness reflecting the conservative role of mind on the time dimension.

Conceptualization as Memory

Concepts of mind have always been closely tied to the role of memory in intelligence. The Lockean theorist, viewing ideas as receptacles, is prone to speak of "memory stores" (Kintsch, 1970, p. 142) in which the material input can be retained for a short-term or long-term period. When subjects are then found to organize their learnable items the Lockean theorist is likely to interpret this organizing capacity as a learned intervening process coming between input and output. One cannot properly name historical developments in less than a generation of time passage, but the writer feels that the reason we find the term *cognitive* virtually preempted by mechanistic theories today—that is, theories which found this term anthropomorphic in the 1930s and 1940s (see Chapter 5)—is because the vast preponderance of evidence has made it clear that human beings *do* organize their so-called input information, and hence a formal-cause emphasis in human learning theories was inescapable.

The present theoretical account of memory follows directly from our view of conceptualization, because it should make no difference whether the stabilizing role of mind is brought to bear in the present, to orient the future, or to turn around and look to the past. In both cases conceptualization at the protopoint and precedent-sequacious meaning-extension takes place. Experience is always more fraught with such logical considerations than classical sensation and perception theory has implied. We now attempt to provide a beginning theory of how logical considerations of inference (implication) enter into both original experience with objects in experience and, thereby, with the memory of such objects.

Limiting our example to visual memory, we begin by observing that visual perception, far from being a question of *tabula-rasa* input, is a matter of *pro-forma* conceptualization involving predications and inferences from the outset. Thus as infants, we all simply infer that the visual field on either side of our eyeblinks is tautologically identical without being taught to do so. This need not be the case, of course, because an apparatus is possible that could slip in a highly similar but not identical picture during the fraction of a second needed to blink one's eye. Yet in the "postblink" (sequacious) position we would simply presume that the pattern observed in the "preblink" position was identical (experienced as a continuation of the precedent pattern). Even in our very first looks at life we are, due to the continuing inferences made concerning the identity of that which is perceived, reconceptualizing our visual field again and again. In one sense we never simply conceptualize anything but always reconceptualize that which we perceive (usually called recognition). In the *act* of placing such fixed identities onto experience we come to know it. Of course the inferences made in such reconceptualization takes place so quickly or concurrently with our visual awareness that we do not think of this time lapse across eyeblinks as a problem in *memory*. However, assume now that we were to extend this lapse of time period across conceptualization or reconceptualization (we use these two terms interchangeably in the remaining pages of this volume). We would *ipso facto* be confronted with the question of so-called memory retention over short or long time periods (Kintsch, 1970).

But we have argued that tautologies function outside of time. What then would be involved in the accuracy of reconceptualizations, either here in the present moment as we look at something before us or as we try to recapture it from a more distant past? Logical learning theory would suggest that we consider this in terms of the relationship between just how reconceptualization at the protopoint was carried out as a precedent, making possible in turn a sequacious meaning-extension to the past—termed *memory*. How much actual organization was framed initially in the conceptualization (the more organization, the richer the meaning-extension, hence the better the memory, etc.)? What other premises are currently being affirmed by the individual in his memory efforts, and how well do these coalesce (pattern) with the organization being sought in recall?

Perfect visual memory would be like standing at a window and verbally describing what one sees on the other side. Yet even if one were to do this, there would be a host of bipolar meanings calling for affirmation in the scene observed on the other side of the windowpane. Hence, if a third party were to (extraspectively) test the accuracy of one's perception in the present, he could well disagree on the essential affirmations of what was being reported as observed through the window. This would not be taken as a problem in memory, of course, because it would be conducted in the immediate present. But what if the person were asked to describe yesterday's window scenes today? The (extraspective) observer might indeed attribute one's arbitrary reconceptualizations to some *failure* in memory.

One might argue that in the typical learning experiment the subject has to meet a criterion of learning, so that the experimenter has assured himself that the subject does indeed see what the experimental task demands that he see. Hence any memory deficit in this previously learned criterion is a real loss and not simply a question of some problem with the original conceptualization. Yet precisely how a subject manages to achieve the experimental learning criterion is not always clear and it need not even mean that he *has* learned anything in the sense of conceptualization. For example, if a subject *now knows* some mnemonic scheme that he can precedently bring to bear as heuristic aid, he might achieve the experimenter's learning criterion (sic) without having learned anything about the material being organized by his already extant mnemonic device. The items the experimenter presumed *were* seen by the subject might have no meaning (not really seen) without this predicating mnemonic scheme.

We can concretize the speculative argument now under development as follows: Assume that there are two points on the time dimension, with A taking place before B. Something takes place at point A, and the individual who witnesses this occurrence is asked to recall it at point B. According to the present view, what A would mean to the individual *at* time A would depend upon the precedent meanings he had affirmed and telosponded to. That is, if a purpose had been intended in the understanding of the individual at A, this would ensure that a precedent-sequacious line of meaning-extension would occur, and therefore the likelihood of recalling the incident would be high. As we have suggested above, memory is tied to the sequacious extension of meanings affirmed as precedents. Binswanger (1963) would suggest that the individual at point A endowed his experience with meaning, and such meanings then frame subsequent reconceptualizations as memories. For perfect memory to occur the individual would have to affirm the *identical* premise at point B. Anything short of this tautological identity across premises at points A and B adversely affects the individual's memory (reconceptualization).

Such tautological identities are difficult to draw across times A and B because circumstances change, so that what has followed in life always influences the grounds for the sake of which one telosponds, both forward *and* backward in time. The meaningful relation between the individual and what he has been asked to recall at B may be lacking or be purely incidental to what he had been intending at A. This is what the gestaltists felt was involved in the Hoffding function (Koffka, 1935, p. 561). Very often the organization resulting from telosponsivity at A has been reoriented or dropped altogether because it was not useful or instructive to the individual as he came to order his life in the intervening period (James's cash value thesis). Finally, memory itself is always inferential, so that just as we distort what is seen presently, we must of necessity distort what we are asked to see in the past.

The Psycho-Logic of Language and the Mind-Body Problem

Our arguments rest heavily upon the concept of meaning and how extensions of meaning may be said to occur in human experience—

bringing more and more of such experience under the range of convenience of some given conceptualization. We have the relational ties of meaning extending tautologically in a precedent-sequacious fashion, and in certain contexts a dialectical opposition as a tautology enters to make diversity out of identity (many in one). Symbols as precedents are expressive of meaning like this because of the analogical variation of the tautology permitting something to stand for something else, to capture the essence of what it is like, but not exactly. The logic of dialectical implication can even turn the "is" into the "is not" in a dream sequence or possibly the supposedly illogical thinking of a psychotic person. To speculate on such matters without confronting the inevitable role of language in human behavior is difficult, and thus we must consider the relationship between what we have called our "psycho-logical" theory of behavior and the human's use of language. We do this even as we recognize that telosponsivity is *not* limited to verbal behavior. Images and affective assessments can act as protopoint premises to influence behavioral patterns in a telic fashion (see Chapter 8).

The Lockean theorists Dollard and Miller (1950) give language a major role in bringing about that human form of behavior known as logic (using the term now in its exclusively demonstrative sense —that is, without regard for the possibility of a dialectical logic). Language (words, sentences, etc.) is another way of speaking about the cue-producing response in mediation (*ibid.*, p. 87), and an individual who lacks such mediational aides is at the mercy of environmental events without being capable of discriminating the useful from the nonuseful. He is likely to behave inconsistently and reflect a "lack of conformity to the rules of logic" (*ibid.*, p. 220). The correction for this state of affairs is proper learning of language, as new input (*ibid.*, pp. 45–46). This view of language as the input materials on which logical orderings are said to depend is another source of the claim made by humanists that mechanists assign no active role to mind. Rather than placing language first and mind second, the humanist believes that mind comes first and language is itself a reflection of the logical patterning of mind. This is, of course, a variation on the theme discussed at the outset of this chapter concerning the proper location of pattern in the changing sequences of behavior. Language reflects the order of mind; it does not make this order possible.

Even a superficial study of word roots and slang expressions teaches one that words are products of the tautological (analogical, metaphorical) capacities of the human mind (via meaning-extensions). The word *attic* devolves from the style of ancient Grecian architecture in Attica. The word *chauvinism* has its basis in an analogy drawn to Nicolas Chauvin, whose showy patriotism and attachment to Napoleon delineates the meaning of this word today as an excessive commitment to one political point of view. The affective side of meaningfulness is reflected here, as it is even more crudely in the slang word *shyster*, which takes meaning from the German-Yiddish word for excrement! Psycho-logically considered, there is no difference between the meaning-extension of a word, relying as it does on some precedent concept which sequaciously extends to other referents (enriching them with this meaning) and the abstract precedents searched for by the thinkers cited in Table 1. The historical thinkers worked back from sequacious extensions to find the abstract precedents, but the general structure of meaning is the same. Both such abstract conceptions and the humblest words bring forward meanings as symbolical expressions, as dialectical implications, or as the grounds for the sake of which further understanding is made humanly possible.

The present view therefore holds that a word is coined to express something—the precedent-sequacious line of development—and it subsequently is used as a convention. That which it expresses is a patterned order (meaning), and this order again comes precedently to engender the coining of the word. Words—maybe most words used by people—lose their precise designation in actual language expression. We have all been surprised by the correct meaning of certain words we use routinely. Most of us fumble along in generalities without grasping the precise meaning of words used by others as well as by ourselves. This is possible because of our analogical capacities to take the circumstances of a communicated statement into consideration and therefore understand (intend) the purpose of another person's statements and vice versa. Hence, even if we do not understand the complete usage or realize that certain usages are literally incorrect but still globally descriptive by strained analogy, we can continue a conversation. Of course misunderstandings also result from such analogical (vague) discourse.

None of this is an argument against the fact that words *follow* logical implications (meaning-extensions). Humans are symbolizing animals because they are tautologizing animals. Mind orders experience through affirming premises at a protopoint and extending tautologically thereby the meaning of the premise to include those experiences that sequaciously follow. This is why in a certain sense *we can only know what we already know!* This theoretical outlook represents a logical and not a sensory phenomenology (Rychlak, 1973, pp. 203 and 513–514). The gestalt psychologists—Wertheimer, Köhler, and Koffka—thought of the Kantian categories of understanding as sensory frames (see Chapter 4). In opposing themselves to Lockeanism the gestaltists took an interest in how humans literally see, hear, and orient themselves by way of native physical equipment to experience reality. But because the gestaltists lacked a dialectical formulation in their construct of proximal stimulation (which might have been thought of as a protopoint needing organizing by mind) there was no real arbitrariness in their theories of mentation. Visual experience as brain physiology itself followed gestalt laws of organization. Since we speak of *grounds* for the sake of which decisions are made in telosponding, the reader may think that the present theory is a form of sensory phenomenology akin to gestalt psychology, which made much of the figure-ground construct. Actually this would be an incorrect characterization.

As a *logical* phenomenology, the present theory considers the Kantian frames of reference (the grounding categories) to function at the level of mind *qua* mind, which is not a process needing housing within the brain structure. The so-called mind-body problem arises in psychology because of the traditional reductive strategies of natural science in which there is an effort to bring all things down to some material- and efficient-cause substrate. A parallel here can be drawn to the phenomenal experience of color vision. We know that colors do not exist *in* things but in our perception of various wave lengths as reflected by the things we perceive. Yet who would deny that as a logical ordering in phenomenal experience things surely are taken as if they were indeed colored. Grass *is* green (to those not color blind), and to stumble onto a field of orange-colored grass would most assuredly upset the logical arrangement within which we move each day. Have the findings on color's source in any way affected the findings of naive experience as ordered according to color? Doubtless our grasp of scientific principles would temper our alarm if a field of orange grass were suddenly to materialize. We would look for possible atmospheric disturbances, or contaminations that might have bent our light source to alter coloration, or whatever.

But the altered meaning of *orange-colored grass* is incidental to the phenomenal necessity of reordering (reconceptualizing) experience according to the perceived coloration. Even when we find the physical reason accounting for the aberration we continue to order and reorder according to the experience of coloration with which our quandary had begun. Nothing has changed, for the logic of fixed color arrangements continues to order our experience regardless of what explanations we arrive at for any changes observed. This is like retaining the structure of a syllogism even though the specific terms we place into this frame as contents can change (see Wittgenstein's propositional variable in Table 1). The question of mind is a comparable one. We must look for the organizing capacities of mind *not* in the architectonic structure of the brain nor in the pattern of electrical firing of neurons in the brain, but in the logic of experience *as* organized, *as* conceptualized, *as* framed meaningfully—which are different ways of expressing the same thing. The mind need not follow the brain, because as a dialectical process, its ordering can be diametrically opposed to the demonstratively framed brain structures (see Penfield, 1975, for clinical-experimental evidence supporting this suggestion; see also Chapter 11, pp. 485–486). Mind is logic, both demonstrative and dialectical logic *in action*. We therefore suggest that the present view is a logical phenomenology, one that recognizes the physical or "body" side to experience but does not expect to find the realm of meaning-extension in such palpabilities except insofar as they enter as meaningful premises into the organizing reconceptualizations of mind (i.e., as contents within these reconceptualizations).

How can psychological science have a mind concept floating above the body in this dualistic fashion, as if it were a stable "meatless" organization directing the palpable cells of the brain "from above" like some grand spiritual force? Tough-minded psychologists dearly love to paint theorists who would see mind independent of body in this manner as misdirected clerics, searching for a concept of soul in the wrong circles. Yet to find theoretical justification for mental conceptualization as something other than brain structure is not difficult if we but add the dialectical conception to the theory of organic evolution. We saw in Chapter 6 how Skinner has used Darwinian theory to justify his operant-contingency theories (p. 261). To see dialectical reasoning as having evolved, through mutation or whatever, to turn the human being back on nature and allow him to affect that environment that used to mold him so exclusively is equally plausible.

As the mechanists now claim, up to some point in the evolutionary ladder an animal may have behaved entirely demonstratively, including following the input-mediation-output sequence at the more advanced levels. Insofar as meaning existed for this animal it was exclusively unipolar as a *sign* function in events. But, when the nervous tissue evolved to some needed level of complexity certain animals could recognize (conceptualize) that they were acting out a sequence of behavior which *could go another way*, even in direct opposition to the so-called natural prompting! Indeed the awareness of alternatives *began* in such opposition. At this point meanings of a bipolar nature arose, and the animal became a symbol-creating rather than a sign-mediating organism. Arbitrariness was born! This development removed the animal from a direct (unipolar) dependence on physical substrates, because the meanings germinating in awareness were no longer one to one with brain physiology but were opened by the immense diversity of dialectical possibilities.

This opening of the mind threw its conceptual abilities into disarray, since an awareness now of many different implications in events existed, essentially forcing the animal to affirm some one among the many possible premises available to it. This made innovations in behavior over the course of life more likely. For example, the animal which was being naturally prompted (efficiently caused) to forage for food in trees or alongside a river bank recognized in this *very prompting* (akin to the Hegelian account of inner contradiction) the alternative possibilities of descending to the ground or moving off into a plain away from the river. In other words, the alternative behavior was *not done* serendipitously; the natural selection at this point was *not* achieved gradually; but it could have been done abruptly (Kierkegaardian leap) and with a cognized plan as an intention—a plan suggested from what was occurring to what could be occurring by way of dialectical or oppositional reasoning.

The necessity of having to predicate its behavior was forced onto this animal in order to stabilize its grasp of events which suddenly took on a myriad of possibilities, bringing its identity as decision-maker into the ongoing process of existence as never before. Experience became premised experience, and behavioral arbitrariness was now always possible because the affirmation of premises was not fixed by body tissues alone but relied upon an understanding of external circumstances, including the attitudes and opinions reflected in the behavior of others. The human person is said to be a social animal, but the reason this is so is because the human intelligence absolutely must have a confident premise on which to proceed—that is, to telospond. The social norm is not some grand input likelihood, which gets funneled into the heads of the masses through external manipulations and reinforcements. The social norm is a mutual "that for the sake of which" (premise) employed in common affirmation by all members of a discernible group (small-to-large in number), lending them a common sense of identity and commitment in life. Because of the fact that norms act as premises, some social theorists have been able to speak of group mentalities, as in *Zeit-geists* and so forth (Becker & Barnes, 1952). In a certain sense this formulation is correct, but we must recognize that group intellects, *which bring on group manipulations*, occur because of the *conformity* of human intelligence to the premises which all individuals in a given group take to be collectively advantageous or the "right way" to look at things.

Norms are not poured into human mental receptacles like milk into a glass. The human intelligence is only too quick to seek and conform to what it wants to presume is a normative certainty. The intelligence opened by dialectical alternatives in evolution wants to close again in the (fixed) certainty of the scientifically truest, best, most beautiful, Divinely revealed, least assailable, and so forth, premises imagineable. Once having fixed such a premise in mind the individual is surely *determined*, as if by the proverbial "Law of Nature." But this taking on or conforming to the premises of normative behavior is *not* a reflection of efficient-cause determinism (see Chapter 6, pp. 243–249). Such behavioral controls are purely telic phenomena, reflecting the dialectical development of peoples, moving from one point of advantage to the next, seeking ever to obtain gains over nature, over others, over themselves.

Thus, although John Watson (1913) recognized "no dividing line between man and brute" (p. 158) in founding behaviorism, we now suggest that there *is* a basis for distinguishing between the lower and higher animals. When this dialectically reasoning animal "emerged" in evolution, it was a mixed blessing—as much an involution as an evolution in nature—for this animal had acquired the capacity to turn back on nature and direct rather than be directed by nature's uniform and graduated course. This transcending capacity, which we know as dialectical reasoning, allowed the higher animal for the first time to *create* alternatives by design, alternatives which were not always to the best end so that the phenomenal possibility of error and failure as well as accuracy and success arose. To call this transcendent judgmental capacity a homunculus or to force it into a spiritual phrasing is to construct a straw-man argument. There is nothing spiritual or mysterious in assuming that a realm of understanding relying upon patterned meanings functions through a form of dialectical logic that is not itself effected by some physical cause in the bodily substrate. We must first understand how this logic is reflected in behavior and then examine its role without prejudice.

A Psychological Conception of Free Will

A psychological interpretation of free will is now possible. We emphasize the psychological here, because too often in discussions of freedom questions enter of physical impossibilities, politics, and the like. We are not free to walk through walls, and in certain political environments we are not free to elect our leadership. But these are not proper topics for a psychological analysis. We have seen in Chapter 6 the behavioristic interpretation of freedom, which amounts to saying that if the individual is not under the total control of present stimuli (input) but rather can modify this current influence thanks to the mediational aids of past stimuli (mediators), he is to that extent "free." We found this efficient-cause account wanting and now offer the following definition:

Freedom of the Will: A popular way of referring to the capacity that human beings have dialectically to alter the meaning (pattern, order, logos, etc.) of premises which are affirmed at the protopoint. Once a premise has been affirmed, the precedent-sequacious meaning-extensions may be adhered to by the individual with rigidity ("will power") so that freedom of the will and (soft) determinism are entirely compatible conceptions.

Although the phrase *freedom of the will* is not a technical description of mental action, we feel it has been sufficiently important in the history of thought to define and discuss it quite openly and in the context of our evolving terminology. The concept of freedom here means free to alter (hence determine) the meanings predicated when confronting environmental circumstances. The concept of will has been tied to such telic concepts as wish, purpose, and desire—usually with the implication of a power exerted to attain the desired end (will power), on the order of our action-intention. There is also the idea of a self-directed effort implied so that a willed behavior is not something done aimlessly (although one can forego such willful intention).

Skinner (1971, p. 14) has argued that a free behavior would be one that had no antecedent cause, but this formulation of the question is wrong on at least two counts. First, there are several types of antecedents; therefore if the humanist argues for teleology in behavior, he not only can but must do so based on the play of certain kinds of antecedents (precedents) in behavior (see our discussion in Chapter 6, Table 3, p. 245). Second, and more to the point, *every* exercise of will seems to be prompted by some environmental "thesis" against which the individual now decides or chooses to press a variant "antithesis." This initial thesis is most assuredly a form of cause (patterning of meaning), although it is not *exclusively* an efficient cause. The antithesis arrived at is not made to happen in a unipolar sense, but it is an essential ingredient in the chain of cause-effect for the human involved. The antithesis affirmed could be in direct opposition to the meaning of the thesis or merely be an alternative formulation. Alternatives are always born in the pole of opposition. We do not simply move back and forth between the extremities of two diametric opposites in behavior. There are gradations of alternatives in between.

As noted in the previous section dealing with the evolution of dialectical reasoning, such an emergence would not have occurred without decided environmental circumstances against which or in support of which an affirmation had to be made. Similarly, we probably come upon our personal willful prerogatives in maturation when we confront environmental circumstances within which we feel a personal inclination to contribute to the patternings of meaning. One has to feel the weight of the given before a willful act can be initiated. The alternative projected might simply be an understanding-intention so that we imagine ourselves in a phantasy existence achieving some end not now "in reality." But fantasied acts of freedom are not action-intentions and so remain mere possibilities until actualized.

Even so, the essential requirement here for a theory of free will is that the person does indeed reason dialectically. If so, a precedent premise that *is* affirmed need not be thought of as the *only* affirmation possible (necessarily affirmed). This is what *soft determinism* means—something less than 100% "cause-effect" in the course of behavior when considered in exclusively efficient-cause steps across time. Demonstrative positions have no need of an affirmation construct, because they hold that all premises are themselves input through and carried along exclusively on the basis of efficient causation. They therefore generate a hard determinism, or so-called 100% determinism, in which no freedom is possible in the sense of "free from necessarily affirming one and only one meaning for the sake of which behavior eventuates."

If we trace the roots of hard determinism in the history of thought, we arrive at two sources: see Becker & Barnes (1952) and Rychlak (1968). The first comes from material-cause theories in which something constructed of a material was recognized to necessarily reflect this material's qualities, as in the case of a wooden versus a marble bench or the offspring of a given animal would have the flesh qualities of that animal, and so on (see Chapter 6, p. 245). The second and more important source of a belief in hard determinism issues from *telic* precedents! As noted in Chapter 1 and also in other sections of this volume, the belief in geometric harmony, the faith in natural lawfulness, and even the confidence in accounting for events through reliable cause-effects over time, stems from the theological view that a Perfect God made this, a perfect universe—albeit one in which we do not always understand everything as it was intended to be. If we now apply the teleological theory of behavior being propounded in this chapter, we would describe this theology as follows: God freely decided to create a universe. He affirmed a plan at the protopoint as a precedent premise that in turn sequaciously (*necessarily*) determined what the world and universe would be like. As a Perfect Being did this designing, the laws promulgated were perfect in their *fixed* regularity (conservative function of the divine intellect, which effectively tautologized the regularities to be seen in its creation). Natural laws are the sequacious enactments of the perfection affirmed by the Deity at the protopoint of His creation!

Modern physics has challenged this precedent theological "myth," so that if a contemporary physicist contends that the world of motion *is* 100% determined, he is likely to be accused of projecting religious prejudices onto his area of study. There is no need to assume such hard determinism in modern physics. The paradoxical reverse is to be seen in modern psychology, where if a contemporary psychologist argues *against* 100% determinism and speaks of freedom in behavior, *he* is likely to be accused of projecting religious prejudices (free will) and mythologies onto *his* area of study. The paradox disappears when we realize that both accusations rest upon the possible use of a teleological conception by the scientist in question. If the physicist places his emphasis on the perfection of events, he appears to be reverting to the sequacious directedness of events believed in by earlier thinkers as supposedly following the creative affirmations of a God. If the psychologist places his emphasis on the arbitrary preliminaries *before* such an affirmation is made, he too appears to be reverting to prescientific accounts—accounts which were earlier combined into such theologies as the one conjectured above.

If we get our theories down properly, there is every justification for saying that a psychologically free being becomes rigidly determined once a premise is fixed. There can be material- and efficient-cause determinisms in behavior as well, of course (see Capter 6). What we can do in life is dependent upon our physical capabilities, natural endowments, and so forth. There is no need to dismiss such verities from our psychological accounts, for they clearly limit the meaning contents of the premises that are brought forward in life. But an interpretation of psychic determinism does *not* require a denial of psychic freedom. Skinner (1971, p. 20) is prone to speak of Freud as a determinist, equating his own operant theory with the determinism of psychoanalysis. Yet nothing could be further from the truth.

Freudian theory rests in part on a dialectical conception of mind as capable of affirming more than one premise for the sake of which behavior might then be intended. Through compromises of such differences, a course of symptomatic behavior is arrived at. But—and this is the important point—psychic determinisms directing such behavior are *without doubt* telosponses! Symptoms take on meanings, for they sequaciously reflect the symbolic expression of a precedent fixation point in psychic development (with a repetition compulsion ensuing). Freudian theory is a telic theory (see Chapter 3, pp. 123–132). Although Skinner's theory also brings in telic factors as reinterpreted mechanisms (see Chapter 6, pp. 255–267), the form of determinism elaborated by operant conditioning—as supposedly rooted in the environment rather than in predication—is entirely on the side of efficient causation. Random behavior issues (is emitted), and the environment supposedly patterns it (in that post-Galilean fashion discussed at the outset of this chapter). This is *diametrically opposite* to the view of behavioral determinism held to by Freud (which was more in the spirit of pre-Galilean description, with precedently fixed patterns determining the libidinal flow of mental energy rather than *vice versa!*).

Summary

Chapter 7 opens with a series of new descriptive terms, which are needed to alter the image of human behavior now in primacy in psychology. A Kierkegaardian conception of change is contrasted with the more customary unidirectional view held to today. This dialectical conception is more qualitative than quantitative, placing emphasis on the stationary and the fixed rather than on the fluctuations in events. The psychological principle selected to account for this fixed aspect of experience is the *tautology*, or a relation of identity in meaning. The analogy and metaphor, as relations of likeness (partial identity), are special cases of the tautology. The role of tautology in human reason is fully discussed.

As an alternative to "response" in behavioral description, we present a definition of the *telosponse*, which is the person's taking on (premising) of an item (image, word, judgmental comparison, etc.), relating to a referent acting as a purpose for the sake of which behavior is then intended. Purpose is the aim of the meaning reflected by an item, as in the point of a definition. An intention is the conceptual understanding of a purpose, which can take the form of a determination to actualize this purpose in behavior or not (understanding-intentions versus action-intentions characterize this difference). Concepts have purpose and human beings have intentions. Meaning-extensions take place in human affairs, and how the order of this extension follows a precedent-to-sequacious succession is shown. A *precedent* meaning goes before others in arrangement, and a *sequacious* meaning is one that flows or extends slavishly the meanings of precedents—as implications, inductions, deductions, and so forth. This ordering of meaning-extension is *not* dependent upon time. Precedent meanings are brought to bear as fixed premises, invoked or affirmed at a protopoint. Mind is then defined as an innate capacity to telospond in relation to patterns of meaning in experience.

Mind serves a conservative role on the time dimension in that the flux of experience is fixed at the protopoint as conceptual premises that are then tautologized through telosponsivity in upcoming experience. The patterned effort to fix experience into certainty or "knowledge" is called thinking, and the conceptualizations employed in this regard are called ideas. To conceptualize is thus to put a frame onto experience, and as such, the frame fixes that which can be known. Dialectic is shown to be a logic of implication, as the diversity it affords in the upcoming experiences of human beings demands that they affirm some given premise for the sake of which they then telospond. Dialectical opposites, in which one pole defines its reverse, are special cases of such tautological identity! Terms like *belief* and *conviction* signify the confidence we have in our affirmations.

The problems of memory are then considered in light of conceptualization. Memory is seen as inferential in the same way that sensory perception is inferential. Time passage is not considered a necessary cause of memory recognitions or reconceptualizations. The central problem is that of reconceptualizing at the protopoint so that what flows sequaciously in meaning-extension recaptures the full experience as memory. Various reasons why reconceptualization (recognition, recall) into the past proves difficult to attain are discussed.

We then consider the role of logic in behavior and how some of the logical principles such as tautology play a role in language expression. Language terms (words) are shown to be reflections of precedent-sequacious meaning expression. Logic comes first and language terms follow, *not* as some behaviorists claim, in the reverse order. A speculative argument is presented which traces how dialectical reasoning might have emerged in the course of organic evolution. The chapter closes with a discussion of free will, which is defined as a popular way of referring to the capacity human beings have dialectically to alter the meaning of premises which are affirmed at the protopoint. Once a premise has been affirmed, the precedent-sequacious meaning-extensions may be adhered to by the individual with rigidity so that freedom of the will and (soft) determinism are entirely compatible conceptions.

References

Becker, H., & Barnes, H. E. *Social thought from lore to science* (2 vols.). Washington, D.C.: Harren, 1952.

Binswanger, L. *Being-in-the-world* (trans. and with a critical introduction by J. Needleman). New York: Basic Books, 1963.

Burtt, E. A. *The metaphysical foundations of modern physical science.* Garden City, N.Y.: Doubleday, 1955.

Dollard, J., & Miller, N. E. *Personality and psychotherapy: An analysis in terms of learning, thinking, and culture.* New York: McGraw-Hill, 1950.

Eves, H. *An introduction to the history of mathematics* (3rd ed.). New York: Holt, Rinehart & Winston, 1969.

Feuer, L. S. *Einstein and the generations of science.* New York: Basic Books, 1974.

Frank, P. *Philosophy of science.* Englewood Cliffs, N.J.: Prentice-Hall, 1957.

Freud, S. A case of successful treatment by hypnotism. In J. Strachey (Ed.), *The standard edition of the complete psychological works of Sigmund Freud.* (Vol. I). London: Hogarth, 1966. Pp. 115–128.

James, W. *The principles of psychology.* In R. M. Hutchins (Ed.), *Great books of the western world* (Vol. 53). Chicago: Encyclopedia Britannica, 1952.

Jung, C. G. *Two essays on analytical psychology.* In H. Read, M. Fordham, & G. Adler (Eds.), *The collected works of C. G. Jung* (Vol. 7). Bollingen Series XX.7. New York: Pantheon Books, 1953.

Kelly, G. A. *The psychology of personal constructs* (2 vols.). New York: Norton, 1955.

Kintsch, W. *Learning, memory, and conceptual processes.* New York: Wiley, 1970.

Koffka, K. *Principles of gestalt psychology.* New York: Harcourt, Brace, 1935.

Kondo, H. *Albert Einstein and the theory of relativity.* New York: Franklin Watts, 1969.

Kuhn, T. S. *The structure of scientific revolutions* (2nd ed.). Chicago: The University of Chicago Press, 1970. (1st ed., 1962.)

Lowrie, W. *A short life of Kierkegaard.* Garden City, N.Y.: Doubleday, 1961.

Magill, F. N., & McGreal, I. P. (Eds.), *Masterpieces of world philosophy* (2 vols.). New York: Salem, 1961.

Nagel, E., & Newman, J. R. *Gödel's proof.* New York: New York University Press, 1958.

Penfield, W. *The mystery of the mind: A critical study of consciousness and the human brain.* Princeton, N.J.: Princeton University Press, 1975.

Russell, B. *Introduction to mathematical philosophy.* London: Allen & Unwin, 1919.

Rychlak, J. F. *A philosophy of science for personality theory.* Boston: Houghton Mifflin, 1968.

Rychlak, J. F. *Introduction to personality and psychotherapy: A theory-construction approach.* Boston: Houghton Mifflin, 1973.

Schwartz, G., & Bishop, P. W. *Moments of discovery: The origins of science.* New York: Basic Books, 1958.

Skinner, B. F. *Beyond freedom and dignity.* New York: Knopf, 1971.

Skinner, B. F. *About behaviorism.* New York: Knopf, 1974.

Voss, J. F. On the relationship of associative and organizational processes. In E. Tulving & W. Donaldson (Eds.), *Organization of memory.* New York: Academic, 1972. Pp. 167–194.

Watson, J. B. Psychology as the behaviorist views it. *Psychological Review*, 1913, **20**, 158–177.

Whitehead, A. N., & Russell, B. *Principia mathematica* (3 vols.; 2nd ed.). Cambridge: The University Press, 1963.

Wightman, W. P. D. *The growth of scientific ideas.* New Haven: Yale University Press, 1951.

Wolman, B. B. Does psychology need its own philosophy of science? *American Psychologist*, 1971, **26**, 877–886.

CHAPTER EIGHT

Foundations for a
Logical Learning Theory

We come now to the framing of a new approach to human learning, based on the teleological image of the person presented in Chapter 7. Although this approach is called *logical learning theory*, we include *both* demonstrative and dialectical forms of logic in this designation. That we believe humans to be logically "correct" or cybernetic in their approach to life should not be presumed. Much of human behavior consists of the so-called illogic of dialectical reasoning. What makes this theory logical is the belief that human beings *do* behave for the sake of an order (logos) which predicates their behavior in a determinate sense. But we also believe that they can effect this ordering of premises *from birth* (circa); if mind is *tabula rasa* at the outset, what is subsequently etched upon it does not rest solely with the hand of experience. The human being helps write the scenario and thereby is necessarily a contributing agent to what will be enacted.

A Neo-Kantian Category of the Mind
for Modern Psychology

If logical learning theory is to constitute a Kantian revolution in the Lockean climate of theory which now permeates psychology, it must come forward with a theoretical construct that acts as Kant had his unlearned categories of the understanding acting in mind. We require some aspect of behavior that can be thought of and then proven to be *pro forma* rather than strictly *tabula rasa*. We need not take over Kantian philosophy *per se* as our psychology, but we must show how in adapting Kant's theoretical style to our own approach, an instructive series of humanistic explanations will follow. In this first section of Chapter 8 we propose one such neo-Kantian category and then relate it to the experimental context.

Emotion versus Affection

No other aspect of behavior has engendered more speculation than emotion. The early psychologists were particularly drawn to the role of what they variously called emotion, feeling, or affection on behavior, as seen in the writings of Brentano (1973), James (1952), or Wundt (1907). Often relegated to a secondary "motivating" function —especially in the drive-reduction learning theories which flourished in the first half of this century—emotions were likely to be given a physiological emphasis because of their tie to bodily sensations (Arnold, 1960, 1970). Yet, at least in the case of human beings, there is often a further motivation to stimulate emotional reactions that are not initially active—for example, in the aesthetic efforts people make via the arts. What then can be said to motivate a motivation for an unrealized emotion? To suggest that this involves yet other emotions merely compounds an already muddled picture. Furthermore, to the human animal an emotion is something beyond simply a physiological reaction or a heightened sense of activation in bodily tempo. *Emotions signify imports.* Even after the flow of a physiological reaction has passed, the recollected (reconceptualized) "feeling" is retained with vividness. One does not need to have love tingling in his breast this moment to say that he does indeed love his child with a total commitment.

Obviously the mind-body issue enters here. We all can think back to some tender period of life and in that very recollection obtain a good feeling. What is the cause here of the engendered mood (body) if not some complex of patterned meanings (mind) as so-called ideas? Even more complexly, how can one be feeling a deep emotion signifying one thing—let us say, hatred—and yet at the very same time *also* feeling either satisfaction or misery in the fact of having such animosity uppermost in one's awareness? Not all individuals enjoy entertaining certain emotions equally well. For some a sexual impulse is sheer joy anytime, while for others it is an embarrassment if not an actual annoyance "depending upon the circumstances." Theories of emotion that rely exclusively on physiological explanations have even more difficulty accounting for such twists and turns of our emotional reactions than they do in accounting for just how many "basic" emotions there supposedly are nestled among the body's organic machinery (love, hate, jealousy, etc.).

How might a Kantian theorist proceed on this question of the emotions? Because there is a mind-body feature involved, he would first take a position on where the emotions might be said to issue from. One must of course be cognizant of one's feelings to experience an emotion; to that extent, emotions make themselves known in mind. They are like characterizations of our feelings. We do not call all mental representations (images, ideas) emotions, nor do we feel emotional in every moment of our waking awareness. Many theorists claim that we are always emoting, in the sense that we constantly feel something in relation to what we know. But at least in commonsensical parlance, to feel an emotion is distinct from, for example, losing oneself in an abstract intellectual activity. Possibly this is merely a question of the extent of one's emotions at the moment. Whatever the case, a Kantian position might suggest that emotional feelings originate in the body and that, insofar as mental activity is concerned, not until the meaning as endowed by mind in the act of conceptualization takes place can we speak of an emotion taking place. In this sense the problem of how many emotions we have or how complexly we "feel" in relation to the circumstances of life depends entirely on the meanings generated in telosponsivity. Conceptualizing stimulations emanating within the body's physiological mechanisms are no different from conceptualizing stimulations emanating from without the body's dermal limits. Indeed the very same physiological stimulations may be conceptualized differently—be "felt" as different emotions—based on the extra-bodily situation in which the individual finds himself (i.e., the meanings he actively conceptualizes).

The drift of this Kantian line surely demands that we have some mental way of referring to the emotional experience or to whatever it is that gets confused with emotional experience. Logical learning theory suggests that we distinguish between affection (mind) and emotion (body). There is a precedent for this in the writings of Titchener (1909), who early distinguished between affection as the "characteristic element in emotion" (p. 277) and emotion proper—which would include all of those distinctive feeling states we name anger, joy, and so forth. Continuing in the vein of his teacher, Wundt, Titchener held that there are only two forms of affections: Either they are pleasant or they are unpleasant (ibid., p. 226). Though he theorized extraspectively and in no way intended a dialectical meaning, the implications for us are clear. Titchener called the pleasant or unpleasant affections sensed in relation to experience "qualities," suggesting thereby that they were reflective of or a part of sensory stimulation, much as varying wavelengths strike us with different hues of color. Although he included judgment in his psychology, Titchener failed to subsume the emotions by this evaluative concept. Logical learning theory does consider affection to involve judgment, as does all telosponsivity, and as a dialectical process, to be seen active in all mental activity. Affective assessments are considered the most abstract of mental telosponsivity possible, as follows:

Affective assessment in its purest manifestation is a transcendental telosponse—that is, an innate capacity to judge (via dialectical division) the meanings of one's concepts, premises, and even telosponses, characterizing them as either positive or negative in meaningfulness. Affective assessment is, however, embodied in *all* telosponsivity, rendering the implicit connotative meaningfulness of the specific (denotative) meanings being extended in mental activity. Affections are purely mental phenomena, ultimately *arbitrary* and up to the person who levels such idiographic judgments from his or her (introspective) perspectives on life. Because the assessment is dialectical, there is no indifference point on the dimension of affective assessment, although there may be ambivalence.

We borrow the concept of transcendence from Kant (1952, p. 229), who in accounting for self-reflexivity in mind held that a human being could turn back on the activities of mind and examine the working of his understanding through the use of a *transcendental dialectic*. Mind could double back on itself, so to speak, and to that extent evaluate its own evaluating capacities. In like fashion, all of those meanings being actively brought to bear in telosponsivity can be evaluated according to a dialectical either-or assessment of positiveness or negativeness. This self-reflexive act is *also* a telosponse, with *its* premising task being that of intending the positive or negative purpose of the mental contents (meanings) under affirmation, conceptualization, and telosponsivity. To say that we can "telospond our telosponses," is therefore not redundant or circular for this is what self-reflexivity implies, as in knowing that we can know (see our discussion of Descartes on this point in Chapter 8, p. 353). Of course there is usually no need to telospond our telosponses because the positive or negative nature of the latter is inherent in our affirmative grasp. We are constantly affectively assessing in reasoning— we know our likes and dislikes without having to enumerate them through a self-reflexive effort. But when asked to assess specifically anything in his or her experience as to its affective quality, the human person can be shown to do so fairly easily. Indeed most people take this process for granted.

There is a Kantian recognition in this construct of affective assessment to the effect that meanings and meaningfulness always "devolve from above" in mental acts (Rychlak, 1973, p. 11). That is, the positiveness or negativeness of meanings being affirmed in telosponsivity are themselves sequaciously determined by the *even more abstract* precedents of affective assessment. If we are now telosponding in some fashion regarding the meanings of symphonic music, for example, we would be cognizant of this or that specific musical theme as it is played. Liking symphonic music in general, we may or may not appreciate the present piece we are listening to. How are we to characterize this personal appraisal? Our definition suggests that it requires a transcendental telosponse to rise above (transcend!) the ongoing telosponsivity of, for example, "I am listening to this symphonic music over the radio" and reveal the precedents which act as background assessments to color our judgment of "I find that I like this piece" or "I find this piece uninteresting." The precedent affection sequaciously colors our continuing experience of listening to the musical score—that is, literally determining our enjoyment of the music. We need not state these assessments, because the routine act of telosponding the musical score "connotes" intrinsically what we think of the piece. We often confuse this connoted significance with an emotional reaction, but logical learning theory contends that emotions are not telosponses. The *meaning* of an emotion is framed telosponsively, but emotion *qua* emotion is not a mental phenomenon; it is physical.

Emotions are rooted in the body. They are triggered by life circumstances quite automatically, and only subsequently do we realize the characterizations this stimulation has put onto our life. It is rarely appreciated that the central point of the James-Lange theory was that having first reacted organically and automatically, we *then* characterize our circumstances via a process termed "the emotions" (see James, 1952, p. 743). Arnold (1970) has termed the emotions "physiological appraisals" (p. 174) of the circumstances in which we find ourselves. An appraisal is a judgment, and so we can say that from birth the child has an unlearned potential to put experience to telic consideration because of his emotional equipment—but not *solely* on the basis of this equipment.

The infant who is pricked by a diaper pin even before language acquisition has an "experience," but the essence of this externally provoked event is that it forces him to judge, to appraise his circumstance. No one denies the truth of an unlearned emotional appraisal in human behavior, because we *do* have innate feelings of a positive or negative quality *vis-à-vis* environmental conditions. But is this unhappy event of a painful physiological appraisal the *cause* of subsequent appraisals made by the child in relation to sharp objects? As this child goes through life confronting nails and thumb tacks and even forks, will he assess the sharpness of such objects due solely to this earlier event with a diaper pin in which he literally felt an emotion of pain or fright and now retains it in an "affective memory" (Arnold, 1970, p. 173)? This is not how we would conceptualize the matter. Affection is something completely different from the physiological reaction of emotion, and comes into play entirely independent of it. A definition of emotion follows:

Emotion refers to the pattern of feelings experienced physiologically by individuals, usually in relation to certain environmental circumstances that seem to provoke them. Insofar as they are physiological appraisals of these life circumstances, emotions are *not arbitrary* but are rather forced onto the individual by the mechanisms of the body. Various emotional moods may be brought about artificially through physiological stimulants (drugs, etc.) or through capturing the environmental situation that naturally provokes them. Emotions are given meaning by the telosponding intellect that conceptualizes and names them. They sometimes provide the basis for and are often confused with affections.

Logical learning theory would therefore hold that even as the child experienced the physical feeling (crude emotion) of pain he was *ordering* (conceptualizing) this experience through an entirely independent, psychological, affective assessment—and that in this ordering of (re)conceptualization the possibility of memorial retention was *created* (see Chapter 7). In other words, the affective assessment acts as a precedent which then sequaciously determines the known through its organizational capacities, aligning meaning-extension accordingly. Assuming now that a child could have conceptualized the meaning of *sharpness* (however idiosyncratically), in his subsequent life he would premise tautologically identical circumstances as affectionally negative. Furthermore he could through analogical forms of meaning-extension, "project into" other life experiences the meaning of sharpness as a kind of negative construct because of some tangential similarity—for example, as between the diaper pin (placed at hip level) and a belt (worn at hip level).

As we do not need to learn what a positive or negative feeling (emotion) *is* we do not have to be instructed in how to behave affectionately. Experience does *not* teach us how to assess affectively, although it does influence the grounds for the sake of which we make our affective assessments. Children reared in culture A eat whale blubber with relish, while children in culture B are revolted by the thought. Even so, this does not prove that the assessment capacity itself is shaped by such cultural considerations. As an aspect of the telosponse, affective assessment begins *with birth*, if not shortly before. Gardner Murphy (1947) tried to make a similar point in his "canalization" (p. 193) construct. Cultures "condition" children in definite ways, but the fact that preferences arise is due to an innate canalizing ability akin to what we have been calling affective assessment in telosponsivity.

Another feature of the affection-emotion distinction is that although these two forms of judgment (mental and physiological) can be concordant, they can *also* be seen to bear an oppositional relationship, one with the other. An unpleasant circumstance, once meaningfully framed, often teaches us to do what is necessary to make it pleasant. The concept of emotion, based as it is on a demonstrative formulation involving unidirectional promptings, fails to capture what actually takes place in behavior of this more dialectical variety. For example, if an individual is "blue" or depressed in the physical sense of a literal feeling, he can reason to the opposite of what is surely now reality and think, "Why not play my favorite music on the stereo? That'll cheer me up." There is no need to have a fleeting emotion—a slight dash of "good feeling"—or a concrete recollection of how once in the past listening to music cured his blue mood before this individual can arrive at his projected intention.

Can we be indifferent toward some item of our experience and to that extent refrain from making an affective assessment of it altogether? As a dialectical conception, affective assessment is not geared to denying this possibility *in principle*. However, as a practical matter, this failure to assess affectively would seem to occur rarely. The affirmation of a premise in conceptualization demands that we take a position concerning the positiveness or negativeness of this premised meaning. Meanings simply *do* take on positive or negative connotations, often revealed in their expressed intonations when the individual speaks about them. What we probably mean by indifference concerning some item of our experience is that we are either not conceptualizing it or that, though conceptualized, it is employed as an understanding-intention and not as an action-intention. But if forced to relate behaviorally to the item in question, we would soon enough be involved in an affective assessment. For example, we are indifferent to the existence of a discarded fishing pole, lying alongside the outer garage wall in our backyard until our beach ball is trapped beyond reach in the limbs of a tree. Suddenly the discarded and indifferent (to us) bamboo shaft takes on a positive valence, as it would have taken on a negative valence were we accidentally to run our power lawnmower into its protruding end. Do these examples establish a unidirectionality in affection, since retrieving beach balls or fouling up lawnmowers are events "in reality" and to that extent unipolar facts?

No. Because the empirical facts are unipolar does not mean we have to think of the reasoning organism as unipolarly directed "by" these facts. We can easily show how the environment influences us by choosing the right examples. Positive and negative reinforcements "in" the environment are especially easy to point to when we choose the extremes. Getting hurt is negative, so think about the times in the past when you were injured, spanked, failed a test, or were fired from a job. Being pleased is positive, so think about the times in the past when you were shown love, scored an academic triumph, or ate a marvelous meal. There are no equivocations about these affective ends of the behavioral dimension, as there are none about our fishing-pole alternatives. But now, what of all the other times? What of all those "in-between" times when the high and low points are not so easily delineated? This is where we usually spend our lives. Can the reader honestly believe that the environmental circumstances were *clearly* positive or negative as he or she went to school, met some new people, spent an evening alone at home, woke up one morning, took a day off, or had a lot to do? If they were not, how can we limit our descriptions of human behavior exclusively to these extrapersonal "facts?"

Reinforcement Value as a Subject-Contributed Variable

Thus far we have been speaking of a theoretical construct in our consideration of affection. A major argument of Chapters 5 and 6 is that we must always have both a theoretical and a methodological grasp of that which we hope to study scientifically. How then are we to put affective assessment to empirical test, and what methodolog-

ical construct would suffice to reflect this human capacity? We propose the term *reinforcement value* for this methodological duty, as
follows:

By *reinforcement value* is meant the operationalizing of affective assessment through asking subjects in experiments to prerate for likability
materials (verbal, pictorial, etc.) which they may be asked to learn or otherwise deal with in an experimental context. We assume that a rating of liking reflects positive affective assessment and a rating of disliking reflects
a subject's negative affective assessment.

In Chapter 9 we trace the development of an extensive research
program which was an attempt to establish the validity of affective
assessment in human behavior through this operationalized measure
of it. The concept of reinforcement is discussed below in Chapter 8
(p. 327). In the present context we want to discuss another aspect of
the reinforcement-value variable, for it can be considered as a methodological construct. Whenever we use the term *reinforcement value*
we are referring to the context of proof. It is a sequacious derivative
of the affective-assessment precedent, reflecting thereby the proper
course of scientific development—that is, from theory to method (see
Chapter 5, pp. 191–192). We have tried to show in previous chapters
how classical learning theories have been cast in exclusively extraspective terms (see Chapters 4, 5, and 6). We have also argued that
this one-sided theory receives much encouragement from the confusion of methodological test with theoretical explanation. When the
traditional experimentalist enters into a relationship with his subject
it does not—or it has not typically—occurr(ed) to him that this may
be a "two-way street" and that just as he is "manipulating variables,"
the subject too may be "manipulating variables."

The canons of scientific objectivity have lent an unreal air of
antiseptic unidirectionality to the influences exerted on the psychological experiment. Yet we have ample evidence from decades of
experience and many explicit studies of the question (e.g., Orne,
1962; Rosenthal, 1966) that *both* experimenter and subject make
contributions to the observed outcome of the study being conducted
—contributions that are never characterized as design factors but
could easily be put in such terms. The subject is virtually always
thinking about his role in first-person terms, asking himself questions like: What is he (the experimenter) up to? What's he trying to
get me to do? What am I getting into here? What's the worth of all

this? What's the trick? But after he conceptualizes in this introspective fashion and completes the research task for the experimenter, his telic performance is taken as further proof of the experimenter's third-person nontelic account of behavior. Logical learning theory holds that the only way in which to rectify this situation and to bring before all psychological researchers the necessity of having to encompass the introspective side of behavior is to formalize an evaluative (hence intentional) variable and assert that it is at play in every experimental study done on human beings. This is how we now view the reinforcement-value variable.

Logical learning theory therefore frankly admits that both the experimenter and the subject make significant contributions to the variables of the experimental relationship. The variables being manipulated by the experimenter can be considered experimenter-contributed variables, and the variables under the manipulation of the subject may be considered subject-contributed variables. Subject-contributed variables can be turned into experimenter-contributed variables, of course, but in making this effort we should never presume that we have exhausted the play of subject-contributed variables in our experiment, and we should never "account for" these introspectively framed variables in an extraspective theoretical description after the fact of data collection. The natural stance of a subject can be framed only in an introspective terminology, whereas experimenters can frame their accounts either introspectively or extraspectively.

But at another level, even the experimenter's experience as a human being conducting research can be understood only introspectively. He brings a theoretical point of view to the data-collecting situation, and though the construct he may be putting to test is extraspective, when we look at him as a logically construing human being we *must* perforce assume the introspective perspective to see things as he does. To assume, as many experimenters do, that the subject's conceptions of the experimental purpose (the design, the experimenter's "game plan") are "chance variations," to be cancelled out by another subject's conceptions is pure fiction. A major aspect of the learning going on in all experiments on humans has to do with the informal study being conducted by the subject as to "what this is all about." The logical learning theorist wants to put the experimenter and the subject on an equal footing, as two human beings participating in a human relationship! In doing so, the account of each participant to the relationship will necessarily be framed from an introspective theoretical perspective because this is the only way that logic can ultimately be said to take place. Logic is not an inevitability; it is not fluctuating "out there," as natural laws are supposed to be doing. Logic is something that is brought to bear out of the thinking of a human being. Logic calls for the logician!

Logical Learning Theory

We next turn to a series of topics relating to logical learning theory. Although of necessity sketchy, the hope is that the reader will find this first formulation of the view stimulating, if not fully instructive.

Learning as Meaning-Extension and the Nature of Reinforcement

Logical learning theory is founded on the unalterable assumption that human beings are meaning-processing animals. Hence at this point in the presentation we once again give the definition of *meaning* and *meaningfulness* already advanced in Chapter 2 (p. 55), elaborated somewhat by our newer terminology:

Meaning refers to the relations between items and their referents as well as to the relations between a user of such meaningful ties and the items he or she employs for the understanding of experience. An *item* can be a verbal language term (letter, word, sentence, etc.) or a purely sensory image (visual, auditory, etc.); its relation to a referent signifies (points to as a purpose) something of import, relevance, or general understanding to the person involved—including conscious and unconscious significations. *Meaningfulness* describes the extent of significance, import, or general understanding that an item has for the individual who intends its purpose. Intended meanings can be grasped conceptually and no more (understanding-intention), acted upon overtly (action-intention), or both.

Meanings are relational ties between items, but logical learning theory insists that such ties are effected not only by chance association, mere repetition, or happenstance. There is a style or strategy in the process of relating one item to a host of others. This notion of meaningful relations, reaching out from one item to make conceptual contact with other items, is captured in the construct of *meaning-extension* (see Spinoza's conception of intelligible extension in Table 1). We have used this term previously without specifically defining it, but now offer the following explanation:

Meaning-extension refers to the precedent-sequacious flow of meaning in the conceptualizations of telosponsivity, commonly referred to as the inductive and deductive knowing of experience. Meanings are extended from premises, framed at fixed protopoints which determine what can be known by the individual based on a psychological principle of tautology [introspectively conceived]. As meaning-extension proceeds, the knowledge framed by the premised meanings of telosponsivity extends its range, and through the tautological identity of dialectical oppositionality as well as through analogical variations, it also changes and alters relations between items and referents as the individual comes to know more about the various meanings of his life experience.

Logical learning theory emphasizes the direct, firsthand acquaintance an individual has with the items—both palpable and abstract—of his life experience. To *know* is to have conceptualized—that is, actively to have put some meaning to use in framing experience. Meanings framed at protopoints and the knowledge framed thereby do not remain unchanged, although a remarkable range of knowledge does seem to have this Parmenidean sameness over the course of a lifetime ("The more things change, the more they remain the same!"). Our knowledge of experience need not be "true," in the sense of meeting some independent criterion of "this, and only this, meaning is the correct one to entertain." Knowledge is earned through actively applying meaningful premises; at this point we can speak of learning taking place.

Since the advent of behaviorism learning has been conceptualized as occurring only when there is an alteration of overt performance, which means that some experimentally preconceived criterion of performance has been attained by an animal or human being. Tied closely to this view is the concept of reinforcement in learning theories. Pavlov's (1927) initial terminology suggested that salivatory behaviors were "made conditional upon" the administration of food powder to the animal in an apparatus designed to evoke and measure the extent of salivation. Reinforcement was subsequently wedded to the habit and drive theories such as those of Watson (1924) and Hull (1952), with the assumption being that habitual behavior was made conditional upon the reduction of drives following behavior's elicitation. Even Skinner's alteration of the response concept (see Chapter 6) did nothing to change this idea of a reinforcement as something that is other than the given behavior under observation but leads to an increased probability that this behavior will be seen to occur. As extraspective formulations, these behavioristic positions have therefore managed to deal with reinforcement concepts which have no basis in meaning or meaning-extension. They have managed to do this because of their tendency—discussed in Chapters 5, 6, and 7—to confound their methodological procedures with their theories of learning (resulting in frequency and contiguity principles being used as the major basis for explanation).

Keeping now strictly on the side of theory (as opposed to method), logical learning theory suggests that to learn is to extend meanings conceptually through what in Chapter 7 (p. 291) we called a conceptualization. To conceptualize is actively to organize experience in some way, to meet it at the level of sensation (input) with a creative capacity to *order* it via patterns that constitute meaning and meaningfulness. A *learning trial* is not a true trial unless the subject has actively employed that which he is attempting to know or put to memory in some organizing fashion. We can see such organizations emerging in the most simple forms of learning, which are just as often not truly new learnings. That is, we can employ an organizing scheme that we have already learned and then submit other items to this frame as if they were under spontaneous ordering when they are not. Probably the most simple ordering here is to employ a sing-song rhythm as precedent in sequaciously organizing a series of items in so-called rote-memory fashion. There are far more intricate memory schemes, of course, which rely upon previously memorized cue words or even the active construing of materials in what William James (1952) called an "ingenious" (p. 437) fashion and in the more popular vein of "memory strengtheners" can even take on bizarre orderings (see, e.g., Lorayne & Lucas, 1974).

From the viewpoint of logical learning theory, when a precedent scheme of this sort is being used, learning may or may not actually eventuate. That is, the sing-song rhythm or the previously learned memory devices are being tautologized—used identically (one) over many different occasions (many)—but not until the individual actively employs that which can be so memorized in a conceptual fashion would new learning be said to have emerged. Memorizing a list of names through a known conceptual scheme is one thing. Coming to know the people who carry these names and meaningfully endowing them with personal understanding and assessments so that they take on significance in one's life is quite another. We address ourselves to the latter form of (meaningful) learning when we say that learning involves active conceptualization and the attendant meaning-extensions of coming to know anything.

What would a reinforcement be in this view? As with our distinction above between affective assessment and reinforcement value, the position of logical learning theory is that reinforcement is a *methodological* construct. We have had theories of reinforcement, of course, as mentioned above. However, the early efforts in psychology to think of reinforcers as bonding agents, somehow cementing the stimulus and response engrams of the nervous system into a chemical unity, have long since fallen from view, and today one is more likely to see the reinforcement construct being used purely as a description of what goes on in the experimental apparatus. So long as the stimulated reinforcement is seen to manipulate the behavior as designed for in the experiment, no further analysis of the reinforcement theory under use is attempted. There may be an implied acceptance of some neo-Hullian drive-reduction thesis or a Skinnerian empirical law of effect, but the major use an experimenter is making of the reinforcement construct is as a gauge of his experimental manipulation. Behavior that can be seen to alter levels is reinforced behavior. Logical learning theory would define learning and reinforcement as follows:

Learning eventuates when through conceptualization a meaning-extension occurs and the individual has more knowledge—that is, an enriched or embellished understanding of the meaning realm initially premised. This knowledge may or may not be "true," as assessed by independent criteria, and it may or may not actually be manifested in overt behavior by the individual learner. Error can be learned! Truth and error are judgments placed upon the learning attained, either by the learner himself or by some other individual, based on some accepted criterion or standard against which what has been learned can be assessed. *Reinforcement* is best thought of as a methodological construct, but theoretically it can relate to the fact that affirmed premises which must then conceptualize meaning actually *do so*. When understanding or action-intentionality is made conditional upon a premise that truly conceptualizes for the individual employing it, we have a reinforcement of this premise. It is likely to be used again and therefore enriched or embellished. Because the premise can entail either positive or negative meanings, the nature of a reinforcement will follow accordingly. Positive reinforcements further meanings that are rooted in positive premises, and negative reinforcements further meanings rooted in negative premises.

Note that we have given a telic interpretation of reinforcement here, essentially equating the phrase *made conditional upon* with *that for the sake of which*. Also, there is a recognition that learning and failing to learn are extraindividual judgments put on a subject's performance in some task situation and that the more accurate truth of the matter could well be that the subject has learned error in seeming not to learn. Based as they are on a demonstrative assumption, the classical learning theories of psychology have always dealt with what *was* learned in behavior—and never with what was *not* learned. Error variance in a methodological test of learning is therefore to be considered the lack of something (control, acquisition, habit formation, etc.). At this point logical learning theory employs its dialectical rationale to suggest that—even acknowledging such things as errors of measurement and fatigue factors in human performance—not all errors reflect a lack of learning on the part of a subject. If a subject can learn to meet the criterion of a teacher or an experimenter, he should also be able to learn *not* to meet it. We do not ordinarily think of such things as misunderstanding directions, failing to follow instructions, or getting the point of a sentence confused as reflecting learning. But just as individuals can reason to unsound albeit "known" conclusions without thereby abandoning logic, so too does logical learning theory contend that they can learn error without abandoning learning (see Nietzsche's notion of the value of *untrue* ideas in Table 1). In fact learning how *not* to learn may be one of the major premises of so-called unmotivated student populations.

It would therefore be wrong for us to conclude that since a premise leading to a successful outcome in actual practice is reinforced (enriched and extended), one that leads to an unsuccessful state of affairs must necessarily be unreinforced (diminished or weakened). If an individual premises a situation as different, strange, impossible, or unknown even if in the abstract he might be capable of doing what is called for, the premise itself can be getting enriched and enlarged (meaning-extension) as the individual does in fact "not know" how to meet the demands of the situation. We could have a case of effective conceptualization through *negative* reinforcement. To consider these failures in performance an instance of nonlearning would be to misconstrue what was taking place from the introspective perspective of the individual learner, even though it met the theoretical understanding of the teacher or experimenter observing the individual perform (refer to our discussion of experimenter-versus-subject-contributed variables). Paraphrasing and enlarging on William James, our theory of reinforcement holds that this is the "cash value" of a premise, paid in positive or negative coin, depending upon the initial investment.

If a subject's premise encompasses meanings that can be considered positive according to *his* (introspective) standards of judgment, the sequaciously flowing reinforcement (effective meaning-extension) will be more likely to be of a positive nature. Negative reinforcements (e.g. criticisms, failures, "bad" outcomes) will not work so effectively in meaning-extension as positive reinforcements. Conversely, if a subject's premises encompass negative meanings (as judged by him), meaning-extension (reinforcements) of a positive type (e.g., compliments, successes, "good" outcomes) will be less likely to affect his performance in the meaning realm defined by those premises. What does "no reinforcement" amount to on this view? This would result when a conceptual profit is not forthcoming. This does not imply that a second-order negative reinforcement need develop through some loss of predictability in the individual's behavior sequence. Certain losses of predictability in this sense can ultimately be elating—for example, when after convincing oneself of the certainty of a serious personal illness, one learns from a physician that all is well.

In such situations the individual will often "not hear" the good news or fail to understand precisely what this entails in his case. Sometimes the patient even feels that the doctor is not telling him the truth. The meaning-extension along a positive line here proves difficult, but once it "sinks in," a changed conceptualization of the future occurs and the patient becomes more open to positive reinforcements as his mood swings upward. This dramatizes our belief that in circumstances where a premise no longer leads to either positive or negative reinforcement in line with the meaning precedently framed, a new conceptualization is likely to take place. This different conceptualization is carried out abruptly (the Kierkegaardian leap) at the *precedent* side of the precedent-sequacious ordering of experience, and a new round of meaning-extension with the attendant reinforcements is then made possible. Logical learning theory holds that reinforcement always follows sequaciously from some precedent *affective* assessment.

Affective Assessment in Premise Affirmation at the Protopoint

In Chapter 7 we saw how, because meanings in life are often bipolar, the individual must affirm some one protopoint meaning at the outset for the sake of which his behavior will then take place. Affirmation is like taking a position on the meanings of life, which in another sense represents an *ordering* (conceptualization) of experience. Affirming "There is the door," we have precedently arranged the direction to be taken when we leave the room and will sequaciously take this route (action-intention) when the time comes. Affirming "That is an act of cowardice and *not* an act of bravery," we have precedently taken on several implications concerning the individual whom we believe has acted in a cowardly way. Once again we have ordered our experience. Though we are less likely to see heroism in the behavior of those whom we typify as cowardly, a coward may after all someday do something heroic; there is always the possibility that such a dialectically opposite meaning-extension will take place as a changed conceptualization.

In both instances were we to be asked, we could probably cite the grounds or reasons for our judgments "There is the door" or "That is an act of cowardice." In formal (demonstrative) logic the ideal is to have such grounds well in mind before rendering a judgment—for example, in knowing what a doorway or a cowardly act means. In actual practice, as humanistically oriented psychologists like to point out, people do not always have such clear grounds for their estimates and beliefs. They frequently act impulsively, let their heart not their brain do their thinking, and to that extent behave emotionally. There are surely times in which an ascendant emotion influences our behavior—literally controls our behavior unidirectionally. However, insofar as a true affirmation has taken place, it is based *not* on emotion but on affection. By a "true" affirmation we mean one in which the position taken, the grounds cited, the alternative selected, *could have gone another way*. We are back to the issue of arbitrariness in behavior discussed in Chapter 7.

We presume that there is a "two-step" feature in human learning. There is the (1) sensational input which via innate sense organs can be ordered or patterned into images and sounds, and there is the (2) active conceptualization of this input through affirmation. This means that sensory input *per se* fails to take on significance until the person has used it as a grounds for the sake of the second step —affirmation in conceptualization. The second step is where affective assessment *always* enters so long as a conceptualization does actually take place. That is, we hold open the possibility that an individual might simply *not* conceptualize some aspect of his potential experience.

Traditional learning theories have referred to this as "attending to" stimulus input, and usually there has been some discussion here of the motivation involved in such attention, suggestions of an incidental form of learning occurring, and so forth. This view of attention is as a nontelic response, a reaction either directly to the stimulus attended to or due to some other stimulation (e.g., a drive stimulus). Logical learning theory contends that the individual really can attend or not attend—be arbitrary hence telic in his behavior by actually choosing the alternative to be affirmed.

What is frequently meant by emotional reasoning is not involved with the emotions at all, but with the affective assessments of affirmed premises. The individual likes to believe X, so he affirms X and not not-X. Granting X, certain meanings follow and as is so often the case in social situations, we interpret things to meet our so-called self-fulfilling prophecies (in this case the meanings implied in premise X). Another form of emotional reasoning involves the finding of reasons after the fact—that is, after we have already taken a position on some question. This is not always so illogical as it may appear initially. If one is truly under the grip of an emotion, taking premises impulsively might indeed lead to illogical or undesired outcomes. But often in interpersonal behavior and even in abstract problem solutions we sense a "feeling" of the right direction to take even though we cannot justify the grounds on which to do so. We "let ourselves go" and proceed intuitively. Here again, rather than emotive feelings prompting this intuition, logical learning theory suggests that the judgment "This feels the right way" is based exclusively on affection. There is no literal feeling emanating from the body to stimulate such lines of intuition, but the "feeling" referred to is like feeling one's way along a darkened passageway, knowing that although one cannot see everything clearly, he is on the right track. Once at the desired goal we can always retrace our steps and find a more thorough justification for how we got there.

The reader must appreciate the Kantian emphasis of logical learning theory. The affective assessment is *not* "out there" in the stimulation of the environment, but rather "in here," in the assessment of that stimulation at the point where a conceptualization or ordering of experience is taking place in the very act of affective assessment! Because an extraspective observer, looking at the individual making affective assessments, can readily guess that he will prefer ice cream to spinach, it is extremely tempting to see the stipulated preference not in the individual's assessment but in the objects assessed. Logical learning theory is an introspective account of behavior, and there is no small amount of confusion generated when we try to make our thinking clear to such extraspectively oriented theoreticians. Although empirical measures of reinforcement value are fairly simply obtained (see Chapter 9), the extraspective theoretician cannot fathom how one can be scientifically precise about such "unobservables" as a person's unique judgments *vis à vis* the stimuli that confront him throughout the days and nights of his life.

The role of affective assessment in learning might be likened to a puzzle solution. When we solve a puzzle the problem is one of identifying the pattern that is at first unconceptualized. Once the pattern *is* conceptualized, there is no need for practice to learn it further. We might spend several trials coming to the solution of the puzzle, trials that could have been cut short if someone had told us what the required pattern had to be. This preliminary knowing of a patterned organization is made possible by affective assessment. When the meaning of an upcoming situation is liked, we have in the very assessment at point 2 already solved our life puzzle. We have taken a position, ordered experience, and now *know* by the very act of assessment what we will affectively know in the meanings of the situation as they unfold. We can of course be completely wrong about what we know here, and we can alter our affective assessments of the meanings as events unfold (though this happens more rarely than most people appreciate). But for the present at least, we have identified the pattern for the sake of which meaning will then be most likely to extend. This pattern is not fixed immutably in the efficient-cause substrate of a material reality. It is at least to some extent up to us how things will eventuate in the ever-recurring puzzles of life.

Active Association in Meaning-Extension

The humanistic psychologist's reference to an *active* role for mind in human behavior frequently prompts the mechanist to exclaim in rebuttal: What can that mean other than the fact that all behavior involves action or motion? As a Lockean, the mechanist does not see the point of calling one view of mind active and a second passive if a principle of association is being employed in both views. But this is what logical learning theory does indeed contend, and we can better understand what is meant here by considering the familiar concept of *association* as employed in psychology. It was adopted from the philosophy of British Associationism as exclusively a question of contiguity and frequency (see David Hume, Table 1; also, Chapter 3). Items that are frequently close together in time become bonded in association and are thereafter seen to occur together. Fundamentally the principle of association has been based on an efficient-cause meaning, as a sort of "hookup" of antecedent-to-consequent which invariably translates into stimulus-to-response (see, e.g., Dollard & Miller, 1950, p. 59). In discussions of meaning the meaningfulness of an item is said to be dependent upon the number of associative ties (frequency thesis) some item has to other items in the "verbal repertoire" of the individual concerned (Underwood & Schulz, 1960, p. 9).

This mechanical—often purely accidental—bonding of one item to another is what humanists consider to be a passive characterization of mental associations. Freud (1960, p. 43) used the concept of association in his therapeutic investigations, but it is totally incorrect to equate his usage with that of the behaviorists. Freud's construct of the mental mechanism was *telic*. Rather than being determined by the frequency or contiguity of this or that input experience, Freudian *psychic* determinism is generated by the telosponsivity of one side of mind which is at all costs seeing that some given purpose (wish) be intended as a form of meaning-extension, even if this extension occurs purely in the symbolical realm (understanding-intention). This is the kind of "action" the humanist wants to capture in speaking of an active intellect.

In an effort to broaden the concept of association in psychology, logical learning theory recommends that we elevate the formal causation that is apparent in all such relational ties and no longer think of this bonding as only occurring across time in antecedent-to-consequent fashion. Associations do not now and never have fortuitously happened through contiguity in human learning. There is always a pattern, a matrix of meaning within which items are brought together. Furthermore not all relations among items can be characterized extraspectively. The concepts of practice and repetition engendered by behavioristic accounts have masked the fact that a subject is not simply "being rehearsed" in the learning context. If learning is a function of practice, we must take a closer look at what is occurring over at the subject's (introspective) perspective in these learning trials. When we take this slant we always find evidence suggesting that the subject who learns is actively bringing to bear on a trial the material we have asked him to learn either as a precedent frame *per se* or as content within some other precedent frame of his preference.

Logical learning theory suggests that there are at least four types of associative bondings that take place in human telosponsivity:

Unqualified Affirmation: The case in which an associative bonding between items is unidirectionally related or one end of a bipolarity is universally identified with some other referent—for example, "X is always Y, X means Y, X is the cause of Y."

Qualified Affirmation: The case in which an associative bonding is said

to occur but without uniformity or universality—for example, "X is sometimes Y, X is occasionally related to Y, X in some circumstances causes Y."

Negative Affirmation: The case in which an associative bonding is universally denied—for example, "X is never Y, X is unrelated to Y, X never
causes Y."

Oppositional Affirmation: The case in which an associative bonding is
universally related through dialectical contradiction—for example, "X is
the reverse of Y, X has a meaning diametrically opposed to Y, X contradicts Y."

Though classical Lockean psychology has recognized that "behaviors" such as negation and qualification occur, the technical
explanation used to account for such associations always comes
down to underlying, unqualified affirmations. Unqualified affirmation
is naturally compatible with the demonstrative outlook, because it
reaches for the clarity of unipolarity (X is X), and the direct communication of what is rather than what is not, is sometimes or is
the opposite of. If we look at the experimental relationship through
the eyes of the typical learning psychologist (i.e., introspectively),
we are likely to see him using unqualified affirmation as his sole
principle of theoretical explanation. Of course he externalizes this
affirmative tie through an extraspective theory—that is, the universality of affirmation is put not in mind, but in external events that
through the contiguity and frequency principles supposedly move
the person's associative processes along as the wind blows the in-
tentionless sand across the beach. Yet once we have acknowledged
that human beings can bring to bear "associations" of such diverse
varieties, the likelihood of mechanizing mentality is greatly diminished.

There are other indications of active intelligence that go unrecognized by psychologists, one type of which we would like to point
to in closing this section. We refer here to the common request made
by a listener for an example of what a speaker is talking about. The
student asks the teacher to concretize what he is saying by citing an
example. Logical learning theory would view this as a reflection of
the sequacious ease with which meaning is extended once a precedent frame is provided for the learner, who then engulfs the example which is provided in terms of his extant knowledge and goes
from there to analogize and disanalogize through our four types of
affirmation until he has satisfied his communicant that he understands what the latter is attempting to convey. As this active
learning process goes on, the individual can even sense that his

conceptualizations are taking hold. He might say, "I am catching on," and if the insights of such conceptualization are especially instructive he might even add, "You have taught me something" or "You have convinced me." If there is no such successful meaning-extension the individual would have failed to learn (in method-talk, fail to have been reinforced). Sometimes this is not the fault of the instructor, of course, because the listener must actively bring his precedents to bear on the topic for meaning to be extended. And, as discussed above, if the affection here is negative, the outcome of the learning may also be negative—that is, not successful (see Chapter 9).

Possibility, Choice, and Psychic Determinism as "Motivation"

Because premises are affectively assessed and in this same process affirmed at a protopoint, the question naturally arises: How does the person come to change his premises? What are the determining factors of choice at the protopoint? Questions such as these are customarily entertained under the concept of motivation, and they are often followed up with queries such as: How do we get the person to change his premises, as in psychotherapy, education, and behavioral manipulation generally? Many psychologists, taking the *control* of the phrase *to control and predict* as a sanction, actually believe that psychology has a social responsibility to devise ways in which to manipulate the behavior of human beings. Logical learning theory interprets the *control* in *control and prediction* as a purely methodological requirement and *no more*. The only social responsibility to be seen here is to submit one's theoretical formulations to proper empirical test! Of course the more we know about human behavior, the greater is our likelihood of influencing people's actions. But the decision actually to influence in this way is extrascientific, and it can be made by any professional group that has some claim on the power structures of social relations (e.g., political leaders, church officials, etc.). Psychological knowledge is not exclusively for psychologists.

The purpose of logical learning theory is to represent a teleological description of behavior which is sufficiently abstract to subsume other theories of behavior, such as those of Freud, Adler, Jung, Rogers, Binswanger, and Boss (see Rychlak, 1973). Just as Dollard and Miller (1950) were able to subsume Freudian conceptions by Hullian learning theory, so too is logical learning theory capable of subsuming other theories of this lower level of abstraction. We have argued in other contexts that Dollard's and Miller's translations of Freudian theory into S-R theory were inadequate (Rychlak, 1973, pp. 387–390), because they took the basically telic meanings of Freud's outlook and twisted them into purely efficient-cause renderings. Due to space considerations we cannot here show how the above humanistic theories are better served by subsumption under the rubrics of logical learning theory, but we do contend that this is the case. And if this be true, there are already a number of ways in which to conceptualize change in behavior through the classical insight and relationship therapies listed. Even so, we must deal with the questions raised in this section in order that the reader understand the general direction taken by logical learning theory on these matters.

Behavioral motivations are to be seen as precedents—the meanings encompassed as so-called grounds for decisions to act. A ground (basis, reason, etc.) for behavior is simply another way of speaking about the premise(s) employed in telosponsivity. If we turn to a consideration of the classical distinction between motivation and learning, a rather interesting aspect of this dichotomy can be delineated. In describing the behavior of lower animals classical learning theorists like Tolman and Hull (see Chapter 4) were always dealing with a literal existing goal. A rat was placed in a T-maze, and while "under motivation" (or not), had to learn to run to the goal box. Behavior was the instrumental motion an animal manifested to attain the goal, and learning constituted a performance in which this goal attainment was actually achieved. There was no need to speak of motivation in the same breath as learning because what was there to be learned at the goal *was* "there for the learning." The goal box was not and never can be a mere possibility in the behavior of the rat, as something that is encompassed in the rat's anticipations (premises) and keeps him going, though it may actually never be there when he winds his way down the maze. *This* kind of motivation, which must of necessity be thought of as defining the end sought, was never to be encompassed in classical learning theory except by way of weak analogies to the T-maze circumstance. The upshot was that hours of food deprivation as a motivation and goal attainment as learning criterion could be kept separate in the thinking of rigorous psychologists.

But how appropriate is it to speak of human beings as either motivated or not motivated to achieve goals in life, as if such goals literally existed down some maze-run of lived time? Trying to make a business run successfully or to cultivate a successful marriage is anything but a sure thing for the person involved in these activities. As we emphasized in Chapter 7 (p. 287), there is no literal end "there" in the telic behavior of human beings, who premise their ends and then *create* them as they work toward them or fail to do so. People even work for ends they know to be impossible of attainment, as in the ethical principles of self-actualization (i.e., we never achieve complete self-realization yet work to do the best we can for such perfection).

Logical learning theory considers false the view of human motivation—nurtured as it is by the chimerical, the risky, the "impossible dream"—as something other than and independent of telosponsiveness. Motivation must be seen as implicit in the conceptualization process, contained in the very premise being affirmed by the individual as he moves toward the ever-recurring future of his life. Motivations are shot through with possibilities, which can be thought of as premised goals that are affirmed tentatively (via qualified affirmation), difficult to conceptualize, or exaggerated in their alternative quality from the more usual goals affirmed. We employ the term *goal* here, but recognize in this usage simply the idea of an end, a "that for the sake of which" reason which is affirmed at the protopoint. We do not contend that all goals exist independently of the motives that prompt them or that motives (drives, impulses, etc.) are what generate the actions in the organism making the attainment of independently existing goals possible. As a clarification of logical learning theory's position on motivation, we offer the following definition:

Motivation: An evaluation or estimation of the relative advantage that a premise (encompassing an intended goal) makes possible in life, leveled by the person affirming this premise or by an observer who presumes to know what is being intended. To understand a specific *motive* (premised advantage) one must know the meanings encompassed in the affirmed premise (predication), how these relate to other people, what the person has affectively assessed in the circumstance, and so on. Advantages for one person in life often hurt other people, and the individual can even consider self-destruction an advantage in some instances. Motivations vary in extent of awareness concerning the person involved. Only a telic animal can be cognizant of motivation in behavior.

We are prompted to speak of our motives in life because of the many possibilities that constantly arise in our experience. The very openness to alternatives in living induces us to affirm a habitual course of behavior (see our related discussion on organic evolution and dialectical reasoning, Chapter 7, pp. 304–305). Having to select among the open possibilities of the future is unsettling so we are "motivated" from the very nature of our dialectical mentality to seek that fixedness of routine termed habit, which itself gives us a certain advantage over the chaos of disorder. A *choice* is an intrusion on this regularity, the necessity of having to take into consideration some break in the pattern of our behavior. Another way of putting this is that the possibilities of existence surface and we must affirm one alternative over another, and naturally wish to maximize our advantage in this affirmation. We are free to see a movie film this evening; now, which one shall it be? When we have settled on one possibility over the other(s), we refer to this as a *decision*, which comes down to an unqualified affirmation of the course of behavior we will follow (often with "second thoughts," to be sure).

Certain behaviors may be engaged in based on an affective assessment to which no verbal justification can be given. We behave and then find the reasons for our behavior afterward. This is not a strike against teleological theory. When choices and decisions are discussed we often put things in an intellectualized either-or phrasing whereby the alternatives are rationally circumscribed. We speak of the choice between movie A and movie B, as if this decision were made solely on the basis of the meaningfulness of the verbally describable content of these films. The person is construed as a kind of cybernetic machine, weighing alternatives. But logical learning theory does not view all choices and affirmed decisions in this light, because the point of affective assessment is to suggest that human beings are often moved by telic evaluations of a sort that are not expressible except in the personal statement, "I just *want* to do this!" or "I do this because it suits me" or "I like doing this." An organism that behaves this way is still a telic organism.

William James (1952, p. 381) properly recognized that purpose and interest are related questions. Every affirmation of the purpose of a concept encompasses the interest we have in this item at the time. In many cases we can stipulate the interest an item holds for us—for example, when we ask that the butter be passed to coat our waiting slice of bread. Yet on other occasions we cannot put our interest value clearly into words, except to say that our preference is to do this or that thing at the time. Our grounds are purely affective assessments, but as telosponses these still reflect a telic line of behavior. There is a logic in affection, a judgment rendered, and behavior that flows thereby is being sequaciously determined for the sake of this precedent affective assessment encompassing the interest of the individual in that which is unfolding and being carried forward.

The image mechanists seem to have of the teleologist is that of a highly idealistic person, one who is overly trusting of rational intelligence and committed to the view that the person is always free to choose spontaneously the course his behavior is to take. Yet, as our discussion of the relationship between freedom and determinism made clear (see Chapter 7, pp. 307–310), there is no need for a telic theory to hold that all people can choose freely to behave spontaneously in *every* circumstance. We must never forget that the determinism of final causation can be just as rigidly determinate as the determinism of efficient causation. When a decision is made, or put in terms of affective assessment, when a telosponsive affirmation of either a positive or negative quality is rendered, there is *no turning back.*

We cannot always intend away "intellectually" a premise that we have affirmed affectionately. We construe the situation facing us negatively, and no amount of self-reproach or coaxing by others can get us to "change our minds" about the likely outcome. This is what we find taking place in so-called psychic determinism (Chapter 6) as well as in the realm of attitude and prejudice formation (Rokeach, 1973). Such biases are usually said to be based on emotion (emotional reasoning), which would make them an efficient-cause determinism. However, logical learning theory contends that it is affective assessment, an arbitrary action *before* being rendered, which fixes the immutability of such conceptual meanings in the course of behavior *after* it has been made. This final-cause determinism is basic to all human behavior, accounting for much of what we call the predictability of behavior.

How then can we "get people to change?" Logical learning theory leaves it up to them, but however they may be said to do so, the mental process will follow the Kierkegaardian leap (Chapter 7). Only through a reordering, reconstruing, reconceptualization, and so forth, which includes an affective reassessment of the meanings to be extended can the individual be said to change his behavior. Alter the precedent meanings (which includes affection), and the sequacious meaning-extensions will take care of themselves. The adage that "time heals all wounds" is a reflection of how altering circumstances can sometimes do this redefining for one. An extended vacation can aid in this reconceptualization. As to psychotherapy, logical learning theory views this as a means through which the individual learns explicit rules of thumb to follow in dealing with a symptom, models the behavior of an affectively positive therapist, or acquires a doctrinaire redefinition of who he or she is as a person. In this connection we must not forget the role of self-conceptualization in psychotherapy (see below). Unsuccessful therapy eventuates when the client's affective assessments of the relationship or the personality theory being used to characterize him are not conducive to learning. Also, emotional promptings enter in to confound the outcome of many therapy series (see Rychlak, 1973).

Some Classical Learning Terminology as
Viewed by Logical Learning Theory

In this section we sample a handful of terms taken from the classical behaviorist and gestalt learning theories, giving the interpretation logical learning theory would have of them. The concepts of operant (p. 259), reinforcement (p. 327), motivation (p. 337), association (p. 333), and habit (p. 338) have essentially already been given such translations.

Repetition, Practice, and Similar Terms. Most behaviorists have assumed that repetition permits the behaving organism to *acquire* learnable materials, usually framed as a new habit formation. Logical learning theory, however, views repetition in terms of the subject's effort to *retain* and extend that which he already possesses. Each trial is an opportunity to bring to bear the already known in order to know further that which is being confronted. Viewed introspectively, repetition is always a continuation, and because the learning criterion is fixed by the experimenter in the nature of the task put to the subject, whether merely one trial (Guthrie, 1952) or several are necessary to accomplish the task makes no difference. At the point when the subject's precedent conceptualization either begins to or does frame-in the task completely, we have learning occurring. Ordinarily the more clear-cut the patterning of the task, the easier is such learning reconceptualized on subsequent occasions; thus a puzzle-solution, whether found in one or several trials, is more easily remembered than a rote task or some less structured task.

Trial and Error. Logical learning theory interprets this introspectively to mean "do something else this time," an inclination the individual may or may not verbalize but is due to his dialectical reasoning capacities. The telosponse here is to behave for the sake of "something else," and these alternatives always begin in the poles of construct opposition. Continuing with our view of repetition, trial and error as practice is what allows such alternatives to take place, even serendipitously.

Generalization. Principles of generalization have been analogized to humans from work on lower animals, in which behavioral responses are extraspectively described as being learned more or less probably to a dimension of stimulation, or stimulations are attached more or less probably to a dimension of responsivity. In this formulation the spread of behavior can always take place automatically, so long as a reinforcing bonding nurtures the generalization along. The behaving organism does not generalize its behavior. Logical learning theory views generalization as a reflection of the principle of tautology in behavior, with the conservative function of mind manifest in this tendency to bring behaviors forward by direct or analogical meaning-extensions across more and more of life's situations.

Discrimination. The principle of discrimination has been used as the obverse of generalization; it also relates to repetition, for the assumption here is that because of repeated trials, a better perception of the stimulus or response is obtained, or depending upon the distribution of reinforcements (frequency thesis), a differential responsivity is established (in time) between two stimuli or two responses. This demonstrative formulation makes discrimination appear to be a linear phenomenon, occurring as generalizations along a unidirectional dimension of difference. Logical learning theory has it that discrimination—as the seeing of differences in events—is best understood in a dialectical either-or framework. Indeed, although not true dialectical reasoning, this is why the logic of the computing machine is binary. Human reason can greatly multiply and contort this either-or divisiveness and even make discriminations in events when objective evidence would suggest that none exists.

Law of Effect. Thorndike (1898) made the consequences of an act appear to be somehow independent of the intentions that might have preceded this act. In looking at behavior exclusively through the extraspective perspective we can usually convince ourselves of the legitimacy of such independence. However, in logical learning theory the point is stressed that all consequences as projected possibilities are contained in the premise at the outset. Any "effects" to be seen in the course of events as a result of such behavior are therefore directly related to the premise as framed. The reformulation of the law of effect by Thorndike clearly supports logical learning theory, for though positive consequences are likely to stamp in habits, negative consequences *do not* always stamp them out. An even more dramatic alteration of the so-called law of habit formation—which was based on the law of effect—was Dunlap's (1928) discovery that a correct response could be learned by practicing the incorrect response (in this case, practicing one's typing errors). Only if we appreciate the dialectical logic in human behavior can such findings make ready sense in our theories of learning.

Principle of Contiguity. This concept has done more than any other to ensure psychology's faith in the role of time on behavior. Items experienced contiguously in time or place (i.e., identical time periods) are associated together more readily than more disparate items. Logical learning theory substitutes the conception of tautology here, insisting on the importance of meaning-extension in both these circumstances. That is, items which follow each other *over time* are not simply being "hooked up" in efficient-cause tandem. They are being patterned as an event or experience by the individual who recalls, "Yes, I remember now. We turned left back there and now we are to follow this road for about a mile and then we will turn right." He might not even recall things explicitly but "feel" (affective assessment) his way forward because he has patterned things in other than purely verbal terms. Similarly, two items experienced immediately together in time are also actively patterned in the telosponsivity of the individual, who readily recalls the totality as, "Oh yes, I remember that vividly because I was just starting my first job when it happened." Logical learning theory discounts the sheer contiguity of such events and emphasizes the obvious formal causation in *both* such incidents.

Needs, Drives. Such constructs are subsumed by the role of emotions and affective assessments in behavior. No one can deny the immense importance of those physically based hedonic tones we all sense as emotions, needs, drives, and so on. However, insofar as they take on distinctive meanings (love, desire, respect, retribution, etc.) logical learning theory suggests that they are conceptualized by the individual's mentality rather than delineated by separate physical mechanisms. The very same hedonic equipment may signal two entirely different emotions, depending upon the individual's characterization and affective assessment of these physical promptings.

Expectancy. The expectancy or level of aspiration construct is interpreted as a premise by the logical learning theorist. Individuals are assumed to be able to see possibilities in events and they can therefore project aspirations or intentions in line with this knowledge. As the meaning of telic suggests, the thrust of mind is ever forward, and human beings therefore quite naturally frame expectancies as a reflection of this telosponsivity.

Transfer. This is usually defined extraspectively as the facilitative (positive) or inhibitory (negative) effect of an antecedent event on a consequent event (considered across time). Theories of (specific) transfer vary, with generalization entering into several of the explanations (Chaplin & Krawiec, 1960). Logical learning theory views transfer introspectively, in terms of precedent-sequacious meaning-extension based on tautology. If events can be brought together into identity (tautology) or partial identity (analogy), obviously a previous circumstance can facilitate behavior in a later circumstance. The latter become a patterned continuation of the former.

Figure and Ground. The remaining concepts in this section are in the realm of gestalt psychology. Viewed in terms of a logical and not a sensory phenomenology (see Chapter 7, p. 303), figure-ground is simply a manifestation of the precedent-sequacious directional flow of meaning. For example, in the work by Rubin on contour, figural contour was found to serve a one-sided function (Koffka, 1935, pp. 181–184). A figure is a figure at the level of proximal stimulation because the ground properties of one's perception always define it inwardly. Grounds define figures but figures never define grounds. Logical learning theory merely extends this into the realm of mental telosponsivity so that, for example, in affirming the antecedent of an *If. . .then. . .* proposition we *necessarily* determine the conclusion drawn as if we were framing the shape of such a figure through its surrounding ground. This is why we chose the language of precedent meanings and their slavishly compliant (sequacious) extensions.

Set, Einstellung, Aufgabe. These gestalt constructs obviously relate to the same issues mentioned above under the expectancy construct. Though they formulated a more introspective theory than the behaviorists, the gestalt psychologists did not capture the element of arbitrariness in thought that logical learning theory does. One is *made* to take on sets based on the organization of his perceptual field—as in Lewin's (1935) demand character conception, for example. And Watt's work on *aufgabe* was typified by a contentless-ness, a lack of appreciation for the *meanings* a subject might be dealing in as he approached the task (see Boring's discussion, 1950,

p. 404). Logical learning theory places more emphasis on the arbitrary aspects of set than the gestaltists would have agreed to.

Closure, Good Shape, Good Continuation, and Pragnanz. Laws of organization such as closure, good shape, good continuation, and so on are related to the general principle of *pragnanz*, which states that all patternings tend to become as well articulated, homogenous, and simple as possible. The view of logical learning theory here would suggest that through tautology and the continuation of a fixed conceptualization to be seen across repetitions, a simplification and clarification would probably occur in meaning-extension. As a conservative aspect of behavior, mental organization in telosponsivity is oriented to fixing the most stable and well-delineated items of knowledge or perception possible. Affirmation might thus very well take this course of clarifying the pattern in its most stable, hence simple, outlines.

Isomorphism. Logical learning theory interprets this construct as something required by the gestalt psychologist to cement his psychological theory to an assumed underlying reality. That is, the gestaltist here tautologizes across the phenomenal and noumenal realms, claiming that the very activities of the electrons in the nervous tissue of the CNS can be said to follow gestalt principles. This is not a proper principle of learning so much as it is an extraspective theory purporting to unite the mental with the physical. As such, it is a daring tautology.

One last point must be added to this limited survey of the directions being taken by logical learning theory. Many of the concepts taken from classical learning theory, such as generalization, discrimination, transfer, practice, and so forth, are strictly speaking, not theoretical but methodological concepts. The close identity of theory and method in classical learning theory has made this appear to be a virtue. But the truth is that there is a greater understanding of these concepts when we are speaking of them in experimental-design terms than when we are speaking of what may actually be taking place in the psychology of the subject under study. The practice has been to consider the concept and neglect the subject. So long as the concept is operationalized, there is no responsibility to consider the subject-contributed variables that may or may not be at play in the experiment. Operational definitions are often weak substitutes for hard and clear thinking. Logical learning theory encourages the psychologist to cultivate his theoretical grasp along with his research expertise and never to let his experimental operations limit his conceptual understanding.

Developmental Factors in Learning: Norms of Behavior

In recent decades the interest in developmental psychology has increased dramatically. There are many who feel that a theory of learning is static or at least not complete unless its formulations are based on a developmental thesis. Psychologists often claim that rather than speculating on the nature of human learning, what we ought to do is study how people *do* learn over the course of the full life span and then we would know about such things firsthand. A popular champion in recent times has been Jean Piaget, who has studied the development of causal conceptualization in children (1930) as well as several other logical features of human beings (e.g., 1952, 1957). Is this not the proper source from which to learn about learning?

Although plausible at first consideration, what this argument overlooks is that certain precedent (model) assumptions are required to organize the developmental theory propounded just as precedents are required to organize *any* theory. A theory of developmental stages that progress one from another is still a *single* viewpoint and to that extent just as static as a theory of learning which attempts to account for learning without introducing developmental conceptions. There is no magic whereby developmental accounts can circumvent the necessity of presuming via a model that the child's learning is either molded exclusively by environmental input, contingent upon successively maturating biological mechanisms, or as in the case of logical learning theory, due to the active intellect that organizes experience from birth. We can find evidence for each of these views, not to mention combinations of these and others as well. To presume that Piaget's data support *only* Piaget's theory is to commit the empiricist's error (see Chapter 7, p. 274). Our hope that logical learning theory will be capable of subsuming other theories of behavior applies equally well to theories of development. Thus when we take an interest in the way that theorists have theorized about development, there will be a need to analyze the theory constructed in terms of some uniform, heuristic, nondevelopmental frame of reference. Precisely here is where logical learning theory can provide the scholar with an alternative to the Lockean formulation.

In presenting logical learning theory, certain speculations about the course of learning over the earliest years of life have been necessary, and thus we might do well to enlarge on a few points. There are noteworthy parallels between logical learning theory and the view of mind held to by William James in his *Principles of Psychology*. Although James (1952) is known for his "stream of thought" (p. 146) ideas and the supposed blooming buzzing confusion of initial experience (p. 318), he also emphasized the "sense of sameness" (p. 299) in conceptualization. Concept-formation, said James (*ibid.*, p. 300), would be impossible without the individual's capacity to see identity in experiences; and he noted that the basis for such principles of identity was at least partially due to the capacity for tautology in human thought (*ibid.*, p. 299). To think of mental concepts as "developing" in some staged or steadily unfolding way was for James an erroneous theory. Developmental advance was always heralded through new conceptualization and not through some kind of development of older conceptions (*ibid.*, pp. 302–303). If we now add to this the Kierkegaardian view of change (refer to Chapter 7, p. 282), logical learning theory's conception of development would be fairly well cricumscribed.

That is, insofar as stages of development can be seen in the conceptual maturation of the child and adult, they would be seen as sequaciously following from the altered premises that growing experience makes possible; and these stages would occur abruptly, as developmental quantum leaps. At the outset of life the infant is probably in a conceptual state of understanding, not unlike what H. S. Sullivan (1953, p. 26) called the prototaxic mode (comparable to the Jamesian blooming and buzzing). However, Sullivan's Yankee Lockeanism encouraged him to view the subsequent stages of verbal-meaning development (parataxic and syntaxic) more in a sociocultural input sense than as a manifestation of the active telosponsivity of the child, who must infer and analogize and extend from rudimentary beginnings to encompass the broader ranges of meaning which life can make available (see Rychlak, 1973, Chapter 8).

Logical learning theory would contend that the early years are notoriously sketchy and difficult to recall (reconceptualize) *not* because of some paucity of input. They are poorly recalled by each of us because this is a period of poor grounding—that is, inadequately framed premises for the sake of which meaning can then be extended in that two-step procedure which we take to be learning (see above). The earliest premising is quite primitive, based primarily on the telosponsivity of raw affective assessments. Emotions move the child, and doubtless there is considerable agreement between the tone or mood of an emotion and the affective assessment made of it in the earliest months of life. But as time passes (irrelevant as it is to learning *per se*), the natural opportunity for increased meaning-extension takes place so that not only does knowing increase dramatically, but a certain leeway develops between the evaluations of one's experience engendered by the emotions and the affective assessments made of the emotions. Put another way, the meanings encompassed in telosponsivity gradually rely less on emotionality and more on affective assessment.

Over this course of development the telosponsive mind of the child is ordering experience (endowing it with meaning). Practice in extending meaning involves not only the exposure to items, but also the "second" step of active conceptualization in extending this meaning (which makes for learning). Such practice is more like noticing experience than it is inputting meanings from experience. Returning to a metaphor employed in Chapter 7, if one sits at a window and gazes at some scene outside, so long as there is an intention to see things outside, there is more and more to be noticed even if the scene is unchanging (e.g., in looking at some complex mural painting through a window—one is enriched by the "practice" of looking at it even though there is a fixed pattern of unchanging meaning depicted there). Similarly, with maturation the child can always notice more and enlarge more on what he can know by way of what he already knows.

Most theories of development point to the influence of the environment by way of sociocultural artifacts such as modeling the "normative" behavior of others (whether in a subcultural identity or more generally among the full culture). Logical learning theory stresses the heavy contribution of conformity to premise affirmation, hence learning among humans. The very openness of conceptualization naturally frightens the child into wanting to know from parents and others what *is* the case in life. Children are also negativistic, of course. But there is a kind of miniature reenactment of what we suggest took place in the developing organisms that came to be human beings, as they sensed their dialectical intelligence emerging in the course of organic evolution. Children take on *most* of the premises of their parents, quite by inferential design. The conformity to such premises by the child is generally apparent until the advent of the teen-age years, at which time a new source of so-called influence often emerges in the peer group. Peer influences are dialectical examinations of the "other side" of the meanings then in preferred ascendance among the parental culture (including most often tastes in music, dress, and heterosexual activities, although many other issues arise as well). The onset here is abrupt, as the so-called developing child can change into a "contradictory" teenager overnight.

Logical learning theory interprets the norm construct in terms of an intrinsic rather than an instrumental value system (Rychlak, 1968, p. 146). Lockean theories invariably press an instrumental value conception in accounting for conformity. The suggestion here is that people of all ages conform to norms because these culturally defined actions are rewarded. A person is repetitively open to reinforcements that occur contiguously to certain of his behaviors, and in this instrumental fashion he is molded according to a statistically frequent habitual pattern of behavior in the society—which is then called the norm of behavior for that particular group.

In opposition to this statistical view of the normal, logical learning theory contends that the person needs and seeks the norm, for it acts as a codified premise for the sake of which he behaves. Norms are intrinsically important to the human situation, for they serve as grounding premises providing not only an ordering for the individual—an important motivation in life—but a sense of identity (a special case of the tautology) for a body of people. The total effect here is a great sense of reassurance and certainty in one's affirmations, a structuring of that openness which is experience that begins in childhood and continues throughout life. From the viewpoint of logical learning theory there is no psychological difference between the scientist's seeking of truth and the average layman's seeking of the latest fashion in clothing or food. Both scientist and layman are trying to ground their premises in the most reassuring (convincing, certain, acceptable, etc.) method possible. Societies do not "program" norms into people. People need these norms as they need the protopoint premises that permit them to behave telosponsively. Of course one can find norms of behavior in other than current cultural products—the Bible, for example—and in basing his or her behavior on this more transcendent, intrinsic grounding, stand against certain conformity pressures of the popular moment. But then, the conformity to religious sanctions must be recognized in such "inner directed" (Riesman, 1953) behavior. In any case the empirical findings of a statistical nature merely reflect the facts of normative influence on behavior. They do not tell us what a norm means to the individual and how it actually enters into his behavior.

The final question we might consider in this section is: What has logical learning theory to say of the undoubted physical changes that take place in maturation and have a bearing on behavior. We have already taken the position that organic evolution, which is surely a type of physical development, probably proceeded in a demonstrative (unidirectional non-Kierkegaardian) fashion until such time that a dialectical intelligence emerged. We see nothing inconsistent in accepting this more conventional view of development as a steady progression through periods or stages in the physical realm of maturation. Of course, insofar as the maturational changes that occur influence the person's conceptualization of his life, we can expect these to engage behavior at the protopoint in the customary fashion. Obviously, due to their immature physical stature and limited experience, children have a narrowed range of alternative premises they might entertain compared to the average adult. The physically handicapped person has special problems of premise affirmation, and so on.

As a psychological theory, logical learning theory cannot presume to speak for theories of physical development. The danger is that we permit physical constructs to limit our thinking concerning what any one individual or class of individuals is capable of achieving in life—whether that be gifted versus retarded or male versus female. There is surely ample evidence from the great number of individuals who have perfected themselves in athletic, artistic, and other intellectual attainments which seem to have been beyond their native endowment to convince us that desire and aspiration are an important ingredient in all types of human performance. Logical learning theory holds that desires as needs and drives are telic factors in behavior, encompassed as such in the premises of telosponsivity, *not* in the physical substrate *per se*.

A Concept of the Self in Human Behavior

We noted above in discussing subject-contributed versus experimenter-contributed variables that a logic calls for the logician. To speak of logical extensions in meaning does not make much sense unless we acknowledge that there is an identity employing these assumptions, inductions, deductions, and conclusions. Thus logical learning theory, like all humanisms, must speak of something called the self.

The Meaning of Self

The word *self* has Anglo Saxon roots meaning the "same" or "identical;" when we say something is self-induced or self-motivated, we usually imply that the same organism did something today along the lines of what it did yesterday. The action may have varied a bit across time (the many), but there was a recognizable continuity nevertheless (the one). The logical learning theorist believes that psychology has erred in trying to construe selves as total organisms (persons), employing thereby all four of the causal meanings in this description. Very likely this is the heritage of the distinguished psychologist Gordon Allport (1937), whose influential trait theory fixed things in the neural substance so that now we feel that a self must also be constituted of something or other. Another problem is that we erroneously believe we must account for the self in efficient-cause terms—which are of course *not* well suited to the description of continuity in events but rather to the change in events.

Mention the term *self* in a conversation among psychologists today and you are likely to prompt questions like: What antecedent factors caused this self to form in the first place? This is frustrating to the self-theorist because one cannot express the meaning of "that which brings to bear an effect" by saying "that which is shaped by antecedent circumstances." Logical learning theory holds that the self is a kind of "logical thrust" from the side of conceptualization which organisms under our observation bring to bear as they "come at" the world in that formal-final-cause sense of the Kantian model. So long as there *are* premised assumptions, biases (Rokeach, 1973), personal constructs (Kelly, 1955), institutionalized paradigms (Kuhn, 1970), and so on, being affirmed by an identity, logical learning theory would argue that they are being expressed by a self. Organisms that bring meaningful premises to bear like this are usefully designated as contributing a self-influence to the course of events, particularly so when they realize that they *are* doing so. With these provisos we can now offer a definition of the self, as follows:

The *self* may be defined as a construct enabling the theorist to conceptualize the contribution made to behavior by an organism which brings meaningful premises to bear from a protopoint. *Behavior* in this context is overt action or covert understanding which has been predicated and styled through self-expression. The term *self* captures the impact or "logical weight" of a precedent meaning (premise), conveying sequacious implications, inductions, deductions, and so on, in the act of telosponsivity. To the extent that a behaving organism *does* (1) precedently and arbitrarily formulate meaningful premises at a protopoint for the sake of which it sequaciously behaves, (2) is conscious of doing so (i.e., has self-awareness), and (3) seeks to improve on the advantages gained from the use of such premises—to that extent can it be said to be self-enhancing in behavior or to be promoting self-realization.

We must move beyond point 1 because we have nothing here different from the usual telosponsivity of human behavior. At this point *self* is a concept more for the observer than for the actor. Infants and very young children are probably telosponding at about this level, and not until later do they begin to be aware of a continuity in such actions and seek thereby to gain some advantage (motivation) in furthering their selves (e.g., goals). Note that there is nothing in this definition to suggest that a something exists to be called the self in the sense that an organ called the liver exists. Nor do we contend that the self acts according to principles that are emergent or otherwise mystical and unamenable to description. The self concept is presented as an introspective formulation, reflecting that sense of orientation and *identity* in behavior which mechanists are prone to consider illusory experience (Immergluck, 1964; Lefcourt, 1973). Just as motion (efficient causality) is not required for the successions of logical or mathematical responding to follow, so are the effects of self-implications on behavior free of impetus considerations, drawing their rationale solely from the patterns and intentions of psychic life. These self-induced features of behavior have a *logical impact* on events.

Of course as selves we are cognizant of the passage of time because of our recognition (reconceptualization) of altering patterns. The seasons of the year present us with an altered patterning of the landscape, as does the shifting location of the sun across the skies each day. We order our lives in terms of such time changes, yet not without also retaining a sense of personal identity and hence continuity at the protopoint of our telosponsivity. Logical learning theory views this capacity to know one's self in the continuity across time as a special case of the principle of tautology. Things may change around us, we may grow wrinkled and grey, yet a kernel of self-identity is tautologized across such ravages of time to reassure us that we are the same person as always. Doubtless at some point self-identities are buttressed by group identities. Knowing who one's group is and its goals can be as important as knowing who one's self is; indeed the individual's selfhood can even be lost in the cohesiveness of group identity (see Table 1, Mead's use of the self-construct).

When we speak of the weight of logic in self-expression, we of course mean *both* dialectical and demonstrative logical progressions. Much of what is called the unreliability of traits or self-concepts in predicting across different situations (Mischel, 1968, 1973) stems from the dialectical ability of the individual to press more than simply one premise at the protopoint in any given circumstance. The next time he comes at the same situation or one similar to it, the individual can precedently switch premises (Kierkegaardian leap), and what sequaciously follows appears as a lack of predictability and hence a strike against the integrity of self-theory. The extraspective theorist presumes that what must be identical across situations is the observed behavior and not some premising identity guiding even differential behaviors from circumstance to circumstance. To prove the latter would require a *post hoc* discussion with the subject, and such after-the-fact examination of what we have called above subject-contributed variables strikes the extraspectionist as an inappropriate scientific procedure. But if we can predict from the outset of our study that what subjects do contra the experimental hypotheses can subsequently be rationalized via a well-controlled interview with them following initial data collection, this prediction is in the spirit of validating evidence. We might thus prove that even though unpredictable in some cases the course of behavior is always self-directed (see Bowers, 1973, for some excellent arguments along this and other lines).

Note that a certain level of self-development is implied in the definition at points 2 and 3, because one can have a greater or lesser awareness of one's function as a premising organism. Though this may be related to the question of development discussed above, logical learning theory does not contend that there need be a uniform progression in this development; also, such a progression can reverse itself and the individual can feel more at sea in life than he had previously. Alfred Adler's (1964) conception of the self emphasized the working-toward-a-goal feature that we have incorporated into our definition. This idea of self-enhancement or self-realization has been central to the ethical theories of history. As scientists, we need not let this tie of self to ethics disturb us, because a mentality that becomes aware of its own influence on the course of events should in time consider the likelihood of improving the relative standing it enjoys among changing circumstances, as per our definition of motivation (refer above). Concepts of perfection no doubt stem from this capacity for human beings to see how their aspirations and directed efforts can improve the quality of life. Of course this does not mean that selves must *always* seek the "higher" or more noble aims of life. Whether all people can work to become whole, self-consistent (Lecky, 1969), or congruent (Rogers, 1961) is an open question. Logical learning theory frankly recognizes that improving one's relative standing among an environment full of possible advantages is hardly limited to brotherly-love behaviors. Surely sometimes this self-induction also takes on a truly "selfish" quality, which means the individual intends to injure or otherwise demean a fellow human being.

The reader must appreciate that logical learning theory does not claim that all behavior is self-induced. The nonteleological formulations of a modern functionalist might hold for much of behavior (see Chapter 4). The presumption is that, as we ascend the phylogenetic scale, a greater likelihood for self-induced behavior is the case. This is due to the increasing employment of dialectical reasoning among higher animals. Stimulus-response psychology seems to fit lower organisms reasonably well, with their more demonstrative behavioral patterns. In light of our history concerning the anthropomorphizing of lower animals, to speak of self-induced factors in subhuman behavior seems a bit foolish. But it is not excessive, and we should not be too intimidated by our history to suggest that the self aspects of behavior could extend below the human level—although surely the telosponsivity here would be limited.

Self-Awareness and Consciousness

The historical search Descartes (1952) made to find the grounds on the basis of which to believe in his own existence is well known. After dismissing various other justifications, he arrived at the famous presumption "I think, therefore I am" (*Cogito ergo sum*). As a mathematician, Descartes' attitude toward the dialectic was very negative (*ibid.*, p. 17), and hence it is not surprising to see that his framing of a self-evident belief in his personal existence was demonstratively phrased. That is, although there is the suggestion here of transcendence in the self-reflexivity of knowing that one thinks, the emphasis is still exclusively on the act of thinking and not on the multiplicity of things that might be thought about *at the same time*. Consequently, as critics have long noted, the precedent meaning encompassing "I think" sequaciously implies that *thinking* exists more clearly than that "I" exist. One might as well say, "I breathe, therefore I exist." Even as a mediating animal, man could be made aware through some form of serendipitous input that his thinking capacity existed without thereby implying that a self-identity in control of this process *also* existed.

However, had Descartes argued dialectically "I think, and realize that I could be thinking quite the reverse many times over, therefore *I* exist" he would have put a more convincing case. In this phrasing the emphasis is taken off thinking *per se* and is placed on the duality of thought management dependent upon the "I." We have argued that a true free will is born in this arbitrary capacity to see alternative assumptions and implications in events. It is the logical weight of a self that chooses (decides, opts, etc.) to affirm "this" alternative rather than "that" alternative—or that has this option in principle—that makes a teleology possible in human behavior. Reasons are then sometimes found after the fact of deciding which direction thought is to take, although as we suggest above, this does not mean a teleology is lost. Here is where affective assessment enters. We could in this case say, "I affectively assess the meaning confronting me positively and realize that I could be assessing it negatively, therefore *I* exist." The affective assessment and the "feeling tone" [sic] this affords acts as a freely willed reason (grounds) for the behavior.

In line with our evolutionary speculations of Chapter 7 (pp. 304–305), we might define *awareness* psychologically as "appreciation of the arbitrariness in experience" or "knowing that something else might be taking place in a life circumstance" (see Table 1, Ducasse's definition of freedom). Simply registering inputs as stimuli and behaving in relation to these promptings does not mean that the animal is aware of its circumstances. Perception is not enough for awareness. To have a grasp of what is taking place demands a broader frame of reference, within which we see not only that which stands before us as reality but (at least some of) the possibilities and likelihoods not yet "there" for perceptual delineation. Telic animals are aware animals because they are constantly looking forward to such *non*literal aspects of experience. And of course even a potentially telic animal is unaware when he cannot organize the developing and unfolding possibilities of a situation in which he finds himself. But through a dialectical intelligence awareness is born.

The consciousness construct has been difficult to agree on in psychology because of a tendency to lump together simple responsivity and awareness into a common designation. If an animal is not asleep and therefore is responsive to external stimulation, it is considered by many to be conscious. There can be no great quarrel with the utility of this description because surely animals reflect altered states of vigilance and responsivity, and therefore a conscious-unconscious distinction seems plausible. However, due to the demonstrative bifurcation (i.e., acceptance of the law of contradiction) this led to, it became theoretically impossible to have these two states in any way *identical* (one among the many). Unconsciousness was now considered a *lack* of consciousness, and an animal was either in one or the other of these two states, but never in both at the same time.

Logical learning theory does not suggest that awareness is something limited to the self. One might be made aware of alternatives in life that have no focal point on selfhood. The person who looks to the skies and sees sunshine but considers the likelihood of rain based on subtle cues in the clouds rimming the horizon is reflecting an awareness, though the point of this is not selfhood. Whether aware or unaware, a person may be functioning consciously; even when aware of certain things, the individual may be unaware of his *self*-contribution in events. Unawareness of this type does not by itself necessarily signify unconsciousness. So long as a person is taking on premises and behaving for the sake of these predications he would be manifesting what our definition would call a self—that is, the weight of logic in a self-induced line of meaning-extension. But note: The definition has this framed as a construct for the utility of the observer. It says nothing about the self literally existing at the point of such telosponsivity in the behavior of others. For the person to develop a self-concept or self-awareness, he must see the contributions he *makes to* experience, depending upon what sort of meanings are affirmed at the protopoint. In this sense the self must be *intended*—that is, the purposive meaning of *self* must be brought to life by the individual, who cultivates it and furthers it or not. Not every conscious being has a high level of self-cultivation.

The more self-awareness an individual has, the more likely is he to appear conscious of his environment. People with so-called strong personalities, who are in command of their faculties, are of this type. They might also be self-centered and even selfish. But consciousness in the sense of vigilance and responsivity is not determined by self-awareness *per se*. We can be conscious without having a high level of self-awareness, and the problem of unconsciousness is therefore a separate issue.

Self-Control, Awareness, and Unconsciousness

We have been arguing for an image of humanity in which there is a self-contributed factor acknowledged in the course of any human behavior. In one sense there is almost no disputing this fact. Even the behaviorists today like to speak of self-control, by which they mean something akin to a Skinnerian view of environments that have been manipulated by persons and in turn control these very same persons. Here is a fine example of this kind of statement, one that shows the typical mediation gambit and theory-method confound as well: "Self-control is exhibited when a person engages in a behavior whose previous probability has been less than that of alternatively available responses. . . . Self-control patterns are usually mediated by symbolic processes and ultimately maintained by external variables" (Thoreson & Mahoney, 1974, p. 22). The person is ultimately controlled by independent variables in the external environment, but he is under self-control insofar as he is aware of these variables (*sic*) and arranges them to control himself. There is no point in repeating our Chapter 7 discussion (pp. 307–310) except to note that in logical learning theory when we speak of self-control *we mean self*-control. If a self is in control, the ultimate role for external factors (not variables) is as encompassed in the premise which the self conceptualizes, affirms, and telosponds in terms of. There is nothing in the research literature to counter such an interpretation of human behavior.

Can we telospond at two or more levels in mind? Can there be unconscious selves that direct the behavior of an individual from outside of self-awareness as most of the classical personality theories have contended? We have already taken a position on this in Chapter 7: dream symbols and themes (p. 289) as well as the dialectical opposite of affirmed meanings (p. 296) can be thought of as potentially exerting an influence on our behavior. However, because the definition of *self* given above emphasizes the eventual development of self-awareness, we would not refer to such unconscious identities in the personality as alternate selves. In fact, for an unconscious affirmation to attain the level of internal consistency and continuity (identity) that the self demands, would be highly unlikely if not impossible. Almost by definition the "other side" of conscious affirmations or the working to consciousness of visual analogues (symbols) in dreams would have to be lacking in that alternativeness that we have said is characteristic of awareness. The telosponsivity of unconsciousness is therefore a kind of mirror-image of conscious affirmation. In the unconscious state we have lost the general awareness of conscious mental states *as well as* the self-awareness within consciousness.

Of course the meanings thus telosponded in unconsciousness can germinate and order into story lines and clearly intentional manifestations of some "hidden" premise which consciousness may have considered and discarded or never have considered at all. It is hidden because the meaning precedently affirmed in unconscious telosponsivity cannot be sequaciously enriched by consciousness any more than what person A thinks can be sequaciously enriched by person B. Not until B takes on the premises of A can this occur, and not until consciousness takes on the premises of unconsciousness can the single person come to understand what meaning is being expressed in his own unconscious mind. It is as if there is an internal semaphore communication being attempted, with the unconscious sphere sending precedent meanings, but the conscious receiving not a sequacious extension of meaning but a flurry of flags, the coding of which has not yet been deciphered by consciousness. Unconscious thoughts are lacking in the quality of awareness, hence they take on a more (hard) deterministic quality. We might say that the unconscious is on the "after affirmation" side of psychic determinism *in every case*—that is, having the quality of determinism following a decision because these contents are always nondecisions, disliked alternatives, and so on, whereas in consciousness we do at times see the "before affirmation" arbitrariness of free will in operation. The unconscious is rigid and unyielding because it is always dealing in post-affirmational materials!

For example, the directing force of hallucinations or delusional systems can be said to take away from self-control in deference to a person's fantasy life. This imaginary material has not always lacked awareness from the outset. Sometimes it can even begin in a self-aware effort to flee the dull routine or the anxiety of an unhappy life. Gradually, however, the person can lose self-awareness—that is, stop conceptualizing his role in the creation of his chimerical fantasies. Sometimes he is in a twilight state on the question, knowing that he had begun all of this "imagined nonsense" but is now losing control over it. To reverse the process and gain self-control involves the cultivation of (1) awareness in consciousness generally and (2) self-awareness in particular. Psychotherapy is aimed at achieving these ends, and even the behavior therapies necessarily devote considerable effort to showing the person how he or she can successfully alter the course of events in daily life. Telling the person that the environment controls his behavior hence he had best look carefully at this environment is surely conducive to both types of awareness. The role of awareness in behavioral manipulation is of primary importance.

Why does mind have such levels of awareness? This question

cannot be answered with assurance, but as a dialectical theory of mentality, logical learning theory would suggest that unconsciousness is a necessary corollary of the affirmation that brings about consciousness. Consciousness telosponds by premising what we think we must do, prefer to do, and so on, and unconsciousness telosponds by premising the reverse—what we must not do, what we "disprefer" to do, and so on. In the same way that we can learn error, mentality can entertain meaning that has *not* been affirmed. That alternatives which were open to behavior and yet not affirmed continue in mind and reappear as viable albeit often troublesome possibilities is probably conducive to survival in the human species. Such unaffirmed alternatives populate our dreams, although quite often what is called a dream is a self-aware affirmation of some wished-for eventuality.[1]

Can there be a direct unconscious affirmation of meaning to parallel the affirmation process that logical learning theory postulates in consciousness? Most of the theoreticians who have accepted the construct of unconsciousness have kept this possibility open, requiring thereby that they have a parallel identity to the self in unconsciousness (e.g., an id, alter-ego, shadow, etc.). Because logical learning theory essentially holds that self-awareness is made possible in the preaffirmation arbitrariness of decision-making, it does not seem consistent to speculate on unconscious identities that supposedly affirm points of view but do not advance self-awareness in so doing. Human beings can always take the opposite position (or an alternative thereby) on *any* question facing them. The unconscious identities that speak out—for example, cases of alternating or multiple personality—invariably show us this clinical picture.

---

[1] Although not suitable for presentation at this point in its speculative development, logical learning theory entertains the possibility that self-awareness may not be limited to consciousness. If we can distinguish between conscious-unconscious as levels of vigilance and responsivity (presumably based on biological factors) *and* conscious-unconscious realms of mental telosponsivity, each with its dialectically arrayed forms of premises readied for affirmation, then what we have termed "awareness in consciousness generally" may simply involve the more reality-bound type of premise—the one likely to be affirmed in the state of vigilance and responsivity (consciousness). Reverse affirmations would then occur in nonvigilant states (unconsciousness) and the self-identity would have altered levels of awareness in the two realms of mentation. In dream states, for example, for the person to ascertain the grounds for the sake of which certain actions are being carried out is difficult but not impossible. Without reality-bound grounds a more bizarre precedent-sequacious line of meaning-extension is enacted. But occasionally one *is* aware that he is having a dream, and to this extent we can appropriately speak of self-awareness.

The emergent personality is dialectically opposite to the original personality, and variations on this theme proceed as new identities multiply. What does this signify? Are these variations on the original personality (i.e., the premises that characterize the original personality) separately affirmed outlooks, or are they dialectically generated developments from the initial conscious affirmation? Logical learning theory takes the latter stance, at least for the present and finds it unfruitful to reify cohesive identities at an unconscious level.

We cannot overestimate the importance logical learning theory places on the human being's capacity to learn that which he does not prefer to learn (i.e., which he has affectively assessed negatively), the learning of error, the processing of information that is unpopular and distasteful even to the self, and so forth. Affirmation at the protopoint is not the end of things but the beginning. Affirmation tells us what direction will be taken (psychic determinism), but awareness demands that the nonaffirmed be known as well. Possibly this is the reason for unconscious behavior (understanding- and action-intentions) emerging. The burden of knowing all that is possible to know, such as the not to be, the unpreferred, the likelihoods but uncertainties, is simply too much for a well-ordered conceptualization to eventuate in conscious thought. Hence certain of these —shall we say too complex, unhappy, defensive, threatening—possibilities are no longer conceptualized, leading to a loss in awareness. Even so, these meanings are not lost to the telosponsivity of mind, and they come back as those one-sided and opinionated views that Jung (1960) called complexes or the undesirable antithetic ideas that Freud (1966) as neophyte theoretician described so well.

Summary

Chapter 8 begins with a distinction between emotion and affection. Although both are evaluations, emotions are seen as rooted in the body and hence best conceptualized in demonstrative terms. Affections are dialectical, completely psychological assessments. Another way of speaking about affective assessment is as a transcendental telosponse—that is, a telosponse in which the individual turns back on his mental processes and evaluates their content in terms of positiveness or negativeness. Affective assessments are arbitrary before being made, whereas emotions are never arbitrary. The methodological counterpart of affective assessment is reinforcement value, which is an operational measure of likability made by the subject of various materials he may be asked to learn or otherwise deal with. A distinction is then drawn between experimenter-contributed and subject-contributed variables, with reinforcement value said to be a subject-contributed variable that usually is uncontrolled in the typical experimental study.

The next topic considered is that of meaning-extension, which refers to the precedent-sequacious flow of meaning in the conceptualizations of telosponsivity. Learning involves the extension of meanings conceptually, and a reinforcement—although best thought of as a methodological construct—can be viewed as successful meaning-extension. When a premise truly conceptualizes experience for the individual, a reinforcement of this premise may be said to have taken place. There are essentially two steps in learning: (1) sensory input as ordered into images, sounds, and so forth by innate sense organs, and (2) the active conceptualization of this input through affirmation. Logical learning theory holds that affective assessment always enters at the second step of this sequence, assuming that the conceptual act does in fact occur.

To bring home the importance of active intellect on behavior, we next introduce a refinement in the concept of association by noting that there are four types of affirmations involved in the association of ideas. These include unqualified, qualified, negative, and oppositional affirmations. We show how a simplistic view of association makes every such bonding of meaningful items in experience an unqualified affirmation when in fact the associative powers of human mentality are not this limited. The problem of motivation, as it relates to the concepts of possibility, choice, and psychic determinism, is discussed. Motivation is defined as an evaluation of the relative advantage a premise affords the individual affirming it. Logical learning theory rejects the classical distinction between learning and motivation. Motivations are always encompassed in the individual's premises, which in turn enter into learning; these are different aspects of the same process and cannot be separated except artificially for the purposes of descriptive analysis.

Classical learning-theory terminology is surveyed, reinterpreting these by way of the rubrics of logical learning theory. Constructs such as trial and error, generalization, discrimination, law of effect, expectancy, figure-ground, and isomorphism are discussed. A major feature of this reinterpretation is evident in that logical learning theory places an introspective theoretical perspective into each of these classical terms. A discussion about the possible role of development factors in learning follows. Although logical learning theory is not formed developmentally, there are certain implications for its tenets in the developmental concept, and these are reviewed. The role of norms on behavior is analyzed in terms of intrinsic versus instrumental value theories. Logical learning theory looks at norms in terms of an intrinsic theory of value.

The final major division of Chapter 8 takes up the question of self-identity in human behavior. The self is defined as a construct enabling the theorist to conceptualize the contribution made to human behavior via a "logical weight" brought to bear on events, one that takes on a continuity and a conscious self-enhancing direction (i.e., seeks advantages) in the flow of life experience. This logical weight involves both dialectical and demonstrative implications, deductions, assumptions, and so forth, brought forward from protopoints and encompassed as premises. Awareness is defined as the appreciation of arbitrariness in experience, and the self-aware individual is said to be the one who knows that he could be thinking (hence doing) otherwise in life, but does as he does for the sake of certain reasons. The closing themes of Chapter 8 include the question of consciousness versus unconsciousness, how this relates to self-awareness, and the role of such factors in self-control.

References

Adler, A. *Social interest: A challenge to mankind.* New York: Capricorn, 1964.

Allport, G. W. *Personality: A psychological interpretation.* New York: Holt, 1937.

Arnold, M. B. *Emotion and personality.* New York: Columbia University Press, 1960.

Arnold, M. B. (Ed.), *Feelings and emotions.* New York: Academic, 1970.

Boring, E. G. *A history of experimental psychology.* New York: Appleton-Century-Crofts, 1950.

Bowers, K. S. Situationism in psychology: An analysis and a critique. *Psychological Review,* 1973, **80**, 307–336.

Brentano, F. *Psychology from an empirical standpoint.* New York: Humanities, 1973.

Chaplin, J. P., & Krawiec, T. S. *Systems and theories of psychology.* New York: Holt, Rinehart & Winston, 1960.

Descartes, R. *Rules for the direction of mind* and *Discourse on method.* In R. M. Hutchins (Ed.), *Great books of the western world* (Vol. 31). Chicago: Encyclopedia Britannica, 1952.

Dollard, J., & Miller, N. E. *Personality and psychotherapy: An analysis in terms of learning, thinking, and culture.* New York: McGraw-Hill, 1950.

Dunlap, K. A revision of the fundamental law of habit formation. *Science*, 1928, **67**, 360–362.

Freud, S. *The psychopathology of everyday life*. In J. Strachey (Ed.), *The standard edition of the complete psychological works of Sigmund Freud* (Vol. VI). London: Hogarth, 1960.

Freud, S. A case of successful treatment by hypnotism. In J. Strachey (Ed.), *The standard edition of the complete psychological works of Sigmund Freud* (Vol. I). London: Hogarth, 1966. Pp. 115–128.

Guthrie, E. R. *The psychology of learning* (rev. ed.). New York: Harper, 1952.

Hull, C. L. *A behavior system*. New Haven: Yale University Press, 1952.

Immergluck, L. Determinism-freedom in contemporary psychology: An ancient problem revisited. *American Psychologist*, 1964, **19**, 270–281.

James, W. *The principles of psychology*. In R. M. Hutchins (Ed.), *Great books of the western world* (Vol. 53). Chicago: Encyclopedia Britannica, 1952.

Jung, C. G. *The structure and dynamics of the psyche*. In H. Read, M. Fordham, and G. Adler (Eds.), *The collected works of C. G. Jung* (Vol. 8). Bollingen Series XX.8. New York: Pantheon, 1960.

Kant, I. *The critique of pure reason*. In R. M. Hutchins (Ed.), *Great books of the western world* (Vol. 42). Chicago: Encyclopedia Britannica, 1952. Pp. 1–250.

Kelly, G. A. *The psychology of personal constructs* (2 vols.). New York: Norton, 1955.

Koffka, K. *Principles of gestalt psychology*. New York: Harcourt, Brace, 1935.

Kuhn, T. S. *The structure of scientific revolutions* (2nd ed.). Chicago: The University of Chicago Press, 1970. (1st ed., 1962.)

Lecky, P. *Self-consistency: A theory of personality*. Garden City, N.Y.: Doubleday, 1969.

Lefcourt, H. M. The function of the illusions of control and freedom. *American Psychologist*, 1973, **28**, 417–425.

Lewin, K. *A dynamic theory of personality*. New York: McGraw-Hill, 1935.

Lorayne, H., & Lucas, J. *The memory book*. New York: Ballantine, 1974.

Mischel, W. *Personality and assessment*. New York: Wiley, 1968.

Mischel, W. Toward a cognitive social learning reconceptualization of personality. *Psychological Review*, 1973, **80**, 252–283.

Murphy, G. *Personality: A biosocial approach to origins and structure*. New York: Harper, 1947.

Orne, M. T. On the social psychology of the psychological experiment: With particular reference to demand characteristics and their implications. *American Psychologist*, 1962, **17**, 776–783.

Pavlov, I. P. *Conditioned reflexes: An investigation of the physiological activity of the cerebral cortex* (trans. by G. V. Anrep). New York: Oxford University Press, 1927.

Piaget, J. *The child's conception of physical causality*. London: Kegan Paul, Trench, Trubner, 1930.

Piaget, J. *The child's conception of number*. London: Routledge & Kegan Paul, 1952.

Piaget, J. *Logic and psychology*. New York: Basic Books, 1957.

Riesman, D. *The lonely crowd.* Garden City, N.Y.: Doubleday, 1953.

Rogers, C. R. *On becoming a person: A therapist's view of psychotherapy.* Boston: Houghton Mifflin, 1961.

Rokeach, M. *The nature of human values.* New York: Free Press, 1973.

Rosenthal, R. *Experimenter effects in behavioral research.* New York: Appleton-Century-Crofts, 1966.

Rychlak, J. F. *A philosophy of science for personality theory.* Boston: Houghton Mifflin, 1968.

Rychlak, J. F. *Introduction to personality and psychotherapy.* Boston: Houghton Mifflin, 1973.

Sullivan, H. S. *The interpersonal theory of psychiatry.* New York: W. W. Norton & Co., Inc., 1953.

Thoreson, C. E., & Mahoney, M. J. *Behavioral self-control.* New York: Holt, Rinehart and Winston, 1974.

Thorndike, E. L. Animal intelligence: An experimental study of the associative processes in animals. *Psychological Review Monograph Supplement,* 1898, No. 8.

Titchener, E. B. *A text-book of psychology.* New York: Macmillan, 1909.

Underwood, B. J., & Schulz, R. W. *Meaningfulness and verbal learning.* Chicago: Lippincott, 1960.

Watson, J. B. *Behaviorism.* New York: Norton, 1924.

Wundt, W. *Lectures on human and animal psychology* (4th ed.). New York: Macmillan, 1907. (1st ed., 1894.)

CHAPTER NINE

The Development and Validation of Logical Learning Theory

Logical learning theory can be considered from two slightly different directions. First, it is a body of technical terminology representing a Kuhnian revolution of the mechanistic human image that is currently accepted in psychology. Basic research on these technical constructs must be carried out in the spirit of the third step of our "line-of-development" progression (see Chapter 5, p. 191). As such validation efforts continue, we expect refinements to occur in the basic technical constructs. Second, logical learning theory is a body of empirical findings that it is hoped will prove instructive regarding human behavior. In this sense, there are "applied" aspects of the point of view to consider. These are findings on various topics that are not necessarily "the" corpus of logical learning theory but rather plausible extensions of the basic theoretical constructs to the teleological image of humanity that it has been formulated to capture. Chapter 9 is organized on the basis of these contrasting focuses of logical learning theory. We begin with a review of the work done on the basic construct of affective assessment and then move to some applications of this measurement to human behavior more generally. Along the way we will discuss theoretical developments and changes. Finally, we will discuss the direction that research is currently taking and the prospects for the future.

A Basic Dimension on Which to Build

Our first challenge was to identify a native capacity of human beings enabling them to influence the course of their learning/behavior independent of environmental influence. We presumed that the person would be telosponding in this native action, which meant that he or she would be framing a meaningful premise and behaving for the sake of this affirmation. Recall that affirmation involves both demonstrative and dialectical strategies in reasoning (see Chapter 7, p. 295). But as we were interested in finding a way to account for the person's unique contribution to the course of behavior, we favored a dialectical conceptualization at this point. The realm of affect drew our immediate interest, because people do seem to evaluate their circumstances according to likes and dislikes—a dialectical contrast if ever there was one. Could a "liking" of something be an affirmation of one end of a bipolar "like-dislike" dimension? This seemed plausible.

Since many psychologists interpret likes and dislikes to be strictly emotional—that is, efficiently and materially caused—"responses," it was necessary to draw the distinction between emotions and affects (see Chapter 8, pp. 315–321). William James (1884) paved the way for a theoretical distinction to be drawn between physical feelings of pleasure/displeasure and what he termed "genuinely *cerebral* forms of pleasure and displeasure" (p. 201) that were more like cognitive judgments of right/wrong than strictly physical feelings. Obviously, the former feelings would involve material-efficient causes, whereas the latter judgments would involve formal-final causes.

Here was our chance to study a truly Kantian "category of the understanding" (Chapter 1, p. 35). People could be said to order their cognitive understanding of experience in terms of like/dislike judgments that they uniquely decided upon for themselves from the very outset of life. They affirmed one end or the other of a dialectical oppositionality concerning whatever it was that they were cognitively processing at the moment. This furthered a continuing discrimination which was in effect the source of the most basic of meaning relations in cognition (from "like to dislike"), much in the sense that the gestaltists referred to the fundamental "differentiation and articulation" of the phenomenal field (see Chapter 4, pp. 158–159). *Affective assessment was part and parcel of human mentation and a clear manifestation of dialectical reasoning.* This was the first hypothesis advanced by logical learning theory. Could it be supported empirically? In due course we turned to the extant literature to see if there were any precedents on which to base our theoretical claim.

Intimations of Affective Assessment in the Literature

We were pleased to learn that there was quite a body of literature on which to draw, although the methodological findings had been understood in biological and mechanical theoretical terms rather than in teleological terms. Findings on affective factors in human behavior have been well documented, dating back at least to Tait (1913), who drew on Wilhelm Wundt's (see Chapter 3, pp. 109–119) theory of emotions to demonstrate empirically that pleasant words were easier to learn than unpleasant words. Tolman (1917) found the same facilitation effect in a study of retroactive inhibition. Occasionally, unpleasant words were learned more quickly than words that were judged "indifferent" by subjects. The unfortunate practice then arose of lumping pleasant and unpleasant (liked versus disliked) words into a single category of "emotional" and comparing ease of learning for these words with words judged to be indifferent (Bunch & Wientge, 1933; Jones, 1929; Lynch, 1932; Smith, 1921).

There followed a host of studies during the 1930s which asked the subject to recall or otherwise learn a list of words that had been prerated by others as to pleasantness (Carter, 1935, 1937; Carter & Jones, 1937; White, 1936; White & Powell, 1936; White & Ratliff, 1934) or that the subject had prerated for himself/herself (Silverman & Cason, 1934; Stagner, 1933; Thomson, 1930). When measurements are taken as averages from samples of subjects and believed to be typical of "all" persons in the sample, we refer to this as *nomothetic* measurement. When measurements are taken from an individual subject and believed to be uniquely typical of this singular person, we refer to this as *idiographic* measurement (after Wilhelm Windelband; see Cassirer, 1944, p. 235). The finding of a learning superiority of pleasant over unpleasant and indifferent words continued to show through these studies, particularly when the prejudgments were handled idiographically.

The general problem of what we take to be affective influence on learning then fell from view for over a decade, until the "perceptual defense" studies rekindled an interest in this area. Work in the modern period has focused primarily on the source of pleasant-unpleasant ratings—an issue that was to bedevil us as we pursued our studies of affective assessment. Typical problems addressed included whether the subject's judgments of pleasant/unpleasant are really a separate process from sheer frequency of contact with a given term, or the number of word-associates that a subject can produce to a positively or negatively toned word-stimulus (Cantor, 1935; Cromwell, 1956; Johnson, Frincke & Martin, 1961; Koen, 1962; Osgood, 1952; Sarbin & Quenk, 1964; Staats, 1959; Zajonc, 1968). These findings suggested that an affective dimension is at work in human learning, one that is often correlated positively with (but still independent from) such frequency measures of subject contact with the learnable items (e.g., words) in question.

The Lockean theoretical model (Chapter 2, pp. 86–88) dominated here, suggesting that a person's likes were due to a history of positive reinforcement for liked things; a person's dislikes were tied to a history of being punished for certain other things. In other words, it was the principle of contiguity (see Chapter 8, p. 342) or frequency of past contact with the item in question that was believed to "really" determine a person's likes and dislikes in the present. To assume that people have a native capacity to render such telosponsive judgments "from birth" was never taken seriously, because it was presumed that any act of (formal-final cause) judgment had itself to be "accounted for" in terms of efficient causation. Logical learning theory begins with the premise that people do indeed have a native capacity to render affective judgments, assessing the items of experience that they are learning even as they come to know them initially. Such assessments then carry over to new learnings, as the principle of tautology suggests (from "liked" to "liked," or *vice versa*; see Chapter 7, p. 278). This (formal-final cause) evaluative capacity is not learned, any more than the capacity to remember past experience is learned.

Research on the Management and Basic Learning Effects of Reinforcement Value

We had now identified a basic dimension—affective assessment—as a presumed Kantian category of innate understanding. People ordered their cognitive processes on the basis of dialectically generated preferences. In line with our arguments of Chapters 5 and 6, we felt it necessary to coin a methodological construct to parallel our strictly theoretical construct of affective assessment. This is how we arrived at the measure known as *reinforcement value* (RV) (see Chapter 8, p. 322). This is an idiographic measurement in which subjects are asked to judge literally anything known or knowable as to its likability. This is accomplished by having the subject rate some item (e.g., a word, design, painting, human image, etc.) on a four-step dimension of preference—i.e., *dislike much, dislike slightly, like slightly,* and *like much* (based on the work of Berg, 1957). It would be possible to obtain nomothetic measures of RV; however, except for a few special research problems (discussed later), we did not pursue this alternative, believing it is most instructive to study what "a" person assesses as liked or disliked rather than relying upon mean (nomothetic) averages of groups of people.

Initially we made use of consonant-vowel-consonant (CVC) trigrams as learnable items. It is possible to control such trigrams (e.g., HIB, LAT, ZOC, PIC, CAX, etc.) for familiarity, frequency of past contact, and the like. Archer (1960), for example, presented all possible trigram combinations to subjects and had them rate each one according to whether it looked like a word, sounded like a word, or could be used in a sentence (possibly as an acronym, etc.). The trigrams were then arrayed from those very familiar, or wordlike, (e.g., POT) to those quite unfamiliar, or unwordlike (e.g., ZOH). It is then not difficult to show that highly familiar trigrams can generate more word associations than trigrams that are less familiar. (POT relates to several words like stove, stew, cook, etc., whereas ZOH lacks such a range of word associates.) Indeed, it is common to refer to this measure as *association value* (AV). The nomothetic AV of any trigram (e.g., SOV) would be the percentage of subjects who believed that it looked like a word, sounded like a word, or could be used in a sentence. To the Lockean theorist, it follows that RV would be due to AV considerations. Zajonc (1968), in particular, had found an "enhancement effect" for exposure, which meant that people tended to like what they had been exposed to. On the other hand, Brickman, Redfield, Harrison, and Crandall (1972) were to find that such enhancement occurred only when the materials exposed to subjects (whether designs, words, etc.) were initially judged by these subjects as neutral or positive in likability (i.e., RV). Disliked materials failed to be enhanced through sheer exposure.

In our first RV studies, we employed CVC trigrams as learnable items. Subjects rated the trigrams (HIB, LAT, ZOC, etc.) on two occasions for likability on the four-step procedure, usually with 24 hours intervening. Note that there is no midpoint on the likability (RV) rating. We are in effect forcing a subject to choose in either of two opposite directions—with "slight" and "much" estimates allowing for a measurement of the extent of liking or disliking. Since subjects shifted their judgments from liked to disliked (and *vice versa*) over repeated tests, we found it necessary to use only the reliably rated items in our learning experiments. Hence, when subjects rate items for RV they *always* do so on two occasions, and we make use of only those items that are rated liked or disliked (preferably "much") on *both* testing occasions.

As the research on pleasantness had suggested, we found immediately that subjects learned their liked trigrams more readily than their disliked trigrams. This finding obtained whether we used mixed lists (i.e., both liked and disliked trigrams included) or unmixed lists (i.e., either all liked or all disliked trigrams included) in paired-associates or serial learning formats, and whether we used trials-to-criterion, recognition, or free recall as our means of testing the rate of learning (Abramson, 1967; Laberteaux, 1968; Rychlak, 1966). We have termed this facility of learning liked over disliked items the *RV-positive effect*, keeping in mind that it is a purely methodological occurrence (i.e., the *effect* explains nothing). Subsequently, Matlin and Stang (1978) were to show that this influence of the positive on learning and memory is pervasive in human experience. These authors referred to this affective preference for the positive as the "Pollyanna principle" and gave it a theoretical, information-processing explanation that— due to its nondialectical framing—considers learnable material of a negative-RV nature as essentially "discarded" (p. 3). There is an important theoretical point to consider here, having to do with the possibility of subjects learning *disliked* items more readily than liked items (an "RV-negative" effect). As dialectical theorists, we would surely expect this alternative to take place in human behavior, and there was some indication of this in the work on pleasantness cited previously. We will return to this question later.

For now, we must take up the matter of what "causes" the RV-positive effect. Is it due to some covert operation of AV? Critics of logical learning theory were pressing this point, and we took various steps to confront it empirically. First, we compared idiographic RV across various levels of nomothetic AV. We drew CVC trigrams from a low, medium, and high level of the Archer (1960) norms. If RV was directly influenced by nomothetic AV, then we should find trigrams high in AV (many subjects see the trigrams as wordlike) performing as "liked" trigrams do in rate of learning. And, conversely, trigrams low in AV (few subjects see the trigrams as wordlike) should be learned primarily as "disliked" trigrams are. Actually, what we found was that idiographic measures of RV functioned equally at all levels of nomothetic AV (Abramson, Tasto, & Rychlak, 1969). Indeed, there was no statistical interaction between nomothetic AV and idiographic RV. These dimensions functioned separately in the learning rate of our subjects. Subjects reflected a clear superiority in their liked over their disliked trigrams, no matter how much nomothetic AV was involved in the trigrams.

The point here is that if human beings do affectively assess even as they cognize experience, then it makes no difference whether their cognitive contents (thoughts, ideas, words, concepts, images, etc.) are familiar, clear, and distinct or strange, vague, and tentative. People must be thought of as affectively choosing in *every* instance as they come to frame a premised meaning. The pattern of experience typifying the meaning may be quite unexpected and unfamiliar, yet whether it strikes the person as positive or negative in RV is not thereby determined. People can like *or* dislike the unexpected and unfamiliar. Research on the visual preference of infants has demonstrated that they prefer to look at curved rather than straight lines, colored rather than uncolored pictures, three-dimensional rather than two-dimensional objects, complex rather than simple patterns, and schematic faces rather than featureless faces (Cohen, 1979). Visual acuity at birth is poor but rapidly improves over the first few months of life. The preferences just noted occur at the very beginning of this improvement in visual acuity. These are the methodological findings. How are we to interpret them? The familiarity-contiguity argument certainly fails, since there *is no* previous history of reinforcement to base such preferences on. At this point, the traditional mechanistic account must fall back on material causation and claim innate visual preferences. This means that the complete theoretical account shifts from mechanistic "inborn" to mechanistic "learned" influences over the life of the child. Logical learning theory takes a more parsimonious view: Infants can affectively assess (telospond), thereby directing *from birth* the course of their cognitive organization based on such telic judgments (however one cares to construe precisely "when" the birth of mentation occurs).

Our next step in the effort to prove that affective assessment is more a cause than an effect of human learning was to confront idiographic AV with idiographic RV. That is, we had the *same* subject rate trigrams for wordlikeness (via Archer's [1960] instruction cited above) and for likability. If AV and RV are separate and distinct measures of cognitive processes then we should be able to find that the subjects' learning facility was independently influenced by each of these dimensions. And so we did. Subjects learned trigrams they considered wordlike more quickly than those they considered unwordlike. Furthermore, within this AV sorting they learned liked trigrams more readily than disliked trigrams (Abramson, Tasto, & Rychlak, 1969). Once again, no statistical interaction between our two measures obtained. It seemed clearer than ever that whatever RV was measuring in the mentation of our subjects was independent of whatever AV was measuring.

Unfortunately, our critics were not so easily convinced. The next line of assault came from the direction of what might be termed the "associative strength" of our trigrams. How could we be so sure that in judging a given trigram as "liked," the subject was not designating for us an item that was prone to call up many associated meanings. That is, in this subject's unique cognizance a liked trigram might stimulate a host of ideas (words, images, etc.), whereas in the case of a disliked trigram few such associations would be generated. And by "generated" our critic meant an automatic, efficient-cause determination of some sort. The obvious way in which to answer this criticism was to give subjects trigrams that they had prerated for RV and to see if they did in fact come up with more word associations for the liked than the disliked trigrams. We did this study and found no consistent relationship between RV and the number of word associations made to the trigram concerned, whether the trigram was from a low, medium, or high level of the Archer (1960) norms (Kubat, 1969). Here again, we cannot "reduce" affective preference to a frequency count.

We enlarged upon the findings of an independence between AV and RV by having groups of subjects make both ratings for the same list of 140 trigrams. We also looked at the reliability of the measures. As we suspected, nomothetic AV was somewhat more reliable over one-week retesting (Pearsonian $r = .85$) than nomothetic RV (Pearsonian $r = .54$). (With 46 subjects in the sample, both of these correlations exceeded the .01 level of significance.) This nomothetic comparison masked the idiographic fact that 19 of the subjects changed from judging a trigram to be wordlike to unwordlike, or *vice versa*, whereas only 13 of the subjects shifted in their RV estimate from like to dislike, or *vice versa* (Tenbrunsel, Nishball, & Rychlak, 1968).

The nomothetic measures of AV and RV reflected a Pearsonian correlation of .45 ($p < .01$, with 100 subjects in the sample). Considered in light of a coefficient of determination, this would suggest that roughly 20–25% of trigrams that a subject rates will be confounded for RV and AV (i.e., a subject will assign liked ratings to wordlike trigrams and disliked ratings to unwordlike trigrams). This is, in fact, what we found when we looked at the 140 trigrams that had been rated by 100 subjects for AV and RV. Thirty-five of these 140 trigrams were confounded in the ratings made by 100 subjects. However, the greatest degree of confounding occurred at the lower levels of the Archer (1960) norms. In other words, the more a trigram began to remind the subject of an actual word, the less likely it was that he or she would confound AV ratings with RV ratings (Tenbrunsel, et al., 1968). This finding supports our contention of an independence of AV and RV, since if the two dimensions were variations of the same thing then the "more" one dimension approached its basic characteristic (i.e., word-likeness) the "more" it should be functioning for the other dimension (i.e., likability).

The final strategy we employed to counter those who would explain RV away via AV involved factor analysis. Critics asked questions such as "How do you know that in saying he or she 'likes' a trigram or an actual word the subject is not telling you that such items are simply easy to learn?" In other words, RV might be a covert way of indexing the subject's perceived difficulty of the item in question. In order to meet this and other objections once and for all, we did several factor analyses in which the same subjects repeatedly rated the same trigrams for various instructions. Thus, subjects rated trigrams based on the typical AV and RV instructions, but they also rated for the following instructions: easy to learn/hard to learn; used often/used rarely; easy to pronounce/hard to pronounce; familiar/unfamiliar. In one factor analysis both trigrams and actual words were used. We also introduced the Osgoodian (1952) dimensions of rating trigrams and words for the meanings of: active/passive, strong/weak, and good/bad. In sum, we found in cross-validating factor analyses that three dimensions were involved in all of these ratings. One was clearly RV, one was clearly AV, and a third was a special kind of "familiarity-for-the-experiment" dimension (Rychlak, Flynn, & Burger, 1979). That is, since subjects usually made six ratings of the same trigrams, instructions such as familiar/unfamiliar or used often/used rarely were predicated by subjects as referring to the task at hand.

The AV factor was loaded by such instructions as word-like/unwordlike and Osgood's active/passive. The RV factor was loaded by such instructions as like/dislike and Osgood's good/bad. The good/bad rating of Osgood (1952) taps what he terms "the evaluation dimension of meaning" (see also Osgood, Suci, & Tannenbaum, 1957). This dimension has proven to be the most salient of the three employed in studies of language systems from all corners of the globe. Interestingly, the easy-to-learn/hard-to-learn instruction failed to load very heavily on any factor, but relatively speaking it was closer to the AV factor than the RV factor.

This completes our survey of the research conducted on the psychometric qualities and basic learning effects of the RV dimension. At this point we had satisfied ourselves that what we were asking subjects to "do" in operationalizing their affective preferences could not be explained away or "accounted for" by the typical measures of meaningfulness that relied upon frequency counts of one sort or another. We took it as "given" that RV was a subject-contributed variable (see Chapter 8, pp. 321–324). It was not the automatic response to previous shapings, but rather a telosponsive action in which a judgment had been rendered and then furthered over the course of the person's life.

Applying the Basic Dimension to Various Theoretical Issues

Now that we had satisfied ourselves that RV could be taken as a dimension separate from other dimensions of measurement based on frequency/contiguity considerations, we could set about applying our metric to various theoretical points of interest. We did precisely this for almost two decades. Over this period of time, we also worked out a more detailed understanding of the telosponsive process. Before turning to a survey of the empirical problems we pursued, we will devote some time to our growing understanding of telosponsivity.

The Role of Predication in Telosponsivity

We have defined affective assessment as a *transcendental telosponse* (see Chapter 8, p. 317), which means that we believe people can turn back reflexively on their ongoing telosponses—that is, on the meanings under affirmation—and render a judgment of what is being premised there. By "reflexively," we mean to rise dialectically above what one is framing in understanding, effectively "turning back" on it from a more abstract perspective. This is what Brentano was referring to in his *secondary* act of consciousness paralleling primary consciousness (see Chapter 3, p. 116). The *terminus* (after Brentano) of such a transcending telosponsive (secondary) act is the meaning being framed telosponsively in ongoing (primary) consciousness. As dialectical reasoners, human beings have the native capacity to transcend from "inside ongoing thought" to "outside ongoing thought," and in this paralleling process render affective assessments of that which we are thinking about at the time. We can also question what we are thinking about, contradict it, and begin to enlarge on what is "not" being thought (telosponded) about.

In the typical RV study, we present a word, concept, or CVC trigram to a subject and ask him or her to render such a judgment (secondary consciousness) even as the item *per se* is being framed cognitively (primary consciousness). In effect, the subject is cognizing something along the lines of "I like X" or "X is something I like." The precise phraseology is not important. Indeed, no actual statement need ever be framed because it is possible to render such evaluations of perceptions, emotions, and so on, without actually putting one's affective assessment into words. Logical learning theory contends that such a process is routine in mentation and that it is difficult, if not impossible, to completely avoid (be indifferent to) one's conceptualizations as framed in primary consciousness. Indifference tends to become mildly negative affection.

Further analysis of telosponsivity suggests that when a statement such as "I like HIB" or "I dislike XIL" is made, this represents in telosponsive terminology an affirmed premise. That is, in order to frame "I dislike XIL" the person must have already considered the opposite possibility ("I like XIL") and opted not to affirm it. Such assessments occur instantaneously, as the person is putting the trigram XIL into cognizance. Telosponsivity involves framing such premises and acting for their sake. In the case of "I dislike XIL," the premise represents an affective assessment, framed from an abstract realm of mind transcending the ongoing task of having to memorize this trigram (XIL). In the ongoing realm of learning (Brentano's primary consciousness), premising also occurs. The person accepts the experimental instruction as a premise, efforts are made to make sense of the trigrams involved in the task, and various heuristic strategies are brought to bear to accomplish the learning task in the tautological manner described in Chapters 7 (p. 276) and 8 (p. 326). But there is also a meaning-extension taking place tautologically within each of these premises, which is wound into the person's line of thought. That is, we have to appreciate that premises encompass predications, which in turn involve meaning-extensions in precedent-sequacious fashion.

For example, if Robert looks out the window before leaving and affirms the premise "It looks like rain today," he will act on this precedent meaning and take along rain gear—especially if he dislikes being rained on. James may find rain refreshing and not take precautionary measures. The precedent meaning and the affective assessment of this meaning (via transcendence by way of secondary consciousness) then determine what will be "done" as Robert's or James's day unfolds. Such precedents have sequacious ramifications.

But there is also a precedent-sequacious line of meaning-extension taking place in the premise "It looks like rain today." The target referent here is "it," which refers to the person's immediate future or "today." The concept of rain acts as the predication of this target referent to endow it with meaning. We might think of the phrase "possible rainy days" as the predicated meaning and "today" as the targeted referent. Many days can be rainy (today, tomorrow, or the day after); hence, it is correct to think of the predicate as broader in its range of meaning than the target referent (today). If we were to picture this premise through the logical demonstration known as Euler circles, we would have a large circle labeled "possible rainy days" and within it a smaller circle labeled "today." Just as we found that the "figure" of the figure-ground relationship went from the broader background to determine the contour of the narrower figure in a one-sided manner (see Chapter 8, p. 343), we now suggest that predication involves moving from a broader predicate meaning to a narrower target meaning. The former meaning extends to and enriches the latter meaning tautologically.

Logical learning theory opposes predication to mediation in accounting for behavior (see Chapter 7, p. 291). *Predication may be defined as an act of affirming, denying, or qualifying certain patterns of meaning in relation to other patterns of meaning.* The qualified, unqualified, and oppositional affirmations of Chapter 8 (pp. 333–334) are concerned with predication. We predicate when we say "Ice cream is tasty"; "Patricia is unattractive"; or "People cannot always be counted on." In each of these examples, the right-hand term serves as a broader referent of meaning encompassing and thereby tautologically lending its meaning to the left-hand term. (Tastiness endows the concept of ice cream, unattractiveness endows Patricia, and unreliability endows people.) As Kant (1952) said, predicates add meaning to what they are related to (p. 181). The complete statement encompassing a predication and its target referent is a *premise*, which can in turn be brought into a line of reasoning. For example, we might use the premise concerning ice cream as a minor premise to the major premise, "I would really enjoy something tasty to eat right now." We would thereby conclude that ice cream will soon be taken in hand by the person framing this sequence of thought.

The more abstract a meaning is, the more items it can take under its range of definition, which is another way of saying that the greater will be its role as a predicate in learning, knowing, recalling, and so forth. The Aristotelian causes, on which we have relied so heavily in this book (especially in Table 1, pp. 8–31), represent abstract predicates, which tautologically endow many concepts with their meanings. There are no other directional requirements of predication except that it always extends meaning from the wider, or broader, to the narrower expanse of meaning. This is a purely formal-cause, *logical* process taking place outside of time considerations in a precedent-sequacious fashion. In the classic major premise "All humans are mortals," the flow of meaning is from right-to-left since mortality is being extended to humanity. But then as we reason along, this premise predicates the further extension of the syllogism. To state the minor premise "This is a human being" further focuses the syllogism, even as the meaning of the major premise at the top of the sequence is being extended downward, until the narrowest premise (conclusion) is reached at the bottom: "*This* human being is a mortal."

Now we have a right-to-left and a top-down flow of precedent-sequacious meaning to complement the left-to-right flow that also takes place in "If . . . then . . ." formulations, such as: "If you do such and thus, then I will be forced to do thus and such." The directional flow of logical orderings is actually irrelevant. The Heraclitian logos (rationale) is not patterned in any one order, except from the broader to the narrower (see Table 1, p. 8). Another way of saying this is that precedent meanings are always broader in reference than sequacious extensions from those meanings. Psychologists have generally presumed that events are determined in a left-to-right fashion, because this is the way that the efficient cause is pictured—as epitomized in the stimulus-response or input-output regularities. Logical learning theorists do not rely upon the concept of time so necessary to behavioristic/mechanistic conceptions (see Chapter 6, pp. 256–260 and Chapter 7, pp. 293–297). We rely upon formal-final causation to predicate our understanding of human behavior and learning.

Returning to affective assessment, it became clear as we worked along that judgments of likability and the consequent sorting of experience into positive and negative RV are based upon an abstract form of predication. It is the person *qua* telosponder who renders the predicate judgment. As we noted earlier in this chapter, the newborn infant definitely seems capable of rendering such assessments. This native capacity to sort out experience based on affective contrasts starts the process of differentiation and articulation that eventuates in meaning (meaning relations, patterns of meaning, etc.). When the person judges or chooses "X" in the affective sense of "I like X," this means that he or she takes a certain form of meaning—liked meaning—from the item (X). X now serves as a predication, extending its liked meaning to the cognizance of the person doing the judging—the "I." The positive RV effect suggests that people will draw meaning from liked items more readily than from disliked items. We have yet to explore the possibility of a reverse RV effect. But the broad range of like-to-dislike, and *vice versa*, provides a predicate context within which the person can begin grasping the meaning of item X.

We sometimes hear a person say: "I don't know much about X [e.g., modern art], but one thing I do know, *I don't like it!*" This is not simply a frivolous remark. We have previously argued that in one sense we must already know something about what it is that we wish to know (see Chapter 7, p. 302). We must have a framing premise encompassing a predication to order our understanding of anything. The dimensional context of affective predications framing "like-dislike," or *vice versa*, does indeed provide us with something *already known* even as we try to learn more about it. As we have demonstrated in the early RV work, it is possible to both like or dislike unknown or meaningless items, such as trigrams low in AV. Sometimes it is the fascination of the unknown item that draws the learner to the task of studying it. Hence, affective assessment as operationalized in RV measures is to be thought of as a broad-ranging form of predication; it pervades experience and begins the process of learning by lending a ready-made dimension/context of meaning to items under further predication through linguistic definitions, examples of use, analogical parallels, and the various heuristic practices of learning. We turn next to our survey of empirical problems in which this growing sense of how affective assessment "works" to facilitate learning was gradually developed.

Reducing or Reversing the RV-Positive Effect

The RV-positive effect was presumed to occur because the human being, employing his or her personal evaluative preferences, establishes a context of meaning in which positive meanings are furthered or extended more readily then negative meanings. In effect, the context meaning was being tautologized to the ongoing understanding of the subject in the learning experiment. What factors entered into this context? Surely, the task *per se* was important. People were instructed to "do" something that they might or might not care to do. Undoubtedly, their general world outlook would be important. Some people view routine daily events as insurmountable obstacles, whereas others move through life with confidence and a taste for the challenging opportunity. Self-evaluations would probably be important. For example, the Rogerian (1970) "positive self-regard" should be relevant, since if a person essentially likes himself or herself the tautologizing of "self" with other liked things should be readily accomplished—thereby enhancing understanding and memory for such things.

But what if a person did not have positive self-regard? According to our line of theorizing, we should find in this case a diminishment of the RV-positive effect, or possibly a complete reversal. Based on such reasoning we conducted learning experiments on samples of acute and chronic mental patients (mixed diagnoses, predominantly schizophrenics) yoked to normal controls on sex, race, and social class (Rychlak, McKee, Schneider, & Abramson, 1971). We had the normals and abnormals idiographically rate trigrams for AV and RV. We found that AV was irrelevant to the learning of our chronic patient sample, but it did function in the acute patient sample (i.e., acute patients learned trigrams they considered wordlike more readily than trigrams they considered non-wordlike). Except for a sex difference in one sample, however, in both chronic and acute samples our patients learned their disliked trigrams significantly faster than their liked trigrams. The female chronic patients did not show a clear reversal of the RV-positive effect, but did have a diminution or flattened performance in which the RV-positive effect was missing. All of our normal subjects reflected the typical RV-positive effect in their learning performance.

We had made a good start. People with mental problems, who might therefore be thought of as predicating life in negative terms, were found to extend meanings in their learning more readily along the negative than the positive. Normals, who might be thought of as having a reasonably positive outlook on life, extended meanings more readily along the positive than the negative. In time, we were to demonstrate the RV-reversal effect on a group of patients suffering from a major depressive disorder, with matched normal controls again performing according to the RV-positive effect (Mosbacher, 1984). But when we work with such global categorizations as diagnostic labels, we fail to pinpoint the more personal aspects of a subject's predications. We need to focus our investigation a bit more.

We therefore conducted several experiments aimed at the possible relationship between self-predication, based on measurements drawn from scales in which the person characterizes himself/herself via predications of a positive or negative flavor (Barron, 1953; Fitts, 1965; Piers & Harris, 1964), and facility in various learning tasks employing trigrams or words in either a paired-associates or free-recall format. As expected, we found that high-school subjects with positive self-predications learned according to the RV-positive effect; those with negative self-predications learned according to the RV-reversal effect (Rychlak, Carlsen, & Dunning, 1974). This finding also carried over to studies on fifth graders (August, Rychlak, & Felker, 1975; August & Rychlak, 1978). Similar studies done on high-school students were in the predicted direction but fell just short of the necessary level of significance (Lappin, 1969; Boland, 1970). Therefore, it seems important to consider the person's affirmed premises concerning his or her strengths and weaknesses (self-confidence, self-regard, etc.).

But it must also be true that even a person with a strong self-image, heralding a positive self-predication, occasionally learns along the negative more readily than the positive. There are areas of life for all of us in which we are ill at ease or must confront the negative. One's predication of an activity in a particular realm of life must enter into one's affective learning style in that realm. To test this belief, we had college subjects identify a positive and a negative realm of life activity. We found that some subjects rated "aggressively competing with others" as an agreeable (liked) challenge, but found "becoming passively intimate with others" a stressful (disliked) activity. Other subjects were found with the reverse predilection. Words were then identified which were consistent with the meanings of aggressive competitiveness (e.g., *incentive, decisive, demanding, excelling*) or passive-intimacy (e.g., *sympathy, pamper, reverence, accepting*). Subjects rated all of the words for RV in the usual manner. As hypothesized, we found that subjects learned according to the RV-positive effect while memorizing words in their agreeable realms, but reflected RV-reversals while memorizing words in their disagreeable realms (Rychlak, Carlsen, & Dunning, 1974).

Another important consideration in affective learning is the task of "memorizing" (recalling, recognizing, etc.)—whether it is liked or disliked, whether the person does well in the task or does poorly, and so forth. Logical learning theory construes what the mechanists call a "reinforcement" as a methodological construct. In its theoretical implications, this construct would involve an affirmation of a premise (encompassing a predication) that would actually "work" (see Chapter 8, p. 327). The meaning that frames an experience accurately conceptualizes the ongoing experience. What is being strengthened or "reinforced" here is the precedent meaning—which can, of course, be negated as well. The person who approaches a closed door on the assumption that it is a room exit is positively reinforced when this portal actually does lead out of the room. On the other hand, if this is the door to a broom closet we would be witnessing a negation or negative reinforcement of the precedent meaning under affirmation. Hence, reinforcements provide information in the form of confirmation and disconfirmation of what is under predication from the outset.

We set out to prove that subjects would adapt their affective learning style according to how they predicated the task—as one that highlights success or highlights failure. We employed a muffled chime in a typical paired-associates learning task. Subjects were assigned to contrasting experimental conditions. In one group, the chime was sounded every time a subject failed to give the second member of a paired associate correctly (e.g., failed to say "HIB" when the other member of the pair, "LAT," was presented initially in a memory-drum apparatus). In the other group, the chime was sounded every time the subject correctly called out the second member of a pair. This was not a typical reinforcement "manipulation" because the experimenter did not control when the chime was sounded. It all depended on the subject's natural learning rate. The trigrams had been prejudged for RV in the usual manner. As expected, we found that in the condition highlighting success (in which the chime sounded following correct anticipations of a pair) the RV-positive effect obtained. However, in the condition highlighting failure (in which the chime sounded following incorrect anticipations), there was a reversal of this order of affective facilitation (Muller & Rychlak, 1979). This finding was cross-validated with the addition of a contrast between idiographic AV and RV in the trigrams employed (Apao, 1976). It was found that only wordlike trigrams entered into the findings on muffled chime sounds and RV.

The influence of task-predication on learning seemed established. Even so, another study was suggested. What if subjects were asked to observe a paired-associates task being performed by models *before* they were required to perform it themselves. Subjects could then rate the task for RV based on how much they would themselves like to perform it. According to logical learning theory, those subjects who find the task likable should learn according to the RV-positive effect; those who find it unlikable should diminish or reverse this affective ordering. This is precisely what we found in a study using this "modeling" design (Rychlak & Marceil, 1986). It seems clear that what a subject affectively premises at the outset of a task enters into the course of his or her ongoing learning in that task.

Affective Assessment as a Native Human Capacity

It is fundamental to logical learning theory that the capacity to render affective assessments is native to the person. As noted previously (p. 370), we reject the thesis that inborn decisions are rendered by nature "for" the individual, even as we accept the thesis that the capacity to render such decisions is inborn. The human being is an evaluating organism "by nature." Affective assessments are in operation at birth, organizing a context of understanding within which learning can proceed. But how can we test this claim? If affective assessment is fundamental to learning then children beginning school should reflect a larger RV-positive effect (we do not expect reversals or diminutions of RV in samples of normal subjects) than children who have already been instructed for some time. That is, we would expect children with experience in learning to have predications other than simply their likes and dislikes of the material presented to them. Using designs and abstract paintings as the target items, we had children across the first six grades attempt to recognize these items following brief initial exposures. Although all subjects reflected an RV-positive effect, in line with our expectations the effect was significantly greater for children (especially boys) in the first grade than for children in the higher grades (Rychlak, 1975a). If RV was the result of shaping through experience, this finding should have been in the reverse direction.

Another source of evidence for the native capacity to render like-dislike judgments is the performance of the mentally handicapped. Lacking so-called "higher" level capacities to memorize and organize cognitively, it is plausible to expect that such individuals would fall back on their innate capacity to affectively assess learnable materials. Using the procedure mentioned previously, in which the task was the recognition of designs and abstract paintings, we had a group of educable mentally handicapped children and teenagers matched with normal controls on group means for mental age (i.e., with disparities in chronological age), as well as chronological age (i.e., with disparities in mental age). As expected, the mentally handicapped subjects reflected a significantly larger RV-positive effect than either the subjects matched with them on mental or chronological age (Woodward, 1978). Closely related to this finding is the prediction we tested in a study of fifth graders, who were asked to learn both concrete words (e.g., *tree*) and abstract words (e.g., *truth*). The abstract words are difficult to memorize because they lack clear-cut (including visual) predications and, therefore, approximate the task facing anyone who must learn relatively unknown materials (akin to the task facing the newborn infant!). In such a circumstance, we expect native affection to play a major role in the learning. And so it was that we found significantly larger RV effects for the abstract than the concrete words (August & Rychlak, 1978).

Another line of evidence to support the innate nature of affective assessment stems from research we conducted on minority subjects in the United States who, it might reasonably be argued, have rejected, neglected, or opted out of a commitment to the intellectualized, schoollike tasks so typical of middle-class values. Of course, this reaction may have been furthered by discriminatory practices of the larger majority. But whatever the reasons may be, we would expect such minority groups to rely more heavily on RV than AV—taking the latter measure to represent intellectualized discriminants that fail to act as predications for minorities, although they might indeed serve this role for the majority. Faced with a memorization task, minority subjects should fall back on affective discriminants (RV) more readily than verbal discriminants (AV) when compared to subjects representing the majority.

Two minority groups were studied. Black subjects were matched with white Anglo-American subjects on a trigram task in which these learnable items were idiographically prerated by all subjects for AV and RV. We found that blacks relied significantly more on RV and less on AV than did their white counterparts (O'Leary, 1969; Rychlak, Hewitt, & Hewitt, 1973). Mexican-Americans were also put through a similar procedure. In contrast to Anglo-Americans, they relied more heavily on RV and less on AV in their learning style (Garza, 1975). A word of caution is in order at this point. It should be apparent that just because we have added a sociocultural theme in these experiments on minorities, it does not follow that affective assessment is itself a sociocultural product. We have not softened our contention that affective assessment is a native endowment of *all* human beings. Affection is not "shaped" behavior; affection is a "shaper" of behavior. It is possible, of course, for cultures or subcultures to encourage their members to behave spontaneously and act on impulse. This in turn could lead to a pattern of relying upon affective factors in ongoing learning. But this does not mean the affective evaluations *per se* are cultural products, anymore than the capacity to perceive and retain experience is a cultural product. A subculture in which individuals are encouraged to perfect their ability to retain experience in memory would probably influence its members to develop mnemonic techniques to facilitate recall. It is the same for affective assessment. Culture influences but does not create such native human capacities.

In an effort to tease out the sociocultural factor in our studies on minorities, we designed a study in which black and white children could be compared across levels of social class. Seventh graders (equated for sex) of both races were drawn from middle- and lower-class families. These children were asked to learn a list of words that had been prerated for RV. It was found that blacks as a group and as a subgroup within the lower socioeconomic level clearly reflected the largest RV-positive effects of the total sample. However, when racial groups were combined and social class was contrasted, it was also true that in general the lower-class subjects relied significantly more on RV than did middle-class subjects (Rychlak, 1975b). Indeed, the middle-class black males were among the least sensitive to RV considerations of the sample. Hence, it is unlikely that the minority findings are due to hereditary (material-) causes. To the extent that any group in the culture identifies with the language discriminants, accepts the demands of school-like tasks (memorization, time pressures, etc.), and ascends the economic ladder, to that extent will AV considerations play a greater role in the group's learning proclivities. In the process, the relative influence of RV will be reduced. But nothing in this progression counters the view of logical learning theory that *affective assessment is a native endowment of human behavior.*

The final way in which we attempted to demonstrate our nativistic view was to test affective factors through brain-lateralization. Gazzaniga (1970, pp. 90–93) worked out an experimental design that made this possible. In this design, subjects are asked to fixate on a point in mid-visual field, and then material is flashed tachistoscopically to the left or right of this point. The brief exposure time of materials (1/5 to 1/100 second) flashed to the right or left does not allow subjects to scan the material exposed to one half of their retina with the other half. Due to the anatomical arrangement of the retina, this means that materials (pictures, words, etc.) exposed to the right visual field register *first* in the left-brain hemisphere, and *vice versa*. Of course, these neural impulses traverse the corpus callosum in milleseconds to bring the other half of the brain into play. But there is an undoubted *order of entry* (formal-cause) factor in this sequence that has a proven effect on the processing of materials. For example, subjects recognized more

CVC trigrams when they were flashed into the left hemisphere first rather than the right hemisphere, and the reverse facilitation occurred when the materials employed were pictorial faces (Hilliard, 1973; Klein, Moscovitch & Vigna, 1976).

The work of Sperry (1968) has taught us that the right hemisphere processes pictorial information, and the left hemisphere processes language information in a large proportion of subjects so tested. It would follow that if we could adapt Gazzaniga's procedure and submit each hemisphere to a learning task in the style of previous research on RV, we could place a given hemisphere in the position of having to conceptualize and affectively assess materials that are *both* routine for it and those that are *not* routine. In this case, we would expect the left hemisphere to reflect a larger RV-positive effect in recognizing pictorial rather than verbal materials flashed to the right visual field in the Gazzaniga procedure. Conversely, we would expect the right hemisphere to reflect a larger RV-positive effect in recognizing verbal rather than pictorial materials that had been flashed to the left visual field. Once again, we rely here on the assumption that when a person is confronting new, abstract, highly difficult material, he or she will increasingly fall back on affective considerations to organize learning. We tested this hypothesis on college subjects, using trigrams and abstract paintings flashed for 1/5th of a second. Subjects had to rate these verbal and pictorial materials for RV, as well as recognize them on a later date. The findings were in line with expectations (Rychlak & Slife, 1984). Hence, when the left hemisphere processes its customary materials (trigrams), it is less reliant on RV distinctions than when it must deal with unaccustomed materials. The same can be said for the right hemisphere, although in this case what is customarily processed (i.e., paintings) is different.

Trying to relate affective assessment to the architectonic structure of the brain strikes some people as inappropriate. Critics think we believe that the "logic" behind logical learning theory is in some ethereal, nonmaterialistic realm; hence, what we have here is an extreme dualism (see Glassman, 1983). Others feel that in tying affection to the brain we must of necessity be "reductionistic," bringing our formal-final cause conception of telosponsivity down to the material-efficient causes of the physical brain structure. We do not accept either of these views. Logical learning theory does not represent a dualism, if dualism means a belief in two paralleling but different realms of existence—mind and body. The dualism of logical learning theory issues from its reliance on dialectical oppositionality. If the brain is found to have dialectical arrangements and processes which enable us to think of a transcending (dialectical) effort to select "this" predication from "that" one, or make it possible to select from among the many other possibilities that germinate in opposition to what is being conceptualized at any moment, then we have ample grounds for a monistic (one substance) formulation set within multiple (contrasting, conflicting) alternatives.

In effect, we are looking to the formal-cause (organizational) features of the brain to teach us something about thought. If such biological patternings and functionings lend themselves to oppositional description, logical learning theorists are at least "on the same wavelength" as our colleagues in the biophysical sciences. We disagree with those who would contend that "the laws of thought are neurophysiological laws, not logical ones" (Bunge, 1980, p. 161). We believe that the laws of thought *are* logical; they are concerned with the patterning of meanings and the drawing of inferences and implications in light of such patternings (predications). The logic of mentation does not "emerge" from the lower level neuronal substrate. The logic of consciousness is not patterned by a one-to-one concordance of neurons strung together in physical union. The patterns that encompass meanings being processed in the neural substrate must be construed as open to alternative formulations by way of a dialectical logic, as well as being fixed into the certainties of a demonstrative logic. In the same way that a hard-wired computer can entertain alternative formulations of the problem put to it, so too can the reasoning human being introduce alternative formulations of the biological patternings of the brain tissue. (Of course, in this case it is the programmer who frames such alternatives, not the computer.) A widely held view among brain researchers today is that the neuronal activity in the cortex does not create the direction that thought takes, but rather reflects the patternings of such thoughts in an instrumental manner (Eccles, 1977, pp. 361–362).

What do we find if we turn to the research evidence on brain structure? Extensive research on the brain reveals that there are two kinds of neurons in operation in cerebral tissue: one that forms excitatory synapses and another that forms inhibitory synapses (Eccles, 1977, p. 232). The corpus callosum has fibers joining brain halves that are in a mirror-image relationship with each other (*ibid.*, p. 241). The prefrontal lobes are in a reciprocal relationship with the limbic system (*ibid.*, p. 349). The brain is anything but a model of cybernetic clarity and simplicity. Indeed, the fundamental organization of nerve fibers is modular, in which up to 10,000 nerve cells are locked together by mutual connectives. Once activated, each of these modules takes electrical power from its neighbor. It appears that the nervous system always works by conflict, "in this case by conflicts between each module and the adjacent modules" (*ibid.*, p. 243). An honest assessment of these facts must surely conclude that none is unduly strained by a dialectical formulation of brain activity.

All we need postulate is that there is a process called for in this conflictual arrangement of nerve cells, whereby a meaningful pattern must be activated from among the many available, and then the significance of this affirmation is brought forward volitionally into overt behavior—at least some of the time. The biological means by which this choice (i.e., telosponsive) process is accomplished has yet to be delineated. But there are some fascinating suggestions already underway in the highly innovative research of Benjamin Libet (1985), who finds that voluntary acts (finger or wrist flexions) are preceded by electrophysiological "readiness potentials" in the cortex. These potentials are brought on preceding spontaneous intentions to act. But what is significant for present considerations is the fact that Libet's subjects are described as being "free *not* to act out any given urge or initial decision to act; and each subject indeed reported frequent instances of such aborted intentions" (p. 530). Libet concluded that subjects may spontaneously receive unconscious prompts to act, but that they always can select and control what will eventuate, "either by permitting or triggering the final motor outcome of the unconsciously initiated process or by vetoing the progression to actual motor activation" (*ibid.*, p. 529).

This sounds very much like dialectical reasoning at work. The physical prompting presents itself to the person "from out of nowhere" (spontaneously, unconsciously, etc.) and the opposite implication, therefore, is delimited to allow for a decision one way or the other—to act or not to act. Obviously, we are still a long way from the psychological aspects of thought. But the duality, conflict, and resultant alternatives open to mentation are what the eminent brain researcher Wilder Penfield (1975) was referring to when he contended that the "mind" (we prefer *logic*) programs its "brain-mechanism" (p. 46). Such patternings of meaning (programs) can be framed one way by person X and in a contradictory way by person Y, even though they have identical brain neuronal networks. Or, the opposing positions can be framed by the *same* person, preliminary to making a choice between them or terminating in confusion and indecision. As long as the biological network is capable of a dialectical rendering in mentation, we are able to describe behavior in this fashion. At the present time, the findings on brain structure and function are very much in line with logical learning theory.

Affective Assessment in Experiments on Learning

We continued to investigate the heuristic properties of affective assessment, making certain that it played a role in learning as depicted by the received view of psychology. In such experiments, we used unselected normals and therefore expected the RV-positive effect to obtain. In a task using words, we found that RV-positive facilitated *primacy effects* (i.e., words at the beginning of a list are easier to recall than words learned later in the list), whereas RV-negative did not do so (Apao, 1979). We demonstrated that affective factors in learning are not simply a matter of "sorting out" the liked items first and then taking up the disliked. Using unmixed lists of trigrams, we established that subjects who learn only lists of liked trigrams will learn such lists more readily than lists of disliked trigrams. Even when we remove trigrams that are learned by subjects and replace them with others in the unmixed list before complete mastery of the list is attained, we continue to see the RV-positive effect taking place in comparison to an unmixed list of RV-negative trigrams treated in the same fashion (David, 1977). Studies such as these demonstrate the ongoing role that affective predication plays in life, where it manifests itself at the outset of learning and continues on as subjects intend to retain that which is under conceptualization.

To establish the implicit heuristic properties of affective assessment, we designed a study in which subjects had prerated trigrams for AV and RV and then were given lists of paired-associates in which these dimensions were counterbalanced (i.e., trigrams that were liked and had word associates were formed into pairs; trigrams that had no word associate but were liked were formed into pairs; and so on.) We then instructed some subjects to make every effort to learn trigram pairs that were wordlike first, and then to go on to learn the unwordlike pairs. Other subjects were instructed to make every effort to learn their liked trigram pairs first, and then to move on to their disliked trigrams. Other groups were given the reverse instruction—to learn unwordlike or disliked pairs first. In this manner we were able to test in the interaction for the relative influence that subjects could exert on AV or RV in the course of their learning. What we found was that subjects *could* influence the AV dimension, but they *could not* influence the RV dimension in their learning rates (Rychlak, 1974). We interpret this to mean that once a subject has predicated materials as liked or disliked, the resultant determination of learning is fixed akin to our interpretation of "will power" in free will (see Chapter 7, p. 307).

As a native capacity fundamental to learning, affective assessment is not under the determination of "something else." When the subject affectively assesses, we believe that he or she *at that point* has taken a certain position on what the meaning of ongoing experience "is." One might feign a "change of heart" in affective preference, trying to like what is unliked, or *vice versa*, but the formal-final cause determination has been set and cannot be altered unless there is a genuine reassessment. We have not yet conducted research on such genuine reassessment, but we do believe that it takes place. Evidence for the saliency and heuristic vitality of affective assessment has been garnered from two studies that examine the impact of drugs on the RV phenomenon. In one study we examined the same psychiatric patients performing in an RV learning task while on and off psychotropic drugs (Rychlak, McKee, Schneider, & Abramson, 1971). In another study we examined both normals and depressed patients while performing an RV learning task under the influence of alcohol, as well as in a sober condition (Mosbacher, 1984). In neither of these studies was the RV performance while in the drugged state altered from the performance while in a normal condition.

If affective assessment serves to organize meaning for the individual then it should be possible to demonstrate such organization in the free recall of words that had been prerated for RV. Bousfield (1953) had designed an experiment in which subjects were given words that shared a common categorization. For example, subjects might be given names of various animals as well as various kinds of vegetables. Presented with a list of such words, all mixed together, subjects were instructed to memorize as many of these words as they could. After a memorization period, these subjects were then asked to recall as many of these words as possible, in any order. Bousfield found that subjects tended to "cluster" words under a common category together. When they recalled one animal they added a few others, then shifted to a handful of vegetables, and back to some animals, until they had exhausted their memories for the materials in question. We reasoned that if subjects categorized according to what might be termed the AV considerations of common word meanings (animals, vegetables, etc.), then they should also categorize—or predicate—according to RV-positive and RV-negative in organizing their recall of items.

If subjects reflected a greater primacy effect for liked than disliked words, as we had already found (Apao, 1979), it should follow that in a free-recall task subjects should cluster their liked words "higher" (initially, first) in the recollection list than their disliked words. We used words relating to names of animals (for example, *elephant* or *hyena*) and professions (*doctor* or *lawyer*) and had subjects prerate these for RV. We found that the subjects clustered not only on the basis of animal/profession words, but also on the basis of liked/disliked words within these categorizations. Furthermore, subjects placed their liked words of either category higher in their recollected lists than their disliked words (Nguyen, 1975). No such predilection could be found for the categories of animals or professions, either of which might be listed higher. Subsequently, we did a study in which white and black subjects were put through this free-recall clustering task, using trigrams that had been prerated for AV and RV. We found clustering along RV and AV for both whites and blacks. However, consistent with the findings discussed previously, we found that the black subjects reflected larger clustering scores on RV relative to AV than did the white subjects (Rychlak, 1976). We also found the RV-positive effect in the clustering of trait ascriptions to other people. That is, liked traits were more likely to be clustered in describing others than disliked traits (Bugaj, 1984).

An important yardstick by which learning effects are measured is often said to be whether they have interlist or transfer effects of some sort or another. Affective assessment has passed this test with flying colors. We have consistently found that a dramatic order-effect takes place if subjects are given successive unmixed lists of materials (trigrams, words, etc.) to learn, one of which is liked and the other disliked (or *vice versa*). What we find is that when subjects move from disliked to liked lists they manifest a dramatic positive nonspecific transfer. We refer to this as "nonspecific" because the trigrams in the two lists are totally different—they do not share any specific characteristics. When subjects move from liked to disliked lists they are much less likely to reflect a positive nonspecific transfer. In one study, all 32 subjects moving from a disliked to a liked list reflected improvement in performance on the second list, whereas only 13 of the 32 subjects moving from liked to disliked lists reflected this improvement (Rychlak & Tobin, 1971). In a follow-up study, we compared idiographic AV and RV to establish that AV failed to have such interlist effects, while RV did indeed bring them about (Rychlak, Tuan, & Schneider, 1974).

The next study deals with the role of affection in the process of meaning-extension during learning. The question we asked was: If we were to have subjects prerate trigrams for AV and RV, is there a way in which we might demonstrate that meaning-extensions from a word-like trigram "to" an unwordlike trigram would follow more readily along an RV-positive than an RV-negative line? We reasoned that if subjects were given paired associates in which one trigram was idiographically meaningful and the other was not, then through practice in memorizing these pairs, a wordlike quality would be extended to the initially unmeaningful trigram of the pair—but only if the two trigrams in the pair were liked! For example, if a subject had found SOX wordlike and ZOM unwordlike, but had rated both of these trigrams as positive in RV, then after learning this pair in a list of such paired associates the likelihood is good that ZOM would acquire wordlikeness by suggesting some meaning to the subject. Presumably, this meaning would have been extended from SOX in consonance with the positive task predication during learning. On the other hand, if SOX and ZOM were both disliked by the subject, even though learning criterion would be reached, the likelihood is diminished that such a negative meaning-extension would take place, given the fact that the task is predicated positively. This is what we predicted, and this is what we found (Rychlak & Nguyen, 1979).

Next we conducted some studies that related to basic learning constructs, such as operant conditioning and modeling. Are people really being "shaped" by such considerations in learning, or is there room for a person to strategize and maneuver "within" such presumed shapings? Psychology has, of course, relied upon the Lockean image of behavior to imply that there are no personally determined contributions to the ongoing course of behavior, such as affective preference (see Chapter 2, pp. 86–88). Affective preferences are themselves the "effects" rather than the "causes" of learned experience. This demonstrative image of the person has been greatly enhanced in the experiments on human behavior conducted by psychologists, where little consideration has been given to the fact that there is a strategizing, negotiating, assumption-taking organism working at the "other end" of the "observer-observed" dimension. Experimental designs have not been advanced which might shed light on the contribution made to the ongoing "controls" of the experiment made by the subject. Hence, what is at heart a product of cooperation between the intentions of the experimenter and the intentions of the subject is made to appear a one-sided, efficient-cause manipulation of the latter by the former. The findings on awareness in conditioning theories have exploded this myth of efficient-cause manipulation (see Chapter 5, pp. 264–267). But the implications of these findings have not been widely disseminated into psychology's experimental designs.

We decided to modify the typical operant conditioning experiment, giving subjects a range of movement "within" the targeted behaviors under so-called manipulation. In the usual operant conditioning study on word-emission, for example, a class of words is targeted relating to some linguistic categorical distinction. Recall from Chapter 5 (p. 265) that Greenspoon (1955) had his subjects state aloud any words that came to mind, and then reinforced them with "mmm hmm" each time they said a plural noun. In other formats subjects might be given words printed on cards and instructed to select some combination, such as uniting verbs with singular rather than plural pronouns (Taffel, 1955). We decided to adapt the latter procedure. Subjects first made RV ratings of a pool of words that combined adjectives and nouns. The aim was to operantly reinforce subjects for a linguistic class—that is, for either nouns or adjectives—but also to provide an alternative within this targeted linguistic category.

Instead of giving just two words on a card, one an adjective and one a noun, we gave our subjects *four* words per card. There were two nouns and two adjectives per card; one of each designation was liked while the other was disliked. In other words, a subject in the experimental group was required to select nouns from the card in order to be "conditioned," but still had the option of selecting the liked rather than the disliked noun. From the start, as we established base rates of word "emission" (i.e., selection) we discovered that subjects would point to their liked words rather than their disliked words. And when conditioning for word category (noun or adjective) began (the reinforcer used was "right"), subjects continued to select their liked over their disliked words to a significant degree (Campbell, 1983). We also found that conditioning did not take place unless subjects were aware of the response-reinforcement contingency (see Chapter 5, pp. 264–267). Our finding was in line with the evidence on this issue presented by Brewer (1974).

The implication we drew from such results is that if people are being shaped in their everyday lives, where alternatives exist that are not defined out of existence by an experimenter's research design, then people are also probably contributing to this *in vivo* shaping in every way possible. And the direction of their contribution is doubtless to bring about their preferred alternative whenever possible. A child being shaped by a parent to behave in the way that the parent desires undoubtedly conforms to this shaping by selecting that which is most desirable to him or her, given the parameters laid down in the shaping. As we have already suggested at many points in this book, the child is also being taught to the opposite of what the parent intends. It is impossible to univocally direct a dialectically reasoning organism regarding everything in experience. Such an organism must be psychologically persuaded rather than automatically manipulated. If the parent is successful in convincing the child that the parental alternative is right and good and to be preferred to its opposite implication, then we might indeed witness a successful shaping. But logical learning theory contends that in this case the child has framed the parental injunction as a liked (valued) premise encompassing certain predications, and now enacts the meaning framed telosponsively as a preferred alternative. In other words, the shaping is not of the efficient-cause (mechanistic) variety but rather of the formal-final cause (teleological) variety.

To concretize this line of theorizing into an empirical test, we decided to introduce RV into the television modeling research design of Bandura, Ross, & Ross (1963a, 1963b). The basic approach here is to expose young children to filmed models who aggress against a "bobo" doll, which is an inflated plastic doll standing about three feet in height. The models used various toys (a jumping rope to strangle the doll, a gun to shoot it, etc.). After observing the filmed acts of aggression, children were left alone to "play" with the bobo doll and the toys. Control subjects who had not seen the aggressive acts on film were also left in the playroom with the same materials. We found that the children who had observed the model aggressing against the doll imitated this behavior nearly twice as often as children who had not experienced such aggressive modeling.

In our adaptation of this procedure, we employed first and second graders as subjects (equally divided by sex) and had them observe 15 different televised acts of modeled aggression toward the bobo doll (strangulation, shooting, punching, spanking with some kind of toy, throwing a toy at the doll, etc.). As each aggressive act was presented on the television screen, the subjects rated it for RV. There were 15 different toys (such as a jumping rope, baton, toy pistol, wooden blocks and toy cars) involved in these actions. The subjects rated the toys for RV independently of the ratings for the aggressive acts. As we left our subjects to be observed in the playroom following observation of the model, we knew both the RV for the toys in the room and the RV for the aggressive acts performed by the model. Control subjects were assigned to the playroom with identical toys and the bobo doll in evidence. The control subjects did not see the modeled aggression, but they did prerate the toys for RV.

We found that the experimental group of subjects, who had witnessed the modeled aggression, performed significantly more aggressive acts against the bobo doll than the control subjects (Slife & Rychlak, 1982). This finding was especially true for the boys in the experimental group. However, the aggressive acts performed by subjects in the experimental group were those which they had prerated positively for RV. Our subjects used only the toys in these aggressive acts that they had judged positive in RV. The children in the control condition also played with their liked toys significantly more often than their disliked toys. In other words, even though children were influenced by the model, they selected their preferred actions and preferred toys to enact the modeled behavior. We interpret our findings, as well as Bandura's to mean that children are astute enough to take over the premise suggested by the demands of the experimental instruction/procedure. Children know that the experimenter is showing them things in order to "give them ideas" of what might be done. They enact the behavior in compliance with these prompting premises, but they also select from among them those items that are idiographically most pleasing to them. In this sense they retain the integrity of their play, playing with what they—not the model—have opted to use.

The final study relates to actual performance in a college course (Slife & Rychlak, 1981). At the outset of a semester, over 200 students about to take introductory psychology were asked to rate descriptions of 19 study topics for RV (e.g., memory, motivation, personality). These were topics around which their introductory course would be organized. As the semester unfolded, all 19 study topics were conveyed to the subjects during lecture and discussion groups, and then examinations were routinely given on each. Before an examination, the subjects rated a five-point scale for how much time they spent studying each of the 19 topics. With study time partialed out, the predicted main effect for RV materialized ($p<.01$), indicating that higher examination grades were obtained for liked than disliked topics. Tests of simple effects revealed that 18 of the 19 study topics reflected this RV-positive effect. In line with our findings on minorities and our theoretical understanding of affective assessment as a native capacity that makes learning possible, students with low overall grade-point averages reflected significantly larger RV-positive effects than students with high grade-point averages ($p<.05$).

Affective Assessment in Experiments on Personality

The final area of research we will consider, before moving to a discussion of the future research called for in logical learning theory, represents what might be loosely termed personality-related experimental designs. In these studies we are moving beyond the "basic" considerations of learning theory per se and into a more applied realm. Psychologists in the applied realm do not anguish over the nature of the learning process on which their theoretical accounts ultimately rest. They may refer to personality as a habit or style of behavior that is learned over the course of life, without feeling that there is any need to worry about "the" theory of learning involved. They may employ teleological "sounding" constructs and even honestly believe that they are dealing in intentionality and agency. In fact, by not examining the underlying learning theory they may be robbing their formulations of all such considerations (if it is a mechanistic, efficient-cause account of learning). We have tried to show empirically that logical learning theory is a viable teleological alternative to the mechanistic learning theories of psychology. It is our belief that the teleological view represented is well suited to personality description and analysis. If so, we should also be able to demonstrate this claim empirically.

First, it is important to demonstrate that affective assessment enters into interpersonal relations. For example, recalling people's names might well be influenced by affective predication. In a simple demonstration of this phenomenon, fifth and sixth graders (of both sexes) were asked to prerate a list of names for RV. Several days later, we gave them five liked and five disliked names to memorize in a free-recall task. We found that RV-positive facilitated recall (Rychlak & Saluri, 1973). In a more complex procedure, we employed college students of both sexes in a paired-associates format and instructed them to assign names to photographs of faces taken from old college yearbooks. Both the names and faces had been prerated for RV. Faces were flashed on a screen, followed by the name, and subjects were required to call out the correct name before it was flashed. As expected, we found that the RV-positive effect influenced the course of learning the names of these faces (Rychlak, Galster, & McFarland, 1972).

This interpersonal-relations theme was carried over to a study of countertransference (Heiskell & Rychlak, 1986). Male medical students were used as subjects. They played the role of "psychotherapist." Male VA patients were used in the role of "therapy client." The veterans were videotaped, giving general information about themselves (background, schooling, work history, etc.) and then took up two specific life concerns—one very positive and one very negative (e.g., job success versus sexual inadequacies). Based on the more general comments, the medical students made RV ratings of the patients in a pretest. Subsequently, each medical student was asked to react verbally to a positive and a negative videotaped statement made by *two* patients—a liked and a disliked patient—as if he were in a therapeutic interview with each patient (adapted from Strupp, 1960). These verbal statements were electronically recorded and later scored for empathy by judges who were unfamiliar with the medical student's RV preferences. (The empathy scale was taken from Truax & Carkhuff, 1967.) We found that the medical students reflected the greatest empathy in their statements when they were responding to the positive life concerns of their liked veterans and *also* to the negative statements of their disliked veterans. Liked veterans were also given better prognoses than disliked veterans.

We move next into the realm of personality assessment. There is much work that could be done in projectives testing as it relates to RV. We have not conducted much research in this area, but a few of our studies are relevant. It should be clear that many of the personality constructs applied to people in both projective and objective (paper-pencil) testing or scaling represent oppositional dimensions. Such dimensions as *introversion-extraversion,* *dominance-submission,* *repression-sensitization,* and *leveler-sharpener* have filled the pages of research on personality throughout this century. Interestingly, in one of our studies we found that subjects preferred to be described along dimensions that were clearly oppositional, rather than those that were not decidedly "either-or" (Gruba-McCallister, 1975). There is a certain logic in this choice. If one is to be characterized, it is probably better to be distinctively different from others. Clear self-delineation demands a certain negation of the other end of the descriptive dimension involved.

In a study on heterosexual preference, we found that male college students recognized pictures of liked female faces at briefer tachistoscopic exposure levels than pictures of their disliked female faces (Rychlak, Galster, & McFarland, 1972). On the other hand, female college students recognized their *disliked* male faces at briefer tachistoscopic exposure levels than their liked male faces. In a study more directly tied to projective assessment, we asked college subjects to write a story in which they completed a beginning sentence, such as "You are driving a car on a long trip" or "You are just getting up in the morning." Subjects had idiographically prerated a number of such sentences for RV, and we selected three liked and three disliked sentences for each subject to work with. For each sentence that one subject considered negative, a matched subject was found who considered it positive in meaning. The completed stories were categorized according to positive, negative, or neutral themes by judges who were blind to the purpose of the study. As predicted by the precedent-sequacious explanations of logical learning theory, stories predicated by liked sentences resulted in positive themes being written. Stories predicated by disliked sentences resulted in negative themes being written (Keedy, 1975).

We extended this predicational thesis to a study of so-called objective test items. We had found in an earlier study of college subjects who showed variations on a personality test that masculine subjects, for example, reflected a positive RV effect in their free-recall learning of masculine verbal materials but *not* in their learning of feminine materials, and *vice versa* (Rychlak, Tasto, Andrews, & Ellis, 1973). These findings were cross-validated using subjects who scored in either an ascendant or submissive direction on a scale, and who were asked to memorize words with these meanings in a free-recall format. The combination of a high score on the personality dimension (ascendant or submissive) and positive RV for the relevant words seemed to suggest the greatest actual learning over time (i.e., subjects tautologized from their self-predications "to" the learnable items very readily in a meaning realm that was consistent with their personality style). We predicted from this earlier work that on any scale of objective personality measurement, subjects who are normal individuals should score highest on personality dimensions which they like. Also, they should manifest this behavior most probably if they score high on a scale *and* like it. A relatively high score on disliked scales should not result in the same level of accurate prediction to an independent criterion of the personality-related behavior in question.

College students of both sexes were given personality descriptions of variables taken from the Edwards (1959) Personal Preference Schedule (PPS) (e.g., *autonomy, dominance, achievement,* etc.). They were asked to rank-order them on the basis of RV (from most to least liked). Later, these subjects were given the PPS. We predicted that they would score higher on their most-liked dimensions than on their most-disliked dimensions. This is what we found (Gruba-McCallister & Rychlak, 1981). In a second study, a group of college students of both sexes was culled from a larger sample of students who had scored either high or low on certain PPS dimensions, which they had also prerated as either liked or disliked. Keep in mind that it is possible to find subjects who score high on disliked scales (e.g., some people are highly passive and dislike this fact), and *vice versa* (some subjects would like to be more passive). Overall, however, we find that the tendency is for RV and personality scores to go together.

As an independent criterion with which we could predict subjects' behaviors, we employed a story-completion test. Subjects read a brief vignette setting the stage for an incomplete story. They were then given the option of selecting—or not selecting—an alternative relating to their personality scores on the PPS. Thus, a story might establish the setting for achievement behavior or for dominant acts, and in selecting an ending from among various alternatives the subject was revealing his or her typical behavior in situations of this type. As we expected, a subject's RV for the personality dimension in question entered into the "predictive power" of the test to the independent criterion of the story-completion test (Gruba-McCallister & Rychlak, 1981). Stated in terms of percentages, it was found that 78% of the subjects who scored high on a personality dimension *and* liked it went on to choose this type of story-completion alternative (e.g., select a dominant alternative if the subject had a high score on dominance plus a positive RV for dominance). Of those subjects who scored high but disliked the personality dimension, only 54% were found to select this behavior as an ending.

Intelligence is related to personality; therefore, we expect to find RV differences showing up in a subject's performance on an IQ test. To test this hypothesis, we made a motion picture film with soundtrack, depicting the administration of a quasi-WISC IQ test (Rumsey & Rychlak, 1978). Seventh and eighth graders of both sexes saw this film, heard the instructions for the verbal subtests of the WISC scale (general information, repeating digits, etc.), had the quasiperformance items demonstrated (assembling cut-up pictures, fitting blocks into a pattern, etc.), and made RV ratings for each in turn. That is, the film allowed time for RV ratings between each subtest presentation. Several days later, these children actually took the intelligence test. We found that our subjects scored roughly five IQ points higher when their prorated IQs were determined on the basis of their liked rather than their disliked subtests ($p < .01$).

We conducted a study on childhood sharing involving RV. In previous studies, researchers had found that children are increasingly altruistic as they mature—that is, more willing to share things as they get older (see Green & Schneider, 1974). We reasoned that although this finding might be true, since RV had not been considered in such research it was entirely possible that the seemingly greater altruism might involve a more sophisticated form of sharing. We contrasted kindergarten and fourth-grade children of both sexes who shared candies that they had idiographically rated for RV. We found that the fourth graders shared more of their candies than the kindergarteners. It was clear that at both age levels children "shared" their least-preferred candies (Mosbacher, Gruen, & Rychlak, 1985). Candies that were highly positive in RV were least likely to be shared by children at both age levels.

Affective assessment was also applied to a problem in impression formation, where we found that even when we had removed considerations of AV from the task of forming an impression, the RV dimension had great heuristic influence in determining what our subjects would think about other people (Bugaj, 1981). We also went beyond the bounds of customary personality study to investigate a psi task. Parapsychological studies are not widely attempted in psychology, not the least of the reasons being that there is no satisafactory theory to explain how it is that a subject might be "in touch" with information at a distance or in a future time. Since it emphasizes formal causation (the *logos*), logical learning theory is amenable to speculations in which an order in experiential events is postulated to account for such otherwise inexplicable occurrences. We have in mind here the sort of order that C. G. Jung (1960) was driving at in proposing his construct of *synchronicity*, or meaningful cross-connections in experience (p. 427). In other words, there may be formal-cause patterns taking place in which the person is unconsciously enmeshed over and above the efficient-cause flow of daily experience. Jung also referred to synchronicity as *acausal orderedness* (*ibid.*, p. 516), which, in our terms, means a formal-cause pattern found within the ebb and flow of natural (efficient-cause) events. This pattern of relationship-uniting events creates a meaning context in which the person may relate to or connect with the non-apparent or overtly non-discernible occurrence.

From the viewpoint of logical learning theory, we would naturally expect affective assessment to play a role in such patternings of what we take to be something akin to a pre-sensory *logos* in experience. Thus it was that we designed an experiment in which subjects first rated a series of slides for RV. These slides presented people doing various things, such as going on a picnic, tending a garden, swimming, working on a car engine, and so forth. The range of activities was broad enough so that subjects could find activities in the pictures which they liked as well as those they disliked. In the actual experimental situation, the RV of these pictures was combined with a relaxed/non-relaxed manipulation. Half of the subjects were given relaxation training before being tested, and half were not so prepared. Subjects were tested in a room two doors away from the room in which their slides were to be flashed onto a screen. There were 30 slides per subject, 15 of which were liked and 15 of which were disliked. Upon being cued, subjects were instructed to say "yes" or "no" if they believed a slide had been flashed. Slides were flashed half of the time, in random order, over 60 trials (i.e., half of the flashes were of slides and half of the flashes were blanks). A control subject, who had not rated these slides for RV, received the same set of slides as the experimental subject to whom he or she was matched.

The findings were merely suggestive (Ballard, 1983). The RV dimension failed to enter into a main effect. However, an unanticipated interaction occurred between relaxation condition and RV ($p < .02$). A combination of relaxation and *negative* RV for the flashed pictures resulted in the experimental subjects identifying more of these slide flashes as correctly taking place than the control subjects. Future work is undoubtedly called for here. We do not present these findings as proving anything at this point. We merely want the record to show that there is no reason why any problem in human (normal or paranormal) behavior cannot be investigated empirically. As we have argued elsewhere in this book (see Chapter 5, pp. 219–221), the only thing holding us back from revolutionizing psychological science is our ability to conceive of proper experimental designs. The scientific method cannot foreclose on parapsychological investigations; only psychologists with closed minds can do this.

Future Research Directions of Logical Learning Theory

The future direction called for in research on logical learning theory concerns the details of the telosponsive process. As a transcendental telosponse, an affective assessment moves from precedents to sequacious meaning-extensions of one sort or another. The dialectical nature of this preferential evaluation is clear, but we need to spell out in greater detail the role of oppositionality in all of human learning. That is, we need to show how oppositionality relates not only to affective assessment, but to the telosponsive process *per se*. As they are elaborations of the telosponsive process, *oppositionality* and *predica-*

tion are the key conceptions now being pursued experimentally in logical learning theory.

Dialectical reasoning hinges on the assumption that people routinely learn and process information bipolarly, contradictorily, and negatively—terms that capture the oppositional nature of certain meanings. Logical learning theory would seem to stand or fall on the single assumption of oppositionality in human learning, for it is from the play of such contrasting and conflicting poles of meaning in experience that agency takes root. People are predicators of their experience because, rather than simply taking in and storing and then putting out a succession of unidirectional influences, as the mediation-model suggests (see Chapter 7, p. 291) they must "take a position on" the implicit alternatives framed by oppositionality—both of an affective (like/dislike) and a conceptual variety. By "conceptual," we mean ideas or sensory impressions framed in such a way as to be communicated by language. The language expresses or reflects the underlying oppositionality (e.g., left/right, true/false). The language does *not* create the oppositionality as a speech convention.

As a first step in broadening our scope of investigation, we designed a study aimed at demonstrating that affective assessment could indeed be shown to organize mentation oppositionally (Rychlak & Williams, 1984). College subjects were asked to prerate for RV words that had antonyms, or opposite meanings. For example, two of the words we used were *active* and *realistic*. If a subject rated these words positively, we would then administer the antonyms *passive* and *idealistic* to the subject as a paired-associates unit in the learning task. If this same subject rated *quiet* and *tense* negatively, we would then administer the antonyms *loud* and *relaxed* in the learning task. (There were several such pairs to be learned in the task.)

The important point is that the subjects had *not* rated the antonyms for RV. They had not seen these antonyms previously in the experiment. A control subject was yoked to each experimental subject. Control subjects learned the same antonyms as the experimental subjects, but they had not done the RV prerating; hence, we did not expect their cognitive organizations to reflect the same patterning as our experimental subjects. Our prediction was that the RV-positive effect would show up among the antonyms being memorized by the experimental subjects in a pattern to the opposite of the preratings. Experimental subjects would learn the opposite of their disliked words more readily than the opposite of their liked words, and *vice versa*. The control subjects would not show such RV effects because we had not indexed their idiographic patterns of affective cognitive organization. Our prediction was substantiated at beyond the .001 level of significance.

It was at this point that we decided the heuristic properties of oppositionality should be demonstrable in studies based on criteria other than affective assessment. We decided to combine oppositionality with predication in a study in which we called on subjects to memorize a list of names in terms of certain personality characterizations. For example, a subject might be asked to learn a series of predications, such as "Charles is quiet; Douglas is outspoken; Michael is outspoken: and Timothy is quiet." Another series might be "Valerie is cautious: Melissa is bold: Sherrie is bold: and Deborah is cautious."

Note that *quiet* and *outspoken* are opposites, as are *bold* and *cautious*. We would expect that these lists would prove easier to learn than a list using the *same* words and names framed as non-oppositional predications—as, for example, "Charles is quiet: Douglas is cautious: Timothy is quiet: and Michael is cautious." The words *quiet* and *cautious* are not opposites; hence, they do not establish that dialectical context of meaning in predication which logical learning theory suggests is basic to mental organization (see p. 377). There were actually eight names to learn in terms of either an oppositional or a non-oppositional array of predications. As predicted, we found that the oppositional organization of predications led to significantly faster ($p < .001$) learning among college students than when the predications were non-oppositional (Rychlak, Williams, & Bugaj, 1986).

That this heuristic benefit of oppositional predication is not limited to actual words was demonstrated in research employing what we had come to call the method of *triassociation*. In contrast to paired-associates learning, which rests upon the efficient-cause assumption that associations connect-up or hook-up automatically, triassociation is based on a formal-cause assumption which views the learner as predicating learnable items in a context of meaning relations. Thus in triassociation (unlike paired-association), we are interested in *three* terms: the left-hand member, the right-hand member, and the intermediate predicational relation of the latter to the former. We systematically vary this intermediate predicational relationship to test its role in learning. In Chapter 8, we took up these varying ways of predicating things by way of unqualified, qualified, negative, and oppositional affirmations (pp. 333–334). We can apply these four types of affirming predicate relations to the task of "associating" trigrams together. Take a CVC trigram like HIB, for example. It would be possible to give it four somewhat different predications as follows: HIB is always VIC; HIB is never QIN; HIB is sometimes YAT; and HIB is opposite JOQ.

We have, in effect, a paired-associates unit with the left-hand member constant and four different right-hand members relating to it—situated in the common predicate position of English syntax. We can now present the left-hand term (HIB) and its four qualifying pre-dications (is always, is opposite, etc.) to subjects via a memory drum or computer screen, and test for the correctness of the right-hand member (VIC, JOQ, etc.) in what is comparable to a paired-associates learning task. This enables us to examine our theory of predication in light of the heuristic pull of oppositionality, as compared to the other predications.

Thus in the "HIB is always VIC" predication, we have the usual form of the major premise of a syllogism—akin to: "A person is always mortal." ("If a person then a mortal.") Of course, the right-hand term is not demonstrably broader in meaning than the left-hand term when we use CVC trigrams, but the syntactic arrangement of terms *per se* should facilitate learning if our theory of predication holds. If we think of Euler circles in this instance, HIB would be placed *within* VIC and therefore nicely framed by the latter's meaning as a universal condition (if HIB then VIC; but not necessarily *vice versa*). This universal relation is not evident on the "HIB is sometimes YAT" predication, where we have a qualified and tentative union of meanings implied. If we think of HIB and YAT as Euler circles, there would only be partial overlap between the two meanings being symbolized (only part of the two circles labeled HIB and YAT would overlap). In this instance, a reasoner is in the semantic state of having to guess when one meaning does frame or imply the other. As for the "HIB is never QIN" predication, in this case the Euler circles would be totally separated from each other. Given this line of theoretical development, it is possible to frame a testable hypothesis: The "is always" predication will be easier to learn than the "is sometimes" and the "is never" predications. The latter predications do not have the enveloping precedent-sequacious ties of meaning that the former predication enjoys.

But what about the "HIB is opposite JOQ" predication? It is not possible to diagram oppositionality through Euler circles. At best, we might think of this relationship as one of parallel and equal circles, meaningfully tied to each other by the fact that each delimits the other. According to logical learning theory, this dialectical relationship is essentially tautological (see Chapter 7, p. 296). That is, the meanings of these parallel circles are at one point "the same," even as there is a *context* within which these contrasts are framed. *Left* delimits and hence "defines" *right*, even as it stands meaningfully apart from *right*, and *vice versa*. Meaning extension here is bidirectional. Therefore, meaning extension is *broadened* as a predicational context, even though there is not the customary enveloping of one term by another. It follows from this broadened context that the heuristic facility of oppositional predication should be equal to or exceed the heuristic qualities of the "is always" predication. As opposite ends of a broader context, HIB and JOQ share a meaning relation that cements them together to the same degree that the "is always" instruction cements HIB to VIC, by enveloping the former in the latter. Both of these forms of predication enjoy a more complete tautological identity than the "is never" and "is sometimes" predications (see Chapter 7, pp. 277–279).

We conducted two experiments using the triassociation design. The trigrams used in the various predicational relations were randomized among the sample, to counter any claim that it was the trigrams rather than the affirmation instructions that influenced the findings. We found that oppositional predication was second to no other instruction in ease of learning. In one study done on college students, the oppositional predication was significantly better ($p < .001$) than all three of the other predications in facilitating learning (Rychlak, Williams, & Bugaj, 1986). Since CVC trigrams lack oppositional stimulus qualities, it is clear that oppositionality *per se* has great heuristic facility in human learning.

Our next venture involved a theoretical analysis of the predicational process as it related to *inference* and *implication*. It is possible to see a role for oppositionality in these two variations on the predicational theme. Inference may be defined as the psychological process whereby we derive conclusions from premises that are presumed true or apparently true (Reese, 1980, p. 252; Runes, 1960, p.146). In the case of an implication, however, we do not extend our line of reasoning from a premise that is quite so certainly known to be true or presumed to be true. Implication has a hypothetical quality about it (Reese, 1980, p. 270). An implication suggests what might be possible but is not known with certainty, or was not affirmed with clarity at the outset in the predications of our premises.

Thus if Mary hears her doorbell ring, she infers that there is someone at the door seeking her presence. On the other hand, if she arrives at the door and no one is there, she may draw the implication that her doorbell was rung in error—or, was it that someone played a joke on her? There are other possibilities as well, none of which Mary takes on as a premise with the confidence and certainty of an inference. It seemed to us that implications always involve some kind of oppositional reasoning. We gain implications from what was not said (but implied), from imagined circumstances that negate what is obviously taking place, from reversals in expectations calling for an explanation (as in Mary's case), and so forth. Inferences are more demonstratively framed than this. Implications must take the complete context of an event into consideration, because something is involved which is not distinctively and unequivocally "the case," but might very well be the case if only we assume the "other" side of things.

To test for the relative contribution of inference and/or implication in human learning, we had college subjects read a series of four vignettes in the lives of four youı.g junior executives, covering one full day in their work lives. Here is the first vignette as presented to our subjects: "In the morning, as they were driving to work, Jason said to Scott, 'I like impulsive women.' Later that day, in a coffee shop near their place of employment, Lori said to Beth, 'I like suggestible men.' All four of these people knew each other very well. Jason had never asked Beth for a date, but he regularly dated Lori. Scott dated Beth often, but he had tried to date Lori several times with no success." After three minutes of reading and studying this vignette, it was removed from our subjects' presence. Another form was given to them on which a number of conditional predications were listed, as follows:

Jason is probably easily influenced.
Lori is probably stubborn.
Beth is probably deliberate.
Scott is probably stubborn.
Beth is probably easily influenced.
Jason is probably spontaneous.
Lori is probably spontaneous.
Scott is probably deliberate.

The subject's task was to agree or disagree with the predications concerning each of the four principals in the vignette. Note that "easily influenced" is synonymous with "suggestible"; "stubborn" is antonymical to "suggestible." If a subject agrees with the predication that Jason is easily influenced, this would represent an inference from the known fact that Lori likes suggestible men and she regularly dates Jason. On the other hand, if a subject agrees with the predication that

Scott is probably stubborn this would represent an implication, based on the fact that he has been unable to secure a date with Lori. We reason to the opposite of Lori's preference to arrive at an implication concerning Scott's personality. There are similar inferences and implications concerning the female personalities. It is also possible to make inferential and implicational errors, to attribute inappropriate personality tendencies to the four principals.

We asked college subjects to perform in this research design (Rychlak, 1986). They read the stories and made their decisions, following up with a "confidence" rating of how certain they were in their agreements or disagreements with the various predications. We found that subjects did indeed draw both appropriate inferences and implications, distinguishing these from inappropriate predications with significantly higher levels of confidence ($p < .001$). Subjects also recalled inferences significantly better than they recalled implications in a follow-up memory task ($p < .001$). Thus, we were able to demonstrate empirically that people do frame differential levels of meaning in predicating their experience.

We have also begun a series of experiments dealing with precedent-sequacious meaning extension. In these designs subjects might be asked to learn various predications concerning a person, such as:

In competition, John is _____
In solving problems, John is _____
When life gets tense, John is _____

The initial phrase (precedent) in these sentences sets the context for the predication of John to follow (sequacious meaning-extension). Subjects are asked to learn a series of these statements, in which the predication of John occupying the blanks either carries forward the meaning inferred in the initial context, negates it, or is unrelated to it. In the noncontradictory condition, the preceding sentences would be completed with the words "active, fast and uptight." In this case, the sequacious meaning would extend one possibility of the precedent context. Competition suggests activity, problem solving is measured in terms of time spent on the task, and uptightness is virtually a synonym for tension. It is also possible to have an experimental condition in which the precedent contextual meaning is contradicted. In this case, we would end the sentences with the words "passive, slow, relaxed." Although we have given the "other side" of what might occur in the three circumstances, we still remain in the meaning-realm under contextual predication. The precedent context establishes a context within which we can "think forward" to the predication of John, as either one way or another *vis à vis* this context.

A third control condition was entered into the design, in which the sentences ended with the words "willing, vague, accepting." Notice that although the control predications categorize John, they "do not follow" readily from their precedent contexts. They do not extend from this context in either a positive or negative sense, as do our experimental conditions. We had college subjects learn predications in the three conditions described. As we predicted, the contradictory and noncontradictory lists were learned at a similar rate, and both were easier to learn than the control lists ($p < .01$). We take this as evidence for the precedent-sequacious nature of telosponsivity.

Studies on cued recall, in which either the subject or the predicate of a sentence is used as "the" cue, are underway. To date, these studies are highly supportive of the view that meaning extends from predicate "to" targeted subject more readily than *vice versa*. Indeed, subjects given lists of words to learn which have antonyms and synonyms can be seen to benefit equally well from antonymical cueing as from synonymical cueing in recall. We find people highly sensitive to oppositional meanings in various circumstances. For example, they can pick out pairs of antonyms as readily as pairs of synonyms when presented with a list of randomly arrayed words. We are greatly encouraged by the steady flow of evidence supporting the contention of logical learning theory that oppositionality is a *basic* feature of the human experience. We look forward to a continuing verification of this fact, since this provides us with the foundation on which to rest our agential image of humanity.

Summary

Chapter 9 presents an overview of the empirical studies conducted to date in support of logical learning theory. It begins with a consideration of the basic dimension of affective assessment, which is operationalized as reinforcement value (RV). This measure of likability is taken as a native human capacity to order experience oppositionally, in terms of what Aristotle called *dialectical reasoning*. To support this claim we found it necessary to establish in various ways that RV is independent of a dimension of meaningfulness based on association value (AV), or the frequency of contiguous contact with verbal or pictorial items in the course of learning. Various studies, ranging from psychometric considerations through learning investigations and even factor analyses, successfully establish that RV cannot be reduced to or explained in terms of AV. The test-retest reliability for RV compares favorably to AV when the measures taken are handled idiographically.

The RV-positive effect occurs when subjects predicate a task, their own abilities in the task, and the contents to be learned in that task as *liked*. In such a circumstance, subjects will learn liked items (e.g., CVC trigrams, words, recognitions of pictures, etc.) more readily than disliked items. However, we discovered in studies conducted on subjects who predicated the task, their personal behavior, or the contents of the task as *disliked* that it is possible to diminish or completely reverse this order of affective learning. In the latter cases, subjects actually memorize, recognize, and recall items (words, trigrams, pictures, etc.) that they dislike at the same rate or even faster than items that they like. Logical learning theory explains this as due to the fact that the precedent meaning (liked, disliked) is being sequaciously extended with greater facility into ongoing learning than its reverse. People telosponding on the basis of liked premises extend more readily along the positive meanings under predication by these premises, and *vice versa*.

Evidence is marshaled to support the view that affective learning style is a native human capacity. Younger children are found to rely more on RV in their learning than older children, supporting the view that this factor makes learning possible rather than being a product of learning. Mentally handicapped individuals rely more on the affective discrimination of RV than normal controls. Minority groups and lower-class populations in general reflect this tendency to rely more on affective (RV) than intellectual (AV) discriminants in their learning styles. We surmise that this occurs because they are not as identified with the culture-bound, intellectual discriminants of their environments. Indeed, we have empirical evidence demonstrating that when a task becomes difficult, as when it becomes increasingly abstract, a learner is prone to fall back on RV discriminants in his or her efforts to master the task. We also find RV effects reflected in the right/left brain organization suggested by split-brain research.

Chapter 9 continues with a survey of experiments that have relevance to traditional learning theories and their experimental results. Thus, we find RV-positive facilitating the classical primacy effect of serial learning. We find clustering effects based on the RV of the material being learned—liked items clustering with liked items, and disliked with disliked. We find interlist effects in which moving from a disliked to liked list facilitates positive nonspecific transfer, but moving in the opposite affective direction inhibits such transfer. In an operant-conditioning format, in which the subject is allowed to influence as well as to be shaped by the procedure, we find that subjects conform to experimental instructions if they are aware of what is to take place; but they also influence the course of this conditioning by selecting what they prefer to be "shaped" into doing by the supposed manipulation. This applies to modeling as well as to operant conditioning. Students do better in study topics that they like than in study topics they dislike, with study time on these topics partialed out. Affective learning style is shown to be resilient to the ingestion of alcohol and psychotropic drugs, as well as to experimental instructions aimed at reversing the RV-positive effect.

Chapter 9 next reviews studies having relevance for personality. Thus, subjects will remember liked names and liked faces more readily than disliked names or faces. In studies relating to interpersonal relations, we found that if a person likes another person then the former will tend to attribute more positive characteristics to the latter. Affective factors can be found in personality assessments of both a projective and an objective variety. If someone scores high on an objective personality dimension (such as dominance) and also finds this dimension positive in RV, the likelihood is about 25% greater that he or she will actually enact this pattern overtly than would a subject with the same score who disliked this dimension. People in general find it easier to learn word meanings that are consistent with their personality predilections, if we take RV into consideration. Thus, an aggressive person will learn liked aggressive words more readily than disliked aggressive words, or passive words of either a liked or disliked quality. Performance on IQ tests is about five points higher on liked subtests than on disliked subtests. Children who share things with others tend to share what they dislike more often than what they like. Impression-formation follows affective lines, and we even found some suggestive evidence that RV might be involved in parapsychological phenomena.

Chapter 9 closes with a survey of researches currently underway, pointing toward the future. Logical learning theory hinges in large measure on the validity of oppositionality in human learning; therefore, the current emphasis is on studies that prove that human mentation is organized oppositionally. It is also important to establish that learning follows the precedent-sequacious course of meaning extension called for by telosponsivity. Several studies are presented in support of such contentions. People learn the opposite meanings of disliked words more readily than the opposite meanings of liked words, and *vice versa*.

Oppositionality proves heuristic in memorizing predications regarding the behavior of others. An analysis of *inference* versus *implication* suggests that the latter phenomenon rests more on oppositionality than the former. Evidence is presented in support of this analysis. The ubiquitous nature of oppositionality in human learning is not difficult to establish. As we progress in the continuing refinement of logical learning theory, we hope to make use of this fact to effect a basic change in how human behavior is understood. A rigorous humanism can supplement—if not supplant—a rigorous mechanism in the psychological theories of the future.

References

Abramson, Y. *Reinforcement value: An idiographic approach to meaningfulness.* Unpublished doctoral dissertation. St. Louis: St. Louis University, 1967.

Abramson, Y., Tasto, D. L., & Rychlak, J. F. Nomothetic vs. idiographic influences of association value and reinforcement value on learning. *Journal of Experimental Research in Personality,* 1969, 4, 65–71.

Apao, W. K. *Affect and memory: Tests of the serial position effect.* Unpublished doctoral dissertation. West Lafayette, Ind.: Purdue University, 1979.

Apao, W. K. *Reinforcement and two kinds of meaningfulness measures in paired-associates learning.* Unpublished master's thesis. West Lafayette, Ind.: Purdue University, 1976.

Archer, E. J. Re-evaluation of the meaningfulness of all possible CVC trigrams. *Psychological Monographs,* 1960, 74, (10, Whole No. 497).

August, G. J., & Rychlak, J. F. Role of intelligence and task difficulty in the affective learning styles of children. *Journal of Educational Psychology,* 1978, 70, 406–413.

August, G. J., Rychlak, J. F., & Felker, D. W. Affective assessment, self-concept, and the verbal learning styles of fifth-grade children. *Journal of Educational Psychology,* 1975, 67, 801–806.

Ballard, J. A. *Affective assessment in a psi task.* Unpublished doctoral dissertation. West Lafayette, Ind.: Purdue University, 1983.

Bandura, A., Ross, D., & Ross, S. Imitation of film mediated aggressive models. *Journal of Abnormal and Social Psychology,* 1963a, 66, 3–11.

Bandura, A., Ross, D., & Ross, S. Vicarious reinforcement and imitative learning. *Journal of Abnormal and Social Psychology,* 1963b, 67, 601–607.

Barron, F. S. An ego strength scale which predicts responses to psychotherapy. *Journal of Consulting Psychology,* 1953, 17, 327–333.

Berg, I. A. Deviant responses and deviant people: The formulation of the deviation hypothesis. *Journal of Counseling Psychology,* 1957, 4, 159.

Boland, G. C. *The relationship of personality adjustment to the learning of material having connotative and associative meaningfulness.* Unpublished doctoral dissertation. St. Louis: St. Louis University, 1970.

Bousfield, W. A. The occurrence of clustering in the free recall of randomly arranged associates. *Journal of General Psychology,* 1953, 49, 229–240.

Brewer, W. F. There is no convincing evidence for operant or classical conditioning in adult humans. In W. B. Weimer & D. S. Palermo (Eds.), *Cognition and the symbolic processes.* Hillsdale, N. J.: Lawrence Erlbaum, 1974.

Brickman, P., Redfield, J., Harrison, A. A., & Crandall, R. Drive and predisposition as factors in the attitudinal effects of mere exposure. *Journal of Experimental Social Psychology,* 1972, 8, 31–34.

Bugaj, A. M. *The role of dialectical meaning in impression formation.* Unpublished master's thesis. West Lafayette, Ind: Purdue University, 1981.

Bugaj, A. M. *Affect and the cognitive organization of social information.* Unpublished doctoral dissertation. West Lafayette, Ind.: Purdue University, 1984.

Bunch, M. E., & Wientge, K. The relative susceptibility of pleasant, unpleasant, and indifferent material to retroactive inhibition. *Journal of General Psychology,* 1933, 9, 157–178.

Bunge, M. *The mind-body problem.* New York: Oxford University Press, 1980.

Campbell, K. A. *Affective assessment and awareness in the operant conditioning of verbal response.* Unpublished doctoral dissertation. West Lafayette, Ind.: Purdue University, 1983.

Cantor, G. N. Children's "like-dislike" ratings of familiarized and unfamiliarized visual stimuli. *Journal of experimental Child Psychology,* 1935, 6, 651–657.

Carter, H. D. Effects of emotional factors upon recall. *Journal of Psychology,* 1935, 1, 49–59.

Carter, H. D. Emotional factors in verbal learning. *Journal of Educational Psychology,* 1937, 28, 101–108.

Carter, H. D., & Jones, H. E. A further study of affective factors in learning. *Journal of Genetic Psychology,* 1937, 48, 126–133.

Cassirer, E. *An essay on man.* Garden City, N. Y.: Doubleday, 1944.

Cohen, L. Our developing knowledge of infant perception and cognition. *American Psychologist,* 1979, 34, 894–899.

Cromwell, R. L. Factors in the serial recall of names and acquaintances. *Journal of Abnormal and Social Psychology,* 1956, 56, 63–67.

David, K. L. *The relationship of replacement condition and an affective dimension of meaningfulness to rate of learning.* Unpublished master's thesis. West Lafayette, Ind.: Purdue University, 1977.

Eccles, J. C. Part II in K. R. Popper & J. C. Eccles, *The self and its brain.* New York: Springer-Verlag, 1977. Pp. 225–421.

Edwards, A. L. *The Edwards Personal Preference Schedule.* New York: Psychological Corporation, 1959.

Fitts, W. H. *Tennessee Department of Mental Health Self-Concept Scale.* Nashville: Counselor Records & Tests, 1965.

Garza, R. T. *Affective and associative meaningfulness in the learning styles of Chicano and Anglo college students.* Unpublished doctoral dissertation. West Lafayette, Ind.: Purdue University, 1975

Gazzaniga, M. S. *The bisected brain.* New York: Appleton-Century-Crofts, 1970.

Glassman, R. B. Free will has a neural substrate: Critique of Joseph F. Rychlak's *Discovering free will and personal responsibility.* Zygon, 1983, 18, 67–82

Green, F. P., & Schneider, F. W. Age differences in the behavior of boys on three measures of altruism. *Child Development,* 1974, 45, 248–251.

Greenspoon, J. The reinforcing effect of two spoken sounds on the frequency of two responses. *American Journal of Psychology*, 1955, 68, 409–416.

Gruba-McCallister, F. P. *The relation of dialectical opposition and an affective dimension of meaningfulness to verbal learning.* Unpublished master's thesis. West Lafayette, Ind.: Purdue University, 1975.

Gruba-McCallister, F. P., & Rychlak, J. F. A logical learning theory explanation of why personality scales predict behavior. *Journal of Personality Assessment*, 1981, 45, 494–504.

Heiskell, T. L., & Rychlak, J. F. The therapeutic relationship: Affective preference and empathic communication. *Journal of Social and Personal Relationships*, 1986, 3, 267–274.

Hilliard, R. D. Hemispheric laterality effects on a facial recognition task in normal subjects. *Cortex*, 1973, 9, 246–258.

James, W. What is an emotion? *Mind*, 1884, 9, 188–205.

Johnson, R. C., Frincke, G., & Martin, L. Meaningfulness, frequency, and affective character of words as related to visual duration threshold. *Canadian Journal of Psychology*, 1961, 15, 199–204.

Jones, H. E. Emotional Factors in learning. *Journal of General Psychology*, 1929, 2, 263–272.

Jung, C. G. Synchronicity: An acausal connecting principle. In H. Read, M. Fordham, & G. Adler (Eds.), *The collected works of C. G. Jung* (Vol. 8). Bollingen Series XX.8. New York: Pantheon, 1960.

Kant, I. *The critique of pure reason.* In R. Hutchins (Ed.), *Great books of the western world* (Vol. 42). Chicago: Encyclopedia Britannica, 1952.

Keedy, N. S. *The relationship between the affective quality of a premise and meaning-extension based upon its affirmation.* Unpublished manuscript. West Lafayette, Ind.: Purdue University, 1975.

Klein, D., Moscovitch, M., & Vigna, C. Attentional mechanisms and perceptual asymmetries in tachistoscopic recognition of words and faces. *Neuropsychologia*, 1976, 14, 55–66.

Koen, F. Polarization, m and emotionality in words. *Journal of Verbal Learning and Verbal Behavior*, 1962, 1, 183–187.

Kubat, W. J. *The reinforcement value of associations made to CVC trigrams.* Unpublished master's thesis. St. Louis: St. Louis University, 1969.

Laberteaux, T. E. *The influence of positive versus negative reinforcement value on mediated paired-associate learning.* Unpublished master's thesis. St. Louis: St. Louis University, 1968.

Lappin, R. W. *Meaningfulness, deviant achievers, and personal adjustment.* Unpublished doctoral dissertation. St. Louis: St. Louis University, 1969.

Libet, B. Unconscious cerebral initiative and the role of conscious will in voluntary action. *The Behavioral and Brain Sciences*, 1985, 8, 529–566.

Lynch, C. A. The memory values of certain alleged emotionally toned words. *Journal of Experimental Psychology*, 1932, 15, 298–315.

Matlin, M., & Stang, D. *The pollyanna principle: Selectivity in language, memory, and thought.* Cambridge, Mass.: Schenkman, 1978.

Mosbacher, B. J. *Depression and alcohol ingestion: A teleological perspective.* Unpublished doctoral dissertation. West Lafayette, Ind.: Purdue University, 1984.

Mosbacher, B. J., Gruen, G. E., & Rychlak, J. F. Incentive value: The overlooked dimension in childhood sharing. *Journal of Genetic Psychology*, 1985, 146, 197–204.

Muller, J. B., & Rychlak, J. F. Reinforcement as positive or negative meaning-extension: An empirical demonstration. *Motivation and Emotion*, 1979, 3, 287–297.

Nguyen, M. L. Clustering in terms of categorization and reinforcement value in ran-
    domly arranged associates. Unpublished master's thesis. West Lafayette, Ind.: Pur-
    due University, 1975.
O'Leary, L. R. The effect of idiographic meaningfulness on the learning of subjects from
    different racial backgrounds, social classes, and ability levels. Unpublished doc-
    toral dissertation, St. Louis: St. Louis University, 1969
Osgood, C. E. The nature and measurement of meaning. Psychological Bulletin, 1952,
    49, 197–237.
Osgood, C. E., Suci, G. J., & Tannenbaum, P. H. The measurement of meaning. Urbana:
    University of Illinois Press, 1957.
Penfield, W. The mystery of the mind. Princeton, N.J.: Princeton University Press, 1975.
Piers, E. V., & Harris, D. B. Age and other correlates of self-concept in children. Journal
    of Educational Psychology, 1964, 56, 81–85.
Reese, W. L. Dictionary of philosophy and religion: Eastern and western thought. At-
    lantic Highlands, N.J.: Humanities Press, 1980.
Rogers, C. R. Toward a modern approach to values: The valuing process in the mature
    person. In J. T. Hart & T. M. Tomlinson (Eds.), New directions in client-centered
    therapy. Boston: Houghton Mifflin, 1970. Pp. 430–441.
Rumsey, J. M., & Rychlak, J. F. The role of affective assessment in intelligence testing.
    Journal of Personality Assessment, 1978, 42, 421–425.
Runes, D. E. (Ed.), Dictionary of philosophy. New York: Philosophical Library, 1960.
Rychlak, J. F. Reinforcement value: A suggested idiographic, intensity dimension of
    meaningfulness for the personality theorist. Journal of Personality, 1966, 34, 311–
    335.
Rychlak, J. F. Intentionally manipulating association value and reinforcement value in
    paired-associates learning. Unpublished manuscript. West Lafayette, Ind.: Purdue
    University, 1974.
Rychlak, J. F. Affective assessment in the recognition of designs and paintings by ele-
    mentary school children. Child Development, 1975, 46, 62–70.
Rychlak, J. F. Affective assessment, intelligence, social class, and racial learning style.
    Journal of Personality and Social Psychology, 1975, 32, 989–995.
Rychlak, J. F. Affective clustering in the verbal learning styles of whites and blacks.
    Unpublished manuscript. West Lafayette, Ind.: Purdue University, 1976
Rychlak, J. F. Inference versus implication in predicating personality. Unpublished
    manuscript. Chicago: Loyola University of Chicago, 1986.
Rychlak, J. F., Carlsen, N. L., & Dunning, L. P. Personal adjustment and the free recall
    of material with affectively positive or negative meaningfulness. Journal of Abnor-
    mal Psychology, 1974, 83, 480–487.
Rychlak, J. F., Flynn, E. J., & Burger, G. Affection and evaluation as logical processes of
    meaningfulness independent of associative frequency. Journal of General Psychol-
    ogy, 1979, 100, 143–157.
Rychlak, J. F., Galster, J., & McFarland, K. K. The role of affective assessment in asso-
    ciative learning: From designs and CVC trigrams to faces and names. Journal of
    Experimental Research in Personality, 1972, 6, 186–194.
Rychlak, J. F., Hewitt, C. W., & Hewitt, J. Affective evaluation, word quality, and the
    verbal learning styles of black versus white junior college females. Journal of Per-
    sonality and Social Psychology, 1973, 27, 248–255.
Rychlak, J. F., & Marceil, J. C. Task predication and affective learning style. Journal of
    Social Behavior and Personality, 1986, 1, 557–564.
Rychlak, J. F., McKee, D. B., Schneider, W. E., & Abramson, Y. Affective evaluation in

the verbal learning styles of normals and abnormals. *Journal of Abnormal Psychology*, 1971, 77, 11–16.

Rychlak, J. F., & Nguyen, T. D. The role of frequency and affective assessment in associative enrichment. *Journal of General Psychology*, 1979, 100, 295–311.

Rychlak, J. F., & Saluri, R. E. Affective assessment in learning of names by fifth- and sixth-grade children. *Journal of Genetic Psychology*, 1973, 123, 251–261.

Rychlak, J. F., & Slife, B. D. Affection as a cognitive judgmental process: A theoretical assumption put to test through brain-lateralization methodology. *The Journal of Mind and Behavior*, 1984, 5, 131–150.

Rychlak, J. F., Tasto, D. L., Andrews, J. E., & Ellis, H. C. The application of an affective dimension of meaningfulness to personality-related verbal learning. *Journal of Personality*, 1973, 41, 341–360.

Rychlak, J. F., & Tobin, T. J. Order effects in the affective learning styles of overachievers and underachievers. *Journal of Educational Psychology*, 1971, 62, 141–147.

Rychlak, J. F., Tuan, N. D., & Schneider, W. E. Formal discipline revisited: Affective assessment and nonspecific transfer. *Journal of Educational Psychology*, 1974, 66, 139–151.

Rychlak, J. F., & Williams, R. N. Affective assessment and dialectical oppositionality in the cognitive processing of social descriptors. *Personality and Social Psychology Bulletin*, 1984, 10, 620–629.

Rychlak, J. F., Williams, R. N., & Bugaj, A. M. The heuristic properties of dialectical oppositionality in predication. *Journal of General Psychology*, 1986, 113, 359–368.

Sarbin, T. R., & Quenk, A. The rationality of nonsense: Intensity of meaning of non-referential verbal units. *Psychological Record*, 1964, 14, 401–409.

Silverman, A., & Cason, H. Incidental memory for pleasant, unpleasant, and indifferent words. *American Journal of Psychology*, 1934, 46, 315–320.

Slife, B. D., & Rychlak, J. F. Affection as a separate dimension of meaningfulness. *Contemporary Educational Psychology*, 1981, 6, 140–150.

Slife, B. D., & Rychlak, J. F. Role of affective assessment in modeling aggressive behavior. *Journal of Personality and Social Psychology*, 1982, 43, 861–868.

Smith, W. W. Experiments on memory and affective tone. *British Journal of Psychology*, 1921, 11, 236–250.

Sperry, R. W. Hemisphere deconnection and unity in conscious awareness. *American Psychologist*, 1968, 23, 723–733.

Staats, A.W. *Meaning and word associations: Separate processes* (Tech. Rep. No. 12; Contract No. 2794 [02]). Tempe: Arizona State University, 1959.

Stagner, R. Factors influencing the memory value of words in a series. *Journal of Experimental Psychology*, 1933, 16, 115–128.

Strupp, H. H. *Psychotherapists in action.* New York: Grune & Stratton, 1960.

Taffel, C. Anxiety and the conditioning of verbal behavior. *Journal of Abnormal and Social Psychology*, 1955, 51, 496–501.

Tait, W. D. The effect of psycho-physical attitudes on memory. *Journal of Abnormal Psychology*, 1913, 8, 10–37.

Tenbrunsel, T. W., Nishball, E. R., & Rychlak, J.F. The idiographic relationship between association value and reinforcement value, and the nature of meaning. *Journal of Personality*, 1968, 36, 126–137.

Thomson, R. H. An experimental study of memory as influenced by feeling tone. *Journal of Experimental Psychology*, 1930, 13, 462–467.

Tolman, E. C. Retroactive inhibition as affected by conditions of learning. *Psychological Monographs*, 1917, 25, No. 107, 1–50.

Truax, C. B., & Carkhuff, R. R. *Toward effective counseling and psychotherapy: Training and practice*. Chicago: Aldine, 1967.

White, M. M. Some factors influencing recall of pleasant and unpleasant words. *American Journal of Psychology*, 1936, 48, 134–139.

White, M. M., & Powell, M. Differential reaction time for pleasant and unpleasant words. *American Journal of Psychology*, 1936, 48, 126–133.

White, M.M., & Ratliff, M. N. The relation of affective tone on the learning and recall of words. *American Journal of Psychology*, 1934, 46, 92–98.

Woodward, K. E. *Affective factors in learning across levels of intelligence*. Unpublished doctoral dissertation. West Lafayette, Ind.: Purdue University, 1978.

Zajonc, R. B. Attitudinal effects of mere exposure. *Journal of Personality and Social Psychology Monograph Supplement*, 1968, 9, (2, Part 2).

CHAPTER TEN

A Logical Learning Theorist's Questions Concerning Alternative Approaches to Rigorous Humanism

Logical learning theory is not the only approach to rigorous humanism that has emerged in recent times. In fact, in the past generation there has been a steady trend in experimental circles of psychology to explain behavior in what is presumed to be an agential or teleological fashion. In Chapter 10 we will review a number of such theories, selecting those that are usually advanced by psychologists as satisfactorily accounting for the teleological side to behavior in a rigorous, experimental context. We will pose certain questions concerning these theories as we review their claims. Our purpose is not to discredit these alternative forms of rigorous humanism, but rather to bring into sharper focus their strengths and weaknesses as viewed from the perspective of logical learning theory. This analysis should help the reader gain a better appreciation of the fundamental issues that may divide those who would favor an agential view of human beings. The more humanistic form of theorizing must surely one day become a major force in psychology. Time is on the humanistic theorist's side, because the truth is that strictly mechanistic formulations are failing to capture the full range of human behavior. Of equal importance, the empirical evidence is continually supportive of agential explantions.

The various rigorous theories—that is, exacting formulations tied to validation—that we will be considering can be grouped into five sections. We begin with the area of causal attribution, move to self theories, and then take up the question of computer analogues before discussing dialectical themes in the study of human beings. We will close with some examples of the ongoing efforts of phenomenologically oriented psychologists to improve on the traditional scientific method used in psychology. As we move through these alternative approaches, we will raise some of the questions considered by logical learning theorists as they contemplate the basic issues that any teleologist should be sensitive to in framing a rigorous humanism.

Causal Attribution

We began this book with a consideration of the four causal meanings that any theorist might employ (see Table 1, pp. 8–31), and we have returned repeatedly to this theme of causal assumptions or predications. Mechanism is predicated on the meanings of material and efficient causation. Teleology is predicated on the meanings of formal-final causation. (We hyphenate these causal meanings because the final cause always encompasses a formal cause as the "that" pattern of meaning or reason "for the sake of which" behavior is enacted.) It is therefore fitting that psychologists should have taken up this question of causation in their examination of human behavior. Evidence for the role of formal-final causation in human reasoning was not difficult to find, but the conclusions drawn from such evidence has not *ipso facto* been supportive of a teleological formulation of human behavior.

Piaget (1930) seems to have been the first researcher to take an interest in human causal reasoning. He studied how children perceived causality by interviewing them at several age levels and asking them what made various things in life happen. Piaget found what he called *adherences* at all ages of development. In four cases out of five, these amounted to formal-final causal formulations of natural events. The child believes that the moon sends him or her dreams, or that the sun is aware of our existence on earth, or that things in the universe are made for our benefit. Rather than concluding that developing human organisms were manifesting their fundamental natures in such speculations Piaget referred to this telic propensity critically, as a "deep and stubborn finalism [i.e., formal-final cause description]" (p. 244). As a child matures such adherences diminish, and Piaget treated this development as a healthy movement away from erroneous description toward the correct (i.e., efficient-cause) way of talking about causation in nature. This suggests the first question that a teleological theorist might raise:

Question 1: Is it possible to advance empirical evidence for a teleological theory, given the historical scientific prejudice against such description?

We have seen in Chapters 1 and 2 how the rise of Newtonian science, which rested on Lockean assumptions, assured that whatever was being studied would be framed in material- and/or efficient-cause terms. We know that scientific investigation has the limitation of necessarily "affirming the consequent" of an "If . . . then . . ." line of propositional reasoning (see Chapter 5, p. 181). Falsification is never achieved without certain theoretical predications framing what is under test. If a theorist is flatly opposed to explanations encompassing formal-final causation, he or she will be unable to find evidence for this kind of account—even if it is "there" for the finding. The steady confounding in psychology of an efficient-cause method with an efficient-cause theory (see Chapter 1, p. 44) leads the logical learning theorist to question whether traditional stimulus-response or more recent input-output theories can be falsified—even in principle! Therefore, we pose Question 1 as a legitimate point of order.

The case for teleology seemed to have taken a more positive turn when Heider (1958) published his highly influential book, *The Psychology of Interpersonal Relations*. Heider's specific aim (p. 14) was to find something worthwhile in the naive descriptions that people advance concerning their everyday experience. He did not spell out the differences between efficient and final causality, but his approach clearly rested on such distinctions, as when he noted that "It makes a real difference . . . whether a person discovers that the stick that struck him fell from a rotting tree or was hurled by an enemy" (*ibid.*, p. 16). Heider spoke of such predications as the "attribution of events to causal sources" (*ibid.*, p. 16). In the process he coined the phrase that was to identify the area of research we are now considering. Much of the terminology used today by rigorous humanists can be traced to Heider, such as his concepts of "thing versus person perception" (*ibid.*, p. 21), "construction of the stimulus" (*ibid.*, p. 44), and "personal versus impersonal causality" (*ibid.*, p. 100).

Heider and Simmel (1944) conducted an experiment in which adult subjects observed a film of two geometrical figures (a triangle and a circle) moving about in what seemed to be a meaningless fashion, *unless* the figures were construed as persons. Viewed as persons, the geometrical forms were soon described by the subjects in ways reminiscent of the anthropomorphizing of Piaget's younger subjects. That is, the geometrical figures were said to be following or chasing one another about the screen. Heider (1958) was to conclude from this observation that "meanings as data . . . are part and parcel of the perceptual process" (p. 45). As the concept of meaning is well suited to a "that [meaning], for the sake of which" a stimulus is framed, things looked encouraging at this point for the teleologist. Meanings were tied to motives which, in turn, were tied to the person's intentions by Heider, as follows: "Psychological processes such as motives, intentions, sentiments, etc., are the core processes which manifest themselves in overt behavior . . ." (*ibid.*, p. 34).

Heider seemed to be construing the person as an agent when he drew his distinction between personal and impersonal causality: "What we have designated as personal causality refers to instances in which p causes x intentionally. That is to say, the action is purposive" (*ibid.*, p. 100). He even included unconscious purposes in this formulation (*ibid.*, p. 100). Impersonal causality was nonpurposive action: ". . . cases of personal causality must be distinguished from effects involving persons but not intentions. The latter are more appropriately represented as cases of impersonal causality" (*ibid.*, p. 101). Had this theoretical distinction between personal and impersonal causality been framed in light of the Aristotelian causal meanings, much confusion in the subsequent experimental literature might have been avoided. As it turned out, even Heider tended to confound telic with nontelic causal description, as in the following quote where he is fleshing out the contribution that might be made to the understanding of a stimulus (for example, to the actions of the geometric figures) by a reasoning human intelligence:

That the valuations of different parts of the stimulus manifold are put together in such a way as to form an integrated impression leads to the assumption of a hierarchy of structures interposed between the stimulus manifold and the resulting impressions, of stages of intervening variables that help us to analyze in a fruitful manner the correlations between the total stimulus field and the total phenomenal field. The parts of the stimulus manifold are evaluated, and these evaluations combine to produce still more encompassing evaluations, and so on—though in considering this process we must never forget that its direction is not all one way, from stimuli to impressions, but that the evaluations or meanings of the higher levels in turn influence the meanings of the lower levels (*ibid.*, p. 50).

This is where the case for agency, for the description of the teleological organism begins to crumble. Notice that Heider mixes Lockean and Kantian models (see Chapter 2, pp. 86–92) in this paragraph. He also confounds methodological terminology, such as intervening variables, with theoretical terminology, such as phenomenal evaluations (see Chapter 4, pp. 168–172). What proves detrimental to teleology in this paragraph is that Heider begins his treatment as a Lockean would, from the lower-level building blocks of perception "to" the higher levels, which *"in turn* influence the meanings of the lower levels [italics added]" (Heider, 1958, p. 50). The result is that what we have here is a mediation, not a predication, model (see Chapter 7, p. 291). The clear suggestion is that the person begins experience as a *tabula rasa.* After a period of time, in which presumably unpredicated learning takes place, the person begins to use earlier inputs to modify ongoing inputs in a pseudo-predicational fashion. This takes us to our second question:

Question 2: Which comes first: The capacity to mediate or the capacity to predicate? Do we learn to predicate, or do we predicate to learn?

Though we have two questions posed for emphasis, they are actually variations on the same theme, which is doubtless the fundamental issue dividing mechanistic from teleological theorizing. Mechanists always want to "account for" telic processes rather than beginning with the assumption of telic processes in human behavior. They begin unhesitatingly with mechanistic assumptions that are equally unaccounted for, such as the capacity to record or encode stimulations (inputs), the serial order in which such promptings are retained (stored) in memory, and the capacity to recall such retentions. But to assume that human beings *begin* a process of learning in which they as agents bring together conceptually what will be known via a predicational process is considered unwarranted speculation. Retaining their extraspective perspective and the Newtonian-Lockean assumptions on which psychological science has been founded, they invariably place the teleologist "one down" by insisting that anything like a predication must be the outcome and not the cause of human learning.

Here is where Heider begins to lose his grip on the teleological reformulation that his brilliant analysis has initiated. As subsequent events were to demonstrate in the recent history of psychology, social and personality psychologists have either transferred Heiderian insights into clearly mechanistic formulations, or they have inadvertently forfeited their teleological explanations to sundry mediation models, thanks to the ongoing confusion over what the word *cause* really means. We will return to this point several times in the remainder of this chapter.

For his part, Heider (1958) clearly seems to have wanted a rigorous humanism to have a place in psychology. Indeed, the writer would suggest that in his frequent references to inference and related dispositional properties in human learning (see pp. 34, 80, 116, 124), Heider was actually trying to explain behavior based upon the logic of a naive individual—the untainted human being who comes at life with certain predications that have great legitimacy. He wanted to base psychology on people's implicit assumptions concerning their everyday experience, and to avoid the temptation to explain away such assumptions prematurely (*ibid.*, p. 295). Heider argued that people made causal attributions in order to "predict and control events" (*ibid.*, p. 146) involving themselves and others. Attribution is defined as ordering proximal stimuli (i.e., the stimuli impinging on our retinas) by way of the invariants and dispositional properties of distal stimuli (i.e., perceived objects in the environment) (*ibid.*, p. 296). The logical learning theorist would suggest that such invariants and dispositional properties are readily understood as predications wound into premises under the affirmation of a telosponsive intelligence. As such they frame the human being's understanding and are *always* involved in behavior. We do not find any contradictions here with anything that Heider has contended. Indeed, we could easily claim Heider as a progenitor of logical learning theory.

Next, it was Michotte's (1963) turn to tackle the question of causation in human perception, and his approach would have warmed Immanuel Kant's heart. Michotte took a position in opposition to David Hume, the British empiricist who had argued that human beings are not natively equipped to see "cause-effect" taking place in the efficient-cause sense (see Chapter 1, p. 43). Michotte (1963) held that human beings do have the innate capacity to see cause-effect (in the efficient-cause sense) when it occurs in experience. People can see one object acting on another, producing changes, and modifying the course of events in the process (p. 15). If we construed what Michotte had to say as Kantians, we would be encouraged to believe that he was talking about a Kantian-like category of the understanding.

Michotte's experiment followed the example of Heider and Simmel (1944). His subjects viewed a film in which a black square and a red square moved about on a white background. The basic motion portrayed one square moving toward and making contact with the other, which to that point in time was stationary. This parallels Hume's well-known analysis of causality in terms of a moving billiard ball striking a stationary billiard ball. However, in the Michotte (1963) experiment two courses of action followed the pictured contact. Sometimes the moving square stopped while the formerly stationary one moved on (called the *launching effect*); at other times both squares moved off in tandem (called the *entraining effect*) (p. 20).

Consistent with the earlier findings of Piaget and Heider-Simmel, Michotte found his subjects constantly anthropomorphizing the moving squares, assigning purposes to what they saw taking place in the film. For example, they would describe one square as having "hit" the other or as "chasing" it. Many claimed they did not see any necessity in the sequence of motion, so that events seemed as if they might stop at the point of contact (*ibid.*, p. 23). This finding alone casts doubt on the assumption that efficient causation was under study. An efficient cause in which the sequence of linear motions is not necessary seems a contradiction in terms. The logical learning theorist would suggest that what these subjects were "seeing" is more akin to formal-final causation than efficient causation. Michotte failed to entertain such alternative possibilities, and pressed the point that he was dealing exclusively with efficient causation. Indeed, he denigrated the telic possibilities of his interesting research: "We all know . . . how frequently people fail to make a distinction between [efficient] 'cause' and 'purpose' [formal-final cause]. We constantly find that children and even adults are satisfied with 'explanations' in terms of purpose, and *attribute* [italics added] to them a causal significance in the sense of 'efficient' causality" (*ibid.*, p. 260). An attitude of this sort by the experimenter surely calls to mind Question 1.

Note that the meaning of "attribute" in Michotte's comments is beginning to shift—from the ongoing effort that Heider envisioned of people trying to control and predict their destinies, to an arbitrary and often erroneous ascription of what people "think" is taking place over and against what is "really" taking place in perceived reality. This shift in meaning is one of the changes that we see taking place in the further development of causal attribution as a theoretical conception.

The next major figure in causal attribution is De Charms (1968), who combined Heider's notion of personal causality with Polanyi's (1964) conception of "personal knowledge" to arrive at what he called "personal causation." Strangely enough De Charms (1968) rejects the concept of causation from the outset of his argument. "*The concept of 'cause' implies more than is ever empirically demonstrated to occur in the physical world between two objects or two events*" (p. 5). He embraced physical reductionism, believing that in the final analysis psychology must rest on physical events. He took it as his goal to "account for the persistent fact that human beings believe themselves to be 'causes'," because "this belief affects their behavior" (*ibid.*, p. 5). De Charms defines his construct as follows: "*Personal causation is the initiation by an individual of behavior intended to produce a change in his environment*" (*ibid.*, p. 6). He returns to the Humean position—attacked by Michotte—to claim that causes are indeed learned regularities based on the fact that humans are motivated to learn about their experience in order to survive:

Human beings, and probably animals too, know without learning about their own simple motives or reasons for acting, and they soon learn to act in a way to satisfy these motives, and along the way they learn that things are caused because *they cause them!* If a child does not learn to cause things to happen he cannot live (*ibid.*, p. 9).

This Humean stress on learning to account for causation brings us to our third question, which deals with the assumptions of the underlying learning theory being called upon to explain behavior:

Question 3: *Is the theory of learning being relied upon to account for an organism's acquired knowledge based on mechanistic or teleological precepts?*

Question 3 is really an extension of Question 2, but it must be singled out as a distinctive issue. Too often we find psychologists speaking of the "learning" through past experience of this or that sort of behavior (beliefs, attitudes, value systems, etc.). Indeed, "past experience" is presumed to mean "past learnings" by most psychologists. Along with the confusion over the meaning of causation, there is considerable ambiguity in the term "learning." The point made by logical learning theory is that a mechanistic formulation of learning *cannot* underwrite a theory of agency. It must necessarily happen that the teleological meanings under espousal will be lost to the mechanism of the learning theory in question. Invariably, this theory will involve some form of mediation model (Question 2). If the learning theory involved is mechanistic then all this can mean is that the person will acquire some form of mediator giving him or her the illusion of agency (see Chapter 8, p. 351). To have a telic account of behavior, the theory accounting for learning must itself be a telic formulation. As a case in point we might now contrast Polanyi's (1964) view of personal knowledge with De Charms' (1968) adaptation of this concept to underwrite his notion of personal causation.

There can be no doubt that Polanyi (1964) is a teleologist and that his understanding of learning would readily adapt to the precepts of logical learning theory. Indeed, along with Heider he could be a progenitor of this approach. Polanyi interprets "personal" to mean something like a tacitly known sense of what is true at the outset of experience, committing the person to a course of action in the telosponsive manner of a premise encompassing a predication regarding that experience (p. 300). This active predication of meaning begins in the very definitions that the person assigns to his or her concepts (*ibid.*, p. 250). It would not be wrong to suggest, as does logical learning theory, that the person must first "know" (affirm a predicating meaning-relation as a premise) in order to know anything else (see Chapter 7, p. 302). Polanyi (1964) assigns definite powers to the intellect for making knowledge possible, such as the capacity for understanding meaning, for believing a factual statement, reflecting on problems, and transcending what is under affirmation to see alternatives in meaning (pp. 263 and 268). Above all, learning is tied to purposivity (*ibid.*, pp. 62, 73, and 120). Aiming his theoretical guns directly at the mechanistic ("objectivist") learning theory of Clark L. Hull (1943), Polanyi had this to say:

For even the most elaborate objectivist nomenclature cannot conceal the teleological character of learning and the normative intention of its study. Its supposedly objective terms still do not refer to purposeless facts but to well functioning things. Something is a "stimulus" only if it succeeds in stimulating. And though "responses" may be meaningless in themselves, the state of affairs called "reinforcement" functions as such by converting at least one particular response into a sign or a means to an end (Polanyi, 1964, pp. 371–372).

How different it is when we consider De Charms' use of personal knowledge. After stating that he is relying upon this conception as employed by Polanyi, De Charms (1968) continues: "One type of personal knowledge, *learned in childhood* [italics added] by all human beings when the baby learns to distinguish himself from others and other things, is the knowledge of personal causation" (p. 10). If personal causation were a type of personal knowledge, then according to Polanyi's treatment this would represent an implicit (tacit) truth to be affirmed by the person as a predication, and not learned in childhood by the person. In terms of Question 2, Polanyi would be suggesting that we predicate personal causation to learn, whereas De Charms has us learning to predicate personal causation.

De Charms has simply not shaken himself loose from traditional theories of learning. Thus, he can say in a Lockean vein that "Knowledge derives originally from sense perception" (*ibid.*, p. 258). There is no Polanyian talk here of framing or predicating this sense perception from the outset of learning. Any such convictions or predicated assumptions are due to the "effects" of previous learning (*ibid.*, p. 265). It would be our suggestion that De Charms interprets "personal" as "private," as the singular experiences learned by the individual over the course of life. There is no role here for an organism actively predicating this experience—except only later, after learning has taken place as a kind of mediator. Of course, De Charms employs terminology that has the sound of agency, as when he says that *"man is the origin of his behavior"* (*ibid.*, p. 271). He also notes that humans can attribute characteristics to others (*ibid.*, pp. 282–283) based upon the learning of certain universal attributes (*ibid.*, p. 268). But there is nothing essentially teleological in this treatment, and we seem to be back in the same situation as with the reinterpretation of Heider. A promising teleological treatment of causation, based on the formal-final conceptualizations of Polanyi, has been lost to the traditional Lockean models of learning embraced by modern psychology (see Chapter 4).

The next development in causal attribution theory came from the work of Jones and Nisbett (1971). These researchers tackled the problem of perspective in describing or accounting for the cause of a line of behavior. They found that actors in situations tend to say the factors in the circumstances facing them are what cause them to behave, whereas observers of these same actors are likely to attribute the cause of the latter's behavior to stable personality traits or habitual dispositions to act in some way, regardless of situational circumstances. This divergence in causal attribution can be reversed through the use of videotape, by having an observer look at things from the viewpoint of the actor, and *vice versa.* The logical learning theorist would see in these data an actor and an observer framing predicate assumptions about what causes are in operation, based on whether these individuals take an introspective or an extraspective theoretical perspective on things.

It appears that in looking "at" the actor in an extraspective manner, the observer is encouraged to predicate material- and/or efficient-cause explanations of what is transpiring. People "over there" behave as they do because they have inborn traits, or they have been shaped by experience to exhibit a repetitive, hence observable, style of behavior. Looking "with" the actor in an introspective manner encourages formal-final cause description, in that now we take into consideration the actor's predication of the circumstances in the context framing this situation. The actor is, after all, confronting a situation; hence, it would be senseless to suggest that what the actor "does" is due to something totally extraneous to this situational context. This is how the logical learning theorist would begin thinking about the data reported by Jones and Nisbett. And in the process there is another question suggested:

Question 4: In referring to contrasting cognitive occurrences such as attributions, are we referring to different fundamental processes of cognition or merely to different contents of a uniform cognitive process?

The distinction between a process and the contents of that process is an important one. It would be easy to overlook the fact that both the observer and the actor in the Jones and Nisbett research were attempting to make sense of the experimental task before them. They were subjects in an experiment, taking on two different roles based upon contrasting perspectives of the same event. Though they framed different causal explanations of this event, we can understand this contrast by considering the common process of cognition within which such predications are framed. The contents of the logical task confronting the observer and the actor are what we must consider, as in our previous discussion. Precisely where does "attribution" enter—as the process of assigning causal or other accounts to experience, or as the specific contents or "attributes" so assigned? Logical learning theory places its emphasis on the process itself over the contents of the process. Telosponsivity is at the core of attribution because it demands that the person "bring to bear" (attribute) some precedent meaning "for the sake of which" experience can be sequaciously known. Contentual differences in such precedents are of interest, but they do not capture the basic (telosponsive) process at play in cognition.

The word attribution takes its roots from "to bestow," and hence it would seem to be highly compatible with this line of teleological theorizing. However, Kelley (1973), one of the chief spokesmen for attribution theory, relied upon information-processing theory to say: "It must be emphasized . . . that attribution theory deals only with the processes by which attributions are derived from informational input" (p. 126). We will be taking up some of the problems that the computer analogue presents for the teleologist later (see p. 455), but for now let us merely observe that Kelley cannot be thinking of attribution as a process of cognition. He has accepted the computer analogue as his cognitive process and now shifts the discussion to a consideration of what that process allows as input material for attribution to participate in. This enables him to speak about manipulating people into having either good or bad attributional information under processing:

. . . through proper manipulation of causes and information about causes, actors can be uniformly led to highly erroneous views about the reasons for their own behavior. . . . Thinking in these terms, eventually we will be able to identify other attributional illusions and to describe the conditions necessary for their production. These will include the illusions of responsibility, whereby a person assumes to an unrealistic degree that he is personally responsible for consequences that other persons would attribute largely to circumstances or luck, and the illusion of external constraint, in which the person attributes to the situation or other persons consequences that are generated by his own behavior (Kelley, 1973, p. 125).

In this formulation, the contents of the predications are fixed upon as the data of importance to be studied. The process whereby such predications are framed is really not under study. This is why attribution theorists can say that the person is not *always* attributing in cognitive processing (see Jones, Kanouse, Kelley, Nisbett, Valins, & Weiner, 1971, p. xii). It all depends upon the mediating cues (Question 2) input by the information processing system. If these cues are of a certain type then attributions will be forthcoming; if not, then no attributions take place. The logical learning theorist would of course dispute this claim. In line with Heider's original speculations, we believe that people must *always* bestow meaning onto existence. As Polanyi has taught us, without this initial affirmation of personal commitment there would be no grasp of existence possible (Question 2).

Because of the continuing tendency to consider the process of attribution a closed issue, the research findings in causal attribution fail to impress anyone with their teleological significance. For example, there is considerable agreement among researchers that when subjects frame causal explanations of items or events this greatly facilitates long-term memory of these cognitive contents (Black & Bern, 1981; Bradshaw & Anderson, 1982; Fisher & Craik, 1980; Sherman & Titus, 1982; Stevenson, 1981). Many of these causal attributions are clearly teleological in nature, which is usually justified as merely "information" concerning plans and goals stored hierarchically in long-term memory (see Black & Bower, 1980; Graesser, Robertson, Lovelace, & Swinehart, 1980). If these researchers were thinking of the *process* of cognition as under study, they might well begin to wonder why the Aristotelian formal-final cause meanings so prominent in the history of Western thought (see Table 1, pp. 8–31) continue to provide great heuristic benefit to the human learner.

This is even more apparent when we consider the empirical finding that when unexpected events arise the subjects confronting these events are all the more prompted to offer causal explanations of the unexpected occurrence (Pyszcynski & Greenberg, 1981; Wong & Weiner, 1981). Is this not highly consistent with the view of the person as a framer of experience, lending order to it when such order is called for? It is in the realm of the unexpected that a bestowal or attribution of order (meaning) is especially called for, so that things might be set right again. Findings such as these strike us as highly consistent with logical learning theory. Yet, a shift in the cognitive process is not to be seen in the research, because this is not what is under "test." The cognitive model of process is not open to change through experimental manipulation, only the contents carried on within it can be so effected. Thus it is that the attribution theorist can continue referring to the "elicitation" (Hastie, 1984, p. 44) of causal reasoning. A meaning-bestowing process is now said to be triggered by events external to it. The efficient cause continues to swamp formal-final cause description in the face of apparent evidence to the opposite (Question 1). Obviously, in a circumstance like this there is little hope for the teleologist. Thus, we leave the area of causal attribution—an area with great promise for rigorous humanism—without much satisfaction.

Self Theories

The next area in which it is often said that teleological explanations are being dealt with is that of self theorizing. Other terms, such as *person* or *personal being*, may be substituted for *self*. However, the essential point is that some consideration is being given to the identity of the individual and, it is assumed by those who theorize in this vein, to agency—or what might suffice as agential descriptions of behavior.

Taking his stance as a cognitive social learning theorist, Mischel (1976) has discussed the self as the person, which for him is tantamount to saying that we have a "behaving organism" (p. 146) under consideration. Although he expresses great reluctance to consider the self as an "extracausal agent" residing in the person with the responsibility of generating causal sequences in behavior (*ibid.*, p. 145), Mischel arrives at some highly teleological-sounding statements. "We [human beings] can actively *select* (choose) the situations to which we expose ourselves, in a sense creating our own environment, entering some settings but not others, making decisions about what to do and what not to do" (*ibid.*, p. 151). Although there is a slight waffle in Mischel's reference to "in a sense" creating our own environments, someone who reads a sentence like this could well draw the implication that we have a teleological account under presentation. This suggests another question to the logical learning theorist:

Question 5: Can a theorist reject formal-final cause description and then go on to employ agential terminology like choice, self-regulation, and purpose without contradiction?

There is an assumption in psychology, stemming in all probability from what we called the "accounting-for" argument in Chapter 4 (pp. 164–168), that it is proper to dismiss telic phraseology in one breath and then to use it in another, possibly with a caveat, a wink, or an "in-quotes" gesture. The logical learning theorist finds this an unacceptable practice, and indeed suggests that when it is carried out the theorist concerned is involved in a contradiction. If a theory cannot stand on its own terminology but must borrow from another theory on a regular—albeit informal—basis, how satisfactory can this theory be? (We anticipate Question 10 here.)

If the person is the self, in what sense can Mischel mean this? In fact, we find the typical subsumption of final-cause terminology by efficient-cause terminology in Mischel's formulations. He speaks of "person variables" and "situation variables," with an ongoing interaction between these two realms of measurable influences, all totaling up to behavior. We have a familiar theory-method confound here (see Chapter 4, pp. 168–172). As examples of person variables Mischel (1976) includes constructing cognitions of behavior, encoding strategies, expectancies, valuations of stimuli, self-regulatory systems, plans, and self-reactions (p. 150). The informal meaning of all such concepts stems *not* from a primary emphasis on material or efficient causation, but from a primary emphasis on formal and final causation. Indeed, as we suggested in Question 3, there is no way in which to justify such terminology based on anything but a teleological learning theory of behavior. Anything other than this results in an "accounting-for" situation, in which we would have to admit frankly that believing that people can choose, self-direct, or plan is an illusion. (Immergluck [1964] and Lefcourt [1973] have properly taken this tack.)

Does Mischel's (1976) avowed cognitive social learning theory (p. 145) rest on telic assumptions? In speaking of variations in self-regulation, he observes that "Individuals differ with respect to each of the components of self-regulation . . . depending on their unique earlier histories or on more recent situational information" (*ibid.*, p. 151). It is soon evident that what we have here is a mediational model, in which early influences and present influences interact with one another to bring about behavior without anything akin to telosponsivity. Mischel even speaks of "strong" situational variables, such as the red or green stoplight signal which tugs at our awareness in the traffic lane, as opposed to the "weak" situational variable of a blank TAT card on which we can project anything we personally desire (*ibid.*, p. 153). The subjects in the attribution research cited previously are obviously looking "at" people, viewing them extraspectively as under the unidirectional thrust of variables from out of the past, as well as coming up against such directing variables in the present. The resultant efficient-cause "interaction" somehow results in the outcome we call behavior.

Mischel does not entertain the theoretical suggestion of logical learning theory that situations are never "situations" until they are predicated as such by the behaving organism. He measures what he observes and assigns part of the observed variance of his measures to the situation and part to the person. But, again, as with the attribution experimenters (Question 4), he does not perceive evidence strongly suggestive of agency as evidence *against* his underlying model of the cognitive process—which is, in fact, akin to an information-processing (computer) model (see Rychlak, 1976, for a detailed analysis of Mischel's theorizing).

For example, Mischel (1979) has found that children can delay rewards if they concentrate on something other than the consummatory delights of such rewards (p. 750). A child can wait for candy longer if he or she avoids thinking about its taste than if this satisfaction is contemplated. Or, the child can turn his/her attention away from candy entirely and effect a longer delay of gratification. Children are also aware of their capacity to plan things in their lives by age ten, if not earlier (*ibid.*, p. 749). The logical learning theorist is excited by such findings, since they are consistent with an agential view of the learning process. But the cognitive social learning theorist views such findings as merely different contents of the interacting, mediational model that represents the underlying learning process.

Bandura's (1977a) social learning theory is also cited by many psychologists as a humanizing view of the person. Surely, his excellent work on the vicarious or observational aspects of human learning has proved a boon to teleological theorists. The logical learning theorist views this modeling of others' behavior as a reflection of the predication process, in which the person frames a verbalized or unverbalized predication in the sense of "I can do what X did," or "I can avoid doing what X did." The formal-final cause aspects of such behavior are clear. Bandura's interpretation of reinforcement as information rather than direct manipulation is also consistent with a predicational model of mind. Even so, Bandura remains a confirmed mediationist, adapting, as did Mischel, the information-processing model to his explanations of behavior (Bandura, 1977b, p. 191). Apparently, in an effort to enrich our understanding of the multiple causes of behavior, Bandura (1978) advanced his conception of "reciprocal determinism," which reminds us of Mischel's (1979, p. 747) reliance upon "interaction." This brings another question to mind:

Question 6: Are concepts such as "mutual interaction" or "reciprocal determinism" specific enough to (a) explain behavior and (b) submit to falsification?

Bandura's (1978) reciprocal interaction is aimed at countering what he takes to be the one-way explanations of behavior employed by theorists like Skinner (1971, p. 211), who believe that the person is unidirectionally acted upon by the environment, and not *vice versa*. Bandura (1978) views determinism as signifying "the production of effects by events" (p. 345), which strikes us as an efficient-cause definition. Logical learning theory views determinism as limiting the alternatives that might occur, and this can be framed in terms of all four of the causal meanings (see Chapter 6, pp. 243–245). In social learning theory, "behavior [B], internal personal factors [P], and environmental influences [E] all operate as interlocking determinants of each other" (Bandura, 1978, p. 346). This is schematized as:

Note the double-headed arrows uniting the three touchpoints of what Bandura describes as psychological functioning. The "self-system" is said to comprise "*structures and subfunctions for perceiving, evaluating, and regulating behavior,* [but it is] *not a psychic agent that controls action* [italics in original]" (*ibid.*, p. 344). We begin with the customary disclaimer against final-cause description (Question 5), but then, as was true of Mischel, we also read statements in Bandura's writings that have the sound of teleology. Thus, he says that people "engage in reflective thought" for innovative action (*ibid.*, p. 345) and that people are self-reactors with capacities for reflective self-awareness (*ibid.*, p. 351). He has found in his research that subjects "improvise on information conveyed by instructions to create their own performance guides" (Bandura & Simon, 1977).

The logical learning theorist would be interpreting such empirical findings to mean that human beings reason dialectically, that they can predicate what the environment presents to them in either "this" or "that" sense. Hence, what eventuates is to this extent up to the person. The question was put to Bandura (by Rychlak, 1979) as to whether or not an additional double-headed arrow in his triangular model was not necessary to account for this seeming transcendent dialectical capacity of people to turn back reflexively on what they know, or are told, and to reason thereby to an alternative by way of such an opposition. Should not the reciprocal interaction model have a looping arrow turning back on the P (person) symbol?

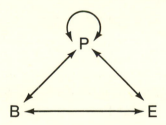

The looping arrow above P symbolizes that aspect of telosponsivity in which it is possible to take a position in opposition to what is being affirmed (premised, predicated, etc.). This loop would account for Bandura's subjects recasting the experimental instructions as it would for self-reflective thought in general. In responding to our query, Bandura (1979) defined reflective thought as "thoughts about one's

thoughts," adding: "By *operating* on what they know, people can derive knowledge about the things that extend beyond their experiences
and *generate* innovative courses of action [italics added]" (p. 439).
The logical learning theorist would like to know what Bandura means
by "operating on" or "generate" in this comment, but it is not difficult
to guess. There is a kind of efficient-cause meaning at play here. This
becomes clearer when Bandura expands on his answer to our query:

In the social learning view, behavior, cognitive and other personal factors, and
environmental influences all operate as interlocking determinants of one another. . . . Within each of the triadic factors there exist, of course, many reciprocal processes. In the action domain, particular movements reciprocally
activate other movement patterns. Similarly, there exist reciprocal spiraling
processes in thought-produced affective reactions. The occurrence of an environmental event likewise reciprocally affects other environmental events
(Bandura, 1979, p. 440).

In other words, Bandura is prepared to state that there are looping
double-headed arrows at *each* point of the triangle:

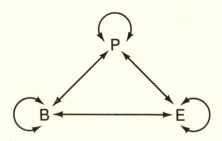

There is nothing unique or transcendent about reflective thought.
It is simply one of the many reciprocal subprocesses that operate within
each of the three constituent factors (i.e., B, P, E). A child skipping
rope (a B function) brings many movements into coordination, so that
as one action (twisting the rope) is undertaken, a second is reciprocally coordinated (leaping from the ground). As a diesel train approaches a crossing, it triggers mechanisms to lower a gate so that we
are unable to drive across the railroad tracks at that crossing. This
would be a case of E reciprocally interacting with itself. And a philosopher turning back on certain assumptions by way of a Brentanoan
secondary consciousness (see Chapter 3, p. 116) would be reciprocally

interacting in the P realm, by way of thinking about his or her thoughts. There is obviously no room for a teleological explanation in this account. Bandura made his feelings known explicitly on this point, when he added:

There is a difference between analyzing cognition as a contributing factor in the reciprocal determination of events and conceptualizing cognition as a psychic agent that orchestrates behavior. Understanding of how people exert some influence over their actions is more likely to be advanced by delineating and exploring the nature of self-regulatory mechanisms than by simply ascribing behavior to a psychic agent (Bandura, 1979, p. 440).

Question 6 asks just how much Bandura has explained in his ever-expanding conception of reciprocal determinism. The logical learning theorist views Bandura as claiming that "behavior is a function of everything," which is on the one hand difficult to dispute and on the other hand impossible to falsify. If the self-system is a mechanism relying upon reciprocal determinations, then on what basis can Bandura say that "Cognitive competencies and perceptual sets affect what information people extract from the environment and how they organize and interpret what they see and hear. *Conceptions* thus give meaning to experiences and are in turn altered by them. *Conceptions* of oneself, of generative skills, and of the physical and social environment are not simply yesterday's passively imprinted stimulus input acting unidirectionally as today's internal efficient causes [italics added]" (*ibid.*, p. 440).

Although the logical learning theorist applauds such statements, how do we justify them in our technical theoretical positions? When we use a word like "conception" and imply that it has arisen in "interaction" with the environment and/or the behavior of a person, what do we mean? Does the environment provide the conceptualization, or is it the person as a conceptualizer who frames the environment in light of this precedent organizer? If we mean the latter, then in what way is the environment "interacting" with the framing conceptualization? We have noted in Chapter 8 (p. 343) that the figure *does not* interact with—hence, reciprocally determine—the framing ground. Contour is one sided, with organization moving from the broader (ground) to the narrower (figural) aspects of the total gestalt. Logical learning theory follows this research finding in its interpretation of the precedent-sequacious nature of telosponsivity. Hence, when the environment is conceptualized, it is brought into awareness by way of the person's (P) conceptual process. The environment is not an aspect of that (grounding) process but a (figural) content "within" that process (Question 4).

To say that two or all three corners of the interaction triangle are involved in the framing of conceptions is not distinctive or explicit enough to explain how behavior actually "works." If we empirically test the "functioning" of conceptions in human behavior and find that they do not function as we had believed, this would have no bearing on reciprocal determinism—anymore than would the reverse finding. Reciprocal determinism would remain, but we would have to find something other than "conceptions" to study in light of the interacting triangle. This would call for additional theoretical constructs to be added, and we know from Bandura's proclaimed opposition to agential explanation that his additions are not likely to enhance a teleological understanding of the self.

The concept of selfhood has a long history in social psychology. The influence of Cooley's (1902) "looking-glass self" has been important. Cooley suggested that we become aware of our selves as objects thanks to our mirrored images from others with whom we relate. We essentially internalize or adopt the perspective of the "other" person in framing our self-image. Sullivan (1962) later referred to these interpersonally generated attitudes as "reflected appraisals" (p. 5). Social psychologists have continued to interpret the self in light of such interpersonally acquired or learned reactions (responses, self-images, etc.) (Wegner & Vallacher, 1980). Unfortunately the emphasis has been placed on the "reflected" rather than on the "appraisal" aspect of our looking-glass selves—that is, to appraise is to judge or to render a value estimate of some sort. Logical learning theorists place affective assessment at the core of human cognition, viewing it as an essential ingredient of agency. In social psychology, this evaluative process has not been taken seriously. The locus of such judgments has been moved to the supraindividual functioning of "norms," to which a person is shaped to comply. This takes us to our next question:

Question 7: Is a socially induced belief, such as a norm or a self-image, the result of a process located supraindividually or individually?

For the logical learning theorist, a norm or a self-image is nothing more than the person's taking on as a premise (encompassing a predication) some content of belief, based on relations with other human beings but situated individually. A norm is akin to a premise held by

an identifiable group or subgroup of human beings, who affirm something in common (e.g., "We are God's chosen people." Or, "Each person has certain inalienable rights."). The norm is not some huge, supraindividual "force" in the sky, dispensing positive or negative
reinforcements to the individual mortals below. Similarly, self-image
would be understood as a premise that others (e.g., parents or peers)
have framed initially concerning the individual, who now takes over
the premise because it offers a way of relating to the others without
conflict. Central to this process on both sides—that of the "other" and
of the person—is the affective process in which judgments are being
rendered. If the individual person assesses the "other" negatively and
himself/herself positively, it is not likely that reflected appraisals will
take hold (see Chapter 9). As theorists such as Sullivan and Jung appreciated, there are also hidden self-images, uniquely framed premises and appraisals of the self that are kept from the view of others.

Social psychologists have not promoted such theories. They have
relied primarily on mechanistic learning theories or information-processing theories. The view of normative behavior or the framing of
self-images has been given an extraspective formulation, in which the
locus of influence is situated supraindividually. Formulations of the
self are often tied to social roles, which are viewed as rules of behavior that are acquired by the person in the social nexus. The self is
often viewed as "a mechanism that brings rules to bear on behavior"
(Vallacher, 1980, p. 35). Mediation theorizing underwrites most of the
explanations at this point. Sometimes the self is equated with a "program" or a "script" which functions to direct the actions of the organism (ibid., pp. 4 and 33). The latter conceptions are, of course,
another reflection of the growing role of the computer analogue in
psychology.

Logical learning theory has the self as an identity which brings
forward the precedent-sequacious process of meaning-extension in
telosponsivity (see Chapter 8, pp. 349–353). Telosponsivity occurs "as
such" from birth. It is only when a theoretician wishes to refer to the
identity (telosponder) affirming the premises encompassed as precedents that we speak of *selves* in logical learning theory. Logical learning theorists concur with the view that the premises framed about
one's self over the course of maturation are taken from the views and
attitudes of others, as well as framed idiosyncratically and even pri-
vately (unconsciously?) by the telosponder. The logical learning theorist always thinks of the self from an introspective theoretical perspec-

tive. As self-theorists, we are trying to see the world through the predications of another person. We identify with the actor in the causal attribution research discussed earlier.

Research findings in social psychology suggest that the self is an important ingredient in the cognitive processes of the person. Words judged for self-descriptiveness are recalled better than words judged on other dimensions, or with respect to other persons (Bower & Gilligan, 1979; Keenan & Baillet, 1980; Markus, 1977; Rogers, Kuiper, & Kirker, 1977). Theoretical explanations of such findings suggest that the self is a schematic program or script of some sort, which "when activated" can process and store information relevant to its stored content. In effect, the self serves as a mnemonic device to enhance the ongoing process of input-mediation-output taking place in the organism's cognition (Bellezza, 1984). Although self-theorists may refer to the contents or outputs of this mediational process as *constructions*, this term relates to the presumption that there are certain readily available cues in long-term memory to which the organism can associate new inputs (Greenwald, 1981). The process is mechanical, not conceptual. Once again, the ultimate source of the cues is the supraindividual nexus (as well as the innate "hardwiring" of the organism).

One does see glimmerings of a logical learning theory in certain aspects of social psychology. Festinger's (1954) social-comparison theory is supportive of the individual as framing grounds for the sake of which behavior is then carried out, rather than as behavior that is simply mediated (Question 2). Bem (1967, 1972) also relied upon logical processes to explain behavior, even as he reinterpreted Festinger's theory. Bem (1972) suggests that inference plays a role in learning and that individuals make inferences about themselves from observing their own overt behavior, as well as the circumstances in which they behave. There is no difference here between whether person A is explaining his/her own behavior or the behavior of person B. Certain grounds must be affirmed regarding why behavior by the self or by others is carried out. Bem tends toward the perspective of the actor, rather than the observer, in making his theoretical explanations. All of this is highly consistent with logical learning theory.

Festinger and Carlsmith (1959) reported some interesting findings on forced compliance. Subjects first engaged in a monotonous task (e.g., placing spools in a tray, dumping them out, and repeating the process again and again). The subjects were then asked to convince another person that this task was actually entertaining. Half of the subjects received $1 for making their persuasive argument, and half received $20. Contrary to what a reinforcement theory would suggest, the subjects who were paid $20 expressed *less* enjoyment in the experiment than those who were paid $1. Bem suggested that the reason this occurred was because if a person receives an excessive extrinsic reward for some obviously meaningless activity, it follows that he/she does not have to justify performing this activity for its intrinsic worth. Hence, the overpaid subject views the money as "the" value obtained, and the meaningless activity can be appropriately judged negatively. On the other hand, the subject who is paid little or nothing must conclude that there is some intrinsic merit to the task over and above the material reward; why else would he/she be engaged in it?

The logical learning theorists finds such experiments very instructive. Undoubtedly, such grounding reasons for doing a task enter into the fixing of premises and the rendering of affective assessments in all aspects of life. This treatment is highly compatible with a teleological explanation of behavior, and, as we shall see below, Deci was to take this style of explanation even further. Of course, as it so often happens in psychology, even though the research findings are amenable to telic explanation and terms such as "inference" are used informally by those who conduct these experiments, it does not follow that the formal explanation will advance the cause of teleology. Gains made in the context of proof can be lost in the context of theoretical interpretation (Question 3).

Harré (1984) has presented an interesting case for selfhood, one which could be viewed in many respects as consistent with logical learning theory. Although he did not conduct empirical research himself, he based his arguments on such research and offered recommendations for further empirical work to back up his analysis (e.g., p. 93). Harré argues that we do not begin life as selves but acquire or learn to be selves through language conventions. His general principle is: "Nothing in the mind that was not first in the conversation" (*ibid.*, p. 116). This suggests a question to the logical learning theorist:

Question 8: *Is language the cause of cognitive processing or its effect?*

It is clear that Question 8 is a variant of Question 4, except that now we are focusing on the precise issue of whether mind is on the effect side of linguistic usage, as Harré suggests, or whether it serves as a cause of such usage. According to logical learning theory, telosponsivity as a cognitive process comes first. It functions in preverbal perception, and through the telosponsive process the individual comes to learn language. Predication is thought of as primarily a semantic (meaning-producing) act of conceptualization, and only secondarily as a syntaxic process of linguistic rule-following. Language is therefore an instrumentality, used in mentation to express ideas continually under formulation by the individual. However, it is also true that human beings affirm lasting linguistic conventions, and such affirmations are carried forward as cultural products reflecting the precedent affirmations of earlier generations. Indeed, it would be impossible to have an interpersonal idiom if an identifiable group or subgroup of individuals failed to affirm a common symbol or sign system. This process of mutual affirmation is akin to the establishing of norms, which encompass the affective preferences of the group. Language therefore encourages by inference and implication the different world views, theories, and other preferences of various social groups.

It is at this point that we begin to have some difficulty distinguishing between these different perspectives on experience and the cognitive process whereby such alternatives are made possible in the first place. If we focus on how language functions in the delineation and characterization of experience, then it is possible to think of language as the cause of cognitive processing rather than the effect (the latter view is that of logical learning theory). After all, can anyone "name" anything that is not *ipso facto* a linguistic expression, and in defining it or elaborating on it are we not immediately involved in a set of grammatical (syntaxic) rules? It is but a short step to conclude that these linguistic conventions and rules of expression are "the" process determining what will be known "within it." To round off such theorizing we are likely to hear of the social organization *per se* as the directing source of influence on how the individual will cognize experience. In recent years, this view of cognitive processing and behavior has been referred to as *social constructionism* (see p. 469) (Gergen, 1985).

Harré (1984) adapts social constructionism to his account of the self (p. 215), which he takes as a kind of linguistic convention that is learned or acquired in the process of becoming a socialized human being:

I claim that the "self" is acquired as a generalization and abstraction of the public person-concept, that is, in use in the public-collective discourse of a community by a slide from one grammatical model to another, initiated by certain social/linguistic practices. As a theoretical concept, "the self" stands in a peculiar relation to "the person." The latter is materially grounded by reference to the human being as a kind of thing, with all kinds of properties. (Harré, 1984, p. 167).

Harré suggests here that we form a theory of our selves by first forming a theory of other persons (*ibid.*, p. 20), and then in time we learn that we have a unique slant on the things that persons "do." Harré seems to believe that people *are* identities (*ibid.*, p. 210), but the point of his self theory is to say that there is no sense referring to selves independently of a socially learned acquisition. Our personal sense of "being" is due to the fact that we believe a theory of our selves "based on our society's working conception of a person" (*ibid.*, p. 26). The agency which flows from the sense of selfhood is a theory as well (*ibid.*, p. 29). The society interprets people to be intentional beings (*ibid.*, p. 85), and this is transmitted to the individual by way of language instruction resulting in a theory of the self. Thus, Harré's basic thesis is summed up as follows:

The basic thesis of this work is that animate beings are persons if they are in possession of a theory—a theory about themselves. It is a theory in terms of which a being orders, partitions and reflects on its own experience and becomes capable of self-intervention and control (Harré, 1984, p. 93).

How does this theory of the person come about? It is encompassed in the very language that the person is taught. For example, in learning the pronoun system and especially the rules for the use of "I" we human beings are being taught a theory of personhood, from which we generalize to our selves. We learn to locate our speech acts in the array of other people and ourselves (*ibid.*, p. 103). Psychological symbiosis is also an important ingredient in this learning. As children we learn from the interdependent union with our mothers that we are supposed to have wishes, needs, and intentions (*ibid.*, p. 105). Drawing much of his argument from Wittgenstein (1953) at this point, Harré (1984) speaks of the learning of "language games" (*ibid.*, p. 105).

To this point the logical learning theorist would be in essential agreement. That is, logical learning theory does not hold that a "self" exists at birth, but only that an identity exists—a logically processing identity framing experience telosponsively. (A theoretician may want to call this identify a "self," but this is purely a semantic matter for other terms could be used as well.) The telosponder does learn in time that he/she is a factor in this process and, through social relations, acquires the self-image or self-predication that Harré is talking about

(see Chapter 8, pp. 349–353). However, the nature of this acquisition—the process of learning—is separate and distinct from the rules
of grammar or the language games eventually learned. It could even
be that such syntactical considerations further the learning of self-predications. But the logical learning theorist keeps the distinction between the *process* of learning and the resultant *content* (linguistic
conventions) of that process clearly in view.

Jenkins (1982), for example, employed the research findings and
descriptive terminology of logical learning theory to explain the psychology of the Afro-American. Jenkins also speaks of the person's
learning of a theory about the self by way of such sociocultural factors
as linguistic conventions and the attitudinal biases often encompassed
therein (p. 30). However, Jenkins *begins* with the assumption of a telic
process (*ibid.*, p. 31), so that when he examines the effects of racial
labeling on black children (*ibid.*, pp. 47–48) he is framing such linguistic influences by a teleological explanation. His references to sociocultural influences do not bear the theoretical weight of explanation at the level of learning (Question 3). Jenkins is therefore never in
the position of Harré, of losing his teleological analysis to an underlying theory of mechanism.

Harré (1984) seems to believe that he has nothing to worry about
in constantly referring to "acquisition" and "learning" as he does (pp.
21, 102–104, and 145). He refers globally to learning as the "privatization of features of public-collective episodes of mutual engagement"
(*ibid.*, p. 137); but this privatization could obviously occur in a purely
mediational fashion (Questions 2 and 3). Indeed, it would be very easy
for a mechanistic theorist to accept everything Harré says about people being shaped by circumstances, and in particular by the linguistic
cues "input" from the environment, *sans* personal intentionality. Of
course, the mechanist would postulate an underlying, efficiently caused
process, in which language would be said to "function" as a content
within that process. Harré's *formal* position leads us to believe that
he views language as this underlying process which determines agency,
person, self, and so on. But we can now appreciate that his continual
stress on learning and acquisition commits him to an *informal* explanation of things as well (see Question 10, below). Unfortunately, this
informal account of the learning process is unexplicated; hence, we
are left wondering whether Harré's fundamental position is a predicational or a mediational model (Questions 2 and 3). Things look better here than when we confronted the theories of Mischel and Bandura, but the teleological potentials in human description are still a

bit hazy. If Harré had relied upon the tenets of logical learning theory, the picture would be clearer.

Deci (1980; with Ryan, 1985) has worked out a position regarding self-determination which is also closely aligned with the goals of logical learning theory in human description. We will rely here on the Deci and Ryan (1985) book since it is a more recent statement of Deci's views. Taking their initial theoretical prompt from White (1959), who argued that organisms are innately motivated to be effective in dealing with their environments, Deci and Ryan (1985) postulated an intrinsic motivation in all behavior, which they defined as follows: "Intrinsic motivation is the innate, natural propensity to engage one's interests and exercise one's capacities, and in so doing, to seek and conquer optimal challenges" (p. 43). Deci and Ryan believe that an explanation of human behavior must include a motivational construct, and as far as they are concerned intrinsic motivation is a "life force or energy" (ibid., p. 8).

Of course, this life force is not like a traditional drive conception, in which there is a mounting thrust in the organism due to some tissue need, followed by a quiescence when the biological deficit is satisfied. Such drive-reduction theories (e.g., Hull 1952) have been widely used in psycholoy to account for the fact that antecedent stimuli become attached to consequent responses. The stimulus-response attachment occurred when a drive was reduced in the behavioral sequence. Deci and Ryan (1985) eschew this style of explanation (p. 32). Instrinsic needs share the fact that they are innate with physical drives, and intrinsic needs may interact with drives in a course of behavior. But intrinsic motivation (prompted by intrinsic needs) reflects a teleological effort, in which the person is doing something "for its own sake, that is, for its inherent interest and the spontaneous affects and cognitions that accompany it" (ibid., p. 66). There is also an extrinsic form of motivation, in which a person's behavior is being carried out for some other reason than the activity per se (ibid., p. 35). This too is teleological, in which case the person is usually doing something in order to obtain a reward for the activity or is following out an order to do something (ibid., p. 66).

The discussion of intrinsic motivation as a natural propensity as well as the obvious stress on final-cause meanings in this concept prompts our next question:

Question 9: Is it the force of an energy or the force of logic that induces behavior in a teleological explanation?

Logical learning theory frames human behavior as innately teleological, but does not construe this intentionality as stemming from some kind of force or energic thrust analogical to needs or drives. People are viewed as moving from precedent meanings to sequacious extensions of these meanings due to the weight or *force* of logic, rather than due to some kind of mounting life energy. Deci and Ryan's metaphor (1985) strikes the logical learning theorist as quasi-biological and, therefore, conceptually closer to traditional drive theory than these authors would prefer. Indeed, their treatment of the self reflects this biological affinity, as in the following: ". . . human beings attempt actively to master the forces in the environment and the forces of drives and emotions in themselves. In mastering these forces, human beings integrate them into the internal, unified structure called self" (p. 8).

The concept of self-determination follows from the distinction between intrinsic and extrinsic motivation. Self-determination arises only when the person is moved to do something for an intrinsic reason, rather than for some reason extrinsic to the behavior under consideration. "When self-determined, one acts out of choice rather than obligation or coercion, and those choices are based on an awareness of one's organismic needs and a flexible interpretation of external events" (*ibid.*, p. 38). It follows from this theory that a person can be more or less self-determining, "implying that when the environment supports self-determination, the person will be more self-determining" (*ibid.*, p. 39). As we look closer at this formulation it becomes clearer that it is aimed at drawing a distinction within teleological behavior rather than explaining teleological behavior *per se*. There is really no fundamental explanation of teleological behavior in Deci and Ryan's account. Self-determination is merely presumed to take place. The fact that Deci and Ryan often refer to self-selection and choice as an "experience" or as "perceived" (*ibid.*, p. 38) can lead one to wonder if they really believe that the person is framing and bringing about this experience or perception teleologically, or whether the person is not reacting to what is done "to" him or her.

In logical learning theory, to speak of being more or less self-determined based upon environmental considerations is to go beyond the basic issue of whether or not people *really are* self-determiners (telosponders). The poor person cannot plan trips to Hawaii over the holidays, and the prisoner cannot opt for his or her daily attire, but what has this to do with whether or not the behaving organism is to be understood in teleological terms? Self-determination is self-determination, or it is not. Restrictions on such determination may occur, but these are secondary considerations which fail to address the fundamental question. As with Harré's account, it would be possible for a mechanist to read Deci and Ryan and to interpret their references to "perceived" (ibid., p. 38) self-determination and the delimitations of the environment on such selfhood (ibid., p. 39) as reflective of a mediation model (Question 2) and as a mechanically learned and environmentally shaped sequence of behavior, explicable in terms of traditional Hullian learning theory. There is a gray area here which is not addressed. We are told that people are agential as a going assumption (ibid., p. vii), but Deci and Ryan lack an explanation like logical learning theory to underwrite this belief.

The research conducted by Deci and Ryan (and others) follows the lead of Festinger and Carlsmith (1959). The typical research experiment on intrinsic motivation involves having subjects perform some task, with experimental subjects receiving an extrinsic reward in the form of a payment whereas control subjects are not paid. Subsequently, subjects are exposed to the task in a free period, where no reward is forthcoming for any subject, and it is observed whether or not subjects will engage in the task. It is usually found that subjects who are paid to do the task are less likely to perform it during the free period than subjects who have not been paid. Thus, subjects paid $1 for each of four puzzles they solved within an allotted time were significantly less likely to work on such puzzles during a free period than control subjects who had not been paid initially (Deci, 1972). In line with Festinger and Carlsmith's results, Calder and Staw (1975) found that subjects who received payments to do some interesting jigsaw puzzles rated these puzzles significantly less enjoyable than control subjects who received no payment.

To account for such findings, Deci and Ryan (1985) began to use descriptive terminology that seems removed from energic conceptualizations. Thus, they framed an instrumental explanation. They noted that if someone works to accomplish something for pay or if a person plays a sport exclusively to "win" in the contest, then the work or the sport activity becomes an instrument to receiving payment or winning (p. 57). As such, the activity is not valued and not pursued for its own sake. The logical learning theorist agrees with this analysis completely. But the question now arises: Is the logic of means (instruments) versus ends related to intrinsic motivation as a cause or an effect? In work on affective assessment (see Chapter 9), which is akin to intrinsic motivation, we have subjects arrange the independent variable in the experimental context. This is where one would ordinarily expect an intrinsic motivation to come into play. However, Deci and Ryan (1985) invariably have their construct manifesting itself as a dependent variable. Does the person perform the task in the free period or not? If he/she does, then we have intrinsic motivation occurring; if he/she does not, then we have extrinsic motivation taking place, and so forth.

To make this point even clearer, we should note that not just "any" task or reward can be used to get the effects reflecting intrinsic motivation. Danner and Lonky (1981) found that the task has to be optimally challenging for the rewards to undermine intrinsic motivation. Ross (1975) and McLoyd (1979) have proven that the rewards will not have this undermining effect if they are undesired or considered nonsalient by the experimental subjects. Fazio (1981) has shown that if children are reminded that they were initially drawn to the task, the undermining effect can be forestalled. For the logical learning theorist, considerations such as these are better understood as the outcome of evaluative acts in logical reasoning than they are as energic propulsions of one sort or another. As the person judges what is worthwhile to do, or to receive as a reward, so too does the person carry through on the logical course of behavior in light of these precedents, resulting in what is now termed an *intrinsic* or *extrinsic energic motivational force*.

Deci and Ryan (1985) also draw a distinction between internally informational and internally controlling forms of behavioral regulation. Only internally informational regulation is self-determination (p. 106). The example they give is of a girl who practices her guitar lessons. If she is practicing out of guilt or anxiety—to please a parent or to avoid a scolding from her instructor—then she would be under internally controlling regulations and not really self-determining (ibid., pp. 106–107). If, on the other hand, she is practicing out of the "satisfaction that would accrue from improving" (ibid., p. 106), she would be under internally informational regulation and hence self-determining. Once again, the logical learning theorist would say that the girl's premises—the predications and affective assessments encompassed therein—are framed by her. She is the telosponder; hence, she is conceptually determining what will eventuate in her behavior regardless of whether this is carried out under the pressure of anxiety or improvement satisfaction. Of course, the distinction made by Deci and Ryan is a legitimate one. They are drawn to a distinction in the content of the telic-process rather than to a fundamental understanding of the process itself (Question 4). Even so, there is much in the empirical and theoretical work of Deci and Ryan to advance the cause of rigorous humanism. As with Harré's work, logical learning theory can co-exist and even cross-fertilize aspects of Deci and Ryan's work.

Computer Analogues

We now come to a realm of theorizing that has been growing by leaps and bounds in psychology. It involves the use of computer constructs as metaphors to characterize or simulate the cognitive process and content of human reason. We have seen several references to computer models in the theories of this chapter. The development of computer or cybernetic models in psychology has represented both good news and bad news for the logical learning theorist. The bad news is that in the cybernetic model there is no room for dialectical reasoning. No thinking machine has ever "thought" dialectically (see Rychlak, 1981, pp. 291–294). We cannot expect much help from the artificial intelligence community in advancing our theory of agency based on dialectical reasoning. But the good news in this so-called cognitive revolution is that the older, mechanistic learning theories of psychology are being neglected and may one day be supplanted entirely. Indeed, the leaders in "cognitive science," as this field is now referred to, frequently make it a point to denigrate traditional learning theories and to advance conceptions that are highly compatible with, if not actually examples of, teleological description.

For instance, Minsky (1968, p. 2) has criticized behaviorism for leading to ineffectual, statistically oriented theorizing. He calls for the use of "meaning" in explaining cognition, arguing that this is not an empty metaphor for the cognitive scientist. In her excellent survey of cognitive science, Boden (1977) has pointed to many examples of what she takes to be teleological explanation. Indeed, she has specifically noted that many of the concepts employed by computer scientists draw their meaning from final causation and not from efficient causation (p. 77). We have highlighted a distinction between the presumed "process" taking place in any account of cognition and the "content" of that process in our discussion of Questions 4 and 8. This distinction becomes especially pertinent in considering computer analogues, for here we have the "hardware" on the one hand, and the "software" on the other. Boden points out that there is no intention on the part of cognitive scientists to reduce the latter to the former:

Contrary to popular opinion, artificial intelligence researchers do *not* interpret their work as supporting the reductionist view, that psychological explanations are in principle dispensable since everything mental is "really" just something happening in the brain. On the contrary, they choose to describe and explain their programs in mentalistic terms (many of which are borrowed from ordinary language, although others are newly coined), because they find it more natural and illuminating to do so than to refer merely to "behavioristic" input-output correlations or to "physiological" details of machine engineering (Boden, 1977, pp. 400–401).

Boden goes on to suggest that artificial intelligence eschews the prediction of quantitatively defined variables that characterize traditional natural science, and to this extent joins hands with humanistic psychology (*ibid.*, p. 404). The view that artificial intelligence is capturing teleological description is widely held today. Although logical learning theorists are pleased by this willingness to entertain teleology as a proper psychological topic, they are not yet ready to applaud the resulting theoretical formulations of cognitive science. The reservations expressed by logical learning theorists go beyond the matter of ignoring dialectical mentation. There is a basic inability on the part of the artificial intelligence community to distinguish between its *formal* model of cognitive processing and its *informal* model of such processing. Teleological descriptions of behavior are always traceable to the informal model and never to the formal model. Thus, we raise the following question:

Question 10: How much reliance can a theory legitimately place upon constructs that are not formally explicated in its explanatory model?

From the viewpoint of logical learning theory, which is situated at the introspective theoretical perspective (see Chapter 1, p. 35), those psychologists who rely upon a computer as a model for human reason frame their formal constructs extraspectively (*ibid.*) and then "sneak in" through the back door other constructs that give an illusion of "accounting for" teleology. For example, in their historically important work, *Plans and the Structure of Behavior*, Miller, Galanter, and Pribram (1960) define a plan as any hierarchical process in the organism that can control the order in which a sequence of operations is to be performed (p. 16). They then go on to state: "A plan is, for an organism, essentially the same as a program for a computer, especially if the program has the sort of hierarchical character described above" (*ibid.*, p. 16).

The next theoretical step is to bring in the TOTE, or sequence of "test-operate-test-exit" that is a built-in cybernetic mechanism relying upon the feedback loop. This mechanism is said to operate both in the reflexes of the body (*ibid.*, p. 26) and in the overt patterns of general behavior (*ibid.*, p. 27). Stimulus and response are considered different aspects of a feedback loop (*ibid.*, p. 30). To this point a mechanist can be entirely at ease. Feedback is a portion of the output returning as input, so that in its strict meaning when a machine is receiving feedback information it is recording at the input end what is already a *fait accompli* at the output end. There is nothing here to suggest that the machine is opting by premising circumstances from the outset, framing the predications of "what means what" as the course of behavior moves along. Yet Miller, Galanter, and Pribram propose that their TOTE unit is a teleological formulation of behavior (*ibid.*, p. 44). As with Bandura, we have a mechanism "accounting for" a teleological process. Intention is defined as the uncompleted parts of a plan whose execution has already begun (*ibid.*, p. 61). There is no formal analysis of the intention to frame a plan, describing the heuristics of how such patterns would be framed. There is an admission by the theorists that their formulation is aimed more at the execution than the formation of a plan (*ibid.*, p. 69). Heuristics is viewed more as a problem of searching among already established alternatives than as an act of creating such alternatives to begin with (*ibid.*, p. 168).

The logical learning theorist thinks of agency as founded upon heuristics. If an organism is merely executing plans (premises, encompassing predications) then in what way can we speak of a teleology taking place? Recall from Chapter 1 (pp. 41–42) that Bacon's attack on Aristotle was precisely on this issue—of whether or not formal/final causation was required in order to describe an extraspectively construed "natural" process. If we can see a TOTE process mechanically carrying itself forward in the bodily reflexes as well as in the more involved behaviors of a human being, what do we add to the account to say that it is also a teleological process? Surely our bodily reflexes do not intend to transmit impulses, nor seek to achieve certain ends. They are automatic mechanisms. To say that such an automatic TOTE process is also a teleological process is akin to saying that leaves exist for the sake of shading fruit on trees. As Bacon noted, the telic phrasing here adds nothing to our understanding of how mechanisms function or leaves grow on trees. In the formal designation of the theory, the teleology plays no role at all. We understand the essentials of the TOTE process quite precisely whether it is, or is not, a teleological process.

Miller, Galanter, and Pribram (1960) speak of a "new freedom" (p. 42) for the theoretical psychologist in the modern tendency to describe machines as purposive, but the truth is that in their case this freedom is not exercised to revolutionize the mechanistic image of human behavior. Their view of behavior continues to be an efficient-cause sequence, guided by the formal-cause patterning of the plan or program; but the machine *qua* agent is nowhere described as framing that plan (the question of heuristics again). Yet, this does not prevent our theorists from speaking of people choosing plans (*ibid.*, p. 63) or making decisions to execute a plan (*ibid.*, p. 65). The statement that the TOTE is a teleological conception followed by such references to choice and decision, beguile us into believing that we have an agential theory under development here. But we do not. Plans are learned (*ibid.*, p. 89) and acquired through practice (*ibid.*, pp. 157–158). No learning theory is given to underwrite what our theorists believe learning entails (Question 3). But there are references to the "associations" (*ibid.*, p. 177) formed in learning plans, to the fact that plans as general frames of reference which can be modified somewhat, are basically remembered rather than created (*ibid.*, p. 178), and that children "acquire their store" (*ibid.*, p. 184) of heuristic strategies through frequent contact with others. One is left with the clear impression that a mechanistic, efficient-cause understanding of learning is being relied upon. If teleology is a formal aspect of the computer analogue, it should be spelled out here. But it is not.

Considered more broadly, study after study in cognitive psychology demonstrates that people attempt to impose order on experience, to "do" something with the materials they are trying to commit to memory. We also hear of the importance of an intention to learn, mnemonic strategies which facilitate retention, and the selective encoding and retrieval of information. Although frequency was used routinely to account for learning in theories of yesteryear, we now know that merely repetitively rehearsing material in rote fashion does not increase the likelihood of recall from long-term memory. Material must be enriched and elaborated by the person so that it becomes more meaningful, and hence is retained (Howard, 1983, pp. 144–145). Yet, it is certainly true that we could write a program in which rote rehearsal *would* increase the likelihood of recall from long-term memory. We could also toss in a highly confused, nonorganized assemblage of items as "the" long-term memory store. Even so, our computer would work as effectively in retrieving such information, learned through rote, as would a computer that works according to a nonrote and well-organized pattern of long-term memory. The disorganized computer program might take a little longer to get things done, but this would be an insignificant drawback.

Thus, it is clear that meaningfulness and heuristic strategies that go beyond rote repetition are not *formal* requirements of the computer analogue. When such findings occur in studies on human beings, they are adapted to the computer process without jeopardizing the integrity of this model (Question 4). Logical learning theorists interpret the findings on organization in human learning and memory as evidence for a process in which the *logos* (formal cause) is central, so that the agent must frame a meaningful pattern as precedent in order to extend such meaning sequaciously into ongoing experience. Boden's previously cited quote (pp. 445–446) suggests another question concerning the precise target of a psychological explanation in the computer analogue:

Question 11: *Where is the psychological process needing explanation located, in the mechanics of the "hardware" or in the logic of the "software"?*

If we are to embrace the computer analogue, are we not left with the choice of asking precisely "where" our analysis is supposed to be offered? As Boden suggests, the student of artificial intelligence is not required to reduce his or her explanation to underlying physical processes. In like fashion, could it be that the psychologist is not called on to stipulate the precise nature of the hardware in order to study the patterned organization of the software? Another way of saying this is that the software aspects constitute a separate and distinct—we would say "logical"—process from the hardware aspects of the computer. The logic of the program becomes embodied in the hardware of the machine. But the ways in which programs are framed, or the strategy of the approach used to the solution of a programming problem, is not fixed by the blueprint layout of the machine parts. The machine does not provide the creative logic of the programmer. Indeed, it is the logic of the machine's creator that made this machine possible in the first place.

Let us now think of the human brain as a hardware item. Hofstadter (1980, pp. 565–568) has observed that even though the substrate neurons in brain activity may be functioning correctly, the thought being carried forward by such physiological mechanisms may be illogical or erroneous. Dreyfus (1979, p. 166) argued that although the network of neurons in the brain constitutes a fixed pattern of associative links, it does not follow that these associated ties can account for the direction that thought takes within these patterns. Indeed, Dreyfus suggested that this neuronal network may be randomly organized to some extent.

It strikes the logical learning theorist that psychologists continually frustrate themselves by attempting to describe software processes, such as the logic of human reason, by drawing metaphors to what are essentially the hardware processes. This frequently occurs because the psychologist is trying to do what Dreyfus said could not be done—that is, to explain the direction that thought takes as a kind of biological necessity running through the brain structure. We see this in so-called network theorizing, where the model of Wyer and Carlston (1979) might be used as an example. According to this network model, memory is organized as a pattern of interconnecting or associated *nodes*. Each concept in the mind is represented by a node, and there are *paths* connecting different nodes. These paths are conceptualized in demonstrative, unidirectional fashion so that if two concepts are associated together, there would have to be two paths— for example, one uniting the word "honest" to "trustworthy," and one going in the opposite direction (pp. 72–73). As there is no implicit dialectical oppositionality on this view, the same dual-associative paths would apply if we had opposite associations under consideration, such as "honest" to "untrustworthy"; except in this case, it is assumed that there is a greater distance between the nodes than would be true of two words with synonymic meaning relations.

As two nodes are frequently encountered in proximity to each other, over the course of experience the associative pathways between these nodes increase in diameter. Highly connected nodes have wide (or thick) pathways between them, and weakly connected nodes have narrow (or thin) pathways between them (*ibid.*, p. 71). One is reminded here of Locke's (1952) allusion to frequently associated ideas as wearing a "smooth path" (p. 249) joining them in the mind. It is significant to note that whereas the Greek theorists like Socrates (Plato, 1952, p. 230) and Aristotle (1952, p. 693) had principles of contrariety or opposition as fundamental ways of associating ideas, the British philosophers, from whom psychology took primary influence, did not include such oppositional formulations. We find principles such as contiguity, repetition, frequency, vividness, similarity, intensity, and inseparability in the writings of people like Locke, Hume, Hartley, and the Mills (Boring, 1950, pp. 191, 197, 224, 229).

The Greeks, who were appreciative of dialectical reasoning, did not see it as possible to stipulate the necessary direction that thought would take. People lived and reasoned their way through a sea of oppositionality; hence, it was always possible to redirect things even though under the prompting thrust of some unidirectional force. On the other hand, since the British philosophers viewed people as dealing exclusively in unidirectionalities (demonstrative reasoning), it followed that such unidirectionalities would not only pattern but direct the necessary course of thought in the process. Invariably, the course of this direction stemmed from past experience, which is translated now into a frequency and contiguity explanation of learning. And so it is that we see this British influence in Wyer and Carlston (1979), who unequivocally state: "*A path between two nodes is directed. Its direction reflects the order in which the concepts have occurred in the relation as it has been encountered* [italics in original]" (p. 72). It strikes the logical learning theorist that we have an involved analogy to some hardware-like biological substructure in network theory, but one that falls back on typical mediational theorizing in the learning process, which supposedly functions among the associated nodes (Questions 2 and 3).

Logical learning theory, on the other hand, is leveled at the logical process that frames not only the program but the very design of the computer, which acts as the instrument of the precedent meanings framing both realms. More to the point of Question 11, the metaphors of logical learning theory should be drawn from the software realm of the total computer enterprise. Computers as hardware are surely not simulating human reason. But in framing a program, in deciding upon a logical strategy, rejecting alternatives formed within opposite possibilities, and then affirming a precedent which is extended into the algorithmic steps as a sequacious flow of meaning, we have the "real thing" taking place rather than a simulation of human reason. This reasoning process is both dialectical and demonstrative in nature. It names a problem and frames a solution to this problem as opposite sides of the same coin. It is agency personified.

Dialectical Themes

There have been and continue to be intimations of dialectical processes taking place in the empirical literature, although these are not always recognized for what they are. That is, the import of oppositional considerations in human behavior is not usually construed as reflecting dialectical reasoning. Almost invariably, when we come across empirically oriented theories in which dialectical considerations are apparent, we find that teleological considerations are not far behind. One of the first dialectical theories which was widely tested empirically was Festinger's (1957) theory of cognitive dissonance. Dissonance was defined as due to the "existence of nonfitting relations among cognitions" (p. 3). Cognition was seen as a process of relating elements of knowledge together (ibid., p. 9); and when such elements were logically inconsistent, a state of dissonance resulted (ibid., p. 2). When such elements were consistent, a state of consonance resulted in the person's cognitive organization (ibid., pp. 2–3). This dissonance-versus-consonance distinction reflected a dialectical face-off, but there is an even more fundamental role for the dialectic in this theory.

Festinger hypothesized that dissonance is "psychologically uncomfortable" (ibid., p. 3). Hence, people will experience a "pressure" to reduce the level of dissonance (ibid., p. 5). We are back to Question 9 here, wondering just what the nature of this pressure would be— analogical to a biological drive or simply reflecting the "weight" of logic. Logical learning theory would, of course, favor the latter interpretation. Unfortunately, Festinger suggested that "dissonance acts in the same way as a state of drive or need or tension" (ibid., p. 18). For example, people who smoke and who must confront the growing evidence that smoking causes lung cancer must deal with this dissonance. They are as if under a drive to reduce this inconsistency in the elements of their cognition. Festinger demonstrated empirically that in this situation the smoker tends to denigrate the empirical evidence supporting the link of smoking to cancer, and often, simply ignores new evidence on this question when it becomes available (ibid., p. 155).

Harking back to our discussion concerning Question 9 (see above), the logical learning theorist finds it unnecessary to explain this empirical finding on smokers in terms of a "drive to reduce dissonance." It seems far more parsimonious to take the more direct strategy of simply noting that as dialectical reasoners human beings have the capacity to revise their contradictory predications through all kinds of conceptual maneuvers. This is essentially a problem in dialectical logic. It does not clarify things to speak in terms of drive-reductions. We must appreciate that Festinger was theorizing during the heyday of drive-reduction theory, as epitomized in Hullian learning theory. This undoubtedly influenced his formulation. But this tendency to construe dialectical cognitions in terms of drives was to continue on into another form of dialectical theorizing.

We refer here to so-called *reactance theory* (Brehm, 1966, 1972; Wicklund, 1974). This formulation of human behavior builds on the insights of Festinger, but focuses more specifically on the agential question of freedom. Of course, reactance theorists do not actually take a position on whether or not people really *are* capable of behavior in a free-will manner. Wicklund (1974, p. 181) claimed that this question is not vital to reactance theory, and Brehm (1966, p. 1) noted that all the reactance theorist must accept is that people "believe" they have freedom to choose alternatives in life. We are back to the issues discussed regarding Question 4. That is, we seem to have an attributional stance being taken by reactance theorists on the matter of free will. People behave "as if" they had agency, attributing personal freedom to themselves whether this is actually the case or not. The essence of reactance theory is that when people believe themselves free to engage in behavior, they will experience a psychological state of reactance when that freedom is threatened or actually eliminated.

The reactance state is described as an arousal (Brehm, 1966, p. 2) or a "motivational state" (Wicklund, 1974, p. 4), forcing the person toward the preservation of his or her freedom. Thus, eighth-grade children who ranked six movies that they might eventually see, only to be told that their second choice was not available, increased their desire to see the eliminated movie (Brehm, 1966 p. 85). Children doing cross-out tasks of two types (A and B), when under persuasion by the experimenter's confederate to do task A opted to the contrary and did task B (*ibid.*, p. 56). There have been many studies done that rely on such a persuasion strategy, and it is interesting to note that the more consideration a subject gives to the persuader's *intention* to influence, the more likely it is that the subject will manifest reactance and behave to the opposite of this intentional effort (Wicklund, 1974, p. 28). Reading through the many studies on reactance, one is brought back to Question 1, which raises the issue of just what sort of evidence the reactance theorist would want in order to begin taking teleological description more seriously than is presently the case.

Surely, we cannot overlook the undoubted role for dialectical oppositionality in reactance theory. It seems a misnomer to call reactance a mounting force or drive calling for reduction in the way that we reduce our physical drives (Question 9). It is clear to the logical learning theorist that reactance is another way of referring to the dialectical logic of seeing to the opposite of what is being "input," particularly as this refers to the intentions of the person or persons conveying such input to the individual. People can reason to the opposite of such pressures, as they can long for what is unattainable. People are—as the Greeks described them—continually swimming through a sea of opposition in life. As our work on affective assessment suggests (see Chapter 9), preferences are also due to dialectical reasoning capacities. It would, therefore, be a simple matter to subsume the core ideas and empirical findings of reactance theory under the rubrics of logical learning theory.

The use of a dialectical ploy to explain behavior, without falling back on an analogy to drives in the style of dissonance and reactance theories, is seen in so-called *reversal theory* (Apter, 1982, 1984). This theory relies on motivational factors in behavior, but rather than stressing organismic homeostasis the conception of *bistability* is employed to explain why it is that people are prompted to behave in various ways. The latter term is borrowed from cybernetics, in which it is suggested that bistable systems involve two—essentially opposite—states under which the system will function at any point in time (Murgatroyd, 1985, p. 3). Rather than describing the person as behaving according to a preferred level of homeostatic balance or according to some singular trait, the reversal theorist posits oppositionally framed states of behavior between which the person "switches" with some frequency, sometimes momentarily. In other words, a person might behave in consonance with or in opposition to a currently elevated drive state. Reversal theory embraces a "principle of inconsistency" (Apter, 1982, pp. 8–9), which declares that the behavior of an individual at any point in time is often inconsistent with the way in which he or she may usually behave.

Thus, a person feeling exhilarated in some circumstance may suddenly find this emotion turning to anxiety, or *vice versa*. The mountain climber, for example, may feel such alternating senses of the experience as he or she ascends the face of a dangerous cliff. The climber's drive or arousal level is not altered here one bit, but the meaning of this elevated emotional state changes depending upon the next step in the climb, recollections of past mishaps or conquests, and so on. Empirical evidence in support of such psychological reversals in meaning during arousal has been advanced in a color-preference task (Walters, Apter, & Svebak, 1982). Reversal theory has been extended to empirical studies of sports, humor, gambling, and stress (see Apter and Fontana, 1985). Such empirical support for what is obviously a theory relying upon dialectical meaning-relations in human behavior is welcomed by the logical learning theorist. The tie to cybernetics is not welcomed, of course, because the seeming role of teleology in this explanation of behavior can be lost to formal designations of the computer analogue (Questions 10, 11).

There is also the unfortunate tendency among reversal theorists to refer to shifts in motivational states as being "triggered" (e.g., Murgatroyd, 1985, p. 9). Thus, rather than viewing the person as having to premise his or her motivational state, lending it meaning in telosponsive fashion, the reversal theorist is likely to see contingencies, frustrations, and levels of satiation as "inducing agents" (ibid.) to bring about this alteration in predication. The logical learning theorist would surely agree that factors in the contingent circumstances, such as one's sense of frustration or one's gratifying feeling of satiation, might provide grounds for a reframing of one's affirmed premises. But the way in which this occurs is not as an efficient-cause triggering of mental events, but rather as a formal-final cause affirmation of a premise, lending the meaning in terms of which a reversal would take place. The teleology of reversal theory is lost when the language of mechanistic psychology is accepted whether this is (or is not) the intention of the theorist using such language (Questions 2 and 3). This brings another question to mind:

Question 12: Who decides what is meaningful in a line of behavior that is being observed as it is enacted—the observer or the actor?

Logical learning theory rests on the assumption that it is always the actor who both conceptualizes what is taking place in ongoing behavior and affectively assesses the significance of the meanings so framed. Hence, to say that contingencies, frustrations, and satiations are involved in the reversal phenomenon is to say that the person qua agent has conceptualized and affectively assessed these psychological meanings. If the person had not framed precisely "when" a contingent set of circumstances in ongoing behavior called for a reversal, there would be no reversal. It is the mountain climber qua agent who decides when the "next" step up the mountain is anxiety laden or exhilarating. Only the person can decide precisely when a state of frustration or satiation takes place in his or her phenomenal awareness. We can, as observers of the person, make educated guesses as to when such states will be present, but the final decision is up to the person. Reversal theory seeks to acknowledge a role for phenomenal description in human behavior (see Apter, 1981). If we could remove the inevitable mechanism that comes along with the use of computer lingo in reversal theory, it seems highly likely that logical learning theory would be compatible with this dialectically based understanding of human behavior.

Lord, Lepper, and Preston (1984) have shown how "considering the opposite" in a social judgment task reduced the level of bias that occurs when experimental subjects do not consider this dialectical alternative. Subjects who were pro or con on the matter of capital punishment read materials containing reports of empirical evidence supporting both sides of this issue. One group of subjects simply read the evidence favoring or rejecting the death penalty without further instructions. A second group was asked to be as unbiased and objective as they could in reading this material, since there were empirical findings in support of and in opposition to their personal opinion. A third group was asked to evaluate the empirical evidence as they read through the material, and to see if they would have given the findings equal weight in supporting or rejecting capital punishment had these results gone in the opposite direction (i.e., from pro to con, or vice versa). All subjects were then retested on their attitudes toward capital punishment.

It was found that subjects in the "consider-the-opposite" condition failed to increase their attitudes (pro or con) regarding capital punishment, but the subjects from the other two groups did precisely this. That is, people who do not consider the opposite are likely to look for and pick up only that which they favor from empirical research that actually lends equal support to both sides of the question at issue. The logical learning theorist views such findings in terms of the precedent-sequacious extension of meanings in telosponsivity. Since one's precedents lend meaning to life, it is not phenomenally "logical" to seek evidence to contradict the predications encompassed therein. However, thanks to the self-reflexivity of dialectical reasoning in which one's assumptions can be put to question, check-mated, and even convincingly countered, there is always a possibility to break free of one's precedent biases (i.e., premised meanings). The experimental instruction to the "consider-the-opposite" group of subjects obviously made this alternative of counter-weighting one's biases more likely to take place. Lord, Lepper, and Preston (1984) go on to explain their finding in light of a "mechanism" (p. 1241) of anchoring accessibility (Question 3).

Another line of research on oppositionality which takes the subject's dialectical reasoning potentials into consideration in a most in-

teresting manner is Howard's (1986; Howard & Conway, 1986) "peanut studies" on volition. College students were given jars containing
precisely sixteen ounces of peanuts. Many different studies were carried out, but the fundamental instruction to a subject was to take the
,jar of peanuts back to his or her room and over the next several weeks
to "eat" or "try not to eat" the contents. Each day, at a prearranged
hour, an experimenter showed up to weigh the peanut jar and to refill
it to precisely sixteen ounces. The ounces of peanuts eaten per 24-
hour period represented the dependent variable in this study. Subjects
were admonished not to share their peanuts with friends, and follow-
up checks were made to prove that experimental instructions were
being followed in this regard. The eat/do-not-eat manipulation was
paralleled by an instruction to keep the jar of peanuts in sight or out
of sight. Hence, a contrast could be drawn between those subjects who
were trying to eat at will and had peanuts in view, versus those who
had peanuts out of sight and were trying to avoid eating them, and so
forth. The in-view/out-of-view instruction paled in significance to the
eat/do-not-eat instruction, which accounted for an enormous amount
of the observed variance (regularly, over 60%).

Howard took this finding as evidence for volitional behavior on
the part of his subjects. Critics, however, were quick to charge that
there is no evidence for volition since Howard had instructed, and
therefore manipulated, the subjects' behavior to begin with. At best,
we have here a finding of "conforming to experimental instructions."
This brings another question to mind:

*Question 13: Is an experimental instruction equivalent to a necessary control
placed on a subject's behavior, or is it a premise that can be accepted or
rejected by the subject in question?*

Howard—as does the logical learning theorist—thinks of people
as framing premises for the sake of which they behave. He thinks of
behavior in a formal/final-cause fashion. A critic of his experiments
would think of people as locked in reciprocal interactions of an efficient-cause nature (Question 6), which means that only a control and
countercontrol image of experimenter-subject relations is possible. In
a highly creative move to counter criticism of his study, Howard adapted
his peanut-eating design to allow for a "free-choice" experimental instruction. Thus, subjects were instructed to decide for themselves
whether or not to follow experimental instructions on a given day.
When told by the experimenter to "eat" they flipped a coin, and, based

on what values they assigned to heads (eat/don't eat) or tails (eat/don't eat), they either followed experimental instructions or negated them by doing precisely the opposite. Once again, the results were clearly supportive of volitional control in subject behavior. Subjects did what they decided to do.

In an even more creative use of oppositionality, Howard "double-crossed" his research assistant in one of the experiments and had a covert understanding with the subjects. Without informing the research assistant (who gave the daily eating instructions and weighed the peanuts), Howard arranged with all of the subjects to "do the opposite" of what the research assistant requested. Thus, when the research assistant asked a subject to eat, he/she tried not to eat, and *vice versa*. Once again, to the chagrin of the research assistant who thought the findings of previous studies had flip-flopped entirely, subjects were controlled by *their* decision which was defined in opposition to the research assistant's directive. The question arises as to whether experimental subjects have been found to behave spontaneously in this dialectically oppositional manner (without having to be told to "do the opposite").

Recall from Chapter 6 (pp. 265–266) that Page (1972) has indeed shown that certain subjects in a verbal operant-conditioning task know what the experimenter is attempting to "shape" in their behavior and do not conform, but do precisely the opposite. It seems ever clearer that rather than being manipulated without choice, human beings under experimental instructions in literally any kind of psychological study are "taking a position on" what they construe or premise to be taking place (Brewer, 1974). What does the experimenter want them to do, and are they willing to do it? To accept the experimental instruction as a premise on which to act, or not—that is the question! This is the fundamental psychological state of an experimental subject. But the critics of research such as Howard's take it as an obvious fact that since he initially instructed his subjects in "what to do," it follows that he was controlling their behavior; or the subjects, due to previous shaping, were simply conforming to experimental instructions without volitional choice. As the stimulus comes before the response and controls it, so too did Howard's instructions as vocal stimulations come before the subjects' observed behavior. Hence, the former has to be seen as necessarily controlling the latter. Efficient-cause determinism has gripped the critic's intellect at this point, and his or her logic seems impeccable.

In posing Question 13, the logical learning theorist turns the tables on Howard's critic and essentially asks: How are we to *falsify* the proposition which states that "Experimental instructions control subject behavior"? As we noted in Chapter 5 (p. 181), in order for a proposition to be falsified we must be able to frame it in such a way as to either support or negate it (a dialectical alternative *par excellence*). Presumably, if what we ask subjects to do "is done" in the experiment to follow, then we have provided support for our proposition. But what would disconfirm this proposition? Presumably, if subjects would not do what we ask them to do. We do offer subjects the opportunity to perform or not perform in an experiment, and many decline to cooperate. The lion's share of our subjects are given credit in their academic courses or they would not participate in our experiments. Unrewarded volunteers are not always easy to find. Yet, in asking potential volunteers to cooperate in our study or not, we are also speaking to them and to that extent making an opening experimental instruction. Their response—to either cooperate or not cooperate—can therefore support the critic's position that we are exerting a control on their behavior no matter which direction it takes.

In the peanut experiments, Howard at least made it possible to contrast the instruction to behave or not behave with other instructions—such as keeping the peanuts in sight or out of sight—as well as running the risk that what subjects said they tried to do might not turn out to be predictive of the amount of peanuts eaten after all. But what has Howard's critic put forward to support the contention of manipulation and mechanism rather than volition and teleology in the experimental findings? Nothing but a confused understanding of what is theory and what is method in the total psychological investigation (see Chapter 4, pp. 168–172). In fact, the mechanistic critic has turned the scientific experiment into a nonobjective, predetermined source of evidence that would make the Lord, Lepper, and Preston (1984) subjects who failed to consider the opposite explanation appear to be excellent models of scientific rigor. It is clear that we cannot foreclose on alternative theoretical explanations of behavior in the very methodological steps that we take to prove our theories empirically. Critics of Howard must first show how their explanation of his findings could be falsified before we take them seriously.

In what is doubtless the most sophisticated empirical investigation of dialectical reasoning to date, Lamiell (1987) and his colleagues (Lamiell, Foss, Larsen, & Hempel, 1983; Lamiell, Foss, Trierweiler, & Leffel, 1983) have examined how it is that people form impressions of other people based upon the latter's scores on a personality scale. The generally held assumption in psychology is that if person A obtains a certain score on some personality scale X, the meaning of this score is derived by comparing it with the scores that persons B, C, D, and so on, obtained on personality scale X (see Kleinmuntz, 1967, p. 45). This normative procedure of assessment is well suited to demonstrative formulations of the measurement process, in which normal curves well-up around a total sample of test scores so that we can locate the relative standing of a single person's score in relation to the total array. Lamiell asks the nomotheticist whether the psychological meaning of this score actually derives from the relative standing of the person in an array, or whether there is not a psychological meaning of the score that is separate and distinct from such measurement—and, which must be understood in a dialectical context. We might incorporate his challenging thought in our next question:

Question 14: Is it possible to make a judgment without first having established an oppositional context of meaning within which the resultant estimate is rendered?

Lamiell's empirical work on impression formation establishes that subjects do not review a series of scores drawn from personality dimensions regarding some target person (whom they are evaluating) and then, by situating the person on each of these dimensions in comparison to the scores of others who have taken the scale, arrive at a statistical estimate as to what the target person is like. Impressions are not formed by normatively relating the scores of person A to the scores of persons B, C, D, and so on. Impressions are formed by deciding how person A presently "is" in regard to the dimension under consideration but might otherwise be in this regard. Person A is, therefore, placed within an oppositionally framed context which defines the dimension under consideration. This context can, of course, be metricized, so that we can speak of scoring in "this" direction (aggressively in behavior) or in "that" direction (non-aggressively or passively in behavior) based upon a subject's answering of scaled questions tapping this overall (passive/ aggressive) meaning. Lamiell's empirical studies, in which he contrasts subjects' ratings of another person based upon a statistical formula framed normatively with a statistical formula of the same ratings framed dialectically, repeatedly support the latter explanation of impression formation.

Cattell (1944) unknowingly made room for such dialectical oppositionality in psychometric measurement when he observed that tests do, after all, provide a restricted framework within which measurement takes place (p. 293). Although Cattell did not think of this framework as oppositional in nature, Lamiell (1987) argues persuasively that this is invariably the case. In other words, though our numerical scale may range unidirectionally from "1 to 100," the only reason such linear measures have value is because they trace a range based upon the conceptual premises of the person who made this scale, which is always found to be nestled in an oppositional context of meaning. The measures gain their psychological meanings (their nonpsychometric meanings) from this dialectical context. The scale designer may confound the mathematical dimension with the psychological dimension, and believe that he or she is tracking a "real" range which exists independent of the psychological construct defining the dimension. This is surely in the realistic traditions of American Lockeanism (see Chapter 4), but we also know from our study of the evolution of science (see Chapter 1) that empirical facts *never* speak for themselves. Therefore, to believe that one's metric is measuring some independent reality, without contributions being made from the construct meanings of the scale builder, is too naive for serious consideration.

What Lamiell reminds us at this point is that constructs are as Kelly (1955) said they were—framed oppositionally. Further, Lamiell (1987) suggests that all human cognition originates in dialectical oppositionality. There is a fundamental issue here, which takes us back to Aristotle's initial distinction between demonstrative and dialectical reasoning. Recall from Chapter 2 (pp. 63–65) that Aristotle made it appear that in a demonstrative frame of thought the reasoner would take on a major premise as "primary and true," implying that a unipolarity of meaning was involved in this cognitive act. Lamiell's criticism implies that although human reasoners may take on certain premises with singular conviction (as "primary and true"), it is also true that they know implicitly what the contradiction or negation of such premised meaning is. Simply because the reasoner is in a demonstrative frame of mind, the dialectical side of things cannot be overlooked, because it is in this context of meaning that demonstrative singularities are actually being singled out. A logical learning theorist would find nothing to dispute in Lamiell's analysis of human cognition.

This brings to a close our consideration of alternative approaches to rigorous humanism, and the reactions that such efforts have prompted in the thinking of the logical learning theorist. There is, however, one more topic that should be examined, particularly because it is often identified with the movement to humanize psychological description. We refer here to the current efforts being made by theorists in the phenomenological-existentialistic tradition to change the method through which psychological research is being carried out.

Phenomenological Methodological Claims

In Chapter 5 (pp. 190–201) we explored why it is that so-called humanistic methods fail as rigorous science. We focused on van Kaam (1969) and Giorgi (1970) in our analysis and concluded that there was no need to revolutionize *scientific method* (if this phrase means the way in which we go about proving our hypotheses). There are surely significant problems with the way in which psychologists approach their topic of study. As we pointed out in the previous section, during our consideration of Howard's experiments, a psychologist is frequently uncertain as to what is his or her *theory* (understandings, assumptive viewpoints, etc.) and what is his or her *method* (steps in proving, validating, etc.) during the over-all practice of science. The logical learning theorist finds it absolutely essential to draw this distinction between the generation of ideas on the one hand and testing of such ideas on the other. In the early history of psychology, this confounding of theory with method resulted in what we have called the S-R bind (see Chapter 4, pp. 172–174), whereby the efficient-cause framework of experimental independent and dependent variables was naively seen as the tracing of S-R laws.

But today there seems to be a rising tide of psychological approaches which are going in the opposite direction—assigning matters that strike the logical learning theorist as purely theoretical to the realm of the methodological. These various approaches go under different names, such as phenomenology (Shapiro, 1985), hermeneutics (Packer, 1985), social constructionism (Gergen, 1985), narrative or thematic analysis (Polkinghorne, 1983, 1986), psychobiography (Runyan, 1982), and qualitative analysis. There are certain themes running through all of these approaches, including the purity criticism (see Chapter 5, p. 193), the emphasis on phenomenal meaning in the study of behavior, and a reliance upon arguments drawn from the philosophy of science that detract from the hegemony of traditional science. Humanistic psychologists are often found in what we might now refer to as the phenomenological tradition. Logical learning theorists would like to find some common ground with the proponents of this tradition of thought, since there are many points of agreement between us. This collaboration is difficult to accomplish because of the dismissal of validation that many of these approaches advocate. In reading the various critiques and recommended alternatives to traditional science, the logical learning theorist is struck by how often they seem to be answerable in light of strictly theoretical formulations. Thus, our question for the phenomenologist at this point is:

Question 15: Is the call for a new method among phenomenologically oriented psychologists actually a call for introspectively framed, teleological theorizing?

When all of the arguments are made, we invariably find that the innovations in "method" proposed by the phenomenologist actually come down to descriptions of human beings from an introspective perspective, enlivened by pronounced teleological formulations. Furthermore, there is nothing in these findings to contradict logical learning theory, which has and continues to be validated in the traditional manner. We can demonstrate our point by taking a closer look at some of the published examples of phenomenological method, beginning with Shapiro (1985). Shapiro makes some excellent arguments against the view that meaning and knowledge are fundamentally linguistic (recall our discussion of Harré's explanation of selfhood in this regard, p. 438). Meanings are phenomenally experienced by the person. They must therefore be studied in this fashion rather than as if they were merely conveyed to the person through cultural shaping in the use of language. The specific "phenomenological method" that Shapiro (1985) proposes to study such phenomena encompasses two steps. The first step is termed the *return*, which means that the subject in the investigation attempts to return to the situation in which the phenomenon (e.g., an emotional state) has been bodily experienced.

Some kind of experimental device to help evoke the phenomenon may be used, such as resituating the person in the key experience (returning to the emotion-provoking context literally or in imagination), holding semistructured interviews, or even having a subject read relevant theoretical accounts of a phenomenon. Since the body has already experienced the phenomenon that is returned to, the return is simply an attempt to recapture those aspects of phenomenal experience that have actually occurred.

When the return is successfully accomplished, the subject moves into the second step of this phenomenal method, in which a "sense

of" the structure of the phenomenon, as already generated by the body
(e.g., the emotional mood), is put into some kind of meaningful
expression. Here is where *reflection* enters the picture. Reflection begins in abstraction; it is an "awareness of awareness" (*ibid.*, p. 24), in
which "there is at once an awareness of that which has been ab-
stracted and of the self implied in that abstraction" (*ibid.*, p. 13). To
accomplish the goal of step two, the person relies on what Shapiro
calls *forming*, which is "a species of behavior with the peculiar prop-
erty of looking at itself" (*ibid.*, p. 139). Forming is not imagination, it
involves an effort to understand the bodily meanings by abstracting
the structure of the phenomenon as originally lived. The phenomenon
is, in effect, "there" in the lived mode of bodily experience. We must
reflect, form, and express what is given to us by lived experience.

What are the data of this method? Shapiro mentions two kinds of
products: schematic diagrams and the framing of relevant metaphors.
After anguishing about how much his method will distort the targeted
experience as actually lived (the purity criticism), Shapiro decides to
demonstrate his method through an examination of ambivalence, including an analysis of his writing of the volume demonstrating the
method (*ibid.*, pp. 171–176). He takes the reader through a reliving of
his bouts of ambivalence over the work of creative writing and draws
schematic diagrams purporting to represent what ambivalence meant
to him as he actually lived it, sitting at his desk. The result is that we
have an interesting analysis of behavior, drafted from an introspective
perspective, in which the themes of self-reflexivity, transcendence, dialectical conflict, and intentionality are prominent. For example, having lost his trend of phenomenal understanding, Shapiro struggles along
in a seemingly losing cause: "Surely, I am just stuck momentarily;
stay with the task, I exhort myself. But I cannot stave off the negativ-
ity. The phenomenon I sought to describe has slipped through my
fingers" (*ibid.*, p. 172).

It would be a simple matter to subsume such descriptive efforts
under the terminology of logical learning theory. We see here the behavior of what is obviously a teleological organism, a behaving human
being with hopes and goals, but suffering the inevitable setbacks and
frustrations of life on the way to attaining hoped-for ends. In subsuming such rich descriptions by the rubrics of logical learning theory, we
would in no way be robbing the content of its humanity. We would
have Shapiro, the human being, rent with dialectically framed meanings, struggling to align certain predications but for some reason unable to find a precedent with the precise sense of what it is that he

wants to express. There is nothing in the fact that logical learning theory has been tested in the traditional scientific context to weaken any of Shapiro's personalized descriptions. And even if someone else were to describe ambivalence in terms unlike those selected by Shapiro or if Shapiro himself were to describe ambivalence in other terms at a later date, this "unpredictability" would not affect the reliability or validity of logical learning theory—which always relates to the fundamental process and not to the shifting contents of this process (Questions 4, 7, and 11).

Shapiro's method obviously rests with procedural evidence (see Chapter 1, p. 45). Science also begins in the common-sense tests of procedural evidence, but then moves to validate its claims through empirical controls and predictions whenever such validation is possible. The point the logical learning theorist makes is that the phenomenological investigation typified by Shapiro can result in rich insights into human behavior; but the resultant findings that rest on procedural evidence can be further supported through alignment with an account of human learning that has been validated in a traditional manner. There is no contradiction here. The phenomenological investigations enrich our understanding of the teleological organism known as a human being. But it is still possible, and indeed highly desirable, to align these insights with more rigorous formulations as long as we have a validated theory that does not rob them of their essential meaning. A distortion of this type occurred in the case of Dollard and Miller (1950), who completely lost the agential meanings of Freudian psychology by subsuming them under mechanistic constructs. (For a teleological presentation of Freud, see Cameron & Rychlak, 1985.)

Another example of a phenomenological method is Giorgi's reformulation or perfection of the approach we discussed earlier (see Chapter 5, pp. 197–201). Unlike Shapiro's method, which is based on a direct revivification of the experimenter's own experience, Giorgi's (1985) method focuses on recorded experiences that have been recalled by other people. For example, the phenomenological investigator might ask a subject to "please describe for me a situation in which you have learned" (p. 8). The subject's description could be electronically recorded and then a transcript made, or it could be written down by the subject in question. In either case, we would have a narrative account—written in the subject's own words—of a past life situation in which he or she believes that learning took place.

The narrative is then submitted to a method involving four steps (ibid., p. 10): (1) the investigator reads the narrative account in order to get a general sense of the whole statement. (2) After the whole meaning is grasped, the investigator goes back to the beginning and reads through the text once more to specifically delineate "meaning units" from within a psychological perspective and with a focus on the phenomenon being researched. (3) Once such meaning units have been identified, the investigator goes through all of the meaning units and expresses the psychological insight contained in them more directly. (4) Finally, the investigator synthesizes all of the transformed meaning units into a "structure of the experience," which is a consistent statement regarding the subject's experience. The structure of experience is, in effect, the ultimate "finding" of the phenomenological method.

As an example of his method, Giorgi presents the case of a father who described a learning situation stemming from a time when he gave one of his sons a revered chess set that had been in his possession for a number of years (*ibid.*, pp. 9–10). The weights which lent stability to the chess pieces were loose, and they could be felt and heard rattling around within them. To his initial chagrin, the father was to learn that his son's delighted acceptance of the set was not based upon an appreciation of the father's "love-of-the-game" motivation in offering the gift, but in the fact that the boy could split the chess pieces open and obtain the weights contained therein. In time, the father came to appreciate the meaning of the gift from the boy's point of view. The father said that he finally understood what St. Thomas Aquinas meant, when he wrote that "the quality of a gift is determined not by the giver's ability to give but by the receiver's ability to receive" (*ibid.*, p. 9).

Giorgi submits the father's narrative account to the four steps of his method, identifying several meaning units, which give prominent attention to the intentions of the father versus the intentions of the boy, the "real" meaning of the gift, and the comprehension of this disparity by the father's capacity to shift perspectives from his view to his son's. The structure of the father's learning experience is synthesized by Giorgi as follows:

Learning, for S [the father], consisted in the clarification of a situation rendered ambiguous because a false assumption did not allow S to see the same situation in terms of different perspectives for different persons. This experience also enabled S to learn a deeper meaning of the philosophical saying he had previously read, but the saying also helped him interpret the situation he had ambiguously lived through (Giorgi, 1985, p. 20).

Once again, it is immediately evident that this finding is readily subsumed—without distortion—by the tenets of logical learning theory. Human beings do indeed lend meaning to their experience through their intentions. The meaning of the gift as predicated by the son was not the same gift that the father had predicated in the act of giving. Intentions are fundamental to all human interactions; hence, the Aquinian insight is profoundly correct. The relationship of a giver and a receiver must be understood dialectically, so that the intentional thrust in the act of gift-giving is never situated exclusively at one pole of the bipolarly meaningful interaction. Nothing prevents us from accepting Giorgi's insightful analysis, even as we also attempt to validate through more traditional steps the learning theory which we believe can subsume his explanations without distortion. Giorgi acknowledges that his phenomenological method relates more to the "context of discovery" than to the "context of verification" (*ibid.*, p. 14). This distinction in the total scientific enterprise dates to Reichenbach (1938). It parallels our distinction between theory or theorizing (discovery), on the one hand, and method or proving things (verification), on the other. Giorgi's method is what we have termed a cognitive or conceptual one, relying upon procedural evidence (Rychlak, 1981, p. 74). It has merit; it has a use. But its findings can be submitted to theoretical analysis and subsumption by a theory that has *also* been submitted to the context of verification. Thus, logical learning theory is based on an image of humanity that is in complete agreement with Giorgi's style of theoretical description.

Our third example of phenomenological method is the hermeneutic inquiry advanced by Packer (1985). This method focuses on the interpersonal in human relations. It is defined as follows: "The hermeneutic method . . . employs a detailed progressive description of episodes of social interchange and gradually articulates more and more of their organization" (p. 1089). As an example of the method, Packer studied the conflicts that develop between college students as they took part in a modified version of the Prisoners' Dilemma Game (Luce & Raiffa, 1957). Although the hermeneutic investigator strives to be free of rational preconceptions (purity criticism), Packer (1985) admits that the investigator must have a preliminary and tentative "preunderstanding" of what is to be studied (p. 1090). The logical learning theorist suggests that this is always the case in human behavior. It is quite impossible for anyone to think (theorize) without a precedent meaning being sequaciously extended into what can be thought. Based on his readings in the phenomenological tradition, Packer selected three different aspects of the social interaction to investigate: the moral status that people ascribed to themselves and others as they interact, the kind of interpersonal intimacy their actions produced or maintained, and the "mythology" of their talk (ibid., p. 1090).

Packer's strategy was to study the transcripts of subjects who spoke, back and forth, in performing the task and commenting on what transpired. Subjects can behave cooperatively or selfishly, either "burning" or getting "burned" and therefore expostulating their co-participants to keep the trust in which they had begun the game. Packer summarized his findings as follows: "The two teams [of subjects] in the conflict, the burned and the burners, understood events very differently, but they were not themselves aware that their understanding was not shared; it was so self-evident that it could not be doubted" (ibid., p. 1091). Packer gradually came to appreciate that these conflicting ways of understanding were based on the emotions following a burning and, at a deeper level, "in the situation people found themselves in at the start of the session as well as in the background of their friendships" (ibid.). Subjects began to deliberate and give fresh accounts of the supposed "facts" taking place in the interaction. They tried to influence their co-participants. In line with logical learning theory, they were seen to move from the more global (precedents) to the specific (sequacious extensions) in framing these alternative accounts of their interactions.

Packer contends that what he did in his research is different from what the typical behavioristic investigator would do with the same subject matter. For example, unlike the behaviorist, he did not use fixed and precisely defined categories of events. Aspects of the interaction were allowed to develop as they were studied. We might remind Packer that this is precisely what Skinner (1956) contended in an examination of his own method of investigation. He (as Newton before him) did not press hypothetical preconceptions upon the data but let the animal's behavior speak for itself. Indeed, Skinner claimed that he avoided the oft-cited canons of logic advanced by John Stuart Mill. Packer (1985) also contended that the conflicts he uncovered among his subjects were not predictable and that he was unable to "model" such conflicts with a computer program or even to recognize the cause involved in them. Even so, he did experience "a greatly increased and differentiated sensitivity to the concerns at work in such conflicts" (p. 1091).

Of course, people's conflicting understandings and reformulations of what transpired in an interaction would be readily explicable in terms of logical learning theory. We might not be able to predict the precise contents (Question 4) of an interpersonal conflict in cross-validating Packer's phenomenological insights, but we surely could predict that conflicts *would* ensue anytime we place human beings in a zero-sum game, whereby to gain advantage a person must take something away from someone else. This seems a perfectly predictable suggestion flowing from the hermeneutic inquiry. But there may be—and doubtless are—unique findings emerging in such hermeneutic efforts. These are insights into the *contents* of human reasoning during interaction with others that would be difficult or impossible to obtain via other theoretical strategies. Once again, there is merit in the hermeneutic analysis, but there is no reason why the insights gained thereby cannot be subsumed and eventually tested empirically within the rubrics of a teleological theory of the person, such as logical learning theory.

We have already seen intimations of social constructionism in our discussion of Harré earlier in this chapter (see p. 438). Gergen's (1985) Chapter 80: Child Abusebrand of social constructionism is fraught with the view that all reports of human experience are "linguistic constructions guided and shaped by historically contingent conventions of discourse" (p. 272). Social constructionism offers no alternative theory of truth to conventional science, but primarily falls back on sociohistorical analysis, which means it rests with procedural evidence. Evidence would not be data-driven and impersonal in the social-constructionist strategy. "Scientific formulations would not . . . be the result of an impersonal application of decontextualized, methodological rules, but the responsibility of persons in active, communal interchange" (*ibid.*, p. 272). To this, we would simply observe that capturing such a responsible human being, interacting in a socio-historical context, is one of the clear aims of logical learning theory. However, as per our discussion of Questions 3, 7, and 8, we want to do this in a teleological and not a mechanistic fashion.

Narrative analysts (Polkinghorne, 1983, 1986) and psychobiographers (Runyan, 1982) strike the logical learning theorist as wanting to recapture the humanity of the human being in their descriptive accounts. As we read through such accounts we are struck by the compatibility between these views and the basic assumptions of logical learning theory. The solution to recapturing real human experience is usually framed in terms of studying the individual (Runyan, 1982, p. 13) or the single person (Carlson, 1971). Runyan (1982) argues that if two studies of the same individual life are made in psychobiographical fashion and they disagree on the interpretation of this life, this need not be viewed as a strike against the validity or reliability of the psychobiographical method. "The position argued for here is that alternative biographical accounts are not necessarily indications of inadequate scholarship, but may reflect different yet supplementary perspectives on the same central figure, and that rigorous critical standards can and should be employed within any given perspective" (p. 36).

Logical learning theorists would agree with this completely. We would also agree with the following: "A crucial dimension of the story of a life, which can be effectively expressed through narrative (and perhaps only through narrative), is the relationship between intentions and actions, and often, the discrepancy between intentions and results" (*ibid.*, p. 68). We can understand how the psychobiographer might find mechanistic learning theories continually frustrating this desire to capture genuine intentionality, unadulterated by the mechanistic lingo which so often accompanies empirical investigation. (Question 3). However, logical learning theory is framed in order to meet the need of those psychologists who would like to tie their thinking into a traditionally validated explanation of human learning that takes intentionality seriously. Hence, we see no reason for the narrative analyst or the psychobiographer to distrust traditional scientific validation. This method of testing hypotheses is a source of support and not an enemy to those who would view the person as an intentional agent.

Conclusion

We conclude that although a tradition of rigorous humanism is well underway, there are several issues left unresolved due to conceptual and terminological ambiguities. The logical learning theorist can find much in this tradition to take support from. We would see Heider (1958) and Polanyi (1964) as important progenitors of rigorous humanism. Deci and Ryan (1985) have done a somewhat better job of capturing this teleological line of explanation than De Charms (1968). Harré (1984) is closer to our outlook than Mischel (1976) or Bandura (1977a). The computer analogue as presently conceived is basically mechanistic, but if we are given the liberty of studying the logic used by the computer's designer or the program writer, logical learning theory may yet be able to bring rigorous humanism into line with information processing.

Festinger's (1957) theory of cognitive dissonance is an obvious example of the line of theorizing we favor. Of course, as drive theories were prominent when Festinger advanced his ideas, he needlessly relied upon such mechanistic remnants to flesh out what is obviously a dialectical formulation of human reason. Reactance theory has these same problems. Thus, we see more potential in Apter's reversal theory than in Brehm's (1972) or Wicklund's (1974) treatment of dialectical reasonings. Although both their research findings are consistent with dialectical reasoning, Howard's (Howard & Conway, 1986) understanding of what took place in his experimental design is surely more in line with logical learning theory than the understanding advanced by Lord, Lepper, and Preston (1984) concerning their experimental design.

Both Jenkins (1982) and Lamiell (1987) represent direct and clear examples of logical learning theory. The logical learning theorist also feels an affinity to phenomenological theorists. Although we have much to agree with in the theoretical accounts of Shapiro (1985), Giorgi (1985), Packer (1985), Polkinghorne (1983), and Runyan (1982), we cannot agree with their methodological claims. Validation must remain a goal of rigorous humanism. We suggest, however, that most of what the phenomenologists seek as students of the human condition is already at their disposal, because the principles of logical learning theory can subsume their teleological accounts without distortion.

Summary

In Chapter 10 we survey a number of alternative approaches to rigorous humanistic theory. Causal attribution is frequently cited as a teleological approach to the description of human behavior. In the basic outlooks of certain causal attribution theorists like Heider and Polanyi this seems to be the case. But other theorists, such as Piaget, Michotte, and De Charms, are not as easily understood as teleologists. Causal attribution theorists tend to frame mediational conceptions of human behavior, and such formulations rob the behaving human being of true agency. Given their tendency to confound theory with method, it is difficult to see how negative empirical evidence can influence psychologists concerning the underlying process of human mentation.

Typically, a psychologist will employ telic "sounding" concepts to describe behavior but then claim that these behavioral patterns are learned through previous experience. When we look closer, we find that the learning theory supposedly at work in previous experience is mechanistic (mediational rather than predicational).

Self theories are in the same predicament. It is not unusual for a self theorist to reject teleology in his or her formal theorizing, only to bring in such meanings informally. Mischel and Bandura are given as examples of theorists who provide an overlay of telic description, yet fail to explicate precisely how their concepts of mutual interaction or reciprocal determinism save them from an efficient-cause account. Socio-psychological theorists who fall back on normative influences seem deeply imbedded in mediational theorizing. Rather than viewing normative behavior as a reflection of predications held in common by a group of people, they seem to search about for supraindividual normative mechanisms to explain how intentions and purposes are shaped into the person. Harré's social constructionism is in this vein, whereby language usage seems to be carrying the sense of identity and agency experienced by human beings. Although Deci and Ryan come closest to the theories of Heider and Polanyi, their commitment to energic conceptualizations clouds the issue somewhat.

Computer analogues are the next topic to be reviewed. Many social scientists believe that the computer will one day serve as a complete model for the description of telic behavior. Computer enthusiasts seem to focus on the hardware as the ultimate metaphor for the mind, yet they repeatedly sneak in informal teleological conceptions when considering the software aspects of the total endeavor. It is difficult to see how a computer could be designed or a program written without some form of logical assumptions being made and alternatives considered before arriving at the end point in a "product." Yet, computer models are focused on the instrumentalities of the mental process with little or no concern for the initiating heuristics of that process. If we are to learn about agency, we most certainly will have to look into the predicated beginnings of mental processing. It is too early to judge how much impact computer science will have on teleology. At this point in time the outlook is not exactly rosy.

Dialectical themes in the literature have been quite encouraging to the logical learning theorist. Festinger's theorizing on dissonance was an excellent beginning in this regard. The findings of reactance theorists like Brehm and Wicklund were also highly supportive of a theory relying upon dialectical human capacities in mentation. However, lacking a proper theory to subsume this ubiquitous human characteristic, dissonance and reactance theorists fall back on arousal conceptions to say why it is that people try to resolve conflicts in outlook or motivational intentions. Apter's reversal theory seems to be getting closer to the real thing, although he draws on questionable cybernetic formulations to make his case. Lamiell's detailed examination of impression formation presents the clearest argument (backed up by evidence) for dialectical reasoning in the literature.

Chapter 10 closes with a consideration of various phenomenological approaches that claim to be going beyond or improving upon the traditional scientific method. It is clear that the approaches exemplified in the work of Shapiro, Giorigi, and Packer have some merit; but there is absolutely no conflict in their insights with the sort of teleological theory proposed here. The suggestion is made that the reason phenomenologically oriented psychologists want a "new" method in their science is because most of those psychologists who employed the standard method have relied solely on mechanistic theory in accounting for their data. The standard method cannot dictate what theory is used to account for such data. If we look carefully we find that the phenomenological methods invariably arrive at descriptions of behavior that are framed introspectively and encompass human teleology. As logical learning theory is similarly construed, the recommendation is made that phenomenologists employ this empirically validated explanation of behavior, even as they specify within its tenets the distinctive contents of mind that a human organism phenomenally experiences.

References

Apter, M. J. The possibility of a structural phenomenology: The case of reversal theory. *Journal of Phenomenological Psychology*, 1981, **12**, 173–187.

Apter M. J. *The experience of motivation: The theory of psychological reversals.* New York: Academic Press, 1982.

Apter, M. J. Reversal theory and personality: A review. *Journal of Research in Personality*, 1984, **18**, 265–288.

Apter, M. J., & Fontana, D. Overview and discussion. In M. J. Apter, D. Fontana, & S. Murgatroyd (Eds.), *Reversal theory: Applications and developments.* Cardiff, Wales: University College Press, 1985. Pp. 179–186.

Aristotle. *On memory and reminiscence.* In R. M. Hutchins (Ed.), *Great books of the western world* (Vol. 8). Chicago: Encyclopedia Britannica, 1952. Pp. 690–701.

Bandura, A. *Social learning theory.* Englewood Cliffs, N.J.: Prentice-Hall, 1977a.

Bandura, A. Self-efficacy: Toward a unifying theory of behavioral change. *Psychological Review*, 1977b, **84**, 191–215.

Bandura, A. The self system in reciprocal determinism. *American Psychologist,* 1978, **33,** 344–358.

Bandura, A. Self-referent mechanisms in social learning theory. *American Psychologist,* 1979, **34,** 439–440.

Bandura, A., & Simon, K. M. The role of proximal intentions in self-regulation of refractory behavior. *Cognitive Therapy and Research,* 1977, **1,** 177–193.

Bellezza, F. S. The self as a mnemonic device: The role of internal cues. *Journal of Personality and Social Psychology,* 1984, **47,** 506–515.

Bem, D. Self-perception: An alternative interpretation of cognitive dissonance phenomena. *Psychological Review,* 1967, **74,** 183–200.

Bem, D. Self-perception theory. In L. Berkowitz (Ed.), *Advances in experimental social psychology* (Vol. 6). New York: Academic Press, 1972. Pp. 4–46.

Black, J. B., & Bern, H. Causal coherence and memory for events in narratives. *Journal of Verbal Learning and Verbal Behavior,* 1981, **20,** 267–275.

Black, J. B., & Bower, G. H. Story understanding as problem solving. *Poetics,* 1980, **9,** 223–250.

Boden, M. A. *Artificial intelligence and natural man.* New York: Basic Books, 1977.

Boring, E. G. *A history of experimental psychology* (2nd ed.). New York: Appleton-Century-Crofts, 1950.

Bower, G. H., & Gilligan, S. G. Remembering information related to one's self. *Journal of Research in Personality,* 1979, **13,** 420–432.

Bradshaw, G. L., & Anderson, J. R. Elaborative encoding as an explanation of levels of processing. *Journal of Verbal Learning and Verbal Behavior,* 1982, **21,** 165–174.

Brehm, J. W. *A theory of psychological reactance.* New York: Academic Press, 1966.

Brehm, J. W. *Responses to loss of freedom: A theory of psychological reactance.* Morristown, N.J.: General Learning Press, 1972.

Brewer, W. F. There is no convincing evidence for operant or classical conditioning in adult humans. In W. B. Weimer & D. S. Palermo (Eds.), *Cognition and the symbolic processes.* Hillsdale, N.J.: Lawrence Erlbaum, 1974. Pp. 1–42.

Calder, B. J., & Staw, B. M. Self-perception of intrinsic and extrinsic motivation. *Journal of Personality and Social Psychology,* 1975, **31,** 599–605.

Cameron, N., & Rychlak, J. F. *Personality development and psychopathology: A dynamic approach* (2nd ed.). Boston: Houghton Mifflin, 1985.

Carlson, R. Where is the person in personality research? *Psychological Bulletin,* 1971, **75,** 203–219.

Cattell, R. B. Psychological measurement: Normative, ipsative, interactive. *Psychological Review,* 1944, **51,** 292–303.

Cooley, C. H. *Human nature and the social order.* New York: Scribner's, 1902.

Danner, F. W., & Lonky, E. A cognitive-developmental approach to the effects of rewards on intrinsic motivation. *Child Development,* 1981, **52,** 1043–1052.

De Charms, R. *Personal causation: The internal determinants of behavior.* New York: Academic Press, 1968.

Deci, E. L. Intrinsic motivation, extrinsic reinforcement, and inequity. *Journal of Personality and Social Psychology,* 1972, **22,** 113–120.

Deci, E. L. *The psychology of self-determination.* Lexington, Mass.: D.C. Heath & Co., 1980.

Deci, E. L., & Ryan, R. M. *Intrinsic motivation and self-determination in human behavior.* New York: Plenum Press, 1985.

Dollard, J., & Miller, N. E. *Personality and psychotherapy: An analysis in terms of learning, thinking, and culture.* New York: McGraw-Hill, 1950.

Dreyfus, H. L. *What computers can't do: The limits of artificial intelligence.* New York: Harper & Row, 1979.

Fazio, R. H. On the self-perception explanation of the overjustification effect: The role of the salience of initial attitude. *Journal of Experimental Social Psychology,* 1981, **17,** 417–426.

Festinger, L. A theory of social comparison processes. *Human Relations,* 1954, **7,** 117–140.

Festinger, L. *A theory of cognitive dissonance.* Evanston, Ill.: Row, Peterson & Co., 1957.

Festinger, L., & Carlsmith, J. M. Cognitive consequences of forced compliance. *Journal of Abnormal and Social Psychology,* 1959, **58,** 203–210.

Fisher, R. P., & Craik, F. I. M. The effects of elaboration on recognition memory. *Memory & Cognition,* 1980, **8,** 400–404.

Gergen, K. J. The social constructionist movement in modern psychology. *American Psychologist,* 1985, **40,** 266–275.

Giorgi, A. *Psychology as a human science: A phenomenologically based approach.* New York: Harper and Row, 1970.

Giorgi, A. Sketch of a psychological phenomenological method. In A. Giorgi (Ed.), *Phenomenology and psychological research.* Pittsburgh: Duquesne University Press, 1985. Pp. 8–22.

Graesser, A. C., Robertson, S. P., Lovelace, E. R., & Swinehart, D. M. Answers to why-questions expose the organization of story plot and predict recall of actions. *Journal of Verbal Learning and Verbal Behavior,* 1980, **19,** 110–119.

Greenwald, A. G. Self and memory. In G. H. Bower (Ed.), *The psychology of learning and motivation* (Vol. 15). New York: Academic Press, 1981. Pp. 201–236.

Harré, R. *Personal being: A theory for individual psychology.* Cambridge, Mass.: Harvard University Press, 1984.

Hastie, R. Causes and effects of causal attribution. *Journal of Personality and Social Psychology,* 1984, **46,** 44–56.

Heider, F. *The psychology of interpersonal relations.* New York: John Wiley & Sons, 1958.

Heider, F., & Simmel, M. An experimental study of apparent behavior. *American Journal of Psychology,* 1944, **57,** 243–259.

Hofstadter, D. R. *Gödel, Escher, Bach: An eternal golden braid.* New York: Vintage Books, 1980.

Howard, D. V. *Cognitive psychology.* New York: Macmillan, 1983.

Howard, G. S. *Dare we develop a human science?* Notre Dame, Ind.: Academic Publications, 1986.

Howard, G. S., & Conway, C. G. Can there be an empirical science of volitional action? *American Psychologist,* 1986, **41,** 1241–1251.

Hull, C. L. *Principles of behavior.* New York: Appleton-Century-Crofts, 1943.

Hull, C. L. *A behavior system.* New Haven: Yale University Press, 1952.

Immergluck, L. Determinism-freedom in contemporary psychology. An ancient problem revisited. *American Psychologist,* 1964, **19,** 270–281.

Jenkins, A. H. *The psychology of the Afro-American: A humanistic approach.* New York: Pergamon Press, 1982.

Jones, E. E., Kanouse, D. F., Kelley, H. H., Nisbett, R. E., Valins, S., & Weiner, B. *Attribution: Perceiving the causes of behavior.* Morristown, N.J.: General Learning Press, 1971.

Jones, E. E., & Nisbett, R. E. *The actor and the observer: Divergent perceptions of the causes of behavior.* Morristown, N.J.: General Learning Press, 1971.

Keenan, J. M., & Baillet, S. D. Memory for personality and socially significant events. In R. S. Nickerson (Ed.), *Attention and performance* (Vol. 8). Hillsdale, N.J.: Erlbaum, 1980. Pp. 651–659.

Kelley, H. H. The processes of causal attribution. *American Psychologist*, 1973, **28**, 107–128.

Kelly, G. A. *The psychology of personal constructs* (2 vols.). New York: Norton, 1955.

Kleinmuntz, B. *Personality measurement: An introduction.* Homewood, Ill.: Dorsey Press, 1967.

Lamiell, J. T. *The psychology of personality: An epistemological inquiry.* New York: Columbia University Press, 1987.

Lamiell, J. T., Foss, M. A., Larsen, R. J., & Hempel, A. M. Studies in intuitive personology from an idiothetic point of view: Implications for personality theory. *Journal of Personality*, 1983, **51**, 438–467.

Lamiell, J. T., Foss, M. A., Trierweiler, S. J., & Leffel, G. M. Toward a further understanding of the intuitive personologist: Some preliminary evidence for the dialectical quality of subjective personality impressions. *Journal of Personality*, 1983, **51**, 213–235.

Lefcourt, H. M. The function of the illusions of control and freedom. *American Psychologist*, 1973, **28**, 417–425.

Locke, J. *An essay concerning human understanding.* In R. M. Hutchins (Ed.), *Great books of the western world* (Vol. 35). Chicago: Encyclopedia Britannica, 1952. Pp. 85–395.

Lord, C. G., Lepper, M. R., & Preston, E. Considering the opposite: A corrective strategy for social judgment. *Journal of Personality and Social Psychology*, 1984, **47**, 1231–1243.

Luce, R. D., & Raiffa, H. *Games and decisions.* New York: John Wiley, 1957.

Markus, H. Self-schemata and processing information about the self. *Journal of Personality and Social Psychology*, 1977, **35**, 63–78.

McLoyd, V. C. The effects of extrinsic rewards of differential value on high- and low-intrinsic interest. *Child Development*, 1979, **50**, 1010–1019.

Michotte, A. E. *The perception of causality.* New York: Basic Books, 1963.

Miller, G. A., Galanter, E., & Pribram, K. H. *Plans and the structure of behavior.* New York: Holt, Rinehart & Winston, 1960.

Minsky, M. L. (Ed.), *Semantic information processing.* Cambridge, Mass.: MIT Press, 1968.

Mischel, W. The self as the person: A cognitive social learning view. In A. H. Wandersman, P. J. Poppen, & D. F. Ricks (Eds.), *Humanism and behaviorism: Dialogue and growth.* New York: Pergamon Press, 1976. Pp. 145–156.

Mischel, W. On the interface of cognition and personality: Beyond the person-situation debate. *American Psychologist*, 1979, **34**, 740–754.

Murgatroyd, S. Introduction to reversal theory. In M. J. Apter, D. Fontana, & S. Murgatroyd (Eds.), *Reversal theory: Applications and developments.* Cardiff, Wales: University College Press, 1985. Pp. 1–19.

Packer, M. J. Hermeneutic inquiry in the study of human conduct. *American Psychologist*, 1985, **40**, 1081–1093.

Page, M. M. Demand characteristics and the verbal operant conditioning experiment. *Journal of Personality and Social Psychology*, 1972, **23**, 304–308.

Piaget, J. *The child's conception of physical causality.* London: Kegan Paul, Trench, Trubner, 1930.

Plato. *Sophist.* In R. M. Hutchins (Ed.), *Great books of the western world* (Vol. 7). Chicago: Encyclopedia Britannica, 1952. Pp. 551–579.

Polanyi, M. *Personal knowledge: Towards a post-critical philosophy.* New York: Harper Torchbooks, 1964.

Polkinghorne, D. *Methodology for the human sciences: Systems of inquiry.* Albany: State University of New York Press, 1983.

Polkinghorne, D. *Narrative knowledge and human science.* Unpublished manuscript. San Francisco: Saybrook Institute, 1986.

Pyszczynski, T. A., & Greenberg, J. Role of disconfirmed expectancies in the instigation of attributional processing. *Journal of Personality and Social Psychology,* 1981, **40,** 31–38.

Reichenbach, H. *Experience and prediction.* Chicago: University of Chicago Press, 1938.

Rogers, T. B., Kuiper, N. A., & Kirker, W. S. Self-reference and the encoding of personal information. *Journal of Personality and Social Psychology,* 1977, **35,** 677–688.

Ross, M. Salience of reward and intrinsic motivation. *Journal of Personality and Social Psychology,* 1975, **32,** 245–254.

Runyan, W. M. *Life histories and psychobiography: Explorations in theory and method.* New York: Oxford University Press, 1984.

Rychlak, J. F. Comments on "The self as the person." In A. H. Wandersman, P. J. Poppen, & D. F. Ricks (Eds.), *Humanism and behaviorism: Dialogue and growth.* New York: Pergamon Press, 1976. Pp. 157–167.

Rychlak, J. F. A nontelic teleology? *American Psychologist,* 1979, **34,** 435–438.

Rychlak, J. F. *A philosophy of science for personality theory* (2nd ed.). Malabar, Fla.: Krieger, 1981.

Shapiro, K. J. *Bodily reflective modes: A phenomenological method for psychology.* Durham, N.C.: Duke University Press, 1985.

Sherman, R. C., & Titus, W. Covariation information and cognitive processing: Effects of causal implications on memory. *Journal of Personality and Social Psychology,* 1982, **42,** 989–1000.

Skinner, B. F. A case history in scientific method. *American Psychologist,* 1956, **11,** 221–233.

Skinner, B. F. *Beyond freedom and dignity.* New York: Knopf, 1971.

Stevenson, R. J. Depth of comprehension, effective elaboration, and memory for sentences. *Memory & Cognition,* 1981, **9,** 169–176.

Sullivan, H. S. *Schizophrenia as a human process.* New York: Norton, 1962.

Vallacher, R. R. An introduction to self theory. In D. M. Wegner & R. R. Vallacher (Eds.), *The self in social psychology.* New York: Oxford University Press, 1980.

van Kaam, A. *Existential foundations of psychology* (Image Books ed.). Garden City, N.Y.: Doubleday, 1969.

Walters, J., Apter, M. J., & Svebak, S. Colour preference, arousal and the theory of psychological reversals. *Motivation and Emotion,* 1982, **6,** 193–215.

Wegner, D. M., & Vallacher, R. R. *The self in social psychology.* New York: Oxford University Press, 1980.

White, R. W. Motivation reconsidered: The concept of competence. *Psychological Review,* 1959, **66,** 297–333.

Wicklund, R. A. *Freedom and reactance.* Potomac, Md.: Erlbaum, 1974.

Wittgenstein, L. *Philosophical investigations.* Oxford, England: Basil Blackwell, 1953.

Wong, P. T. P., & Weiner, B. When people ask "why" questions, and the heuristics of attributional search. *Journal of Personality and Social Psychology,* 1981, **40,** 650–663.

Wyer, R. S., & Carlston, D. E. *Social cognition, inference, and attribution.* Hillsdale, N.J.: Erlbaum, 1979.

CHAPTER ELEVEN

Summations, Reactions, and Reaffirmations

In this closing chapter we summarize what has transpired over the preceding ten chapters. Because there are objections to the general thrust of humanistic psychology, we then take up some of the reactions and questions most often called to our attention. The discussion is brought to a close by delineating the tenets of a rigorous humanistic psychology.

What Have We Accomplished?

We began with a review of Western intellectual history in terms of the four causal meanings—a metaphysical framework which emerged quite spontaneously in the knowledge of mankind. Aristotle gave these concepts a name, but he did not have to "think them up." The ideas presented in Table 1 (pp. 8–31) were then taken as the data of a study in which our goal was to capture the kind of organism which could have proffered them, keeping as close to the meaning of these formulations as possible. That is, we took what was included in Table 1 *seriously,* feeling that a psychology should not dictate what was or was not characteristic of its data.

We found that there were many ideas in Table 1 that simply could not be expressed without the full panoply of causation subsuming their meaning. No psychological scientist who wishes to speak for the organism of Table 1 can do so if he or she limits descriptive conceptualization to one, two, or even three of the *four* causal meanings. Even if such limitation is called for in the descriptive explanations of natural science, to limit the causal meanings employed by the human beings cited in Table 1 in explaining *their* behavior is consciously and arbitrarily to distort psychology's professional calling. The problem facing us, then, was to frame a psychology that could subsume the humanly generated concepts of Table 1.

We discovered that to do so involved a recognition of the precedents in thought. If we took these to be predicate assumptions concerning the nature of experience (reality, etc.), then it was possible to think of human behavior in telic terms. Surely, Table 1 establishes that teleological formulations are heavily represented in the history of thought. Having committed ourselves to *all* of the ideas in our historical survey, we had to find some of our own precedents which might help aid our understanding of the telic intelligence. An analysis of meaning soon established that a belief in the human person's dialectical (in addition to demonstrative) reasoning ability could help in this effort. The remarkable fact that not only the causal meanings but the demonstrative-dialectical contrast in meaning could be found in Eastern as well as Western thought, with no evidence of cultural transmission, lent a historical weight of conviction (procedural evidence) to our efforts. There was nothing here to weaken the contention that human beings reason by nature in a dialectical fashion.

While developing these themes we also established why neither the dialectic nor the final-cause description of human behavior which it makes possible is employed in modern natural science. Due to historical confrontations between deity teleology and the empirical approach of science, a Baconian material- and efficient-cause restriction was put on the causes of Table 1—first, in the description of nonhuman events and then of human events as well (even though Bacon never intended to dismiss formal-final cause description in art, ethics, metaphysics, etc., each of which can be thought of as a manifestation of human nature). The rise of mathematics with its attendant law of contradiction also served to remove dialectical formulations from the list of acceptable theoretical precedents in the conceptualization of the human condition. The inevitable (because sequacious) outcome of these ground-rule restrictions on the theoretical predications of psychology was a mechanistic human image.

We traced the course of mechanistic theoretical development in psychology, contrasting the leading thinkers of our profession in terms of so-called Lockean and Kantian models—so named because these two philosophers epitomized the contrast in outlook that we have seen occurring across the ages and in different cultural milieus. There can be no doubt but that psychology has institutionalized the Lockean model as its reigning paradigm. Even the historical debate between structuralism and functionalism in psychology was found to be a pseudo-confrontation, insofar as the basic paradigm of these two schools is concerned. The naive empiricist attitude which Lockeanism has encouraged in psychology has led to a serious confounding of what is literally observed in an empirical study with how one accounts for what is observed. The S-R bind or efficient-cause stranglehold that this attitude has placed on psychological theorizing has yet to be loosened. Physical scientists today bring humanizing features into their *formal* theoretical accounts of how they practice their profession. It is obvious that the physical sciences have conceptually surpassed psychology on its home ground.

In opposition to this outmoded Newtonian view of science and the mechanistic image of humanity it prompts, we called next for a revolution in theory, but not in method. A psychology of rigorous humanism was held possible if we retained the classical and unchanging logic of validation in science, but altered the form of the hypothesis put to test by this method. Taking a "middle road," we spurned the efforts to change the control-and-prediction method of science as well as the more pernicious—because insidious—efforts to account for telic behavior in nontelic theoretical formulations. A sensible revolution was called for, in which we would strive to keep our theoretical terminology clear and distinct from our methodological terminology. Several examples of this terminological confusion are given, and an effort was made to explain clearly what we mean by determinism and freedom in human behavior. In this discussion we suggested that the evidence now accruing in rigorous experimentation does *not* validate an exclusively efficient-cause interpretation of determinism. If the telic hypothesis is put to the data on conditioning of human behavior, there is no doubt that the latter confirms the former.

We moved next into a teleological interpretation of behavior, in which it was necessary to introduce some new terminology, the most basic of which was the *telosponse*. It is absolutely essential to find a term that contradicts the simplistic meaning of *response*, without denying the fact that behavior takes place within a time frame. Telosponsive behavior takes place, but it works at the initiating point of a course of events, moving precedently and sequaciously across the passage of time without being itself a function of time. Using this basic concept, we then could subsume all of the behaviors represented in Table 1, as well as the core argument in the Kuhnian conception of a scientific revolution. Such revolutions occur conceptually, brought on initially when some phenomenon cannot be understood as a sequacious meaning-extension from the precedent paradigm (i.e., it "doesn't follow"); hence, a new precedent must be delineated that is more in consonance with the observed facts, which in turn are created (made possible) by the new conceptualizations of the changed paradigm.

This process of revolutionizing science is merely one example of the fact that human beings order their understanding of experience in terms of something else. They must have—and constantly seek—the grounding frame for the sake of which their behavior takes place or can be rationally understood, altered, reinterpreted, and so on. In the same way that scientists may disagree over what they empirically see taking place in their most rigorous experimental framework, so too do humans constantly diverge and take contrasting (dialectically generated) positions on the "right" way of viewing things, behaving, handling their interpersonal relations, and so on. The most difficult aspect of human relations must surely be finding a common ground on which to proceed. Morale suffers among group members to the extent that a family, a professional society, or a nation lacks such predications in common.

As an initial statement of a humanistic psychology to accommodate this view of the person, we then proceeded to a description of logical learning theory (LLT). This theory is sufficiently abstract to subsume both the mechanistic and the telic formulations of behavior *as proffered by* the scientists who propound them. The tenets of logical learning theory do not dispute the mechanistic formulations of inanimate nature, but suggest that many hidden telic behaviors occur within the experimental designs of classical laboratory psychology. We can understand both historically and practically why psychologists who previously embraced behavioristic principles now welcome the machine metaphor of cybernetics. They believe that this keeps them in step with their colleagues in the physical sciences. The irony is that this leaves no one to claim the humanity of the scientist—the organism that designs the cybernetic machine and writes its programs—as a legitimate topic of scientific investigation. Logical learning theory is one attempt to fill this void.

The presentation moves on to a review of the research conducted on LLT. As an example of the kind of revolution needed in psychology, the prediction is made that teleological formulations based on LLT can be brought to bear in research designs that have been initially framed to test nontelic theory and, even on such unfriendly ground, can be *proven to hold*. After a full generation of work on LLT, predictions based upon its tenets continue to receive experimental validation. In full recognition of the unavoidable limitations of validation or falsification (due to the affirming-the-consequent fallacy encompassed in this logical sequence), the logical learning theorist is nevertheless greatly encouraged and looks to the future for additional support in the rigorous context of empirical validation.

The human image which validly emerges in research on LLT is that of a telosponsive organism, capable of both arbitrariness and rigid determinism in its behavior, furthering meanings for the sake of which it behaves in both preferred and nonpreferred directions. Life experience is ordered by an agent known as the person or self, who actively conceptualizes from the protopoint. Much of what is predictable in this organism's behavior stems from the fact that these introspective orderings into meaning are either known or can be guessed at by an extraspective observer who, for the sake of this insight, forecasts its *logical* (precedent-sequacious) direction. The individual's telic determination is graphed or tracked by the mathematical (formal-cause) determinism of statistical prediction. But by not letting such methodological tracking serve as our theory of explanation, we can appreciate the *self*-determined nature of behavior that makes such regularities possible. Furthermore, we can see in the error variance a "something" and not a "lack of something." Error is not only chance fluctuation from a substrate hence predictable reality. Error has as much subject-contributed determination as does the tracked and then predicted performance (see Rychlak, 1976, for a discussion of tracking versus identity in human behavior).

Finally, we examined a number of alternative approaches to rigorous humanism, raising questions about the constructs advanced and the methodological designs employed. We found that there are several approaches consonant with logical learning theory. There are other approaches that do not stand up to the requirements of a teleological explanation. It was our feeling that the lion's share of modern phenomenological approaches to the description and study of behavior could be easily subsumed by the rubrics of logical learning theory, which would in turn give these views a tie to empirical validity that many of them now lack. All in all, the future of rigorous humanism looks bright. If the lessons of history have been framed correctly and our recommended solutions are reasonably sound, we can call LLT a truly revolutionary alternative in psychology (Rychlak, 1984). What has been our experience with this self-styled revolution?

The Convolutions of Our Revolution

No one can step up and proclaim a revolution in the conceptual realm of science. As presented by Kuhn, a scientific revolution emerges when the practitioners of that science gradually come to see that there are inconsistencies and inadequacies in the (precedent) paradigm that has been predicating their efforts. But what happens when a body of scientists does not acknowledge such inconsistencies (assuming they exist); or, acknowledging them informally, decides that they are not worth formalizing within the basic terminology of the discipline? Kuhn did not consider this possibility, yet this is what seems to be happening in psychology. To say "look, your conception of humanity is at variance with the human image as known since the beginnings of thought" is hardly to suggest an anomaly to the mechanistic psychologist, who takes pride in being tough minded. He or she replies: "Well, so what? That is what science is *supposed* to do strip the human being of fancied capacities and present behavior in its true nature, unadorned by anthropomorphic claptrap." Others with this mind set say, "Look, I believe that behavior is purposive and that we are agents, but I also believe it is necessary for us to study the mechanisms that bring this about." (See Bandura's statement to this effect in Chapter 10 p. 433.) Still other psychologists have not really thought about such questions, which means they continue to support a tradition of nontelic human description.

Logical learning theory has had a limited influence to date. Both Jenkins' (1982) analysis of the Afro-American experience and Lamiell's (1987) empirical study of impression formation draw upon the insights of LLT (see Chapter 10, pp. 440 and 459). But in the main, the impact of LLT has been minimal. There are probably several reasons for this fact. First, LLT has not been a fully explicated, cohesive body of principles which could be pointed to as distinctive. The concepts are distinctive enough, but as they are continually under development they come across more as a global "alternative outlook" than an "alternative system." The second problem is that logical learning theorists have interpreted the findings of experiments conducted by traditional learning theorists differently, but they have not always been able to frame experiments that could confront and embarrass traditional theoretical explanations. The logical learning theorist does not hope for "crucial" experiments, of course, but it is just not easy to design experiments that clearly support *only* one point of view. Indeed, it is a tenet of LLT that alternative explanations of empirical "facts" are to be expected and accepted as the inevitable outcome of a dialectically reasoning intelligence (see p. 503).

This leads to the third, and most important, drawback to LLT— that is, its basic opposition to the Lockean view of mechanism in psychological description. We believe that there is a Kuhnian anomaly involved in this opposition and that LLT is therefore in a revolutionary posture in opposition to the received view of psychology (Rychlak, 1984). There is simply no way in which a teleological understanding of behavior can be subsumed by a mechanistic understanding of behavior. Another way of putting this is that the efficient-cause meaning can never predicate the meaning of final causation. Once the logical learning theorist is understood as calling for a *formal* telic description of behavior, centuries of historical debate and disagreement over free will and related agential conceptions are brought into the confrontation. Deity and natural teleologies get mixed into the discussion, when in fact all LLT purports to deal with is a human teleology. But such historical confounding so muddies the waters that it becomes very difficult to communicate the specifics of the LLT challenge to potential adopters of the viewpoint. Too often, the logical learning theorist is cast in the role of supporting vitalistic, spiritualistic, or theistic concepts that are irrelevant to the conceptual revolution in the human image that is at stake.

There are colleagues who believe that the strategy followed in LLT, whereby we first construe the person as an agent and then conduct research to support this view, places the cart before the horse. They say: "Let the evidence speak for itself": or "Rather than fixing our minds first let's look at the results of experimentation" or "This calls for a new experiment to be done, not a new theory to be written." We have tried to demonstrate why this naively empirical approach to science is untenable. We cannot find something unless we are willing to predicate its possible occurrence *before* we begin the empirical search. This writer began RV research in 1959, believing that should an experiment be designed "tightly" and evidence garnered rigorously, a professional peer would entertain the theory as a legitimate statement, worthy of scientific consideration. Even if this theory would be dismissed on first contact, surely as more data were accrued in support of its claims, the referees of our profession who sit on journal or granting boards would take the necessary time to assess such empirical findings in order to understand what the total approach was driving at.

How naive this view is! How right Kuhn was in his analysis! What one *actually* learns is that a psychologist trained in one school of thought finds it professionally impossible to look at findings in another way. Logical learning theory requires an effort on the part of colleagues to look at things in quite a different way indeed. There have also been some errors in the choice of terminology by logical learning theorists that have not helped LLT gain acceptance. For example, the use of the term *reinforcement value* in operationalizing affective assessment has probably added to the difficulty of understanding the drift of LLT research. To speak of reinforcement "values" and not mean some kind of food reward, shock, or empirically tracked fluctuation in performance is to tamper with a hallowed theoretical—actually, a methodological!—construct. That is, no one really has a satisfactory theory of reinforcement today, but we all understand the research designs employed by those who first studied the reinforcement of behavior. Nevertheless, by using such terminology logical learning theorists have undoubtedly confused their colleagues. In recent years, the phrase "reinforcement value" has been avoided because of this confusion. Of course, we never want to forget the reason for having both a theoretical and a methodological term to describe the concept of our interest (i.e., to keep method free and clear of theory, and *vice versa*).

An unexpected source of confusion and disagreement stemmed from the use of verbal-learning experimental designs and paraphernalia. Although we entered this area of research believing that it was an acceptable (if complex) branch of psychological science, we were shocked to learn that so many psychologists, even tough-minded ones, were prepared to dismiss evidence issuing from a paired-associates study. There has been a steady trend to what is termed "ecological" (life-like) research strategies in the study of verbal behavior. Although this development is to be applauded, the fact remains that we can still learn something about human reasoning from traditional laboratory experiments, employing memory drums and memory tasks. Yet too many psychologists seem to believe that there can be no worthwhile evidence issuing from such experimental designs, *ever!*

As if this were not trouble enough, the psychologists who typically embraced verbal-learning data found it impossible to accept RV as anything short of all those things we tried to prove in Chapter 9 that it was *not*—that is, frequency related, an experimental artifact, or a redundant measure of "something else." Even when we presented evidence to the opposite and referred the journal referee to our earlier work, we found that such colleagues simply dismissed all that had gone before without examination and repeatedly raised old questions. One particularly obstinate editor never did get past the "How can you be sure RV isn't a frequency measure?" stage. We have no doubt that if we referred him to Chapter 9, he would still consider the picture dark enough on this question to reject an RV-study. Another editor, with a sense of humor, frankly admitted that some of the problem with letting the LLT viewpoint stand "as is" in a write-up stemmed from the "negative RV" the members of his review board had for LLT. There is nothing personal in such editorial decisions; these editors and their staffs were doing the best job possible under the circumstances and given their paradigmatic predications. It is difficult to believe in a Popperian principle of falsification while living through such experiences. But believe in it we do. We also believe in the humanity of fellow scientists, who have intentions and wishes regarding their theories no matter what the evidence may suggest concerning alternative theories.

There is no single study in psychology that, totally by itself, is worth singling out as an unassailable collection of facts establishing some theoretical position *all at once*. We can fault the design, results, or interpretation of *any* research report. This fact is magnified for the more innovative research line because the referee is naturally brought up short as the theoretical language and conceptualization begins to shift from the familiar to the unfamiliar. In the case of RV research, we heard many times that the supposed research design did not *necessarily* test the theory behind it. This is actually a principle of LLT, in recognition of the affirming-the-consequent of an "If . . . then . . . " proposition fallacy (see Chapter 5, p. 181). But to the critic this becomes grounds for dismissing out of hand the evidence actually accrued. If the evidence *could* be accounted for another way it must be so accountable; hence, the theory as espoused (being unusual) is unreliable if not flatly invalid! At the very least, this would dictate that the "going paradigm" should not be tampered with, because there is strength in numbers and why not stay with the predominant position? This is the way in which many of our critics seemed to have reasoned. It is especially easy to think this way when the findings of any one study on RV are not immense, in the sense of a mean difference between experimental conditions; or, the p-level cited is not extreme.

The sheer power of a score value in the mean difference between groups can sometimes bear a hypnotic influence. Better to have a 10-score-points mean difference at the .05 level than a 2-score-points mean difference at the .01 level of significance. But even this is not infallible, for there are tough minded psychologists who make a virtue of the p-level *per se*. It is not unusual for a psychologist to consider .05 findings "weaker" than .01 findings, which in turn are considerably "weaker" than .001 findings. This reification of the logic of statistics is pernicious. If a critic has both the mean-difference and the p-level to consider, through a self-styled claim of "rigor" he or she can say "these are not very impressive results," when in fact the results amount to cross-validations of a line of theorizing that has been reaching all manner of statistically significant levels over a twenty-year period. Minute differences and .05 levels that are cross-validations of a series of experiments can be taken as a whole and, indeed, recalculated to high p-levels. But there can be no such understanding of the total if the point of view under consideration has been ignored by the psychologist reviewing the single study. In the latter case, each study is reviewed as if it were a new beginning. This has been the fate of LLT on countless occasions.

The unrealistic expectation for each experimental design to result in huge numerical differences at high p-levels is impossible to sustain when we enter the more subtle areas of research, particularly if it is done ecologically in a real-life setting. Of necessity, we must look for cross-validation of small but significant differences which may not look like much standing alone, but will gain in merit—and statistical significance—due to the consistency reflected over a series of developing research. We easily forget that a p-level is not a probability statement of the likelihood that findings will cross-validate in the real world of data collection. Experience with a series of studies on some topic soon teaches the researcher that .001 level findings often fail to cross-validate at this or any conventional level of significance; whereas a .05 finding, which stands up at even the .10 level (or *vice versa*) across different samplings, has much more to say for the theory under test in the long run.

Reactions and Questions

Over the years a number of objections have been raised and observations rendered concerning the shortcomings of LLT. In this section we review twelve of the more commonly heard reactions in a question-answer format. So that we may refer back to the numbered questions of Chapter 10 without confusion, the practice followed in this section will be to assign letters to the reactions and objections advanced by critics of LLT.

A) Why a "learning" theory? Learning theories are passé in psychology. Nevertheless, I am a personality (social, clinical, etc.) psychologist and have no interest in learning theory. I have my own theories to consider.

It is mildly shocking to discover how many psychologists openly dismiss learning theories today. Some of these rejections are based on the belief that modern cognitive theories somehow supplant the older learning theories; but many psychologists disdain all learning theories *per se*, believing that their professional responsibility is in "another realm" of explanation. As encompassed in our consideration of Question 3 in Chapter 10 (see p. 422), the reason we select human learning to focus on is to confront the extant explanations of learning at their own level of abstraction—views such as the Hullian, Skinnerian, interactive, etc.—and to offer thereby a teleological accounting of how it is that people manifest regularities in their behavior. What psychologists who raise Question A fail to realize is that even though they may concoct their clinical or sociopsychological theories, when it comes right down to the details of how behavior "works" there will be a definite tendency to account for such details through traditional mechanistic terminology.

This may not bother the psychologist in question. After all, if we can use terms like *purpose, choice,* and *intention* to describe people, what difference does it make if the underlying learning theory is a mechanical one? All that matters is that we can proceed to use telic meanings in our broader understanding. This is *not* all that matters to the logical learning theorist, who feels that it is essential to be as "ecologically" correct in the basic understanding of human behavior as possible. Telic terminology is not something to be "accounted for," but rather something to be taken seriously because it happens to represent the truth concerning how people behave (insofar as anything scientifically tested can be said to be "true").

B) Why must there be new jargon introduced, such as telosponse, precedent, sequacious, and so forth? This just turns people away from the ideas being expressed.

For over ten years an effort was made to use the language of traditional learning theories, as well as common-sense terms like *purpose* and *intention*. The problem was that our colleagues lost the teleology to the formal terminology of traditional learning theory; and when common-sense terms were used, they were viewed as informal statements having no serious weight of their own (see Question 10, Chapter 10, p. 446). It was painfully obvious that we needed new terminology stating exactly what we meant, and which could be clearly opposed to the language of mechanism. Our dilemma proved to be a special instance of the insights of LLT, because we were learning that there is no alternative to framing new terminology. All theoretical terms take meaning from precedents in sequacious fashion. Hence, if we use a term that takes meaning from efficient-cause precedents, it follows necessarily (sequaciously) that when we employ that term we will be expressing the efficient-cause meaning and not the final-cause meaning we are striving to convey. This is at least one of the reasons why our concept of reinforcement value has led to confusion (see p. 485).

The most difficult problem facing the teleologist is the fact that psychology has traditionally taken an extraspective theoretical stance in framing mediational theories (see Question 2, Chapter 10, p. 419). This means that even when they use informal terms, such as *purpose* and *intention*, most psychologists think of such meanings as variant forms of mediation—as the content of a cognitive process rather than as an alternative process of cognition (see Question 4, Chapter 10, p. 425). The meaning of a *predication*, an act of relating items together in meaningful organization from the point of view of a conceptualizing intelligence, is simply never an issue in such an understanding of cognition. If we now want to advance a predicational model from the introspective perspective, we are totally unable to do so. We are blocked by the limitations of our professional language, based as it is on an accepted model of cognition. Cognitive processing is always mediation and never predication. This is why the logical learning theorist requires his or her own terminology, to capture a process that simply does not exist in the present psychological lexicon.

C) *Logical learning theory is based on a circularity, because it contends that learning is possible only after it has already taken place.*

This objection rests on the assumption that learning occurs in the process of acquisition as graphed in a curve of learning. Logical learning theory contends that the process being graphed reflects the conceptualization, which is brought forward as a fixed given over (and within) time. The experimenter defines what (the criterion of) learning is, but since much of the subject's performance within the so-called error variance of the graphing procedure is premised behavior, it is held by LLT to be just as much a part of the learning process as is the line eventually traced. One of the first things the subject must learn (premise) is the ground rules the experimenter expects him or her to follow and then must comply with these or not (see Question 13, Chapter 10, p. 457). The graphing of such learning is "after the (conceptual) fact," but this does not make the explanation of learning circular. The measurement process must be decided on beforehand in line with experimental predictions; but in the scientific method, data are necessarily recorded in *post hoc* relationship to what has occurred in learning after sampling has been completed according to plan, subjects have attained their arbitrary criterion levels, and so forth.

D) If people have fixed premises that endow their experience with meaning, why would learning ever take place? Would not all people be rigid and inflexible?

Research evidence over the developmental years or through the course of psychotherapy is hardly indicative of great changeability in the behavior of human beings. Logical learning theory contends that insofar as people *are* unchangeable this rigidity is due to the telic determinism made possible through fixed premises—premises that have endowed life with meaning and, therefore, are very difficult to dismiss without some dramatic quantum leap taking place in experience. Whether a person changes or not, the contention of LLT is that we can determine the reasons for such eventualities only through a proper understanding of the premises being affirmed at the period of life under consideration. Psychologists who deny the role of premises in behavior have serious theoretical and methodological problems to confront, because the unequivocal drift of findings on human behavior demonstrates that awareness and intention are central features of this process, and that even erroneous premises can be brought to bear in experimental efforts with success (see Chapter 6, pp. 264–270). To continue pretending that something like telosponsivity is inconsistent with the facts on human behavior grossly misrepresents the empirical literature.

E) Is it good to base a psychology on innate factors such as affective assessment? Isn't this a concession to material-cause determinism? Don't you have to agree that in time biology is the ultimate cause of, and will account for, telosponsivity?

We must not confuse the structural ordering of physique, including all aspects of genetic patterning, with the ordering and patterning of mentation. As a *logical* theory of behavior, LLT contends that human intelligence lends pattern and order to events based on an inherited capacity to behave in this way. The logic (*logos* = order) made possible by the innate physical structure is no more determined solely by this palpable structure than is the patterning of human behavior determined solely by the fact that all people have the same general physical structure. There are vast differences, both intra- and intercul- turally, in the way people walk, talk, in what they do, how they play out their lives. To say that people innately affectively assess the ex- periential contents they bring into premises concerning the meaning of life is not to say that the resultant orders (meanings) are *themselves* innately determined. The determination here is not primarily mate- rial-formal but formal-final, albeit granted that the reason a body which can make judgments (orderings) of this sort exists is due to the mate- rial-cause determination of biological heredity. But the orderings-into- judgment have nothing to do with this material substance. If people were constituted of flour and apple juice rather than flesh and blood, the logical process they use to learn would remain unaffected (see Questions 9 and 11, Chapter 10, pp. 441 and 449).

The critic who believes that human logic is secondary to the ne- cessity of first studying the organic structure of the eye, ear, brain, etc., might well ponder whether it would be possible to learn anything about such physical structures without a presumption of logical order. Does not the biologist/physiologist approach his or her study based on some predicate assumption, organize the facts, and arrive at conclu- sions in the manner of a logical process? If we were to take away this logical framework, would it be possible to have a "biology" to reduce logic to? The logical learning theorist believes that the presumption of a biological substrate to logic is problematic. Someone should be studying this logical process because it has definite implications for all human behavior, including the scientific behavior of biologists.

F) *Where do affective assessments come from?*

This is the most frequently raised question by colleagues. What it *really* asks is: "Can you explain affective assessment in efficient-cause terms?" or "Could you tell us the efficient cause of the judgments made in affection?" To answer "No" to this reformulated question is a simple matter, believing as we do that a formal/final-cause construct is a legitimate explanation unto itself. But when one frames the issue in these terms, the logical learning theorist seems to be saying to the critic, "No, I don't know where these assessments come from; they are a mystery." Rather than take the more frank and sophisticated route and cast the issue in theory-construction terms, we have learned from experience that the best way to deal with this question is by answering in the following vein: We are born with the innate capacity to affectively assess (Question E), as we are born with the capacity to remember what we input from experience. Experience influences the grounds for making affective assessments. In this sense we can say that affective assessments come from "past experience."

However, it must not be assumed that past experience has itself gone without the predicate judgments of affective assessment. Affective assessments and their influence on the contents of the mind are not "produced" by experience, but make such experience possible by organizing it into the peculiar meaning that it has for the person concerned. We are back once again to Questions 4 (p. 425) and 11 (p. 449) of Chapter 10. Those who would view affective assessment as the product of past experience are predicating their view on the assumption that a cognitive *content* is under consideration rather than a cognitive *process*. Such theorists do not ask where the memory comes from, because they recognize this as a basic assumption of their (precedent) model, which attempts to explain all cognitive contents as previous inputs that have been stored in memory and, hence, can serve in the present as mediators (see Question 2, Chapter 10, p. 419). It follows logically (i.e., sequaciously) that if there is something like an affective preference "in" the cognitive process of memory at this point in time, it must have "come from" somewhere.

We noted in our discussion of Question 7 (Chapter 10, p. 434) that normative influences can be seen in terms of holding a common predication rather than as some huge reinforcement mechanism in the cultural heavens, manipulating all those who live below in efficient-cause fashion. The same point has relevance here. People live within a unified culture, taking on premises in common because this orders their existence and unites them into adaptive units with high morale. This means that there is little or no friction over what is to be "believed in" or taken on as a true predication. Children reared in this uniform setting are naturally going to take on the grounds for the sake of which their parents and then their peers have behaved. This is not always perfectly the case, of course, so that we have social outcasts and iconoclasts in every generation. But in the main, such sociocultural "shapings" take place. Logical learning theory demonstrates that the nature of such shaping is *not* as advertised in mechanistic accounts. People share common predications, they render common affective assessments, and they conform all the more to these commonalities as long as they find some advantage in the enriched meanings of their social group. This conformity rests on telic capacities, which are unlearned because they represent a process—not the content—of a process (see Chapter 10, Question 4 and 7, pp. 425 and 434).

G) *How do other sciences view the prospects of a teleological description of behavior? Do we run the risk of being ostracized from the scientific community if we reintroduce final causes?*

We have at various points throughout this volume presented evidence from other branches of science which suggests that our fellow scientists might be more ready to accept teleology than we psychologists now appreciate. The final answer probably comes down to who shall decide what the definition of science is. We have noted how Bacon's restrictions in natural-science description were extended from inanimate to animate nature. Yet, Bacon also said that final causation was relevant to theoretical description in metaphysics, the arts, and ethics. This is precisely the responsibility of a psychology of human behavior. It must account for an animal in nature that reflects its interests in artistic creations, morality, and the play of ideas in thought. Here is an unoccupied role in the sciences, one which a psychologist would be best qualified to fill. Furthermore, considering scientists' increased awareness of themselves as active "participators" in the creation of knowledge, any psychologist who decides to fill this role based upon the tenets of a rigorous humanism would seem to be on solid ground (see Prigogine & Stengers, 1984; Zukav, 1979).

H) *Psychologists are supposed to "control and predict behavior." Logical learning theorists claim that people are "free" agents. How can psychology remain a science and also hold that people are free to do as they please in behavior?*

This is a continuation of Question G, having to do with the definition of science. It is probably a measure of the ease with which psychologists have confounded their theories with their methods that so many of them continue to believe that their professional role is *literally* to "control and predict" behavior. This phrase—control and prediction—is central to the scientific method of validation. We accrue validating evidence to the extent that we control circumstances, prescribing a succession of events beforehand which we have come to believe will test our theoretical proposition, predicting the course of this alignment as our experimental hypothesis (Rychlak, 1981, p. 77). This telosponsive sequence is flawed by the affirming-the-consequent fallacy (see Chapter 5, p. 181); but it nevertheless forces us to put our ideas "on the line" in an open, objective, and repeatable test of validity. We move from complete reliance on a coherence interpretation of truth (procedural evidence and common sense) to a reliance on a correspondence theory of truth in practicing the scientific method.

But there is nothing in scientific practice which demands that we literally control people's lives, nor must our predictions always come out exactly as expected. In fact, due to the logical flaw implicit in validating evidence, even when we have predicted behavior with 100% accuracy, this does *not* mean we necessarily understand why it is true that such accuracy in prediction obtains. Sir Isaac Newton once admitted frankly that, though his concept of gravity predicted real events marvelously well, he did not know very much about its actual nature (Wightman, 1951, p. 101). We also make perfect predictions on the wrong assumptions; we learn after the fact how our good fortune actually came about.

Assuming that we do learn through the control-and-prediction sequence of validation that people are more likely to buy a product in a brightly packaged container than a dull one and we put this knowledge to use, precisely how are we "controlling" those who now reach for our attractive container? Have we somehow flipped the toggle switches of their minds so that they "respond" as efficiently caused "effects" to our manipulative interventions? Or, have these telosponding organisms rendered an affective assessment—based on discernible aesthetic grounds—and made a choice which is best understood in a formal- /final-cause sense? It should be clear to even the novice in research methodology that the "observed data" cannot decide this question for us. Psychology merely takes the mechanistic alternative out of a Newtonian tradition of reductive explanation.

According to LLT, if we want to predict what people might do in any situation, we have to sample in some direct or indirect manner just how they personally (introspectively) premise the situation we have in mind. If the situation calls for aggressive action and we know with certainty that our subject avoids confrontations with others, expressing the attitude that it is anxiety-provoking to have to force oneself on others, it is unlikely that he or she would change premises in this situation. Hence, we would expect the precedent non-aggressivity to extend sequaciously to the aggressive situation. The result would obviously be a so-called prediction of low probability for manifesting overt aggression. By asking this subject the right kinds of "objective" questions on a personality scale beforehand or gleaning from the subject's interpretations of a "projective" test item (an inkblot or a picture) the affection he or she has for certain behaviors in certain situations, we can extrapolate such an estimate given that our measuring instruments are reliably constructed.

Personality measures "predict behavior" because they capitalize on the precedent-sequacious nature of telosponsivity. Even though several factors enter, the person *always* creates the "criterion" behavior or the "dependent-variable" measurement along which we array him or her in relation to others whom we have also measured. We are not sampling a genetic pool. We are not sampling a reinforcement history. It would be much easier to predict behavior if such delineable and nondialectical aspects of behavior were being sampled. We are sampling meanings (patterns) that have been wound into life premises for the sake of which people behave. The resultant observed behavior is an instrumentality brought about sequaciously, thanks to the precedent affirmations of meanings tapped by the objective or projective instrument used. Therefore, the problem of accurate test prediction involves tapping the right premises for the right situation and finding out which of these subjects would truly want to take on and further his or her behavior.

Psychologists "control and predict" behavior in the context of verification or proof. As a methodological phrase, "control and prediction" makes sense. All scientists do this in validating hypotheses. But trouble begins to develop when we make purely theoretical claims about how "best" to shape people's lives or how their behavior is supposedly the result of natural laws which direct all things. There is no contradiction between human agency and predictability. We sometimes forget that in the "free-will" phraseology the second term refers to predictable, iron-clad determination that certain ends will come about. Rather than being an enemy to the "control and prediction" of behavior, LLT provides a clear explanation of precisely how scientists employ this phrase in methodological endeavors, as well as how people can be construed in predictable fashion without turning them into machines.

I) By acknowledging the affirming-the-consequent of an "If . . . then . . ."
proposition fallacy in science, you must now admit that the RV research conducted proves nothing with certainty for all time. Why then should we bother doing research at all?

The reason we do research is not simply to counter the views of our theoretical opponents in the description of behavior. We always appreciate that though we have evidence for our theory, the "other side" could probably explain it away in some fashion. (This goes both ways, of course.) But validation is important within our own line of thinking. It is important because only through such evidence can we become assured that our ideas actually stand up when we are not there to twist and contort them into the flow of behavior, as if they were relevant when they were not. But even more importantly, if we want others to begin looking at events as we do, we have a responsibility to transfer our ideas into methodological designs so that they can "get their hands wet" by plunging into the practical demonstration of that which we contend. Nothing is more convincing to our potential supporters than seeing that what we predict will happen actually does take place.

In LLT we say that a scientist is someone who moves to validate his or her theoretical contentions "some of the time," leaving open how often this is done (sometimes 100% and sometimes only 5% of the time, "depending"). Obviously, someone else—a student or colleague—could also accomplish this empirical testing for the theoretical scientist concerned. But if such tests are never made and if the results of such tests do not influence the theoretical generation under development, we would contend that this person is not scientific though he or she may be of immense importance in other realms of knowledge. It is always the types of *evidence* (and not the theories) used that stamp a body of knowledge as either scientific or nonscientific.

J) Humanistic psychology alienates comparative psychology.

If this is true, and we do not believe it to be so, the blame should be laid at the feet of those natural scientists who insist on uniformly keeping all behavioral description efficiently causal. This reductive requirement was taken as a predication because it seemed to promote a parsimonious line of theoretical description in psychology. We suggest an alternative principle of parsimony later. But more fundamentally, we wonder if a telic account at the human level actually downgrades the importance of comparative psychological study. If one looks into the literature of comparative ethology, for example, one can see that there is just as great a range of "pro-versus-con" attitudes concerning the acceptability of telic description in this speciality as there is in psychology (see Lorenz's [1970] critical analysis, pp. 351–370).

In recent years there has been a mushrooming interest in the question of animal awareness and purposivity (Burghardt, 1985; Dennett, 1983; Gallup, 1982; Griffin, 1981; Walker, 1983). The unidirectional demonstrative assumptions of organic evolution play a central role in this line of theorizing. The principle of retaining a continuity in the description across increasingly more complex levels of behavior has been especially important. The result is that we now have a virtual tradition of mediation theorizing (see Question 2, Chapter 10, p. 419). Dialectical oppositionality is not viewed as an aspect of the growing complexity in evolving animals. Even if it were, to retain the continuity of description from lower to higher organisms, we would undoubtedly find the natural duality of dialectic lost in the need to retain a demonstrative singularity and uniformity across all levels.

Dialectical reasoning can be seen as a so-called emergent on the ladder of organic evolution, but even in this case we would need to find some linkages with animals below the level of the human being. Since dialectical reasoning is seen as fundamental to telosponsivity, making the choice between "this" and "that" (i.e., "non-this") behavioral action possible, it follows that we would like to have evidence for oppositionality in the behavior of at least some animals other than *Homo sapiens*. There is no reason why we might not find early glimmerings of dialectical reasoning in such cases.

Of course, telosponsivity is an introspective construct, and it is surely difficult to obtain this perspective in work on lower animals. A subtle but equally difficult obstacle to learning about dialectical reasoning in lower animals is that no modern experimenters have taken this bidirectional cognitive process seriously. We cannot find what we do not look for. Both of these obstacles to discovering a continuity in dialectical reasoning across the animal kingdom are highlighted in an interaction that Patterson (1978) reports in her hand-signing work with the gorilla Koko. The problems associated with studying chimpanzees and gorillas using the hand speech of the deaf are well known, and this is not the context in which to contest whether or not these apes are "really" communicating with their trainers. But as an example of the failure to see what might be taking place before the observer's eyes, Patterson tells of Koko's disobedience and capacity to "play jokes" on her trainers:

She [Koko] seems to relish the effects of her practical jokes, *often* [italics added] responding exactly opposite to what I ask her to do. One day, during a videotaping session, I asked Koko to place a toy animal under a bag, and she responded by taking the toy and stretching to hold it up to the ceiling (Patterson, 1978, p. 443).

It does not require a stretch of the imagination to see in Koko's frequent behavioral negations of her trainer's intent an animal that is "taking a position" on what is being conveyed through hand signs rather than "responding" to them without such predication. Koko's behavior is consonant with telosponsivity. However, Patterson will never "observe" Koko's oppositionality as evidence for dialectical reasoning because she lacks a precedent theoretical framework making this evidence possible when it is manifest. Such observations would not be lost on the logical learning theorist. So, we do not accept the charge that a rigorous humanism would alienate comparative psychology; indeed, the logical learning theorist would find certain research on lower animals of great interest.

K) *Logical learning theorists employ an* ad hominem *argument when they insist on looking at the theorist's predications, the assumptions made by his or her school of thought, etc. Scientists cannot be concerned with such "personal" factors. They must deal in hard evidence alone.*

An *ad hominem* argument is one in which a position is rejected because of extraneous and irrelevant factors concerning the opponent "as a person." For example, if moved by religious considerations to argue for free will, the free-will argument fails because of this biasing motivation. A critic who believes that we employ *ad hominems* in LLT would presumably hold that in challenging the material-efficient cause predications of natural scientists, we are discrediting what they have accrued as hard data simply because they refuse to see but *two* causal meanings in the play of these data. Critics of LLT claim that as long as evidence is accrued for what these theories suggest, we have to deal with the empirical data as recorded and not dispel them by arguments from the precedent assumptions made before data were sought.

If LLT's only challenge to traditional natural-science description was to dismiss its evidence based on the narrow range of causation predicated in such a study, this criticism would have merit. But if, as we have demonstrated in this book, the evidence proffered by natural-science psychologists can be shown to subvert telic proofs (see Chapter 4, pp. 172–174) and a body of alternative data are presented to challenge such nontelic accounts of behavior (see Chapter 9), to contend that we are waging an *ad hominem* argument is entirely erroneous. The scientist who holds that the data are self-evident has probably already lost the case for humanism; because, as we have seen, the scientific method *per se* is a poor analogue for the "discovery" of anything but efficient-cause regularities (the S-R bind).

In another sense, however, we must admit that humanistic psychologists cannot entirely avoid an interest in the *ad hominem* tactic. Bias, sophistry, and related human characteristics of this variety surely should not be defined out of existence in humanistic psychology. We do not want to employ such arguments in our psychological experimentation, but neither do we want to pretend that they do not take place or that scientists in their personal outlooks are free of such irrelevancies. Humanistic psychology will always take a deep interest in the *hominem*.

L) Logical learning theory is unable to predict the direction that an intention will take. Simply calling one intention "understanding" and a second "action" does not salvage the inability of LLT to predict behavior. How can we have a scientific theory that admits from the outset its inability to predict events?

The last question we consider is probably taken by the critics of teleology as the *coup de grâce* for this approach to behavioral study. It is based on a definition of science which stresses prediction above knowledge. We have tried to show that scientists can predict something that they fail to understand (see Frank, 1957, Chapter 2, for the best discussion of this in the literature). If prediction is an aspect of evidential demonstration—as in the control and prediction of validation—there is no need for any science to presume from the outset that it will someday predict everything! A science which takes as a premise that everything is predictable has already precluded the possibility that some things may not be predictable, or that there are different forms of prediction possible. Such a science would not be objective, for it would be blind to certain alternatives suggested by the data.

In psychology those who believe that their mission is to "predict all behavior, all of the time" do so because they elevate their methodological skills above their responsibilities as theoreticians. They have turned psychologists into actuaries and have succeeded in propounding the mythology that actuarial prediction suffices for scientific evidence, when it clearly does not! As discussed in Chapter 6, one can study the identity behaving within the actuarial rule and find thereby that the reason the rule "works" is because of the premises this identity (self) brings forward, given the logic of the situation being confronted (final-cause determinism).

We do not deny that our willingness to assign responsibility to the individual means that at some point in the course of behavioral description we may say that the behavior is up to the person. We can give odds that the person will choose this way or that, but what he or she actually does is *in principle* not determined by our actuarial rule but by the person's decision (i.e., affirmed premise within a context of dialectical oppositionality). There is no other way for a free-will psychology to operate. Either one accepts a final-cause construct as the legitimate cause of behavior in at least some situations, or one does not. If the person patterns his or her brain processes in thinking about experience (see Chapter 9, p. 384) and conceptualizes that which he or she "behaves for the sake of" within a context of meaning with certain probabilities, then we must hold open the possibility that any one person may order the meanings (energic brain processes) *against the observed odds*. Put in other terms, the person may frame a situation in which we psychologists have empirically garnered data defining base rates for what is likely to occur as a "completely different" situation, thereby dialectically negating/invalidating our base rates. If we knew the person's precedent characterization of the situation, we could then successfully predict his or her behavior with some facility; but as long as he or she is a dialectical reasoner, we cannot always know the person's framing premise beforehand.

Practically speaking, the loss in prediction here is more than offset by the benefit received in knowing what "most people" will premise in this or that situation. (Psychometric tests doubtless capitalize on this factor as well.) The unusual orderings (premises) are swallowed up in the error variance. As a rigorous humanistic psychology LLT can predict behavior; it can be expected to predict about as much behavior as mechanistic psychology. But some of the predictions made by the humanistic psychologist in the experimental context will be of the following variety: "We predict that the person will base his or her course of behavior on an idea (predication) about what should be done in the experiment, even when what he or she then does is *incorrect* from the viewpoint of the experimental design." By proper examination of the error variance, we expect to improve prediction of behavior through an examination of why it was that the subject who failed to meet experimental expectations actually did so. This is, in effect, what Page (1972) did in his studies of subject awareness and cooperation (see Chapter 6, pp. 265–266). He improved prediction and provided support for dialectical reasoning at the same time.

Tenets of a Psychology of Rigorous Humanism

In full appreciation of the fact that LLT may not survive in the future of rigorous humanistic psychologies, we would like to conclude by giving ten tenets that logical learning theorists hope will be encompassed by any outlook that professes to speak for this image of human behavior. We trust that the rigorous humanisms of the future will advance the following beliefs.

1. *The precise nature of theory is different from the nature of method; and to attain the former from the latter is impossible in principle.*

Unless we take as precedently true that theory and method are two somewhat different enterprises, the efficient-cause frame of scientific method will continue to be entitized into our theoretical descriptions of behavior. Once this distinction is accepted, the responsibility of psychological scientists broadens. Not only must psychologists then garner scientific evidence, but they must continually refine their thinking and examine their assumptions concerning any "empirical account" they proffer concerning such data.

2. *Extraspectively framed methods are compatible with theories that are framed introspectively.*

The attitude of "I can only say in my scientific account what I have observed in my method" has led to a tautological rephrase of the experimental design in the discussion to follow. Though admirable as a starting point, "sticking to the facts" can mean that one refuses to get over into the perspective of the facts to see what may be going on there. Although improper for some aspects of scientific description, one can frame introspective theoretical formulations to describe the human being. It is perfectly logical to frame first-person accounts of behavior as we observe this behavior from a third-person perspective aimed at removing our influence in what transpires. We can look at "that behavior over there" for evidential reasons but explain the predicted course of events as "my" behavior in a theoretical sense (i.e., what *I* would do in *that* circumstance).

3. *It is profitable to view two or more identities—the experimenter's and the subject's—as contributing to every experimental finding on human beings.*

If we conceptualize a subject in an experiment as a noncontributing participant in the course of events, then obviously a humanistic account of his or her behavior will be difficult, if not impossible, to achieve. Experimental evidence now establishes beyond doubt that this passive view of the subject is fallacious. We must accept that in every experiment on humans there is an identity, which brings forward what we have called subject-contributed variables to the course of events. Recognizing the identity of the experimenter is also important, because in this way we remind ourselves that experimenters speak from certain points of view and that they have paradigmatic presumptions about what they can see in their data. Research experimentation on human beings is, therefore, a *relationship* between two identical organisms, each of whom has a "say" in the outcome. This takes us to our next point.

4. *Considered on introspective theoretical grounds, the principle of parsimony dictates that any descriptive formulation applicable to the experimenter must be applicable to the subject, and* vice versa.

Psychologists are accustomed to speaking of the importance of a parsimonious explanation of behavior. They never realize that parsimony in the physical sciences relates exclusively to extraspective accounts. Considered extraspectively, it makes good sense "parsimoniously" to describe human behavior in identical terms to the behavior of lower animals, which translates into material- and efficient-cause concepts. But what of introspective theory? In this case, we must obviously relate the (human) experimenter to the (human) subject and insist that the behavioral account of one person match up with the behavioral account of the other. If we look at how all experimentalists speak about *their* (introspectively framed) scientific behavior, what do we find?

The experimentalist thinks of himself or herself as proceeding on the basis of hypotheses which are drawn analogically from models of various types. These hypotheses are then tested through a series of rigorously prearranged steps which meet the experimenter's evaluative standards, and the resultant data are submitted to mathematical tests that rest on self-evident assumptions (e.g., the central limit theorem). The p-level employed is entirely arbitrary. The experimentalist is only too willing to describe his or her behavior in this manner. Yet, when he or she records the description of the empirical facts under observation, we hear nothing about analogical assumptions, prearrangements, evaluations, or arbitrary standards of judgment. The human organism "in the apparatus" or "in the research design" comes out as the tail end of an efficient-cause reinforcement history! Surely this is a most *unparsimonious* manner in which to proceed as a scientist. Henceforth, humanists will ask on the grounds of introspective theoretical parsimony that psychologists describe both their own and their subject's behavior in identical fashion.

5.   *In principle, there are N possible explanations for any observed factual pattern—experimental or otherwise.*

Though almost no theoretical physicist today is naive enough to assume that an *experimentum crucis* is possible—much less desirable—too many psychologists still harbor this eighteenth-century dream. Method will never suffice for theory. Although we may put down rules of thumb for theoretical descriptions such as our "new parsimony," no psychologist should delude himself or herself into believing that a method can be devised that will allow us to settle, once and for all time, which theory is representative of the nature of anything! More than one theory can—and always will—be true about the same observation. Even so, we should continue to submit our theories to the test of validation. This tenet is not framed to justify a flight from experimentation. We cannot have a rigorous humanism unless we put our ideas to empirical test in a properly designed experiment.

6.   *The word "control" in the phrase "control and prediction" refers to both the logic of experimental design and the subsequent manipulations carried out in the experimental context.*

The concept of controlling behavior has been given too narrow a definition in discussions of method. It is presumed that only an efficient-cause control is meant, when in fact the *logic* of scientific discovery—that is, the aligning of premises, the seeking of measurements, the testing of predicted results, and the drawing of conclusions—is heavily weighted with the meanings of formal and final causality. Even if scientists deny that they reason teleologically (employing final causation in the meaning of their behavior), they surely cannot deny that they follow ordered steps of logic; and logic is not an efficiently caused succession of events. Hence, at least some of the control in our control-and-prediction definition of validating evidence is *logical* control. This simply means we are never observing only efficient causes in our scientific procedures. We are observing what we have logically prearranged to see, and this is a succession of events that might easily be influenced by both our own and our subject's (precedent-to-sequacious) logic.

7. *To encourage broader conceptualizations by psychological theorists, it would be helpful to lengthen the line of development from theory to methodological test.*

Psychology suffers as much from a conscious effort to *avoid* conceptualizing data as it does from so-called loose conceptualization in wild theorizing. If there was a time when psychologists theorized wildly (and we doubt it), that time has surely long past. A conceptual research effort cannot be done successfully unless the psychologist and those who later review his or her work for publication accept the fact that a *logical line of development* is possible from the background conceptualization to the empirical test generated. This line can be lengthened a bit, as long as our logical controls remain clear and rigorous. By trying to see theory in method—in the experimental design—psychologists have guaranteed that conceptual innovation will never take place. It is not legitimate to dismiss an experimental study on the grounds that it failed to test its entire paradigm "at once" or that only a logical derivative of the background paradigm was tested in the actual experiment. Since validation is patterned on efficient causality, all that one can "see directly" as a paradigm in this ordering of events is the precedent Lockean model. To claim that this paradigm is the only one possible in evidence generated by scientific method is to *forego* true objectivity.

8. *Confine the use of the term "variable" to methodological discussion and remove it entirely from theoretical discussion.*

We must flatly deny that psychologists study variables. They study that which their theoretical predilections suggest are relevant to their professional interests. Once they have moved to the job of proving that which they believe, their theoretical ideas are brought to evidential life as variables. To speak of our constructs as variables once we have left the methodological context of verification serves no purpose and is actually detrimental to objectivity.

9. *In the realm of theory, readmit formal- and final-cause constructions as legitimate explanations in their own right.*

Humanistic psychology is impossible to attain without teleological description of behavior. This requires that we return to a style of description that has been disowned and ridiculed in natural science for over three centuries. Scientists threw out telic description 350 years ago for good and proper reasons. It created problems it could not solve, and those it did solve were achieved repressively. But we are untrue to our missions as twentieth-century scientists if we must, like sheep herded along by the weight of seventeenth-century history, continue to press a restriction on our theoretical descriptions which has been negating the person's humanity in the face of rigorous evidence to the opposite. The dialectic as metaconstruct provides a useful rationale for the telic description of human behavior.

10. *Distinguish between humanistic and humanitarian approaches to psychology.*

The growth of humanism in psychology would be encouraged if we could—once and for all time—dispel the view that one must be a humanitarian to propound a humanistic psychology. Because teleology has been associated in the history of thought with theology, moral philosophy, and ethics, an unfortunate contemporary development is the presumption that a humanist must argue for the more uplifting, quasi-religious side to man. Some psychologists who might honestly prefer to give a humanistic theory serious consideration in their work are dissuaded from doing so because of the "goody-goody" connotation of humanism. Humanism has been identified with encounter groups and social reforms of various types. It has sometimes been framed in an emotionalized manner by dewey-eyed advocates ready to press the *purity criticism* (see Chapter 5, p. 193) on any characterization put forth by an observer of behavior.

As we propose to use the term, *humanism* in psychology is a purely technical aspect of any theory under espousal. Humanists employ teleology in their description of a person's behavior. Mechanists do not bring such final-cause conceptions into their explanations. Humanitarians, however, whether of a humanistic or a mechanistic persuasion, are in the profession of psychology at least in part to improve the lot of humankind—either by raising the person's level of self-worth in a conceptual sense (e.g., Rogers, 1961) or by raising the person's level of material satisfaction in some managed fashion (e.g., Skinner, 1971). This distinction between the humanitarian and the humanist has the advantage of removing those unfair *ad hominems* Skinner and other behaviorists have had to confront, such as "fascist," "cruel," or "enemy of the person's dignity." One may disagree with the image of the person underwriting operant conditioning in behavioral modification, but surely the intent of such efforts is no less humanitarian than the sharing and caring of an existential encounter of the "me-thou" variety. In fact, behavior-modification advocates often use the term *humanistic* to modify their approaches, when they should more properly be using the term *humanitarian* (see Chapter 6). But the point is that one can be a humanist without having to bear the weight of sociopolitical or psychotherapeutic advance on one's shoulders.

We do not ask the reader to accept any type of humanitarian premise in order to do the work of a humanistic psychologist. We welcome the iconoclast and the misanthrope, as long as these individuals are prepared to submit their notions to rigorous empirical test. The aim is to be tough-minded without being close-minded. Let no one badger, cajole, or intimidate us into basing our theories on anything but what we personally take to be a suitable beginning model for the human condition. The scientific methodological devices are "there" for those who are ready to put forward the effort to prove what they theoretically believe in. We hope that this book aids the humanistic cause by framing a more satisfactory language of description to be used in this regard.

Summary

Chapter 11 is a summary of the book's total argument. We offer an interpretation of what has been accomplished, respond to several questions raised concerning the shortcomings of LLT, and then reaffirm those tenets of rigorous humanistic psychology that have emerged in the preceding chapters.

References

Burghardt, G. M. Animal awareness: Current perceptions and historical perspectives. *American Psychologist*, 1985, 40, 905–919.

Dennett, D. C. Intentional systems in cognitive ethology: The "Panglossian paradigm" defended. *Behavioral and Brain Science*, 1983, 6, 343–355.

Frank, P. *Philosophy of science*. Englewood Cliffs, N.J.: Prentice-Hall, 1957.

Gallup, G. G., Jr. Self-awareness and the emergence of mind in primates. *American Journal of Primatology*, 1982, 5, 237–248.

Griffin. D. R. *The question of animal awareness: Evolutionary continuity of mental experience* (2nd ed.). New York: Rockefeller University Press, 1981.

Jenkins, A. H. *The psychology of the Afro-American: A humanistic approach*. New York: Pergamon Press, 1982.

Lamiell, J. T. *The psychology of personality: An epistemological inquiry.* New York: Columbia University Press, 1987.

Lorenz, K. *Studies in animal and human behavior* (Vol. 1). Cambridge, Mass.: Harvard University Press, 1970.

Page, M. M. Demand characteristics and the verbal operant conditioning experiment. *Journal of Personality and Social Psychology,* 1972, 23, 304–308.

Patterson, F. Conversations with a gorilla. *National Geographic,* 1978, 154, 438–465.

Prigogine, I., & Stengers, I. *Order out of chaos: Man's new dialogue with nature.* New York: Bantam Books, 1984.

Rogers, C. R. *On becoming a person.* Boston: Houghton Mifflin, 1961.

Rychlak, J. F. Personality theory: Its nature, past, present and—future? *Personality and Social Psychology Bulletin,* 1976, 2, 209–224.

Rychlak, J. F. *A philosophy of science for personality theory* (2nd ed.). Malabar, Fl.: Krieger, 1981.

Rychlak, J. F. Logical learning theory: Kuhnian anomaly or medievalism revisited? *The Journal of Mind and Behavior,* 1984, 4, 389–416.

Skinner, B. F. *Beyond freedom and dignity.* New York: Knopf, 1971.

Walker, S. *Animal thought.* London: Routledge & Kegan Paul, 1983.

Wightman, W. P. D. *The growth of scientific ideas.* New Haven: Yale University Press, 1951.

Zukav, G. *The dancing wu li masters: An overview of the new physics.* New York: Bantam Books, 1979.

GLOSSARY

Affective Assessment, Affection: A transcendental telosponse—an innate capacity to judge (via dialectical division) the meanings of one's concepts, premises, and even telosponses, characterizing them as either positive or negative in meaningfulness. In contrast to emotions, affections are purely mental phenomena, ultimately *arbitrary* and up to the person who levels such idiographic judgments from his or her (introspective) perspective on life. Because the assessment is dialectical, there is no indifference point on the dimension of affective assessment, although there may be ambivalence. See also Emotions, Meaningfulness, Reinforcement Value, Telosponse, Transcendental Dialectic.

Affirmation: A special case of the telosponse in which one pole of a bipolar conception is precedently framed (presumed, held to be the case, "believed in," chosen, etc.). Affirmation also encompasses the framing of meaningful unipolarities in sensory experience by tautological means ("That is that." "That is a tree." "I recognize that face."). Affirmation can be further analyzed into unqualified, qualified, negative, and oppositional varieties. See also Meaning-extension, Premise.

Affirming the Consequent: A logical error growing out of an "If . . . then . . ." course of reasoning. It takes place when we reason "If A then B," and subsequently affirm "B" to conclude "Therefore A." In science it arises when we reason "If my theory [A] is true then my experimental data [B] will array as predicted" and subsequently affirm "My experimental data array as predicted" to conclude "Therefore, my theory is [necessarily] true." The theory is "true" with the proviso that an alternative theory might *in principle* also be validated by the observed data. See also Affirmation.

Agent, Agency: An agent is capable of behaving in consonance with, in addition to, in contradiction of, or without regard for sociocultural and/or biological stimulations. See also Final Cause, Introspective Theoretical Perspective, Teleology.

Analogy: Analogies are a special case of the tautology, in which only part of the identity between meaningful items obtains. There is always the disanalogous portion of the relationship to consider. Dialectical reasoning is reflected in the drawing of analogies. See also Dialectical Reasoning, One and Many Thesis, Tautology.

Arbitrary Behavior: Behavior that is telically determined due to frequent or unexpected shifting of the grounds "for the sake of which" action is then intended. Behavior continues to be premised but the meaning under affirmation and extension has been changed. See also Awareness, Dialectical Change, Freedom of the Will, Protopoint.

Association Value: A metric of meaningfulness based on a frequency theory of some form—for example, the number of associative bondings connecting to a verbal item or the number of people in a population who recognize an item as wordlike. See also Reinforcement Value

Awareness: Appreciation or cognizance of the arbitrariness in experience—knowing that something might be taking place in a life circumstance other than what is now occurring. See also Agent, Arbitrary Behavior, Dialectical Change.

Behavior: A global reference to the overt and covert activities of organisms, including the various physiological and biological functions of life. Behavioral descriptions in psychology vary: Some employ predominantly material- and efficient-cause meanings, and others introduce the formal- and final-cause as equally important.

Cause(s):   Derived from the Greek word aitia, which means the responsible factor in any descriptive understanding of the nature of things, including behaviors, physical bodies, and thoughts. The four causes include the material, efficient, formal, and final. These meanings serve as the predicates of literally anything in existence. They are highly abstract precedents from which meaning-extension occurs in human thought. See also Efficient Cause, Final Cause, Formal Cause, Material Cause, Meaning-extension, Precedent.

Choice: A nontechnical way of referring to the affirmation of bipolar conceptions. Arbitrariness and alternatives in behavior must necessarily arise due to the nature of telosponsivity. See also Affirmation, Freedom of the Will.

Conceptualize: Actively to organize experience in some way, to meet it at the level of sensory input with a creative capacity to order such sensations via patterns which constitute meaning and meaningfulness. See also Affirmation, Meaning, Meaning-extension, Meaningfulness, Pro Forma.

Decision: According to logical learning theory, decision is an unqualified affirmation in which the individual comes down to a specific course of (purposive) behavior which he or she then intends (action-intention). *See also* Affirmation, Intention.

Demonstrative Meaning: A way of describing meaning in which meaning relations are said to bear the characteristics of singularity, linearity, unidirectionality, and noncontradiction. *See also* Demonstrative Reasoning, Dialectical Meaning, Meaning.

Demonstrative Reasoning: Aristotle's construct in which it is claimed that the major premise in a line of logical reasoning is "primary and true" rather than simply opinion. *See also* Dialectical Reasoning.

Determine, Determinism: Refers to the limitation or setting of limits on events, including behavior. Framed in terms of antecedents (or precedents) and consequents (or sequacious events), *four* types of determinism can be described, depending upon which of the causes we wish to emphasize in our account. *See also* Cause.

Dialectic, Dialectical: *See* Dialectical Meaning.

Dialectical Change or Alternatives: Oppositional alternation of the pattern of precedent events, thereby affecting changes in meaning "for the sake of which" sequacious events occur. This can be contrasted with the linear, unidirectional change of efficient causation. Dialectical change relies on the formal- and final-cause meanings, introducing the *vehicle* for a reconstruction through the organism's capacity to reason oppositionally. *See also* Dialectical Meaning, Precedent Meaning, Sequacious Meaning.

Dialectical Meaning: A way of describing meaning in which meaning relations are said to bear the characteristics of oppositionality, duality, relationality, contradiction, and arbitrariness. There is often a uniting of opposites or contradictions into a new totality, described most frequently as the synthesis of a thesis and an antithesis. *See also* Demonstrative Meaning.

Dialectical Reasoning: Aristotle's construct in which it is claimed that the major premise in a line of logical reasoning is based on opinion (point of view, bias, choice, etc.) rather than on a fixed, primary, and true meaning. *See also* Demonstrative Reasoning.

Efficient Cause: Any concept used to account for the nature of things (including behavior) based on the impetus in a succession of events over time. Explanations of behavior based on energy pushes, gravity attractions, and the machine-like flow of "motion" are usually thought of in efficient-cause terms. *See also* cause(s).

Emotions: Bodily feelings that can act as physiological grounds for the appraisal of an organism's circumstances at any given point in time. Emotions are never arbitrary and can be thought of in nontelic terms. *See also* Affective Assessment.

Empiricist's Error: The tendency to accept what we observe and record in the experimental context as *necessarily* explaining (completely describing) what is taking place there. The most serious outcome of this error is when scientists confound their methods with their theories. *See also* Method, Theory.

Extraspective Perspective, of Theory: Framing theoretical explanations of things and/or events in the third person, from the convenience of an observer. Extraspective theory describes "that, it" rather than "I, me." Extraspection is the natural outlook for validation, but it is always possible to test introspective theory through validation by taking the line of development into consideration. *See also* Introspective Perspective, of Theory.

Final Cause: Any concept used to account for the nature of things (including behavior) based on the assumption that there is a reason, end, or goal "for the sake of which" things exist or events are carried out. Explanations that rely on the person's intentions, aims, or aspirations are final-cause descriptions of behavior. *See also* Cause(s), Teleology.

Formal Cause: Any concept used to account for the nature of things (including behavior) based on their patterned organization, shape, design, or order. Explanations of behavior emphasizing the style or type of behavioral pattern taken on are formal-cause descriptions. *See also* Cause(s).

Freedom of the Will, Free Will: A popular, nontechnical way of referring to the capacity human beings have to alter dialectically the meaning (pattern, order, logos, etc.) of premises that are affirmed at the protopoint. Before affirmation we can speak of freedom, and after the protopoint affirmation, we can speak of will (power). *See also* Affirmation, Dialectical Change or Alternatives, Protopoint.

Ground(s): The reference point or "that on the basis of which" or "for the sake of which" a telosponse is enacted. Grounds are necessary aspects of telosponsivity, which is made possible when the person who, utilizing such grounds, assesses (evaluates, judges, assumes, believes, etc.) the meaning encompassed and behaves accordingly. *See also* Meaning, Predication, Premise, Telosponse.

Homunculus: The "little person" who supposedly must be concocted to explain how it is that agency can occur in human behavior.

Teleologists are criticized for putting this smaller "being" within the human being, in order to "steer" or "direct" the psychic mechanism. This criticism rests on the invalid assumption that only "blind" efficient causes take place in human behavior. Telosponsive organisms need no homunculus to direct them about, but can "run themselves." *See also* Agent, Telosponse.

Humanism: A theory of behavior in which—knowingly or unknowingly—the theorist employs telic constructs. This is purely a technical theory-construction matter to be decided upon by analysis of the theory under consideration. *See also* Humanitarianism, Mechanism, Teleology.

Humanitarianism: A theory of behavior relying upon *either* mechanistic or humanistic formulations that seeks to improve the lot of humanity in some way—for example, by viewing people as more positively endowed with potentials, or to somehow improve their material status through behavioral manipulations of one sort or another. *See also* Humanism, Mechanism.

Idea: A repetitive patterning of meaning brought forward tautologically to extend what is predicated. This is essentially a Kantian view of the idea in which it is said to be *pro forma*, in opposition to the Lockean idea of a receptacle of the mind beginning in a *tabula rasa* state and then being "ordered from without." *See also* Kantian Model, Lockean Model, Meaning, *Pro Forma*, *Tabula Rasa*.

Identity: Refers to a continuity in mentation over time, and may be considered a variant definition of "self." *See also* Agent, Self.

Idiographic: An approach to the description of things (including behavior) based upon what is distinctive and unique about a single country, individual person, and so forth. The idiographic (*idios* = one's own) description always tries to capture what is individually distinctive about its subject matter. The study of history employs idiographic description. *See also* Nomothetic.

Intention: Behaving "for the sake of," hence enlivening or creating the purposive meaning of a concept in words, images, intellectual or affective assessments, and so on. Such intended meanings can relate to overt behavior (*action-intentions*) or be restricted to rational cognizance (*understanding-intentions*). Intentionality is as pure an expression of final-causation as possible. *See also* Cause, Final Cause, Ground, Purpose, Telosponse.

Introspective Perspective, of Theory: The framing of theories of things and/or events in the first person, from the outlook of an identity acting within them. Introspective theory refers to "I, me" rather than to "that, it." *See also* Extraspective Perspective, of Theory.

Kantian Model: The minority position in current psychology concerning a "model of the person." The significant features of this model are dialectical as well as demonstrative reasoning, *pro-forma* intellect, noumenal versus phenomenal experience, meaningful understanding, transcendence, and predication rather than mediation. *See also* Lockean Model.

Knowledge, Known: The "broadly conceptualized," hence fixed and repetitive (constant), grasp of experience permitting individuals to further meanings to their advantage in life. Although usually framed in a positive sense, knowledge of the limitations facing one in life is also possible. *See also* Conceptualize, Mind, Reason.

Law of Contradiction or Noncontradiction: The view that "A is not non-A" or that something cannot both be and not be. This assumption predicates demonstrative reasoning. *See also* Demonstrative Meaning, One and Many Thesis.

Learning: As viewed in logical learning theory, learning occurs when a meaning-extension is useful, and an individual thereby has an enriched understanding of experience based on the meaningful conceptualization he or she premised at the outset. This increase in knowledge may not be "true" as assessed by independent criteria—that is, people can "learn error." *See also* Logical Learning Theory, Reinforcement.

Lockean Model: The currently ascendant paradigm or "model of the person" in psychology. The significant features are demonstrative reasoning, *tabula-rasa* intellect, simple-to-complex ideas, constitutive mentality, mediation, and empirical determination of all that mind represents. *See also* Kantian Model.

Logical Learning Theory: A teleological (humanistic) formulation of learning which rests on both demonstrative and dialectical types of logical explanation. The question of its application to lower (subhuman) organisms is left open, but there is no intent to deny telic behavior below the level of the *homo sapien*.

Material Cause: Any concept used to account for the nature of things (including behavior) based on an assumed underlying, unchanging *substance* that constitutes them or "makes them up." Explanations of behavior based on genetic transmission or chemical elements are examples of material-cause description. *See also* Cause(s).

Meaning: A relationship between "poles" or points of reference, which in turn creates patterns with purposive and, thereby, intentional features. As a relationship, meaning can be analyzed in terms of its tautological unipolarities or bipolarities, extraspective or introspective formulations, and sign or symbolic functions. *See also* Intention, Purpose, Sign, Symbol.

Meaning-extension: The precedent-sequacious flow of meaning in the conceptualizations of telosponsivity, commonly referred to as the *inductive* and *deductive* knowledge of experience. As meaning-extension proceeds, the knowledge framed by the premised meanings of telosponsivity extends its range; and through the tautological identity of dialectical oppositionality as well as through analogical variations, it also changes and alters relations between items and referents as the individual comes to know more about the various meanings of his or her life experience. *See also* Dialectical Change or Alternatives, Meaning, Meaningfulness, One and Many Thesis.

Meaningfulness: The extent of significance, import, or general understanding an item or its referent has for the individual. Meaningfulness is thus a measure or metric of the extent of meaning—that is, clarity, centrality, import, value, and so on—the item holds for the individual or part-personality (e.g., ego, id) structure. Traditional measures of meaningfulness have rested on the frequency thesis (association value), but there are also nonfrequency metrics of meaningfulness (reinforcement value). *See also* Affective Assessment, Association Value, Reinforcement Value.

Mechanism: A theory of behavior in which—knowingly or unknowingly—the theorist fails to use telic constructs. This is purely a *technical* theory-construction matter to be decided upon by analysis of the theory under consideration. *See also* Humanism, Humanitarianism.

Mentation: Refers to what takes place when a person may be said to be thinking. In logical learning theory, mentation is used to stress the fact that a cognition is taking place, but that this is not simply the processing of information. Rather, mentation involves the initiating premises, the grounds, and the heuristics of thought that are influenced by an agent actively framing the direction that cognitive processing is taking. *See also* Affirmation, Agent, Ground, Meaning-extension, Predication, Premise.

Method: The means or manner of determining whether a theoretical construct or proposition is true or false. Methods follow theories, though one can work back from sequaciously defined methodological events to a new or modified precedent theory. Methods are vehicles for the exercise of evidence. There are two general types: (1) *cognitive* (or conceptual) method, which makes use of procedural evidence, and (2) *research* method, which uses validating evidence in addition to procedural. *See also* Theory.

Mind: The innate capacity to telospond in relation to ("for the sake of") patterns of meaning in experience, as well as to create these patterns anew through dialectical reasoning. Mind is fundamentally conservative, so that the flux of experience is fixed at the protopoint in conceptual premises which are then tautologized through telosponsivity in upcoming experience. The patterned effort to fix experience into certainty or knowledge is called *thinking*, and conceptualizations employed in this effort are called *ideas*. *See also* Dialectical Reasoning, Idea, Telosponse.

Model: A patterned structure or stylized means of conceptualization which the theoretician uses to order his or her thinking, or to bring it into agreement with an existing line of thought. *See also* Ground, Precedent

Motivation: According to logical learning theory, this is an evaluation of the relative advantage a premise (encompassing an intended "goal") makes possible in life, leveled by the person affirming this premise or by an observer who presumes to know what is being intended. To understand a specific *motive* (i.e., premised advantage, gain, reward, etc.) one must know the meanings encompassed in the affirmed premise, how these relate to other people, what the person has affectively assessed in the circumstance, and so on. *See also* Affirmation, Premise, Meaning-extension.

Nomothetic: An approach to the description of things (including behavior) based upon what is generally the case. The nomothetic approach relies upon common laws *(nomos* = law) which describe everything exactly the same way for all time. Unique distinctions are minimized and common trends are focused upon. The study of astronomy employs nomothetic description. *See also* Idiographic.

Objective: Refers to meanings that transcend the individual who propounds these relationships and hence may be grasped or understood by all individuals who seek to understand the meaning at issue. *See also* Meaning, Subjective.

One and Many Thesis: The view that all events are united (ordered meaningfully) and thus must necessarily be arbitrarily distinguished, one from the other. This assumption predicates dialectical reasoning. *See also* Arbitrary Behavior, Dialectical Change or Alternatives, Law of Contradiction.

Precedent: Refers to the ordering of meaning without regard for time considerations. A precedent meaning is one that goes before others in logical order or arrangement and establishes via the principle of tautology the course and nature of meanings which follow it (telic determination). *See also* Protopoint, Sequacious, Tautology.

Predication: The cognitive act of affirming, denying, or qualifying certain patterns of meaning in relation to other patterns of meaning. Predication always proceeds from a broader range of (precedent) meaning to a (sequaciously) narrower, targeted range of meaning. The resultant tie of meanings standing as a statement is referred to as a *premise*. *See also* Precedent, Premise.

Premise: A statement of meaning consisting of a predication through which human mentation is carried out. Premises need not be objectively "true," but when held to with conviction they can be taken by the person as "facts." *See also* Precedent, Predication.

Procedural Evidence: The kind of evidence which issues from the cognitive or conceptual method. We rely on procedural evidence (proof) when we believe in something because of its plausibility or consistency with common sense. This is sometimes called *theoretical proof*, but it is best not to mix theory and method language. *See also* Validating Evidence.

Pro Forma: For the sake of a form, organization, order, and so on, which when considered relationally is *meaning*. In logical learning theory this phrase is used to suggest that human mentation, rather than being *tabula rasa* and hence ordered exclusively by experiential input, contributes order (meaning) "to" experience. *See also* Freedom of the Will, Kantian Model, Meaning, Meaning-extension, Precedent, Protopoint, *Tabula Rasa*.

Protopoint: Refers to the anchoring point of meaning-extension at which affirmations are made. The terms *precedent* and *sequacious* refer to the ordering of meaning-extension at *any* point in the course of intentional behavior—for example, over the full course of a deductive or inductive line of thought. But the *initiating* point at which a *proforma* intelligence grounds its understanding or intends its purposes is the protopoint. In one sense this is the "first precedent" for any one line of intentionality, but all protopoint affirmations are sequaciously implied by ever more abstract conceptions. If there are "universals" in human intelligence, they would represent the ultimate protopoints of reason (as in Plato's Realm of Being). *See also* Freedom of the Will, Premise, Precedent, Self, Sequacious.

Purity Criticism: The charge that theoretical constructs sometimes force their descriptive referents (whatever is being described or explained) into arbitrary and distorted meanings, losing the essence of what should be captured meaningfully. The construct predetermines what will be stated about the object or action to which it is being implied rather than allowing the object or action to be understood in its "pure" nature. Purity criticisms range from mere cautions of this possibility to highly aggressive rejections of "all theory" in favor of a "spontaneous illumination" sent to the theoretically unprejudiced observer of the data *qua* data.

Purpose: The "aim of the meaning" of a concept, which is brought to mental existence by the intentional behavior of a telic organism. Purpose focuses on the formal-cause aspect of telosponsive behavior. When such patterned organizations that have an aim (point, significance, end, etc.) are intended by a conceptualizing organism, we can speak of the combined process as a telosponse. *See also* Intention, Telosponse.

Reason, Reasoning: Finding the grounds "for the sake of which" behavior (events, "happenings") may now be taking place, or, "should" ("could," "might") be taking place. *See also* Ground, Idea, Mentation, Mind.

Reinforcement: Best understood as a methodological design or as a stage in such a design. Logical learning theory would consider reinforcement as occurring when the learner's affirmations of meanings into premises (via predication) are successfully extended into ongoing experience. Thus, when understanding- or action-intentionality is made conditional upon a premise that truly (effectively, helpfully) conceptualizes for the individual employing it, we have a *reinforcement* of this premise taking place. It is likely to be used again and therefore enriched or embellished (learned). Positive reinforcements further meanings that are rooted in positive premises, and negative reinforcements further meanings that are rooted in negative premises. *See also* Affirmation, Learning, Predication, Premise.

Reinforcement Value: The operationalized measure (metric) of affective assessment achieved by asking subjects to prerate for likability materials (linguistic, pictorial, etc.) which they may be asked to learn or otherwise deal with in an experimental context. It is assumed that a rating of liking reflects positive affective assessment and a rating of disliking reflects a subject's negative affective assessment. Considered from its background theory, reinforcement value is a nonfrequency measure of meaningfulness. *See also* Affective Assessment, Association Value.

Self: A logical learning theory demands that there be a logician—an agent or identity—who brings forward the "logical weight" of meaning-extension in what is commonly called an inductive or deductive fashion. The *self* captures this identity feature of telosponsivity. To the extent that a behaving organism (1) *does* precedently and arbitrarily formulate meaningful premises at a protopoint "for the sake of which" it sequaciously behaves, (2) is conscious of doing so (i.e., has self-awareness), and (3) seeks to improve on the advantages gained from the use of such premises, to that extent can it be said to be self-enhancing in behavior or to be promoting self-realization. See *also* Affirmation, Agency, Meaning-extension, Telosponse.

Self-Reflexivity, Reflexivity: The capacity that human mentation has to turn back on itself, and therefore to know that it is knowing. See *also* Transcendental Dialectic.

Sequacious: Refers to the ordering of meaning without regard for time considerations. A sequacious meaning is one that follows or flows logically from the meanings of precedents, extending these in a *necessary* sense according to the principle of tautology (telic determination). Sequacious meaning-extension can be purely or partially tautological (i.e., analogical, metamorphical, etc.). See *also* Meaning-extension, Precedent, Tautology.

Sign, Signalizing Meaning: A nontelic formulation which holds that words are associated "stand-ins" for environmental items. Based on the frequency and contiguity of past experience, they are bonded together as input to mind totally without intention. See *also* Association Value, Mediation Model, Symbol.

S-R Bind: Limiting one's theoretical conceptions to an efficient-cause frame. This limitation is especially harmful to psychology when theorists fail to distinguish between their theories and their methods (of establishing proof), for then the independent-dependent variable (method) tandem is confounded with the stimulus-response (theory) tandem. See *also* Method, Purity Criticism, Theory.

Subjective: Refers to meanings that are somehow private, difficult, or impossible to circumscribe. Hence, the meanings are incapable of being extended beyond the behavior of the individual who has affirmed them. See *also* Meaning, objective.

Symbol, Symbolizing Meaning: A telic formulation which holds that words express the intentions of independently formulated ideas. See *also* Sign, Telosponse.

Tabula Rasa: The view that mind is as a "smoothed tablet" at birth and that all it subsequently manifests in mentation is input or etched upon it by external experience. *See also* Idea, Lockean Model, Pro Forma.

Tautology: A relation of identity, considered either extraspectively as redundant analytically true statements or introspectively as the premised meaning being extended from what *is* known to what *can be* known. Examples of tautology range from the repetitive rigidity of the stereotype to the partial identities of analogy, metaphor, allegory, synecdoche, and so on. Even more complexly, pure dialectical relations are tautological because one pole of the meaning necessarily delimits, hence enters into, the definition of the other, accounting for the One and Many Thesis. *See also* Analogy, Demonstrative Reasoning, Dialectical Reasoning, One and Many Thesis.

Teleology, Telic: The view that events are predicated according to plan, design, or assumption—that is, based upon purposive meanings—and therefore directed to some intended eventuality. In psychology this generates a humanistic rather than a mechanistic conception of behavior. *See also* Humanism, Humanitarianism, Intention, Meaning, Purpose.

Telos: The Greek word for end, goal, or grounding reason for the sake of which things exist, or an event (e.g., behavior) takes place. *See also* Final Cause, Ground(s), Teleology, Telosponse.

Telosponse: Taking on (premising, predicating) of a meaningful item (e.g., image, word, judgmental comparison) relating to a referent acting as a purpose for the sake of which behavior is then intended. Telosponsivity is the global term, subsuming intentionality and purposivity, which makes teleological description possible in logical learning theory. Human beings do not "learn" to telospond. It is an aspect of their very nature, a description of a process occurring in mind rather than how mind has been molded into performing from some other process. *See also* Intention, Mentation, Mind, Purpose.

Theory: A series of two or more constructions (abstractions, concepts, items, images, etc.) which have been hypothesized, assumed, or even factually demonstrated to bear a certain relationship, one to the other. *See also* Method.

Transcendental Dialectic: The Kantian conception suggesting that human reason can rise above and observe its own cognitive (conceptual) processes, permitting thereby a self-reflexivity in thought. *See also* Dialectical Reasoning, Kantian Model.

Unconscious Behavior: Logical learning theory views this as a kind of mirror-image telosponsivity in which the opposite or reverse of affirmations made with awareness are brought into play without the benefit of such alternative understanding. This makes unconscious behavior very literal and unbending (psychic determinism). *See also* Affirmation, Awareness, Telosponse.

Will: A telic conception which relies upon the necessity of a sequacious meaning-extension, brought forward in behavior as an intention. A willed action suggests a psychic determination, an intended end *(telos)* which the person wants to happen. *See also* Free Will, Intention, Sequacious, Teleology, Telosponse.

BIBLIOGRAPHY

Abramson, Y. *Reinforcement value: An idiographic approach to meaningfulness.* Unpublished doctoral dissertation. St. Louis: St. Louis University, 1967.

Abramson, Y., Tasto, D. L., & Rychlak, J. F. Nomothetic vs. idiographic influences of association value and reinforcement value on learning. *Journal of Experimental Research in Personality,* 1969, **4,** 65–71.

Adams, D. K. The inference of mind. *Psychological Review,* 1928, **35,** 235–252.

Adams, D. K. Note on method. *Psychological Review,* 1937, **44,** 212–218.

Adler, A. *Social interest: A challenge to mankind.* New York: Capricorn, 1964.

Alexander, F. G., & Selesnick, S. T. *The history of psychiatry: An evaluation of psychiatric thought and practice from prehistoric times to the present.* New York: Harper & Row, 1966.

Allport, G. W. *Personality: A psychological interpretation.* New York: Holt, 1937.

Allport, G. W. Personalistic psychology as a science: A reply. *Psychological Review,* 1946, **53,** 132–135.

Angell, J. R. The relations of structural and functional psychology to philosophy. *Philosophical Review,* 1903, **12,** 203–243.

Angell, J. R. The province of functional psychology. *Psychological Review,* 1907, **2,** 61–91.

APA Monitor, April 1974, **5** (4). Washington, D.C.: American Psychological Association, 1974.

Apao, W. K. *Reinforcement and two kinds of meaningfulness measures in paired-associates learning.* Unpublished master's thesis. West Lafayette, Ind.: Purdue University, 1976.

Apao, W. K. *Affect and memory: Tests of the serial position effects.* Unpublished doctoral dissertation. West Lafayette, Ind.: Purdue University, 1979.

Apter, M. J. The possibility of a structural phenomenology: The case of reversal theory. *Journal of Phenomenological Psychology,* 1981, **12,** 173–187.

Apter, M. J. *The experience of motivation: The theory of psychological reversals.* New York: Academic Press, 1982.

Apter, M. J. Reversal theory and personality: A review. *Journal of Research in Personality,* 1984, **18,** 265–288.

Apter, M. J., & Fontana, D. Overview and discussion. In M. J. Apter, D. Fontana, & S. Murgatroyd (Eds.), *Reversal theory: Applications and developments.* Cardiff, Wales: University College Press, 1985. Pp. 179–186.

Archer, E. J. Re-evaluation of the meaningfulness of all possible CVC trigrams. *Psychological Monographs,* 1960, **74** No. 10 (Whole No. 497).

Aristotle. *Metaphysics.* In R. M. Hutchins (Ed.), *Great books of the western world* (Vol. 8). Chicago: Encyclopedia Britannica, 1952. Pp. 499–626.

Aristotle. *On memory and reminiscence.* In R. M. Hutchins (Ed.), *Great books of the western world* (Vol. 8). Chicago: Encyclopedia Britannica, 1952. Pp. 690–701.

Aristotle. *Physics.* In R. M. Hutchins (Ed.), *Great books of the western world* (Vol. 8). Chicago: Encyclopedia Britannica, 1952. Pp. 257–355.

Aristotle. *Posterior analytics.* In R. M. Hutchins (Ed.), *Great books of the western world* (Vol. 8). Chicago: Encyclopedia Britannica, 1952. Pp. 95–137.

Arnold, M. B. *Emotion and personality.* New York: Columbia University Press, 1960.

Arnold, M. B. (Ed.), *Feelings and emotions.* New York: Academic Press, 1970.

August, G. J., & Rychlak, J. F. Role of intelligence and task difficulty in the affective learning styles of children. *Journal of Educational Psychology,* 1978, **70,** 406–413.

August, G. J., Rychlak, J. F., & Felker, D. W. Affective assessment, self-concept, and the verbal learning styles of fifth-grade children. *Journal of Educational Psychology,* 1975, **67,** 801–806.

Bakan, D. Learning and the principle of inverse probability. *Psychological Review,* 1953, **60,** 360–370.

Bakan, D. Learning and the scientific enterprise. *Psychological Review,* 1953, **60,** 45–49.

Bakan, D. A reconsideration of the problem of introspection. *Psychological Bulletin,* 1954, **51,** 105–118.

Bakan, D. Clinical psychology and logic. *American Psychologist,* 1956, **11,** 655–662.

Ballard, J. A. *Affective assessment in a psi task.* Unpublished doctoral dissertation. West Lafayette, Ind.: Purdue University, 1983.

Bandura, A. *Principles of behavior modification.* New York: Holt, Rinehart & Winston, 1969.

Bandura, A. Behavior theory and the models of man. *American Psychologist,* 1974, **29,** 859–869.

Bandura, A. Self-efficacy: Toward a unifying theory of behavioral change. *Psychological Review,* 1977, **84,** 191–215.

Bandura, A. *Social learning theory.* Englewood Cliffs, N.J.: Prentice-Hall, 1977.

Bandura, A. The self system in reciprocal determinism. *American Psychologist,* 1978, **33,** 344–358.

Bandura, A. Self-referent mechanisms in social learning theory. *American Psychologist,* 1979, **34,** 439–440.

Bandura, A., Ross, D., & Ross, S. Imitation of film mediated aggressive models. *Journal of Abnormal and Social Psychology,* 1963, **66,** 3–11.

Bandura, A., Ross, D., & Ross, S. Vicarious reinforcement and imitative learning. *Journal of Abnormal and Social Psychology,* 1963, **67,** 601–607.

Bandura, A., & Simon, K. M. The role of proximal intentions in self-regulation of refractory behavior. *Cognitive Therapy and Research,* 1977, **1,** 177–193.

Barron, F. S. An ego strength scale which predicts responses to psychotherapy. *Journal of Consulting Psychology,* 1953, **17,** 327–333.

Bartlett, F. C. *Remembering.* Cambridge: The University Press, 1932.

Bartlett, F. C. *Thinking.* New York: Basic Books, 1958.

Becker, H., & Barnes, H. E. *Social thought from lore to science* (2 vols.). Washington, D.C.: Harren, 1952.

Bellezza, F. S. The self as a mnemonic device: The role of internal cues. *Journal of Personality and Social Psychology*, 1984, **47**, 506–515.

Bem, D. Self-perception: An alternative interpretation of cognitive dissonance phenomena. *Psychological Review*, 1967, **74**, 183–200.

Bem, D. Self-perception theory. In L. Berkowitz (Ed.), *Advances in experimental social psychology* (Vol. 6). New York: Academic Press, 1972. Pp. 4–46.

Berg, I. A. Deviant responses and deviant people: The formulation of the deviation hypothesis. *Journal of Counseling Psychology*, 1957, **4**, 159.

Bergmann, G., & Spence, K. Operationism and theory in psychology. *Psychological Review*, 1941, **48**, 1–14.

Binswanger, L. *Being-in-the-world* (translated and with a critical introduction by J. Needleman). New York: Basic Books, 1963.

Black, J. B., & Bern, H. Causal coherence and memory for events in narratives. *Journal of Verbal Learning and Verbal Behavior*, 1981, **20**, 267–275.

Black, J. B., & Bower, G. H. Story understanding as problem solving. *Poetics*, 1980, **9**, 223–250.

Blumenthal, A. L. A reappraisal of Willhelm Wundt. *American Psychologist*, 1975, **30**, 1081–1088.

Boden, M. A. *Artificial intelligence and natural man*. New York: Basic Books, 1977.

Boland, G. C. *The relationship of personality adjustment to the learning of material having connotative and associative meaningfulness*. Unpublished doctoral dissertation. St. Louis: St. Louis University, 1970.

Boneau, C. A. Paradigm regained? Cognitive behaviorism restated. *American Psychologist*, 1974, **29**, 297–309.

Boring, E. G. Mind and mechanism. *American Journal of Psychology*, 1946, **54**, 173–192.

Boring, E. G. *A history of experimental psychology* (2nd ed.). New York: Appleton-Century-Crofts, 1950.

Boss, M. *Psychoanalysis and daseinsanalysis*. New York: Basic Books, 1963.

Bousfield, W. A. The occurrence of clustering in the free recall of randomly arranged associates. *Journal of General Psychology*, 1953, **49**, 229–240.

Bower, G. H., & Gilligan, S. G. Remembering information related to one's self. *Journal of Research in Personality*, 1979, **13**, 420–432.

Bowers, K. S. Situationism in psychology: An analysis and a critique. *Psychological Review*, 1973, **80**, 307–336.

Bradshaw, G. L., & Anderson, J. R. Elaborative encoding as an explanation of levels of processing. *Journal of Verbal Learning and Verbal Behavior*, 1982, **21**, 165–174.

Bransford, J. D., & Franks, J. J. The abstraction of linguistic ideas. *Cognitive Psychology*, 1971, **2**, 331–350.

Brehm, J. W. *A theory of psychological reactance*. New York: Academic Press, 1966.

Brehm, J. W. *Responses to loss of freedom: A theory of psychological reactance*. Morristown, N.J.: General Learning Press, 1972.

Brentano, F. *Psychology from an empirical standpoint*. New York: Humanities, 1973.

Breuer, J. Theoretical selection, section III. In J. Strachey (Ed.), *The standard edition of the complete psychological works of Sigmund Freud* (Vol. II). London: Hogarth, 1955. Pp. 185–251.

Breuer, J., & Freud, S. On the Psychical mechanism of hysterical phenomena: Preliminary communication. In J. Strachey (Ed.), *The standard edition of the complete psychological works of Sigmund Freud* (Vol. II). London: Hogarth, 1955. Pp. 1–17.

Brewer, W. F. There is no convincing evidence for operant or classical conditioning in adult humans. In W. B. Weimer & D. S. Palermo (Eds.), *Cognition and the symbolic processes*. Hillsdale, N.J.: Lawrence Erlbaum, 1974. Pp. 1–42.

Brickman, P., Redfield, J., Harrison, A. A., & Crandall, R. Drive and predisposition as factors in the attitudinal effects of mere exposure. *Journal of Experimental Social Psychology*, 1972, **8**, 31–34.

Bridgman, P. W. *The way things are*. Cambridge, Mass.: Harvard University Press, 1959.

Broadbent, D. E. Flow of information within the organism. *Journal of Verbal Learning and Verbal Behavior*, 1963, **2**, 34–39.

Bronowski, J. *The common sense of science*. Cambridge, Mass.: Harvard University Press, 1958.

Bugaj, A. M. *The role of dialectical meaning in impression formation*. Unpublished master's thesis. West Lafayette, Ind.: Purdue University, 1981.

Bugaj, A. M. *Affect and the cognitive organization of social information*. Unpublished doctoral dissertation. West Lafayette, Ind.: Purdue University, 1984.

Bugental, J. F. T. Humanistic psychology: A new break-through. *American Psychologist*, 1963, **18**, 563–567.

Bunch, M. E., & Wientge, K. The relative susceptibility of pleasant, unpleasant, and indifferent material to retroactive inhibition. *Journal of General Psychology*, 1933, **9**, 157–178.

Bunge, M. *The mind-body problem*. New York: Oxford University Press, 1980.

Burghardt, G. M. Animal awareness: Current perceptions and historical perspectives. *American Psychologist*, 1985, **40**, 905–919.

Burtt, E. A. *The metaphysical foundations of modern physical science* (rev. ed.). Garden City, N.Y.: Doubleday, 1955.

Calder, B. J., & Staw, B. M. Self-perception of intrinsic and extrinsic motivation. *Journal of Personality and Social Psychology*, 1975, **31**, 599–605.

Caldwell, W. Professor Titchener's view of the self. *Psychological Review*, 1898, **5**, 401–408.

Caldwell, W. The postulates of a structural psychology. *Psychological Review*, 1899, **6**, 187–191.

Calkins, M. W. A reconciliation between structural and functional psychology. *Psychological Review*, 1906, **13**, 61–81.

Calverton, V. F. The rise of objective psychology. *Psychological Review*, 1924, **31**, 418–426.

Cameron, N., & Rychlak, J. F. *Personality development and psychopathology: A dynamic approach* (2nd ed.). Boston: Houghton Mifflin, 1985.

Campbell, D. T., & Stanley, J. C. *Experimental and quasi experimental designs for research*. Chicago: Rand McNally, 1963.

Campbell, K. A. *Affective assessment and awareness in the operant conditioning of verbal response*. Unpublished doctoral dissertation. West Lafayette, Ind.: Purdue University, 1983.

Cantor, G. N. Children's "like-dislike" ratings of familiarized and unfamiliarized visual stimuli. *Journal of Experimental Child Psychology*, 1935, **6**, 651–657.

Carlson, R. Where is the person in personality research? *Psychological Bulletin*, 1971, **75**, 203–219.

Carter, H. D. Effects of emotional factors upon recall. *Journal of Psychology*, 1935, **1**, 49–59.

Carter, H. D. Emotional factors in verbal learning. *Journal of Educational Psychology*, 1937, **28**, 101–108.

Carter, H. D., & Jones, H. E. A further study of affective factors in learning. *Journal of Genetic Psychology*, 1937, **48**, 126–133.

Cassirer, E. *An essay on man.* Garden City, N.Y.: Doubleday, 1944.

Cassirer, E. *The problem of knowledge.* New Haven: Yale University Press, 1950.

Cattell, R. B. Psychological measurement: Normative, ipsative, interactive. *Psychological Review*, 1944, **51**, 292–303.

Chan, W.-T. Chinese theory and practice, with special reference to humanism. In C. A. Moore (Ed.), *The Chinese mind: Essentials of Chinese philosophy and culture.* Honolulu: University of Hawaii Press, 1967. Pp. 11–30.

Chan, W.-T. The story of Chinese philosophy. In C. A. Moore (Ed.), *The Chinese mind: Essentials of Chinese philosophy and culture.* Honolulu: University of Hawaii Press, 1967. Pp. 31–76.

Chaplin, J. P., & Krawiec, T. S. *Systems and theories of psychology.* New York: Holt, Rinehart & Winston, 1960.

Cohen, L. Our developing knowledge of infant perception and cognition. *American Psychologist*, 1979, **34**, 894–899.

Colaizzi, P. F. An analysis of the learner's perception of learning material at various phases of a learning process. *Review of Existential Psychology and Psychiatry*, 1967, **7**, 95–105.

Colaizzi, P. F. *Reflection and research in psychology: A phenomenological study of learning.* Dubuque, Iowa: Kendall/Hunt, 1973.

Conant, J. B. *Modern science and modern man.* Garden City, N.Y.: Doubleday Anchor, 1952. (Originally published, New York: Columbia University Press, 1929.)

Cooley, C. H. *Human nature and the social order.* New York: Scribner's, 1902.

Creelman, M. B. *The experimental investigation of meaning: A review of the literature.* New York: Springer, 1966.

Cromwell, R. L. Factors in the serial recall of names and acquaintances. *Journal of Abnormal and Social Psychology*, 1956, **56**, 63–67.

Cronbach, L. J. Beyond the two disciplines of scientific psychology. *American Psychologist*, 1975, **30**, 116–127.

Danner, F. W., & Lonky, E. A cognitive-developmental approach to the effects of rewards on intrinsic motivation. *Child Development*, 1981, **52**, 1043–1052.

Darwin, C. R. *The descent of man.* In R. M. Hutchins (Ed.), *Great books of the western world* (Vol. 49). Chicago: Encyclopedia Britannica, 1952.

Datta, D. M. Epistemological methods in Indian philosophy. In C. A. Moore (Ed.), *The Indian mind: Essentials of Indian philosophy and culture.* Honolulu: University of Hawaii Press, 1967. Pp. 118–135.

David, K. L. *The relationship of replacement condition and an affective dimension of meaningfulness to rate of learning.* Unpublished master's thesis. West Lafayette, Ind.: Purdue University, 1977.

De Charms, R. *Personal causation: The internal determinants of behavior.* New York: Academic Press, 1968.

Deci, E. L. Intrinsic motivation, extrinsic reinforcement, and inequity. *Journal of Personality and Social Psychology*, 1972, **22**, 113–120.

Deci, E. L. *The psychology of self-determination.* Lexington, Mass.: D.C. Heath, 1980.

Deci, E. L., & Ryan, R. M. *Intrinsic motivation and self-determination in human behavior.* New York: Plenum Press, 1985.

DeNike, L. D. The temporal relationship between awareness and performance in verbal conditioning. *Journal of Experimental Psychology*, 1964, **68**, 521–529.

Dennett, D. C. Intentional systems in cognitive ethology: The "Panglossian paradigm" defended. *Behavioral and Brain Science*, 1983, **6**, 343–355.

Descartes, R. *Rules for the direction of mind and Discourse on method.* In R. M. Hutchins (Ed.), *Great books of the western world* (Vol. 31). Chicago: Encyclopedia Britannica, 1952.

Dollard, J., & Miller, N. E. *Personality and psychotherapy: An analysis in terms of learning, thinking, and culture.* New York: McGraw-Hill, 1950.

Dreyfus, H. L. *What computers can't do: The limits of artificial intelligence.* New York: Harper & Row, 1979.

Dulany, D. Awareness, rules, and propositional control: A confrontation with S-R behavior theory. In T. R. Dixon & D. L. Horton (Eds.), *Verbal behavior and general behavior theory.* Englewood Cliffs, N.J.: Prentice-Hall, 1968.

Dulany, D. E. The place of hypotheses and intentions: An analysis of verbal control in verbal conditioning. In C. W. Eriksen (Ed.), *Behavior and awareness: A symposium of research and interpretation.* Durham, N.C.: Duke University Press, 1962. Pp. 102–129.

Dunlap, K. A revision of the fundamental law of habit formation. *Science*, 1928, **67**, 360–362.

Ebbinghaus, H. *Memory: A contribution to experimental psychology.* New York: Dover, 1964.

Eccles, J. C. Part II in K. R. Popper & J. C. Eccles, *The self and its brain.* New York: Springer-Verlag, 1977. Pp. 225–421.

Eddington, A. *A philosophy of physical science.* Ann Arbor: University of Michigan Press, 1958.

Edwards, A. L. *The Edwards Personal Preference Schedule.* New York: Psychological Corporation, 1959.

Edwards, P. (Editor-in-Chief) *The encyclopedia of philosophy* (8 vols.). New York: Macmillan and Free Press, 1967.

Einstein, A. Ernst Mach. *Physikalische Zeitschrift*, 1916, **17**, 101–104.

Einstein, A. *Essays in science.* New York: Philosophical Library, 1934.

Engels, F. *Dialectics of nature.* Moscow: Progress, 1966.

English, H. B., & English, A. C. *A comprehensive dictionary of psychological and psychoanalytical terms.* London: Longmans, Green, 1958.

Evans, R. I. *B. F. Skinner: The man and his ideas.* New York: Dutton, 1968.

Evans, R. I. *Dialogue with B. F. Skinner.* New York: Praeger, 1981.

Eves, H. *An introduction to the history of mathematics* (3rd ed.). New York: Holt, Rinehart & Winston, 1969.

Farber, I. E. The things people say to themselves. *American Psychologist*, 1963, **18**, 185–197.

Fazio, R. H. On the self-perception explanation of the overjustification effect: The role of the salience of initial attitude. *Journal of Experimental Social Psychology*, 1981, **17**, 417–426.

Fehl, N. E. *History and society*. Hong Kong: Chung Chi College Publication, 1964.

Fernberger, S. W. Behavior versus introspective psychology. *Psychological Review*, 1922, **29**, 409–413.

Festinger, L. A theory of social comparison processes. *Human Relations*, 1954, **7**, 117–140.

Festinger, L. *A theory of cognitive dissonance*. Evanston, Ill.: Row, Peterson, 1957.

Festinger, L., & Carlsmith, J. M. Cognitive consequences of forced compliance. *Journal of Abnormal and Social Psychology*, 1959, **58**, 203–210.

Feuer, L. S. *Einstein and the generations of science*. New York: Basic Books, 1974.

Fisher, R. P., & Craik, F. I. M. The effects of elaboration on recognition memory. *Memory & Cognition*, 1980, **8**, 400–404.

Fitts, W. H. *Tennessee Department of Mental Health Self-Concept Scale*. Nashville, Tenn.: Counselor Recordings & Tests, 1965.

Forbes, R. J., & Dijksterhuis, E. J. *A history of science and technology* (2 vols.). Baltimore: Penguin Books, 1963.

Frank, P. *Philosophy of science*. Englewood Cliffs, N.J.: Prentice-Hall, 1957.

Frazer, J. G. *The new golden bough* (abridged by T. H. Gaster). Great Meadows, N.J.: Phillips, 1959.

Freud, S. *The interpretation of dreams*. In J. Strachey (Ed.), *The standard edition of the complete psychological works of Sigmund Freud* (Vols. IV & V). London: Hogarth, 1953.

Freud, S. *The origins of psycho-analysis, letters to Wilhelm Fliess, drafts and notes: 1887–1902*. New York: Basic Books, 1954.

Freud, S. The psychotherapy of hysteria. In J. Strachey (Ed.), *The standard edition of the complete psychological works of Sigmund Freud* (Vol. II). London: Hogarth, 1955. Pp. 254–305.

Freud, S. On narcissism: An introduction. In J. Strachey (Ed.), *The standard edition of the complete psychological works of Sigmund Freud* (Vol. XIV). London: Hogarth, 1957. Pp. 67–102.

Freud, S. Some general remarks on hysterical attacks. In J. Strachey (Ed.), *The standard edition of the complete psychological works of Sigmund Freud* (Vol. IX). London: Hogarth, 1959. Pp. 227–234.

Freud, S. The psychopatholgy of everyday life. In J. Strachey (Ed.), *The standard edition of the complete psychological works of Sigmund Freud* (Vol. VI). London: Hogarth, 1960.

Freud, S. The aetiology of hysteria. In J. Strachey (Ed.), *The standard edition of the complete psychological works of Sigmund Freud* (Vol. III). London: Hogarth, 1962. Pp. 182–221.

Freud, S. The neuro-psychoses of defense. In J. Strachey (Ed.), *The standard edition of the complete psychological works of Sigmund Freud* (Vol. III). London: Hogarth, 1962. Pp. 41–61.

Freud, S. A case of successful treatment by hypnotism. In J. Strachey (Ed.), *The standard edition of the complete psychological works of Sigmund Freud* (Vol. I). London: Hogarth, 1966. Pp. 115–128.

Freud, S. Project for a scientific psychology. In J. Strachey (Ed.), *The standard edition of the complete psychological works of Sigmund Freud* (Vol. I). London: Hogarth, 1966. Pp. 283–397.

Gallup, G. G., Jr. Self-awareness and the emergence of mind in primates. *American Journal of Primatology*, 1982, **5**, 237–248.

Garza, R. T. *Affective and associative meaningfulness in the learning styles of Chicano and Anglo college students.* Unpublished doctoral dissertation. West Lafayette, Ind.: Purdue University, 1975.

Gazzaniga, M. S. *The bisected brain.* New York: Appleton-Century-Crofts, 1970.

Gergen, K. J. The social constructionist movement in modern psychology. *American Psychologist*, 1985, **40**, 266–275.

Giorgi, A. *Psychology as a human science: A phenomenologically based approach.* New York: Harper & Row, 1970.

Giorgi, A. Toward phenomenologically based research in psychology. *Journal of Phenomenological Psychology*, 1970, **1**, 75–98.

Giorgi, A. Phenomenology and the foundational problems of psychology. In W. J. Arnold & J. K. Cole (Eds.), *Nebraska symposium on motivation* (Vol. 22). Lincoln: University of Nebraska Press, 1975.

Giorgi, A. Sketch of a psychological phenomenological method. In A. Giorgi (Ed.), *Phenomenology and psychological research.* Pittsburgh: Duquesne University Press, 1985. Pp. 8–22.

Glassman, R. B. Free will has a neural substrate: Critique of Joseph F. Rychlak's *Discovering free will and personal responsibility. Zygon*, 1983, **18**, 67–82.

Graesser, A. C., Robertson, S. P., Lovelace, E. R., & Swinehart, D. M. Answers to why-questions expose the organization of story plot and predict recall of actions. *Journal of Verbal Learning and Verbal Behavior*, 1980, **19**, 110–119.

Green, F. P., & Schneider, F. W. Age differences in the behavior of boys on three measures of altruism. *Child Development*, 1974, **45**, 248–251.

Greenspoon, J. The reinforcing effect of two spoken sounds on the frequency of two responses. *American Journal of Psychology*, 1955, **68**, 409–416.

Greenwald, A. G. Self and memory. In G. H. Bower (Ed.), *The psychology of learning and motivation* (Vol. 15). New York: Academic Press, 1981. Pp. 201–236.

Griffin, D. R. *The question of animal awareness: Evolutionary continuity of mental experience* (2nd ed.). New York: Rockefeller University Press, 1981.

Gruba-McCallister, F. P. *The relation of dialectical opposition and an affective dimension of meaningfulness to verbal learning.* Unpublished master's thesis. West Lafayette, Ind.: Purdue University, 1975.

Gruba-McCallister, F. P., & Rychlak, J. F. A logical learning theory explanation of why personality scales predict behavior. *Journal of Personality Assessment*, 1981, **45**, 494–504.

Guthrie, E. R. *The psychology of learning* (rev. ed.). New York: Harper, 1952.

Haigh, G. V. Letter to the editor. *Psychology Today*, 1969, **3**, 4.

Harré, R. *Personal being: A theory for individual psychology.* Cambridge, Mass.: Harvard University Press, 1984.

Hastie, R. Causes and effects of causal attribution. *Journal of Personality and Social Psychology*, 1984, **46**, 44–56.

Hebb, D. O. What psychology is about. *American Psychologist*, 1974, **29**, 71–79.

Heider, F. *The psychology of interpersonal relations.* New York: John Wiley & Sons, 1958.

Heider, F., & Simmel, M. An experimental study of apparent behavior. *American Journal of Psychology,* 1944, **57,** 243–259.

Heiskell, T. L., & Rychlak, J. F. The therapeutic relationship: Affective preference and empathic communication. *Journal of Social and Personal Relationships,* 1986, **3,** 267–274.

Helmholtz, H. von. Treatise on physiological optics. In T. Shipley (Ed.), *Classics in psychology.* New York: Philosophical Library, 1961.

Hess, E. H. Attitude and pupil size. *Scientific American,* 1965, **212,** 46–54.

Hilgard, E. R., & Bower, G. H. *Theories of learning.* New York: Appleton-Century-Crofts, 1966.

Hilliard, R. D. Hemispheric laterality effects on a facial recognition task in normal subjects. *Cortex,* 1973, **9,** 246–258.

Hofstadter, D. R. *Gödel, Escher, Bach: An eternal golden braid.* New York: Vintage Books, 1980.

Howard, D. V. *Cognitive psychology.* New York: Macmillan, 1983.

Howard, G. S. *Dare we develop a human science?* Notre Dame, Ind.: Academic Publications, 1986.

Howard, G. S., & Conway, C. G. Can there be an empirical science of volitional action? *American Psychologist,* 1986, **41,** 1241–1251.

Hull, C. L. Mind, mechanism, and adaptive behavior. *Psychological Review,* 1937, **44,** 1–32.

Hull, C. L. *Principles of behavior.* New York: Appleton-Century-Crofts, 1943.

Hull, C. L. *A behavior system.* New Haven: Yale University Press, 1952.

Hume, D. *An enquiry concerning human understanding.* In R. M. Hutchins (Ed.), *Great books of the western world* (Vol. 35). Chicago: Encyclopedia Britannica, 1952. Pp. 446–509.

Immergluck, L. Determinism-freedom in contemporary psychology: An ancient problem revisited. *American Psychologist,* 1964, **19,** 270–281.

Irwin, F. W. *Intentional behavior and motivation: A cognitive theory.* Philadelphia: Lippincott, 1971.

James, W. What is an emotion? *Mind,* 1884, **9,** 188–205.

James, W. *The principles of psychology.* In R. M. Hutchins (Ed.), *Great books of the western world* (Vol. 53). Chicago: Encyclopedia Britannica, 1952.

Jaspers, K. *The great philosophers.* New York: Harcourt, Brace & World, 1962.

Jenkins, A. H. *The psychology of the Afro-American: A humanistic approach.* New York: Pergamon Press, 1982.

Jenkins, J. J. Remember that old theory of memory? Well, forget it! *American Psychologist,* 1974, **29,** 785–795.

Johnson, R. C., Frincke, G., & Martin, L. Meaningfulness, frequency, and affective characters of words as related to visual duration threshold. *Canadian Journal of Psychology,* 1961, **15,** 199–204.

Jones, E. *The life and work of Sigmund Freud: The formative years and great discoveries* (Vol. 1). New York: Basic Books, 1953.

Jones, E. E., Kanouse, D. F., Kelley, H. H., Nisbett, R. E., Valins, S., & Weiner, B. *Attri-*

bution: Perceiving the causes of behavior. Morristown, N.J.: General Learning Press, 1971.

Jones, E. E., & Nisbett, R. E. The actor and the observer: Divergent perceptions of the causes of behavior. Morristown, N.J.: General Learning Press, 1971.

Jones, H. E. Emotional factors in learning. Journal of General Psychology, 1929, 2, 263–272.

Jung, C. G. Psychology and alchemy. In H. Read, M. Fordham, & G. Adler (Eds.), The collected works of C. G. Jung (Vol. 12). Bollingen Series XX.12. New York: Pantheon Books, and London: Routledge & Kegan Paul, 1953.

Jung, C. G. Two essays on analytical psychology. In H. Read, M. Fordham, & G. Adler (Eds.), The collected works of C. G. Jung (Vol. 7). Bollingen Series XX.7. New York: Pantheon Books, 1953.

Jung, C. G. Symbols of transformation. In H. Read, M. Fordham, & G. Adler (Eds.), The collected works of C. G. Jung (Vol. 5). Bollingen Series XX.5. New York: Pantheon Books, 1956.

Jung, C. G. Psychology and religion: West and east. In H. Read, M. Fordham, & G. Adler (Eds.), The collected works of C. G. Jung (Vol. 11). Bollingen Series XX.11. New York: Pantheon Books, and London: Routledge & Kegan Paul, 1958.

Jung, C. G. The structure and dynamics of the psyche. In H. Read, M. Fordham, & G. Adler (Eds.), The collected works of C. G. Jung (Vol. 8). Bollingen Series XX.8. New York: Pantheon Books, 1960.

Jung, C. G. Synchronicity: An acausal connecting principle. In H. Read, M. Fordham, & G. Adler (Eds.), The collected works of C. G. Jung (Vol. 8). Bollingen Series XX.8. New York: Pantheon Books, 1960.

Kant, I. The critique of pure reason. In R. M. Hutchins (Ed.), Great books of the western world (Vol. 42). Chicago: Encyclopedia Britannica, 1952. Pp. 1–250.

Kausler, D. H. Continuity of processes across variants of recognition learning. In R. L. Solso (Ed.), Theories in cognitive psychology: The Loyola symposium. New York: Wiley, 1974. Pp. 45–75.

Keedy, N. S. The relationship between the affective quality of a premise and meaning-extension based upon its affirmation. Unpublished manuscript. West Lafayette, Ind.: Purdue University, 1975.

Keenan, J. M., & Baillet, S. D. Memory for personality and socially significant events. In R. S. Nickerson (Ed.), Attention and performance (Vol. 8). Hillsdale, N.J.: Erlbaum, 1980. Pp. 651–659.

Kelley, H. H. The processes of causal attribution. American Psychologist, 1973, 28, 107–128.

Kelly, G. A. The psychology of personal constructs (2 vols.). New York: Norton, 1955.

Kintsch, W. Learning, memory, and conceptual processes. New York: Wiley, 1970.

Klein, D., Moscovitch, M., & Vigna, C. Attentional mechanisms and perceptual asymmetries in tachistoscopic recognition of words and faces. Neuropsychologia, 1976, 14, 55–66.

Kleinmuntz, B. Personality measurement: An introduction. Homewood, Ill.: Dorsey Press, 1967.

Koen, F. Polarization, m and emotionality in words. Journal of Verbal Learning and Verbal Behavior, 1962, 1, 183–187.

Koffka, K. Principles of gestalt psychology. New York: Harcourt, Brace, 1935.

Köhler, W. Gestalt psychology today. In M. Henle (Ed.), *Documents of gestalt psychology*. Berkeley: University of California Press, 1961. Pp. 1–15.

Köhler, W. Psychological remarks on some questions of anthropology. In M. Henle (Ed.), *Documents of gestalt psychology*. Berkeley: University of California Press, 1961. Pp. 203–221.

Kondo, H. *Albert Einstein and the theory of relativity*. New York: Franklin Watts, 1969.

Kubat, W. J. *The reinforcement value of associations made to CVC trigrams*. Unpublished master's thesis. St. Louis: St. Louis University, 1969.

Kuhn, T. S. Logic of discovery or psychology of research? In I. Lakatos & A. Musgrave (Eds.), *Criticism and the growth of knowledge*. Cambridge: The University Press, 1970. Pp. 1–23.

Kuhn, T. S. *The structure of scientific revolutions* (2nd ed.). Chicago: The University of Chicago Press, 1970. (1st ed., 1962.)

Kuo, Y. Chinesse dialectical thought and character. In J. F. Rychlak (Ed.), *Dialectic: Humanistic reationale for behavior and development*. Basel, Switzerland: S. Karger AG, 1976. Pp. 72–85.

Kuo, Z. Y. The fundamental error of the concept of purpose and the trial and error fallacy. *Psychological Review*, 1928, **35**, 414–433.

Laberteaux, T. E. *The influence of positive versus negative reinforcement value on mediated paired-associate learning*. Unpublished master's thesis. St. Louis: St. Louis University, 1968.

Lamiell, J. T. *The psychology of personality: An epistemological inquiry*. New York: Columbia University Press, 1987.

Lamiell, J. T., Foss, M. A., Larsen, R. J., & Hempel, A. M. Studies in intuitive personology from an idiothetic point of view: Implications for personality theory. *Journal of Personality*, 1983, **51**, 438–467.

Lamiell, J. T., Foss, M. A., Trierweiler, S. J., & Leffel, G. M. Toward a further understanding of the intuitive personologist: Some preliminary evidence for the dialectical quality of subjective personality impressions. *Journal of Personality*, 1983, **51**, 213–235.

Langer, S. K. *Philosophy in a new key*. New York: Penguin Books, 1948.

Lappin, R. W. *Meaningfulness, deviant achievers, and personal adjustment*. Unpublished doctoral dissertation. St. Louis: St. Louis University, 1969.

Lecky, P. *Self-consistency: A theory of personality*. Garden City, N.Y.: Doubleday, 1969.

Lefcourt, H. M. The function of the illusions of control and freedom. *American Psychologist*, 1973, **28**, 417–425.

Levy, L. H. *Psychological interpretation*. New York: Holt, Rinehart & Winston, 1963.

Lewin, K. *A dynamic theory of personality*. New York: McGraw-Hill, 1935.

Libet, B. Unconscious cerebral initiative and the role of conscious will in voluntary action. *The Behavioral and Brain Sciences*, 1985, **8**, 529–566.

Locke, J. *An essay concerning human understanding*. In R. M. Hutchins (Ed.), *Great books of the western world* (Vol. 35). Chicago: Encyclopedia Britannica, 1952. Pp. 85–395.

Lorayne, H., & Lucas, J. *The memory book*. New York: Ballantine, 1974.

Lord, C. G., Lepper, M. R., & Preston, E. Considering the opposite: A corrective strategy for social judgment. *Journal of Personality and Social Psychology*, 1984, **47**, 1231–1243.

Lorenz, K. *Studies in animal and human behavior* (Vol. 1). Cambridge, Mass.: Harvard University Press, 1970.

Lowrie, W. *A short life of Kierkegaard.* Garden City, N.Y.: Doubleday, 1961.

Luce, R. D., & Raiffa, H. *Games and decisions.* New York: Wiley, 1957.

Lynch, C. A. The memory values of certain alleged emotionally toned words. *Journal of Experimental Psychology,* 1932, **15,** 298–315.

MacCorquodale, K., & Meehl, P. E. On a distinction between hypothetical constructs and intervening variables. *Psychological Review,* 1948, **55,** 95–107.

Mach, E. *The science of mechanics.* Chicago: Open Court, 1893.

Magill, F. N., & McGreal, I. P. (Eds.), *Masterpieces of world philosophy* (2 vols.). New York: Salem, 1961.

Mahoney, M. J. *Cognition and behavior modification.* Cambridge, Mass.: Ballinger, 1974.

Maltzman, I. Theoretical conceptions of semantic conditioning and generalization. In T. R. Dixon & D. L. Horton (Eds.), *Verbal behavior and general behavior theory.* Englewood Cliffs, N.J.: Prentice-Hall, 1968. Pp. 291–339.

Mancuso, J. C. Dialectic man as a subject in psychological research. In J. F. Rychlak (Ed.), *Dialectic: Humanistic rationale for behavior and development.* Basel, Switzerland: S. Karger AG, 1976. Pp. 113–125.

Markus, H. Self-schemata and processing information about the self. *Journal of Personality and Social Psychology,* 1977, **35,** 63–78.

Marrow, A. J. *The practical theorist: The life and work of Kurt Lewin.* New York: Basic Books, 1969.

Marx, K. *Capital.* In R. M. Hutchins (Ed.), *Great books of the western world* (Vol. 50). Chicago: Encyclopedia Britannica, 1952. Pp. 1–393.

Maslow, A. H. Eupsychia, the good society. *Journal of Humanistic Psychology,* 1961, **1,** 1–11.

Maslow, A. H. *The farther reaches of human nature.* New York: The Viking Press, 1971.

Masterman, M. The nature of a paradigm. In I. Lakatos, & A. Musgrave (Eds.), *Criticism and the growth of knowledge.* Cambridge: The University Press, 1970. Pp. 59–89.

Matlin, M., & Stang, D. *The pollyanna principle: Selectivity in language, memory, and thought.* Cambridge, Mass.: Schenkman, 1978.

McDougall, W. Prolegomena to psychology. *Psychological Review,* 1922, **29,** 1–43.

McDougall, W. Purposive or mechanical psychology? *Psychological Review,* 1923, **30,** 273–288.

McGuire, W. (Ed.), *The Freud/Jung letters.* Bollingen Series XCIV, Princeton, N.J.: Princeton University Press, 1974.

McLoyd, V. C. The effects of extrinsic rewards of differential value on high- and low-intrinsic interest. *Child Development,* 1979, *50,* 1010–1019.

Meehl, P. E., & MacCorquodale, K. On a distinction between hypothetical constructs and intervening variables. *Psychological Review,* 1948, **55,** 95–107.

Michotte, A. E. *The perception of causality.* New York: Basic Books, 1963.

Miller, D. L. The meaning of explanation. *Psychological Review,* 1946, **53,** 241–246.

Miller, G. A., Galanter, E., & Pribram, K. H. *Plans and the structure of behavior.* New York: Holt, Rinehart & Winston, 1960.

Miller, N. E., & Dollard, J. *Social learning and imitation.* New Haven: Yale University Press, 1941.

Minsky, M. L. (Ed.), *Semantic information processing*. Cambridge, Mass.: MIT Press, 1968.

Mischel, T. Wundt and the conceptual foundations of psychology. *Philosophical and Phenomenological Research*, 1970, **31**, 1–26.

Mischel, W. *Personality and assessment*. New York: Wiley, 1968.

Mischel, W. Toward a cognitive social learning reconceptualization of personality. *Psychological Review*, 1973, **80**, 252–283.

Mischel, W. The self as the person: A cognitive social learning view. In A. H. Wandersman, P. J. Poppen, & D. F. Ricks (Eds.), *Humanism and behaviorism: Dialogue and growth*. New York: Pergamon Press, 1976. Pp. 145–156.

Mischel, W. On the interface of cognition and personality: Beyond the person-situation debate. *American Psychologist*, 1979, **34**, 740–754.

Moore, C. A. Introduction: The comprehensive Indian mind. In C. A. Moore (Ed.), *The Indian mind: Essentials of Indian philosophy and culture*. Honolulu: University of Hawaii Press, 1967. Pp. 1–18.

Moore, C. A. Introduction: The humanistic Chinese mind. In C. A. Moore (Ed.), *The Chinese mind: Essentials of Chinese philosophy and culture*. Honolulu: University of Hawaii Press, 1967. Pp. 1–10.

Mosbacher, B. J. *Depression and alcohol ingestion: A teleological perspective*. Unpublished doctoral dissertation. West Lafayette, Ind.: Purdue University, 1984.

Mosbacher, B. J., Gruen, G. E., & Rychlak, J. F. Incentive value: The overlooked dimension in childhood sharing. *Journal of Genetic Psychology*, 1985, **146**, 197–204.

Muller, J. B., & Rychlak, J. F. Reinforcement as positive or negative meaning-extension: An empirical demonstration. *Motivation and Emotion*, 1979, **3**, 287–297.

Murgatroyd, S. Introduction to reversal theory. In M. J. Apter, D. Fontana, & S. Murgatroyd (Eds.), *Reversal theory: Applications and developments*. Cardiff, Wales: University College Press, 1985. Pp. 1–19.

Murphy, G. *Personality: A biosocial approach to origins and structure*. New York: Harper, 1947.

Nagel, E., & Newman, J. R. *Gödel's proof*. New York: New York University Press, 1958.

Nakamura, H. *Ways of thinking of Eastern peoples*. Honolulu: East-West Center Press, 1964.

Neisser, U. *Cognitive psychology*. New York: Appleton-Century-Crofts, 1967.

Nguyen, M. L. *Clustering in terms of categorization and reinforcement value in randomly arranged associates*. Unpublished master's thesis. West Lafayette, Ind.: Purdue University, 1975.

Nikhilananda, S. Concentration and meditation as methods of Indian philosophy. In C. A. Moore (Ed.), *The Indian mind: Essentials of Indian philosophy and culture*. Honolulu: University of Hawaii Press, 1967. Pp. 136–151.

O'Leary, L. R. *The effect of idiographic meaningfulness on the learning of subjects from different racial backgrounds, social classes, and ability levels*. Unpublished doctoral dissertation. St. Louis: St. Louis University, 1969.

Oppenheimer, R. Analogy in science. *American Psychologist*, 1956, **11**, 127–135.

Orne, M. T. On the social psychology of the psychological experiment: With particular reference to demand characteristics and their implications. *American Psychologist*, 1962, **17**, 776–783.

Osgood, C. E. The nature and measurement of meaning. *Psychological Bulletin*, 1952, **49**, 197–237.

Osgood, C. E., Suci, G. J., & Tannenbaum, P. H. *The measurement of meaning*. Urbana: University of Illinois Press, 1957.

Packer, M. J. Hermeneutic inquiry in the study of human conduct. *American Psychologist*, 1985, **40**, 1081–1093.

Page, M. M. Demand characteristics and the verbal operant conditioning experiment. *Journal of Personality and Social Psychology*, 1972, **23**, 304–308.

Palmer, R. E. *Hermeneutics*. Evanston, Ill.: Northwestern University Press, 1969.

Patterson, F. Conversations with a gorilla. *National Geographic*, 1978, **154**, 438–465.

Pavlov, I. P. *Conditioned reflexes: An investigation of the physiological activity of the cerebral cortex* (translated by G. V. Anrep). New York: Oxford University Press, 1927.

Penfield, W. *The mystery of the mind: A critical study of consciousness and the human brain*. Princteon, N.J.: Princeton University Press, 1975.

Pepper, S. C. *World hypotheses*. Berkeley: University of California Press, 1970.

Piaget, J. *The child's conception of physical causality*. London: Kegan Paul, Trench, Trubner, 1930.

Piaget, J. *The child's conception of number*. London: Routledge & Kegan Paul, 1952.

Piaget, J. *Logic and psychology*. New York: Basic Books, 1957.

Piaget, J., Inhelder, B., & Szeminska, A. *The child's conception of geometry*. New York: Harper Torchbooks, 1964.

Piers, E. V., & Harris, D. B. Age and other correlates of self-concept in children. *Journal of Educational Psychology*, 1964, **56**, 81–85.

Plato. *Sophist*. In R. M. Hutchins (Ed.), *Great books of the western world* (Vol. 7). Chicago: Encyclopedia Britannica, 1952. Pp. 551–579.

Polanyi, M. *Personal knowledge: Towards a post-critical philosophy*. New York: Harper Torchbooks, 1964.

Polkinghorne, D. *Methodology for the human sciences: Systems of inquiry*. Albany: State University of New York Press, 1983.

Polkinghorne, D. *Narrative knowledge and human science*. Unpublished manuscript. San Francisco: Saybrook Institute, 1986.

Popper, K. R. *The logic of scientific discovery*. New York: Basic Books, 1959.

Popper, K. R. Normal science and its dangers. In I. Lakatos & A. Musgrave (Eds.), *Criticism and the growth of knowledge*. Cambridge: The University Press, 1970. Pp. 51–58.

Prigogine, I., & Stengers, I. *Order out of chaos: Man's new dialogue with nature*. New York: Bantam Books, 1984.

Pyszczynski, T. A., & Greenberg, J. Role of disconfirmed expectancies in the instigation of attributional processing. *Journal of Personality and Social Psychology*, 1981, **40**, 31–38.

Raju, P. T. Metaphysical theories in Indian philosophy. In C. A. Moore (Ed.), *The Indian mind: Essentials of Indian philosophy and culture*. Honolulu: University of Hawaii Press, 1967. Pp. 19–40.

Rancurello, A. C. *A study of Franz Brentano*. New York: Academic, 1968.

Reese, W. L. *Dictionary of philosophy and religion: Eastern and western thought.* Atlantic Highlands, N.J.: Humanities Press, 1980.

Reichenbach, H. *Experience and prediction.* Chicago: University of Chicago Press, 1938.

Rieff, P. *Freud: The mind of the moralist.* New York: Viking, 1959.

Riegel, K. F. Dialectic operations: The final period of cognitive development. *Human Development,* 1973, **16,** 346–370.

Riesman, D. *The lonely crowd.* Garden City, N.Y.: Doubleday, 1953.

Roberts, W. T. *Instrumental effects of causal constructs.* Unpublished master's thesis. West Lafayette, Ind.: Purdue University, 1974.

Rogers, C. R. *Client-centered therapy.* Boston: Houghton Mifflin, 1951.

Rogers, C. R. *On becoming a person: A therapist's view of psychotherapy.* Boston: Houghton Mifflin, 1961.

Rogers, C. R. Toward a modern approach to values: The valuing process in the mature person. In J. T. Hart & T. M. Tomlinson (Eds.), *New directions in client-centered therapy.* Boston: Houghton Mifflin, 1970. Pp. 430–441.

Rogers, C. R., & Skinner, B. F. Some issues concerning the control of human behavior: A symposium. *Science,* 1956, **124,** 1057–1066.

Rogers, T. B., Kuiper, N. A., & Kirker, W. S. Self-reference and the encoding of personal information. *Journal of Personality and Social Psychology,* 1977, **35,** 677–688.

Rokeach, M. *The nature of human values.* New York: Free Press, 1973.

Rosenthal, R. *Experimenter effects in behavioral research.* New York: Appleton-Century-Crofts, 1966.

Ross, M. Salience of reward and intrinsic motivation. *Journal of Personality and Social Psychology,* 1975, **32,** 245–254.

Rumsey, J. M., & Rychlak, J. F. The role of affective assessment in intelligence testing. *Journal of Personality Assessment,* 1978, **42,** 421–425.

Runes, D. D. (Ed.), *Dictionary of philosophy.* New York: Philosophical Library, 1960.

Runyan, W. M. *Life histories and psychobiography: Explorations in theory and method.* New York: Oxford University Press, 1984.

Russell, B. *Introduction to mathematical philosophy.* London: Allen & Unwin, 1919.

Russell, B. *Wisdom of the west.* Garden City, N.Y.: Doubleday, 1959.

Rychlak, J. F. Reinforcement value: A suggested idiographic, intensity dimension of meaningfulness for the personality theorist. *Journal of Personality,* 1966, **34,** 311–335.

Rychlak, J. F. *A philosophy of science for personality theory.* Boston: Houghton Mifflin, 1968. (2nd ed., Malabar, Fla.: Krieger, 1981.)

Rychlak, J. F. Lockean vs. Kantian theoretical models and the "cause" of therapeutic change. *Psychotherapy: Theory, Research and Practice,* 1969, **6,** 214–222.

Rychlak, J. F. The human person in modern psychological science. *British Journal of Medical Psychology,* 1970, **43,** 233–240.

Rychlak, J. F. Communication in human concordance: Possibilities and impossibilities. In J. H. Masserman & J. J. Schwab (Eds.), *Man for humanity: On concordance vs. discord in human behavior.* Springfield, Ill.: Charles C. Thomas, 1972. Pp. 91–101.

Rychlak, J. F. *Introduction to personality and psychotherapy: A theory-construction approach.* Boston: Houghton Mifflin, 1973.

Rychlak, J. F. *Intentionally manipulating association value and reinforcement value in paired-associates learning*. Unpublished manuscript. West Lafayette, Ind.: Purdue University, 1974.

Rychlak, J. F. Affective assessment in the recognition of designs and paintings by elementary school children. *Child Development*, 1975, **46**, 62–70.

Rychlak, J. F. Affective assessment, intelligence, social class, and racial learning style. *Journal of Personality and Social Psychology*, 1975, **32**, 989–995.

Rychlak, J. F. A humanist looks at psychological science. In W. J. Arnold & J. K. Cole (Eds.), *Nebraska symposium on motivation* (Vol. 22). Lincoln: University of Nebraska Press, 1975.

Rychlak, J. F. *Affective clustering in the verbal learning styles of whites and blacks*. Unpublished manuscript. West Lafayette, Ind.: Purdue University, 1976.

Rychlak, J. F. Comments on "The self as the person." In A. H. Wandersman, P. J. Poppen, & D. F. Ricks (Eds.), *Humanism and behaviorism: Dialogue and growth*. New York: Pergamon Press, 1976. Pp. 157–167.

Rychlak, J. F. (Ed.), *Dialectic: Humanistic rationale for behavior and development*. Basel, Switzerland: S. Karger AG, 1976.

Rychlak, J. F. Is a concept of "self" necessary in psychological theory, and if so why? In A. H. Wandersman, P. J. Poppen, & D. F. Ricks (Eds.), *Humanism and behaviorism: Dialogue and growth*. Elmsford, N.Y.: Pergamon Press, 1976. Pp. 121–143.

Rychlak, J. F. The multiple meanings of dialectic. In J. F. Rychlak (Ed.), *Dialectic: Humanistic rationale for behavior and development*. Basel, Switzerland: S. Karger AG, 1976. Pp. 1–17.

Rychlak, J. F. Personality theory: Its nature, past, present and—future? *Personality and Social Psychology Bulletin*, 1976, **2**, 209–224.

Rychlak, J. F. A nontelic teleology? *American Psychologist*, 1979, **34**, 435–438.

Rychlak, J. F. Logical learning theory: Kuhnian anomaly or medievalism revisited? *The Journal of Mind and Behavior*, 1984, **4**, 389–416.

Rychlak, J. F. *Inference versus implication in predicating personality*. Unpublished manuscript. Chicago: Loyola University of Chicago, 1986.

Rychlak, J. F., Carlsen, N. L., & Dunning, L. P. Personal adjustment and the free recall of material with affectively positive or negative meaningfulness. *Journal of Abnormal Psychology*, 1974, **83**, 480–487.

Rychlak, J. F., Flynn, E. J., & Burger, G. Affection and evaluation as logical processes of meaningfulness independent of associative frequency. *Journal of General Psychology*, 1979, **100**, 143–157.

Rychlak, J. F., Galster, J., & McFarland, K. K. The role of affective assessment in associative learning: From designs and CVC trigrams to faces and names. *Journal of Experimental Research in Personality*, 1972, **6**, 186–194.

Rychlak, J. F., Hewitt, C. W., & Hewitt, J. Affective evaluation, word quality, and the verbal learning styles of black versus white junior college females. *Journal of Personality and Social Psychology*, 1973, **27**, 248–255.

Rychlak, J. F., & Marceil, J. C. Task predication and affective learning style. *Journal of Social Behavior and Personality*, 1986, **1**, 557–564.

Rychlak, J. F., McKee, D. B., Schneider, W. E., & Abramson, Y. Affective evaluation in the verbal learning styles of normals and abnormals. *Journal of Abnormal Psychology*, 1971, **77**, 11–16.

Rychlak, J. F., & Nguyen, T. D. The role of frequency and affective assessment in associative enrichment. *Journal of General Psychology,* 1979, **100,** 295–311.

Rychlak, J. F., & Saluri, R. E. Affective assessment in learning of names by fifth- and sixth-grade children. *Journal of Genetic Psychology,* 1973, **123,** 251–261.

Rychlak, J. F., & Slife, B. D. Affection as a cognitive judgmental process: A theoretical assumption put to test through brain-lateralization methodology. *The Journal of Mind and Behavior,* 1984, **5,** 131–150.

Rychlak, J. F., Tasto, D. L., Andrews, J. E., & Ellis, H. C. The application of an affective dimension of meaningfulness to personality-related verbal learning. *Journal of Personality,* 1973, **41,** 341–360.

Rychlak, J. F., & Tobin, T. J. Order effects in the affective learning styles of overachievers and underachievers. *Journal of Educational Psychology,* 1971, **62,** 141–147.

Rychlak, J. F., Tuan, N. D., & Schneider, W. E. Formal discipline revisited: Affective assessment and nonspecific transfer. *Journal of Educational Psychology,* 1974, **66,** 139–151.

Rychlak, J. F., & Williams, R. N. Affective assessment and dialectical oppositionality in the cognitive processing of social descriptors. *Personality and Social Psychology Bulletin,* 1984, **10,** 620–629.

Rychlak, J. F., Williams, R. N., & Bugaj, A. M. The heuristic properties of dialectical oppositionality in predication. *Journal of General Psychology,* 1986, **113,** 359–368.

Saksena, S. K. Relation of philosophical theories to the practical affairs of men. In C. A. Moore (Ed.), *The Indian mind: Essentials of Indian philosophy and culture.* Honolulu: University of Hawaii Press, 1967. Pp. 19–40.

Sarbin, T. R., & Quenk, A. The rationality of nonsense: Intensity of meaning of nonreferential verbal units. *Psychological Record,* 1964, **14,** 401–409.

Sarton, G. *Introduction to the history of science* (4 vols.). Baltimore: Williams and Wilkins, 1927. (Reprinted, 1968.)

Schrödinger, E. *Science theory and man.* New York: Dover, 1957.

Schwartz, G., & Bishop, P. W. *Moments of discovery: The origins of science.* New York: Basic Books, 1958.

Shapiro, K. J. *Bodily reflective modes: A phenomenological method for psychology.* Durham, N.C.: Duke University Press, 1985.

Sherif, M., & Hovland, C. I. *Social judgment: Assimilation and contrast effects in communication and attitude change.* New Haven: Yale University Press, 1961.

Sherman, R. C., & Titus, W. Covariation information and cognitive processing: Effects of causal implications on memory. *Journal of Personality and Social Psychology,* 1982, **42,** 989–1000.

Silverman, A., & Cason, H. Incidental memory for pleasant, unpleasant, and indifferent words. *American Journal of Psychology,* 1934, **46,** 315–320.

Skaggs, E. B. The limitations of scientific psychology as an applied practical science. *Psychological Review,* 1934, **41,** 572–576.

Skinner, B. F. The concept of the reflex in the description of behavior. *Journal of General Psychology,* 1931, **5,** 427–458.

Skinner, B. F. *The behavior of organisms: An experimental analysis.* New York: Appleton-Century, 1938.

Skinner, B. F. Are theories of learning necessary? *Psychological Review*, 1950, **57**, 193–216.

Skinner, B. F. A case history in scientific method. *American Psychologist*, 1956, **11**, 221–233.

Skinner, B. F. *Beyond freedom and dignity.* New York: Knopf, 1971.

Skinner, B. F. *About behaviorism.* New York: Knopf, 1974.

Slife, B. D., & Rychlak, J. F. Affection as a separate dimension of meaningfulness. *Contemporary Educational Psychology*, 1981, **6**, 140–150.

Slife, B. D., & Rychlak, J. F. Role of affective assessment in modeling aggressive behavior. *Journal of Personality and Social Psychology*, 1982, **43**, 861–868.

Smith, W. W. Experiments on memory and affective tone. *British Journal of Psychology*, 1921, **11**, 236–250.

Solso, R. L. (Ed.), *Theories in cognitive psychology: The Loyola symposium.* New York: Wiley, 1974.

Spence, K. W. The postulates and methods of "behaviorism." *Psychological Review*, 1948, **55**, 67–78.

Spence, K. W. *Behavior theory and conditioning.* New Haven: Yale University Press, 1956.

Sperry, R. W. Hemisphere deconnection and unity in conscious awareness. *American Psychologist*, 1968, **23**, 723–733.

Spielberger, C. D., Berger, A., & Howard, K. Conditioning of verbal behavior as a function of awareness, need for social approval, and motivation to receive reinforcement. *Journal of Abnormal and Social Psychology*, 1963, **67**, 241–246.

Staats, A. W. *Meaning and word associations: Separate processes* (Tech. Rep. No. 12; Contract No. 2794 [02]). Tempe: Arizona State University, 1959.

Stagner, R. Factors influencing the memory value of words in a series. *Journal of Experimental Psychology*, 1933, **16**, 115–128.

Stevens, S. S. The operational definition of psychological concepts. *Psychological Review*, 1935, **42**, 517–527.

Stevenson, R. J. Depth of comprehension, effective elaboration, and memory for sentences. *Memory & Cognition*, 1981, **9**, 169–176.

Strupp, H. H. *Psychotherapists in action.* New York: Grune & Stratton, 1960.

Sullivan, H. S. *The interpersonal theory of psychiatry.* New York: Norton, 1953.

Sullivan, H. S. *Schizophrenia as a human process.* New York: Norton, 1962.

Suppes, P. The place of theory in educational research. *Educational Researcher*, 1974, **3**, 3–10.

Suzuki, D. T. *The essentials of Zen Buddhism.* New York: Dutton, 1962. (Edited and with an introduction by B. Phillips.)

Taffel, C. Anxiety and the conditioning of verbal behavior. *Journal of Abnormal and Social Psychology*, 1955, **51**, 496–501.

Tait, W. D. The effect of psycho-physical attitudes on memory. *Journal of Abnormal Psychology*, 1913, **8**, 10–37.

Takakusu, J. Buddhism as a philosophy of "thusness." In C. A. Moore (Ed.), *The Indian mind: Essentials of Indian philosophy and culture.* Honolulu: University of Hawaii Press, 1967. Pp. 86–117.

Tenbrunsel, T. W., Nishball, E. R., & Rychlak, J. F. The idiographic relationship between association value and reinforcement value, and the nature of meaning. *Journal of Personality*, 1968, **36**, 126–137.

Thomson, R. H. An experimental study of memory as influenced by feeling tone. *Journal of Experimental Psychology*, 1930, **13**, 462–467.

Thoreson, C. E., & Mahoney, M. J. *Behavioral self-control*. New York: Holt, Rinehart & Winston, 1974.

Thorndike, E. L. Animal intelligence: An experimental study of the associative processes in animals. *Psychological Review Monograph Supplement*, 1898, No. 8.

Thurstone, L. L., & Chave, E. J. *The measurement of attitude*. Chicago: The University of Chicago Press, 1929.

Titchener, E. B. *An outline of psychology*. New York: Macmillan, 1897.

Titchener, E. B. *A text-book of psychology*. New York: Macmillan, 1909.

Titchener, E. B. The postulates of a structural psychology. In T. Shipley (Ed.), *Classics in psychology*. New York: Philosophical Library, 1961. Pp. 224–243. (Originally published in *Philosophical Review*, 1898, **7**, 449–465.)

Titchener, E. B. *Systematic psychology: Prolegomena*. Ithaca, N.Y.: Cornell University Press, 1972.

Tolman, E. C. Retroactive inhibition as affected by conditions of learning. *Psychological Monographs*, 1917, **25**, No. 107, 1–50.

Tolman, E. C. *Purposive behavior in animals and men*. New York: Appleton-Century-Crofts, 1967.

Truax, C. B., & Carkhuff, R. R. *Toward effective counseling and psychotherapy: Training and practice*. Chicago: Aldine, 1967.

Tulving, E. Subjective organization in free recall of "unrelated" words. *Psychological Review*, 1962, **69**, 344–354.

Underwood, B. J. Individual differences as a crucible in theory construction. *American Psychologist*, 1975, **30**, 128–134.

Underwood, B. J., & Schulz, R. W. *Meaningfulness and verbal learning*. Chicago: Lippincott, 1960.

Untersteiner, M. *The sophists*. New York: Philosophical Library, 1954.

Vallacher, R. R. An introduction to self theory. In D. M. Wegner & R. R. Vallacher (Eds.), *The self in social psychology*. New York: Oxford University Press, 1980.

van Kaam, A. *Existential foundations of psychology* (Image Books ed.). Garden City, N.Y.: Doubleday, 1969.

Voss, J. F. On the relationship of associative and organizational processes. In E. Tulving & W. Donaldson (Eds.), *Organization of memory*. New York: Academic, 1972. Pp. 167–194.

Walker, S. *Animal thought*. London: Routledge & Kegan Paul, 1983.

Walters, J., Apter, M. J., & Svebak, S. Color preference, arousal and the theory of psychological reversals. *Motivation and Emotion*, 1982, **6**, 193–215.

Waters, R. H. Morgan's canon and anthropomorphism. *Psychological Review*, 1939, **46**, 534–540.

Waters, R. H. Mechanicomorphism: A new term for an old mode of thought. *Psychological Review*, 1948, **55**, 139–142.

Watson, J. B. Psychology as the behaviorist views it. *Psychological Review*, 1913, **20**, 158–177.

Watson, J. B. *Behaviorism*. New York: Norton, 1924.

Watson, R. I. Psychology: A prescriptive science. *American Psychologist*, 1967, **22**, 435–443.

Watsons, R. I. *The great psychologists* (3rd ed.). Philadelphia: Lippincott, 1971.

Wegner, D. M., & Vallacher, R. R. *The self in social psychology*. New York: Oxford University Press, 1980.

Weiss, A. P. The mind and the man within. *Psychological Review*, 1919, **26**, 327–334.

Wertheimer, M. *Productive thinking*. New York: Harper, 1945.

White, M. M. Some factors influencing recall of pleasant and unpleasant words. *American Journal of Psychology*, 1936, **48**, 134–139.

White, M. M., & Powell, M. Differential reaction time for pleasant and unpleasant words. *American Journal of Psychology*, 1936, **48**, 126–133.

White, M. M., & Ratliff, M. N. The relation of affective tone on the learning and recall of words. *American Journal of Psychology*, 1934, **46**, 92–98.

White, R. W. Motivation reconsidered: The concept of competence. *Psychological Review*, 1959, **66**, 297–333.

Whitehead, A. N. *The function of reason*. Boston: Beacon, 1958.

Whitehead, A. N., & Russell, B. *Principia mathematica* (3 vols.; 2nd ed.). Cambridge: The University Press, 1963.

Wicklund, R. A. *Freedom and reactance*. Potomac, Md.: Lawrence Erlbaum, 1974.

Wiener, P. P., & Noland, A. (Eds.), *Roots of scientific thought*. New York: Basic Books, 1957.

Wightman, W. P. D. *The growth of scientific ideas*. New Haven: Yale University Press, 1951.

Winter, J. E. The postulates of psychology. *Psychological Review*, 1936, **43**, 130–148.

Wittgenstein, L. *Philosophical investigations*. Oxford, England: Basil Blackwell, 1953.

Wolman, B. B. Does psychology need its own philosophy of science? *American Psychologist*, 1971, **26**, 877–886.

Wong, P. T. P., & Weiner, B. When people ask "why" questions, and the heuristics of attributional search. *Journal of Personality and Social Psychology*, 1981, **40**, 650–663.

Woodward, K. E. *Affective factors in learning across levels of intelligence*. Unpublished doctoral dissertation. West Lafayette, Ind.: Purdue University, 1978.

Woodworth, R. S., & Sheehan, M. R. *Contemporary schools of psychology* (3rd ed.). New York: Ronald, 1964.

Wundt, M. *Die Wurzein der deutschen Philosophie in Stamm und Rasse*. Berlin: Junker and Dunnhaupt, 1944.

Wundt, W. *Lectures on human and animal psychology* (4th ed.). New York: Macmillan, 1907. (1st ed., 1894).

Wundt, W. Contributions to the theory of sensory perception. In T. Shipley (Ed.), *Classics in psychology*. New York: Philosophical Library, 1961.

Wundt, W. *The language of gestures*. Paris: Mouton, 1973.

Wyer, R. S., & Carlston, D. E. *Social cognition, inference, and attribution*. Hillsdale, N.J.: Erlbaum, 1979.

Yerkes, R. M. Concerning the anthropocentrism of psychology. *Psychological Review*, 1933, **40**, 209–212.

Zajonc, R. B. Attitudinal effects of mere exposure. *Journal of Personality and Social Psychology Monograph Supplement*, 1968, **9**, (2, Part 2).

Zukav, G. *The dancing wu li masters: An overview of the new physics.* New York: Bantam Books, 1979.

AUTHOR INDEX

SUBJECT INDEX